Installing, Configuring, and Administering Microsoft® Windows® 2000 Professional

Exam 70-210

Installing, Configuring, and Administering Microsoft® Windows® 2000 Professional

Exam 70-210

First Edition

Kenneth C. Laudon, Series Designer
Robin L. Pickering

The Azimuth Interactive MCSE/MCSA Team
Carol G. Traver, Series Editor
Ken Rosenblatt
Russell Polo
David Langley
Kevin Jensen, MCSE
Howard Kunkel, MCSE
Mark Maxwell

PEARSON
Prentice
Hall

Upper Saddle River, New Jersey, 07458

Senior Vice President/Publisher: Natalie Anderson
Acquisitions Editor: Steven Elliot
Marketing Manager: Steven Rutberg
Senior Editorial Project Manager: Kristine Lombardi Frankel
Assistant Editor: Allison Williams
Editorial Assistant: Jasmine Slowick
Editorial Assistant: Jodi Bolognese
Marketing Assistant: Barrie Reinhold
Media Project Manager: Joan Waxman
Production Manager: Gail Steier de Acevedo
Editorial Production Project Manager: Tim Tate
Associate Director, Manufacturing: Vincent Scelta
Manufacturing Buyer: Tim Tate
Art Director: Pat Smythe
Design Manager: Maria Lange
Interior Design: Kim Buckley
Cover Design: Jill Little
Associate Director, Multimedia: Karen Goldsmith
Manager, Multimedia: Christy Mahon
Full Service Composition: Azimuth Interactive, Inc.
Quality Assurance: Digital Content Factory Ltd.
Printer/Binder: Banta Book Group, Menasha
Cover Printer: Phoenix Color Corporation

Credits and acknowledgments borrowed from other sources and reproduced, with permission, in this textbook appear on appropriate page within text.

Microsoft® and Windows® are registered trademarks of the Microsoft Corporation in the U.S.A. and other countries. Screen shots and icons reprinted with permission from the Microsoft Corporation. This book is not sponsored or endorsed by or affiliated with the Microsoft Corporation.

10 9 8 7 6 5 4 3 2 1
0-13--42209-X

To our families,
for their love, patience,
and inspiration.

Brief Contents

Contents

Welcome to the Laudon MCSE/MCSA Certification Series!

You are about to begin an exciting journey of learning and career skills building that will provide you access to careers such as Network Administrator, Systems Engineer, Technical Support Engineer, Network Analyst, and Technical Consultant. What you learn in the Laudon MCSE/MCSA Certification Series will provide you with a strong set of networking skills and knowledge that you can use throughout your career as the Microsoft Windows operating system continues to evolve, as new information technology devices appear, and as business applications of computers continues to expand. The Laudon Certification Series aims to provide you with the skills and knowledge that will endure, prepare you for your future career and make the process of learning fun and enjoyable.

Microsoft Windows 2000 and the Networked World

We live in a computer networked world—more so than many of us realize. The Internet, the world's largest network, now has more than 400 million people who connect to the Internet through an estimated 300,000 local area networks. About sixty percent of these local area networks are using a Windows network operating system (the other networks use some version of UNIX Netware or other network operating system). About 95% of the one billion personal computers in the world use some form of Microsoft operating system, typically some version of Windows. A growing number of handheld personal digital assistants (PDAs) also use versions of the Microsoft operating system called Microsoft CE. Most businesses—large and small—use some kind of client/server local area network to connect their employees to one another, and to the Internet. In the United States, the vast majority of these business networks use a Microsoft network operating system—either an earlier version called Windows NT, or the current version called Windows 2000.

The Laudon MCSE/MCSA Certification Series prepares you to participate in this computer networked world, and specifically for the world of Microsoft Windows 2000 Professional client operating system and Windows 2000 Server (a network Operating system).

Laudon MCSE/MCSA Certification Series Objectives

The first objective of the Laudon MCSE/MCSA Certification Series is to prepare you to pass the MCSE/MCSA certification exams and to receive certification. Why get certified? As businesses increasingly rely on Microsoft networks to operate, employers want to make sure their networking staff has the skills needed to plan for, install, and operate these networks. While job experience is an important source of networking knowledge, employers increasingly rely on certification examinations to ensure their staff has the necessary skills. The MCSE/MCSA curriculum provides networking professionals a well-balanced and comprehensive body of knowledge necessary to operate and administer Microsoft networks in a business setting.

There is clear evidence that having the MCSE/MCSA certification results in higher salaries, and faster promotions, to individual employees. Therefore, it is definitely in your interest to obtain certification even if you have considerable job experience. If you are just starting out in the world of networking, certification can be very important for landing that first job.

A second longer-term objective of the Laudon MCSE/MCSA Certification Series is to help you build a set of skills and a knowledge base that will prepare you for a career in the networking field. There is no doubt that in the next five years Microsoft will issue several new versions of its network operating system, and new versions of Windows client operating system. In the next five years—and thereafter—there will be a steady stream of new digital devices that will require connecting to networks. Most of what you learn in the Windows 2000 Laudon Series will provide a strong foundation for understanding future versions of the operating system.

The Laudon Series teaches you real-world job-related skills. About 90% of the work performed by MCSE/MCSAs falls into the following categories according to a survey researcher (McKillip, 1999):

- Analyze the business requirements for the system architecture.
- Design a system architecture solution that meets business requirements.
- Deploy, install, and configure the components of the system architecture.

- Manage the components of the system architecture on an ongoing basis.
- Monitor and optimize the components of the system architecture.
- Diagnose and resolve problems regarding the components of the system architecture.

These are precisely the skills we had in mind when we wrote this Series. As you work through the hands-on instructions in the text, perform the instructions in the simulated Windows 2000 environment on the CD-ROM, and complete the problem solving cases in the book, you will notice our emphasis on analyzing, designing, diagnosing, and implementing the Windows 2000 software. By completing the Laudon MCSE/MCSA Certification Series, you will be laying the foundation for a long-term career based on your specialized knowledge of networks and general problem solving skills.

Preparing you for a career involves more than satisfying the official MCSE/MCSA objectives. As you can see from the list of activities performed by MCSE/MCSAs, you will also need a strong set of management skills. The Laudon MCSE/MCSA Certification Series emphasizes management skills along with networking skills. As you advance in your career, you will be expected to participate in and lead teams of networking professionals in their efforts to support the needs of your business firm. You will be expected to describe, plan, administer, and maintain computer networks, and necessarily, to write about networks and give presentations to other business professionals. We make a particular point in this Series of developing managerial skills such as analyzing business requirements, writing reports and making presentations to other members of your business team.

Who Is the Audience for This Book?

The student body for the Laudon MCSE/MCSA Certification Series is very diverse, and the Series is written with that in mind. For all students, regardless of background, the Series is designed to function as *a learning tool first*, and, second, as a compact reference book that can be readily accessed to refresh skills. Generally, there are two types of software books: books aimed at learning and understanding how a specific software tool works, and comprehensive reference books. This series emphasizes learning and explanation and is student-centered.

The Laudon MCSE/MCSA Certification Series is well suited to beginning students. Many students will just be starting out in the networking field, most in colleges and training institutes. The Series introduces these beginning students to the basic concepts of networking, operating systems, and network operating systems. We take special care in the introductory chapters of each book to provide the background skills and understandings necessary to proceed onto more specific MCSE/MCSA skills. We cover many more learning objectives and skills in these introductory lessons than are specifically listed as MCSE/MCSA objectives. Throughout all Lessons we take care to *explain why things are done*, rather than just list the steps necessary to do them. There is a vast difference between understanding how Windows 2000 works and why, versus rote memorization of procedures.

A second group of students will already have some experience working with networking systems and Windows operating systems. This group already has an understanding of the basics, but needs a more systematic and in-depth coverage of MCSE/MCSA skills they lack. The Laudon MCSE/MCSA Certification Series is organized in such a fashion that these more experienced students can quickly discover what they do not know, and can skip over introductory Lessons quickly. Nevertheless, this group will appreciate the emphasis on explanation and clear illustration that we emphasize throughout.

A third group of students will have considerable experience with previous Microsoft operating systems such as Windows NT. These students may be seeking to upgrade their skills and prepare for the Windows 2000 MCSE/MCSA examinations, and they may be learning outside of formal training programs as self-paced learners, or in distance learning programs sponsored by their employers. The Laudon MCSE/MCSA Certification Series is designed to help these students quickly identify the new features of Windows 2000, and to rapidly update their existing skills.

Laudon Series Skills and MCSE/MCSA Objectives

In designing and writing the Laudon Certification Series, we had a choice between organizing the book into chapters composed of MCSE/MCSA domains and objectives, or organizing the book into chapters composed of skills needed to pass the MCSE/MCSA certification examinations (a complete listing of the domains and objectives for the relevant exam will be found inside the front and back covers of the book). We chose to organize the book around skills, beginning with introductory basic skills, and building to more advanced skills. We believe this is a more orderly and effective way to teach students the MCSE/MCSA subject matter and the basic understanding of Windows network operating systems.

Yet we also wanted to make it clear just exactly how the skills related to the published MCSE/MCSA objectives. In the Laudon Series, skills are organized into Lessons. At the beginning of each Lesson, there is an introduction to the set of skills covered in the Lesson, followed by a table that shows how the skills taught in the Lesson support specific MCSE/MCSA objectives. All MCSE/MCSA objectives for each of the examinations are covered. And at the beginning of each skill discussion, the exact MCSE/MCSA objective relating to that skill is identified.

We also recognize that as students approach the certification examinations, they will want learning and preparation materials that are specifically focused on the examinations. Therefore, we have designed the MCSE/MCSA Interactive Series (on CD ROM) to follow the MCSE/MCSA domains and objectives more directly. Students can use these tools to practice answering MCSE/MCSA examination questions, and practice implementing these objectives in a realistic simulated Windows 2000 environment.

What's Different about the Laudon Series—Main Features and Components

The Laudon MCSE/MCSA Certification Series has three distinguishing features that make it the most effective MCSE/MCSA learning tool available today. These three features are: a graphical illustrated 2-page spread approach, a skills-based systematic approach to learning MCSE/MCSA, and an interactive *multi-channel learning pedagogy*.

Graphical illustrated approach. First, the Laudon Series uses a graphical illustrated approach in a convenient *two-page spread format* (see illustration below). This makes learning easy, effective and enjoyable.

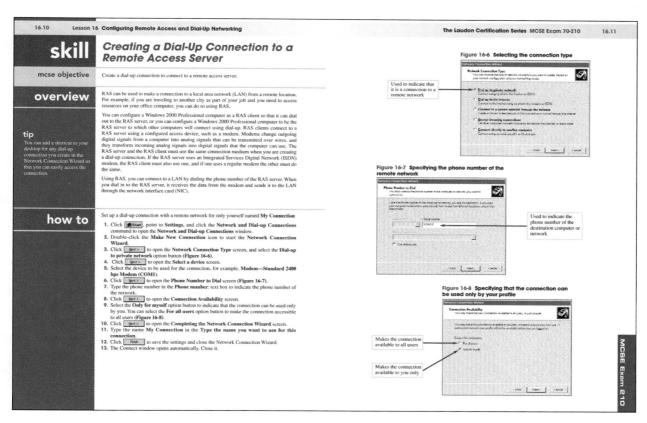

Each two page spread is devoted to a single skill. For each skill, on the left-hand side of the two-page spread there is a *conceptual overview* explaining what the skill is, why it is important, and how it is used. Immediately following the conceptual overview is a series of *How To Steps* showing how to execute the skill. On the right hand side of the two-page spread are screen shots that show you exactly how the screen should look as you execute the skills. The pedagogy is easy to follow and understand.

In addition to these main features, each two page spread contains several *learning aids*:

■ *More:* a brief section that explains more about how to use the skill, alternative ways to perform the skill, and common business applications of the skill.

■ *Tips:* hints and suggestions to follow when performing the skill placed in the left margin.

■ *Caution:* brief sections that tell you about the pitfalls and problems you may encounter when performing the skill placed in the left margin.

At the end of each Lesson students can test their and practice their skills using three end of Lesson features:

■ *Test Yourself:* a multiple choice examination that tests your comprehension and retention of the material in the Lesson.

■ *Projects: On Your Own:* short projects that test your ability to perform tasks and skills in Windows 2000 without detailed step-by-step instructions.

■ *Problem Solving Scenarios:* real-world business scenarios where you are required to analyze or diagnose a networking situation. The case generally requires you to write a report or prepare a presentation.

Skills-based systematic approach. A second distinguishing feature of the Laudon MCSE/MCSA Series is a *skills-based systematic approach* to MCSE/MCSA certification by using five integrated components:

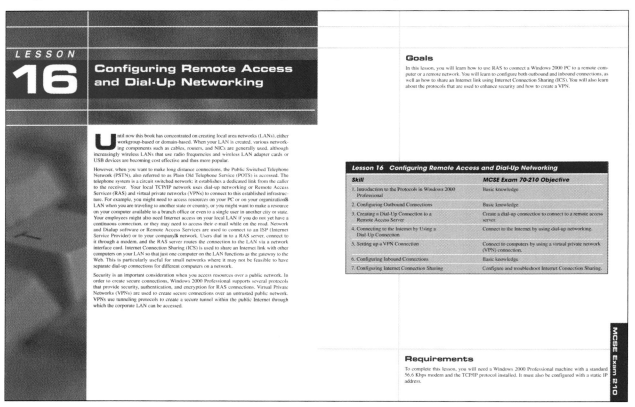

■ Main Book organized by skills.

■ Student Project Book for practicing skills in realistic settings.

■ Examination Guide organized by MCSE/MCSA domains and objectives to practice answering questions representative of questions you are likely to encounter in the actual MCSE/MCSA examination.

■ Interactive multimedia CD ROM organized by MCSE/MCSA domains and objectives that allows students to practice performing MCSE/MCSA objectives in a simulated Windows 2000 environment.

■ Powerful Web site that provides additional questions, projects, and interactive training.

Within each component, the learning is organized by skills beginning with the relatively simple skills and progressing rapidly through the more complex skills. Each skill is carefully explained in a series of steps and conceptual overviews describing why the skill is important.

The CD ROM is especially useful to students who do not have access to a Windows 2000 network on which they can practice skills, and it is useful to all students who want to practice MCSE/MCSA skills efficiently without disturbing an existing network. Together these five components make the Laudon Certification Series an effective learning tool for students, increasing the speed of comprehension and the retention of knowledge.

Interactive media multi-channel learning. A third distinguishing feature of the Laudon MCSE/MCSA Certification Series is *interactive media multi-channel learning*. Multi-channel learning recognizes that students learn in different ways, and the more different channels used to teach students, the greater the comprehension and retention. Using the MCSE/MCSA Interactive Series CD ROM, students can see, hear, read, and actually perform the skills needed in a simulated Windows 2000 environment on the CD ROM. The CD ROM is based directly on materials in the books, and therefore shares the same high quality and reliability. The CD ROM and Web site for the book provide high levels of real interactive learning—not just rote exam questions—but realistic opportunities to interact with the Windows 2000 operating system and to actually practice skills in the software environment without having to install Windows 2000 or build a network.

Supplements Available for This Series:

1. Test Bank

The Test Bank is a Word document distributed with the Instructor's Manual (usually on a CD). It is distributed on the Internet to Instructors only. The purpose of the Test Bank is to provide instructors and students a convenient way for testing comprehension of material presented in the book. The Test Bank contains forty multiple choice questions and ten true/false questions per Lesson. The questions are based on material presented in the book, and are not generic MCSE questions.

2. Instructor's Manual

The Instructor's Manual is a Word document distributed to Instructors only that provides instructional tips, answers to the Test Yourself questions and the Problem Solving Scenarios. The IM also includes an introduction to each Lesson, teaching objectives, and teaching suggestions.

3. PowerPoint Slides

The PowerPoint slides contain images of all the conceptual figures and screenshots in each book. The purpose of the slides is to provide the instructor with a convenient means of reviewing the content of the book in the classroom setting.

4. Interactive Study Guide

The Interactive Study Guide is a Web-based Pearson learning tool that contains ten multiple choice questions per Lesson. The purpose of the Interactive Study Guide is to provide students with a convenient on-line mechanism for self-testing their comprehension of the book material.

About This Book

Exam 70-210 Installing, Configuring, and Administering Microsoft Windows 2000 Professional

This book covers the subject matter of Exam 70-210. The focus in this book is on the Windows 2000 Professional operating system. You will learn about a variety of tools that are used to implement, configure and administer the Windows 2000 operating system such as the Microsoft Management Console, Task Scheduler, Control Panel, and the Registry. You will also learn about network protocols, especially TCP/IP (Transmission Control Protocol/Internet Protocol). You will be introduced to the Domain Name System (DNS) which is the hierarchical name service used on the Internet as well as by Microsoft's network operating system.

You will learn about the following specific knowledge domains:

- Installing Windows 2000 Professional.
- Implementing and Conducting Administration of Resources.
- Implementing, Managing, and Troubleshooting Hardware Devices and Drivers.
- Monitoring and Optimizing System Performance and Reliability.
- Optimizing and Troubleshooting Performance of the Windows 2000 Professional Desktop.
- Implementing, Managing, and Troubleshooting Network Protocols and Services.
- Implementing, Configuring, Managing, and Troubleshooting Local Security Policy.

How This Book Is Organized

This book is organized into a series of Lessons. Each Lesson focuses on a set of skills you will need to learn in order to master the knowledge domains required by the MCSE/MCSA examinations. The skills are organized in a logical progression from basic knowledge skills to more specific skills. Some skills—usually at the beginning of Lessons—give you the background knowledge you will need to understand basic operating system and networking concepts. Most skills, however, give you hands-on experience working with Windows 2000 Professional and Server. You will follow step-by-step instructions to perform tasks in the software.

At the beginning of each Lesson you will find a table that links the skills covered to specific exam objectives. And for each skill presented on a 2-page spread the MCSE/MCSA objective is listed.

The MCSE/MCSA Certification

The MCSE/MCSA certification is one of the most recognized certifications in the Information Technology world. By following a clear cut strategy of preparation you will be able to pass the certification exams. The first thing to remember is that there are no quick and easy routes to certification. No one can guarantee you will receive a certification—no matter what they promise. Real-world MCSE/MCSAs get certified by following a strategy involving self-study, on the job experience, and classroom learning either in colleges or training institutes. Below are answers to frequently asked questions that should help you prepare for the certification exams.

What Is the MCP Program?

The MCP program refers to the Microsoft Certified Professional program that certifies individuals who have passed Microsoft certification examinations. Certification is desirable for both individuals and organizations. For individuals, an MCP certification signifies to employers your expertise and skills in implementing Microsoft software in organizations. For employers, MCP certification makes it easy to identify potential employees with the requisite skills to develop and administer Microsoft tools. In a recent survey reported by Microsoft, 89% of hiring managers said they recommend a Microsoft MCP certification for candidates seeking IT positions.

What Are the MCP Certifications?

There are today seven different MCP certifications. Some certifications emphasize administrative as well as technical skills, while other certifications focus more on technical skills in developing software applications. Below is a listing of the MCP certifications. The Laudon MCSE/MCSA Certification Series focuses on the first two certifications.

- *MCSA:* Microsoft Certified Systems Administrators (MCSAs) administer network and systems environments based on the Microsoft Windows® platforms.
- *MCSE:* Microsoft Certified Systems Engineers (MCSEs) analyze business requirements to design and implement an infrastructure solution based on the Windows platform and Microsoft Server software.
- *MCDBA:* Microsoft Certified Database Administrators (MCDBAs) design, implement, and administer Microsoft SQL Server™ databases.
- *MCT:* Microsoft Certified Trainers (MCTs) are qualified instructors, certified by Microsoft to deliver Microsoft training courses to IT professionals and developers.
- *MCAD:* Microsoft Certified Application Developers (MCADs) use Microsoft technologies to develop and maintain department-level applications, components, Web or desktop clients, or back-end data services.
- *MCSD:* Microsoft Certified Solution Developers (MCSDs) design and develop leading-edge enterprise-class applications with Microsoft development tools, technologies, platforms, and the Windows architecture.
- *Microsoft Office Specialist:* Microsoft Office Specialists (Office Specialists) are globally recognized for demonstrating advanced skills with Microsoft desktop software.
- *MCP:* Microsoft certified Professionals

What Is the Difference Between MCSA and MCSE Certification?

There are two certifications that focus on the implementation and administration of the Microsoft 2000 operating system and networking tools: MCSA and MCSE. The MCSA credential is designed to train IT professionals who are concerned with the management, support, and troubleshooting of existing systems and networks (see diagram below).

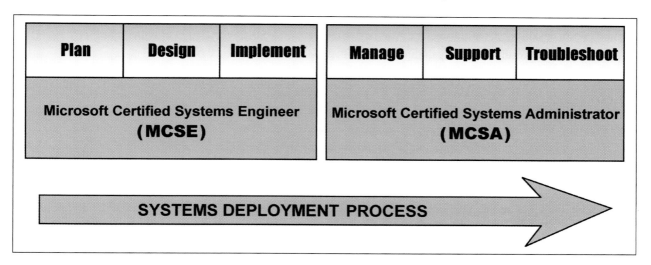

MCSA prepares you for jobs with titles such as systems administrator, network administrator, information systems administrator, network operations analyst, network technician, or technical support specialist. Microsoft recommends that you have six to twelve months experience managing and supporting desktops, servers and networks in an existing network infrastructure.

The MCSE credential is designed to train IT professionals who are concerned with the planning, designing, and implementation of new systems or major upgrades of existing systems. MCSE prepares you for jobs with titles such as systems engineer, network engineer, systems analyst, network analyst, or technical consultant. Microsoft recommends that you have at least one year of experience planning, designing and implementing Microsoft products.

What Does the MCSA Require?

MCSA candidates are required to pass a total of four exams: three core exams and one elective exam. The list below shows examinations that are included in the MCSA track.

Core Exams (3 Exams Required)

(A) Client Operating System (1 Exam Required)

- *Exam 70-210:* Installing, Configuring, and Administering Microsoft Windows 2000 Professional **or**
- *Exam 70-270:* Installing, Configuring, and Administering Microsoft Windows XP Professional

(B) Networking System (2 Exams Required)

- *Exam 70-215:* Installing, Configuring, and Administering Microsoft Windows 2000 Server **and**
- *Exam 70-218:* Managing a Microsoft Windows 2000 Network Environment

Elective Exams (1 Exam Required)

- *Exam 70-028:* Administering Microsoft SQL Server 7.0
- *Exam 70-081:* Implementing and Supporting Microsoft Exchange Server 5.5
- *Exam 70-086:* Implementing and Supporting Microsoft Systems Management Server 2.0
- *Exam 70-088:* Implementing and Supporting Microsoft Proxy Server 2.0
- *Exam 70-214:* Implementing and Administering Security in a Microsoft Windows 2000 Network
- *Exam 70-216:* Implementing and Administering a Microsoft Windows 2000 Network Infrastructure
- *Exam 70-224:* Installing, Configuring, and Administering Microsoft Exchange 2000 Server
- *Exam 70-227:* Installing, Configuring, and Administering Microsoft Internet Security and Acceleration (ISA) Server 2000, Enterprise Edition
- *Exam 70-228:* Installing, Configuring, and Administering Microsoft SQL Server 2000 Enterprise Edition
- *Exam 70-244:* Supporting and Maintaining a Microsoft Windows NT Server 4.0 Network

As an alternative to the electives listed above, you may substitute the following third-party certification combinations for an MCSA elective:

CompTIA Exams: *CompTIA A+* and *CompTIA Network+*
                      CompTIA A+ and *CompServer+*

What Is the MCSE Curriculum?

MCSE candidates are required to pass a total of seven exams: five core exams and two elective exams. The list below shows the examinations that are included in the MCSA track.

Core Exams (5 Exams Required)

(A) Client Operating System (1 exam required)

- *Exam 70-210:* Installing, Configuring, and Administering Microsoft Windows 2000 Professional
  or
- *Exam 70-270:* Installing, Configuring, and Administering Microsoft Windows XP Professional

(B) Networking System (3 Exams Required)

- *Exam 70-215:* Installing, Configuring, and Administering Microsoft Windows 2000 Server
- *Exam 70-216:* Implementing and Administering a Microsoft Windows 2000 Network Infrastructure

- *Exam 70-217:* Implementing and Administering a Microsoft Windows 2000 Directory Services Infrastructure

(C) Design (1 Exam Required)

- *Exam 70-219:* Designing a Microsoft Windows 2000 Directory Services Infrastructure
- *Exam 70-220:* Designing Security for a Microsoft Windows 2000 Network
- *Exam 70-221:* Designing a Microsoft Windows 2000 Network Infrastructure
- *Exam 70-226:* Designing Highly Available Web Solutions with Microsoft Windows 2000 Server Technologies

Elective Exams (2 Exams Required)

- *Exam 70-019:* Designing and Implementing Data Warehouses with Microsoft SQL Server™ 7.0
- *Exam 70-028:* Administering Microsoft SQL Server 7.0
- *Exam 70-029:* Designing and Implementing Databases with Microsoft SQL Server 7.0
- *Exam 70-056:* Implementing and Supporting Web Sites Using Microsoft Site Server 3.0
- *Exam 70-080:* Implementing and Supporting Microsoft Internet Explorer 5.0 by Using the Microsoft Internet Explorer Administration Kit
- *Exam 70-081:* Implementing and Supporting Microsoft Exchange Server 5.5
- *Exam 70-085:* Implementing and Supporting Microsoft SNA Server 4.0
- *Exam 70-086:* Implementing and Supporting Microsoft Systems Management Server 2.0
- *Exam 70-088:* Implementing and Supporting Microsoft Proxy Server 2.0
- *Exam 70-214:* Implementing and Administering Security in a Microsoft Windows 2000 Network
- *Exam 70-218:* Managing a Microsoft Windows 2000 Network Environment
- *Exam 70-219:* Designing a Microsoft Windows 2000 Directory Services Infrastructure
- *Exam 70-220:* Designing Security for a Microsoft Windows 2000 Network
- *Exam 70-221:* Designing a Microsoft Windows 2000 Network Infrastructure
- *Exam 70-222:* Migrating from Microsoft Windows NT 4.0 to Microsoft Windows 2000
- *Exam 70-223:* Installing, Configuring, and Administering Microsoft Clustering Services by Using Microsoft Windows 2000 Advanced Server
- *Exam 70-224:* Installing, Configuring, and Administering Microsoft Exchange 2000 Server
- *Exam 70-225:* Designing and Deploying a Messaging Infrastructure with Microsoft Exchange 2000 Server
- *Exam 70-226:* Designing Highly Available Web Solutions with Microsoft Windows 2000 Server Technologies
- *Exam 70-227:* Installing, Configuring, and Administering Microsoft Internet Security and Acceleration (ISA) Server 2000 Enterprise Edition
- *Exam 70-228:* Installing, Configuring, and Administering Microsoft SQL Server 2000 Enterprise Edition
- *Exam 70-229:* Designing and Implementing Databases with Microsoft SQL Server 2000 Enterprise Edition
- *Exam 70-230:* Designing and Implementing Solutions with Microsoft BizTalk® Server 2000 Enterprise Edition
- *Exam 70-232:* Implementing and Maintaining Highly Available Web Solutions with Microsoft Windows 2000 Server Technologies and Microsoft Application Center 2000
- *Exam 70-234:* Designing and Implementing Solutions with Microsoft Commerce Server 2000
- *Exam 70-244:* Supporting and Maintaining a Microsoft Windows NT Server 4.0 Network

What About Windows XP and Windows 2003 Server?

Windows XP and Windows Server 2003 are the latest releases of Microsoft's family of operating systems. In early 2003 Microsoft began releasing the full requirements for the MCSE and MCSA examinations on Microsoft Windows Server 2003. The MCP program will offer an upgrade path consisting of one or two exams that will enable current MCSEs and MCSAs on Windows 2000 to update their respective certification to the Windows Server 2003 track. You should check with the Microsoft Certification Program official Web site at **http://www.microsoft.com/traincert/mcp/default.asp** for the latest information. Microsoft recommends that until the software and examination requirements are released, individuals should continue to pursue training and certification in Windows 2000 because the skills acquired for Windows 2000 are highly relevant to, and provide a solid foundation for, Windows 2003 Server. To retain certification, MCSEs and MCSAs on Windows 2000 will *not* be required to pass Windows 2003 Server exams. If you are training on a Windows 2000 network for Windows 2000 certifications, you should continue to do so.

Do You Need to Pursue Certification to Benefit from This Book?

No. The Laudon MCSE/MCSA Certification Series is designed to prepare you for the workplace by providing you with networking knowledge and skills regardless of certification programs. While it is desirable to obtain a certification, you can certainly benefit greatly by just reading these books, practicing your skills in the simulated Windows 2000 environment found on the MCSE/MCSA Interactive Series CD ROM, and using the online interactive study guide.

What Kinds of Questions Are on the Exam?

The MCSE/MCSA exams typically involve a variety of question formats.

(a) Select-and-Place Exam Items (Drag and Drop)

A select-and-place exam item asks candidates to understand a scenario, and assemble a solution graphically on screen by picking up screen objects and moving them to their appropriate location on screen to assemble the solution. For instance, you might be asked to place routers, clients, and servers on a network and illustrate how they would be connected to the Internet. This type of exam item can measure architectural, design, troubleshooting, and component recognition skills more accurately than traditional exam items can because the solution—a graphical diagram—is presented in a form that is familiar to the computer professional.

(b) Case Study-Based Multiple Choice Exam Items

The candidate is presented with a scenario based on typical Windows installations and then is asked to answer one or several multiple choice questions. To make the questions more challenging several answers may be correct and you will be asked to choose all that are correct. The Laudon Certification Series Test Yourself questions at the end of each Lesson give you experience with these kinds of questions.

(c) Simulations

Simulations test your ability to perform tasks in a simulated Windows 2000 environment. A simulation imitates the functionality and interface of Windows 2000. The simulation usually involves a scenario and you will be asked to perform several tasks in the simulated environment, including working with dialog boxes and entering information. The Laudon Certification Series Interactive Media CD-ROM gives you experience working in a simulated Windows 2000 environment.

(d) Computer Adaptive Testing

A computer adaptive test (CAT) attempts to adapt the level of question difficulty to the knowledge of each individual examinee. An adaptive exam starts with several easy questions. If you get these right, more difficult questions are pitched. If you fail a question, the next questions will be easier. Eventually the test will discover how much you know and what you can accomplish in a Windows 2000 environment.

You can find out more about the exam questions and take sample exams at the Microsoft Web site:
http://www.microsoft.com/ traincert/mcp/default.asp.

How Long is the Exam?

Exams have fifty to seventy questions and last anywhere from 60 minutes to 240 minutes. The great variance in duration is due to variation in the requirements for specific exams (some exams have many more requirements than others), and because the adaptive exams take much less time than traditional exams. When you register for an exam, you will be told how much time you should expect to spend at the testing center. In some cases, the exams include timed sections that can help for apportioning your time.

What Is the Testing Experience Like?

You are required to bring two forms of identification that include your signature, including one photo ID (such as a driver's license or company security ID). You will also be required to sign a non-disclosure agreement that obligates you not to share the contents of the exam questions with others, and you will be asked to complete a survey. The rules and procedures of the exam will be explained to you by administrators. You will be introduced to the testing equipment and you may take an exam tutorial intended to familiarize you with the testing equipment. This is a good idea. You will not be allowed to communicate with other examinees or with outsiders during the exam. You should definitely turn off your cell phone when taking the exam.

How Can You Best Prepare for the Exams?

Prepare for each exam by reading this book, and then practicing your skills in a simulated environment on the CD ROM that accompanies this series. If you do not have a real network to practice on, and if you do not build a small network, the next best thing is to work with the CD ROM. Alternatively, it is very helpful to build a small Windows 2000 network with a couple of unused computers. You will also require experience with a real-world Windows 2000 network. An MCSE/MCSA candidate should at a minimum have at least one year of experience implementing and administering a network operating system in environments with the following characteristics: a minimum of 200 users, five supported physical locations, typical network services and applications including file and print, database, messaging, proxy server or firewall, dial-in server, desktop management, and Web hosting, and connectivity needs, including connecting individual offices and users at remote locations to the corporate network and connecting corporate networks to the Internet.

In addition, an MCSE candidate should have at least one year of experience in the following areas: implementing and administering a desktop operating system and designing a network infrastructure.

Where Can You Take the Exams?

All MCP exams are administered by Prometric and VUE. To take exams at a Prometric testing center call Prometric at (800) 755-EXAM (755-3926). Outside the United States and Canada, contact your local Prometric Registration Center. To register online with Prometric, visit the *Prometric Web site, www.prometric.com*. Register by telephone at any VUE location worldwide by calling the registration center nearest you. To register online with VUE, visit the *VUE Web site, www.vue.com*.

How Much Does It Cost to Take the Exams?

In the United States exams cost $125 US per exam as of January, 2002. Certification exam prices are subject to change. In some countries/regions, additional taxes may apply. Contact your test registration center for exact pricing.

Can You Take the Exam More Than Once?

Yes. You may retake an exam if you do not pass at anytime. But if you do not pass the second time, you must wait fourteen days. A 14-day waiting period will be imposed for all subsequent exam retakes. If you have passed an exam, you cannot take it again.

Where Can I Get More Information about the Exams?

Microsoft Web sites are a good place to start:

MCP Program (general): **http://www.microsoft.com/traincert/mcp/default.asp**

MCSE Certification: **http://www.microsoft.com/traincert/mcp/mcsa/default.asp**

MCSA Certification: **http://www.microsoft.com/traincert/mcp/MCSE/MCSA/default.asp**

There are literally thousands of other Web sites with helpful information that you can identify using any Web search engine. Many commercial sites will promise instant success, and some even guarantee you will pass the exams. Be a discriminating consumer. If it was that easy to become an MCP professional the certification would be meaningless.

Acknowledgments

A great many people have contributed to the Laudon MCSE/MCSA Certification Series. We want to thank Steven Elliot, our editor at Prentice Hall, for his enthusiastic appreciation of the project, his personal support for the Azimuth team, and his deep commitment to the goal of creating a powerful, accurate, and enjoyable learning tool for students. We also want to thank David Alexander of Prentice Hall for his interim leadership and advice as the project developed at Prentice Hall, and Jerome Grant for supporting the development of high-quality certification training books and CDs for colleges and universities worldwide. Finally, we want to thank Susan Hartman Sullivan of Addison Wesley for believing in this project at an early stage and for encouraging us to fulfill our dreams.

The Azimuth Interactive MCSE/MCSA team is a dedicated group of technical experts, computer scientists, networking specialists, and writers with literally decades of experience in computer networking, information technology and systems, and computer technology. We want to thank the members of the team:

Kenneth C. Laudon is the Series Designer. He is Professor of Information Systems at New York University's Stern School of Business. He has written twelve books on information systems and technologies, e-commerce, and management information systems. He has designed, installed, and fixed computer networks since 1982.

Carol G. Traver is the Senior Series Editor. She is General Counsel and Vice President of Business Development at Azimuth Interactive, Inc. A graduate of Yale Law School, she has co-authored several best-selling books on information technology and e-commerce.

Kenneth Rosenblatt is a Senior Author for the Series. He is an experienced technical writer and editor who has co-authored or contributed to over two dozen books on comptuer and software instruction. In addition, Ken has over five years experience in designing, implementing, and managing Microsoft operating systems and networks.

Robin L. Pickering is a Senior Author for the Series. She is an experienced technical writer and editor who has co-authored or contributed to over a dozen books on computers and software instruction. Robin has extensive experience as a network administrator and consultant for a number of small to medium-sized firms.

Russell Polo is the Technical Advisor for the Series. He holds degrees in computer science and electrical engineering. He has designed, implemented, and managed Microsoft, UNIX, and Novell networks in a number of business firms since 1995. He currently is the Network Administrator at Azimuth Interactive.

David Langley is an Editor for the Series. David is an experienced technical writer and editor who has co-authored or contributed to over ten books on computers and software instruction. In addition, he has over fifteen years experience as a college professor, five of those in computer software training.

Kevin Jensen is a Technical Consultant and Editor for the Series. He is a systems consultant, trainer, administrator, and independent technical editor. Kevin's industry certifications are MCSE on Windows 2000, Microsoft Certified Trainer (MCT), Certified Novell Engineer (CNE), Certified Netware Instructor (CNI), and Certified Technical Trainer (CTT). Kevin has specialized in enterprise network management, design, and interoperability between different network operating systems.

Howard Kunkel is a Technical Consultant and Editor for the Series. His industry certifications include MCSE on Windows 2000, and MCP on Exchange Server 5.5 and SQL 7.0 Administration. He also is certified for IBM e-servers xSeries. His other industry certifications are CompTIA A+, Network+, and Certified Document Imaging Architect (CDIA). His industry experience includes being a Network Field Engineer for a Fortune 500 company for three years. Howard also teaches these subjects at a local community college.

Mark Maxwell is a Technical Consultant to and Editor for the Series. He has over fifteen years of industry experience in distributed network environments including TCP/IP, fault tolerant NFS file service, Kerberos, Wide Area networks, and Virtual Private Networks. In addition, Mark has published articles on network design, upgrades, and security.

Quality Assurance

The Laudon MCSE/MCSA Certification Series contains literally thousands of software instructions for working with Windows 2000 products. We have taken special steps to ensure the accuracy of the statements in this series. The books and CDs are initially written by teams composed of Azimuth Interactive Inc. MCSE/MCSA professionals and writers working directly with the software as they write. Each team then collectively walks through the software instructions and screen shots to ensure accuracy. The resulting manuscripts are then thoroughly tested by an independent quality assurance team of MCSE/MCSA professionals who also perform the software instructions and check to ensure the screen shots and conceptual graphics are correct. The result is a very accurate and comprehensive learning environment for understanding Windows 2000 products.

We would like to thank the members of the Quality Assurance Team for their critical feedback and unstinting efforts to make sure we got it right. The members of the team are:

Dan DiNicolo is an independent tech editor, technical trainer, consultant, and author. Dan has worked on a variety of training, consulting, and authoring projects for enterprise-level clients worldwide. Dan's professional certifications include Microsoft Certified Systems Engineer (MCSE), Microsoft Certified Trainer (MCT), Cisco Certified Networking Associate (CCNA), and Cisco Certified Design Associate (CCDA). His main areas of expertise include network administration, network security, enterprise internetworking, and directory services design.

Mike Aubert is an experienced technical editor and technical author. Mike has also worked as an independent consultant and engineer on a variety of enterprise-level projects for clients in the United States. Mike's professional certifications include Microsoft Certified Systems Engineer (MCSE), Microsoft Certified Database Administrator (MCDBA), Microsoft Certified Solution Developer (MCSD), as well as MCSA and MCAD. His main areas of expertise include network engineering and security, directory services design, database administration, and solution architectures, including Microsoft.NET.

Other Books in the Laudon MCSE/MCSA Certification Series

Installing, Configuring, and Administering Microsoft® Windows® 2000 Server Exam 70-215
ISBN 0-13-142211-1

Implementing and Administering a Microsoft® Windows® 2000 Network Infrastructure Exam 70-216
ISBN 0-13-142210-3

Implementing and Administering a Microsoft® Windows® 2000 Directory Services
Infrastructure 70-217   ISBN 0-13-142208-1

Managing a Microsoft® Windows® 2000 Network Environment Exam 70-218

Designing Security for a Microsoft® Windows® 2000 Network Exam 70-220

Installing, Configuring, and Administering Microsoft® Windows® XP Professional Exam 70-270

Installing, Configuring, and Administering Microsoft® Windows® 2003 Server Exam 70-275

1

Introducing Windows 2000 Professional

Welcome to Windows 2000, Microsoft's multipurpose family of operating systems. Windows 2000 is used throughout the world by large and small corporations to build and administer corporate networks that can contain thousands of client user workstations. Windows 2000 and UNIX are the major corporate operating systems in use today.

Windows 2000 builds on Microsoft's earlier Windows operating system, combining many of the benefits of Windows 98 and Windows NT 4.0. The Windows 9.x operating systems concentrated on compatibility with older devices and the ability to perform well on systems without much memory. With Windows 2000, Microsoft decided to sacrifice these features in order to improve security and reliability. New features in Windows 2000 emphasize tighter security and strong central administrative controls for corporate networks, as well as improvements to the user interface. The most significant new feature is Active Directory. All of the information about how a server-based network is structured and organized is stored in Active Directory. Users access it to identify and locate resources on a network, such as users and groups, printers and computers. Active Directory serves as a central repository for network objects and as a central administrative site so that network administrators do not have to individually manage multiple servers.

Windows 2000 features, such as the customized Start menu, make the operating system more user-friendly. Dialog boxes have been updated, Wizards added, and many AutoComplete fields and most recently used lists have been added as a time-saving convenience for users. Enhanced hardware support including improved power management and Plug and Play capabilities, and support for a number of new devices and buses has also been included. An improved file management system is another key feature of Windows 2000. In terms of scalability, Windows 2000 supports small workgroups as well as larger domain-based networks with thousands of clients. In this way, Windows 2000 can fulfill the networking needs of both small and large corporations.

Goals

In this lesson, you will learn about the various versions of the Windows 2000 operating systems, as well as the key features of Windows 2000 Professional. You will also learn about both the workgroup and the domain networking models.

Lesson 1   Introducing Windows 2000 Professional

Skill	Exam 70-210 Objective
1. Introducing the Windows 2000 Family of Operating Systems	Basic knowledge
2. Introducing Windows 2000 Features and Enhancements	Basic knowledge
3. Identifying the Range of Supported Hardware	Basic knowledge
4. Introducing Windows 2000 Enhanced File Management Features	Basic knowledge
5. Introducing Windows 2000 Security Features	Basic knowledge
6. Introducing Workgroups and Domains	Basic knowledge

Requirements

There are no special requirements for this lesson.

skill 1

Introducing the Windows 2000 Family of Operating Systems

exam objective

Basic knowledge

overview

Windows 2000 is a multipurpose operating system that supports client/server networks (called domain-based networks), as well as peer-to-peer or workgroup networks. Windows 2000 is actually a family of closely integrated products that make up the Windows 2000 environment (**Figure 1-1**).

◆ **Windows 2000 Professional** is the primary Microsoft desktop operating system. It is used by businesses and organizations both large and small. Windows 2000 Professional combines the most useful and powerful features of Windows 98 with the best aspects of the Windows NT 4.0 Workstation operating system. It provides a user-friendly interface, a secure network-client environment, enhanced Plug and Play capabilities, improved power management features, and support for a broad range of hardware devices. Users can easily manage their system's hardware and software requirements and conserve power when they are not working. All of these features make Windows 2000 Professional a good fit for the corporate desktop. Using only Windows 2000 Professional, small businesses can create a workgroup or peer-to-peer network in which workstations can communicate with one another and share resources. Windows 2000 Professional can be used to its fullest potential when connecting to and interacting with a centralized domain-based Windows 2000 network. MCSE Exam 70-210 and this book focus on this operating system.

◆ **Windows 2000 Server** is an operating system for client/server networks. It can be used for Web servers as well as for file, print, and application servers. It has all of the features of Windows 2000 Professional along with a complete set of services based on Active Directory (AD). Active Directory services involve the management of users, groups, security services, and network resources. Windows 2000 Server provides a wide range of administrative features along with improved security and directory services. Centralized server-based networks that combine Windows 2000 Professional client computers and Windows 2000 Servers allow network administrators to perform software updates and configure multiple workstations from a single location. Unlike its Windows 9.x predecessors, Windows 2000 Professional can take advantage of the automated network connectivity, desktop configuration, and software installation features of Windows 2000 Server that make it simple for users to set up their own workstations without any help from technical staff. Microsoft claims that total cost of ownership (TCO) for a network can be dramatically reduced when the centralized services available in Windows 2000 Server are used in conjunction with Windows 2000 Professional clients. Network administrators on a Windows 2000 network can more easily manage network resources such as file and print servers, and shared folders, files, and printers using Active Directory services. In addition to its many security features which provide for the protection of files and folders and the auditing of file, folder, and network access, Windows 2000 Server can handle up to 15,000 user connections and supports the use of extremely large databases which can have more than 5000 simultaneous users.

◆ **Windows 2000 Advanced Server** is a more powerful version of Windows 2000 Server that enables the use of multiple processors in large sophisticated corporate networks. Windows 2000 Advanced Server has the improved scalability required for global corporations. With enhanced features for both Network Operating Systems (NOS) and the Internet, it can be used to host high-end network applications.

◆ **Windows 2000 Datacenter Server** has even greater power and functionality than Windows 2000 Advanced Server. This product is ideal for data warehousing on a large scale. It is also used for econometric analysis and simulation-based applications in science and engineering. Datacenter Server can support up to 32 processors and 64 GB of RAM.

tip

Microsoft recommends that workgroup networks contain fewer than 10 computers.

Figure 1-1 Products in the Window 2000 environment

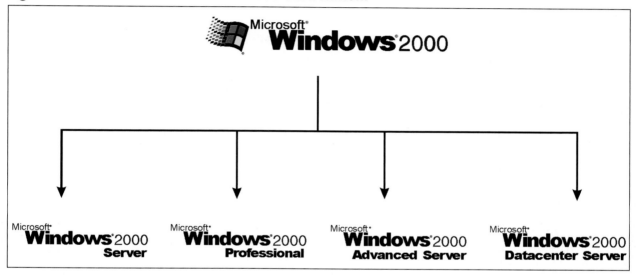

skill 2

Introducing Windows 2000 Features and Enhancements

exam objective   Basic knowledge

overview

The features and enhancements in the Windows 2000 family of products (**Figure 1-2**) include:

◆ **Reduced total cost of ownership:** Microsoft claims that Windows 2000 lowers the total cost of ownership (sometimes referred to as TCO) of corporate networks by using technologies that enable automatic installation and upgrading of the operating system and applications. Automation reduces the burden for technical support personnel. Windows 2000's familiar interface, interactive help, and Wizards also enable users to successfully tackle many support tasks themselves, reducing the need for professional network technicians.

◆ **Security:** The Windows 2000 operating systems incorporate a variety of enhanced security features, in particular, the Kerberos authentication protocol (**Figure 1-3**). Files and folders can also now be encrypted using the Encrypting File System (EFS). The TCP/IP protocol, which is the core protocol for the Internet, is also improved, and communications can be made more secure using Internet Protocol Security (IPSec) and Layer 2 Tunneling Protocol (L2TP). Windows 2000 supports multiple hardware-based authentication systems such as smart cards. There are many options for the stronger authentication of users before they can access resources or data from a computer or the network. Windows 2000 also has the ability to perform system audits and impose secure access to files, directories, printers, and other resources.

◆ **Multiprocessing, multitasking, and multithreading:** The Windows 2000 operating systems support multiprocessing, multitasking, and multithreading.

- *Symmetric multiprocessing (SMP)* enables a system to use any available processor. This contributes to the even distribution of system load and application needs across available processors. In SMP, each central processing unit (CPU) is equal, they share common memory and disk input/output resources, and process threads can be scheduled on any processor. This is in contrast to asymmetric multiprocessing in which processors are specialized, for example, for network processes, input/output processes, or graphics/video. In asymmetric multiprocessing, one CPU does the work for the system, while the other CPUs service user requests. Windows 2000 Professional can support up to two CPUs, Windows 2000 Server up to four CPUs, Windows 2000 Advanced Server up to eight CPUs, and Windows 2000 Datacenter up to 32 CPUs. When several CPUs are available, a number of different applications can run concurrently on different processors. Priority levels for each processor can be set so that more important programs will be allocated more CPU capacity.

- Windows 2000 operating systems also support *preemptive multitasking* for system processes and programs. In preemptive multitasking, the computer runs multiple programs at the same time by allocating CPU time among the various applications. It can preempt or block an application that is currently running a process in order to run another process from a different application. The operating system essentially creates a timetable for how long one task in a multithreaded program, or a complete single-threaded program, will be allowed to access the CPU. Tasks can be preempted when they have taken up too much CPU time or when a more important application sends a request for attention. Preemptive multitasking is used by Windows 9.x and NT, as well as Windows 2000.

- *Multithreading*, in which a single application creates several execution threads that can carry on simultaneously, is also supported. For example, you can perform a spell check in Microsoft Word at the same time that the program executes a background process such as repagination. The term "threads" refers to units of code that the operating system can schedule to run. When multiple execution threads can run at the same time and the computer is also configured for SMP, threads can be executed simultaneously on different CPUs, greatly improving the

Figure 1-2 Windows 2000 features and enhancements

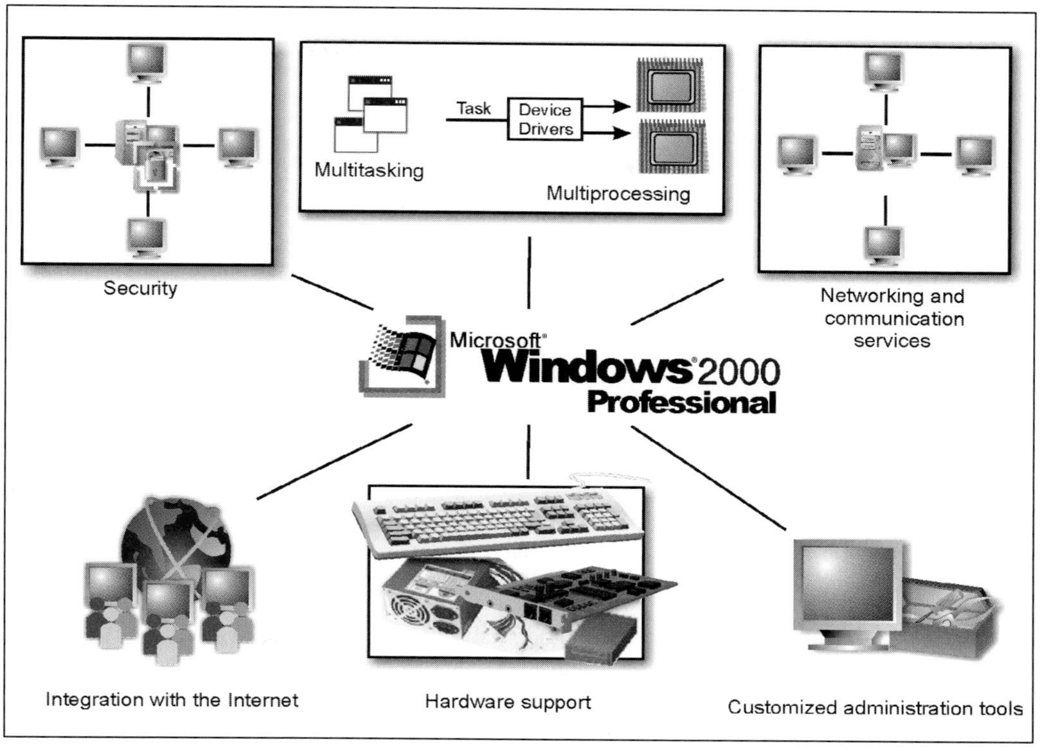

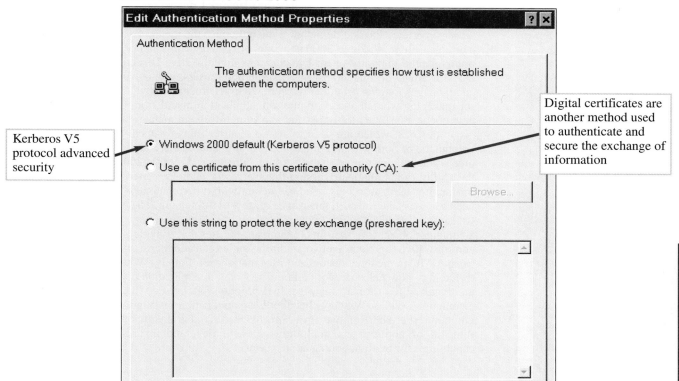

Figure 1-3 The Kerberos V5 protocol, the default authentication method for Windows 2000

Kerberos V5 protocol advanced security

Digital certificates are another method used to authenticate and secure the exchange of information

skill 2

Introducing Windows 2000 Features and Enhancements (cont'd)

exam objective

Basic knowledge

overview

speed of application processes and enabling both multiple foreground and multiple background tasks to run concurrently.

◆ **Connectivity:** Windows 2000 operating systems support a variety of network protocols, such as TCP/IP (Transmission Control Protocol/Internet Protocol), NetBEUI (NetBIOS Enhanced User Interface), DLC (Data Link Control), and AppleTalk, as well as providing connectivity with Novell NetWare and UNIX systems **(Figure 1-4)**. Windows 2000 operating systems also support dial-up networking.

◆ **Hardware support:** Windows 2000 operating systems support Plug and Play, a set of specifications developed by Intel that allows a computer to automatically detect and configure a hardware device and install the appropriate device drivers. Windows 2000 operating systems also support the Universal Serial Bus (USB) standard, which allows a single port to support up to 127 peripheral devices and enables you to connect and disconnect devices without shutting down or restarting your computer **(Figure 1-5)**. While earlier versions of Windows such as Windows 98 supported Plug and Play, it is much expanded in Windows 2000. The IEEE 1394 high-performance serial bus, also known as FireWire, is also supported, allowing VCRs and camcorders to be connected to a Windows 2000 PC. DVDs, digital scanners, and cameras are also supported. The Control Panel includes utilities for configuring scanners and cameras. Furthermore, additional monitors can be added to expand the desktop as long as either AGP (Accelerated Graphics Port) or PCI (Peripheral Component Interconnect) adapters are used.

◆ **Greater Ease of Use:** Windows 2000 features an enhanced user interface that makes the operating system easier to use and control. Ease of use features include:
  - A Start menu that enables you to display the most frequently accessed applications while hiding the less frequently used applications.
  - More user-friendly dialog boxes, many of which automatically complete fields for you as you are entering data (Auto Complete).
  - Several new Wizards, notably the Network Connection Wizard **(Figure 1-6)**.
  - Personalized menus that hide commands that have not been recently used until you click the double-arrow at the bottom of the menu.

◆ **Manageability:** Windows 2000 networks offer many conveniences for network administrators, beginning with Active Directory. As noted, **Active Directory** is the central database for a network that stores information about users, groups, and access permissions, and manages logging on to the network. Active Directory provides a centralized method for managing workstation configuration, application installation, network resources, and network access. Other tools that add to a straightforward managerial environment include group policies, which are used to set up security rules for local workstations, network computers, or both. Group policies that are implemented at the network level are configured in the administrative tools in Active Directory. Windows 2000 computers also have the ability to automatically assign themselves IP addresses even if a network server is offline. For users who only need to interact with other computers on a LAN and do not need to access the Internet, this can be quite a useful feature. The Microsoft Management Console, or MMC also adds to the manageability of the operating system. MMC is simply a container object for "snap-ins," which are utilities that provide an interface and a set of administrative functions. Network administrators can add the snap-ins they use most often to an MMC to create a customized managerial tool. Finally, Windows Installer Package technology now helps network administrators with application deployment by providing an organized file format (.msi) that lists program functions so that they can manage user installation options. Windows Installer is an application installation technology that now augments the Add/Remove Programs Wizard. It also ensures the complete and safe removal of applications, including registry files, and is useful for its diagnostic capabilities for malfunctioning applications.

Figure 1-4 Network protocols for connectivity with non-Microsoft networks

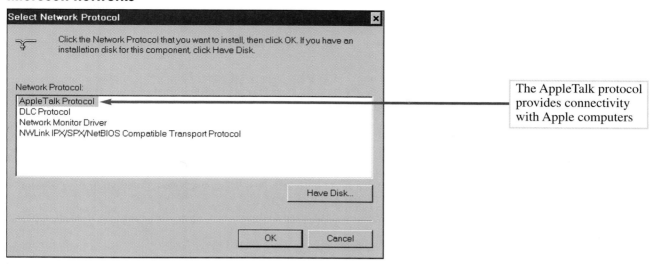

The AppleTalk protocol provides connectivity with Apple computers

Figure 1-5 USB controllers in the Device Manager

Windows 2000 supports both USB and Plug and Play

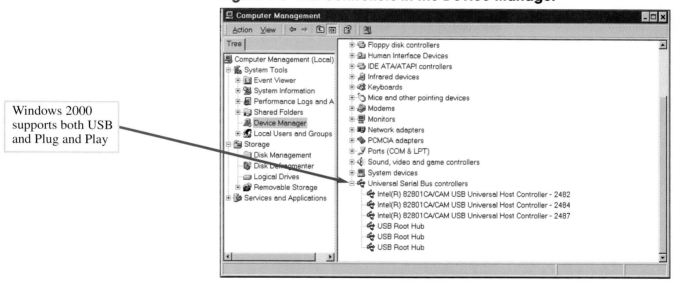

Figure 1-6 The Network Connection Wizard

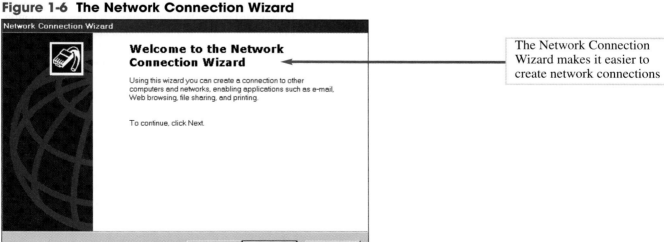

The Network Connection Wizard makes it easier to create network connections

skill 3

Identifying the Range of Supported Hardware

exam objective

Basic knowledge

overview

While Windows 2000 Professional supports thousands of hardware devices, including some of the latest technologies such as infrared devices, digital cameras and scanners users cannot assume that a device supported by earlier versions of Windows will necessarily work correctly. Every hardware device on a system should be systematically checked against the **Hardware Compatibility List (HCL)** to determine whether it will work with Windows 2000 Professional. You can find the HCL on the Windows 2000 CD-ROM, or for the most recent version go to the following Web address: **www.microsoft.com/Windows2000/server/howtobuy/upgrading/compat/default.asp**.

The hardware support in Windows 2000 Professional has been improved to include several new or enhanced features **(Figure 1-7)**.

◆ **Add/Remove Hardware Wizard:** You use the **Add/Remove Hardware Wizard** to add, delete, upgrade, and troubleshoot computer peripherals **(Figure 1-8)**. You can also stop the operation of devices or remove devices that are malfunctioning.

◆ **Win32 Driver Model (WDM)**: WDM is a common model for device drivers supported across the Windows 98 and Windows 2000 operating systems platforms. WDM supplies a cohesive architecture for device drivers that provides for cross-platform power management and supports Plug and Play capabilities. WDM was designed to function as a bridge between Windows 98 and Windows 2000 because drivers for certain components in Windows NT 4.0 and Windows 2000 are not compatible with Windows 98.

◆ **Plug and Play support:** Plug and Play gives Windows 2000 Professional the capability to configure newly connected hardware automatically and dynamically, to load the appropriate drivers, to register device notification events, and to use removable and changeable devices.

◆ **Power Options:** You can use the Power Options program in the Control Panel window to reduce the power consumption of the monitor and hard disks with additional settings for the entire system. You do this by choosing a power scheme, which is a collection of settings that manages the power usage of a computer. You can create your own power schemes or use the ones provided **(Figure 1-9)**. Windows 2000 Professional supports two power management standards, the older standard, APM (Advanced Power Management), which is found on pre-1999 computers that were equipped with a power management system, and the newer standard, ACPI (Advanced Configuration and Power Interface), which allows users to control power management settings more precisely. Improved power management using the ACPI standard makes Windows 2000 Professional a practical operating system for notebook computers, more so than its predecessor Windows NT. Power Management options include:

  • **Hibernation:** You can use the **Hibernation** option to save the contents of your computer's memory before shutting down your system. When you restart your system, your files and documents will be open on your desktop just as you left them.

  • **Standby:** You can use the **Standby** option to shut off power to hardware components that are not in use such as the monitor or hard drive, while maintaining power to the computer's memory so that your work is not lost.

Figure 1-7 New Windows 2000 hardware support features

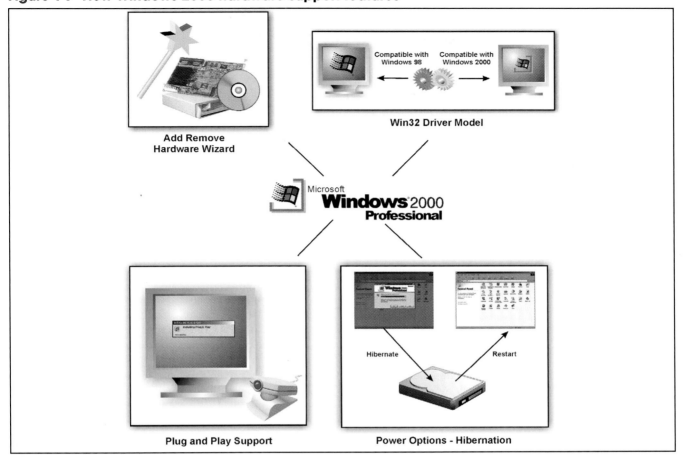

Figure 1-8 Using the Add/Remove Hardware Wizard to troubleshoot a device

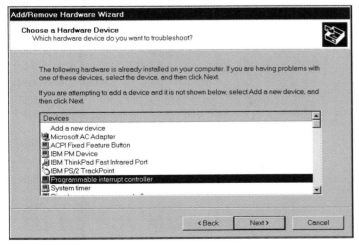

Figure 1-9 Creating a power scheme for a laptop computer

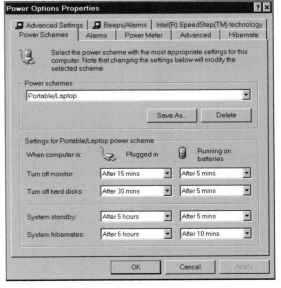

skill 4

Introducing Windows 2000 File Management Features

exam objective

Basic knowledge

overview

Windows 2000 Professional offers a number of facilities (**Figure 1-10**) that make it easier to manage your files. File management features include:

◆ **The NTFS file system:** An advanced file system designed for use specifically within the Windows NT and Windows 2000 operating systems. It supports file system recovery, large storage media, long file names, file encryption, and disk quotas.

◆ **POSIX (Portable Operating System Interface for UNIX) subsystem:** POSIX is a standard set by the Institute of Electrical and Electronics Engineers (IEEE). This standard defines a set of operating-system services. Programs that adhere to the POSIX standard can easily be transported from one system to another.

◆ **The FAT32 file system:** A derivative of the File Allocation Table (FAT) file system. The **File Allocation Table** is a list maintained by the operating system that keeps track of the status of various segments of disk space used for file storage. FAT32 supports smaller cluster sizes than FAT, which results in more efficient space allocation on FAT32 drives. FAT32 is compatible with all Windows operating systems since the second version of Windows 95. To ensure compatibility with the first release of Windows 95 and DOS, Windows 2000 Professional also supports the FAT file system.

◆ **Disk Defragmenter utility:** A tool to help improve disk performance on heavily used systems (**Figure 1-11**). Defragmentation is the process of rewriting various parts of a file to contiguous sectors on a hard disk to increase the speed of file access and retrieval. The **disk defragmenter utility** optimizes stored data and unused space to help ensure that all related components of files and programs are placed in contiguous sectors of the hard disk. This means the processor does not have to spend excess time locating them during execution.

◆ **Backup utility:** Windows 2000 Professional provides a **Backup utility** to prevent the accidental loss of data due to hardware or software failure. You can use this utility to schedule automatic backups at regular intervals. The Backup utility can be used with a variety of storage media such as tape drives, logical drives, Zip disks, and CD-ROMs.

Figure 1-10 Windows 2000 file management features

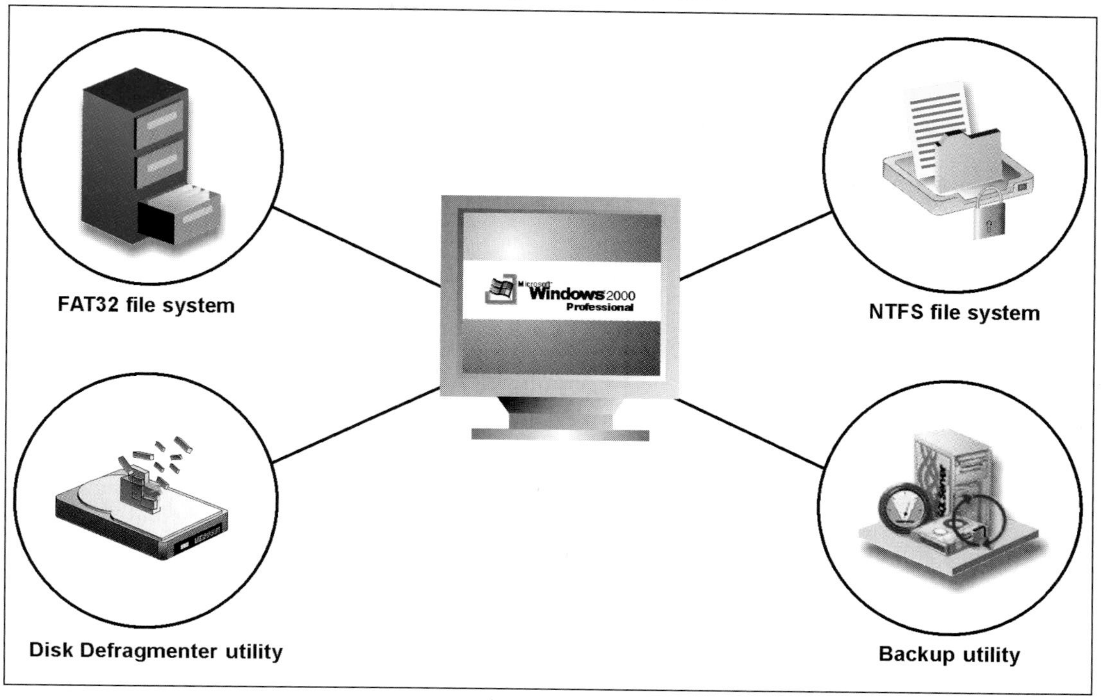

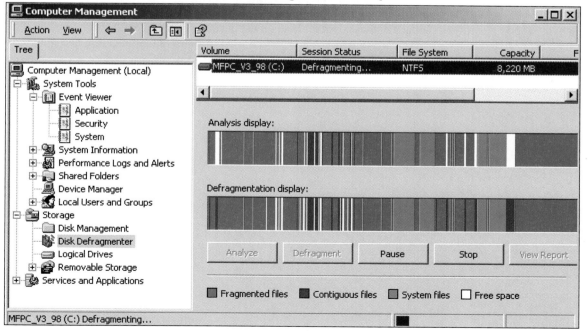

FAT32 file system

NTFS file system

Disk Defragmenter utility

Backup utility

Figure 1-11 The Windows 2000 Disk Defragmenter utility

skill 5

Introducing Windows 2000 Security Features

exam objective

Basic knowledge

overview

The new features of Windows 2000 Professional relating to system security **(Figure 1-12)** include:

◆ **Kerberos V5:** This is an Internet standard security protocol for handling the authentication of user or system identity. With Kerberos V5, passwords that are sent across network lines are encrypted, not sent as plain text. Kerberos V5 is the primary security protocol for domains in the Windows 2000 operating system. It can be used to prevent a user from logging on to more than one system on a network using the same user name and password. This network authentication protocol uses powerful cryptography. Clients must prove their identity to a server, and vice versa, providing a more secure network connection.

◆ **Encrypting File System (EFS):** Using Windows 2000 Professional, users can now encrypt files on a hard disk **(Figure 1-13)**. Data is scrambled so that no one can access the file or folder unless they have a file recovery certificate and a private key. EFS encrypts data using a cryptographic key pair: a public key and a private key. Data is encrypted using a session key (file encryption key – FEK). The session key is then encrypted with the user's public key and later decrypted with the user's private key. Either the owner of the file or a user account that has been designated as a recovery agent for the file can simply log on with the correct user name and password in order to decrypt the file. The NTFS file system supports EFS.

◆ **Internet Protocol Security (IPSec):** IPSec is used to encrypt Transmission Control Protocol/Internet Protocol (TCP/IP) traffic to ensure that communications within an intranet are more secure. Typically used to support VPNs (Virtual Private Networks), IPSec provides the highest level of Internet security currently possible. IPSec is a security addition to the IP protocol, that when enabled, protects communications so that no one except the receiver can read what is sent over the network.

◆ **Smart card support: Smart cards** are credit card-sized devices that are used to store passwords, public and private keys and other types of identifying data. You can attach a smart card reader to a Windows 2000 computer and use it to make certificate-based authentication possible. Users must have a personal identification number (PIN) for the smart card. Smart cards are often used to transfer identification and other confidential information between systems. With the help of smart cards, you can reduce the risks involved in transmitting sensitive information over the network.

Figure 1-12 Windows 2000 security features

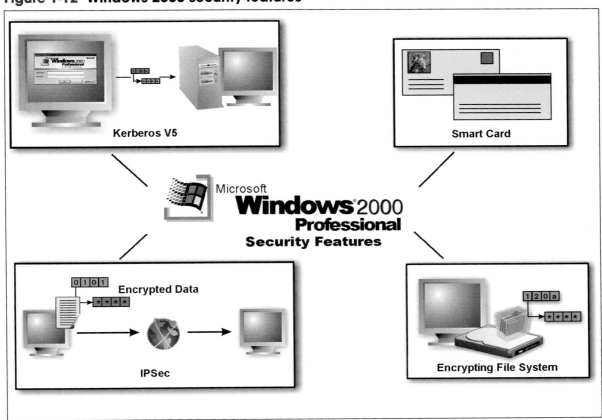

Figure 1-13 Using EFS to encrypt a folder on an NTFS disk

Selecting this check box will encrypt a folder's contents using EFS

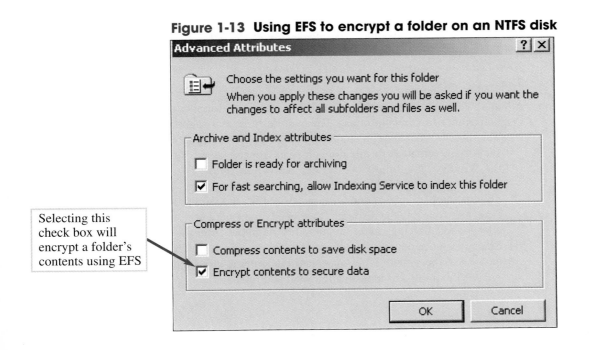

skill 6

Introducing Workgroups and Domains

exam objective

Basic knowledge

overview

The Windows 2000 operating system supports both workgroups and domains, the two basic network model types that enable users to share common resources.

A **workgroup (Figure 1-14)** is a logical group of computers that are interconnected, generally over a local area network (LAN). Workgroups allow users to easily share information and resources. A workgroup is also referred to as a **peer-to-peer network**. In a peer-to-peer network, all the computers in a workgroup share resources as equals, without a dedicated server. The main design features of workgroups are:

◆ The administration of user accounts and resource security in a Windows 2000 workgroup is decentralized. Each computer on the network maintains a **local security database**. This database lists user accounts and resource security information for the computer on which the database resides. All information about users, groups and permissions is stored in the local security database. Each computer user can share resources such as printers and folders with other users on the network. They can also control access to resources stored on their computer by setting access permissions for groups or individual users.

◆ In order for a user to gain access to any computer in the workgroup, he or she must have a user account on every computer. Furthermore, in order to maintain complete access to all computers on the network, if you make changes to a user account, you must update each computer in the workgroup with the changed information. If you forget to add a new user account on one of the computers in a workgroup, the new user will not be able to log on to that computer or access resources from it.

There are several advantages to using Windows 2000 workgroups to share resources:

◆ It does not require a computer running Windows 2000 Server to store information.

◆ Workgroups are relatively simple to design and implement. Unlike a domain, it does not require extensive planning and administration.

Limitations: A workgroup model is practical only in smaller environments where the computers are located in close proximity **(Figure 1-15)**. Microsoft recommends less than 10 computers. If you require a more scalable network that includes machines located in different geographic locations, you must use Windows 2000 domains. (***Note:*** *If all computers on a network are running Windows 2000 Professional, the only type of network option available is a workgroup. To implement a domain-based model, one of Windows 2000 Server, Windows 2000 Datacenter Server, or Windows 2000 Advanced Server is required to function as a domain controller.*)

A Windows 2000 **domain (Figure 1-16)** is a logical grouping of network computers that share a central **directory database**. The main features of a domain are:

◆ The directory database, also referred to as *the Directory*, contains all user account and security information for the domain. This directory constitutes the database portion of the Windows 2000 directory service, known as *Active Directory*. One of the notable new components of Windows 2000, Active Directory stores information about network objects such as users and groups, printers, and computers. Users access Active Directory to locate the resources they need on the network. Active Directory now stores all network directory data, functionality migrated from the Registry in Windows NT. Since the entire network directory is stored on a single database rather than on multiple databases, the system is more structurally robust, offering extensibility which allows greater flexibility for modifications and additions.

Figure 1-14 Windows 2000 workgroup

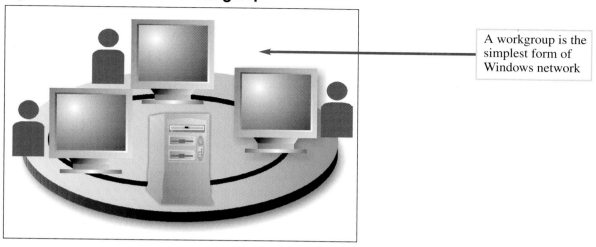

A workgroup is the simplest form of Windows network

Figure 1-15 A Windows 2000 workgroup with 3 computers

A workgroup is suitable for 10 computers or fewer

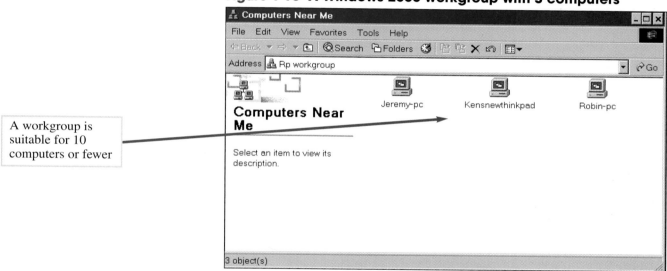

Figure 1-16 Windows 2000 domain

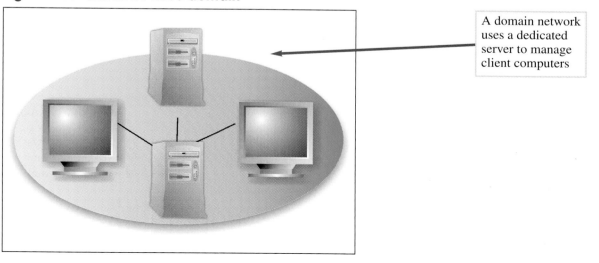

A domain network uses a dedicated server to manage client computers

skill 6

Introducing Workgroups and Domains *(cont'd)*

exam objective

Basic knowledge

overview

♦ All domains have a **domain controller**. A domain controller is a server on which the Directory resides. As noted above, this service must be run on one of the server versions of Windows 2000. This server manages security-related aspects of user/domain interactions. In a Windows 2000 domain, all domain controllers are equals, doing away with the concept of primary and backup domain controllers used in Windows NT.

♦ The computers in a domain can be in close physical proximity on a LAN, or can be located in different corners of the world using a WAN. These systems can use various media for communication, such as dial-up lines, Integrated Services Digital Network (ISDN) lines, fiber optic lines, frame relay connections, satellite connections, or leased lines.

The two main advantages of a domain are:

♦ Security and administration are centralized.

♦ It provides a single logon process for users to gain access to network resources, such as file, print, and application resources for which they have permissions.

more

A Windows 2000 domain consists of three kinds of computers (**Figure 1-17**):

♦ **Domain controllers running Windows 2000 Server:** In a domain, when you create a user account, the Windows 2000 operating system records it in Active Directory, which resides on the domain controller. When a user logs on to a computer in a specific domain, a domain controller checks the directory for authentication of the user name and password, as well as any log on restrictions. This process helps prevent unauthorized access to computing resources. The domain controller performs this check by using the name specified by the user during the logon process. If a domain has multiple domain controllers, when you make changes to the Active Directory on one domain controller, they are automatically replicated to all other domain controllers in the domain.

♦ **Member servers running Windows 2000 Server:** A computer that is not a domain controller for a Windows 2000 domain but that is running the Windows 2000 Server operating system is referred to as a member server. Member servers do not authenticate users, but are used to provide shared resources, such as printers and folders. These servers participate in a domain, but do not store a copy of the Active Directory database. Permissions are set locally for resources that reside on a member server, allowing users to connect to the server and use its resources.

♦ **Client computers running Windows 2000 Professional:** These are the computers that comprise the end user desktop environment. These computers allow users to access domain resources.

Figure 1-17 Domain controller and Windows 2000 client computers in a Windows 2000 domain

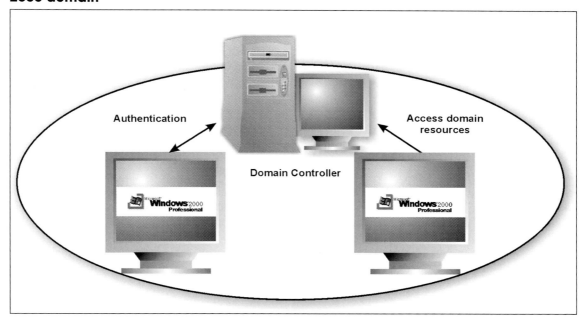

Summary

◆ Windows 2000 is a multipurpose operating system that supports client/server (domain-based networks) as well as peer-to-peer networks (workgroups). Workgroup networks and domain networks are the two networking models that can be used to share common resources.

◆ Windows 2000 Professional, Windows 2000 Server, Windows 2000 Advanced Server and Windows 2000 Datacenter Server are the four versions of the Windows 2000 platform developed by Microsoft.

◆ General features and enhancements provided by Windows 2000 Professional include reduced total cost of ownership, enhanced security, support for symmetric multiprocessing, multitasking and multithreading, support for a variety of network protocols, Plug and Play hardware support, and greater ease of use (customized start menu, and user-friendly dialog boxes).

◆ Windows 2000 supports thousands of different hardware devices. However, it is not necessarily the case that a device that works with Windows 95, Windows 98, or even Windows NT will be supported by Windows 2000 Professional. Every hardware device on a system should be systematically checked against the Hardware Compatibility List (HCL) to determine conclusively whether it will work with Windows 2000 Professional.

◆ File management features in Windows 2000 Professional include the NTFS file system, FAT 32 file system, disk defragmentation utility, and backup utility. The new NTFS file system is an advanced file system designed for use specifically within the Windows 2000 operating system. It supports file system recovery, large storage media, long file names, file encryption, and disk quotas which control disk usage by network users.

◆ Kerberos V5, IPSec, EFS, and smart card support are some of the new security features of Windows 2000 Professional. Kerberos V5 is the primary security protocol for domains in the Windows 2000 operating system. Internet Protocol Security (IPSec), which is typically used to support virtual private networks, is a security addition to the IP protocol, that when enabled, protects communications so that no one except the receiver can read what is sent over the network. EFS allows files and folders on NTFS disks to be encrypted. Smart cards are credit card-sized devices that are used to store passwords, public and private keys and other types of identifying information. A smart card reader can be attached to a Windows 2000 computer and used to make certificate-based authentication possible.

◆ The Windows 2000 operating system supports both the workgroup and domain network models. In a workgroup, the administration of user accounts and resource security is decentralized and each computer on the network maintains a local security database that stores information about users, groups and permissions on the network.

◆ A Windows 2000 domain is a logical grouping of network computers that share a central directory database. The directory database, which contains user accounts and security information for the domain, constitutes the database portion of the Windows 2000 directory service known as Active Directory. Active Directory, which is one of the notable new components of Windows 2000, stores information about network objects on a domain-based network. Users access the Active Directory to locate the resources, such as users and groups, printers, and computers that they need on the network.

Key Terms

Active Directory	File Allocation Table (FAT)	Plug and Play
Add/Remove Hardware Wizard	Hardware Compatibility List (HCL)	Smart card
Backup utility	Hibernation	Standby
Directory database	Internet Protocol Security (IPSec)	Win32 Driver Model (WDM)
Disk defragmenter utility	Kerberos V5	Windows 2000 Advanced Server
Domain	Local security database	Windows 2000 Datacenter Server
Domain controller	Member server	Windows 2000 Professional
Enrypting File System (EFS)	NTFS file system	Windows 2000 Server
FAT32 file system	Peer-to-peer network	Workgroup

Test Yourself

1. The Windows 2000 Professional operating system: (Choose all that apply)
   a. Can function with five processors.
   b. Supports automatic private IP addressing.
   c. Supports Plug and Play functionality.
   d. Supports asymmetric multiprocessing.

2. Which Windows 2000 operating systems feature allows a single port to support up to 127 peripheral devices and enables you to connect and disconnect devices without shutting down or restarting your computer?
   a. The Universal Serial Bus (USB) standard
   b. Kerberos V5

c. Active Directory

d. Virtual private network support

3. What must you do to ensure that hardware devices are compatible with Windows 2000 Professional?

   a. Nothing, all devices that work with Windows 95, Windows 98, or even Windows NT will work well with Windows 2000 Professional.

   b. Check the Hardware Compatibility List (HCL) to determine conclusively whether they will work with Windows 2000 Professional.

   c. You must have an IT professional install and configure any pre-1999 devices.

   d. Make sure that they use the Win32 Driver Model.

4. Which of the following statements about the enhancements in Windows 2000 Professional are true? (Choose all that apply.)

   a. The Add/Remove Programs Wizard is used to add, remove, and repair peripheral devices.

   b. Windows 2000 lowers the total cost of ownership by using technologies that enable automatic installation and upgrading of the operating system and applications.

   c. Windows 2000 Professional supports only the Advanced Configuration and Power Interface (ACPI) for managing power consumption.

   d. The Windows 2000 operating systems support symmetric multiprocessing (SMP), preemptive multitasking, and multithreading.

5. Which of the following hardware support options in Windows 2000 Professional has the capability to configure the installed hardware automatically and load the appropriate drivers?

   a. Win32 Driver Model

   b. Add/Remove Hardware Wizard

   c. Plug and Play support

   d. Install and drive support

6. Which of the following file-related options in Windows 2000 Professional ensures that all the related components of files and programs are placed in contiguous sectors of the hard disk?

   a. NTFS file system

   b. FAT 32 file system

   c. Disk Defragmenter utility

   d. Backup utility

7. Which protocol uses encryption to support the secure exchange of data packets in the IP (Internet Protocol) layer?

   a. Encrypting File System

   b. Kerberos V5 Protocol

   c. Internet Protocol Security (IPSec)

   d. Smart card support

8. Which of the following are features of Windows 2000 workgroups? (Choose all that apply.)

   a. Simple to design and implement.

   b. Require a computer to run a Windows 2000 Server to hold centralized security information.

   c. A workgroup model is practical only in smaller environments where the computers are located in close proximity.

   d. Support client/server relationships.

9. Which of the following statements about Windows 2000 domains are true? (Choose all that apply.)

   a. They provide centralized administration and security.

   b. They provide multiple logon processes.

   c. A directory database contains user accounts and security information for the domain.

   d. A domain controller is a client on which Active Directory resides.

Problem Solving Scenarios

You are working for TechStaff, Inc., a small start-up company that provides job placement services for information technology specialists. TechStaff has ten employees with plans to expand to 15-20 within the next year. Currently, the office has eight PCs from various manufacturers running Windows 98 and a peer-to-peer network. The network supports two different printers, a scanner, and all the employees use personal digital assistants. Colleen Williams, the founder of the company, is concerned that the Windows 98 network does not have the capacity to scale up as the organization grows, and that there is very poor file and communications security. She has asked you for recommendations and a report. Write a report for Colleen identifying the features of Windows 2000 that make it an appropriate solution and your recommendations for a new network.

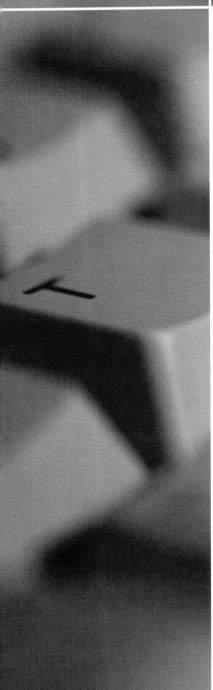

2 Installing Windows 2000 Professional

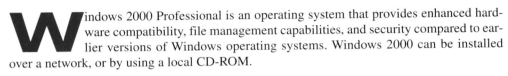

Windows 2000 Professional is an operating system that provides enhanced hardware compatibility, file management capabilities, and security compared to earlier versions of Windows operating systems. Windows 2000 can be installed over a network, or by using a local CD-ROM.

For a smooth and successful installation, certain pre-installation tasks should be completed before you start. Computers on most networks have different configurations depending on their use. To specify variations in configuration at the time of installation, installation scripts are used. To create and modify scripts for a customized installation of the operating system, you can use the Windows 2000 Setup Manager Wizard. The wizard enables you to input user settings during installation. It then creates an answer file that contains information about the settings that will be used in the installation process. This answer file is used to generate another file that will be used to configure the computer. This type of installation is called an unattended installation. The computer is set up with Windows 2000 Professional, and other applications if desired, with no user intervention.

Manual installation of Windows 2000 Professional on multiple computers in an organization with identical configurations can be a tedious and time-consuming task. Creating a disk image of the Windows 2000 Professional installation and copying this image to the other computers makes multiple installations simpler. A utility called Sysprep is used to prepare the system for duplication, also referred to as cloning. Sysprep does not perform the actual duplication. A third-party utility must be used to duplicate the master disk image onto the target computers. Sysprep makes sure that the security identifiers (SIDs) are unique on each of the target computers. It also initiates a Mini-Setup Wizard, which can be used on each of the targets to enter computer-specific information such as the user name, domain name, and time zone. Sysprep is included on the Windows 2000 operating system CD in the **\Support\Tools\Deploy.cab** folder.

You can also perform remote installations of the operating system using the Remote Installation Service (RIS). In RIS installation a client computer is booted up, an image of the operating system is located, and the image is downloaded and installed. RIS helps you to simplify image management for client computers. It also supports recovery of the operating system in the event of system failures.

If you are currently using Windows 95, 98, ME, or NT 4.0 Workstation, you can upgrade the existing operating system on the computers in your network to Windows 2000. You can use the Windows 2000 Readiness Analyzer to generate a compatibility report about the current hardware and software on a system.

Microsoft periodically releases utilities and patches that contain error correction or improvements on widely used applications. These items are packaged together in the form of service packs. Using Windows 2000 Professional, you can install these service packs at the same time as you are installing the operating system, unlike previous versions of the operating system where service packs had to be installed separately.

Goals

In this lesson, you will learn about the tasks that must be performed before you can install Windows 2000 Professional. You will use a CD-ROM to install Windows 2000 Professional and also install the operating system over a network. You will learn how to resolve setup problems, log on, and work with Setup Manager. You will also learn how to use the System Preparation tool and Windows 2000 Server Remote Installation Services to perform remote installations on client computers. Finally, you will learn how to configure Remote Installation Services, upgrade previous versions of Windows to Windows 2000 Professional and install service packs.

Lesson 2   Installing Windows 2000 Professional

Skill	Exam 70-210 Objective
1. Identifying Pre-installation Tasks	Prepare a computer to meet upgrade requirements.
2. Installing Windows 2000 Professional Using a CD-ROM	Perform an attended installation of Windows 2000 Professional.
3. Installing Windows 2000 Professional over a Network	Perform an attended installation of Windows 2000 Professional.
4. Resolving Problems Encountered During Setup	Troubleshoot failed installations.
5. Logging On to Windows 2000 Professional	Basic knowledge
6. Using the Windows 2000 Setup Manager	Perform an unattended installation of Windows 2000 Professional. Create unattended answer files by using Setup Manager to automate the installation of Windows 2000 Professional.
7. Using the System Preparation Tool	Perform an unattended installation of Windows 2000 Professional. Install Windows 2000 Professional by using the System Preparation Tool.
8. Performing Remote Installation on Client Computers	Perform an unattended installation of Windows 2000 Professional. Install Windows 2000 Professional by using Windows 2000 Server Remote Installation Services (RIS).
9. Configuring Remote Installation Services	Perform an unattended installation of Windows 2000 Professional. Install Windows 2000 Professional by using Windows 2000 Server Remote Installation Services (RIS).
10. Upgrading Previous Versions of Windows to Windows 2000 Professional	Upgrade from a previous version of Windows to Windows 2000 Professional.
11. Deploying Service Packs	Deploy service packs.
12. Installing Service Packs	Apply update packs to installed software applications.

Requirements

To complete this lesson, you must have administrative rights, a distribution server, a domain, and a computer running Windows 2000 Professional that is connected to a network.

skill 1

Identifying Pre-installation Tasks

exam objective

Prepare a computer to meet upgrade requirements.

overview

Before you install Windows 2000 Professional, you should plan carefully and perform a number of checks to ensure that the installation proceeds without delays and bottlenecks. When you install, you can either upgrade an existing OS or do a clean installation of Windows 2000 Professional. You can upgrade from Windows 95, 98, ME, or NT 4.0 Workstation. This will retain a number of settings including your desktop settings, user account and password information, and general computer and network configuration settings. Choose the upgrade option if you want to keep the Registry settings that allow you to run applications that are already installed.

You will choose a clean installation on computers with blank hard drives, when you want to overwrite an existing OS, or if you are going to create a dual-boot system in which the user will select the OS to use at startup. You can create a dual-boot system on machines that have Windows 95, 98, NT 3.51 Workstation, and NT 4.0 Workstation installed. If you choose to overwrite an existing OS, you will have to reinstall all applications, reconfigure any customized settings, and recreate user account and password data. Following the guidelines outlined below will help ensure a successful installation:

◆ Check Microsoft's minimum hardware requirements list **(Table 2-1)** to make sure that the hardware on your computer is sufficient to install Windows 2000 Professional.

◆ If the computer meets the minimum hardware requirements, make sure all of your hardware devices are included on the **Hardware Compatibility List**. Only devices listed on the HCL are guaranteed to be compatible with Windows 2000 Professional. If you use a hardware device that isn't on the HCL, you might encounter problems during and after installation. A copy of the HCL is provided in the file called HCL.txt, which is in the Support folder on the Windows 2000 CD, or you can view the most current copy on the Internet at the URL **http://www.microsoft.com/windows2000/server/howtobuy/ upgrading/compat/default.asp (Figure 2-1)**.

◆ Check for software compatibility on the Microsoft Web site at **http://ww.microsoft.com/ windows2000/server/howtobuy/upgrading/compat/default.asp**. Click the **Software** button to open a Web page where you can search for a particular application, a category of applications (for example data processing software), or download a complete list of compatible applications.

◆ Check to make sure the computer has the most recent BIOS (basic input/output system). The HAL (Hardware Abstraction Layer) that is installed is dependent upon the type and version of the BIOS.

◆ Run your virus scanning software, correct any problems, and then disable this software if it is BIOS-based. BIOS-based virus scanning software can impede an installation because it will react badly when the Setup program accesses the partition table on the hard disk.

◆ Find out how many partitions are on the hard disk of your computer and the file system with which they are formatted. (A **partition** is a part of your hard disk drive that has been formatted to act as a logically separate unit of storage.)

◆ Decide which file system you want to use for the installation partition.

◆ Select the domain or workgroup that your computer will join if it is to be a part of a network.

caution

When you install the operating system on a partition that already contains data, all existing files will be overwritten.

Table 2-1   Hardware requirements for installing Windows 2000 Professional

Component	Requirement
CPU	Pentium compatible, 133 MHz +
Memory	64 MB RAM
Hard disk space	Recommended: Total: 2 GB Free space: 650 MB minimum (This space is needed to store the system files.)
Networking	Network adapter card
Display	• Video Display Adapter (VDA) • Monitor with Video Graphics Adapter (VGA) resolution or higher
Other devices	Recommended: CD-ROM drive 12 x or faster, unless you are installing Windows 2000 Professional over a network
Accessories	Keyboard and mouse or other pointing devices

Figure 2-1 Search for compatible hardware devices

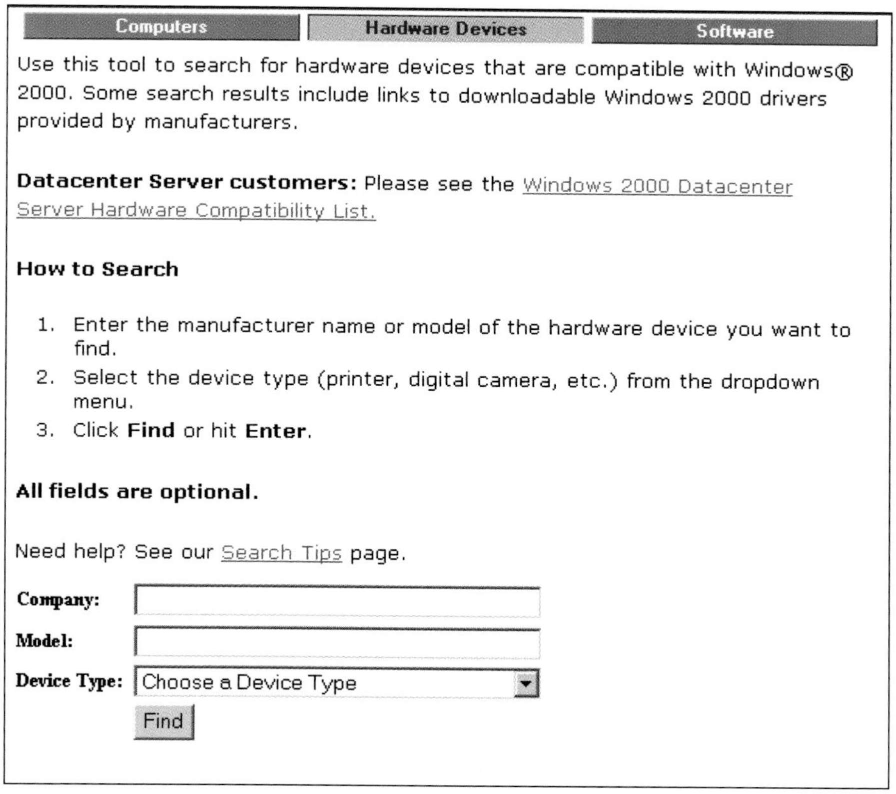

Computers	Hardware Devices	Software

Use this tool to search for hardware devices that are compatible with Windows® 2000. Some search results include links to downloadable Windows 2000 drivers provided by manufacturers.

Datacenter Server customers: Please see the Windows 2000 Datacenter Server Hardware Compatibility List.

How to Search

1. Enter the manufacturer name or model of the hardware device you want to find.
2. Select the device type (printer, digital camera, etc.) from the dropdown menu.
3. Click **Find** or hit **Enter**.

All fields are optional.

Need help? See our Search Tips page.

Company: [   ]

Model: [   ]

Device Type: [Choose a Device Type ▾]

[Find]

skill 1

Identifying Pre-installation Tasks
(cont'd)

exam objective

Prepare a computer to meet upgrade requirements.

overview

During installation, you will select one of the following partition options according to the configuration of your computer's hard disk:

◆ **Unpartitioned hard disk:** Create a partition for the installation files and then choose the size you want for this partition.

◆ **Existing partition with enough free space:** You can install Windows 2000 Professional on an existing partition if it has enough free space or you can create a new partition for the installation files if there is sufficient unpartitioned disk space. You can also delete an existing partition to create enough space, and then create a partition large enough for the installation files.

After installing Windows 2000 Professional on a partition, you must partition the remaining disk space to make it usable. Data cannot be stored until the disk is partitioned and formatted. The preferred method for formatting a disk is to use the Disk Management administrative tool after the installation process is complete rather than during setup, although this is possible.

According to the guidelines provided by Microsoft, the disk partition on which you install Windows 2000 must have 1 GB or more of free disk space. While this may be adequate in some situations, using a larger partition is highly recommended because the operating system alone consumes 650 MB of disk space. This will allow for scalability, leaving room for updates and operating system tools or files that may be required later.

Next, you must select a file system for the Windows 2000 partition. Partitions can be formatted with any one of three file systems: NTFS, FAT, or FAT32 (**Figure 2-2**). A description of these file systems is provided below:

◆ **NTFS:** This is the file system recommended by Microsoft because it offers many benefits, including security at both the file and folder levels, compression for individual files and folders rather than just an entire drive, increased performance on large drives, and support for much larger disk and file sizes. NTFS 5, the new version of the file system (NTFS 4 was used for NT Workstation 4.0), also includes encryption, disk quotas, and support for mount points. Quotas are used to restrict the amount of disk space a user can consume on a particular partition or volume. Encrypted files provide additional security by preventing any user but the owner or the recovery agent (typically, the Administrator's account) from opening them. Mount points are used to create a path to a physical disk that points to a folder on a physical disk that acts as an entry to another partition. This means that you can add a second hard drive and, rather than labeling it the D: drive, you can assign it to a folder on the C: drive. Users will not have to access the D: drive to use the new storage space. Instead, what they will see is an extremely large new folder on a drive that is already familiar. NTFS also supports dynamic disks, which are divided into dynamic volumes. This storage method is superior to the partition-based storage on a basic disk because you can create an unlimited number of volumes on each disk. You use the Disk Management utility to create dynamic volumes.

◆ **FAT and FAT32:** Unlike NTFS, the FAT and FAT32 file systems do not allow you to control access to individual files. On FAT and FAT32 disks, you can only control access to shared folders. However, if you want to set up your computer for dual booting, in many cases you should format the system partitions as FAT or FAT32. When you configure a computer for dual booting, you can choose between one or more operating systems when you turn the computer on. The operating systems will be saved in different OS folders, which can be on the same partition or on different partitions. Generally, it is recommended that you install each operating system on a separate drive or on its own partition. This approach will prevent errors that can occur because each of the operating systems installs its own files into certain shared folders. Files installed by one OS may not work under the other OS; for example, files in the Common Files, Accessories, and Program

tip

The only operating systems you can use to access data from a hard disk that has been formatted with NTFS are Windows 2000 and Windows NT.

Figure 2-2 Types of file systems supported by Windows 2000

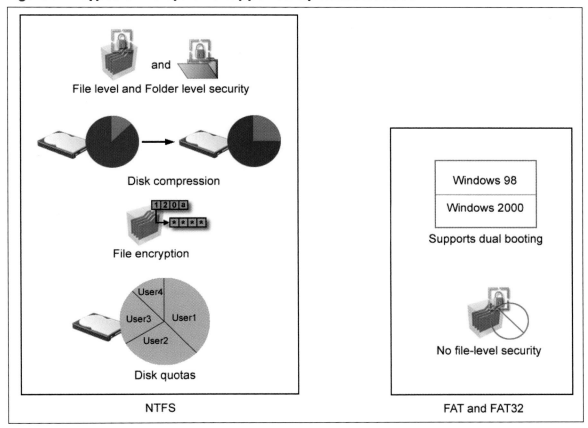

skill 1

Identifying Pre-installation Tasks
(cont'd)

exam objective   Prepare a computer to meet upgrade requirements.

overview

Files folders, as well as those in the Microsoft Internet Explorer and the Microsoft Outlook Express folders. You will want to format the disks with FAT or FAT32 because, generally, you will want to be able to read and write to other partitions, no matter which operating system you are presently using. As a Windows 2000 user, you likely will want to take advantage of such features as Encrypting File Systems (EFS) and disk quotas, which are available only on NTFS partitions. This creates a dilemma on many dual-boot systems. If you convert a partition to NTFS, only Windows 2000, Windows XP, and now Windows NT 4.0 with the latest service pack can read from and write to Windows 2000 NTFS volumes or partitions.

To create a dual-boot with either Windows 95 or Windows NT, the most important consideration is that you must install the earlier operating system first. When creating a dual-boot configuration with Windows 98 and Windows 2000, either operating system can be installed first. If you want to configure a multiple-boot situation in which you will have Windows 9x, Windows NT, and Windows 2000, first install Windows NT, then Windows 9x, and Windows 2000 last. In a dual-boot situation with Windows 95 OSR2 or Windows 98, the primary partition can be formatted as either FAT or FAT32. FAT32 is recommended. For a dual-boot with earlier versions of Windows 95, the primary partition must be FAT.

The Windows 2000 Setup program will automatically format the hard disk with FAT if the disk is smaller than 2 GB, and with FAT32 if it is larger than 2 GB. However, you can format another drive with NTFS.

You must also choose the type of network security group you will be using at the time of installation. Network security groups can be either workgroups or domains.

♦ **Workgroup:** A workgroup is a logical grouping of networked computers that share resources without a dedicated server (**Figure 2-3**). Workgroups are used for small groups of approximately 10 computers. You must join either a workgroup or a domain during installation, although you can change a workgroup or domain membership later. To add a computer to an existing workgroup during installation, you must enter the name of the workgroup you want to join. You can also create a new workgroup during the installation.

♦ **Domain:** A domain consists of computers that are logically networked together for a similar purpose, regardless of their physical location. These logical groups share a central directory database. The directory database stores the user accounts and security information for the domain (**Figure 2-4**). During installation, you can join a domain, add your computer to an existing domain, or you can add a computer to a domain after installation. In order to join a domain, your computer must have an account in the domain you want to join. You can create the account during installation if you have administrative privileges for the domain. You will have to enter the name and password for the administrative account. The Domain Administrator can also create a computer account for you before you begin the installation. In addition, you must ask your Domain Administrator to provide you with the DNS (Domain Name System) name for the domain you want to join. An example of a DNS domain name is techsoft.com. Techsoft is the organization's DNS identity. Finally, when you join a domain, there must be at least one domain controller and one DNS server online in the domain you want to join.

Figure 2-3 Workgroup

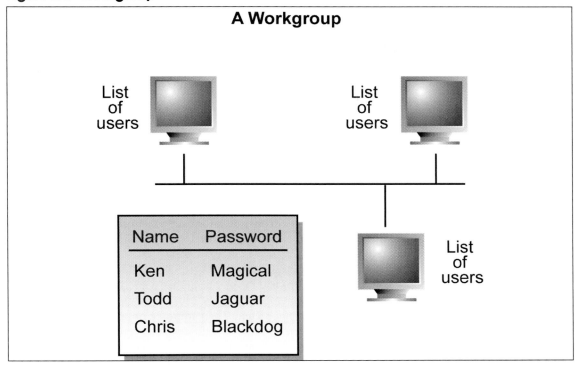

Figure 2-4 Domain

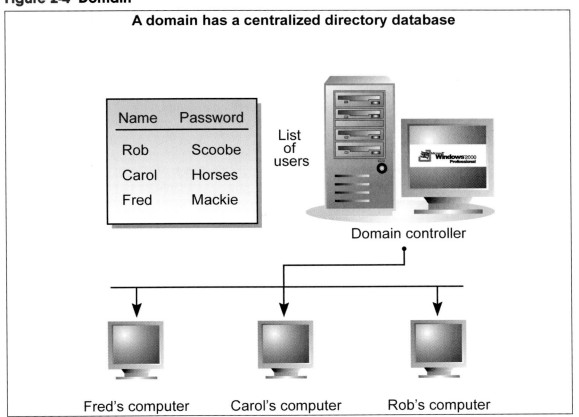

<table>
<tr><td>

skill 2

</td><td>

Installing Windows 2000 Professional Using a CD-ROM

</td></tr>
</table>

exam objective

Perform an attended installation of Windows 2000 Professional.

overview

After you have completed the pre-installation tasks, you are ready to install Windows 2000 Professional on your computer. You can install the operating system from a CD-ROM or over a network. Booting a CD-ROM involves the following four stages:

1. **Running the Setup program:** This is the basic **setup** stage, in which a rudimentary version of the operating system is loaded into the memory of the computer. You accept the licensing agreement, create the installation partition and choose the file system for it, or select an existing partition as the installation partition.

2. **Running the Setup Wizard:** This is the graphical phase of installation, in which the Setup Wizard prompts you to provide information that is required to complete the installation. You will interact with the GUI interface in the Setup Wizard to perform the following tasks:
   • Selecting the regional settings
   • Entering your name and the organization's name
   • Entering the Product Key
   • Entering the computer name: The **computer name** (also known as the **NetBIOS name**) can contain no more than 15 characters and it must be unique. The same name cannot be given to another computer, workgroup, or domain. On a domain-based network, the NetBIOS name will appear in Active Directory as an object. It will be used in the UNC (Universal Naming Convention) path you will use to create connections to shared resources.
   • Entering the password of the Administrator's account
   • Selecting the modem dialing information
   • Selecting the date and time settings

3. **Installing Windows Networking Components:** Although the Setup Wizard is still running, this is considered the third stage of setup. The operating system attempts to detect the network card and copies a number of network software files to your computer. You enter the networking settings you want, either the typical setup, which includes installing Client for Microsoft Networks, File and Printer Sharing, and TCP/IP (Transmission Control Protocol/Internet Protocol), or a custom setup. These networking-related files, which you will learn more about in succeeding chapters, will be used to send and receive files on the network. You will also join either a workgroup or a domain and the Setup program will install and configure the networking components.

4. **Completing the Installation:** In the final stage, the Setup program copies files onto the hard disk, registers the components, and configures the computer. The Installing Components screen shows the progress of the installation of various files including the Fax Service, Indexing Service, games, and accessories. Next, the Performing Final Tasks screen displays the progress of installing the Start-menu items, registering the components, saving the configuration, and removing the temporary files. Finally, the computer is restarted and the installation is complete.

how to

Install Windows 2000 Professional using a CD-ROM.

1. Insert the **Windows 2000 Professional CD-ROM** disk into the CD-ROM drive of your computer. The **Microsoft Windows 2000 CD** message box **(Figure 2-5)** prompts you to upgrade your system to Windows 2000.

2. Click [Yes] to open the **Welcome to the Windows 2000 Setup Wizard**. You will be prompted to specify whether you want to upgrade to Windows 2000 or install a new copy of Windows 2000 **(Figure 2-6)**.

Figure 2-5 Microsoft Windows 2000 CD message box

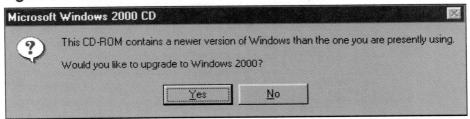

Figure 2-6 Windows 2000 Setup Wizard Welcome screen

skill 2

Installing Windows 2000 Professional Using a CD-ROM *(cont'd)*

exam objective

Perform an attended installation of Windows 2000 Professional.

how to

3. Click the **Install a new copy of Windows 2000 (clean install)** option button. Then, click
   `Next >` . The **Licensing Agreement** opens.
4. Click the **I Accept this agreement** option button to accept the licensing terms and then
   click `Next >` . The **Your Product Key** screen opens.
5. Enter the 25-character product key number for Windows 2000 Professional (**Figure 2-7**).
   The product key is provided with the Windows 2000 Professional CD.
6. Click `Next >` . The **Select Special Options** screen opens. Here, you can customize the
   language, installation, and accessibility options for the setup. You do not need to modify
   the default settings. Click `Next >` .
7. If the drive you are installing the operating system on is not currently formatted with
   NTFS, the **Upgrading to the Windows 2000 NTFS File System screen** will open.
   Select the **Yes, Upgrade my drive** option button, if desired, and click `Next >` .
8. Setup will load the information and determine the files that must be copied for the installation. After the information is loaded, Setup will copy the installation files to your
   computer and restart your computer. Restarting the computer enables Setup to inspect the
   hardware configuration and load the installation files to your computer. The Setup program prepares Microsoft Windows 2000 Professional to run on your computer.
9. Press the **[Enter]** key to continue the installation. The **Welcome to Setup** screen displays
   three options:
     - To set up Windows 2000 now, press ENTER
     - To repair a Windows 2000 installation, press R
     - To quit Setup without installing Windows 2000, press F3.
10. Press **[Enter]**. The next screen displays a list of the existing partitions and unpartitioned
    space on the computer and offers the following three choices (**Figure 2-8**):
      - To set up Windows 2000 on the selected item, press ENTER.
      - To create a partition in the unpartitioned space, press C.
      - To delete the selected partition, press D.
11. Press **[Enter]** to select the default C: partition. Setup will examine your disks, copy files
    to the Windows 2000 installation folders, and reboot the computer. If you are converting
    the drive to NTFS, the conversion process will take place and the computer will reboot
    again.
12. When the computer restarts, Windows 2000 Professional Setup resumes and the
    Welcome to Windows 2000 Professional screen opens. Setup then detects and installs
    devices such as your keyboard and mouse. The computer screen may flicker during this
    process. (**Figure 2-9**).
13. Next, the **Regional Settings** screen opens. Here, you can customize Windows 2000 for
    different regions and languages.
14. Accept the default settings and click `Next >` . The **Personalize Your Software** screen
    opens. Here you can personalize your software by providing information about yourself
    and your organization (**Figure 2-10**).
15. After you have entered the required information, click `Next >` . The **Computer Name
    and Administration Password** screen opens.
16. Type the computer name, for example, **comp1**, in the **Computer name** text box. The
    computer name will be entered in all capital letters. This is the NetBIOS name for the
    computer. It cannot contain more than 15 characters, and it cannot be the same as the
    name given to any other computer, workgroup, or domain. This computer name will
    appear as an object in Active Directory on a domain-based network.
17. Type a password, for example, **adminpass**, in the **Administrator password** and
    Confirm password text boxes. You will need to remember this password in order to have
    administrative rights on the computer.

Figure 2-7 The Your Product Key dialog box

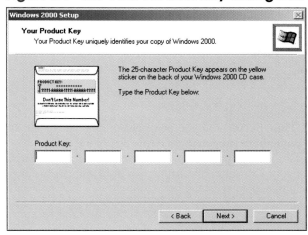

Figure 2-8 Selecting a partition for Windows 2000

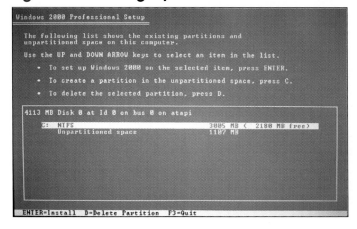

Figure 2-9 Installing Windows 2000 components

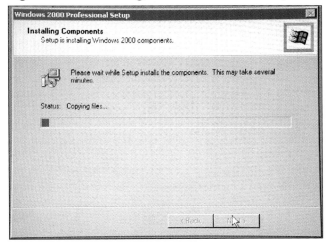

Figure 2-10 The Personalize Your Software dialog box

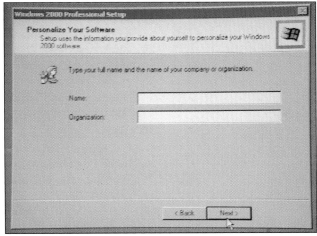

skill 2

Installing Windows 2000 Professional Using a CD-ROM *(cont'd)*

exam objective   Perform an attended installation of Windows 2000 Professional.

how to

18. Click `Next >`. The **Date and Time Settings** dialog box opens. Make sure that the **Automatically adjust clock for daylight saving changes** check box is selected.

19. Set the correct date and time and click `Next >`. The **Networking Settings** screen opens. Setup now installs the network software that enables you to communicate with other computers, networks, and the Internet.

20. After the networking components are installed, click `Next >` to go to the second screen of the Networking Settings window.

21. Here you can select typical or custom settings for configuring the networking settings. When you select the typical settings, you can create your network connections using **Client for Microsoft Networks, File and Printer Sharing for Microsoft Networks**, and the **TCP/IP** protocol with automatic addressing. If you choose custom settings, you can manually configure the networking components. Click the **Custom settings** option button and click `Next >`. The **Networking Components** dialog box opens. You must select the networking components so that your computer can connect to other computers.

22. Accept the default components and click `Next >`. The **Workgroup or Computer Domain** dialog box opens. Here you must specify whether your computer will join a workgroup or a domain.

23. If you are on a domain-based network, accept the default selection **Yes, make this computer a member of the following domain** and type the domain for your computer, for example, **Domain1**. If your computer is not on a network, or is on a network without a domain, select that option and enter a workgroup name.

24. Click `Next >`. The **Join Computer to Domain** dialog box opens **(Figure 2-11)**. Type a user name, for example, **Usr1**, in the User name text box. You will be prompted for the name and password for the Administrator account in the domain you are joining. This will be used to create a computer account in the domain for your new Windows 2000 Professional system.

25. After you have entered the required information, click `OK`. The **Installing Components** screen opens while the Setup program installs the Windows 2000 components.

26. After the components are installed, click `Next >`. The **Performing Final Tasks** screen opens **(Figure 2-12).** The final tasks include installing the **Start** menu items, registering the components, saving the settings, and removing any temporary files.

27. After these tasks are completed, click `Next >`. The next screen informs you that you have successfully completed the Windows 2000 setup.

28. Remove the installation CD and click `Finish` to restart your computer. After the reboot, the **Welcome to the Network Identification Wizard** screen will display.

29. Click `Next >`. The **Users of This Computer** screen opens. Here, you can choose to have the system automatically log on the same user each time (the user name that was entered on the Personalize Your Software screen), or to require each user to enter a name and password in order to use the computer. Select the **Users must enter a user name and password to use this computer** option button.

30. Click `Next >`. The **Completing the Network Identification Wizard** screen indicates that you have successfully completed the process. Click `Finish`.

31. In the **Log On to Windows** dialog box, type: **administrator** in the **User name** text box. Type the password you created in step # 17, **adminpass**, in the **Password** text box. Press **[Enter]**.

32. The **Getting Started with Windows** dialog box opens. Clear the check mark from the **Show This Screen At Startup** check box and click **Exit** to close the dialog box.

Figure 2-11 Joining a Workgroup or Domain

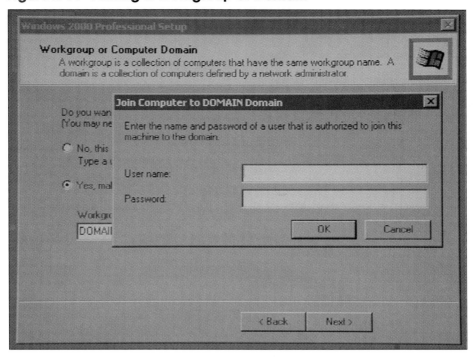

Figure 2-12 The Performing Final Tasks screen

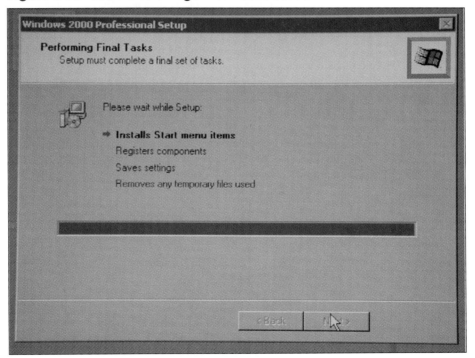

skill 3

Installing Windows 2000 Professional over a Network

exam objective

Perform an attended installation of Windows 2000 Professional.

overview

To install Windows 2000 Professional over a network, you must first connect to a distribution server and then run the Setup program. The **distribution server** is a network file server that contains the Windows 2000 Professional installation files. In order to install Windows 2000 Professional over a network, you must adhere to the following pre-setup requirements (**Figure 2-13**):

◆ **Creating a distribution server:** A distribution server contains a set of distribution folders that store the installation files from the **i386** folder on the Windows 2000 Professional CD-ROM. It is a good idea to create more than one set of distribution folders if you have many computers on which to install the operating system, or if you must perform many installations at the same time. To create a distribution server, log on to the server as an administrator, create a distribution folder, and copy the contents of the i386 folder on the installation CD to the folder. If you have applications, drivers, or utilities that you want Setup to copy to the target computers, create a subfolder named **OEM** and place the executable files for these programs in the **OEM** subfolder. Setup will copy all files in this directory to a temporary directory during the setup process. Then, you must share the distribution folder so that it can be accessed on the network. To do this, right-click the distribution folder, select **Properties** to open the Properties dialog box for the folder, and open the **Sharing** tab of the dialog box. Select the **Share this folder** option button, and enter a name for the shared folder in the **Share name** list box. You can also install Windows 2000 Professional on systems with different hardware configurations by using one set of distribution folders. This set of folders is used with files that contain the inputs required for the Setup program. These files are referred to as the **answer files**. They contain information about how the computer will interact with the network and are used to generate a file that will be used to configure the computer during installation.

◆ **Creating a FAT partition on the target computer:** After creating a distribution server, you must format the partition on the target computer. To do so, you must first create a 650 MB (preferably larger, at least 1GB) partition on the computer and then format the partition with the FAT file system.

◆ **Creating a client boot disk:** A network client is a software application that enables your computer to connect to the distribution server. If you are installing Windows 2000 Professional on a computer with no operating system, you must boot the computer from a system boot disk that includes a network client so that the target computer can connect to the distribution server.

tip

You can use the network installation method to install Windows 2000 Professional concurrently on multiple computers after you have created or located a distribution server.

how to

Install Windows 2000 Professional over the network.

1. Boot the target computer.
2. Connect to the shared folder on the distribution server that contains the Windows 2000 Professional installation files.
3. If you are installing Windows 2000 Professional on a target computer running a Windows 3.x operating system, run the **Winnt.exe** file. If you are installing Windows 2000 Professional on a target computer running Windows 95, 98, NT 4.0 (or NT 3.5), or 2000 operating system, run the **Winnt32.exe** file. You can locate the Winnt.exe and Winnt32.exe files in the shared folder on the distribution server. Running Winnt.exe from the shared folder results in the following:
   • Creation of the temporary folder Win_nt.~ on the target computer
   • Copying of the Windows 2000 installation files from the shared folder on the distribution server to the Win_nt.~ folder on the target computer

Figure 2-13 Pre-setup requirements for installing Windows 2000 over a network

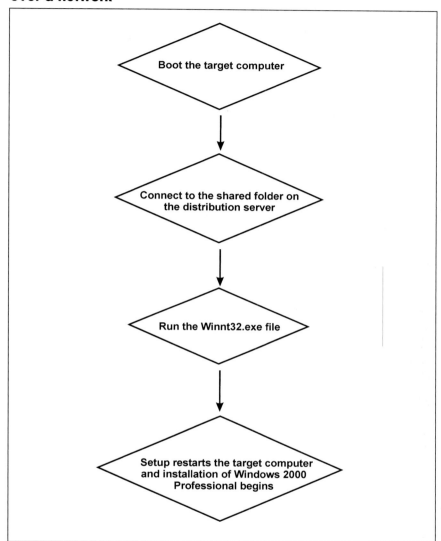

skill 3

Installing Windows 2000 Professional over a Network *(cont'd)*

exam objective

Perform an attended installation of Windows 2000 Professional.

how to

4. Setup restarts the computer and the installation of Windows 2000 Professional begins. The subsequent installation process is identical to that used in installation with a CD-ROM.

more

caution

Most of the command-line switches for Winnt32.exe and Winnt.exe have similar functionality with a different syntax. Thus, it is important to know the difference between them.

Installing Windows 2000 Professional from a CD-ROM and installing it over the network differ only in the method of locating the installation files. To perform a network installation, you first locate and connect to the shared distribution folder, which contains the files from the i386 folder from the installation CD. After you locate and run either Winnt.exe or Winnt32.exe, the installation process is identical. You can modify a server-based installation by changing the way in which the Winnt32.exe and Winnt.exe files run the setup process. To do so, you can use the command line switches to customize the installation process.

Table 2-2 provides a list of the switches that are used with the Winnt32.exe file. **Table 2-3** provides a list of the switches that are used with Winnt.exe.

Table 2-2   Switches used for Winnt32.exe

Switch	Description
/checkupgradeonly	Used to verify whether the computer qualifies for an upgrade to Windows 2000 Professional. This switch also creates a report for upgrade installations.
/copydir:folder_name	Used to create an additional folder within the systemroot folder. Windows 2000 system files are copied to this folder.
/copysource:folder_name	Used to create an additional folder within the systemroot folder. Setup deletes the files created using this switch once the installation is complete.
/cmd:command_line	Used to allow the user to execute a command before the final phase of Setup.
/cmdcons	Used to install the Recovery Console.
/debug[level] [:file_name]	Enables you to create a debug log at the specified level. It creates the C:\Winnt32.log at level 2 (the warning level) by default.
/m:folder_name	Forces Setup to copy the replacement files from other locations. If the replacement files are on the computer, this switch asks Setup to use those files and not the files from the default location.
/makelocalsource	Used to copy all of the installation files to the local hard disk. You can use these files later if the CD-ROM drive is not available for installation.
/noreboot	Used to prevent Setup from restarting the computer when the file copy phase of Setup is over. Thus, the user is allowed to enter a command, if required, before completing setup.
/s:source_path	Used to determine where the Windows 2000 Professional installation files source is located. To copy files from multiple paths simultaneously, you use separate/s switches for all source paths.
/syspart:drive_letter	Used to copy the Setup startup files to the hard disk. The drive specified for installation is marked as the active drive. To install Windows 2000 Professional on another computer, you can install this drive on that computer and the Setup program will start from the next phase on that computer. Note that you cannot use the /syspart switch without the /tempdrive switch.
/tempdrive:drive_letter	Used to place temporary files on the specified drive. Windows 2000 Professional is installed on the same drive.
/unattend[number]	Used to perform an unattended installation.
[:answer_file]	Used to give custom specifications to the Setup program. If an answer file is not specified, Setup takes the user settings from the previous installation.
/udf:id[,udf_filename]	Used to specify an identifier (ID) used by the Setup program. Setup uses this ID to find out how an answer file is changed by a Uniqueness Database File.

Table 2-3   Switches used with Winnt.exe

Switch	Description
/a	Provides accessibility options.
/e[:command]	Used to specify a command to be executed on the completion of the GUI mode Setup program.
/r[:folder]	Used to specify an optional folder, which will be retained after installation.
/rx[:folder]	Used to specify an optional folder, which is copied to the hard disk. However, this folder is deleted by Setup after installation.
/s[:sourcepath]	Used to specify where the source files for Windows 2000 Professional are located. The syntax for this path is: **x:\[path] or \\server\share\ [path]**
/t[:tempdrive]	Used to specify the drive that will store temporary files. Windows 2000 Professional is installed on that drive.
/u[:answer file]	Used to perform an unattended setup using an answer file.
/udf [id],[UDB_filename]	Used to specify an identifier that Setup will use to modify the answer file. You can configure a Uniqueness Database File (udf) and tell Setup to use this file to override values in the answer file. The identifier tells Setup which values in the UDB file to use. If no UDB file is entered, you will be prompted to insert a disk containing the $Unique$.udb file.

skill 4

Resolving Problems Encountered During Setup

exam objective

Troubleshoot failed installations.

overview

Despite following the hardware requirements, checking the HCL, and inspecting all compatibility issues, you may still encounter installation problems. You can use several information files, called **log files**, which are generated during the setup process, to help you to troubleshoot installation problems. These files contain information about the installation process. The action log (**Figure 2-14**) and the error log (**Figure 2-15**) are particularly valuable.

◆ **Action log:** The action log, which is stored in the **Setupact.log** file, contains information about the events that transpired during Setup, including the copying of files, the creation of registry entries, and any errors that might have occurred. Each event is recorded as it happened. Log files are created during the **GUI** phase of setup. These files are located in the directory in which Windows 2000 Professional is installed. The four log files that are created are: **Setupact.log**, **Setuperr.log**, **Setupapi.log**, and **Setuplog.txt**.

◆ **Error log:** The error log, which is stored in the **Setuperr.log** file, stores a description of the errors that have occurred and an entry indicating the magnitude of each error.

more

In addition to the action and error log files, the following device-specific or component-specific log files may also be created (**Windir** is the command to display names and paths of Windows directories):

◆ **Windir\comsetup.log:** Registers the **Optional Component Manager** and **Com+** setup routines.

◆ **Windir\mmdet.log:** Registers multimedia device installation information and the port range for each device.

◆ **Windir\setupapi.log:** Registers an entry when a line from an **.INF** file is executed and error information if the execution was unsuccessful.

◆ **Windir\debug\netSetup.log:** Registers information about joining a domain or a workgroup, including the network computer name, workgroup, and domain validation.

Other problems you may encounter include media errors and CD-ROM drives that are not supported by Windows 2000. These problems can usually be solved by replacing the CD-ROM you are using with a new one or replacing the CD-ROM drive. If you do not want to replace an unsupported CD-ROM drive, you can also simply use the network installation method and later add the adapter card driver for the CD-ROM drive, if available. If you find that you have insufficient disk space, simply create a new partition using the free space available on the hard disk or reformat one of the available partitions to create more space. If the dependency service doesn't start, make sure that you have installed the correct protocol and network adaptor in the **Network Settings** dialog box in the Setup Wizard, that the network adapter has the been configured correctly, and that the computer has a unique name on your network. If you cannot connect to a domain controller, check to see if the DNS server and the domain controller are online and running, and make sure that you have entered the correct domain name. If you cannot locate a domain controller, you must create and join a workgroup and join the domain after installation. Finally, if the operating system will not install or start, check to see if all hardware has been detected and confirm that it is all on the Hardware Compatibility List.

Figure 2-14 Action log

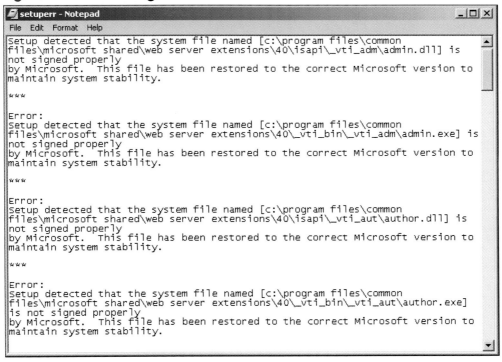

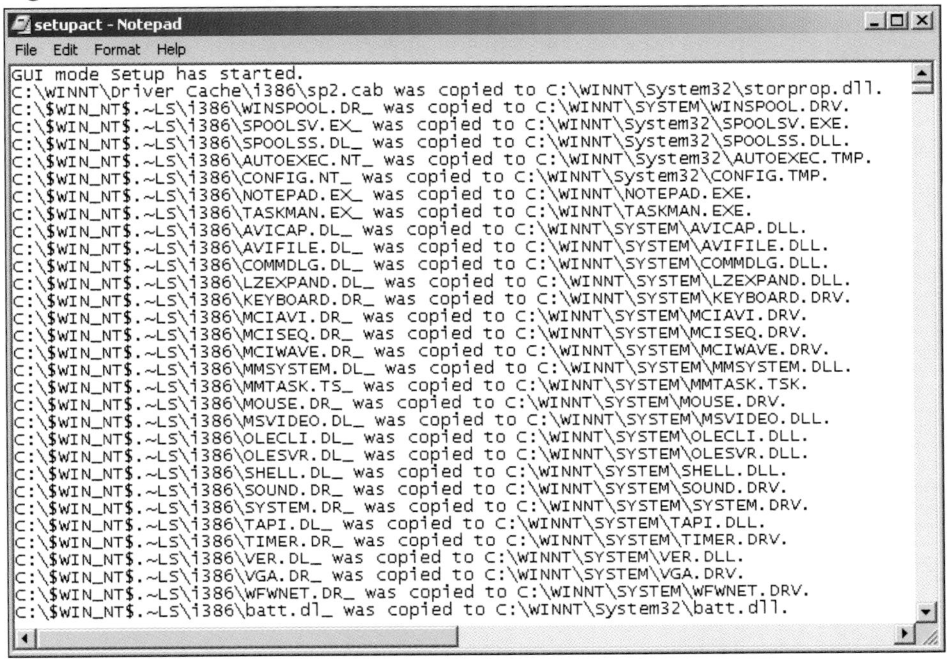

Figure 2-15 Error log

skill 5

Logging On to Windows 2000 Professional

exam objective

Basic knowledge

overview

After you have installed Windows 2000 Professional, you must log on to the computer to access the data and resources on the system. Windows 2000 uses logon authentication for network security purposes and so that each user can have his or her own system preferences and private documents saved in a separate location. Logon authentication simply involves entering a user name and password in the **Log On to Windows** dialog box. Windows 2000 Professional uses the user name and password to verify the authenticity of a user, so that only a valid user can access the resources and data on a computer or network. **Table 2-4** describes the options available in the **Log On to Windows** dialog box.

how to

Log on to a local computer running Windows 2000 Professional.

1. Turn on the computer. The **Log On to Windows** dialog box opens (**Figure 2-16**). How this dialog box looks will depend on whether it was last used in its normal state or in its expanded state, and whether or not the computer belongs to a domain. If the **Options** button was selected by the last person to log on to the computer, the **Shutdown** button and **Log on using dial-up connection** check box will be shown (**Figure 2-17**). If the computer belongs to a domain, in the **Log on to** list box you can either select *computername* (this computer) to log on locally, or you can select the domain name to which the computer belongs to log on to the domain .
2. Type a user name in the **User name** text box and a password in the **Password** text box (**Figure 2-18**). Windows 2000 Professional sends this information to the security subsystem of the computer. It then compares the logon information to the user information in the local security database to validate the authenticity of the user (ID). The user's identification for the local computer is referred to as the **access token.** It contains the user's security settings and allows the user to gain access to system resources and to perform specific system tasks such as modifying the system date.
3. If the user account is valid and the information matches the information stored in the local security database, Windows 2000 Professional creates an access token for the computer and the user is able to log on.

more

There are actually two separate logon processes on a Windows 2000 network. There is the process by which you access the local computer at which you are physically located, and the process by which you access network resources. If you log on locally but need to access a resource on another network computer, you will have to establish a network connection with that server. When you attempt to establish this connection, the user name and password that you used to log on locally are submitted. Another authorization process must take place to make sure that the Access Control List (ACL) for the resource you are attempting to use gives you permission to access it. As long as this authorization is granted, you will not be aware that this second authentication process is occurring. However, if the account name you used to log on locally does not have permission for this resource, you will be prompted to enter the user name and password for an account which does have permission for this resource.

When the computer belongs to a domain, the Log on to list box will include the name of the local computer, the name of the domain to which the computer belongs, and the names of all other trusted domains. If you log on to a domain, the user name and password you use to log on with will be used to authenticate you to network resources.

Table 2-4   Options in the Log On to Windows dialog box

Option	Description
User name	A unique name assigned by an administrator. In order to log on to a domain, you must provide a user name so that you can log on to Windows 2000 Professional.
Password	A password is assigned to each user account. Users must enter their respective passwords in the Password text box so that Windows 2000 Professional can authenticate their accounts. Passwords are case sensitive and appear as asterisks (*) on the screen.
Options	This button is used to expand the Log On to Windows dialog box so that you can access the Log on using dial-up connection check box and the Shutdown button, and the Log on to list box if the computer belongs to a domain.
Log on using dial-up connection	This option permits a user to connect to a domain server using dial-up networking, so that he or she can log on and work from a remote location.
Shutdown	This option closes all files, saves all operating system data, and prepares the computer to be turned off.
Log on to list box	This list box will be included when your computer belongs to a domain. You can either log on locally or you can select a domain name to log on to a domain.

Figure 2-16 Log On to Windows dialog box

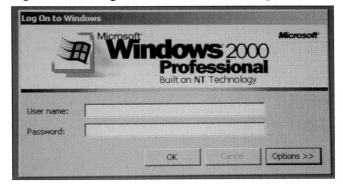

Figure 2-17 Log On to Windows dialog box (expanded)

Figure 2-18 User name and password entered

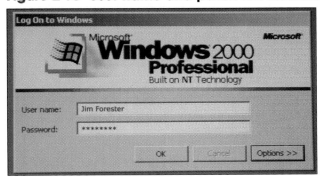

skill 6

Using the Windows 2000 Setup Manager

exam objective

Perform an unattended installation of Windows 2000 Professional. Create unattended answer files by using the Setup Manager to automate the installation of Windows 2000 Professional.

overview

Before you perform an unattended installation of Windows 2000 Professional, you must set up the automatic install environment and create customized **installation scripts** using the Windows 2000 Setup Manager. Installation scripts specify variations in the hardware configurations of the computers depending upon their role and use.

You can also create and modify answer files using the Windows 2000 Setup Manager. Setup Manager asks you a series of questions and, as a result, a script is created for a customized installation of Windows 2000. The answer files provide the responses to the questions that the Setup program asks.

In order to create customized installation scripts and answer files, you must copy the Windows 2000 Setup Manager Wizard to your hard disk. First, you must open the **Deploy.cab** (or **Deploy**) file on the Windows 2000 Professional CD. It is stored in the **Tools** sub-folder in the **Support** folder. Next, double-click the **Deploy** file to open the Deploy window. Select all of the files, right-click them, and select the **Extract** command on the shortcut menu **(Figure 2-19)**.

After the files are extracted, you can use the Setup Manager to either create a new answer file, create an answer file that duplicates the configuration of the computer you are using, or to modify an existing answer file. When you create a new answer file, you must select from among three types of answer files, depending on the type of installation. You can either use the Sysprep utility along with an image replication tool to create a duplicate of the computer configuration that will be copied to other systems on the network, the Remote Installation Services (RIS) to install Windows 2000 Professional on computers with no operating systems, or you can perform an unattended installation. If you create an answer file that duplicates the configuration of the computer you are using, you can customize the level of user interaction with the Setup program.

Setup Manager has an easy-to-use graphical interface that will help you to create and modify answer files and UDFs (Uniqueness database files) that will contain all of the necessary computer-specific and user-specific data. Using Setup Manager, application setup scripting is straightforward and a distribution folder for the installation files is automatically created.

tip

Create the destination folder before you begin. You cannot create folders during the extraction process.

how to

Create unattended answer files by using Setup Manager.

1. Log on as an **Administrator** and insert the **Windows 2000 Professional CD** in the **CD-ROM** drive.
2. Right-click ⊞**Start** and select the **Explore** command on the shortcut menu to open **Windows Explorer**.
3. Click the **C:** drive.
4. Click **File** on the **Menu** bar, point to **New**, and select the **Folder** command to create a new folder on the C: drive.
5. Type **Deploy** to replace the default name for the folder. You will use this folder to store the files that have been extracted from the **Deploy.cab** file on the Windows 2000 Professional CD. Double-click the **CD-ROM drive** icon in Windows Explorer to display the contents of the CD-ROM in the right pane.
6. Double-click the **Support** folder to open the **Support** window.
7. Double-click the **Tools** folder to open the **Tools** window.
8. Double-click the **Deploy** file **(Figure 2-20)** to open the **Deploy** window.
9. Open the **Edit** menu and click the **Select All** command to select all of the files in the window.
10. Right-click any file and click the **Extract** command on the shortcut menu. The **Browse for Folder** window opens.
11. Double-click the **C:** drive to save the extracted files.
12. Click the **Deploy** folder and then click ⬚ OK ⬚. Windows 2000 Professional copies the selected files to the Deploy folder.

tip

To select all of the files in the Deploy.cab file, hold down the **[Ctrl]** key and select each of the files listed. If the file icons are listed in one column, you can also select the files by clicking the first file in the list, holding down the **[Shift]** key and then clicking the last file in the list.

Figure 2-19 The Deploy window

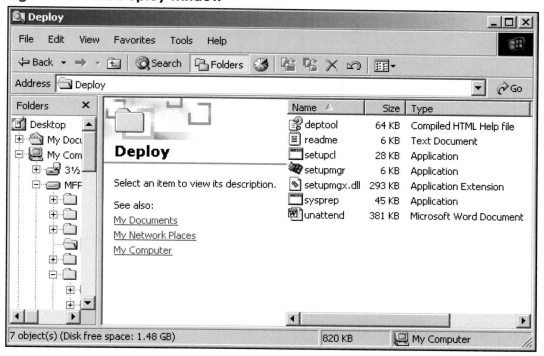

Figure 2-20 The Deploy file in the Tools window

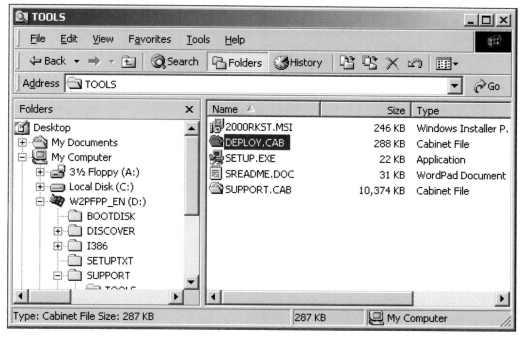

skill 6

Using the Windows 2000 Setup Manager (cont'd)

exam objective

Perform an unattended installation of Windows 2000 Professional. Create unattended answer files by using the Setup Manager to automate the installation of Windows 2000 Professional.

how to

13. After Windows 2000 Professional has finished copying the files to the Deploy folder on your system's **C:** drive, open the Deploy folder to view the copied files.
14. Double-click the **Readme** file to read its contents.
15. Open the Deploy folder in Windows Explorer.
16. Double-click **Setupmgr.exe** in the Deploy folder to start the **Windows 2000 Setup Manager Wizard**.
17. Click `Next >`. The **New Or Existing Answer File** dialog box opens.
18. Make sure that the **Create a new answer file** option button is selected, as shown in **Figure 2-21**.
19. Click `Next >`. The **Product To Install** dialog box opens.
20. Make sure that the **Windows 2000 Unattended Installation** option button is selected. Click `Next >`. The **Platform** dialog box opens.
21. Make sure that the **Windows 2000 Professional** option button is selected. Click `Next >`. The **User Interaction Level** dialog box opens.
22. Select the **Fully automated** option button, as shown in **Figure 2-22**.
23. Click `Next >`. The **License Agreement** opens.
24. Click the **I Accept the terms of the License Agreement** check box and then click `Next >`. The **Customize The Software** dialog box opens.
25. Enter your name in the **Name** text box and your organization name in the **Organization** text box. Click `Next >`. The **Computer Names** dialog box opens.
26. Type the computer name, **PRO2**, in the Computer name text box and click `Add`.
27. Repeat this step to add **PRO3** and **PRO4** to the list of computer names. These names appear in the **Computers to be installed** list box, as shown in (**Figure 2-23**).
28. Click `Next >`. The **Administrator Password** dialog box opens.
29. Make sure that the **Use the following Administrator password (127 characters maximum)** option button is selected and type the password, **password 2**, in the **Password** and **Confirm Password** text boxes.
30. Click `Next >`. The **Display Settings** dialog box opens. Click `Next >` to accept the default settings. The **Network Settings** dialog box opens.
31. Select the **Custom Settings** option button and then click `Next >`. The **Number Of Network Adapters** dialog box opens.
32. Make sure that the **One network adapter** option button is selected. Click `Next >`. The **Networking Components** dialog box opens.
33. Click `Next >` to accept the default settings. The **Workgroup Or Domain** dialog box opens.
34. Click `Next >` to accept the default settings. The **Time Zone** dialog box opens.
35. Select the appropriate time zone and click `Next >`. The **Additional Settings** screen opens.
36. Make sure that the **Yes, edit the additional settings** option button is selected. Click `Next >`. The **Telephony** dialog box opens.
37. Provide the appropriate information for the **What Country/Region Are You In?, What area (or city) code are you in?, If you dial a number to access an outside line, what is it?**, and **The phone system at this location uses** fields.
38. Click `Next >`. The **Regional Settings** dialog box opens.
39. Click `Next >` to accept the default settings. The **Languages** dialog box opens.
40. Click `Next >` to accept the default settings. The **Browser And Shell Settings** dialog box opens.
41. Click `Next >` to accept the default settings. The **Installation Folder** dialog box opens.
42. Select the **This folder** option button and type **W2000Pro** in the **This folder** text box, as shown in **Figure 2-24**.

Figure 2-21 New or Existing Answer File dialog box

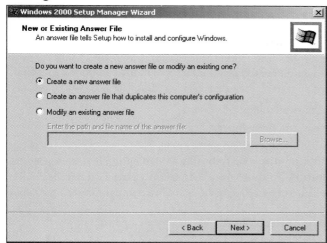

Figure 2-22 The Fully automated option button in the User Interaction Level dialog box

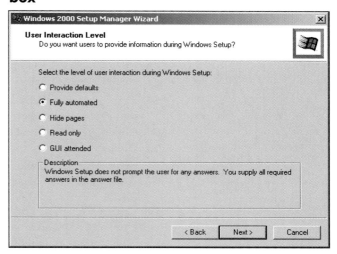

Figure 2-23 Computer Names dialog box

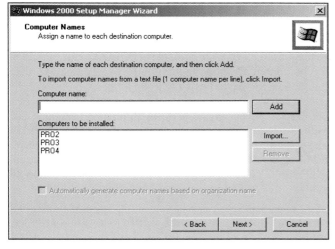

Figure 2-24 Installation Folder dialog box

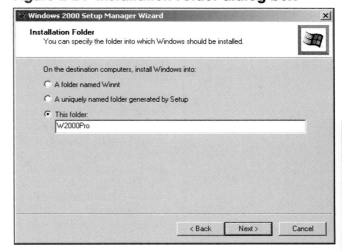

skill 6

Using the Windows 2000 Setup Manager (cont'd)

exam objective

Perform an unattended installation of Windows 2000 Professional. Create unattended answer files by using the Setup Manager to automate the installation of Windows 2000 Professional.

how to

43. Click [Next >]. The **Install Printers** dialog box opens.
44. Click [Next >]. The **Run Once** dialog box opens.
45. Click [Next >]. The **Distribution Folder** dialog box opens.
46. Make sure that the **Yes, create or modify a distribution folder** option button is selected.
47. Click [Next >]. The **Distribution Folder Name** dialog box opens (**Figure 2-25**).
48. Click [Next >] to accept the default settings. The **Additional Mass Storage Drivers** dialog box opens.
49. Click [Next >]. The **Hardware Abstraction Layer** dialog box opens.
50. Click [Next >]. The **Additional Commands** dialog box opens.
51. Click [Next >]. The **OEM Branding** dialog box opens.
52. Click [Next >]. The **Additional Files Or Folder** dialog box opens.
53. Click [Next >]. The **Answer File Name** dialog box opens.
54. Type the path for the answer file, **C:\Deploy\Unattend.txt** in the **Location and file name** text box, as shown in **Figure 2-26**.
55. Click [Next >]. The **Location Of Setup Files** dialog box opens.
56. Click [Next >] to accept the default settings. The **Copying File** screen opens. The **Setup Manager** copies distribution files to your computer hard disk (**Figure 2-27**).
57. After the files are copied, the **Completing the Windows 2000 Setup Manager Wizard** screen opens.
58. Click [Finish]. Three new files now appear in the Deploy folder: **Unattend.bat, Unattend.txt**, and **Unattend.udf** (**Figure 2-28**). The Setup Manager has also created a folder called **Win2000dist** on the hard disk of your computer (**Figure 2-29**).
59. Open Unattend.txt and review its contents. Open Unattend.udf using either Word or Notepad and review its contents. When you have finished, close all open windows.

more

A utility called **Sysdiff** is used with the Setup Manager to perform automated installation of applications on client systems. Actually, the preferred method for automating application installation is to use the scripting and installation routines for those applications. However, you can use the Sysdiff tool to install applications that do not support scripted installation. Sysdiff is included on the CD-ROM that comes with the Windows 2000 Professional Resource Kit, which you must purchase.

Use Sysdiff to create before and after "snapshots" of your machine and to capture application installation files. The changes and necessary installation files are written to a "difference file," which is later used to install applications on other machines. Sysdiff uses two files, **Sysdiff.exe** and **Sysdiff.inf**. Sysdiff.inf (sysdiff.zip) can be downloaded from the Windows 2000 Download site at **ftp://ftp.microsoft.com/reskit/win2000**.

First, copy these two files to the \Winnt directory on the machine that you will use to deploy the application installation package. This "baseline station" should have a clean installation that can include the latest update service pack. Then open the command prompt and type: **sysdiff /snap [snapshot_filename]**, where **snapshot, filename** is the name of the snapshot file you will create. Next, install any software applications you want to include and make any desired system configuration changes. Then run sysdiff from the command prompt again, but use the /diff switch: **sysdiff /diff snapshot_filename [diffname]**, where **diffname** is the name of the difference file you will create. The difference file will contain all changes that the application installations made to the computer. Finally, install Windows 2000 Professional on the target computers, and on each target computer, run: **sysdiff /apply [diffname]** to add the files in the difference file. You can apply the difference file to new installations as part of an unattended setup or at any time after initial installation is complete. Installation packages created in Windows NT 4 cannot be installed on a Windows 2000 computer.

Figure 2-25 Distribution Folder Name dialog box

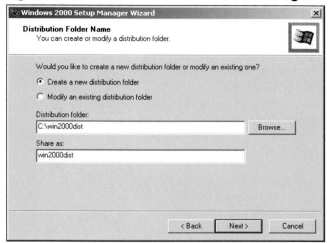

Figure 2-26 Answer File Name dialog box

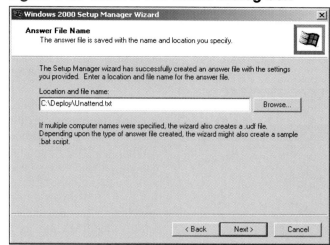

Figure 2-27 Copying Files screen

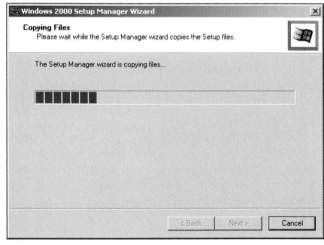

Figure 2-28 New files in the Deploy window

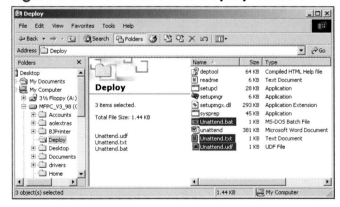

Figure 2-29 Win2000dist folder

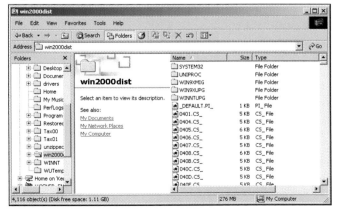

skill 7   *Using the System Preparation Tool*

exam objective

Perform an unattended installation of Windows 2000 Professional. Install Windows 2000 Professional by using the System Preparation Tool.

overview

As a Network Administrator, you may work with a group of computers with identical hardware configurations. Installing Windows 2000 Professional individually on each of these computers would be a tedious task. You can use the **System Preparation tool (SysPrep.exe)** in Windows 2000 Professional to prepare a hard disk so you can create a disk image of the Windows 2000 Professional installation. Then you can transfer that image to multiple computers with the same hardware configuration. The System Preparation tool works in conjunction with a third-party disk-imaging application such as Symantec Ghost or PowerQuest DriveImage. The tool removes computer-specific information, such as the computer name and security identifier (SID), so that you can safely transfer the image created with the disk-imaging software to other computers. This tool helps you create as many "carbon copies" of the distribution model as you require. Each hard drive will include the OS and all applications that those workstations will need.

Before you use the System Preparation tool, you must prepare a distribution model computer. The distribution model machine cannot be a member of a domain. It must be a member of a workgroup, and you must leave the administrator password blank. First, perform a clean installation of Windows 2000 Professional and configure it as desired. Then copy the necessary files from the Deploy.cab file as outlined in the previous skill. Next, log on as the Administrator, and install all of the applications you will use on the network and all necessary update packs. This is the installation you will use to create what is called the **master disk image**. The master disk image will be transferred to the hard disks of the target computers to create clones of the distribution model.

Next, run Sysprep.exe from the Sysprep folder **(Figure 2-30)**. The Windows 2000 Professional System Preparation Tool dialog box will advise you that security parameters are going to be changed, and will prompt you to shut down the computer. The **Sysprep.exe** file is the main Sysprep executable file. The syntax to run Sysprep.exe is as follows:

Sysprep.exe [/quiet] [/nosidgen] [/pnp] [/reboot]

Table 2-5 explains the meaning of the various switches.

The primary function of the System Preparation tool is to remove the SID (security identifier) from the distribution model computer. If this were copied to the clone computers and you had the same SID on a group of computers on the network, it would cause major network security problems. SysPrep ensures that a unique SID will be created the first time one of the clone computers is booted up. It also installs a Mini-Setup Wizard on the distribution model computer so that, when a clone computer is booted up for the first time, the user will be prompted to accept the licensing contract and enter the Product ID, regional settings, user name, company name, network configuration, workgroup or domain, and time zone. The Mini-Setup program includes Plug and Play detection capability. This capability is necessary if the clones do not have the same hardware as the distribution model computer. The distribution model computer and the clone computers must have the same hardware abstraction layer (HAL), hard disk controller, boot device, and Ntoskrnl.exe. Ntoskrnl.exe, the microkernel file, creates a Registry key that contains information about the hardware components on a computer during the boot process. HAL is the layer that sorts out the differences between hardware components, presenting to the operating system a standard-looking set of computer hardware. The hard disk controller is an interface between the hard disk and the operating system. The mass-storage controllers (either IDE or SCSI) must also be identical.

Due to Windows 2000's Plug and Play functionality, other hardware devices such as network adapters, sound cards, modems, and video cards do not have to be the same. However, if any device drivers for hardware devices on the clone computers are not included in Drivers.cab,

caution

Disk duplication will only be successful if the master disk image computer and the clone computers have the same basic hardware (hardware abstraction layer or HAL), hard disk controller, power management, and number of processors.

Figure 2-30 Sysprep.exe and Setupcl.exe in the Sysprep folder

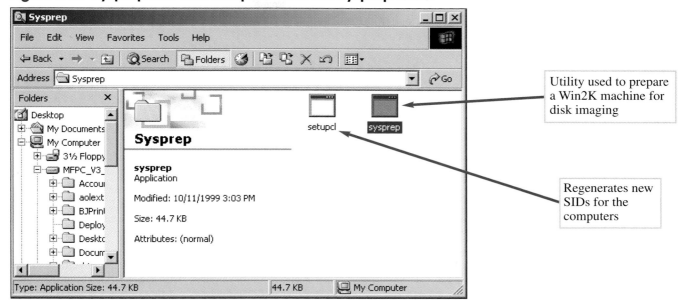

Utility used to prepare a Win2K machine for disk imaging

Regenerates new SIDs for the computers

Table 2-5 Switches used by System Preparation Manager	
Switches	**Description used by System Preparation Manager**
/quiet	Runs Sysprep in quiet mode. This switch stops the confirmation dialog boxes from displaying while Sysprep runs on the distribution model computer. It is used when you want to automate Sysprep by adding it to the GuiRunOnce key in the Unattend.txt file.
/pnp	Forces a full device detection on the target computer. This switch is optional. Use it when non-Plug and Play devices that cannot be dynamically detected exist on the target systems.
/reboot	Enables a reboot of the master computer after the image has been created instead of shutting down and then starting the Mini-Setup Wizard. Use this switch for auditing the system and verifying that Mini-Setup is operating correctly.
/nosidgen	Runs Sysprep without generating any security ID. This switch is useful for the Administrator who doesn't intend to clone the computer on which Sysprep is running.

skill 7

Using the System Preparation Tool
(cont'd)

exam objective

Perform an unattended installation of Windows 2000 Professional. Install Windows 2000 Professional by using the System Preparation Tool.

overview

you must either install them on the distribution model computer before you run Sysprep, or you must ensure that the uninstalled drivers are available on the clone computers when you first boot them so that they can be detected and installed.

The master disk image can be saved on a shared network drive or on a CD-ROM. After you have transferred the master disk image to the clone computers, you can turn them on to initiate the Mini-Setup Wizard. You also can create a Sysprep.inf file so that the Mini-Setup Wizard can run without any user intervention. It will include the answers to all questions posed by the wizard. Before you run Sysprep, use the Setup Manager Wizard (**Setupmgr.exe** from the **Deploy.cab** file) to create a Sysprep.inf answer file **(Figure 2-31)** that you can use to provide unique information for the target computers, including network and regional settings. When the Mini-Setup Wizard runs, it looks for the **Sysprep.inf** answer file **(Figure 2-32)** in the Sysprep folder on the distribution model's root drive and runs it if located. You also can save the Sysprep.inf answer file on a floppy and insert it in the clone computer right after the boot loader appears. If you use a Sysprep.inf answer file, three files: **Sysprep.exe**, **Setupcl.exe, and Sysprep.inf**, must all be saved in the same subfolder. Setupcl.exe is the utility that regenerates new SIDs for the computers.

how to

Use the **System Preparation** tool.

1. If you actually were going to mass deploy Windows 2000 Professional, and you wanted to prepare a hard disk so that you could create a disk image, you first would perform a clean installation of the OS on a computer that was not a member of a domain, leaving the administrator password blank.

2. Next, log on as an **Administrator** and install and customize applications such as Microsoft Office or other business-specific programs that your target computers will need. You also can install any device drivers the clones may need that are not included in **Drivers.cab** (or not installed by the answer file if you have created one).

3. It is often recommended that you now use a third-party auditing tool to audit the system and verify that the image configuration is correct. Do not overwrite any system files when you audit. Sysprep cannot detect or restore system files that the auditing utility may have changed. It is all right to reboot as many times as needed during the auditing process.

4. When your audit is complete, delete any files or folders that the auditing utility added to the hard drive.

5. Open Windows Explorer. Create a new folder on your **%systemroot%** (usually **C:**) named **Sysprep**. Open the **Deploy** folder (extracted files from Deploy.cab) and move the **Sysprep.exe** and **Setupcl.exe** files to the Sysprep folder. If you used the Setup Manager Wizard to create a Sysprep.inf file, it must also be moved to this folder. You can create the Sysprep folder and store Sysprep.inf in it when you run the **Setup Manager Wizard (Figure 2-33)**.

6. Run Sysprep.exe. The Windows 2000 System Preparation Tool message box **(Figure 2-34)** warns you that running Sysprep may modify some of the security parame-

**Figure 2-31 Using the Setup Manager to create a
Sysprep answer file**

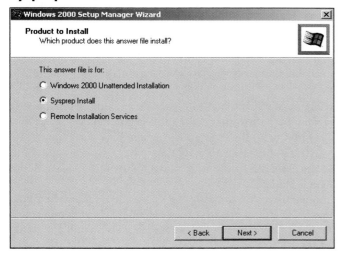

**Figure 2-32 The Sysprep folder after running
the Setup Manager**

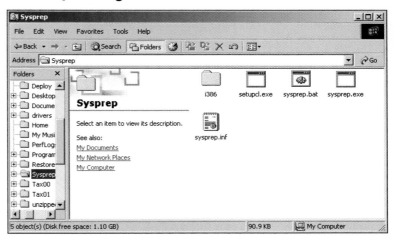

**Figure 2-33 Creating the Sysprep folder and
Sysprep.inf with the Setup Manager**

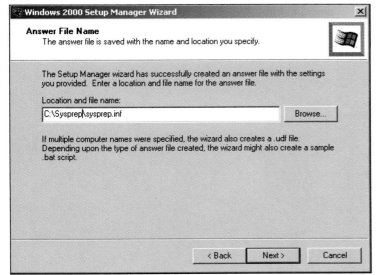

skill 7

Using the System Preparation Tool
(cont'd)

exam objective

Perform an unattended installation of Windows 2000 Professional. Install Windows 2000 Professional by using the Perform Disk Duplication System Preparation Tool.

how to

ters on the computer. ACPI computers will automatically shut down. Otherwise, a dialog box will open to let you know that it is safe to shut down the computer.

7. The hard disk of the computer is now programmed to run Plug and Play detection, create new security identifiers (SIDs) (because Setupcl.exe has been copied to %systemroot%\SYSTEM32 and will run at the next boot), and run the Mini-Setup Wizard the next time the system is started.

8. Now you are ready to use an imaging utility to create the master disk image. Copy the image to a shared folder or onto a CD-ROM. The next time you boot up this computer, or any of the clones that were created from the master disk image, the system will detect and re-catalog the Plug and Play devices.

9. When the clone computers are booted up, first Plug and Play detection will take place. Then, the Mini Setup Wizard will run. Users will be prompted to accept the EULA (End-User License Agreement), enter their name and organization, join a workgroup or a domain, enter regional settings, enter TAPI (Telephony Application Program Interface) information, and choose the networking protocols and service to install. If you used a Sysprep.inf file **(Figure 2-35)**, only dialog boxes containing information that was not included in the .inf file will appear.

10. Finally, the local Sysprep folder containing Sysprep.exe, Sysprep.inf, and Setupcl.exe will be deleted, the computer will restart, and the logon dialog box will display.

Figure 2-34 Windows 2000 System Preparation Tool message box

Figure 2-35 Example of a Sysprep.inf answer file

skill 8

Performing Remote Installation on Client Computers

exam objective

Perform an unattended installation of Windows 2000 Professional. Install Windows 2000 Professional by using Windows 2000 Server Remote Installation Services (RIS).

overview

RIS can eliminate much time and effort on the part of administrators by enabling them to create an image of the operating system that can be downloaded and installed automatically by client computers on a network. In a **remote installation**, the administrator connects to a Windows 2000 Server called the **Remote Installation Server** (or **RIS server**), which stores the RIS image. RIS images, usually referred to simply as images, are copies of the Windows 2000 installation files. An installation of Windows 2000 Professional, free of user interaction, can then be performed from a central location.

caution

In order to perform a remote installation, you must have a Windows 2000 Server computer and the computers on the network must support remote boot.

RIS is not included with Windows 2000 Professional. It comes with Windows 2000 Server, Advanced Server and Datacenter Server. The RIS server can be either a member server or a domain controller. The RIS clients must have either a PXE (Pre-Boot Execution Environment) capable BIOS, a network card with remote boot functionality (PXE version .99c or higher), a regular PCI (Peripheral Component Interconnect) bus network card that is supported by RBFG (Remote Boot Disk Generator) program, or an RIS boot disk, which you can create using the Windows 2000 Remote Boot Disk Generator (RBFG.EXE).

Specific network services must also be available on the network, although they do not have to be on the RIS server. For example, there must be a DNS (Domain Name System) server because RIS needs the DNS service in order to locate the Active Directory and the client computer accounts. A DHCP (Dynamic Host Configuration Protocol) server is also necessary so that client computers that boot from a network card can get an IP (Internet Protocol) address. An IP address is needed in order for client computers to communicate with the RIS server on the network. If you have routers that do not support DHCP/BOOTP message relaying, you will either need a DHCP server or a DHCP relay agent on the same subnet as the RIS clients. It can either be a Windows NT 4.0 server or a Windows 2000 server. Active Directory Services must also be running so that the RIS servers and RIS clients can be located. Active Directory will also handle RIS configuration settings and client installation options.

RIS must be installed on a separate partition from the system partition (the one on which Windows 2000 Server is installed). This partition must have enough space to store the RIS software and images and must be formatted with NTFS. This NTFS volume must then be shared.

how to

Install **RIS** on a computer running Windows 2000 Server.

1. Log on as an **Administrator** and insert the **Windows 2000 Server CD** in the **CD-ROM** drive.
2. Open the **Control Panel** window and double-click the **Add/Remove Program**s icon to open the **Add/Remove Programs window (Figure 2-36)**.
3. Click **Add/Remove Windows Components** to initiate the **Windows Components Wizard**.
4. Select the **Remote Installation Services** check box in the **Components** list box **(Figure 2-37)**.

Figure 2-36 Add/Remove Programs window

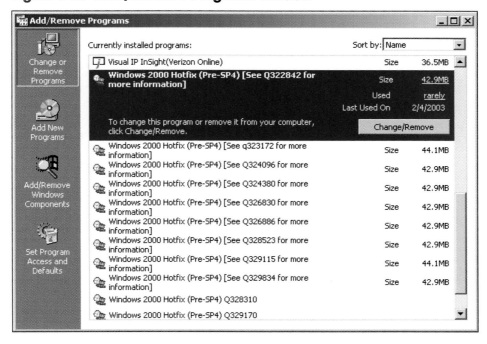

Figure 2-37 Installing Remote Installation Services

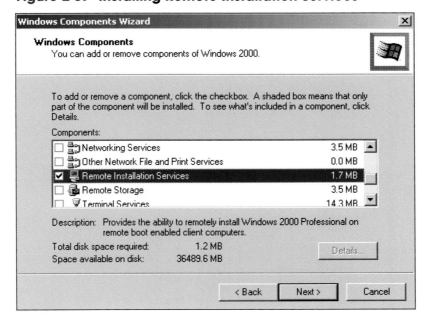

skill 8

Performing Remote Installation on Client Computers *(cont'd)*

exam objective

Perform an unattended installation of Windows 2000 Professional. Install Windows 2000 Professional by using Windows 2000 Server Remote Installation Services (RIS).

how to

5. Click [Next >]. This starts the installation of **Remote Installation Services**, as shown in **Figure 2-38**.
6. When the installation is complete, the **Completing the Windows Components Wizard** screen opens **(Figure 2-39)**.
7. Click [Finish]. The **System Settings Change** dialog box informs you that you must reboot your system before the new settings will take effect.
8. Remove the Windows 2000 Server CD and click [Yes].

more

The RIS server stores the installation images that are used by client computers to download and install Windows 2000 Professional. These images are of two types:

- CD-based
- RIPrep

CD-based images are created from the Windows 2000 Professional installation CD and stored on the RIS server. You can use answer files to customize these images.

RIPrep images are created by taking a snapshot of a preconfigured computer and storing it on the RIS server. These images can also include application installations. An RIPrep image is created by two systems: the source computer, (the computer that contains the basic operating system and applications) and the RIS server.

tip

The Remote Installation Preparation Wizard runs when the source computer is ready. Type \\RIS Server Name\reminst\admin\i386\Riprep.exe to run this wizard.

Figure 2-38 The Windows Components Wizard

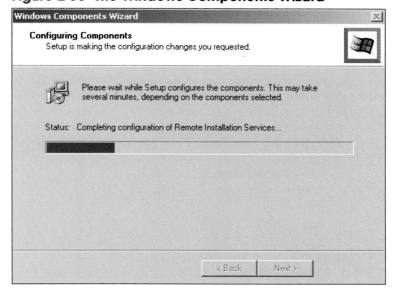

Figure 2-39 Completing the Windows Components Wizard

skill 9

Configuring Remote Installation Services

exam objective

Perform an unattended installation of Windows 2000 Professional. Install Windows 2000 Professional by using Windows 2000 Server Remote Installation Services (RIS).

overview

After you have installed Remote Installation Services, you must configure them to meet your requirements. First, the path to the remote installation folder location must be entered. This folder will not already exist. You will enter the drive letter where you installed RIS (remember, this drive must be formatted with NTFS), and the name for a new folder, which will be created as part of the configuration process. Next, the RIS server must be configured to support the RIS client computers. Finally, you must enter the path to the installation source files. The RIS server can be a:

- Domain controller
- Member server

caution

In order for a member server to be an RIS server, it must be a member of the domain in which the target computers are members.

how to

Configure Remote Installation Services.

1. After installing **RIS**, log on as an **Administrator**. The **Microsoft Windows 2000 Configure Your Server** window opens. If the Configure Your Server window does not open, open the **Control Panel**, double-click **Add/Remove Programs** and select **Add/Remove Windows Components**. Under **Setup Services**, select **Configure Remote Installation Services**. Then click the **Configure** button. Skip the second and third steps and go on to the fourth step.
2. Click **Finish Setup**. The **Add/Remove Programs** window opens, prompting you to **Configure Remote Installation Services (Figure 2-40)**.
3. Click ⬚ Configure ⬚ . The **Remote Installation Services Setup Wizard** opens.
4. Insert the **Windows 2000 Professional CD** in the **CD-ROM** drive of the server. The **Microsoft Windows 2000 CD** dialog box opens.
5. Click **Exit**. The **Welcome** screen for the **Remote Installation Services Setup Wizard** opens **(Figure 2-41)**.
6. Read the Welcome screen and click ⬚ Next > ⬚ . The **Remote Installation Folder Location** dialog box opens.

Figure 2-40 Configure Remote Installation Services in the Add/Remove Programs window

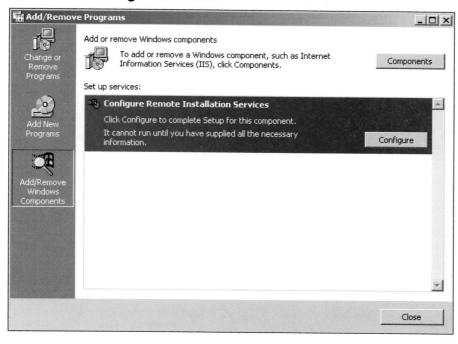

Figure 2-41 The Remote Installation Services Setup Wizard

skill 9

Configuring Remote Installation Services (cont'd)

exam objective

Perform an unattended installation of Windows 2000 Professional. Install Windows 2000 Professional by using Windows 2000 Server Remote Installation Services (RIS).

how to

7. In the path text box, type **D:\RemoteInstall (Figure 2-42)**. Note that you must enter a drive letter that is appropriate for your system. It must be a pre-existing NTFS drive with at least 300 MB of free space on the computer on which you installed RIS. The folder does not have to be pre-existing; it will be created as part of the configuration process.
8. Click [Next >]. The **Initial Settings** page opens.
9. Select the **Respond to client computers requesting service** check box and click [Next >]. The **Installation Source Files Location** dialog box opens.
10. Type the path to the installation source files, **x:\i386**, in the given text box, where **x** represents the drive letter for your CD-ROM drive.
11. Click [Next >]. The **Windows Installation Image Folder Name** page opens.
12. Click [Next >] to accept the default name of **Win2000.pro**. The **Friendly Description And Help Text** page opens.
13. Click [Next >] to accept the default friendly description and help text. The **Review Settings** page opens.
14. Review the information and click [Finish]. The RIS setup program creates the remote installation folder, copies the RIS files and the Windows installation files, updates the Client Installation Wizard screen files, creates a new unattended Setup answer file, creates the Remote Installation Services (RIS), updates the Registry, and starts the necessary Remote Installation Services.
15. Click **Done** when the tasks are completed.
16. Close all open windows and dialog boxes.

more

The most important thing to understand about RIS is that it only comes with the Windows 2000 Server editions and that networks which do not have at least one Windows 2000 server cannot use it. Also remember that DNS must be running on a network server in order for RIS to locate Active Directory and the client computer accounts, and DHCP must be running so that computers with bootable network cards can be assigned an IP address. Client computers must have a BIOS version that supports PXE (Pre-Boot Execution Environment), a PXE network interface card, or a regular PCI (Peripheral Component Interconnect) network interface card that is supported by the Remote Boot Disk (Floppy) Generator (RBFG) program. PXE enables a workstation to boot from a server on a network before it boots the operating system on its hard drive. If the BIOS of the client computer or its network adapters don't support PXE, you can create and use an RIS boot disk to start the RIS client computers. Run the Windows 2000 Remote Boot Disk Generator (RBFG.EXE), which is stored on the RIS server to create the RIS boot disk.

If neither the BIOS nor the network interface card in the client computer supports PXE, you can use the Windows 2000 Remote Boot Disk Generator (RBFG.EXE) to create a boot disk or boot floppy that will mimic the PXE boot process. To create a boot floppy for a remote client, you use the following command at the command prompt on the RIS Server:
◆ The path to create a boot disk is: **\RemoteInstall\Admin\i386\Rbfg.exe.**
◆ Alternatively, you can double-click **Rbfg.exe** in the **\RemoteInstall\Admin\i386** folder to create the boot floppy.

Figure 2-42 Remote Installation Folder Location screen

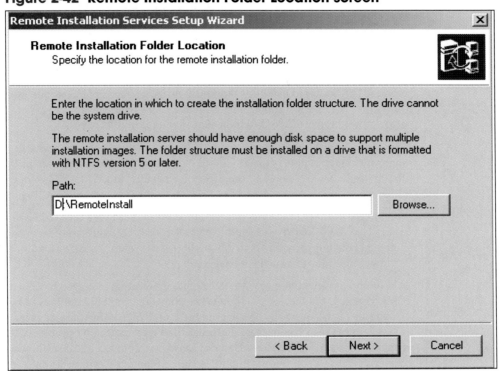

skill 10

Upgrading Previous Versions of Windows to Windows 2000 Professional

exam objective

Upgrade from a previous version of Windows to Windows 2000 Professional.

overview

When you upgrade from a previous version of Windows 2000, you should first generate a report that identifies the system components that are compatible with Windows 2000 Professional. You can do this by running the **Windows 2000 Readiness Analyzer.** This utility runs by design during system upgrades; however, it is a good practice to discover hardware-related problems before the upgrade so that you can preempt any potential problems. To generate a hardware compatibility report, you can use one of two methods. You can either use the **checkupgradeonly switch** with the Winnt32 command (**Winnt32/checkupgradeonly**) or you can run **Chkupgrd.exe**. When you use the checkupgradeonly switch, you start the Setup program and check for compatible hardware and software, but Setup stops and produces the report. The Chkupgrd.exe utility instantly produces the report, but this utility is not included on the Windows 2000 Professional CD-ROM. It can be downloaded at: **http://www.microsoft.com /windows/download/default.asp**.

The compatibility report is generated as a text document, which you can view in the %systemroot% folder which is usually in the WINDOWS folder for Windows 9x upgrades. When you upgrade NT 3.51 or 4.0, the report is saved in the Winnt32.log in the %systemroot% folder.

In addition to identifying the compatibility of the hardware and software, the compatibility report lets you know if you need to upgrade your software and it identifies any additional changes you might need to make so that the system functions without problems after Windows 2000 Professional is installed.

caution

Third-party network protocols and client software that do not have an updated version in the i386 Winntupg folder on the Windows 2000 CD-ROM should also be removed.

You should not encounter any problems with applications that you have installed on Windows NT 3.51 and 4, but there are certain applications that should be removed before you upgrade. Among those are antivirus applications and disk quota software, because the upgrade from NTFS 4 to NTFS 5 has instituted changes that may cause you problems. Any custom power management software and tools should also be removed because they are now irrelevant. Windows 2000 Professional includes the Advanced Configuration and Power Interface (ACPI) and Advanced Power Management (APM) to perform these functions.

how to

Upgrade from a previous version of Windows to Windows 2000 Professional.
1. Insert the **Windows 2000 Professional CD-ROM** disk into the CD-ROM drive of your computer. The **Microsoft Windows 2000 CD** message box **(Figure 2-43)** prompts you to upgrade your system to Windows 2000.
2. Click [Yes]. The **Welcome to the Windows 2000 Setup Wizard** screen prompts you to specify whether you want to upgrade to Windows 2000 or install a new copy of Windows 2000 **(Figure 2-44)**.
3. Make sure that the **Upgrade to Windows 2000 (Recommended)** option button is selected. Click [Next >]. The **Licensing Agreement** opens.
4. Click the **I Accept this agreement** option button to accept the licensing terms and click [Next >]. The **Your Product Key** dialog box opens.
5. Enter the 25-character product key number for Windows 2000 Professional **(Figure 2-45)**. The product key comes with the Windows 2000 Professional CD.
6. Click [Next >]. The **Select Special Options** dialog box opens. You can customize language, installation, and accessibility options. For this installation, you do not need to modify the default settings.

Figure 2-43 Microsoft Windows 2000 CD message box

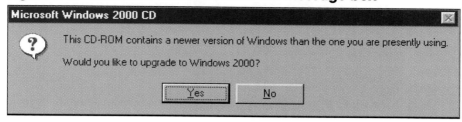

Figure 2-44 Windows 2000 Setup Welcome screen

Figure 2-45 The Your Product Key dialog box

skill 10

Upgrading Previous Versions of Windows to Windows 2000 Professional (cont'd)

exam objective

Upgrade from a previous version of Windows to Windows 2000 Professional.

how to

7. Click [Next >]. Setup will load information and determine which files must be copied for the installation. After the information is loaded, Setup will copy the installation files to your computer and restart your computer. Restarting the computer enables Setup to inspect the hardware configuration and load the installation files to your computer. The Setup program now prepares Microsoft Windows 2000 Professional to run on your computer.

8. Press the **[Enter]** key to continue the installation. Setup will prompt you to select a file system (**Figure 2-46**).

9. Press the **[Enter]** key to accept the default selection. Setup will examine your disk and install Windows 2000 Professional on the drive where there is enough disk space by copying files to the Windows 2000-installation folder. When the process is complete, the Welcome to **Windows 2000 Professional** screen opens. Setup then detects and installs the Windows 2000 components on your system (**Figure 2-47**).

10. After all of the components are installed, click [Next >]. The **Regional Settings** dialog box opens. Here you can customize Windows 2000 for different regions and languages.

11. Accept the default settings and click [Next >]. The **Personalize Your Software** dialog box opens. Here, you can personalize your software by providing information about yourself and your organization (**Figure 2-48**).

12. After you have entered the required information, click [Next >]. The **Computer Name and Administration Password** dialog box opens.

13. Type the computer name and the administrative password that you want to use in order to have administrative rights on the computer.

14. Click [Next >]. The **Date and Time Settings** dialog box opens.

15. Set the correct date and time for your computer and click [Next >]. **The Networking Settings** dialog box opens. Setup now installs network software so that you can communicate with other computers, networks, and the Internet.

16. After the networking components are installed, click [Next >] to go to the second screen of the Networking Settings dialog box.

17. You can select either typical or custom settings for configuring your networking settings. When you select the typical settings, you can create your network connections using the **Client for Microsoft Networks**, **File and Print sharing for Microsoft Networks**, and the **TCP/IP** transport protocol with automatic addressing. However, if you choose custom settings, you can manually configure the networking components. Click the **Custom settings** option button and click [Next >]. The **Networking Components** dialog box opens. Here, you select the networking component that will enable your computer to connect to other computers.

18. Accept the default components and click [Next >]. The **Workgroup or Computer Domain** dialog box opens. You must specify whether you want your computer to join a workgroup or a domain.

19. Accept the default selection **Yes, make this computer a member of the following domain** and type the domain name for your computer, **Domain1**.

20. Click [Next >]. The **Join Computer to DOMAIN Domain** dialog box opens (**Figure 2-49**). Enter your name and password.

21. After you have entered the required information, click [OK]. The **Installing Components** screen opens while Setup installs the Windows 2000 components.

Figure 2-46 Selecting a partition for Windows 2000

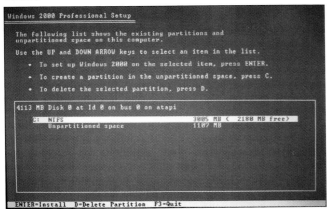

Figure 2-47 The Installing Components screen

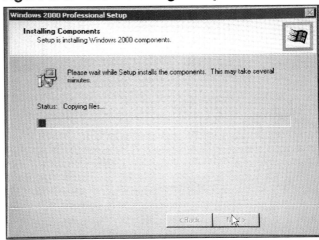

Figure 2-48 Personalize Your Software dialog box

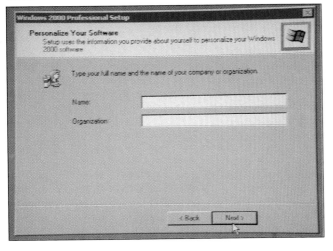

Figure 2-49 Joining a workgroup or domain

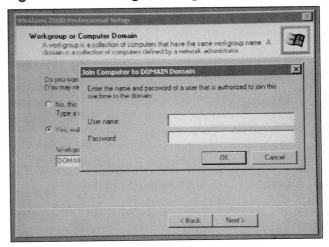

skill 10

Upgrading Previous Versions of Windows to Windows 2000 Professional (cont'd)

exam objective

Upgrade from a previous version of Windows to Windows 2000 Professional.

how to

22. After the components are installed, click [Next >]. The **Performing Final Tasks** screen opens **(Figure 2-50)**. The final tasks include installing the **Start** menu items, registering the components, saving the settings, and removing any temporary files.
23. After these tasks are completed, click [Next >]. The next screen informs you that you have successfully completed the Windows 2000 Setup.
24. Click [Finish]. This will restart your computer. After the reboot, the **Welcome to the Network Identification Wizard** screen will display.
25. Click [Next >]. The **User account** dialog box opens. Enter the user account name, for example **user3**.
26. Click [Next >]. The **Access level** dialog box prompts you to provide the level of access you want to grant to the user.
27. Accept the default selection and click [Next >]. The **Completed Networking** screen indicates that you have successfully upgraded your computer to Windows 2000 Professional.

more

The process of upgrading computers running Windows NT versions 3.51 and 4.0 is similar to that of computers running Windows 95 or 98. You can log on to a Windows 2000 network from a computer running Windows NT 3.51 or Windows NT 4.0 that does not meet the hardware compatibility requirements for Windows 2000 Professional. However, logging on from such a computer will prevent you from taking advantage of many of the Windows 2000 Professional features.

Figure 2-50 The Performing Final Tasks screen

skill 11 *Deploying Service Packs*

exam objective

Deploy service packs.

overview

You need to completely understand the deployment process to ensure the successful deployment of service packs. The deployment process has the following phases (**Figure 2-51**):

◆ **Choosing an installation method:** There are various methods you can use to install service packs. For example, an **Update installation** is used to install only service packs, an **Integrated installation** is used to install service packs along with the installation of Windows 2000 Professional, and a **Combination installation** is used to install service packs with a variety of other components.

◆ **Identifying the deployment tools and files:** You must determine the necessary deployment tools and files after you select the installation method. These tools and files are listed below:

- Unattend.txt
- Cmdlines.txt
- Microsoft Windows Installer Service
- Microsoft Systems Management Server (SMS)
- Determining upgrade options: You also need to determine the upgrade paths and platforms, Update Installation Platforms and Integrated Installation Platforms, before deploying the service packs.

◆ **Checking space requirements:** You must have adequate free hard disk space before you install a service pack to ensure that the service pack functions correctly. The space required for the installation files is temporary and does not contribute to the total space requirement, but you will need adequate space for the uninstallation files and for installation files and settings that are changed during service pack installation. You also need sufficient space to test the deployment on your system to ensure that the service packs are functioning properly after the installation. You must also evaluate application compatibility for applications that were designed to run on Windows 95 or Windows NT 4.0.

Figure 2-51 The deployment process

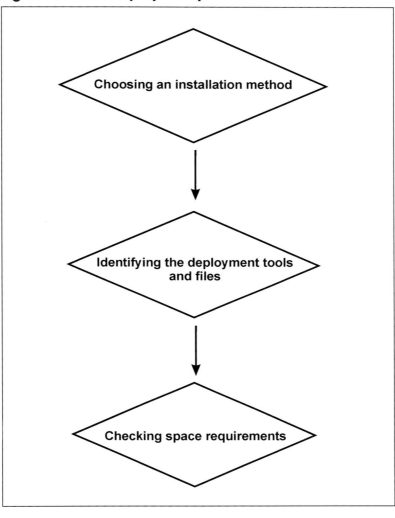

skill 12

Installing Service Packs

exam objective

Apply update packs to installed software applications.

overview

Sometimes Microsoft releases update patches for various applications that are widely in use. For example, there may be SMTP updates for Outlook Express or security updates for Internet Explorer. Updates can be bundled together and packaged with the Windows 2000 CD-ROM in the form of service packs. Service packs are a set of utilities or file updates bundled together. Updates can include new code, error corrections, or service-specific configuration settings from Microsoft. The purpose of updates is to correct or hide the deficiencies of the original product.

All previous versions of the Windows operating system required a separate installation for service packs. In fact, if you reconfigured the operating system by adding a particular service, you would have to reinstall the existing service packs. One of the significant changes in Windows 2000 Professional is that you can perform **slipstreaming** of service packs. This simply means that the service pack is put on the distribution server so that when Windows 2000 Professional is installed over the network the service pack is installed simultaneously.

To install a service pack on a computer, you must run **Update.exe**. Running Update.exe replaces the existing Windows 2000 Professional files with the appropriate new files from the service pack **(Figure 2-52)**. Some of the Windows 2000 files that are typically replaced with new service pack files are:

- layout.inf
- dosnet.inf
- txtsetup.sif
- driver.cab (in case any drivers are changed)

Windows 2000 Professional automatically recognizes when a service is added or removed from your system and copies the required files from either the Windows 2000 installation files or from the service pack install location.

tip

The name of the executable may vary depending on which version of the Windows Professional operating system you are using.

more

Upgrade packs that include one or more .dll files to improve an application's compatibility with Windows 2000 are also released from third party vendors. These types of files are most often used when you upgrade an older version of Windows to Windows 2000 so that you can update existing applications rather than having to reinstall them. Microsoft's Software Development Kit (SDK) provides information to vendors on how to design upgrade packs. In the graphical phase of installation, software upgrade packs can be integrated into the setup process. Open the **WIN9XUPG** subfolder in the **I386** directory to see the upgrade packs already installed on your computer.

A user with administrative rights can deploy a service pack onto a single workstation by simply double-clicking the executable file. Another method is to first extract the executable file by running **Update.exe** with the **/x** switch. After the file is extracted, you can use Update.exe with the various switches shown in **Table 2-6**. If you run Update.exe in Quiet or Unattended Setup mode (**/q** or **/u** switch), you must also use the **/o** switch to ensure that OEM-supplied files are updated, or else the HAL and disk miniport drivers will not be updated. To apply a service pack to a master disk image, use: **Update.exe/Slip**.

Figure 2-52 The Windows 2000 Service Pack Setup Wizard

Table 2-6   Command-line parameters for Update.exe

Switch	Description
/u	Use Unattended Setup mode
/f	Force other applications to close at shutdown
/n	Do not back up files for uninstall
/o	Overwrite OEM files without prompting
/z	Do not restart the computer when the installation completes
/q	Quiet mode 3/4 with no user interaction required
/s:folder_name	Use integrated installation mode 3/4 to a distribution server location

Summary

◆ Windows 2000 is an operating system that provides enhanced compatibility, file management capabilities, and security compared to earlier versions of Windows.

◆ Performing certain pre-installation tasks enables you to avoid problems you may encounter while installing Windows 2000 Professional.

◆ Pre-installation tasks include determining the hardware requirements, cross-checking the hardware compatibility list, creating disk partitions, and determining the file system you will use.

◆ Windows 2000 Professional can be installed from a CD or over a network.

◆ When installing Windows 2000 Professional on a large number of computers, it is preferable to use the over-the-network installation method.

◆ Prerequisites for installing Windows 2000 Professional over a network:

  • Creating a distribution server
  • Creating a FAT partition on the target computer
  • Installing a network client

◆ Computers on most networks do not have identical configurations. To specify variations in hardware configurations, you must use installation scripts. Using the Windows 2000 Setup Manager Wizard, you can create a script for a customized installation of Windows 2000 Professional.

◆ You use disk duplication to create a master disk image of the Windows 2000 Professional installation that is copied to multiple computers with the same hardware configuration on the network.

◆ You use the System Preparation tool, Sysprep.exe, to prepare a computer's hard disk for disk imaging. The System Preparation (SysPrep) tool works in conjunction with a third-party, disk-imaging application. It removes computer-specific information, such as the computer name and security identifier (SID), so that the image that is created can be transferred to the other computers.

◆ Remote Installation can be used to install Windows 2000 Professional on client computers by connecting to a server running installation services, known as Remote Installation Services (RIS).

◆ If you are currently using Windows 95, 98, ME, or NT 4.0 Workstation, you can upgrade to Windows 2000 Professional. The Windows 2000 Readiness Analyzer is used to generate a compatibility report about the current hardware and software on a system.

◆ Using Windows 2000 Professional, you can install service packs at the same time as the operating system, saving time that would have been spent installing the service packs separately.

Key Terms

Access token
Action log
Answer file
checkupgradeonly switch
Chkupgrd.exe
Computer name (NetBIOS name)
Distribution server
Error log
Hardware Compatibility List
Installation script
Log files

Master disk image
Mini-Setup wizard
Partition
Remote installation
Remote Installation Server (RIS server)
Setup
Setup Wizard
Slipstreaming
Sysdiff
System Preparation tool

System service
Update.exe
Windir
Windir\comsetup.log
Windir\debug\netSetup.log
Windir\mmdet.log
Windir\setupapi.log
Windows 2000 Readiness Analyzer
Winnt.exe
Winnt32.exe

Test Yourself

1. You are a system administrator in Software Perfects Inc. Three employees have joined the Applications department. You need to install Windows 2000 Professional on their systems. They have joined as Senior Software Developers and in order to develop a certain project they require different hardware from the rest of the employees in their organization. Which of the following options would you use to specify the hardware variations at the time of Windows 2000 Professional installation?
a. Answer file
b. Installation scripts
c. Action log
d. Distribution server

2. To prepare for disk imaging, which of the following would you need to use?
a. Deploy folder
b. Sysdiff.exe file
c. System Preparation tool
d. Winnt32.exe

3. At the time of master disk generation, if you need to install Windows 2000 without any user intervention, you use the:
a. Sysprep.inf file
b. Sysdiff.exe file
c. Mini-setup wizard
d. Winnt.exe file

4. As an administrator of a software company, GenX Inc., you are required to install Windows 2000 Professional on three computers with blank hard drives. Which of the following options will you use to install Windows 2000 Professional from a central location?
   a. HAL
   b. SID
   c. RIS
   d. i386

5. To locate the Active Directory and client computer accounts on a network, RIS relies on a service called:
   a. DNS
   b. DHCP
   c. Active Directory
   d. RIPrep

6. To configure RIS you need:
   a. A remote installation folder
   b. Installation scripts
   c. Sysprep.exe
   d. RBFG.EXE

7. To replicate the PXE process, you need to use the:
   a. Boot floppy
   b. Remote Boot Disk Generator
   c. Noreboot command
   d. Convert command

8. The files that are replaced when you install a new service pack are: (Choose all that apply.)
   a. Sysprep.inf
   b. Txtsetup.sif
   c. Sysdiff.exe
   d. driver.cab
   e. Winnt.exe file

9. Which of the following pre-installation tasks do you need to complete before installing Windows 2000 Professional? (Choose all that apply.)
   a. Selecting a file system
   b. Accepting the license

   c. Selecting the domain or work group that you want to join
   d. Ensuring that the hardware of your computer is included on the HCL
   e. Selecting the modem dialing information

10. Installing Windows 2000 Professional from a CD-ROM consists of four stages. One of these stages is:
    a. Identifying the hardware requirements.
    b. Determining the way in which you want to partition the hard disk of the computer on which you need to install Windows 2000 Professional.
    c. Identifying a file system that will be used by the installation partition.
    d. Running the Setup wizard after the installation files are copied.

11. To install Windows 2000 Professional over the network, you need to connect to: (Choose all that apply.)
    a. RIS server
    b. DNS server
    c. Distribution server
    d. Answer files

12. When you access the Network Settings dialog box to confirm that you have installed the correct protocols and network adapter, you are providing a solution to which of the following Setup problems?
    a. Media errors
    b. Insufficient disk space on a computer
    c. Failure to connect to the domain controller
    d. Failure of the dependency service to start

13. Which of the following operating systems requires an additional step to be performed in order to be upgraded to Windows 2000 Professional?
    a. Windows 95
    b. Windows NT 3.1
    c. Windows NT Workstation 3.51
    d. Windows 98

Projects: On Your Own

1. Install the Windows 2000 Setup Manager.
   a. Log on as an **Administrator** and insert the **Windows 2000 Professional CD** in the CD-ROM drive.
   b. Open the **Windows Explorer** window and create a folder named **Deploy** in the **C** drive of your system.
   c. Access the **CD-ROM** drive.
   d. Open the **Support** window.
   e. Open the **Tools** window.
   f. Open the **Deploy** window.
   g. Select **all files** in this window.
   h. Extract these files into the **Deploy** folder on your hard disk partition.

   i. Access the **Deploy** folder on your hard disk partition and view the extracted files.
   j. Close all the windows that you have accessed.

2. Create a master disk image using the System Preparation Tool.
   a. Log on as an **Administrator**.
   b. Access the **Windows Explorer** window.
   c. Access the **Windows 2000 System Preparation Tool** message box.
   d. Perform the steps to continue working as guided by the **System Preparation Tool Wizard**.
   e. Shut down your computer.

3. Configure Remote Installation Services.

   a. Log on as an **Administrator**.

   b. Access the **Add/Remove Programs** window.

   c. Access the **Remote Installation Services Setup Wizard**.

   d. Insert the **Windows 2000 Professional CD** in the **CD-ROM** drive of the server.

   e. Start the **Remote Installation Services Setup Wizard**.

   f. Read the information on the **Welcome** screen and then access the **Remote Installation Folder Location** page.

   g. Specify the path as **D:\RemoteInst**.

   h. Access the **Initial Settings** page.

   i. Select the **Respond to client computer** check box.

   j. Access the **Installation Source Files Location** page.

   k. Specify the path to the installation source files.

   l. Access the **Windows Installation Image Folder Name** page.

   m. Accept the default name of **Win2000.pro.**

   n. Accept the default **friendly description and help** text.

   o. Review the information and then click the **Finish** button. Your system will perform certain tasks.

   p. Click the **Done** button when the tasks are completed.

   q. Close any open windows.

Problem Solving Scenarios

1. You work as the Assistant Network Administrator for Northern Casualty Insurance, a regional commercial insurance agency. The agency has several departments, each with a different set of computers and networks. Some departments use Windows 95 without any network, while other departments use Windows 98 in small workgroups. Each of the Windows 98 departments has proprietary software that the insurance agents do not want to give up. Your job is to work with the Network Administrator to devise a plan for upgrading the company's 300 workstations into a single, coherent company network.

Specifically, the Network Administrator has asked you to prepare a PowerPoint presentation describing in general terms the steps required for a remote, unattended installation of a Windows 2000 domain network. This network must be able to run existing proprietary software used in some offices that operates only with Windows 98. You also will need to decide whether to do an upgrade or perform a clean install, and to justify the reasons for doing so. **Note**: The CEO has told the Network Administrator to minimize disruption to the business while making this transition.

3 Managing Hardware Devices

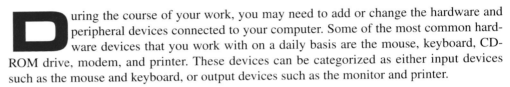

During the course of your work, you may need to add or change the hardware and peripheral devices connected to your computer. Some of the most common hardware devices that you work with on a daily basis are the mouse, keyboard, CD-ROM drive, modem, and printer. These devices can be categorized as either input devices such as the mouse and keyboard, or output devices such as the monitor and printer.

While these hardware devices enable you to work with data, removable media allows you to store data or to backup and archive data on alternatives to the hard drive such as CD-ROMs, DVDs, floppy disks, and tapes. Using removable media to store infrequently used data helps you to save hard disk space.

You may also need to exchange data with computers that are not on your network. Modems are used to exchange data between computers on the Internet using telephone lines. Modems are also used to connect computers to devices such as fax machines. Infrared light is used to connect a digital camera to a computer, whereas external communication lines called buses are used to connect a Web camera to a computer.

These devices must interact with the operating system in order to process data. Windows 2000 Professional uses programs called device drivers to enable interaction with hardware devices. Device drivers serve as the translators for the OS, converting commands from an application into commands that the device can understand and process. A database of device drivers is installed along with the Windows 2000 Professional operating system. However, you may need to upgrade these drivers periodically when the manufacturers distribute newer versions or if the device is not functioning properly.

Windows 2000 Professional includes Plug and Play functionality. Any new Plug and Play devices you add to your system will be detected and the settings will be configured automatically after the device driver is located and installed. However, if the system is unable to locate the required driver in the driver database because it was not included with the OS, you will be prompted to install the driver. After the driver is installed, the hardware device will be configured automatically.

As you take on different kinds of tasks, you may also need to install new software on your system. Windows 2000 Professional uses digitally signed system files to ensure that any new software you install does not overwrite the existing system files. This protects your system against data corruption and general system failures.

Goals

In this lesson, you will learn how to install, configure, and manage devices on your computer such as fax, removable devices, I/O devices, multimedia hardware, modems, IrDA, wireless devices, USB devices, network adapters and video adapters. You will also learn how to update device drivers on your system.

Lesson 3   Managing Hardware Devices

Skill	Exam 70-210 Objective
1. Configuring I/O Devices	Implement, manage, and troubleshoot input and output devices. Monitor, configure, and troubleshoot I/O devices, such as printers, scanners, multimedia devices, mouse, keyboard, and smart card reader.
2. Configuring and Monitoring Removable Media Devices	Implement, manage, and troubleshoot disk devices. Install, configure, and manage DVD and CD-ROM devices. Monitor and configure removable media, such as tape devices.
3. Adding a Modem	Install, configure, and manage modems.
4. Configuring Fax Devices	Configure and troubleshoot fax support.
5. Updating Device Drivers	Update drivers.
6. Managing Driver Signing	Manage and troubleshoot driver signing.
7. Managing Universal Serial Bus and Multimedia Devices	Install, configure, and manage USB devices. Monitor, configure, and troubleshoot multimedia hardware, such as cameras.
8. Installing Network Adapters	Install, configure, and troubleshoot network adapters.
9. Installing Video Adapters	Install, configure, and troubleshoot a video adapter.
10. Installing Infrared Data Association (IrDA) Devices	Install, configure, and manage Infrared Data Association (IrDA) devices. Install, configure, and manage wireless devices.
11. Configuring Multiple Processing Units	Monitor and configure multiple processing units.

Requirements

To complete this lesson, you will need a computer with Windows 2000 Professional installed on it. You will also need a modem, a scanner, a Web camera, a fax modem, and a CD-ROM. A second processor is optional for Skill 11.

skill 1

Configuring I/O Devices

exam objective

Implement, manage, and troubleshoot input and output devices. Monitor, configure, and troubleshoot I/O devices, such as printers, scanners, multimedia devices, mouse, keyboard, and smart card reader.

overview

caution

Make sure that the I/O devices that you use are included on the Hardware Compatibility List (HCL).

Devices such as the mouse and keyboard that are attached to a computer externally are known as peripheral devices. Peripheral devices can be divided into input or output (I/O) devices. Input devices such as the mouse, keyboards, joystick, and scanners are used to provide input data to a computer. Processed data is redirected to the output devices, such as the monitor and printer. Most I/O devices are Plug-and-Play devices. This means that whenever you attach an I/O device to your computer, Windows 2000 Professional automatically detects the device. Then, the OS installs the drivers for the device from the driver database on the system and installs the device. Many vendors choose to certify their drivers with Microsoft and have their drivers included in the driver database.

Often, when you attach an I/O device to a computer, an icon for that device will be placed in the Control Panel window. However, this is not always the case. For example, if you attach a FireWire device (used to connect VCRs and camcorders to a PC) or a USB hard drive, no additional icon for these devices will be added to the Control Panel. Some icons, such as those for the mouse, keyboard, and modems, are shown in the Control Panel window by default. Double-click an icon to install, configure, or troubleshoot the respective device.

In this skill, we will focus on configuring the mouse. You can install or configure a mouse in the **Mouse Properties** dialog box. The Mouse Properties dialog box generally contains five tabs: **Buttons**, **Pointers**, **Motion**, **Hardware**, and **Wheel Settings**, although this can vary with the make and model. **Table 3-1** describes the tabs and the settings you can configure on each tab.

how to

Configure your mouse to open any item on a single click and change the acceleration speed of the pointer.

1. Click 🏁 **Start**, point to **Settings**, and click **Control Panel** to open the **Control Panel** window.
2. Double-click the **Mouse** icon to open the **Mouse Properties** dialog box.
3. In the **Files and Folders** section, click the **Single-click to open an item (point to select)** option button (**Figure 3-1**).
4. Click the **Motion** tab.
5. In the **Acceleration** section, click the **Medium** option button to modify the mouse point acceleration (**Figure 3-2**).
6. In the **Snap to default** section, select the **Move pointer to the default button in dialog boxes** check box.
7. Click ⬚ OK ⬚ to apply the changes and close the Mouse Properties dialog box. You have configured the mouse to open any item on a single click and modified the speed of the pointer to medium. You can return to the default settings if you are uncomfortable with the new settings.
8. Close the **Control Panel**.

more

The I/O devices attached to your system may malfunction occasionally due to various setting problems. If the wheel on your mouse is not functioning properly, open the **Hardware** tab in the Mouse Properties dialog box. In the **Devices** section, select the mouse you are using and click **Properties**. On the **Advanced Settings** tab, change the **Wheel Detection** setting to **Assume Wheel is Present**.

Table 3-1   Tabs in the Mouse Properties dialog box

Properties Tab	Description
Buttons	You can configure your mouse for left-handed or right-handed use, set single-click or double-click preferences, and set the double-click speed. In the Double-click speed section, you can test the double-click speed for your mouse.
Pointers	You can specify the look and feel for the mouse pointer. The shape of the pointer acts as a visual cue to indicate the process taking place. For example, the hourglass icon ⧗ indicates that the computer is processing an event such as opening an application or a file.
Motion	You can set the speed and acceleration with which the mouse pointer moves on your screen. You can also set Snap To Default to program the mouse pointer to move automatically to the default button in dialog boxes.
Hardware	You can troubleshoot and access the port configuration, advanced settings, driver details, resource settings, and power management settings for the mouse.
Wheel Settings	If the mouse you have installed includes a wheel, you can adjust how many lines at a time will scroll for each notch you roll on the wheel.

Figure 3-1 Configuring mouse properties

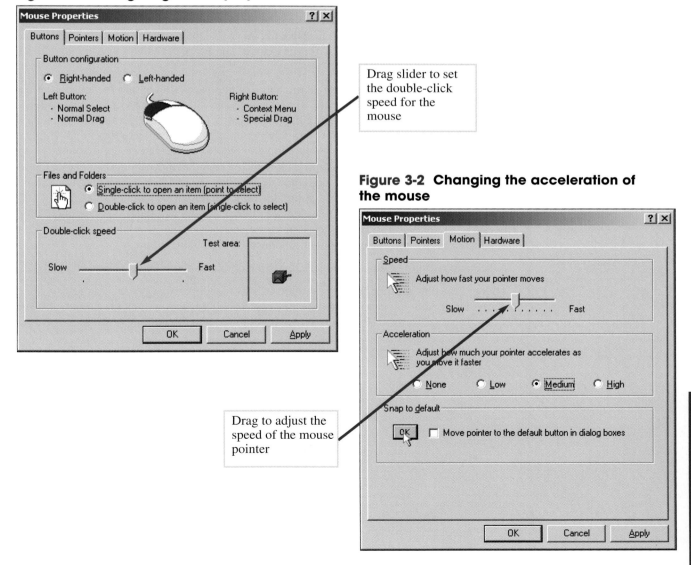

Drag slider to set the double-click speed for the mouse

Figure 3-2 Changing the acceleration of the mouse

Drag to adjust the speed of the mouse pointer

skill 2

Configuring and Monitoring Removable Media Devices

exam objective

Implement, manage, and troubleshoot disk devices. Install, configure, and manage DVD and CD-ROM devices. Monitor and configure removable media, such as tape devices.

overview

You can also connect **removable media** devices to a computer. Common removable multimedia devices include CD-ROMs, DVDs, MIDI (Musical Instrument Digital Interface), scanning hardware, and tape devices. CD-ROMs and DVDs are used to store and view large amounts of data and multimedia. Tape devices are still the most commonly used media for data backups, although today many large organizations are replacing tape systems with RW-DVDs for data archiving. The most commonly used tape devices are DAT (Digital Audio Tape), 8mm cassettes, quarter-inch cartridges, and DLTs (Digital Linear Tape).

CD-ROMs and Digital Video Discs (DVD) are used for audio/video data storage, are user-friendly, and are supported by all Windows platforms. Windows 2000 Professional uses the **Compact Disk File System (CDFS)** to read and write to CD-ROMs and the **Universal Disk Format** file system **(UDF)** to access DVD drives.

You can configure and manage removable media devices in the **Properties** dialog box for the device. To open the Properties dialog box for a media device, right-click **My Computer** on the desktop, click **Properties**, and open the **Hardware** tab in the **System Properties** dialog box **(Figure 3-3)**. Click the **Device Manager** button to open the Device Manager window. The media devices are listed under the **Disk drives** node. Double-click the media device name to open the **Properties** dialog box for the device. The Properties dialog box for the device contains the following tabs:

General: Lists the type of the device, the name of the manufacturer, and the location of the device. It also shows the status of the device, indicating whether the device is working properly. You can also configure the device usage for a particular hardware profile . You can click Troubleshooter... to troubleshoot any problems with the device **(Figure 3-4)**. The Troubleshooter presents a series of questions for you to answer about the malfunctioning device. The answers you give will direct you to the information that is relevant to the problem. One main task you will often be asked to perform is to check the HCL (Hardware Compatibility List) to make sure that the device is supported by Windows 2000. You will often be prompted to make sure that the appropriate drivers are installed and functioning properly. You may also be prompted to perform such actions as checking general or SCSI (small computer system interface) connections, cables and ID conflicts.

Disk Properties: Contains options specific to the device that you are managing.

Driver: Contains information about the device driver that is currently loaded on your system. On the Driver tab you can uninstall or update a driver. When you click the **Update Driver** button, the **Add/Remove Program Wizard** will guide you through the process of updating the drivers.

Figure 3-3 The System Properties dialog box

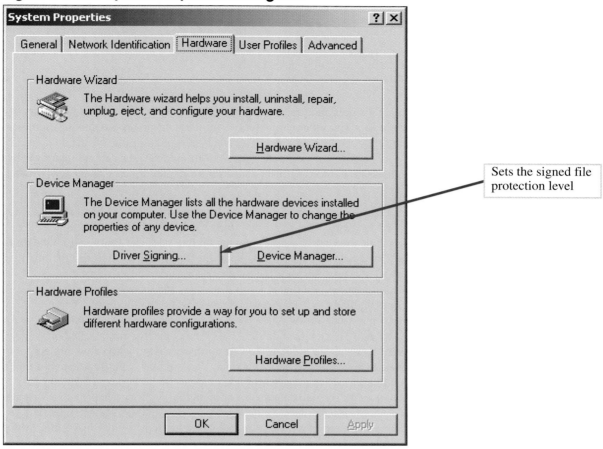

Sets the signed file protection level

Figure 3-4 Modifying the properties for a removable media device

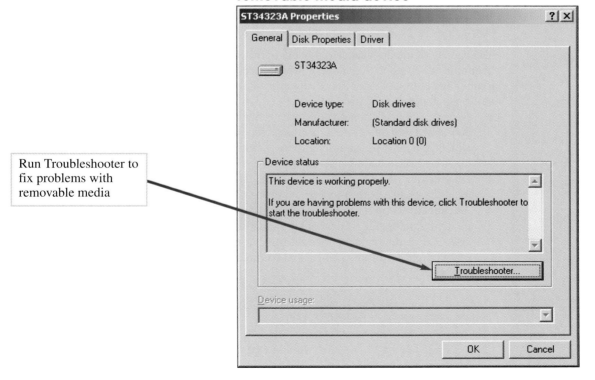

Run Troubleshooter to fix problems with removable media

skill 3

Adding a Modem

exam objective

Install, configure, and manage modems.

overview

A computer stores and processes data in digital format and uses binary digits to communicate internally and with other computers. A **modem** enables two computers to communicate with each other over telephone lines. The binary information sent by the computer is converted to analog signals by that computer's modem in order to transfer the data over telephone lines. When the data is received, it is converted from analog back to binary by the modem of the receiving computer.

If you add a modem to your computer that supports Plug and Play, it should be automatically identified by your system and the correct drivers installed. To add a modem that does not support Plug and Play to your computer, double-click the **Phone and Modems Options** icon in the **Control Panel** window to open the **Phone and Modem Options** dialog box. The Phone and Modems Options dialog box contains the following tabs:

- ◆ **Dialing Rules:** On this tab you can enter, add, or edit your geographical location, area codes, calling cards features, and more. When you dial a number, the information specified on this tab assists Windows 2000 Professional in establishing links to the number.
- ◆ **Modems:** This tab contains a list of all modems that are installed on your system (**Figure 3-5**). You can use the **Add** and **Remove** buttons to add a new modem to your system or remove an already installed modem. You can also click the **Properties** button to configure the properties for any installed modems in the **Properties** dialog box.
- ◆ **Advanced:** This tab contains a list of all the TAPI service providers that are available for telephony applications. You can add or remove TAPI service providers from the list or configure the properties for the telephony service providers using the **Add**, **Remove**, and **Configure** buttons.

When you click the **Add** button on the **Modems** tab, the **Add/Remove Hardware Wizard** will guide you through the installation process. You can either choose the modem to be installed, or have the system automatically detect the modem. If the modem is not automatically detected, or you want to choose the modem, select the **Don't detect my modem; I will select it from a list** check box in the **Install New Modem** dialog box. Then, follow the instructions in the Wizard to complete the installation.

You can configure any installed modem in the Properties dialog box for that modem. On the **Modems** tab, select the modem whose properties you want to access, and click the **Properties** button to open the **Properties** dialog box. The Properties dialog box for each modem contains the following tabs:

- ◆ **General:** This tab consists of three sections: **Speaker Volume**, **Maximum Port Speed**, and **Dial Control**. In these sections, you can set the speaker volume and the speed at which programs transmit data to the modem, and configure the modem to wait for the dial tone before dialing a given number.
- ◆ **Diagnostic:** This tab is used to troubleshoot the modem. You can view information about the performance of the modem and modify the modem settings.
- ◆ **Advanced:** Using this tab, you can configure any additional settings for initializing your modem. Additional settings for your modem can be found in the modem manual. You can also change the default modem settings, which may include call and data connection preferences, hardware settings, and terminal preferences.

how to

Configure a modem already installed on your system to wait for the dial tone before it starts dialing, and set the port speed to 57600.

1. Open the **Control Panel** window.
2. Double-click the **Phone and Modem Option**s (**Figure 3-6**) icon to open the **Phone and Modem Options** dialog box.

Figure 3-5 Selecting the modem

Figure 3-6 Phone and Modem Options icon in Control Panel

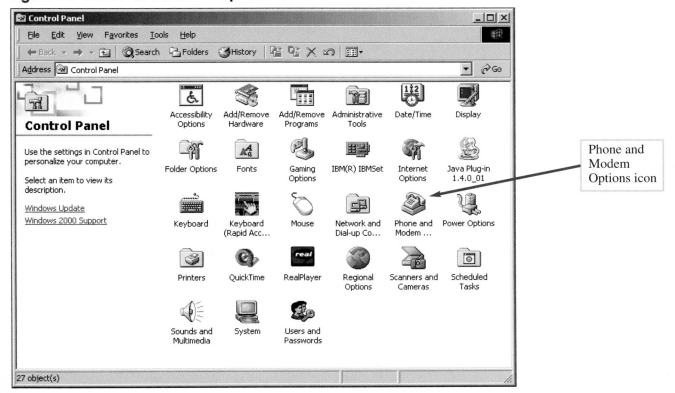

skill 3

Adding a Modem (cont'd)

exam objective

Install, configure, and manage modems.

how to

3. Click the **Modems** tab to display the list of installed modems in the Modem section.
4. Select a modem, for example, the **Motorola Premier 33.6 Desktop Plug and Play** modem and click [Properties] to open the **Properties** dialog box for the modem. The **General** tab opens by default.
5. In the **Maximum Port Speed** section, click the list arrow and select **57600** as the port speed for transmitting data.
6. In the **Dial Control** section, the **Wait for dial tone before dialing** check box is selected by default (**Figure 3-7**). This will program the modem to detect the dial tone before it begins dialing out.
7. Click [OK] to apply the changes and close the dialog box.

more

If you are unable to install a modem or encounter any other problems, check the following:
◆ Check that the modem or cables are not faulty or that the connections are not loose.
◆ Check the Hardware Compatibility List (HCL) on the Microsoft Web site (**Figure 3-8**) to see if the modem you are trying to install is compatible with your system.
◆ Check that the COM port that the modem is using is recognized by Windows 2000. Double-click the **Ports** icon in the Device Manager to list all ports currently in use. If your COM port is on the list, Windows 2000 is recognizing it. If your COM port appears in the list with an exclamation point (!) in a yellow circle, or a red X, there may be a hardware conflict or a disabled modem device.

Figure 3-7   Modem properties dialog box

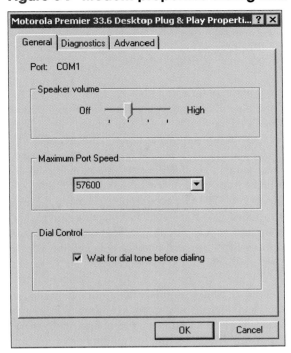

Figure 3-8   Microsoft hardware compatibility list

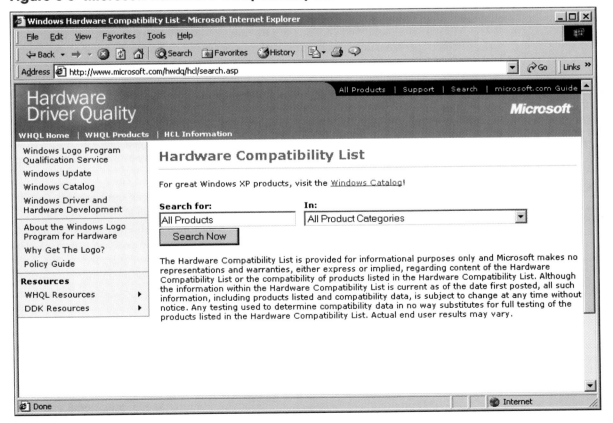

skill 4

Configuring Fax Devices

exam objective

Configure and troubleshoot fax support.

overview

One of the most commonly used hardware devices today is a fax modem. A fax modem is a Plug and Play device, so when you attach a fax modem, Windows 2000 Professional should detect it at startup and install it automatically. The OS will also install the Windows NT fax driver and the Fax Service. The Windows NT fax driver will be stored in the Printers folder as a printer named Fax. If Windows 2000 Professional does not detect the device at startup, you can run the Add/Remove Hardware Wizard. The Wizard will search for and install the device and its drivers. You can access this Wizard in the Control Panel. After the Fax Service has been installed, you must start it. You start the Fax Service through the Services node in the Computer Management console. Right-click **My Computer** and click **Manage** to open the **Computer Management console**. Expand the **Services and Applications** node, and click **Services** to display a list of the services on the computer in the Details pane. Then, either right-click **Fax Service** and click **Start**, or double-click **Fax Service** to open the **Fax Service Properties (Local Computer)** dialog box. In the **Service Status** section, click the **Start** button. Documents that you want to fax will be sent to the fax driver in the Printers folder. Faxes are received as TIFF (tagged image file format) images. They can be opened and read in **Microsoft Office Document Imaging** or in any other utility that can view TIFF files. The default behavior is for the TIFF file to be sent to the **Received Faxes** folder, but you can also save a received fax in a different folder, send it directly to a print device, or send it as an e-mail.

When you install a fax device, Windows 2000 Professional adds the fax icon to the **Control Panel** window. Double-click the **Fax** icon to open the **Fax Properties** dialog box. On the **User Information** tab **(Figure 3-9)** you enter the information for the cover page. On the **Cover Pages** tab, you can use the **Cover Page-Fax Cover Page Editor** to create a personalized cover page. The **Status Monitor** tab is used to configure the behavior when faxes are sent or received, for example, whether an icon will display on the taskbar or a sound will play to notify you that a fax is being sent or received. In order to receive a fax, you must be logged on as an administrator. The **Advanced Options tab (Figure 3-10)** will then be visible in the Fax Properties dialog box. On the Advanced Options page, you can **Add a Fax Printer**, open the **Fax Service Management Help**, or click the **Open Fax Service Management Console** button to open the **Fax Service Management** console.

The Fax Service Management console has two nodes: **Devices** and **Logging**. To configure the properties for an attached fax device, select the **Devices** node, right-click the device in the Details pane, and select **Properties** to open the Properties dialog box for the specific device. On the **General** tab, you enable or disable the sending and receiving of faxes. The **Enable send** option is selected by default, but you must manually configure the device to receive faxes. On the **Received Faxes** tab, you have three options for managing incoming faxes. You can save the fax to a local folder, send it directly to a print device or send it to a local e-mail inbox.

To configure the Fax Service on the local computer, right-click **Fax Service on Local Computer** in the Fax Service Management window and click **Properties** to open the **Fax Service on Local Computer Properties** dialog box. On the **Security** tab, you can set various permissions (See Lesson 10) for users on the system to submit, view, and manage fax jobs, services, and devices. On the General tab, you can configure the following services:

◆ Fax properties include the number of rings before the fax device answers automatically, priority settings for sending faxes, and settings for the event log. You can also set the number of times a computer should retry to send a document if the first attempt fails, and you can prevent personal cover pages from being sent.

Figure 3-9 The Fax Properties dialog box

Information about the person who is sending the fax

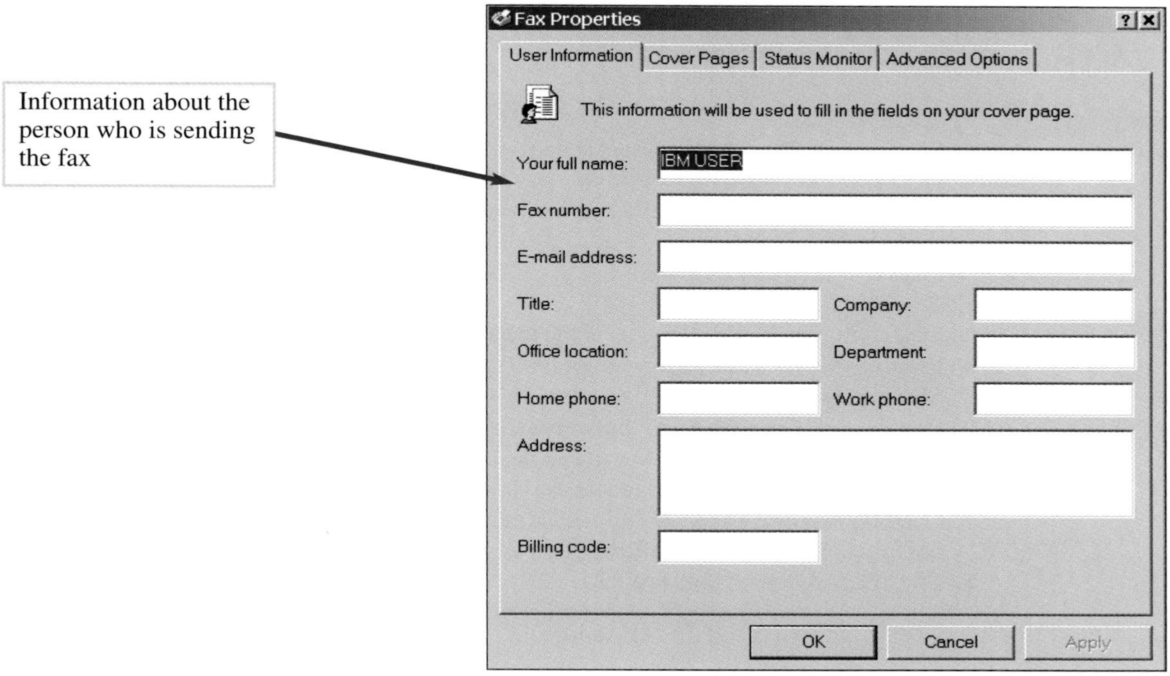

Figure 3-10 Advanced Options tab in the Fax Properties dialog box

Here you can view the fax devices you have installed and modify their properties

Provides help related to fax devices

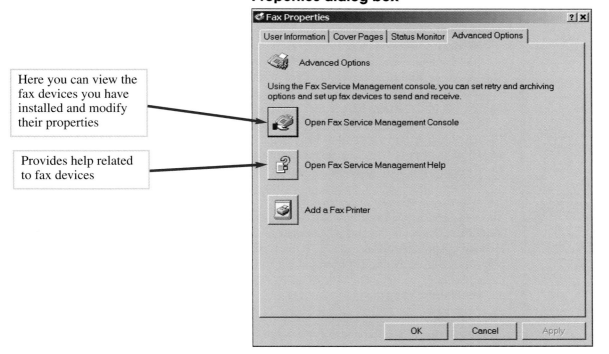

skill 4

Configuring Fax Devices (cont'd)

exam objective

Configure and troubleshoot fax support.

overview

◆   Security includes selecting users and assigning permissions to them to use the fax service on a network.
◆   The path for the folder indicates where the sent and the received documents will be saved.

how to

Start and configure the Fax Service on the local computer and configure a fax device.
1. Right-click **My Computer** and click the **Manage** command to open the **Computer Management** console.
2. Double-click **Services and Applications** to expand the node. Click **Services**.
3. Locate and right-click **Fax Service** in the list of services in the Details pane. Click **Start** on the context menu to start the fax service. Close the Computer Management console.
4. Open the Control Panel. Double-click the **Fax** icon to open the **Fax Properties** dialog box. By default, the **User Information** tab opens.
5. Click the **Advanced Options** tab.
6. Click the **Open Fax Service Management Console** button to open the **Fax Service Management** console.
7. Right-click the **Fax Service on Local Computer** node and then click the **Properties** command in order to open the **Fax Service on Local Computer Properties** dialog box (**Figure 3-11**). By default, the **General** tab opens.
8. In the **Number of retries** text box in the **Retry Characteristics** section, type: **4**.
9. In the **Minutes between retries** text box, type: **5**.
10. Click ⬚ OK ⬚ to close the Fax Service on Local Computer Properties dialog box.
11. In the **Fax Service on Local Computer** console tree, click the **Devices** node to display a list of all fax devices currently installed on the system in the Details pane.
12. Right-click the device you want to configure, for example, **Lucent Technologies Soft Modem AMR**, and click **Properties** on the context menu to open the Properties dialog box for the device.
13. Select the **Enable receive** check box in the **Receive** section to enable the fax device to receive faxes.
14. Type **4** in the **Rings before answer** spin box to program the device to start receiving faxes after four rings (**Figure 3-12**).
15. Click ⬚ OK ⬚ to apply the changes and close the dialog box.
16. Close the Fax Service Management console.
17. Close the **Fax Properties** dialog box and the **Control Panel**.

more

You can send a fax from any Windows-based application such as **Microsoft Word** or **WordPad.** Open the document you want to fax and click the **Print** command on the **File** menu to open the **Print** dialog box. In the **Printer** section, select the fax device instead of a print device in the **Name** list box, and click either ⬚ Print ⬚ or ⬚ OK ⬚ , depending on the application you are using. The **Send Fax Wizard** is initiated and will guide you through the process of sending the fax.

You can monitor the status of your fax in the **Fax Monitor** dialog box. To display the **Fax Monitor** dialog box automatically every time a fax is sent or received, double-click the **Fax** icon in the **Control Panel** window, and click the **Status Monitor** tab. Select the **Display the Status Monitor** check box, and click ⬚ OK ⬚ . The Fax Monitor will display the current status for the fax, record the fax events, and allow you to interrupt a fax call or disable manual answering for the next call.

Figure 3-11 Fax Service on Local Computer Properties dialog box

The number of times to attempt to resend a fax after the first attempt has failed

The minimum number of minutes between each attempt

The number of days an unsent fax remains in the fax queue

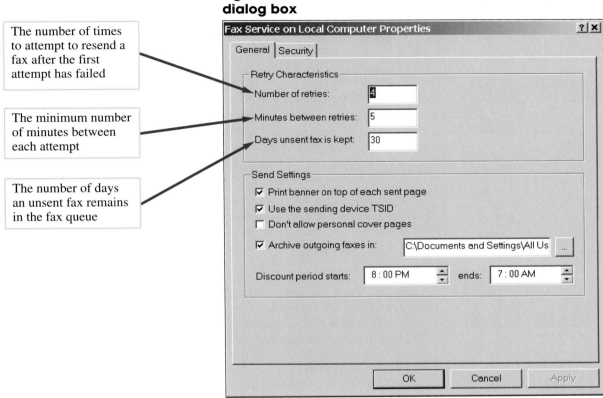

Figure 3-12 Properties dialog box for a specific fax device

Select number of rings before fax device starts receiving fax

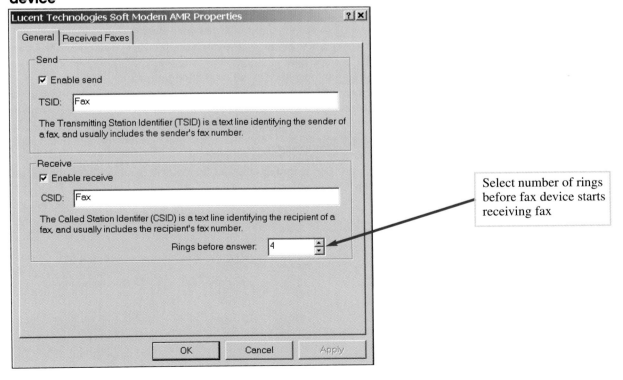

skill 5 *Updating Device Drivers*

exam objective

Update drivers.

overview

A **device driver** is software that enables a specific device such as a printer, modem, or network card to communicate with the computer. For example, to establish network connections using a modem, you need serial port drivers. Windows 2000 Professional includes the built-in drivers required for installing and configuring many commonly used devices. If you are installing a newer version of a device, adding new functionality to a device, or fixing device errors, you must update the drivers on your system.

You will also need to update a driver if the manufacturer of the hardware device has released a newer version. Moreover, some devices may contain additional features that can be enabled only if you update the driver. You can also upgrade drivers if the device is not functioning properly. You update device drivers in the **Device Manager**.

how to

Update the drivers for the modem attached to your system.

1. Right-click the **My Computer** icon on the desktop and click the **Manage** command to open the **Computer Management** console.
2. Click the **Device Manager** node to display all of the devices that are currently installed on the system. Alternatively, you can click **Start**, point to **Settings**, click **Control Panel**, and double-click **System** to open the **System Properties** dialog box. On the **Hardware** tab, click the **Device Manage**r button to open the Device Manager.
3. Double-click **Modems** to display the modems installed on the computer.
4. Right-click the modem name, for example, **Actiontec V.92 PCI Lite SV**, and click the **Properties** command to open the **Properties** dialog box for the modem.
5. Click the **Driver** tab.
6. Click Update Driver... to open the **Upgrade Device Driver Wizard (Figure 3-13)**.
7. Click Next > to open the **Install Hardware Device Drivers** screen.
8. Click the **Display a list of the known drivers for this device so that I can choose a specific driver** option button.
9. Click Next > to open the **Install New Modem** screen.
10. Click the **Show all hardware for this device class** option button to display the **Manufacturers** list. In the **Models** list, the corresponding models for the selected manufacturer are displayed (**Figure 3-14**). If you need to upgrade the drivers from a disk, you can click Have Disk... . This will allow you to select the path to the manufacturer's files so that they can be copied to the hard drive.
11. Click the appropriate manufacturer and the computer model from the **Manufacturers** and **Models** lists, respectively.

Figure 3-13 Displaying the drivers available on the computer

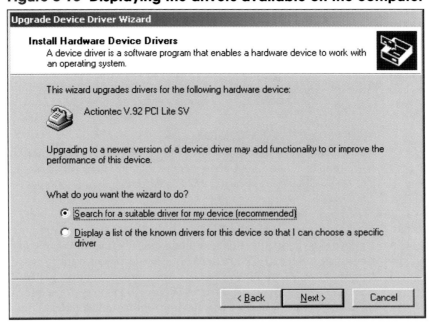

Figure 3-14 Selecting a driver

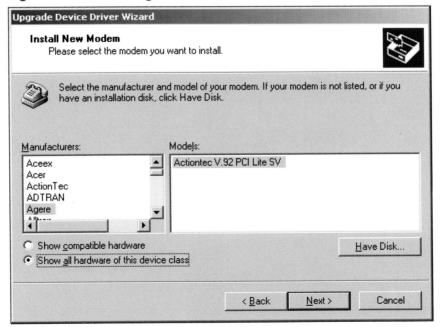

skill 5

Updating Device Drivers (cont'd)

exam objective

Update drivers.

how to

12. Click [Next >] to display the **Start Device Driver Installation** screen.
13. Click [Next >] to display the **Completing the Upgrade Device Driver Wizard** screen.
14. Click [Finish] to complete the update procedure.
15. **Close** the modem **Properties** dialog box. The **System Settings Change** dialog box prompts you to restart the system so that the changes can take effect.
16. Click [Yes] to restart the system and apply the settings.

more

You can also use **Windows Update** on the Start menu to connect to the **Microsoft Windows Update** page at **http://windowsupdate.microsoft.com**. When you connect to the site for the first time, a **Security Warning** will ask you if you want to install and run the **Windows Update V4 Control**. When you click **Yes**, ActiveX controls will be downloaded to your computer. Next, click **Scan for updates (Figure 3-15)** to perform a scan of the software environment on your PC. Finally, click **Review and install updates**. Windows Update will create a catalogue of the latest updates available for your computer's operating system, software, and hardware (**Figure 3-16**). The list will be ranked to let you know if the update is critical or just recommended and may also include security updates and Internet and multimedia updates. This Web site is primarily intended for OS service packs, but you can also update some drivers using this method. If an updated driver is available, you can follow a set of prompts to install it. You must use Internet Explorer to perform this operation because the system scan will not work with non ActiveX browsers such as Netscape.

Windows Update is a convenience for individual users, allowing them to keep their PCs up to date with the latest patches and fixes. However, network administrators may want to control what updates are downloaded on network computers to maintain system conformity for network technicians and troubleshooters. You can disable Windows Update by setting a Group Policy (See Lesson 12).

Figure 3-15 Using Windows Update to scan for updates

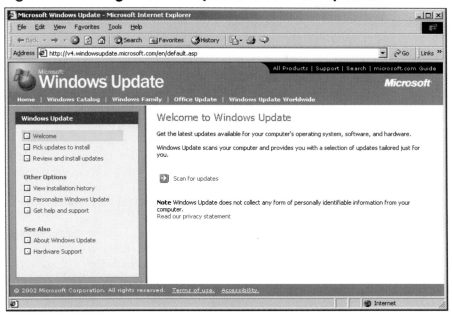

Figure 3-16 Reviewing and installing updates

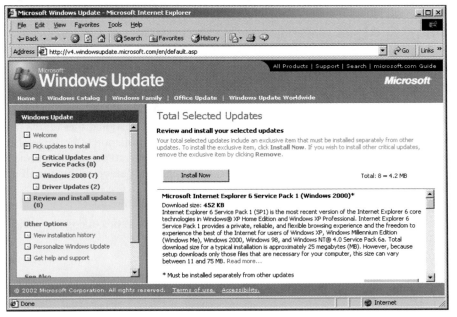

skill 6 *Managing Driver Signing*

exam objective

Manage and troubleshoot driver signing.

overview

Microsoft uses digital signatures to assure users that the drivers they are using have been tested for quality and are safe for installation. A digital signature on a file certifies that the file is from the correct source, typically the hardware manufacturer or Microsoft. Windows 2000 Professional provides several ways of protecting digitally signed files.

◆ The **Windows File Protection** utility in Windows 2000 Professional prevents the replacement of protected system files such as those files ending in **.sys**, **.dll**, **.ocx**, **.ttf**, **.fon**, and **.exe**. It detects any attempt by other programs to replace or move a protected system file. The Windows File Protection utility checks the digital signature on the file to determine if the correct Microsoft version is being installed. If an attempt is made to replace a digitally signed file, Windows 2000 Professional writes an event to the event log to record the file replacement attempt.

◆ The **System File Checker** utility scans and verifies the versions of all protected system files. If a protected file has been overwritten, the correct version of the file is retrieved from the **%systemroot%\system32\dllcache** folder. The **sfc** command can be run from the **Command Prompt**. To open the Command Prompt, click [🏳 Start], point to **Programs**, point to **Accessories**, and click the **Command Prompt** command. The syntax for the System File Checker is:

sfc [/scannow] [/scanonce] [/scanboot] [/cancel] [/quiet] [/enable] [/purgecache] [/cachesize=x]

The parameters for the syntax are described in **Table 3-2**.

The **File Signature Verification** utility is used to identify unsigned files on your computer and display the related information such as the file's name, location, last modification date, file type, and the file's version number.

how to

Set driver signing options to block the installation of unsigned files.

1. Log on as an **Administrator**.
2. Open the **Control Panel** window.
3. Double-click the **System** icon to open the **System Properties** dialog box.
4. Click the **Hardware** tab to display the hardware setting options. (**Figure 3-17**).
5. Click [Driver Signing...] to open the **Driver Signing Options** dialog box.
6. Click the **Block – Prevent installation of unsigned files** option button in the **File signature verification** section to prevent the installation of unsigned drivers (**Figure 3-18**).
7. Make sure that the **Apply setting as the system default** check box is selected in the **Administrator option** section to apply the default setting for all users who log on to the computer.
8. Click [OK] to apply the changes and close the **Driver Signing Options** dialog box.
9. Click [OK] to close the **System Properties** dialog box. Close the Control Panel.

Table 3-2   Syntax for System File Checker

Parameter	Description
/scannow	Scans all protected system files immediately.
/scanonce	Scans all protected system files once.
/scanboot	Scans all protected system files every time the computer restarts.
/cancel	Cancels all pending scans of protected system files.
/quiet	Replaces all incorrect file versions without prompting the user.
/enable	Returns Windows File Protection to default operation. When the System File Checker detects an incorrect version of a file, it prompts the user to restore protected system files.
/purgecache	Purges the Windows File Protection file cache and scans all protected system files immediately.
/cachesize=x	Sets Windows File Protection file cache size.

Figure 3-17   Selecting the driver signing option

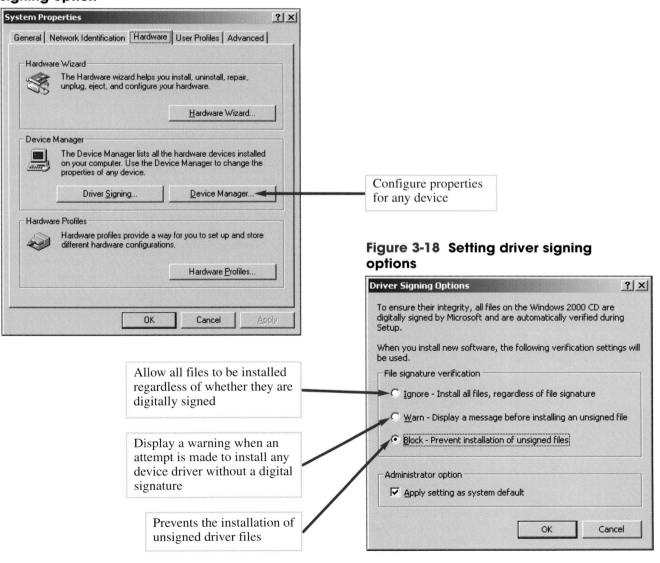

Configure properties for any device

Figure 3-18   Setting driver signing options

Allow all files to be installed regardless of whether they are digitally signed

Display a warning when an attempt is made to install any device driver without a digital signature

Prevents the installation of unsigned driver files

skill 7

Managing Universal Serial Bus and Multimedia Devices

exam objective

Install, configure, and manage USB devices. Monitor, configure, and troubleshoot multimedia hardware, such as cameras.

overview

Universal Serial Bus (USB) is an external communication bus that is used to transfer data among the components in a computer system. USB lets you install devices such as keyboards, joysticks, and tape drives. It provides a faster and more manageable alternative to serial and parallel ports for devices such as keyboards and mice, and is expected to completely replace them in the future. USB is a better alternative to older I/O standards because all USB devices use the same kind of I/O connector so that you will no longer need different types of cables and connectors. USB technology also allows you to install multimedia devices such as scanners, audio players, CD-ROM drives, Web cameras, and speakers. It is supported by the WDM (Windows Driver Model) in Windows 2000. Using one USB controller, you can attach a maximum of 127 USB devices simultaneously (with one or more USB hubs) to a single computer.

USB is a Plug and Play bus that supports **hot swapping** (also called **hot plugging**), which means that you can add and remove devices while the computer is running and have the operating system automatically recognize the change. USB moves the Plug and Play functionality for these peripheral devices outside the computer so that internal cards do not have to be added to the motherboard and the system does not have to be reconfigured. If USB is supported by the BIOS, you will find the **Universal Serial Bus controllers** in the Device Manager. You can configure and manage a USB device in the **Properties** dialog box for the device. You open the **Properties** dialog box by double-clicking the USB device name in the Universal Serial Bus controller node. The **Properties** dialog box for each USB controller contains the following tabs:

◆ **General:** This tab lists the device type and device status. On this page you can run the troubleshooter if the device is not working properly and disable the USB device.

◆ **Advanced:** Each USB controller has a fixed amount of bandwidth, which the attached devices share. On this tab, you can distribute bandwidth among the devices connected to the USB controller.

◆ **Driver:** On this tab you can view the driver properties and remove or upgrade the drivers for the USB device.

◆ **Resources:** On this tab, you can view the device resources that are currently assigned to the USB controller and the settings for each resource. The four types of device resources are: the **input/output (I/O) port**, the **direct memory access (DMA) channel**, the **interrupt request (IRQ) line**, and the **memory address**.

how to

Install and configure a Web camera.

1. Shut down the computer, plug the Web camera into the USB port, and restart the system. The **Found New Hardware** message box opens and the system updates the drivers for the Web camera. This may take several minutes.
2. The **Found New Hardware Wizard** opens.
3. Click [Next >] to open the **Install Hardware Device Drivers** screen.
4. Click the **Search for a suitable driver for my device (recommended)** option button in the **What do you want the wizard to do?** section (**Figure 3-19**).
5. Click [Next >] to open the **Locate Driver File**s screen. The system will ask you to specify the path for the drivers (**Figure 3-20**).
6. Click [Next >]. The system will search the driver database for the drivers for the Web camera.
7. Click [Finish] to apply the settings and exit the Wizard. You will be prompted to restart your computer.
8. Click [Yes]. When the computer restarts, the device will be configured with the default settings and available for use.

Figure 3-19 Installing hardware device drivers

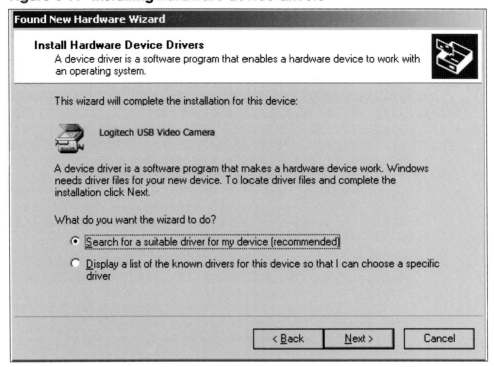

Figure 3-20 Locate Driver Files screen

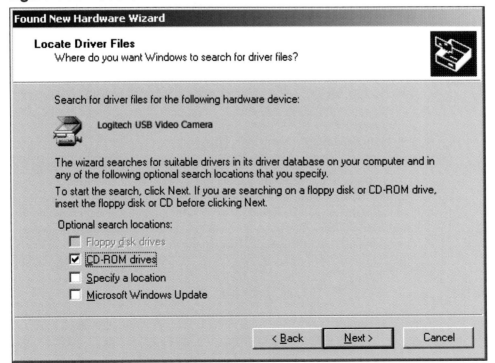

skill 8

Installing Network Adapters

exam objective

Install, configure, and troubleshoot network adapters.

overview

Many network adapter models and the protocols and services that use adapter hardware are supported by Windows 2000 Professional. Although **network interface cards (NICs)** are crucial communications tools that are needed to connect computers to a network, they are just as simple to install as any other hardware device. First, you must install the NIC into a bus slot in the motherboard and attach the network cable to it. If the NIC is Plug and Play compatible and the driver is included in the driver.cab file from the Windows 2000 Professional installation CD, the device will be automatically detected and installed. If the device driver is not in the driver database, you may be prompted to insert the installation CD-ROM or third party diskette. If the NIC is not Plug and Play compatible, you will have to run the Add New Hardware Wizard from the Control Panel and follow the prompts to select the make and model.

You configure NICs in either the network connection **Properties** dialog box or in the **Device Manager**. To open the network connection Properties dialog box, first open the **Control Panel** and double-click the **Network and Dial-up Connections** icon to open the Network and Dial-up Connections window. Then, right-click the icon for connection you want to configure (usually the **Local Area Connection** icon) and click the **Properties** command (**Figure 3-21**). Click [Configure] to open the **Properties** dialog box for the network card. The network card Properties dialog box contains the following tabs:

◆ **General:** On this tab you can view the manufacturer details for the network card. You can also enable or disable the device and run the troubleshooter.

◆ **Advanced:** The contents of this tab are specific to the adapter that you are configuring. In the **Property** list, choose the property you want to modify and change the entry in the **Value** list box to the appropriate setting (**Figure 3-22**). You may find settings to select a regular Ethernet plug or a Fast Ethernet Plug, to select full or half-duplex communications, or to transfer error-checking calculations to the NIC. This is recommended because it will transfer error-checking from the main CPU to the NIC, freeing system resources.

◆ **Driver:** On this tab, you can view information about the drivers being used by the network adapter including the manufacturer, date of manufacture, and digital signer. You can also use the Update Driver Wizard to upgrade the driver.

◆ **Resources:** On this tab, you can view the device resources and settings currently assigned to the selected device. Improper settings can disable the hardware and cause the computer to malfunction.

◆ **Power Management:** On this tab, you can program the computer to turn off the network card to save power or to bring the computer out of standby to respond to a network event.

To configure a NIC from the Device Manager, open the **Control Panel** and double-click the **System** icon to open the **System Properties** dialog box. Next, open the **Hardware** tab and click the **Device Manager** button to open the Device Manager window. Expand the **Network adapters** node to view the NICs installed on the computer. Right-click the NIC you want to configure and click **Properties** to open the Properties dialog box for the NIC.

caution

Only users who have expert knowledge of computer hardware and device resources should change resource settings.

Figure 3-21 The Local Area Connection Properties dialog box

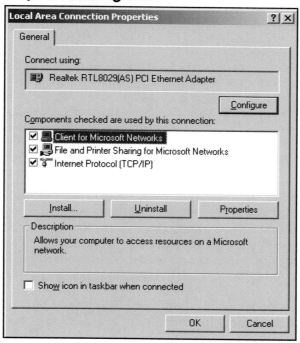

Figure 3-22 Configuring NIC properties

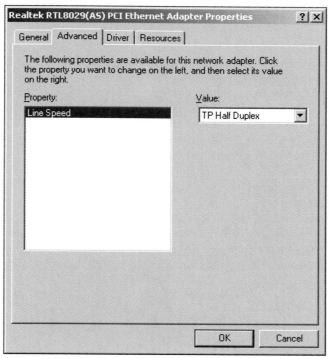

skill 9   *Installing Video Adapters*

exam objective

Install, configure, and troubleshoot a video adapter.

overview

A **video adapter** is an expansion board that plugs into a computer to give it display capabilities such as color and a choice of different resolutions. Modern video adapters contain memory so that RAM is not used for storing displays. Video adapters are also called video cards, video boards, video display boards, graphics cards, and graphics adapters. Most computers manufactured today have built-in video adapters. If a computer does not have a built-in video adapter, you can attach one to the motherboard. The video adapter can then be installed using the Plug and Play method or the Add/Remove Hardware Wizard.

You can configure and manage video adapters on the **Settings** tab in the **Display Properties** dialog box. Right-click any free space on the desktop and click the **Properties** command to open the Display Properties dialog box. On the Settings tab, you can modify the color and screen area settings. You can also solve any problems related to the screen display by clicking Troubleshoot... . On the **Advanced** tab, you can change the font size, select the color profile for your monitor, and extend the desktop to span multiple monitors.

how to

Change the color of your monitor to High color (16 bit).
1. Right-click any free space on the desktop and click the **Properties** command to open the **Display Properties** dialog box **(Figure 3-23)**.
2. Click the **Settings** tab to view the options for changing the monitor display.
3. Click the list arrow on the **Colors** list box and select the **High Color (16 bit)** option.
4. In the **Screen Area** section, move the slider to change the screen area to **1024 by 768** pixels.
5. Click Apply to apply the changes. A message box warns you that it will take a few seconds for the settings to be applied and prompts you to apply the settings.

more

If you encounter problems when you install a video adapter on your system, refer to **Table 3-3**, which lists some common problems and their solutions. If the screen of your computer goes blank when you start up Windows 2000 Professional after configuring the video adapter, you should reboot the system. When the system displays the **Starting Up** progress bar or the message **Please select the operating system to start**, press the **[F8]** key on your keyboard. The **Windows 2000 Advanced Options** menu will open. Select the **Last Known Good Configuration** option to boot the machine. You can also try restarting the computer in either Safe mode or VGA mode (Enable VGA Mode command on the Windows 2000 Advanced Options menu). When Windows 2000 boots into either Safe or VGA (video graphics array) mode, it uses a basic set of drivers, including a VGA adapter with low resolution and a limited number of colors. In Safe mode, you will generally be able to view the screen so that you can open the Display Properties dialog box and fix the settings to make the monitor work again. VGA mode is specifically designed for instances of corruption or incompatibility with the currently installed video driver.

Figure 3-23 Changing the display properties

Display Properties dialog box showing the Settings tab with:

Display:
Plug and Play Monitor on SiS 5598/6326

Colors: High Color (16 bit)

Screen area: 1024 by 768 pixels

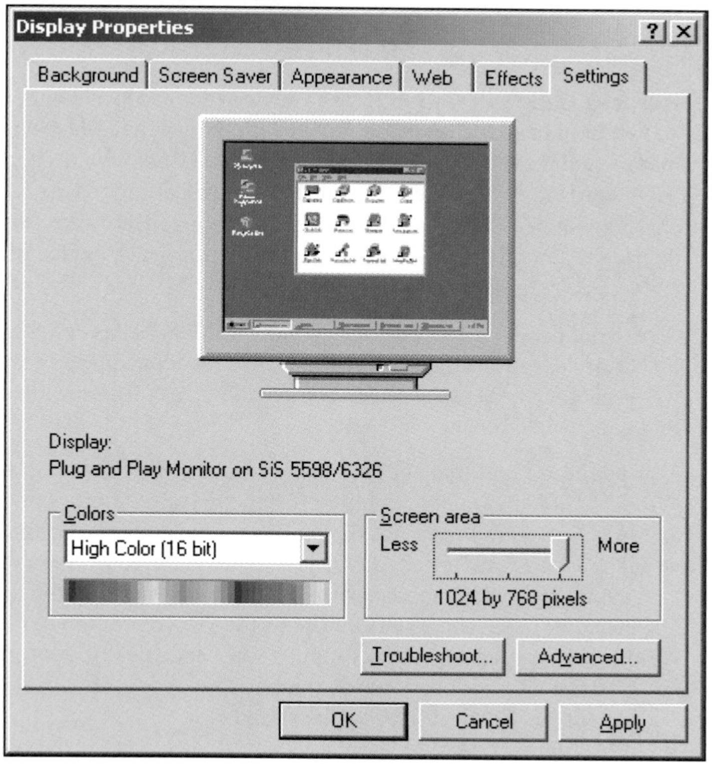

Table 3-3	Common Problems encountered while installing video adapters
Problem	**Solution**
The video adapter is not supported by Windows 2000 Professional.	Check the Hardware Compatibility List or the manufacturer of the video adapter.
Video Mode is not supported by the Video driver.	Select the 640 by 480 screen resolution and 16 bit color from the Display Properties dialog box.
You have the wrong driver for the adapter.	To locate the correct video driver, check the documentation for the video adapter.

skill 10

Installing Infrared Data Association (IrDA) Devices

exam objective

Install, configure, and manage Infrared Data Association (IrDA) devices.

overview

Infrared Data Association (IrDA) devices communicate with computers using infrared light and without using cables. Computers with built-in IrDA hardware such as Infrared Ports automatically detect and install infrared devices. Users who do not have computers with built-in IrDA hardware can attach a serial IrDA transceiver to a serial COM Port to allow the synchronous transmission of data. The Add/Remove Hardware Wizard is used to install infrared devices if a computer does not have an internal IrDA device or if the device is not automatically detected and installed.

After you install an IrDA device, Windows 2000 Professional adds the **Wireless Link** icon to the **Control Panel** window. The Wireless Link icon appears on the desktop and on the taskbar when another IrDA transceiver comes into range. This enables the transfer of data over the infrared connection.

You configure and manage wireless devices in the **Wireless Link** dialog box. To open the Wireless Link dialog box, double-click the **Wireless Link** icon in the **Control Panel** window. The Wireless Link Properties dialog box contains the following tabs (**Figure 3-24**):

◆ The **File Transfer** tab allows you to decide if you want a wireless link icon to display on the taskbar when another wireless device comes into range. It also allows you to specify whether other computers can send files to your computer over the wireless link connection. If you allow other computers to send files to your computer, you can display the transfer status when your computer is receiving files. You can also set a default location where the received files can be stored.

◆ The **Image Transfer** tab allows you to designate if the wireless link will be allowed to transfer images from a camera to your computer. If you allow the transfer of images, you can choose the location of the folder where the files are to be saved. You can also specify that Windows Explorer automatically open the folder after the images have been copied.

◆ The **Hardware** tab displays a list of the wireless devices installed, the names of the manufacturers, and the physical location of the file. Using the options on this tab, you can troubleshoot problems associated with a wireless device and change the properties for the device. Click [Properties] to open the **Properties** dialog box for a wireless device (**Figure 3-25**). The functions of the tabs on the Properties dialog box for an infrared device are described in **Table 3-4**.

more

If you are unable to set up communication between two infrared devices, for example a computer and a digital camera, you must:

◆ Make sure that you have installed the infrared device properly by checking the properties for the device in the **Properties** dialog box.

◆ Check the placement of the two devices. They should be facing each other and not more than three feet apart. If the devices are properly placed, an icon for an infrared device will display on the taskbar.

◆ Check that the device is compatible with Windows 2000 Professional by referring to the Hardware Compatibility List.

Table 3-4	Functions of various tabs on the Properties dialog box of an Infrared device
General	The General tab displays the information about the device that you have selected and the status of the device. You can click the Troubleshooter button to receive help in solving problems with the device. You can also set the device usage (either enabled or disabled) for the device.
IrDA Settings	This tab displays the current setting for the maximum speed at which the infrared device can transfer data. The speed can be changed according to the specifications for the device.
Driver	This tab displays the details, such as the manufacturer's name, for the driver for the infrared device. You can also uninstall or upgrade drivers here.
Resources	This tab displays the device resources that are currently assigned to the selected device and the settings for each resource. Improper resource settings can cause your computer to malfunction. Therefore, only users who have expert knowledge of computer hardware and device resources should change these settings.

Figure 3-24 Configuring the properties for a wireless link

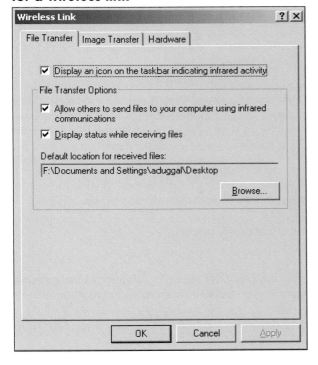

Figure 3-25 The Properties dialog box for an infrared device

skill 11

Configuring Multiple Processing Units

exam objective

Monitor and configure multiple processing units.

overview

Multiprocessing occurs when two or more CPUs carry out one or more processes simultaneously. Each processing unit works on a different set of instructions or on different parts of the same process. You can use a multiprocessor system to provide scalability and increased speed of access to network resources and services. Generally, a multiprocessor system will only be configured on a server, but some graphics-intensive applications, scientific analysis programs or engineering design software may require added CPU power on a client system. You can improve the performance of a system for use by applications such as these by distributing the workload between the two processors.

tip

The Hardware Abstraction Layer (HAL), a hardware-specific operating system component, provides support for multiprocessors.

You can upgrade your system from a uniprocessor to a multiprocessor system if there is an expansion slot available. Then, you can either reinstall Windows 2000 Professional over itself or you can upgrade the drivers to convert the configuration of your system from single processor to multiple processors. You use the Device Manager to upgrade the HAL for SMP (symmetric multiprocessing). You will probably have more luck performing a fresh installation of Windows 2000. However, you can follow the steps in the **How to** section to update the drivers. (***Note:*** *This exercise is optional and should not be performed unless you have installed a second CPU. Your system may be severely compromised if you upgrade to a HAL that supports two processors when only one is installed.*)

caution

Windows 2000 does not support Asymmetric Multiprocessing (ASMP), a process in which each processor can operate on an independent task.

If this method does not work, perform a fresh installation of Windows 2000 Professional. If you install Windows 2000 Professional on a computer that already has two processors, Setup should automatically detect both processors and install the correct HAL. When you add a second processor on the other hand, a different HAL is used for SMP, resulting in a completely different method of handling the hardware attached to your system.

When a second processor is installed on your system, you can use the Performance console to monitor the system, which is now a Symmetric Multiprocessing System (SMP). To open the Performance console, click the **Performance** icon in the **Administrative Tools** window.

how to

Update the driver for the computer for multiprocessor support.
1. Open the **Device Manager** window.
2. Double-click **Computer**.
3. Double-click the model name of your computer, for example, **Advanced Configuration and Power Interface (ACPI) PC,** and then click the **Properties** command to open the **Properties** dialog box for the computer.
4. On the **Driver** tab, click the **Update Driver** option button to open the **Upgrade Device Driver Wizard**.
5. Click [Next >] to open the **Install Hardware Device Drivers** screen.
6. Click the **Display a list for the known drivers for this device so that I can choose a specific driver** option button and click [Next >] to open the **Select a Device Driver** screen (**Figure 3-26**).
7. Click the **Show all hardware of this device class** option button to display the list of computer models (**Figure 3-27**).
8. Click the model name of your computer in the **Models** list and click [Next >]. The **Start Device Driver Installation** screen opens.
9. An **Update Driver Warning** dialog box may open if Windows cannot verify that the driver you want to install is compatible with your hardware. If you are sure the driver is compatible with your hardware, click **Yes**.
10. Click [Next >] to open the **Completing the Upgrade Device Driver Wizard** screen.
11. Click [Finish] to complete the process. You must restart the system to implement the changes.

Figure 3-26 Displaying the list of drivers

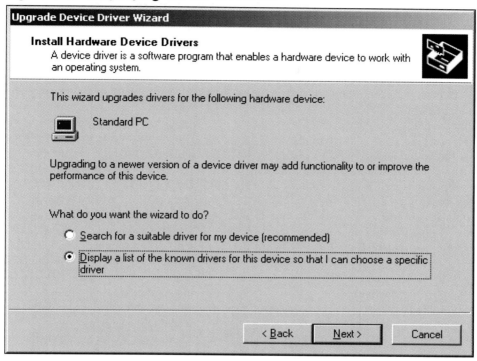

Figure 3-27 Selecting the manufacturer and model

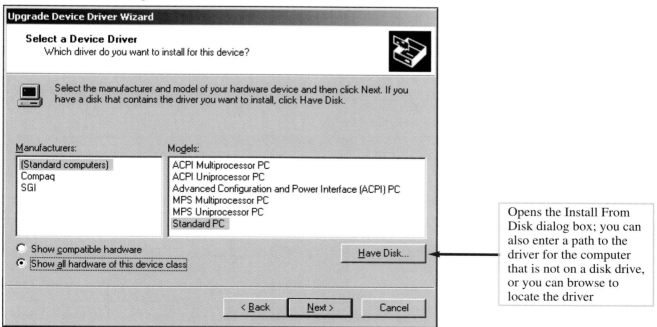

Opens the Install From Disk dialog box; you can also enter a path to the driver for the computer that is not on a disk drive, or you can browse to locate the driver

Summary

- Plug and Play devices are installed automatically by Windows 2000 Professional.
- Devices installed on your system can be managed using the Device Manager.
- Input devices such as the mouse, keyboard, joystick, and scanners are used to provide input data to a computer. Processed data is redirected to the output devices such as the monitor and the printer.
- Before installing a mouse on your system, make sure that the drivers for the mouse are compatible with Windows 2000 Professional.
- When you plug in a mouse, Windows 2000 Professional automatically detects this new hardware and installs the drivers.
- Removable media are devices such as the CD-ROM, DVD, and tape devices that can be removed from your system without having to shut down the system.
- Removable media is used to store data in alternative storage devices other than the hard drive.
- A DVD is a removable device that is commonly used to store large amounts of multimedia data.
- A modem converts analog signals to digital signals and vice versa, making it possible for data to be transferred over telephone lines.
- You can configure the modems installed on your system in the Properties dialog box for that modem.
- You must be careful when selecting your modem speed. If you select a high speed for your modem and the speed of the Internet service provider is slow, you may have problems with your connections to the Internet.
- The fax support feature is enabled only when you install a fax device.
- Device drivers are software that enables a specific device, such as a printer, modem, or network card, to communicate with Windows 2000 Professional computers.
- Windows 2000 Professional has built-in drivers for installing and configuring commonly used devices.
- The Windows File Protection feature checks the digital signature of the file to determine if the correct Microsoft version is being installed.
- The System File Checker utility scans and verifies the versions of all protected system files.
- Universal Serial Bus (USB) is an external communication bus that is used to transfer data among the components of a computer system.
- USB allows you to install multimedia devices such as scanners, audio players, CD-ROM drives, Web cameras, and speakers.
- Network interface cards (NICs) enable you to be connected to the network.
- A video adapter is an expansion board that plugs into a computer and provides display capabilities such as color and a choice of different resolutions.
- IrDA devices communicate with computers using infrared light.
- After an IrDA device is installed on a computer, Windows 2000 Professional adds the Wireless Link icon to the Control Panel window.

Key Terms

Compact Disk File System (CDFS)
Device driver
Device Manager
Hot swapping (hot plugging)

IrDA protocols
Modem
Multiprocessing
Network Interface Card (NIC)
Protocol binding

Removable media
Universal Disk Format (UDF)
Universal Serial Bus (USB)
Video adapter

Test Yourself

1. Which of the following devices is used to store data offline?
   a. UDF
   b. NIC
   c. Modem
   d. DVD

2. A NIC is used to:
   a. Connect to the network.
   b. Configure dial-up options.
   c. Store data on removable media.
   d. Upgrade drivers.

3. You are working as an administrator of a Windows 2000 Professional network environment. One of your team members is facing problems in starting the fax service on his system. He reports that the Control Panel does not display the fax icon. Which of the following may be the cause of this problem?
   a. No fax device is physically attached to the computer.
   b. Supporting fax software is not present.
   c. Windows 2000 Professional registry files are corrupt.

4. Which of the following options is used to configure a fax modem by means of the Dialing Rules tab of the Phone and Modem Options dialog box?
   a. Local dial-up settings
   b. Number of rings before the fax is answered
   c. Number of retries
   d. Fax recipients

5. Which of the following options in the Computer Management console will you use to upgrade drivers?
   a. Hardware Resources
   b. Disk Management
   c. Device Manager
   d. System Information

6. Which of the following is used to install devices such as keyboards, joysticks, and tape drives, and provides a faster and more manageable alternative to serial and parallel ports for devices, such as keyboards and mice?
   a. Parallel port
   b. COM port
   c. Serial port
   d. Universal Serial Bus

7. If you are unable to use the wheel of your mouse, which of the following tabs in the Mouse Properties dialog box, enables you to modify the wheel settings?
   a. Buttons
   b. Motion
   c. Wheel Settings
   d. Hardware

8. You have configured an AGP video adapter on a Windows 2000 Professional computer. Which of the following options is used to change the frequency of the display?
   a. Adapter tab on the Display Adapter Advanced Options dialog box
   b. Monitor tab on the Display Adapter Advanced Options dialog box
   c. Device Manager in the Computer Management console
   d. Services and Application node in the Computer Management console

9. Which of the following is used to install an IrDA device on a computer running Windows 2000 Professional?
   a. Device Manager
   b. Wireless Link program in Control Panel
   c. Add/Remove Programs icon in Control Panel
   d. Add/Remove Hardware icon in Control Panel

10. If you upgrade the drivers for a single processor computer to multiple processor, which of the following is likely to happen?
    a. There will be no change in the functioning of the computer.
    b. The computer will stop functioning.
    c. The computer will be upgraded to a multiple processor computer.
    d. The first processor will be disabled and the second processor will be enabled.

11. The SFC [/quiet] syntax of the System File Checker is used to:
    a. Scan all files for digital signature each time the system is rebooted.
    b. Cancel all pending scans of protected system files.
    c. Replace all incorrect file versions without prompting the user.
    d. Return Windows File Protection to default operation.

12. In the Mouse Properties dialog box, which of the following tabs can be used to set the double-click speed for the mouse?
    a. Pointer tab
    b. Motion tab
    c. Wheel Settings tab
    d. Buttons tab

13. In the Phone and Modem Options dialog box, which of the following tabs can be used to set the speed at which programs transmit data to the modem?
    a. General
    b. Dialing Rules
    c. Advanced
    d. Diagnostic

14. You can assign the Direct Memory Access channel to a USB device.
    a. True
    b. False

Projects: On Your Own

1. Configure a fax device to assign permissions to a user and to receive faxes on the second ring.
   a. Open the **Fax Properties** dialog box.
   b. Open the **Advanced Options** tab.
   c. Open the **Fax Service Management** window.
   d. Open the **Fax Service on Local Computer Properties** dialog box.
   e. Click the **Security** tab.
   f. Select a user
   g. Assign the user permission to submit and view fax jobs. Deny the user permission to manage fax jobs.
   h. Double-click the **Devices** node in the **Fax Service on Local Computer** console tree.
   i. Open the **Properties** dialog box for the device.
   j. Set the device to receive faxes on **2** rings.

2. Configure your mouse to open an item on a double-click action.
   a. Open the **Control Panel** window.
   b. Open the **Mouse Properties** dialog box.
   c. Set the mouse properties to double-click to open an item.

Exam 70-210

3. Configure a modem installed on your system to wait for the dial tone before it starts dialing and set the port speed to 115200.

   a. Open the **Control Panel** window.

   b. Open the **Phone and Modem Options Property** dialog box.

   c. Select a modem on the **Modems** tab.

   d. Access the **Plug and Play Properties** dialog box.

   e. Click the list arrow and select **115200** as the port speed in the **Maximum Port Speed** section.

   f. Select the **Wait for dial tone before dialing** check box in the **Dial Control** section.

Problem Solving Scenarios

1. You are working as the Network Administrator at Nationwide Trucking, a transportation company that specializes in long distance moving of heavy construction equipment. Nationwide is located in Moline, Illinois, but has regional offices in Sacramento, Austin, Minneapolis, and Albany. The marketing manager would like to be able to hold virtual meetings with his marketing staff located in the regional offices. Currently the marketing manager uses telephone conference calling but he would like to switch to Microsoft's NetMeeting software using a Web camera. He has asked you to configure a web camera on his Windows 2000 desktop computer using his USB port to enable video conferencing. Once you have accomplished this, he has asked that you write down the steps you have taken to install the Web camera so other regional offices can also install them. Create a series of PowerPoint slides that provide instructions for employees in the regional offices (if you wish you can include screenshots in your answer).

2. Beryl Williams, an advertising representative at Pique Fashion Design, Inc. in New York City, uses a modem to connect to the Internet. A few weeks after she purchased a new modem, the manufacturer sent her an email notice that a new set of modem device drivers had just been released and that, in order to ensure proper operation of her modem, she should install the new drivers on her system. She has asked you to install the new drivers and to write a memo indicating the steps you followed to do so.

Working with the Control Panel

In Windows 2000 Professional, the Control Panel is used to customize many different system settings to suit users' tastes and needs. For example, you may want to change the screen resolution, screen colors, language support, or keyboard and mouse functionalities. In the Control Panel, you can configure many different options to control the basic functionality and administration of your system.

The Control Panel includes the following utilities. The System and Display utilities are most commonly used.

◆ System: You can use the System program to manage hardware profiles, configure system devices, optimize system performance, and configure the system for startup and recovery.
◆ Regional Options: You can configure multiple-language support on your computer and designate location-specific settings, such as the currency that will be used in monetary calculations, and the date and time.
◆ Accessibility Options: This program is used to configure a system for users with visual, auditory, or physical impairments. For example, you can configure the system to display visual effects or captions when the computer makes a sound, or you can use the MouseKeys setting to allow users to control the pointer using the number pad instead of the mouse.
◆ Display: You can use the Display program to define and modify the screen resolution, color scheme, color resolution, and other properties that affect the appearance of the desktop and application interfaces. You can also set up a multiple display to expand the size of your desktop across more than one monitor.

In the Control Panel, you will also find the Power Options utility, which is used to configure the power management functions in the Windows 2000 environment. The contents of this dialog box will vary depending on the particular power-saving features of the computer. Typically, however, it allows you to implement or create power schemes that will dictate when to turn off the monitor and hard disk, when to put the computer into Standby mode, and when to put it into Hibernate mode (if you so choose). Power-saving capabilities are particularly important when you are using a laptop or notebook computer in order to help you to extend the life of the computer's battery. The PCMCIA (Personal Computer Memory Card International Association) or PC card is another important mobile computer hardware device. These card devices are used to change laptop configurations by adding memory, a NIC, modem, or portable hard drive. Card services do not have a utility in the Control Panel. The operating system automatically carries out most of the functions that are needed to administer PC card support. The main thing you will need to know about configuring card services is that you should make sure that the system stops using the PC card before you remove it.

Goals

In this lesson, you will learn to configure hardware profiles, optimize system performance, and set parameters for system startup and recovery, language and locale support, and display properties. You will also learn to customize the accessibility options, manage power consumption, and configure PC card services.

Lesson 4: Working with the Control Panel

Skill	Exam 70-210 Objective
1. Configuring Hardware Profiles	Manage hardware profiles.
2. Tuning System Performance	Optimize and troubleshoot performance of the Windows 2000 Professional desktop.Optimize and troubleshoot application performance. Optimize and troubleshoot memory performance.
3. Specifying System Startup and Recovery Settings	Optimize and troubleshoot performance of the Windows 2000 Professional desktop.
4. Customizing Language and Locale Support	Configure support for multiple languages or multiple locations. Enable multiple-language support. Configure multiple-language support for users. Configure local settings. Configure Windows 2000 Professional for multiple locations.
5. Customizing the Accessibility Options	Configure and troubleshoot accessibility services.
6. Setting Display Properties	Implement, manage, and troubleshoot display devices. Configure and troubleshoot desktop settings.
7. Configuring Multiple Displays	Implement, manage, and troubleshoot display devices. Configure multiple-display support.
8. Configuring Power Options	Implement, manage, and troubleshoot mobile computer hardware. Configure Advanced Power Management (APM).
9. Configuring Card Services	Implement, manage, and troubleshoot mobile computer hardware. Configure and manage card services.

Requirements

To complete this lesson, you will need a computer running Windows 2000 Professional. The computer should be connected to a network. You will also need a laptop and, to complete Skill 7, multiple monitors and PCI or AGP video adapters.

skill 1

Configuring Hardware Profiles

exam objective

Manage hardware profiles.

overview

The typical hardware requirements for a computer include a CPU, RAM, hard disk, sound card, and probably a network card. In addition to this standard equipment, you may need other hardware, such as a multimedia card and speakers. You can easily install these devices on your system; however, when you install additional hardware devices, each time you boot your computer the system tries to establish a connection with each device, even when you do not need to use them. This can adversely affect system performance. Using Windows 2000, you can prevent this by creating hardware profiles.

Hardware profiles enable you to set up and store different hardware configurations for your computer. A hardware profile contains configuration information about computer hardware or devices. It notifies the computer at startup about the devices to be used and the type of settings for each device. Usually, client desktops will not change hardware configurations; however, mobile computers may do so frequently. Although you could depend on Plug and Play to detect hardware changes at startup, this can increase the amount of time it takes the computer to boot up, and not all of your hardware devices may be Plug and Play compatible. If the OS tries to detect devices that are not present, startup will be considerably delayed while Windows waits a set time period for those devices to respond before deciding that they are not attached.

Multiple hardware profiles are most commonly required for mobile computers. While working with a mobile computer at home, the office, or other sites, you often need to enable or disable network support, docking stations, modems, and monitors.

To create different types of hardware profiles, you use the System Properties dialog box. Each system has a default hardware profile named **Profile 1**. To create a new hardware profile, you must first make a copy of Profile 1 for security reasons and then modify it according to your requirements. Although, by default, new hardware profiles are named **Profile 2** or **Profile 3**, depending on the number of existing profiles, you can easily rename them.

caution

You must be logged on as a member of the Administrators group in order to make changes to hardware profiles.

how to

Create a new hardware profile for a laptop.
1. Click **Start**, point to **Settings**, and click **Control Panel** to open the **Control Panel** window.
2. Double-click the **System** icon to open the **System Properties** dialog box.
3. Click the **Hardware** tab (**Figure 4-1**).
4. Click Hardware Profiles... to open the **Hardware Profiles** dialog box (**Figure 4-2**).
5. Click **Profile 1 [Current]** and then click Copy... to make a copy of the default profile. The **Copy Profile** dialog box opens with the default name **Profile 2** shown for the new profile.
6. Click OK . The new hardware profile is listed in the **Available hardware profiles** list box.
7. Click Properties to open the **Profile 2 Properties** dialog box.
8. Select the **This is a portable computer** check box (**Figure 4-3**) to specify that you are using a portable computer, a laptop.
9. Click OK to save the settings.

more

If there are two or more hardware profiles on your computer, Windows 2000 Professional will prompt you to select one at startup. You can specify a default profile that Windows 2000 Professional will automatically initiate after the specified number of seconds during startup. If you do not want to select a profile, Windows 2000 can, by default, select the first profile as the default profile. To do this, select the **Select the first profile listed if I don't select a profile in** option button. Then, in the **Seconds** spin box, enter the number of seconds your computer should wait before selecting the default profile.

Figure 4-1 Hardware tab in System Properties dialog box

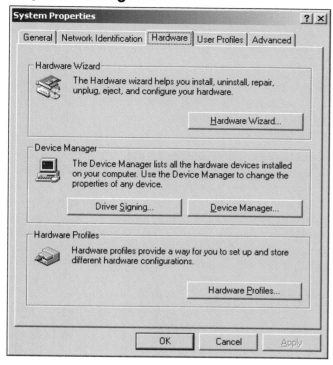

Figure 4-2 Hardware Profiles dialog box

Figure 4-3 Properties of the new profile

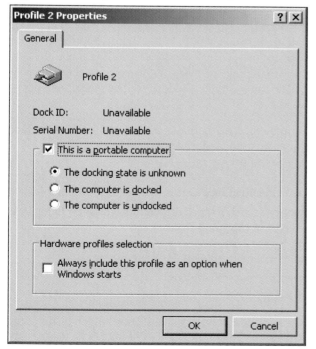

skill 2

Tuning System Performance

exam objective

Optimize and troubleshoot performance of the Windows 2000 Professional desktop. Optimize and troubleshoot application performance. Optimize and troubleshoot memory performance.

overview

You can optimize your system's performance by configuring the application response and the virtual memory settings in the **Performance Options** dialog box to meet the requirements of your individual system. The Performance Options dialog box can be accessed on the Advanced tab in the System Properties dialog box.

Application response: The **application response setting** is used by Windows 2000 Professional to distribute microprocessor resources between programs that are being executed simultaneously on the system at any given point in time. Programs are categorized as either active foreground programs or background programs. If you select the **Applications** option button in the **Performance Options** dialog box, more processor resources will be allocated to the foreground program than the background program **(Figure 4-4)**. This option is generally used for client workstations where more resources are required for the program running in the foreground. On the other hand, if you select the **Background services** option button, all programs will receive equal amounts of processor resources. This option is generally used for servers such as an e-mail server, which is generally only needed for background processing. If your system is often used as a file, print, or e-mail server, you should change the application response option to background services.

Virtual memory: **Virtual memory** is defined as temporary storage, composed of a paging file, pagefile.sys, used by a computer to run programs that need more memory than is available at any given point in time. For example, programs could have access to 4 GB of virtual memory on a computer's hard drive, even if the computer has only 32 megabytes of RAM. The program data that does not currently fit in the computer's memory is saved in the paging file. Virtual memory enables you to run larger and/or more applications than is normally possible with physical memory. Windows 2000 Professional uses the **Virtual Memory Manager (VMM)**, to coordinate the use of physical memory and virtual memory. You can improve virtual memory somewhat by moving the paging file to a faster drive or by making the initial size and the maximum size of the paging file the same. This will make access to virtual memory faster by reducing fragmentation of the swap file. However, system performance will not be significantly increased because memory performance will only be slightly improved. Since physical memory is up to 1000 times faster than virtual memory, installing more physical memory (RAM) is a more productive way to improve memory performance. Making the paging file's initial size and maximum size the same is typically done for machines using heavy applications, for example, a database server.

caution

Selecting Background services may slow down system performance for foreground applications.

caution

You are required to log on as an Administrator to change the paging file size.

how to

Set both the initial size and the maximum size of the paging file to 136 MB to reduce fragmentation in the swap file and improve memory performance.

1. Open the **System Properties** dialog box, if necessary.
2. Click the **Advanced** tab.
3. Click ⟦ Performance Options... ⟧ to open the **Performance Options** dialog box (**Figure 4-4**).
4. Click ⟦ Change... ⟧ in the **Virtual memory** section to open the **Virtual Memory** dialog box.
5. In the **Initial size (MB)** text box, type **136 (Figure 4-5)**.
6. In the **Maximum size (MB)** text box, type **136**.
7. Click ⟦ Set ⟧ to set the initial and maximum sizes of the paging file to 106 MB.
8. Click ⟦ OK ⟧ to close the **Virtual Memory** dialog box.
9. Click ⟦ OK ⟧ to close the **Performance Options** dialog box.

more

The **Virtual Memory** dialog box also contains the **Registry size** section, which displays the current size of the registry. As new software is added the number of entries in the registry increases. When software is uninstalled, not all registry keys are deleted. You can use the Registry size section to specify the maximum possible size to which the Registry can grow.

Figure 4-4 Performance Options dialog box

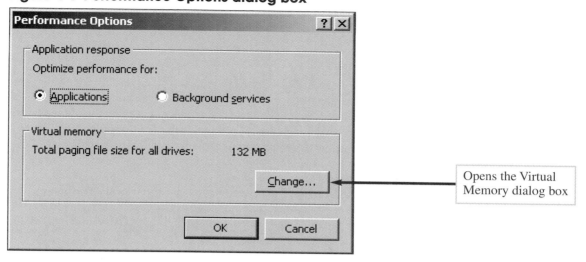

Opens the Virtual
Memory dialog box

Figure 4-5 Virtual Memory dialog box

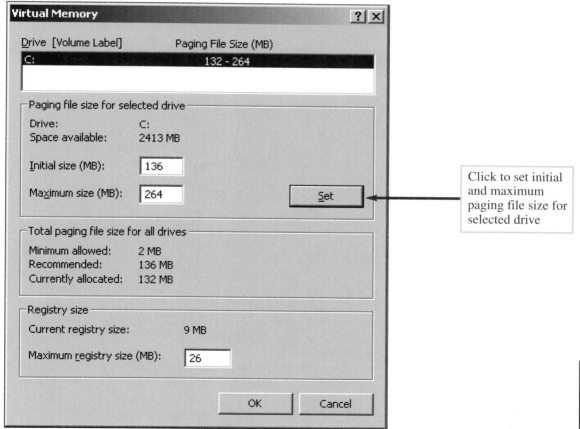

Click to set initial
and maximum
paging file size for
selected drive

skill 3

Specifying System Startup and Recovery Settings

exam objective

Optimize and troubleshoot performance of the Windows 2000 Professional desktop.

overview

When you have installed multiple operating systems on your computer, you may want to specify a particular operating system as the default so that it will be initialized automatically each time you start your computer. Alternatively, you might want to be able to choose one of the installed operating systems at startup. In the **Startup and Recovery** dialog box you can set or change the default operating system options. You can also select the course of action to be followed in case the system stops unexpectedly. The Startup and Recovery dialog box is divided into two sections:

◆ **System Startup:** In this section you can specify which operating system you want as the default at startup and the number of seconds the system should wait during startup before the default operating system initializes. During the waiting period, the user can choose a specific operating system.

◆ **System Failure:** In this section you can control the actions Windows 2000 Professional will take when a system failure occurs. To set the system failure options, you must be logged on as a member of the **Administrators** group. You can configure Windows 2000 Professional to perform any of the following actions in the event of a system failure:

- Write an event to the system log.
- Send an administrative alert.
- Automatically reboot the system.
- Write debugging information.

You can specify the kind of debugging information Windows 2000 Professional will write to the specified dump file, Memory.dmp. **Table 4-1** describes the four options for writing debugging information.

how to

Limit the duration of display for the list of operating systems to zero seconds so that the default operating system will be started without any boot delay. Set the system properties so that, if a system failure occurs, an alert will be sent to the administrator and an entry will be made in the system log giving a brief description of the problem.

1. Open the **System Properties** dialog box, if necessary.
2. Click the **Advanced** tab (**Figure 4-6**).
3. Click ⬚Startup and Recovery...⬚ to open the **Startup and Recovery** dialog box.
4. In the **Display list of operating systems for** spin box, type **0** (**Figure 4-7**). The default setting is 30 seconds.
5. In the **System Failure** section, make sure that the **Write an event to the system log** check box is selected. If a system failure occurs, this will create an entry in the system log.
6. Make sure that the **Send an administrative alert** check box is selected. This will send an alert message to the system administrator informing him or her of the system failure.
7. Make sure that the **Automatically reboot** check box is selected. This will restart the system in case of a system failure.
8. In the **Write Debugging Information** spin box, select the **Small Memory Dump (64 KB)** option. This will record the minimum information about the system problem on the system log.
9. Click ⬚OK⬚ to apply the changes and close the dialog box.
10. Click OK to close the **System Properties** dialog box. Close the **Control Panel**.

Table 4-1 Options for writing debugging information in the dump file

Write Debugging Information Option	Function
None	No information is written to the dump file.
Small Memory Dump	A minimum amount of useful information is written to the dump file. This option requires a paging file of a 2 megabyte (MB) paging file on the boot volume and Windows 2000 Professional must create a new file each time there is a system failure. A history of these files is maintained in the small dump directory named %SystemRoot%\minidump.
Kernel Memory Dump	Kernel memory is written to the dump file. Kernel memory is a part of the operating system that is loaded first and remains in the main memory. This enables faster recording of information in a log when the system stops unexpectedly. You must have 50MB to 800MB available in the paging file on the boot volume, depending on the amount of RAM on your computer. The more RAM you have the less space you will need for the paging file.
Complete Memory Dump	The entire contents of the system memory are written to the dump file when a system failure occurs. The system must have a paging file on the boot partition that is large enough to store the physical RAM plus 1 MB.

Figure 4-6 Advanced tab in System Properties dialog box

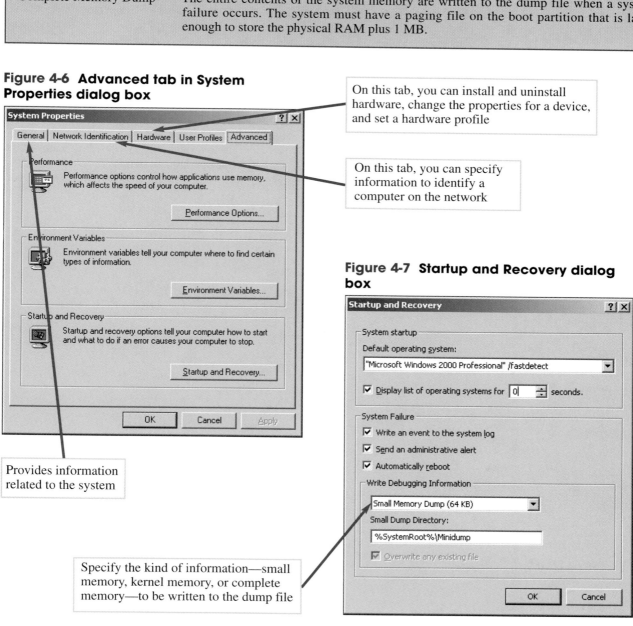

On this tab, you can install and uninstall hardware, change the properties for a device, and set a hardware profile

On this tab, you can specify information to identify a computer on the network

Provides information related to the system

Figure 4-7 Startup and Recovery dialog box

Specify the kind of information—small memory, kernel memory, or complete memory—to be written to the dump file

skill

Specifying System Startup and Recovery Settings *(cont'd)*

exam objective

Optimize and troubleshoot performance of the Windows 2000 Professional desktop.

more

In the **System Properties** dialog box, you can also specify the environment variables. Environment variables provide system and user environment information, such as drives, paths, or file names. All of the various initialization parameters and paths for globally used variable parameters are also stored as environment variables. Since applications use some common variables across the platform to interpret behavior or data in an OS, these variables must be stored in a common place where they are accessible to all. To display the **Environment Variables** dialog box, click [Environment Variables...] on the **Advanced** page in the System Properties dialog box. There are two types of environment variables (**Figure 4-8**):

- ◆ **User variables for <username>:** User environment variables are personalized settings for different users using the same system. For example, users may have defined personal settings such as a particular desktop pattern or display colors or menu options in a specific application. The paths to the locations of application files are also stored as environment variables. Thus, user environment variables differ for each user and are loaded according to the user who logs on to the system. Users can add, delete, or edit their user environment variables to suit their specific requirements.
- ◆ **System variables:** The Setup program in Windows 2000 Professional configures the system environment variables during installation. These variables contain information such as the path used by the Windows 2000 Professional registry files. For example, the **TEMP** environment variable indicates where the operating system stores temporary files, while the **ComSpec** environmental variable indicates the path for the **Command Prompt** executable file.

caution

System environment variables can only be added, changed, or deleted by an administrator.

Figure 4-8 Environment Variables dialog box

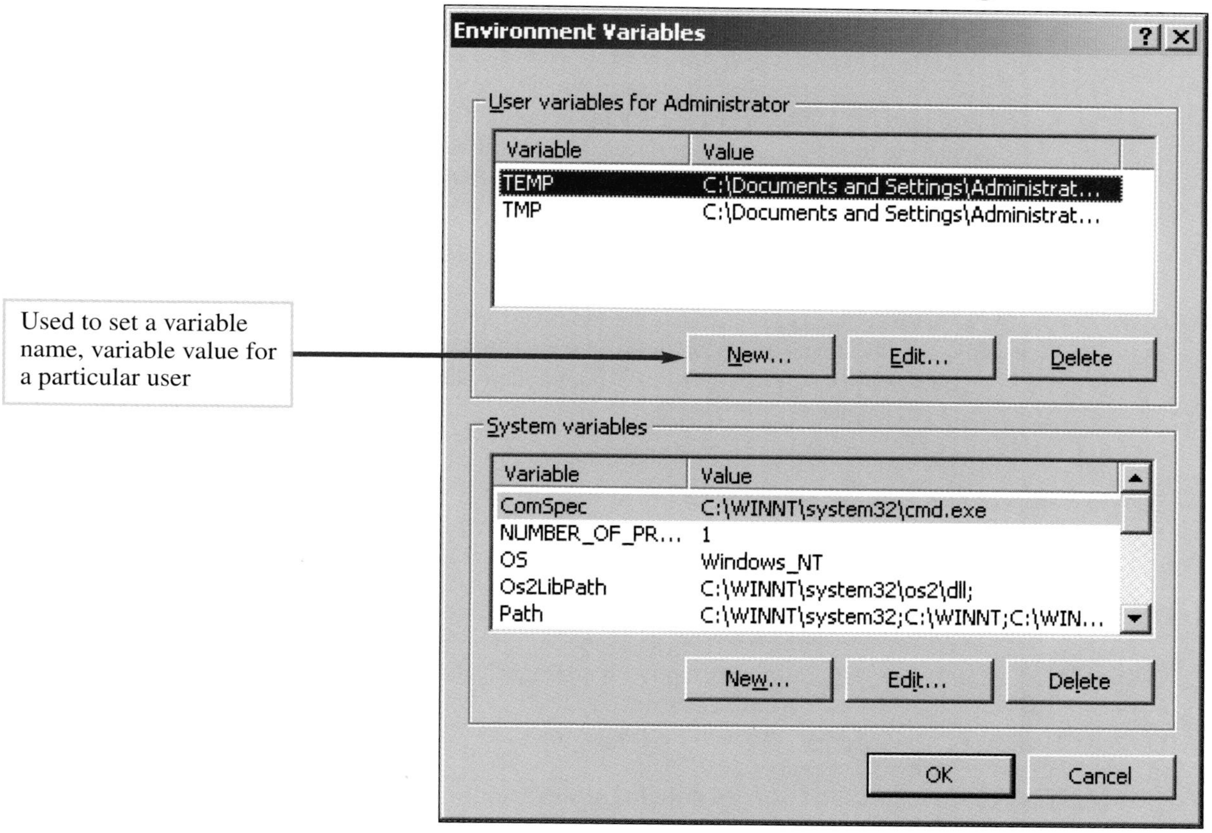

Used to set a variable name, variable value for a particular user →

| Environment Variables | ? ✕ |

User variables for Administrator

Variable	Value
TEMP	C:\Documents and Settings\Administrat...
TMP	C:\Documents and Settings\Administrat...

[New...] [Edit...] [Delete]

System variables

Variable	Value
ComSpec	C:\WINNT\system32\cmd.exe
NUMBER_OF_PR...	1
OS	Windows_NT
Os2LibPath	C:\WINNT\system32\os2\dll;
Path	C:\WINNT\system32;C:\WINNT;C:\WIN...

[New...] [Edit...] [Delete]

[OK] [Cancel]

skill 4

Customizing Language and Locale Support

exam objective

Configure support for multiple languages or multiple locations. Enable multiple-language support. Configure multiple-language support for users. Configure local settings. Configure Windows 2000 Professional for multiple locations.

overview

When you use Windows 2000 Professional, you can customize your desktop for multiple languages and locations. In the English version, users can view, edit, and print information in several languages. In the Translated version, users can access menus, help files, dialog boxes and file system components in multiple languages. The MultiLanguage version allows bilingual users to switch back and forth between several language interfaces, which is particularly useful for employees of multinational companies that have offices and customers in numerous countries. The MultiLanguage version of the OS uses a single worldwide executable file that supports Arabic, Hebrew, and most European and East Asian languages. Rather than having to use a different translated version of Windows for each language, you can install Windows 2000 with the MultiLanguage Pack to support multilingual document editing and the deployment of multiple language interfaces. The MultiLanguage Pack is available to customers who participate in the Microsoft Open License Program and to Select and Enterprise agreement customers.

On the English language version, you can configure your system to display and sort numbers, currency, and the date and time according to the location you select. To specify the language you want to use, you must add the required input locales. When you add an input locale, a keyboard layout or Input Method Editor (IME) for that language is also added. Keyboard layouts or IMEs are designed to accommodate the special characters and symbols used in different languages.

To customize the language and local support for your desktop, you use the **Regional Options** dialog box (**Figure 4-9**). This dialog box contains several tabs where you can specify each language you need your computer to support, the current locale, and any additional locales you need supported. You can also modify input locales to alter keyboard layouts. A brief description of each tab is given in **Table 4-2**.

how to

Configure your desktop to support both English and German.

1. Log on as an **Administrator**.
2. Click [**Start**], point to **Settings**, and click **Control Panel** to open the Control Panel window.
3. Double-click the **Regional Options** icon to open the **Regional Options** dialog box (**Figure 4-9**).
4. Click the **Input Locales** tab .By default, **English (United States)** is the only language displayed in the **Input language** list box. In order to support another language on your system, you must add another locale.
5. Click [Add...] to open the **Add Input Locale** dialog box.
6. Click the **Input locale** list arrow to view a list of available input locales. Select the **German (Germany)** option (**Figure 4-10**).

Table 4-2   Tabs in the Regional Options dialog box

Tab	Offers options that enable you to:
General	Select multiple languages and view the current locale setting. You can also standard configure settings to be used by your system for specific locales.
Input Locales	Add additional locales and configure multiple language support.
Numbers	Configure the appearance of numbers, including the decimal symbol, the number of places after a decimal, the digital grouping symbol, and the measurement symbol.
Currency, Time, Date Tabs	Configure the way currency, time, and date are displayed.

Figure 4-9 The Regional Options dialog box

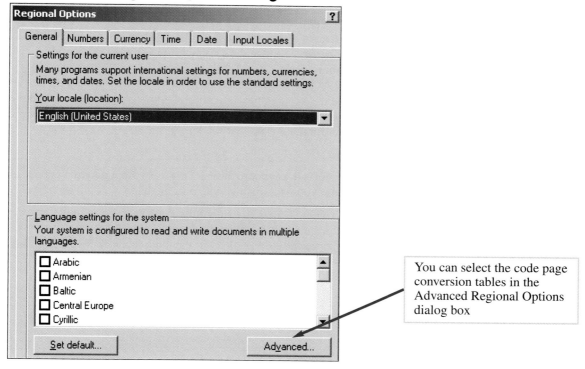

You can select the code page conversion tables in the Advanced Regional Options dialog box

Figure 4-10 Adding a new input locale

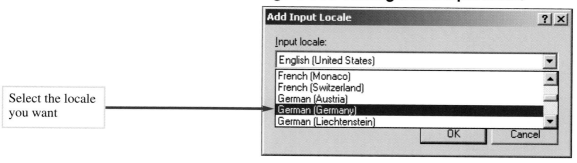

Select the locale you want

skill 4

Customizing Language and Locale Support *(cont'd)*

exam objective

Configure support for multiple languages or multiple locations. Enable multiple-language support. Configure multiple-language support for users. Configure local settings. Configure Windows 2000 Professional for multiple locations.

how to

7. Click [OK] to close the dialog box. The selected language, **German (Germany)** is displayed in the **Input language** list box, along with the default language **English (United States) (Figure 4-11)**.
8. The **Enable indicator on taskbar** check box at the bottom of the Input Locales tab is selected by default.
9. Click [Apply] to apply the new settings. A language/locale indicator, **EN,** is shown on the Taskbar **(Figure 4-12)**.
10. Click [OK] to close the Regional Options dialog box.
11. To switch to the German locale, click **EN** on the Taskbar. A menu listing the locales you have configured appears **(Figure 4-13)**. Click the **German (Germany)** command to switch to the **German** locale.
12. After changing the locale, you will find that some characters have a different appearance when you type them. For example, if you press the [-] key, a German character [ß] is displayed on the screen. This indicates that the internal layout of the keyboard has changed to suit the German locale.

more

Each language has a default keyboard layout, but many languages support alternative keyboard layouts. Even if you work mainly with one language, you can try other layouts.

You can use a different input locale for each program you use. For example, you can use one input locale to create documents using **WordPad** and another input locale at the **Command Prompt**. To do this, open the program and select the input locale to be used for that program by using the locale indicator on the Taskbar.

Figure 4-11 Input locales available on the system

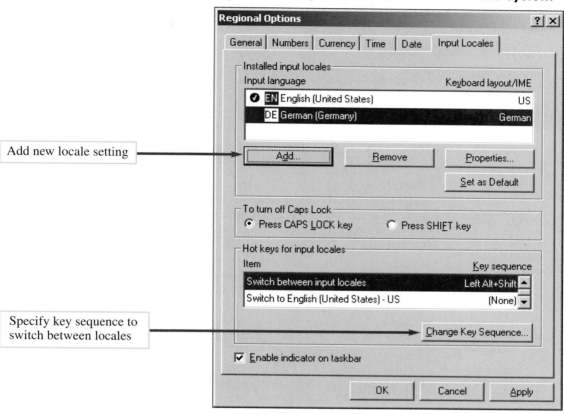

Add new locale setting

Specify key sequence to
switch between locales

**Figure 4-12 Indicator
representing the current
input locale**

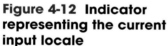

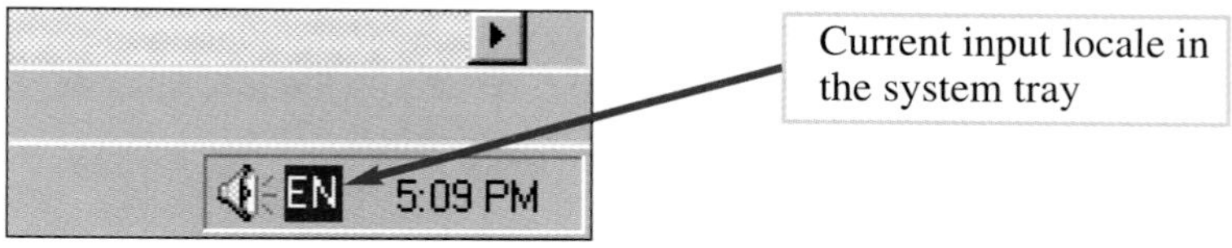

Current input locale in
the system tray

Figure 4-13 Switching the locale

All added locales
will be visible

skill 5

Customizing the Accessibility Options

exam objective

Configure and troubleshoot accessibility services.

overview

You can customize your computer to meet your special visual, auditory, or mobility needs in the **Accessibility Options** dialog box. This dialog box has five tabs: Keyboard, Sound, Display, Mouse, and General (**Figure 4-14**). A brief description of the functions you can configure on each of these tabs is given below.

On the **Keyboard** tab you can configure the following support:

◆ **StickyKeys:** To use a multiple-key combination, such as **[Ctrl]+[Alt]+[Delete]**, normally you must press the required keys simultaneously. For people who find it difficult to press more than one key at a time, such as those with arthritis, you can set the StickyKeys function so that they can perform the same action by pressing one key at a time.

◆ **FilterKeys:** This function adjusts the response of your keyboard to your actions. For example, normally if you press a key on the keyboard and hold it down, multiple instances of the character are inserted until you release the key. With the FilterKeys function activated, the character will appear only once regardless of how long you hold down the key. You can also adjust the length of time a key must be pressed before the keystroke is accepted. The FilterKeys function should be used carefully, however, because a key press can be ignored after a letter has been entered once, even when the character is intended to be displayed twice in succession, such as in the word "succeed."

◆ **ToggleKeys:** Activating the ToggleKeys function configures your computer to emit sounds when certain locking keys are pressed. For example, the computer will make a high-pitched sound each time the **[Caps Lock]**, **[Num Lock]**, or **[Scroll Lock]** keys are toggled on. Similarly, each time these keys are toggled-off, the computer will make a low-pitched sound.

The **SoundSentry** function on the **Sound** tab can be extremely helpful for the hearing impaired. It programs Windows 2000 Professional to generate visual warnings when the system's built-in speaker plays a sound. The visual warning is in the form of a flash on a part of the screen when the user performs an action that causes a sound to be generated. You can specify the part of the screen where you want the warning to appear, either in the caption bar, the active window, or the entire desktop. You can also set the **ShowSounds** function to display captions to replace the speech and sounds generated by programs.

caution

You must be logged on as an administrator or have administrative permissions in order to perform these tasks.

On the **Display** tab, you can set the display to use high contrast color schemes that are specially designed to improve the legibility of text. For example, you can make the color scheme black on white, white on black, or any other color scheme you prefer.

On the **Mouse** tab, you can set the **MouseKeys** function so that users can perform mouse functions using the numeric keypad. The arrow keys on the numeric keypad located at the extreme right of your keyboard can be used to control the pointer movement and actions on the screen. Before you set the MouseKeys function, you must deactivate the **NumLock** key. If you encounter problems implementing this function, verify that NumLock has been deactivated and try again.

On the **General** tab, you can configure settings related to automatic resetting, notification, SerialKey devices, and administrative options (**Figure 4-15**). **Table 4-3** contains a description of each of these functions.

how to

Configure accessibility options so that the numeric keypad can be used instead of a mouse, and change the display settings to provide a high contrast of black text on a white background.

1. In the **Control Panel** window, double-click the **Accessibility Options** icon to open the **Accessibility Options** dialog box.

Figure 4-14 Accessibility Options dialog box

Figure 4-15 The General tab in the Accessibility Options dialog box

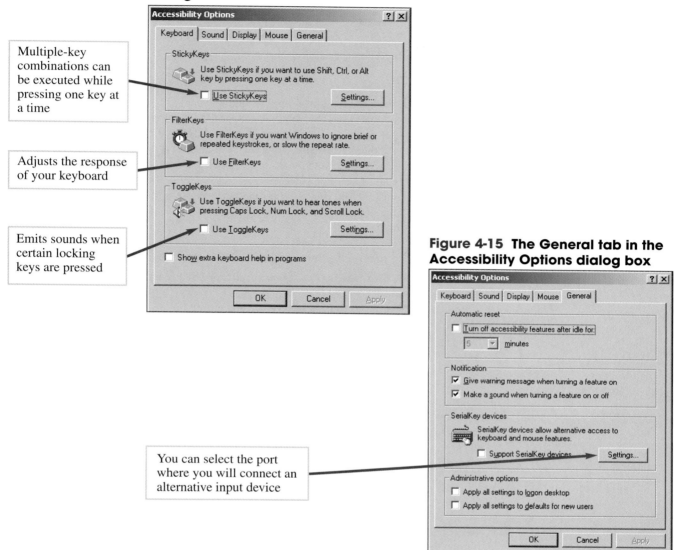

Multiple-key combinations can be executed while pressing one key at a time

Adjusts the response of your keyboard

Emits sounds when certain locking keys are pressed

You can select the port where you will connect an alternative input device

Table 4-3	Options on the General tab
Options	**Description**
Automatic Reset	Deactivates all the accessibility functions, except the SerialKeys device, after the computer has been idle for a specified time. The SerialKeys device is designed for people who are unable to use the computer's standard keyboard and mouse.
Serial Key devices	Allows alternative access to keyboard and mouse functions. SerialKey devices are designed for people who are unable to use the computer's standard keyboard and mouse. Selecting the Support SerialKey devices check box activates SerialKey support and you can attach an alternative input device to your computer's serial port. These devices are also referred to as augmentative communicative devices.
Administrative options	Program the system to apply the newly configured accessibility options as the default settings for a particular user and/or for all new users.

skill 5

Customizing the Accessibility Options *(cont'd)*

exam objective

Configure and troubleshoot accessibility services.

how to

2. Click the **Mouse** tab to display the options on the tab.
3. Select the **Use MouseKeys** check box to activate the numeric pad on your keyboard to control the mouse pointer on the screen (**Figure 4-16**) and click the [Apply] button. The MouseKeys indicator is displayed at the bottom right of the screen (**Figure 4-17**).
4. To confirm that the MouseKeys function has been activated, press the up arrow key on the numeric keypad. The cursor on the screen moves up in the same way it would if you were using a mouse. Hold down the **[Ctrl]** key and press the up arrow key again. The cursor moves up more quickly.
5. Click the **Display** tab.
6. Select the **Use High Contrast** check box.
7. Click [Settings...] to open the **Settings for High Contrast** dialog box.
8. Click the **Black on white** option button (**Figure 4-18**) and then click [OK] to confirm the selection.
9. Click [OK] in the **Accessibility Options** dialog box to apply the changes. **Figure 4-19** displays the Black on white high contrast color scheme.
10. Reopen the **Accessibility Options** dialog box and remove any settings you do not want to retain. Close the dialog box.

more

In addition to the accessibility functions, there are many other desktop settings in Windows 2000 Professional that are configured through the **Control Panel**, such as **Fax Services**, **Internet Options**, and **Phone and Modem Options**. You can configure these settings by double-clicking the relevant icon in the Control Panel, opening the relevant tab, and configuring the required settings.

A few accessibility related problems that you may encounter, along with their solutions, are listed below:

1. If the accessibility options you have set are not working, make sure that the **Turn off accessibility features after idle for** <specified> **minutes** check box on the **General** tab in the **Accessibility Options** dialog box is not selected.
2. If the text is appearing in the white on black contrast, that is, the text is white and the background is black, make sure that the **White on black** option in the **Settings for High Contrast** dialog box is not selected. You must open the **Display** tab on the **Accessibility Options** dialog box and click the **Settings** button to open this dialog box.
3. If the standard keyboard and mouse are not working and you have checked that there are no loose connections, make sure that the Support SerialKey devices check box on the General tab is not selected.

Figure 4-16 The Mouse tab in the Accessibility Options dialog box

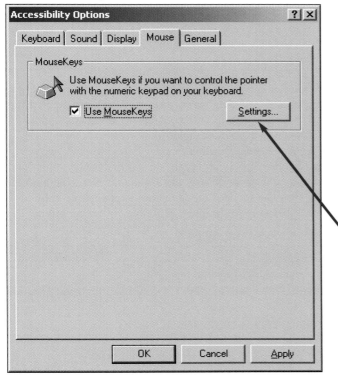

Figure 4-17 The System Tray displaying the MouseKeys indicator

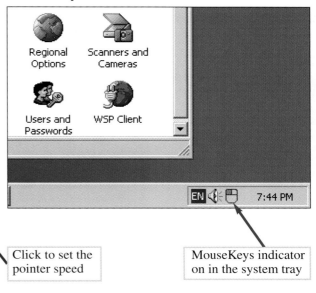

Click to set the
pointer speed

MouseKeys indicator
on in the system tray

Figure 4-18 Changing the High Contrast setting

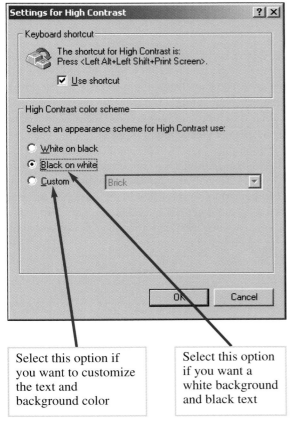

Figure 4-19 The Black on white High Contrast color scheme

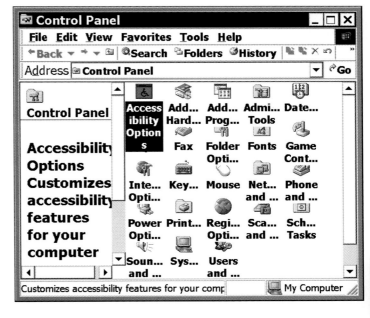

Select this option if
you want to customize
the text and
background color

Select this option
if you want a
white background
and black text

skill 6

Setting Display Properties

exam objective

Implement, manage, and troubleshoot display devices. Configure and troubleshoot desktop settings.

overview

You can also modify the display properties for your computer such as the screen resolution, color depth, and background colors. To configure the display properties, you use the **Settings** tab on the **Display Properties** dialog box. The Settings tab contains the following options:

◆ **Colors:** Provides a list of color depths available for the display adapter.

◆ **Screen Area:** Enables you to set the screen resolution.

◆ **Troubleshoot:** Enables you to diagnose display problems.

◆ **Advanced:** Enables you to configure the properties for the display adapter to support the multiple display feature. The options on the Advanced tab are explained in **Table 4-4**. **Adapter, Monitor**, and **Troubleshooting** options are available for all monitors. The other features are monitor-dependent.

how to

Change the screen area for your computer to **1024 by 768** pixels.

1. Double-click the **Display** icon in the **Control Panel** window to open the **Display Properties** dialog box.

2. Click the **Settings** tab.

3. In the **Screen area** section, drag the slider towards the left to change the resolution to **1024 by 768** pixels **(Figure 4-20)**.

4. Click [Apply]. The Display Properties message box informs you that Windows will apply the new desktop settings.

5. Click [OK]. The **Monitor Settings** message box prompts you to confirm the new setting.

6. Click [Yes] to change the desktop setting.

more

Troubleshooting Display Settings:

◆ Changing the screen resolution: There may be times when you are not able to view graphics on the monitor properly. Some of the graphics may be only partly visible because they extend beyond the screen area. You can change the resolution of the screen to view a graphic in its entirety. A higher screen resolution reduces the size of objects on your screen and increases the size of your desktop. Your monitor and the drivers for the video adapter determine whether you can change your screen resolution.

◆ Changing the refresh frequency of your monitor: If your screen seems to flicker, causing distortion and disturbance, increase the refresh setting for your screen to a higher rate. The default refresh frequency setting is 60 Hertz, but your monitor may support a higher setting. Check your manufacturer's documentation for information regarding the settings your monitor supports. A higher refresh frequency will reduce the flickering, but choosing a setting that is too high for your monitor can make your display unusable and cause damage to your hardware.

Table 4-4   Options in the Graphics Controller Properties dialog box

Tab	Option group	Description
General	Display	Displays the font size for the current monitor. You can set the font size to a predefined small or large font, or you can set a custom font size.
	Compatibility	Specifies the action to be taken after you have changed the display settings. You can select any of the three options: • Restart the computer before applying the new display settings. • Apply the new display settings without restarting. • Display a prompt to restart the computer before applying the new display settings.
Adapter	Adapter Type	Provides information about the type of video adapter used on your system. This includes information about the manufacturer and model number and about the device status, resource settings, and whether there are any conflicting devices.
	Adapter Information	Provides information about the video adapter. This includes information such as the video chip type, DAC type, memory size, and BIOS.
	List All Modes	Lists all the compatible modes for your video adapter. You can select the resolution, color depth, and refresh frequency in a single step.
Monitor	Monitor Type	Provides information about the monitor your system is using. You can also access the display Troubleshooter to diagnose display problems. The troubleshooter asks you to do one of the following: • Restart: Restart your computer if you have changed any hardware settings and you want those changes to take effect immediately. • Reinstall Drivers: Upgrade the device drivers for the device with which you are encountering problems. When you select this option, the Update Device Driver wizard will take you step by step through the upgrade process. • Troubleshooter: Start the Hardware troubleshooter if there is a hardware conflict or a problem listed under the Device status option on the General tab.
	Monitor Settings	You can set the refresh rate frequency.
Troubleshooting	Hardware Acceleration	You can gradually decrease the display hardware's acceleration so that you can segregate and fix display problems.
Color Management		You can select the color profile for your monitor.

Figure 4-20 Changing the resolution

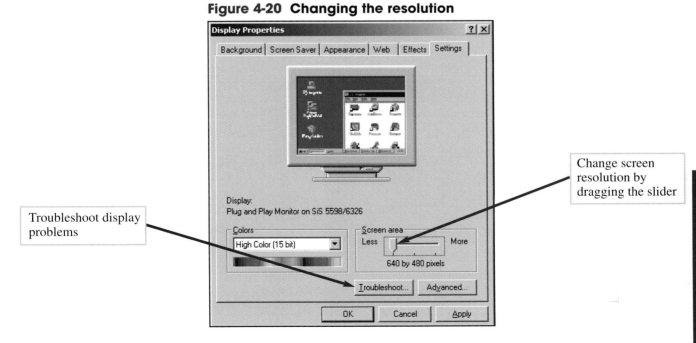

Troubleshoot display problems

Change screen resolution by dragging the slider

skill 7 — *Configuring Multiple Displays*

exam objective

Implement, manage, and troubleshoot display devices. Configure multiple-display support.

overview

You can configure your computer for **multiple displays** to expand the size of your desktop to more than one monitor (**Figure 4-21**). A maximum of ten monitors can be connected to create a desktop large enough to hold multiple displays. For example, if you want to view the contents of a Microsoft Excel spreadsheet without having to scroll, you can set up a multiple display to stretch the spreadsheet across three or four monitors.

how to

Install additional monitors. (Activity 1)

Requirements:

- ◆ Peripheral Component Interconnect (PCI) or Accelerated Graphics Port (AGP) video adapter for each monitor.
- ◆ A multiple-display compatible onboard adapter set as VGA. The motherboard adapter always becomes the secondary display adapter when you add a display adapter.
- ◆ Windows 2000 Professional completely set up before installing another adapter. (Windows 2000 Professional Setup will disable the default display adapter if it detects another display adapter.)

1. Shut down the computer.
2. Insert an additional **Peripheral Component Interconnect (PCI)** or **Accelerated Graphics Port (AGP)** video adapter into an available slot.
3. Plug your additional monitor cable into the display adapter.
4. Restart the computer. Windows 2000 will detect the new video adapter and install the appropriate drivers.
5. Click **Start**, point to **Settings**, and click **Control Panel** to open the Control Panel window.
6. Double-click the **Display** icon to open the Display Properties dialog box.
7. Click the **Settings** tab.
8. Click the **Monitor** icon that represents the monitor you want to use in addition to your primary monitor.
9. Click the **Extend my Windows desktop onto this monitor** check box (**Figure 4-22**).
10. Select the color depth and resolution for the secondary display.
11. Click **OK** to drag items across the screen onto alternate monitors.

Arrange multiple monitors. (Activity 2)

1. On the Settings tab in the Display window, click **Identify** (**Figure 4-23**) to display a large number on each of your monitors, showing which monitor corresponds with each icon.
2. Drag the Monitor icons to positions that represent how you want to move objects from one monitor to another, and click **OK** to view the changes.

If you encounter problems with a multiple-display configuration, such as output failure on the secondary displays, you can try various solutions. For example, if you are unable to see the output on the secondary displays, open the **Display Properties** dialog box, select the device, and verify that you are using the correct video driver. Then restart your computer to make sure that the secondary display starts. If it does not start, open the Device Manger and check the status of the device. If the device is operating correctly, try switching the order of the adapters in the slots on the motherboard. If the **Extend Windows Desktop Onto This Monitor** check box is not presented, open the **Display Properties** dialog box, select the secondary display instead of the primary one, verify that the secondary display adapter is supported, and verify that Windows 2000 Professional can detect the secondary display. If a particular application will not display on the secondary display, first run the application on the primary display, then use full-screen mode to run the application (i.e., maximized). Finally, to find out if the problem is chiefly related to multiple-display support, disable the secondary display.

tip

You can resize a window to stretch it across more than one monitor.

tip

If you are using two monitors and you want to move objects from one monitor to the other by dragging left and right, place the respective monitor icons side by side. To move objects between monitors by dragging up and down, place the icons one above the other.

Figure 4-21 Multiple displays

Figure 4-22 Extending the desktop

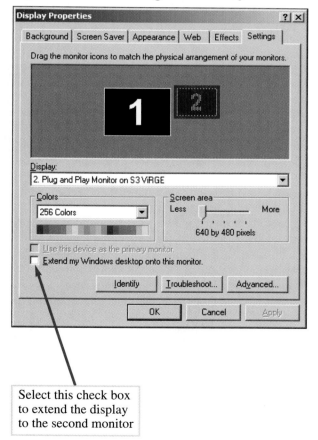

Select this check box
to extend the display
to the second monitor

Figure 4-23 Identifying the monitors

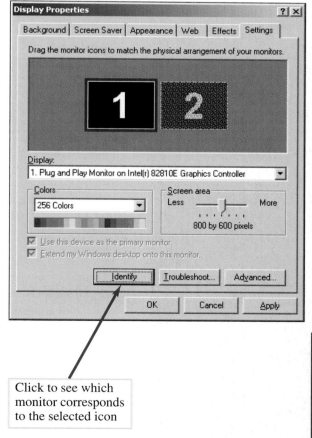

Click to see which
monitor corresponds
to the selected icon

skill 8

Configuring Power Options

exam objective

Implement, manage, and troubleshoot mobile computer hardware. Configure Advanced Power Management (APM).

overview

Windows 2000 Professional supports two power management standards, **Advanced Power Management** (APM) and **Advanced Configuration and Power Interface (ACPI)**. These standards are used to control and manage power consumption. APM is the older standard and it may be all that the hardware in older computers supports. You use the **Power Options** utility in the **Control Panel** to configure the APM or APCI power settings. If the APM tab is there, your computer supports this standard. If APM is not yet turned on, select the **Enable Advanced Power Management** check box. Windows 2000 Professional supports APM version 1.2, but Windows 2000 Server does not support APM at all. Only administrators can turn APM on or off. ACPI is the newer standard. It improves power management capabilities considerably. To find out if your computer's hardware supports this standard, open the **Control Panel**, double-click the **System** icon, open the **Hardware** tab and click the **Device Manager** button. Then expand the **Computer** icon and read the label. If it says Advanced Configuration and Power Interface (ACPI), ACPI Uniprocessor PC, or ACPI Multiprocessor PC, your computer supports the standard. If it says Standard PC, MPS Uniprocessor, or MPS Multiprocessor, it does not.

The Power management features in Windows 2000 are primarily designed for laptop computers so that you can optimize the life span of the battery, although they can also be used to reduce the amount of energy consumed by a desktop computer. You configure either the APM or ACPI power management settings in the Power Options program (**Figure 4-24**), which has the following tabs:

caution

You must be a member of the Administrators group in order to configure power options.

◆ **Power Schemes:** The Power Schemes tab provides you with options to switch off the monitor and hard disk when you are temporarily not using your system. This conserves energy when the system is not in use. You can use the **Power Options Properties** dialog box (**Figure 4-25**) to configure power schemes. However, first you must make sure that your system supports automatically switching off the monitor and hard disk.

◆ **Advanced:** The Advanced tab is used to designate if a power management icon will display in your system tray. When you select the **Always show icon on the task bar** check box (**Figure 4-26**), an icon will appear in the system tray. If you select a standby option on the Power Schemes tab, you can configure your computer to ask for a password when it is taken out of standby.

◆ **Hibernate:** Hibernate mode can also be used to conserve energy while you are not working on your system. When you configure your system to Hibernate, it saves your current system state to your hard disk and then shuts down the system when you are not working. The contents of memory are saved to a disk file. When you restart your system, the operating system gets this information from the disk file and returns the computer to its previous state. Any program that was running before the hibernation will automatically restart and any network connections will be restored. To configure the Hibernate mode, click the **Hibernate** tab in the Power Options Properties dialog box and select the **Enable hibernate support** check box.

◆ **APM:** The APM tab is available if your system supports this standard. If it does, you can use it to reduce the energy consumption of your system. It also displays the battery status information for your system. Windows 2000 Professional supports **APM 1.2**. To configure APM, click the **APM** tab in the Power Options Properties dialog box and select the **Enable Advanced Power Management Support** check box. APM is present only in Windows 2000 Professional and not in Windows 2000 Server.

◆ **UPS:** The UPS (**Uninterruptible Power Supply**) tab is used to configure backup battery power for the system. This protects the system from a sudden loss of electrical power. The battery power gives you enough time to shut down your system safely and save all your current work. The UPS is physically connected to a system's serial port, allowing the asynchronous transmission of data. The information on whether your system is

Figure 4-24 APM power management tab

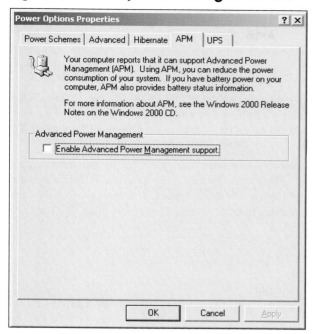

Figure 4-25 Power Schemes tab

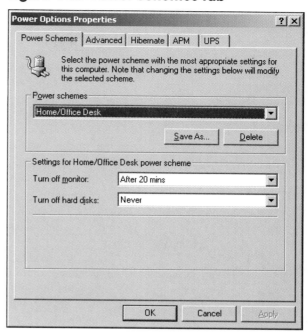

Figure 4-26 Showing the Power Options icon on the taskbar

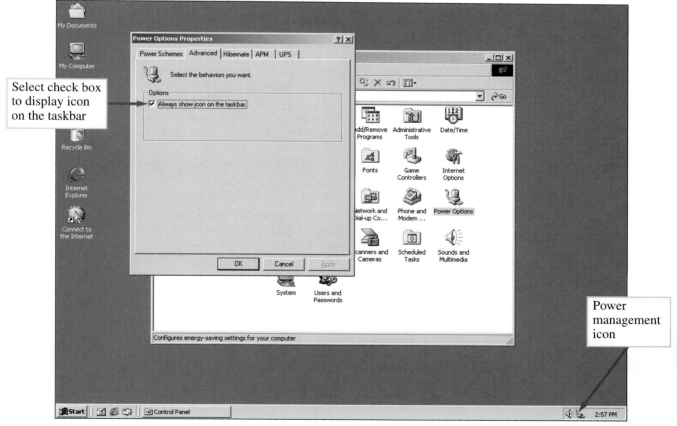

skill 8

Configuring Power Options (cont'd)

exam objective

Implement, manage, and troubleshoot mobile computer hardware. Configure Advanced Power Management (APM).

overview

running on UPS or on power supply appears on the UPS tab in the Power Options dialog box. The **UPS** tab is used to configure the behavior of your system in the event of a power loss. If you do not have a UPS device installed on your computer, there will not be a UPS tab on the Power Options dialog box.

The Power Options dialog box can also contain other tabs with additional capabilities, depending on the computer. Additionally, the Power Options utility provides a feature to warn the user when the power of the battery is below the critical level. You can easily change the battery level at which the alarm or message is to be activated. This ensures that you can save your data on time and shut down the system.

how to

Configure the Power options on a laptop.

1. Log on to the system as an **Administrator**.
2. Click **Start**, point to **Settings**, and click **Control Panel** to open the **Control Panel** window.
3. Double-click the **Power Options** icon 🔋 to open the **Power Options Properties** dialog box.
4. Select the **Portable/Laptop** option in the **Power schemes** list box, as shown in **Figure 4-27**.
5. In the **Plugged in** section, click the **After 15 mins** option in the **Turn off monitor** list box. This programs the monitor to automatically switch off after 15 minutes when it is not in use.
6. In the **Plugged in** section, click the **After 30 mins** option in the **Turn off hard disks** list box. This programs the hard disk to automatically switch off after 30 minutes when it is not in use click **Save As...** .
7. In the **Running on batteries** section, select **After 3 mins** in both the **Turn off monitor** list box and the **Turn off hard disks** list box. Then click **Save As** to save the scheme. This opens the **Save Scheme** dialog box.
8. Type **Laptop Settings** as the name of the power scheme in the **Save this power scheme as** text box.
9. Click **OK** to close the **Save Scheme** dialog box.
10. Click **Apply** to apply the saved scheme to the system.
11. Open the list box in the **Power schemes** section to make sure that your newly created power scheme is on the list.
12. Now click the **Hibernate** tab, as shown in **Figure 4-28**.
13. Select the **Enable hibernate support** check box on the **Hibernate** tab and click **Apply** .
14. Now, click the **APM** tab. If the APM tab is not displayed in the **Power Options Properties** dialog box, skip steps 14 and 15.
15. Select the **Enable Advanced Power Management Support** check box and click **Apply** .
16. Click **OK** to close the **Power Options Properties** dialog box. You have now successfully configured Power options.
17. Close the **Control Panel**.

tip

A system that supports ACPI does not display the APM tab in the Power Option Properties dialog box.

Figure 4-27 Setting power schemes

Power Schemes tab provides different power settings for a system

Switches off the monitor after a specified time

Switches off the hard disk after a specified time

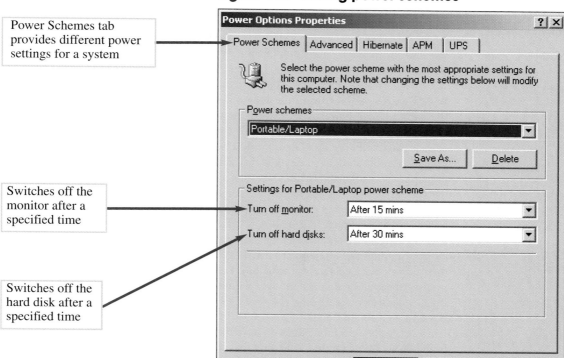

Figure 4-28 Enabling hibernate support

Allows you to turn on hibernate mode on a computer

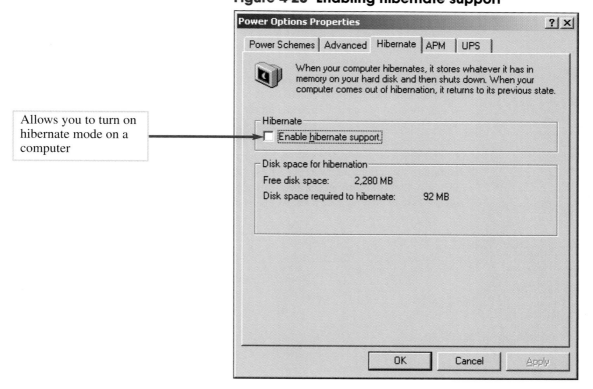

skill 9

Configuring Card Services

exam objective

Implement, manage, and troubleshoot mobile computer hardware. Configure and manage card services.

overview

PCMCIA (Personal Computer Memory Card International Association) card devices or PC cards are mainly found on laptop computers, although you might occasionally find a desktop computer with one. They are used to add a network interface card (NIC), a modem, or occasionally, memory to a laptop, or to connect to a portable hard drive, among other things. They are credit card-sized devices that are inserted into an expansion slot or a port and are immediately recognized by the operating system without you having to shut down and restart the system. When you disconnect PC cards, you simply need to notify the operating system that you are unplugging or ejecting them, and you do not need to reboot for the new configuration to be operational. This ability to insert and remove PC cards while the computer is running is referred to as hot swapping and it makes it very convenient for users to quickly change the configuration of a laptop. The two keys to this technology are Plug and Play support and the ACPI power management standard. Plug and Play was designed to allow computer users to disconnect and reconnect devices without the need to install and uninstall the corresponding device drivers, reallocate resources, or reboot the computer. It works best with the ACPI power management standard because ACPI computers can dynamically reconfigure PC cards. However, some APM machines do have the same functionality. Dynamic reconfiguration is a term closely related to hot swapping that refers to the ability of the operating system to automatically detect and configure devices when they are plugged in with no need to reboot. When you remove a PC card device, the best practice is simply to double-click the Unplug or Eject Hardware icon in the system tray **(Figure 4-29)** to open the corresponding dialog box where you can use the Stop button to stop the device driver for the device **(Figure 4-30)**. This dialog box is also used to stop the device drivers for all removable devices, preventing system errors or possible data loss that could occur when you do not allow the system to complete any processes in progress, clear the related buffers, and disable the drivers and any dependent services.

The operating system software that is used to manage PC cards is referred to as card services and it is automatically installed when you install Windows 2000 Professional on a desktop computer that has a PCMCIA expansion slot, or on a HAL supported notebook or laptop computer. Three types of PCMCIA card standards are currently available. Type I cards are generally used to add memory to a laptop. Type II cards are used to add modems or NICs, and Type III cards are generally used to connect a portable hard drive. These cards also differ in their thickness, ranging from a width of up to 3.3 mm for a Type I card, up to 5.5 mm for Type II, and up to 10.5 mm for a Type III card. When the card services software is installed on a computer, the operating system carries out most of the functions that are needed to administer PC card support, without the need for any user intervention. The Unplug or Eject Hardware dialog box is all you will need to use to make sure that the system stops using the PC card before you remove it.

**Figure 4-29 The Unplug or Eject Hardware icon
in the system tray**

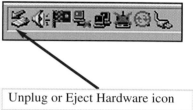

Unplug or Eject Hardware icon

Figure 4-30 The Unplug or Eject Hardware dialog box

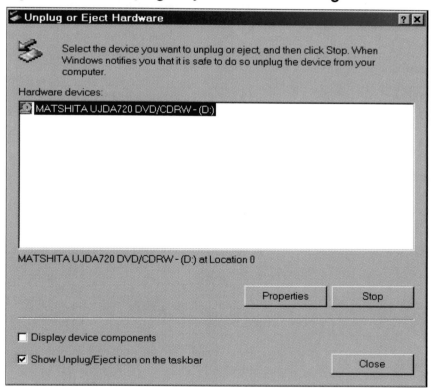

Summary

◆ In the Control Panel, you can configure a system according to your requirements. It contains some basic programs including the System, Regional Options, Accessibility Options, and Display utilities.

◆ The System program is used to optimize your system performance by:
- Creating and managing different hardware profiles for your computer.
- Configuring the application response settings to distribute microprocessor resources between foreground and background programs.
- Configuring the virtual memory settings by adjusting the size of the paging file and setting the maximum size for the registry.
- Setting the system startup settings.
- Designating the actions the system should perform in the event of a system failure.
- Configuring the user and system environment variables.

◆ The Regional Options program is used to customize your system to support multiple languages and locations. You can configure the system to display and sort numbers, currency, date and time according to the location you select.

◆ The Accessibility Options program is used to customize your computer to meet special visual, auditory, or mobility needs. You can configure the keyboard, sound, display, and mouse settings according to your requirements.

◆ The Display program helps you to define, modify, and troubleshoot the display properties for your computer such as the screen resolution, color depth, background colors, and other display features.

◆ The multiple-display feature allows you to expand the size of your desktop across more than one monitor.

◆ Windows 2000 Professional supports two power management standards, Advanced Power Management (APM) and Advanced Configuration and Power Interface (ACPI). These standards are used to control and manage power consumption.

◆ You use the Power Options dialog box to configure power scheme options and to manage the power consumption of a system.

◆ PCMCIA (Personal Computer Memory Card International Association) card devices or PC cards are credit-card-sized devices that are inserted into an expansion slot or a port, mainly on laptop computers, although some desktop computers now have them. They are used to add memory, a network interface card (NIC), or a modem to a laptop, or to connect to a portable hard drive. They are immediately recognized by the operating system without you having to shut down and restart the system. When you disconnect the cards, you simply need to notify the OS that you are unplugging or ejecting them and you do not need to reboot for the new configuration to be operational.

◆ This ability to insert and remove PC cards while the computer is running is referred to as hot swapping.

◆ Dynamic reconfiguration is a term closely related to hotswapping that refers to the ability of the OS to automatically detect and configure devices when they are plugged in, with no need to reboot.

Key Terms

ACPI (Advanced Configuration and Power Interface)
APM (Advanced Power Management)
Application response setting
FilterKeys
Hardware profiles
MouseKeys

Multiple displays
PCMCIA (Personal Computer Memory Card International Association) card
Power options
Power schemes
ShowSounds

SoundSentry
StickyKeys
ToggleKeys
UPS
Virtual memory
Virtual Memory Manager (VMM)

Test Yourself

1. Which of the following utilities will you use to specify the devices, and their configuration settings, that should be loaded during system startup?
   a. Device Manager
   b. Hardware Profiles dialog box
   c. Hardware Wizard
   d. Computer Management snap-in

2. Which of the following dialog boxes or tabs would you use to specify the default operating system in case you have multiple operating systems installed on your system?
   a. Startup and Recovery
   b. Virtual Memory
   c. Hardware Profiles
   d. User Profiles

3. Which of the following settings do you specify in the Startup and Recovery dialog box? (Choose all that apply.)
   a. System environment variables
   b. Wait time before the default operating system is loaded
   c. Method for writing the debugging information to the dump file
   d. Application response time
   e. Paging file size

4. Which of the following program options in the Control Panel enables you to customize your desktop settings for multiple languages and locations?
   a. Accessibility Options
   b. Regional Options
   c. Power Options
   d. Display Options

5. Which of the following functions can you use to perform the same action by pressing one key after the other, instead of holding down multiple keys simultaneously?
   a. FilterKeys
   b. StickyKeys
   c. ToggleKeys
   d. SoundSentry

6. Which of the following command sequences will you use to specify the option to start the Magnifier utility automatically at login?
   a. Start → Programs → Accessories → Accessibility → Magnifier
   b. Start → Programs → Accessories → System Tools → Character Map
   c. Start → Programs → Accessories → Accessibility → Utility Manager
   d. Start → Programs → Accessories → System Tools → Getting started

7. Which of the following statements about a hardware profile are true? (Choose all that apply.)
   a. Notifies the system about the type of settings to be used for the devices.
   b. Notifies the system about the desktop environment settings to be loaded in the system.
   c. Optimizes a system's performance.
   d. Specifies the actions that the system should perform in the event of a system failure.

8. Which of the following is used to distribute microprocessor resources between programs that are being executed simultaneously on a system at a given point in time?
   a. Registry
   b. Virtual memory
   c. Application response
   d. System environment variables

9. Which of the following options, available for writing the debugging information, requires the system to have a paging file on the boot partition that is large enough to store the physical RAM plus 1 MB?
   a. Small Memory Dump
   b. Kernel Memory Dump
   c. Complete Memory Dump
   d. None of the above

10. You have configured your system to enable you to perform mouse functions using the numeric keypad. However, you are facing a problem implementing this function. To resolve the problem, you should ensure that the: (Choose all that apply.)
    a. ToggleKeys function is enabled.
    b. MouseKeys function is activated.
    c. Numlock key is deactivated.
    d. StickyKeys function is activated.

11. You are the Administrator of Excel Inc. and you want to configure the power options on your system to shut off the monitor after the machine has been idle for a specific time period. To do this, you open the Power Option program in the Control Panel and you find that it does not display the APM tab. Which of the following statements provides a correct explanation? (Choose all that apply.)
    a. The system does not have an APM-compliant system board.
    b. The system board is ACPI-compliant.
    c. APM is disabled in the BIOS.
    d. There is no UPS device system installed on the computer.

12. Which of the following writes all of the contents of memory to a file on the hard disk and then turns the power to the computer off?
    a. APM
    b. Power Schemes
    c. Hibernate
    d. Caching

Projects: On Your Own

1. Create a new hardware profile on your system with the name **hardware_nu** and configure your system to wait for you to select a hardware profile during startup.
   a. Open the **Hardware Profiles** dialog box through the **System** program in the **Control Panel**.
   b. Create a copy of the default profile and name it **hardware_nu**.
   c. In the **Hardware profiles selection** section, click the **Wait until I select a hardware profile** option button.

2. Configure your system so that every time there is a system failure, your network administrator receives an alert.
   a. Access the **System Properties** dialog box through the **Control Panel** and click the **Advanced** tab.
   b. Open the **Startup and Recovery** dialog box.

c. In the **System Failure** section, ensure that the **Send an administrative alert** check box is selected.

3. Configure your system in such a way that a flash is visible in the active window each time the system generates a sound.

a. Display the **Sound** tab in the **Accessibility Options** dialog box through the **Control Panel**.

b. In the **SoundSentry** section, click the **Settings** button to open the **Settings for SoundSentry** dialog box.

c. In the **Settings for SoundSentry** dialog box, select the visual warning option **Flash the active window**.

Problem Solving Scenarios

1. The number of complaints about slow computers, poor network response times, and frequent network crashes at Delphi Engineering—a small highway engineering firm in Minden, Nevada—is reaching unusual levels. Delphi's Systems Administrator has asked you to figure out what's wrong and fix the problem. You suspect one issue is that many of the workstations—all of which use Windows 2000—were previously used as servers, and may not be optimized for the kind of intensive desktop programs being used. You believe it may be helpful to increase the size of virtual memory being used because several of the older machines have limited RAM. You are not sure about the network crashing frequency, duration, or time to recover. Outline in a memo or PowerPoint slides the steps you will take to optimize the performance of Delphi's desktop workstations and improve the reporting of system failures.

2. DigitalForge Media, Inc., specializes in creating corporate presentations and Web-related graphic and multimedia material. The firm's chief graphic designer, Harry Bridges, recently injured his left hand in a skiing accident. Unfortunately, Harry was working on a very important project for the firm. Harry is left-handed and has a cast on his left hand, but he can still use his fingers freely to hold a pencil and draw. He requests that you install a tabulet on his system so he can work without having to use the mouse. He also wants you to change the keyboard functionality so he does not have to hold down the ALT key simultaneously with other keys to use various functions in his graphics software. To practice, log on to your Windows 2000 client and use the Accessibility Options dialog box through the Control Panel to activate the Support SerialKey devices feature so Harry can use a tabulet and pen as input devices instead of a mouse. Change the keyboard to use StickyKeys. Write a memo describing the steps you have taken.

5 Managing Data Storage

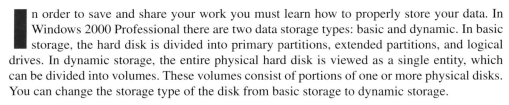

In order to save and share your work you must learn how to properly store your data. In Windows 2000 Professional there are two data storage types: basic and dynamic. In basic storage, the hard disk is divided into primary partitions, extended partitions, and logical drives. In dynamic storage, the entire physical hard disk is viewed as a single entity, which can be divided into volumes. These volumes consist of portions of one or more physical disks. You can change the storage type of the disk from basic storage to dynamic storage.

Effective data storage involves more than storing data in volumes. You must compress data, assign disk quotas, and perform disk maintenance such as deleting files that are no longer needed and organizing your hard disk for effective data storage. NTFS compression allows you to store large amounts of data on a hard disk by compressing entire volumes, folders, sub-folders, and files. Using Windows 2000 Professional, you can also limit the disk space assigned to specific users or groups by assigning disk quotas so that users will not be able to consume excess disk space.

You can also improve file access speed by using the Disk Defragmenter utility to organize the files on the hard disk into continuous clusters, rather than having them scattered over the hard disk. NTFS compression produces a self-defragmenting file system, but you will still need to run the Disk Defragmenter occasionally to optimize the speed with which the system locates and retrieves files.

Goals

In this lesson, you will learn how to create a simple volume, upgrade a basic disk to a dynamic disk, assign disk quotas, compress and manage files and folders, and use the Disk Defragmenter to organize a hard disk.

Lesson 5   Managing Data Storage

Skill	Exam 70-210 Objective
1. Introducing Storage Types	Configure and manage file systems. Configure file systems by using NTFS, FAT32, or FAT. Monitor, configure, and troubleshoot volumes.
2. Upgrading a Basic Disk to a Dynamic Disk	Monitor and configure disks.
3. Creating Volumes	Monitor, configure, and troubleshoot volumes.
4. Identifying the Properties of a Disk	Basic knowledge
5. Converting File Systems	Convert from one file system to another file system.
6. Introducing Disk Quotas	Monitor and configure disks.
7. Introducing NTFS Compression	Configure, manage, and troubleshoot file compression.
8. Copying and Moving Compressed Files and Folders	Configure, manage, and troubleshoot file compression.
9. Optimizing Hard Disk Performance	Optimize and troubleshoot disk performance.

Requirements

To complete the skills in this lesson, you will need a computer with Windows 2000 Professional installed and a disk with free disk space to create volumes and partitions.

skill 1

Introducing Storage Types

exam objective

Configure and manage file systems. Configure file systems by using NTFS, FAT32, or FAT. Monitor, configure, and troubleshoot volumes.

overview

A storage type is a pattern or format in which data is stored on a hard disk. In order to store any kind of data on a hard disk, you must partition and format the hard disk. The tasks involved in setting up a hard disk for data storage are as follows:

◆ Initialize the disk with a storage type
◆ Create partitions on a basic disk or volumes on a dynamic disk
◆ Format the disk with a specific file system such as FAT, FAT32, or NTFS

Windows 2000 Professional supports the basic and dynamic storage types.

◆ **Basic storage** is the method of dividing a hard drive into partitions, which function as logically separate units of storage (**Figure 5-1**). Partitions are used to store different types of information separately (such as user data and applications). All versions of Microsoft Windows, MS-DOS, and Windows NT support basic storage. A disk initialized for basic storage is referred to as a basic disk and it can contain two types of partitions:

  • **Primary partition:** This type of partition can be created using the unallocated space on a basic disk. Windows 2000 Professional uses a primary partition, called an **active partition**, to boot the machine. Only one partition on a single hard disk drive can be designated as an active partition. Primary partitions are created only on basic disks and cannot be partitioned further. You can isolate different types of data by using multiple partitions.

  • **Extended partition:** This type of partition can be created from any free space that is left after the primary partitions have been set up. You can create only one extended partition on a basic disk. Extended partitions are divided into segments in which each segment forms a logical drive. On a basic disk, you can create up to four primary partitions or three primary partitions and an extended partition.

◆ **Dynamic storage**, which is only supported by Windows 2000 Professional and Server, uses volumes instead of partitions. A disk that you initialize for dynamic storage is referred to as a **dynamic disk**. There is no limit on the number of volumes a dynamic disk can contain. A volume can consist of parts of one or more physical disks (**Figure 5-2**). When you create a dynamic disk by upgrading a basic disk, the partitions are changed to volumes. Additional volumes can then be created from any leftover free space. Dynamic storage is free from the constraints that apply to basic storage. For example, unlike in basic storage, the volumes on a dynamic disk, except the boot volume and system volume, can be sized and resized without restarting Windows 2000 Professional. The disk configuration data is stored on the drive rather than in the operating system, which is beneficial because it supports drive recovery if the operating system becomes corrupt. On a dynamic disk, you can create the following volumes:

  • **Simple volume:** This kind of a volume contains disk space from a single disk. You can extend a simple volume to include unallocated space on the same disk. However, you cannot extend either the boot volume or the system volume. A simple volume is not fault tolerant. **Fault tolerance** is the ability of a computer or operating system to respond to a crisis without losing data.

tip

A physical disk must be either basic or dynamic. Both storage types cannot be used on one disk. However, you can use both types of disk storage in a multi-disk system.

caution

Before creating a partition, make sure that the drive has only three primary partitions, or two primary partitions and an extended partition.

Figure 5-1 Basic storage

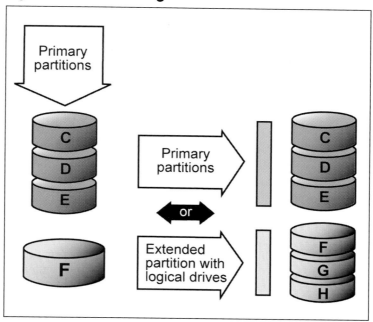

Figure 5-2 Dynamic storage

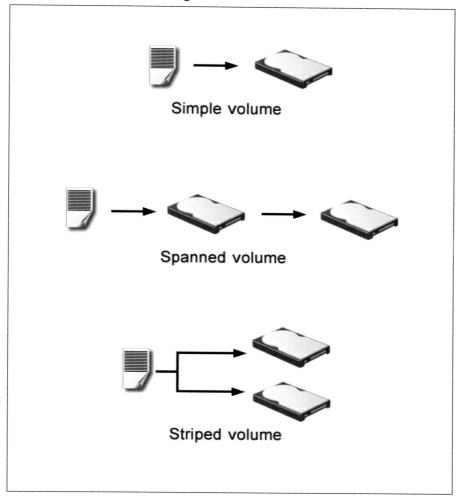

skill 1

Introducing Storage Types (cont'd)

exam objective

Monitor, configure, and troubleshoot volumes. Configure file systems by using NTFS, FAT32, or FAT. Monitor, configure, and troubleshoot volumes.

overview

tip

If you want to dual boot Windows 2000 Professional with Microsoft Windows 95 or MS-DOS, the active partition must be formatted as FAT because Windows 95 cannot read a partition formatted with FAT32 or NTFS.

- **Spanned volume:** This volume can include disk space from up to 32 disks. Starting from a spanned volume on the first disk, Windows 2000 Professional writes data, disk by disk, on each disk included in the spanned volume. A spanned volume is also not fault tolerant. Therefore, data in the entire volume is lost if any disk in the spanned volume fails.
- **Striped volume:** This volume combines areas of free space from multiple hard disks. The maximum number of hard disks that can be included in a logical striped volume is also 32. In a striped volume, data is written evenly across all of the disks so that it is added to each disk at the same rate. All hard disks in a striped volume perform the same functions as a single hard disk. Thus, Windows 2000 Professional can issue and process I/O commands simultaneously on all hard disks. This increases the speed of the system. Like simple and spanned volumes, striped volumes do not provide fault tolerance. Thus, if one disk in a striped volume fails, the data in the entire volume will be lost.

After you have decided on the storage type and created the necessary partitions or volumes, you must format the disk using one of the file systems supported by Windows 2000 Professional, **NTFS, FAT,** or **FAT32.** You should use the NTFS file system if you need partitions that feature file-level and folder-level security, disk compression, disk quotas, or encryption. NTFS is the most commonly used file system because it supports these features.

more

When a new basic disk is added to the computer, the space on the new disk can be divided into partitions. In the **Disk Management** snap-in, right-click the unallocated space where you want to create the partition and click **Create Partition (Figure 5-3)**. In the **Create Partition Wizard,** click ⟨ Next > ⟩. In the **Select Partition Type** window, click the **FAT, FAT32,** or **NTFS** option button to select the file system format (**Figure 5-4**). Follow the subsequent instructions in the Wizard to complete the process of creating a partition. You can also manage disks on a remote computer on the network. For example, you can create partitions as long as the remote computer is running Windows 2000 Professional and is a member of the same domain as your computer. To manage disks in a domain or on a remote computer, you must be a member of either the **Administrators** or **Server Operators** group on the remote computer.

Figure 5-3 Creating a partition

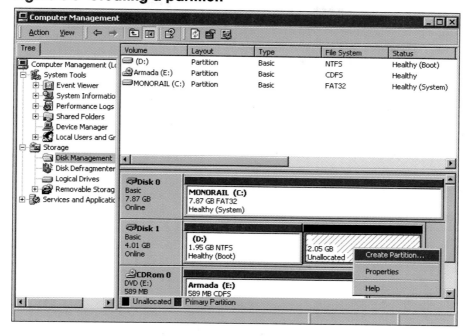

Figure 5-4 Selecting a partition type

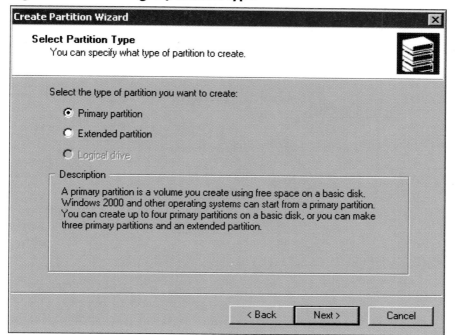

skill 2

Upgrading a Basic Disk to a Dynamic Disk

exam objective

Monitor and configure disks.

overview

Windows 2000 Professional uses basic storage to initialize a hard disk by default. However, you may want to convert a basic disk to a dynamic disk to take advantage of the additional features offered by dynamic disks. For example, if you are working on an important project and the basic disk you are working on becomes corrupt, you may end up losing data. Using a dynamic disk, you can duplicate the hard disk on one or more hard disks. This process is referred to as **disk mirroring** and it will ensure that you do not lose data.

Other important features of dynamic disks are:

◆ Fault tolerance
◆ Disk striping
◆ Extending volumes without restarting the computer

You can upgrade a basic disk to a dynamic disk using the **Disk Management** snap-in. Before upgrading, you need to make sure that:

◆ All programs running on the hard disk are closed.
◆ There is at least 1 MB of free space on the hard disk.
◆ The disk to be upgraded has been backed up.

When you convert a basic disk to a dynamic disk, the existing partitions on the basic disk are converted to simple volumes. A dynamic disk can be changed to a basic disk, but if you do so, you will lose all of the data stored on that disk.

caution

Dynamic disks are unique to Windows 2000 Professional and are not recognized by other operating systems.

how to

Convert a basic disk to a dynamic disk.

1. Right-click **My Computer** and click **Manage** to open the **Computer Management** console.
2. Click the **Disk Management** snap-in under **Storage**.
3. In the lower-right pane of the **Computer Management** window, right-click the disk that you want to upgrade, for example, **Disk 1 (Figure 5-5)**.
4. Click the **Upgrade to Dynamic Disk** command to open the **Upgrade to Dynamic Disk** dialog box **(Figure 5-6)**.
5. Click ⬚ OK ⬚ to open the **Disks to Upgrade** dialog box **(Figure 5-7)**.
6. Click ⬚ Upgrade ⬚. The **Disk Management** message box opens, warning you that once you upgrade to a dynamic disk you will not be able to boot previous versions of Windows from any volume on this disk **(Figure 5-8)**.
7. Click ⬚ Yes ⬚ to confirm the upgrade of the disk. The **Upgrade Disks** message box informs you that file systems on any of the disks to be upgraded will be dismounted.
8. Click ⬚ Yes ⬚. The **Confirm Message** box notifies you that a reboot will take place to complete the upgrade process.
9. Click ⬚ OK ⬚ to finish the process of upgrading.

more

Besides changing the storage type that your system uses, you can also add new disks to a computer running Windows 2000 Professional. You can install a new disk by attaching the disk to your computer and clicking the **Rescan Disks** command in the **Action** menu.

Figure 5-5 Upgrading a disk

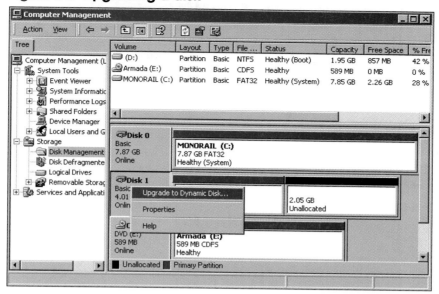

Figure 5-6 The Upgrade to Dynamic Disk dialog box

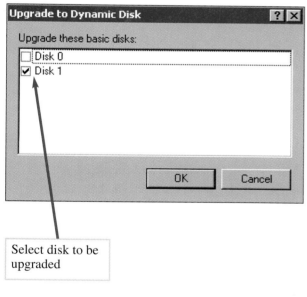

Select disk to be upgraded

Figure 5-7 Checking the details of disks that can be upgraded

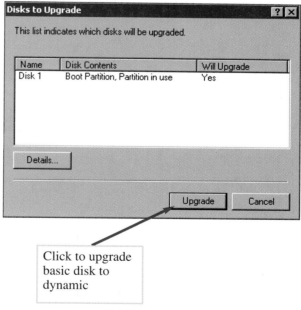

Click to upgrade basic disk to dynamic

Figure 5-8 Disk Management message box

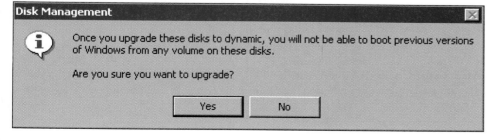

skill 3

Creating Volumes

exam objective

Monitor, configure, and troubleshoot volumes.

overview

Before deciding on the type of file system that you want, you should consider which volume type best suits your needs for efficient utilization of disk space and performance. A simple volume consists of disk space from a single disk. However, it can be extended to include any available free space on the disk. To create a simple volume, you can format the hard disk with FAT, FAT32, or NTFS. However, you can extend a volume only if the hard disk is formatted with NTFS.

how to

Create a simple volume.

1. Click **Start**, point to **Settings**, and click the **Control Panel** command to open the Control Panel window.
2. Double-click the **Administrative Tools** icon to open the Administrative Tools window.
3. Double-click the **Computer Management** icon to open the Computer Management console.
4. Click the **Disk Management** snap-in under **Storage** in the **Computer Management** window.
5. In the lower-right pane of the **Computer Management** window, right-click the unallocated space on the dynamic disk where you would like to create the volume and select the **Create Volume** command (**Figure 5-9**).
6. The **Create Volume Wizard** is initialized and the first screen **Welcome to the Create Volume Wizard** opens.
7. Click **Next >** to display the **Select Volume Type** screen.
8. The **Simple volume** option button is selected by default (**Figure 5-10**). Click **Next >** to display the **Select Disks** screen.
9. In the **For selected disk** spin box, type **6** to specify the disk size (**Figure 5-11**).
10. Click **Next >** to display the **Assign Drive Letter or Path** screen.
11. The **Assign a drive letter** option button is selected by default. Enter **F:** in the spin box if necessary.
12. Click **Next >** to display the **Format Volume** screen. The **Format this volume as follows** option button is selected by default.
13. In the **Formatting** section, select **FAT32** in the **File system to use** list box.
14. Make sure that **Default** is selected in the **Allocation unit size** list box.
15. Type **SimpleVol** in the **Volume label** text box to enter a label for the volume (**Figure 5-12**).
16. Select the **Perform a Quick Format** check box.
17. Click **Next >** to display the final screen, **Completing the Create Volume Wizard**. This screen displays the settings that you have selected.
18. Click **Finish** to complete the process of creating a simple volume.

more

The process of creating a spanned volume or a striped volume is similar to the process of creating a simple volume. In the **Disk Management** snap-in, right click the **Dynamic** disk where you want to create the striped or spanned volume and then click the **Create Volume** command. In the **Create Volume Wizard**, click **Next >**, click either the **Striped Volume** or the **Spanned Volume** option button, and follow the remaining instructions in the Wizard.

Figure 5-9 Selecting unallocated space on the dynamic disk to create a volume

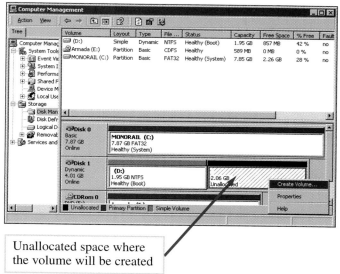

Unallocated space where the volume will be created

Figure 5-10 Selecting the Volume Type

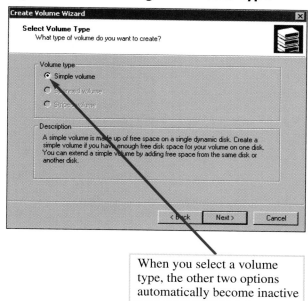

When you select a volume type, the other two options automatically become inactive

Figure 5-11 Selecting the disk where the volume will be created

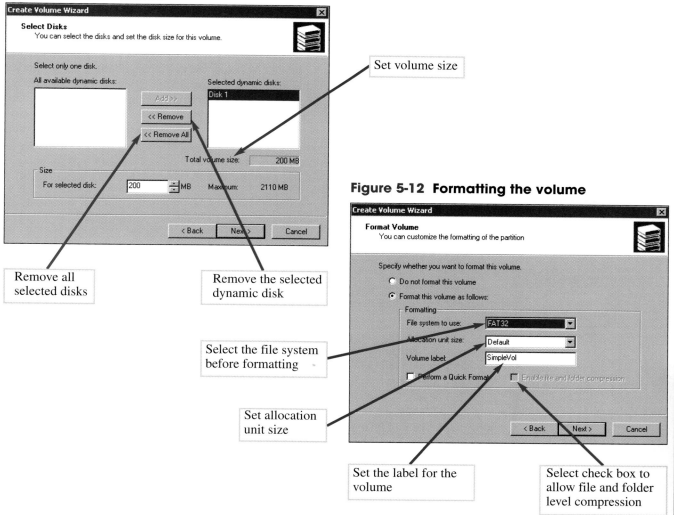

Remove all selected disks

Remove the selected dynamic disk

Set volume size

Select the file system before formatting

Set allocation unit size

Figure 5-12 Formatting the volume

Set the label for the volume

Select check box to allow file and folder level compression

skill 4

Identifying the Properties of a Disk

exam objective

Basic knowledge

overview

Before installing new software on your system, you should determine the amount of free space available on the disk so that you can make sure that there is enough disk space to install and run the software. **Disk properties**, which are the attributes of your hard disk, can be found in the **Properties** dialog box.

The **General** tab in the Properties dialog box provides information on the volume label, type of disk, type of file system, and the disk usage. In this window, you can also run the **Disk Cleanup** utility to remove deleted, temporary, and downloaded files.

Use the **Tools** tab to perform volume error checking, backup, and disk defragmentation.

Use the **Hardware** tab to check the properties of the physical disks and troubleshoot physical disk problems.

The **Sharing** tab allows you to set the network shared volume parameters and permissions.

The **Security** tab provides NTFS access permissions.

Use the **Quota** tab to set user quotas for NTFS volumes.

how to

Use the **Disk Cleanup** utility in the **Properties** dialog box.

1. Click the **Disk Management** snap-in under **Storage** in the **Computer Management** console.
2. In the lower-right pane of the Computer Management window, right-click the **SimpleVol (F:)** drive and click the **Properties** command **(Figure 5-13)** to open the Properties dialog box. Review the properties of SimpleVol (F:) **(Figure 5-14)** and close the Properties dialog box
3. Right-click the **(C:)** drive and select **Properties**. Click Disk Cleanup... . The **Disk Cleanup** message box opens, and the system calculates the amount of space that can be freed.
4. Select all of the check boxes in the **Files to delete** list box in the **Disk Cleanup for (C:)** dialog box **(Figure 5-15)**. You can view the details for the files selected in the **Files to delete** list box by clicking the View Files button.
5. Click **OK** to delete the files.
6. Click OK to close the **Disk Cleanup** dialog box.
7. Close the Computer Management console.

caution

When you run the **Disk Cleanup** utility, the scanning process can take several minutes. It is best to run this utility when the machine is not in use.

more

You can use the **Refresh** and **Rescan Disks** commands on the **Action** menu in the **Computer Management** window to update the information in the **Disk Management** snap-in.

◆ Using the **Refresh** command, you can update the drive letter, file system, volume, and removable media information.
◆ Using the **Rescan Disks** command, you can update the hardware information in the **Disk Management** snap-in and scan the attached disks for any disk configuration changes. You can also use this command to update information on removable media, basic volumes, file systems, and drive letters.

caution

Rescanning disks may take several minutes, depending on the number of hardware devices installed.

Figure 5-13 Viewing the Properties for SimpleVol (F:)

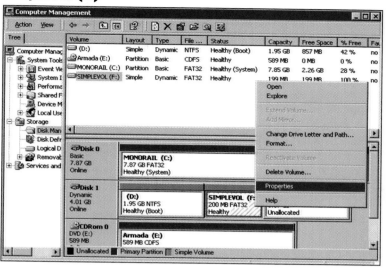

Figure 5-14 Properties dialog box for a disk

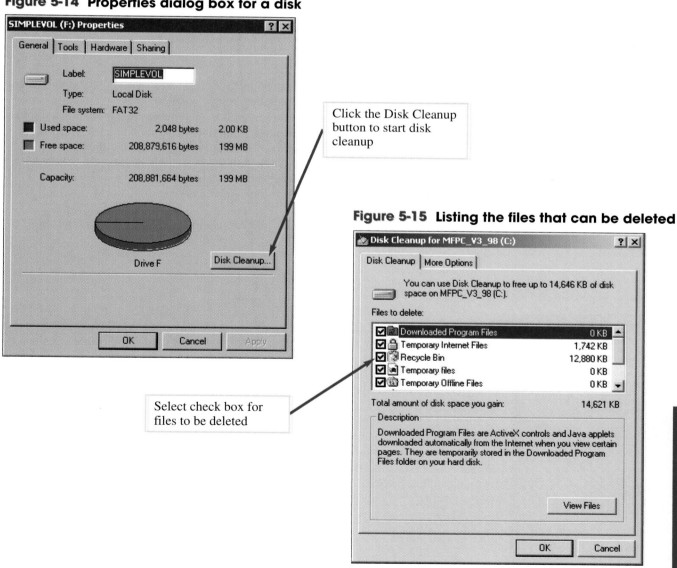

Click the Disk Cleanup button to start disk cleanup

Select check box for files to be deleted

Figure 5-15 Listing the files that can be deleted

skill 5

Converting File Systems

exam objective

Convert from one file system to another file system.

overview

Windows 2000 Professional supports the FAT, FAT32, and NTFS file systems. The FAT (File Allocation Table) formatting structure provides backward compatibility with other operating systems, such as DOS, Windows 3.1x and Windows for Workgroups, thus allowing upgrades from other operating systems to Windows 2000. Under Windows 2000, FAT supports volumes up to 4 GB in size, while the updated version, FAT32, supports volumes up to 2 TB in size. The FAT file system is most efficient for volumes smaller than 256 MB, and can contain 512 entries in the root directory. However, FAT does not support file-level compression and has no file security capabilities. FAT32 can provide adequate functionality for a desktop station, but it is not usually used with servers.

NTFS supports large volumes, is most efficient for volumes larger than 512 MB, and can contain unlimited entries in the root directory. It also has capabilities for file-level compression and security, and you can set disk quotas to restrict users to a specific amount of space on a drive.

caution

FAT and FAT32 can be upgraded to the NTFS format without data loss. However, to convert from NTFS to FAT, you will have to back-up the data on the volume, delete the volume, recreate it, format it, and then restore the data from the backup.

how to

Convert a **FAT** partition to **NTFS**.
1. Click **⊞Start**, point to **Programs**, point to **Accessories**, and click the **Command Prompt** command to open the **Command Prompt** window.
2. Type **convert f:/fs :ntfs /v** and press **[Enter]**. The **/V** indicates that the command should be run in **verbose mode.** In verbose mode, all of the messages generated during the conversion are displayed (**Figure 5-16**). Note that if you have a dual-boot system, only Windows 2000, XP, and NT 4.0 with the lastest service pack applied can read from and write to Windows 2000 NTFS volumes or partitions.
3. Enter **SimpleVol** as the current volume label and press **[Enter]** to perform the conversion.
4. Type **Exit** and press **[Enter]** to exit the command prompt window and return to the Windows 2000 desktop.

caution

You cannot convert the active drive. If you only have a C: drive, the Convert utility will warn you that it cannot gain exclusive access to the drive and will ask you if you want to schedule the conversion for the next time the system starts.

more

Both FAT16 and FAT32 are referred to as FAT unless it is important to differentiate between the two. The FAT file system, and in most cases, the FAT32 file system, can also be used if you want to be able to dual boot the system with Windows 2000 and another operating system. However, NTFS is the preferred file system because it supports larger volumes, file level compression and security, and many other useful features. The Convert utility used in the exercise converts your disk while maintaining all of the files on the disk. However, it is still recommended that you back up the drive before the conversion. You can also reformat a volume or partition in the Disk Management snap-in by right-clicking the volume and selecting **Format** on the context menu (**Figure 5-17**). The **Format (drive letter)** dialog box will open (**Figure 5-18**). In the **File system** list box, select the format you want and click **OK**. A warning dialog box will caution you that formatting will erase all data on the volume (**Figure 5-19**).

Figure 5-16 Convert command in the Command Prompt window

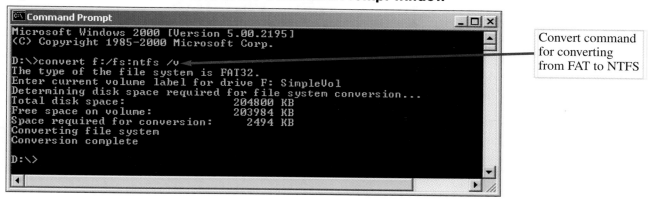

Convert command
for converting
from FAT to NTFS

Figure 5-17 Converting a drive in the Disk Management snap-in

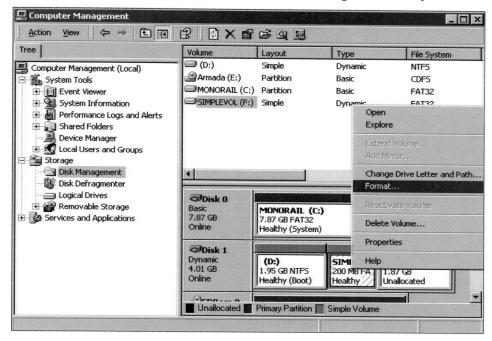

Figure 5-18 Formatting a volume

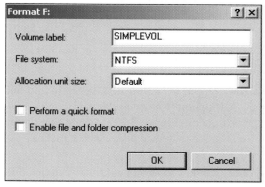

Figure 5-19 The Format warning message

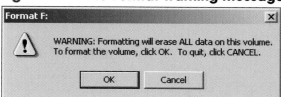

skill 6

Introducing Disk Quotas

exam objective

Monitor and configure disks.

overview

When users are asked to back up their important data on a central machine, they will often dump their entire data load onto that machine. This can drastically decrease the available space on the disk. Disk quotas enable you to track and control disk usage on a per-user, per-volume basis. The number of files and folders owned by a user determines their disk space allotment.

Windows 2000 Professional collects information about disk usage for all users who have files and folders on a volume.

caution

Disk quotas can be applied only to Windows 2000 NTFS volumes.

You set disk quotas on the **Quota** tab in the **Properties** dialog box for an NTFS volume or partition. You can set two values: the **disk limit** and the **warning level**. The disk limit designates the amount of space a user is allowed to use and the warning level sets the storage level at which a warning will be issued to the user. For example, if a user's disk space requirement generally does not exceed 60 MB, you can set the disk limit for a particular volume to 60 MB and the warning level to 55 MB. When the user's storage capacity exceeds 55 MB, a warning will be issued. The user can then either delete some files to free space or ask the administrator to increase the quota limit.

By default, Windows 2000 Professional allows only members of the **Administrator** group to view and modify quota settings. The disk quotas you assign are based on the sizes of uncompressed files, so take this into account when determining the appropriate storage requirement for a user.

how to

Limit the disk space of the drive to **20 MB** and set the warning level to **16 MB** for the **Guest** account.

tip

Right clicking **Start** and selecting Explorer will also open the **Windows Explorer** window.

1. Click [Start], point to **Programs,** point to **Accessories,** and click **Windows Explorer** to open the Explorer **window**.
2. Click the **My Computer** icon, right-click **F:** drive in the left panel, and click the **Properties** command to open the Properties dialog box on the **General** tab.
3. Click the **Quota** tab to display the options for setting disk quotas. By default, disk quotas are disabled.
4. Select the **Enable quota management** check box.
5. Select the **Deny disk space to users exceeding quota limit** check box. This will send an "out of disk space" message when users exceed the limit. To track and generate hard disk usage information without preventing users from saving data, you can clear the **Deny disk space to users exceeding quota limit** check box.
6. Type **20** in the **Limit disk space to** text box.
7. Type **16** in the **Set warning level to** text box.
8. Specify the unit size by clicking the list arrows ▼ on the **Limit disk space to** and **Set warning level to** list boxes and selecting the MB option (**Figure 5-20**).
9. Click [Apply]. The **Disk Quota** message box opens (**Figure 5-21**) to warn you that if you enable disk quotas, the volume will be rescanned to update disk usage statistics.
10. Click [OK] to enable disk quotas.
11. Click [Quota Entries...] in the **Setting Disk Quotas** window to open the **Quota Entries For Local Disk** window.
12. Click **Quota** on the Menu bar and click the **New Quota Entry** command (**Figure 5-22**) to open the **Select Users** dialog box.
13. Select the **Guest** user account in the **Name** list, and click [Add].

Figure 5-20 Setting Disk Quotas

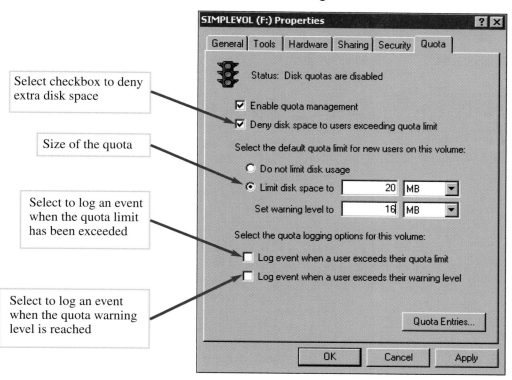

Select checkbox to deny extra disk space

Size of the quota

Select to log an event when the quota limit has been exceeded

Select to log an event when the quota warning level is reached

Figure 5-21 Disk Quota message box

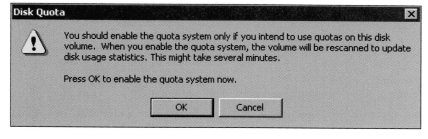

Figure 5-22 Quota entries for window

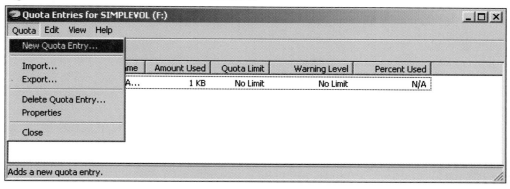

skill 6

Introducing Disk Quotas (cont'd)

exam objective

Monitor and configure disks.

how to

14. Click [OK] to open the **Add New Quota Entry** dialog box (**Figure 5-23**).
15. Type **10** in the **Limit disk space to** text box.
16. Type **8** in the **Set warning level to** text box.
17. Select the MB unit size in on the **Limit disk space to** and **Set warning level to** list boxes.
18. Click [OK] to open the **Quota Entries** window (**Figure 5-24**).
19. Close the **Quota Entries** window.
20. Click [OK] to close the **Properties** dialog box.
21. Close Windows Explorer.

more

The guidelines for assigning disk quotas are listed below:

◆ Log on as the Administrator when you need to install additional Windows 2000 Professional components and applications so that the disk space that you use is not deducted from the disk quota limit for your user account.

◆ Set restrictive limits for all user accounts. However, you can modify these limits according to the requirements of the users. For example, you can increase the limit for users who need to store large files.

◆ Delete the disk quota entries for users who are not currently storing files on a volume and thus not using the allocated space. However, if a user currently has files stored on the volume, you must either delete those files or move them elsewhere before you can delete the quota entry for a user account.

◆ You do not have to deny disk space to users as you did in the exercise. Instead, you can set disk quotas simply to keep an eye on how much space users are consuming. Then, you can periodically check the Quota Entries window. If a user has exceeded the warning level, a yellow warning symbol will appear in the Status column. If a user has exceeded the quota, a red circle with an exclamation point will immediately inform you that the user is above the limit (**Figure 5-25**). You can either increase the disk space allotment for the user, set the deny disk space to users exceeding limit option, or inform the user that he or she must delete some files or store new documents elsewhere.

Figure 5-23 Setting a quota entry for a user

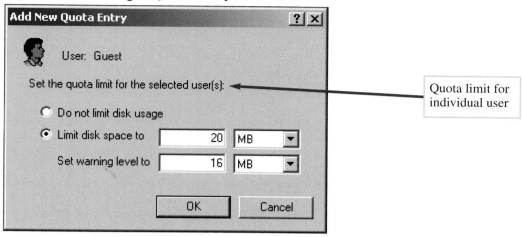

Quota limit for
individual user

Figure 5-24 Quota entry set for the Guest account

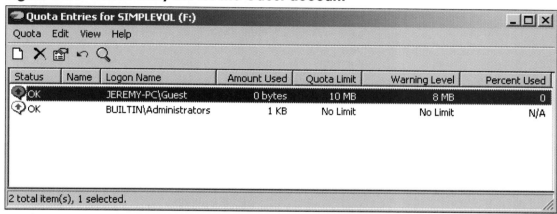

Status	Name	Logon Name	Amount Used	Quota Limit	Warning Level	Percent Used
OK		JEREMY-PC\Guest	0 bytes	10 MB	8 MB	0
OK		BUILTIN\Administrators	1 KB	No Limit	No Limit	N/A

2 total item(s), 1 selected.

Figure 5-25 Quota entry status

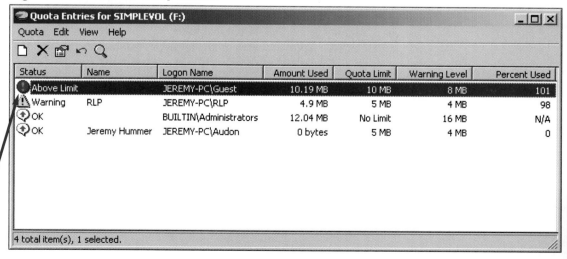

Status	Name	Logon Name	Amount Used	Quota Limit	Warning Level	Percent Used
Above Limit		JEREMY-PC\Guest	10.19 MB	10 MB	8 MB	101
Warning	RLP	JEREMY-PC\RLP	4.9 MB	5 MB	4 MB	98
OK		BUILTIN\Administrators	12.04 MB	No Limit	16 MB	N/A
OK	Jeremy Hummer	JEREMY-PC\Audon	0 bytes	5 MB	4 MB	0

4 total item(s), 1 selected.

Status of quota limit—
whether it is OK, has
exceeded the warning
level, or exceeded the
quota level

skill 7

Introducing NTFS Compression

exam objective

Configure, manage, and troubleshoot file compression.

overview

You can use **NTFS compression** to compress files and folders such as Word or other Office documents and bitmaps to conserve disk space. All NTFS files and folders have a compression state, either compressed or uncompressed. Compressed files and folders exhibit the following features:

◆ **Display color:** Compressed files and folders can be displayed in a different color to distinguish them from uncompressed files and folders.

◆ **Space allocation:** Disk space in NTFS volumes is allocated according to the uncompressed file size. For example, if there is enough space in the NTFS volume for you to store a compressed file, but there is not enough space to store that file in the uncompressed format, when you try to copy the file to the disk you will receive an error message stating that there is not enough disk space available for the file.

◆ **Access to compressed files and folders by applications:** Compressed NTFS files are automatically uncompressed when accessed by Microsoft Windows-based or MS-DOS based applications. For example, when an application such as **Microsoft Excel** opens a compressed file, the file is automatically uncompressed by the NTFS file system. When the file is closed or saved, it is again compressed.

tip

Right clicking Start and selecting Explore will also open the Windows Explorer window.

how to

Compress a folder in an **NTFS** volume and change the display color of the compressed folder.

1. Create a folder called **Compfolder** on the C: drive.
2. Right-click the **Compfolder** folder and click the **Properties** command to open the **Compfolder Properties** dialog box.
3. Click `Advanced...` to open the **Advanced Attributes** dialog box.
4. Select the **Compress contents to save disk space** check box in the **Compress or Encrypt attributes** section (**Figure 5-26**).
5. Click `OK` to close **Advanced Attributes** dialog box and display the **Properties** dialog box for the folder.
6. Click `Apply`. The **Confirm Attribute Changes** dialog box opens prompting you to specify whether you want to apply the change to only the selected folder or to all of the subfolders and files within that folder.
7. Click the **Apply changes to this folder, subfolders and files** option button (**Figure 5-27**).
8. Click `OK` to close the **Confirm Attribute Changes** dialog box.
9. Click `OK` to close the **Properties** dialog box for the folder.
10. Next, you need to change the display color for the compressed folder. Right-click `Start` and click the **Explore** command.
11. Open the **Tools** menu and click the **Folder Options** command to open the **Folder Options** dialog box.
12. Click the **View** tab.
13. In the **Advanced Settings** list box, select the **Display compressed files and folders with alternate color** check box (**Figure 5-28**).
14. Click `OK` to apply the changes. The names of the compressed files and folders are displayed in blue in the **Windows Explorer** window.

more

To troubleshoot file compression, you may have to recompress or remove file compression from the file, or restore the backup of a file that was damaged due to compression.

Figure 5-26 Setting the Compress attribute

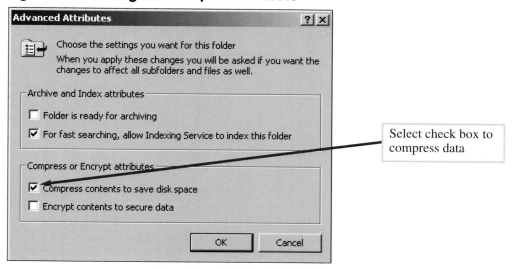

Select check box to compress data

Figure 5-27 Confirming attribute changes

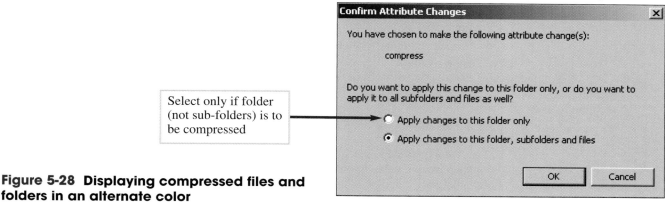

Select only if folder (not sub-folders) is to be compressed

Figure 5-28 Displaying compressed files and folders in an alternate color

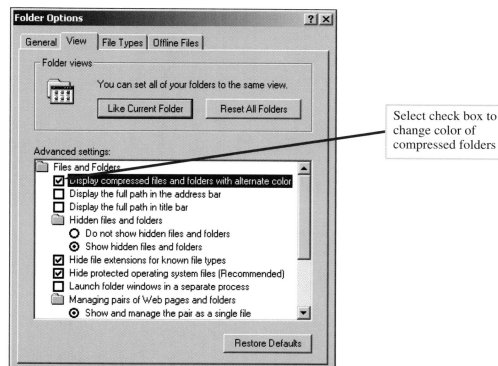

Select check box to change color of compressed folders

skill 8

Copying and Moving Compressed Files and Folders

exam objective

Configure, manage, and troubleshoot file compression.

overview

While working with a compressed file, you might need to copy it on to another machine or move it from its original location. When you copy or move a file, the compression state of the file depends on whether you are copying or moving the file from a different location within the same NTFS volume, between two NTFS volumes, or between NTFS and FAT volumes.

Changes in the compression state of a file or folder are different depending on the situation (**Figure 5-29**):

◆ When a file is copied from one location to another within an NTFS volume or between two NTFS volumes, it inherits the compression state of the target folder.

◆ Moving a file or folder within an NTFS volume does not change the compression state of the file or folder. The file or folder retains its original compression state. For example, if you move a file or folder within the same volume, it retains its original compression state, either compressed or uncompressed. However, if you move it to another volume, it will inherit the attribute of the destination folder.

◆ You can compress only NTFS files. Thus, when you move or copy a compressed file or folder from an NTFS volume to a FAT volume or to a floppy disk, Windows 2000 uncompresses the file or folder automatically.

more

When compressing files and folders, choose appropriate file types because some file types can be compressed to a larger extent than others. For example, .zip, .cab, .gif, and .jpg files are already compressed while **bitmap** files can be compressed to less than 50 percent of their original size and application files can often be compressed to less than 75 percent of their original size.

Compress static data and not files that are frequently changed because compressing and uncompressing files is a waste of system time. Copying a compressed file may affect the performance of the system because Windows 2000 Professional must first uncompress the file, copy it, and then compress it again, using valuable system resources.

Figure 5-29 Copying compressed files and folders

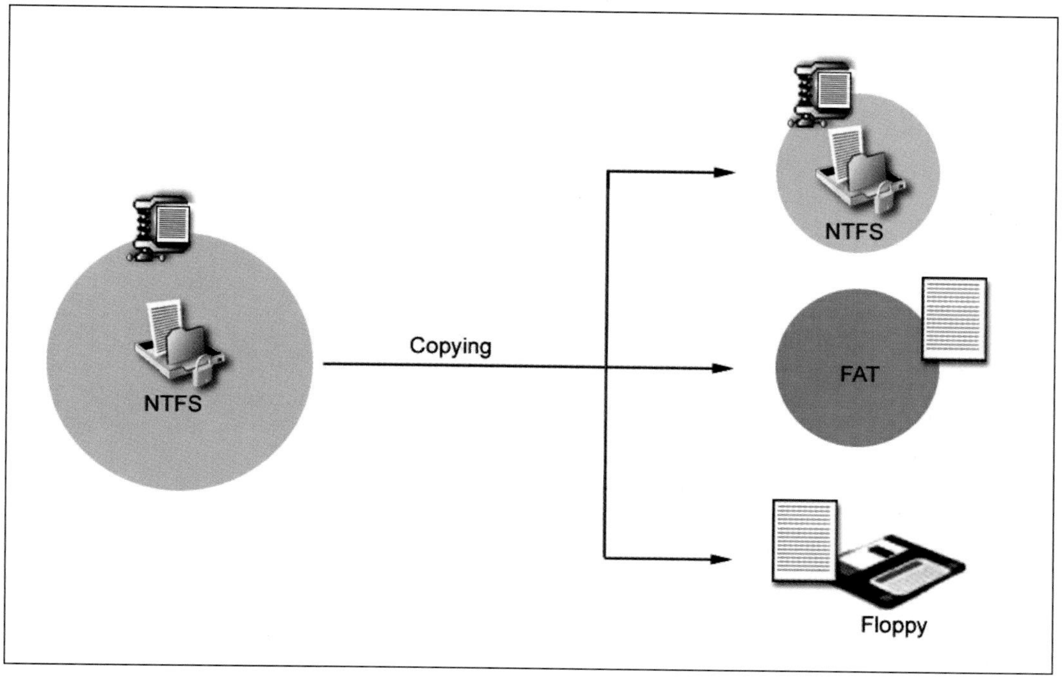

skill 9 *Optimizing Hard Disk Performance*

exam objective

Optimize and troubleshoot disk performance.

overview

When you save files and folders in Windows 2000 Professional, they are saved in the first available space on the hard disk by the hard disk controller chip. This causes file and folder fragmentation as pieces or fragments of large files are stored on different parts of the hard disk. As data becomes increasingly scattered over different parts of the hard disk, the computer takes longer to access files, leading to a general deterioration in system performance. The computer takes longer to create new files and folders because free space is also scattered on the hard disk. You can use the **Disk defragmenter** utility to reorganize the files on the hard disk. The Disk Defragmenter rearranges files and unused space moving the segments of each file and folder to one location so that they occupy a single, contiguous space on the hard disk. This process of finding and consolidating files and folders, called **defragmentation,** enables the system to access files quickly and makes programs run faster.

tip

You can defragment **FAT** and **FAT32,** as well as **NTFS** volumes.

The **Disk Defragmenter** window is divided into three parts:

◆ **Partitions to analyze and defragment:** Lists the volumes that you can view and defragment. It also provides details such as the type of **File System,** amount of **Free Space,** and drive **Capacity**.

◆ **Analysis display:** Provides a graphical depiction of how the selected volume is fragmented.

◆ **Defragmentation display:** Provides a constantly-updating representation of the volume during defragmentation.

how to

Analyze a volume to determine its fragmentation level and defragment it using the **Disk Defragmenter**.

1. Right-click ▓Start and click **Explore** to open the **Windows Explorer** window.
2. Right-click the **C:** drive and click the **Properties** command to open the **Properties** dialog box for the **C:** drive.
3. Click the **Tools** tab **(Figure 5-30)**.
4. Click Defragment Now... to open the **Disk Defragmenter** window **(Figure 5-31)**.
5. Click Analyze . The system analyzes the fragmentation state of the disk. When the analysis is complete, the the **Analysis Complete** dialog box opens.
6. It will either be recommended that you defragment or that the volume does need defragmenting **(Figure 5-32)**.
7. Click View Report to open the **Analysis Report** dialog box **(Figure 5-33)**, which displays information about the fragmented files.
8. Click Defragment to start the defragmenting process **(Figure 5-34)**.
9. After the disk is defragmented, the **Defragmentation Complete** message box will display.
10. Click Close to close the Defragmentation Complete message box.
11. Click OK to close the Disk Defragment window.

more

Run the **Disk Defragmenter** only when your computer is not being used extensively. Defragmentation can adversely affect the time it takes to access other disk-based resources. It is a good practice to defragment your local hard disk at least once a month to prevent the accumulation of fragmented files, and also before installing large applications. Analyze the volume and defragment it if necessary to ensure faster installation and to speed up access to resources.

Figure 5-30 The Tools tab in the Properties dialog box

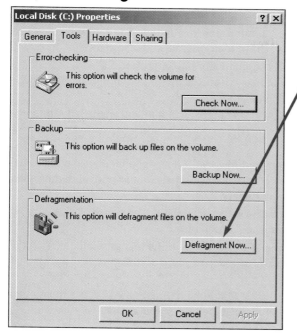

Click the Defragment Now button to start the defragmenting process

Figure 5-31 The Disk Defragmenter

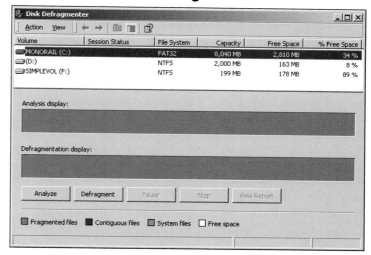

Figure 5-32 Analyzing the fragmentation of the disk

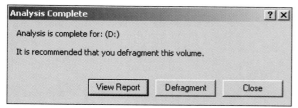

Figure 5-33 The Analysis Report dialog box

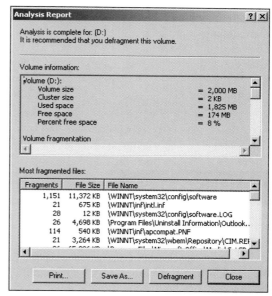

Figure 5-34 Defragmenting the Disk

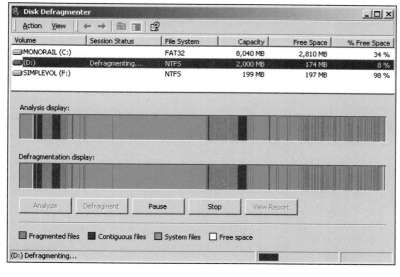

Summary

- There are two storage types—basic and dynamic.
- Basic storage or a basic disk can have primary partitions, extended partitions, and logical drives.
- Dynamic storage or a dynamic disk can be divided into simple, spanned, or striped volumes.
- Disk Cleanup is used to free space on hard drives.
- Before upgrading a basic disk to a dynamic disk, make sure that 1 MB of free disk space is available and that all running programs are closed.
- FAT provides backward compatibility with other operating systems, thus allowing upgrades from other operating systems to Windows 2000.
- NTFS is preferred over FAT because it supports file-level compression and security, larger volumes, and other useful features.
- Reverting from a dynamic disk to a basic disk will result in the loss of data.
- Disk quotas can be assigned only in Windows 2000 Professional or Server on an NTFS volume or partition.

- NTFS compression can reduce some types of files to nearly half of their original size.
- NTFS automatically uncompresses files when they are accessed by Microsoft Windows-based or MS DOS-based applications.
- Windows 2000 Professional automatically uncompresses a file or folder copied or moved to a FAT folder.
- Compressed files and folders can be displayed in a different color to distinguish them from uncompressed files and folders.
- Preferably, static data should be compressed to avoid performance degradation.
- The Disk Defragmenter utility rearranges the files on the hard disk in order to increase the speed of access and retrieval.
- A hard disk should be defragmented once a month and also before installing large applications.

Key Terms

Active partition	Disk properties	Logical drives
Basic storage	Disk quotas	NTFS compression
Defragmentation	Disk striping	Primary partition
Disk cleanup	Dynamic disk	Simple volume
Disk defragmenter	Dynamic storage	Spanned volume
Disk limit	Extended partition	Striped volume
Disk mirroring	Fault tolerance	Verbose mode

Test Yourself

1. You have 3 hard disks of 2 GB each on your Windows 2000 Professional computers. You want to save data sequentially on your hard disk, that is, the first hard disk should be filled before the system starts writing on the second disk, and so on. What kind of a volume will you format the hard disk with?
   a. Simple
   b. Spanned
   c. Striped
   d. Mirrored

2. The compression state of a file or folder does not change when you:
   a. Move a file or folder within an NTFS volume.
   b. Copy a file or folder between NTFS volumes.

   c. Copy or move a file or folder to a FAT volume.
   d. Copy or move a file or folder to a floppy.

3. Your computer is being used as the backup computer for your team. You want to limit the amount of data that can be stored on your computer by the team. However, the Properties dialog box does not show the Quota tab. The reason could be that: (Choose all that apply.)
   a. It is not an NTFS volume.
   b. You are not logged on as an Administrator.
   c. You are not viewing the properties for a volume or partition.
   d. The operating system is not configured properly.

4. As the System Administrator of a company, you need to set up and configure new training software on the computers in the training room. At present, the computers in the training room are running Windows 98. However, the prerequisite for installing new software is that the computer should be running Windows 2000. The users want to use both Windows 98 and Windows 2000 and to be able to access all of the files on their computers while using either operating system. You also want to provide them with optimum performance of the system. What should you do?
   a. Create and format a FAT32 Partition.
   b. Create and format an NTFS volume.
   c. Create and format a FAT16 Partition.
   d. Configure Windows 2000 Professional to enable disk compression.
   e. Configure Windows 2000 Professional to implement dynamic volumes.

5. Which of the following volumes does Windows 2000 Professional support? (Choose all that apply.)
   a. Striped volumes
   b. Mirrored volumes
   c. Spanned volumes
   d. Striped volumes with parity

6. Which of the following disks can be upgraded to dynamic disks?
   a. Disks on laptops
   b. Disks that have less than 1 MB free disk space
   c. Disks that are part of a striped set
   d. Disks that are part of a volume set

7. Which of the following statements are true for disk quotas?
   a. Quotas are set for individuals and not groups.
   b. You can implement quotas on FAT volumes.
   c. By default, quotas are enabled for all volumes.
   d. Administrator group is exempt from quota limit.
   e. You cannot configure guest accounts for disk quotas.

Projects: On Your Own

1. Create a volume.
   a. Log on as **Administrator**.
   b. Access the **Disk Management** option.
   c. Right-click the unallocated disk space on the lower right pane.
   d. Initialize the **Create Volume Wizard**.
   e. Create a **Simple** volume.
2. Defragment a disk.
   a. Log on to **Explorer**.
   b. Access the **Properties** dialog box.
   c. Access the **Tools** tab.
   d. Access the **Defragment** tab.
   e. **Defragment** drive **C:**.
3. Use the Disk Cleanup utility.
   a. Log on to **Explorer**.
   b. Access the **Properties** dialog box.
   c. Click the **Disk Cleanup** Tab.
   d. Run the utility on drive **C:**.

Problem Solving Scenarios

The Financial Manager at Market Forecasts, Inc., a market forecasting firm, complains that his employees are experiencing long delays in accessing and saving files on the server. Employees create detailed financial spreadsheets and MS Word documents for the companies they analyze, and these files are frequently updated. The employees also store a large library of financial research documents on the file server. Each of these documents is accessed infrequently, and they are all read-only. The Financial Manager has asked you to find out what is wrong. After interviewing the employees, you discover that they frequently save updated spreadsheets as new files with the current date, keeping copies of each day's work as a new file. Old files are supposed to be deleted after two weeks, but often are not. Disk space on the file server is being consumed at an alarming rate. Moreover, the frequent writing to and deleting from the disk is causing files to be saved on different sectors of the disk. Outline the steps you would take to improve the efficiency of data storage on the server.

6 Installing and Configuring Network Protocols

A protocol is a set of rules and conventions for sending information over a network. These rules manage the content, format, timing, sequencing, and error control for messages exchanged among network devices. The protocol explains how the clients and servers on a network must arrange data in order to deliver it to other computers on the network and how they can interpret data that is delivered to them. In addition, computers on a network must "speak the same language" in order for data transfers to be possible. Windows 2000 Professional supports several protocols that networks follow when transferring data. The main protocol is TCP/IP (Transmission Control Protocol/Internet Protocol), which is the core protocol for the Internet. TCP/IP is a scalable and routable protocol. It is scalable because it can be used for both large and small networks, and data can be transferred across networks and between computers using different operating systems with widely varying structural designs. TCP/IP is a routable protocol because it ensures that data can cross a router, which is a special computer used to transfer data between networks. Networking protocols today are put into practice as a suite of protocols. A protocol suite is a combination of several different networking applications and services that function jointly to make network communications possible. The protocol suite outlines the stages involved in packaging data so that it can be sent and received on the network. Each packet of data must be correctly formatted, ordered, compressed, and checked for errors. Therefore, each computer on a network must be configured with the same protocol suite if intercommunication between them is required.

If your network uses computers running Microsoft operating systems and you must access the resources on servers running a version of Netware that predates 4.0, you must use the NWLink protocol. Netware 4.0 servers and above support TCP/IP. NWLink can also be used in an exclusively Microsoft environment; however, you will not be able to use Active Directory because it is only compatible with TCP/IP. If a Microsoft client needs to access file and print resources on a NetWare server, Client Service for NetWare (CSNW), the redirector that is compatible with NetWare, must also be installed. Alternatively, you can install Novell's redirector, Novell Client for Windows 2000.

Network bindings are used to set the order in which the protocols that are configured on a system will be used. When a network connection is initiated, the bindings set the order in which the system will attempt to use protocols to establish links.

In addition to TCP/IP and NWLink, Windows 2000 Professional supports several other protocols such as NetBEUI (NetBios Enhanced User Interface), DLC (Data Link Control), and AppleTalk, as well as Network Monitor driver 2, which makes it easier to capture data using the Network Monitor utility.

Goals

In this lesson, you will learn how to configure TCP/IP to use a static IP address, troubleshoot TCP/IP problems, and install the NWLink protocol. You will also learn about other protocols supported by Windows 2000 Professional, and how to configure network bindings.

Lesson 6 Installing and Configuring Network Protocols

Skill	Exam 70-210 Objective
1. Introducing the TCP/IP Protocol	Basic knowledge
2. Configuring TCP/IP to Use a Static IP Address	Configure and troubleshoot the TCP/IP protocol.
3. Introducing WINS and DNS	Basic knowledge
4. Troubleshooting TCP/IP Problems	Configure and troubleshoot the TCP/IP protocol.
5. Installing NWLink on a System	Basic knowledge
6. Introducing Other Protocols Supported by Windows 2000 Professional	Basic knowledge
7. Configuring Network Bindings	Optimize and troubleshoot network performance.
8. Optimizing and Troubleshooting Network Performance	Optimize and troubleshoot network performance.

Requirements

A system with Windows 2000 Professional installed on it.

skill 1

Introducing the TCP/IP Protocol

exam objective   Basic knowledge

overview

TCP/IP (Transmission Control Protocol/Internet Protocol) is a set of protocols that enables you to route messages over a network. A message is broken down into packets before it is transmitted. Although the packets can follow different routes, they generally follow one common path. When the packets reach their destination, TCP/IP uses a sequencing function to ensure that they are reassembled in the correct order to recreate the original message. It also includes procedures for acknowledging the delivery of the correct packets and for requesting that lost or damaged packets be resent.

TCP/IP defines the rules for connecting networks to each other and for communication between computers on a network. These rules are used to correct errors, manage the routing and delivery of data, and to control all aspects of data transmission. Protocols within the TCP/IP protocol suite also provide logon, file, and print services and other services such as FTP (File Transfer Protocol), Telnet, and DNS (Domain Name Service).

TCP/IP is suitable for most large networks because it is supported by most operating systems and multiple hardware configurations. It provides an infrastructure that is cross-platform, client/server based, scalable, dependable, and time-tested. IP is a routable protocol, meaning that it can be used to send packets across a router so that messages can leave a physical network. Since a domain-based Windows 2000 network uses the TCP/IP protocol suite, understanding how a TCP/IP network operates is the equivalent of understanding how an Active Directory-based network functions.

From a conceptual standpoint, the TCP/IP suite can be viewed as consisting of four layers **(Figure 6-1)**:

◆ Application
◆ Transport
◆ Internet
◆ Network Interface

Application layer: This layer is used by applications to gain access to the network. The application layer is at the top of the conceptual model. It includes many standard TCP/IP utilities and services such as FTP, Telnet, and DNS.

Transport layer: This layer sets up communication sessions between computers and makes sure that messages are reassembled in the correct sequence without errors, and with no data duplication or data loss. The transport protocol used depends upon the method chosen to deliver the data. It is a function of the standards associated with the type of data transmission. There are two types of transport layer protocols:

◆ **Transmission Control Protocol (TCP):** TCP is used to establish a connection between two hosts so that they can exchange streams of data. Whereas IP handles packets, TCP handles streams of data. TCP establishes the connections between sending and receiving computers and provides connection-oriented communications. Connection-oriented communications require the sender and the receiver to establish a channel. The term "channel" refers to any communication path between two computers or devices. It can refer to the physical medium such as the wires or network cables, or to the virtual circuits that act as a direct connection. Virtual circuits are connections between two hosts, usually on a packet-switching network, through which they can communicate as though they have a dedicated connection, when in fact the packets may be following a very different

Figure 6-1 The four layers in the TCP/IP suite

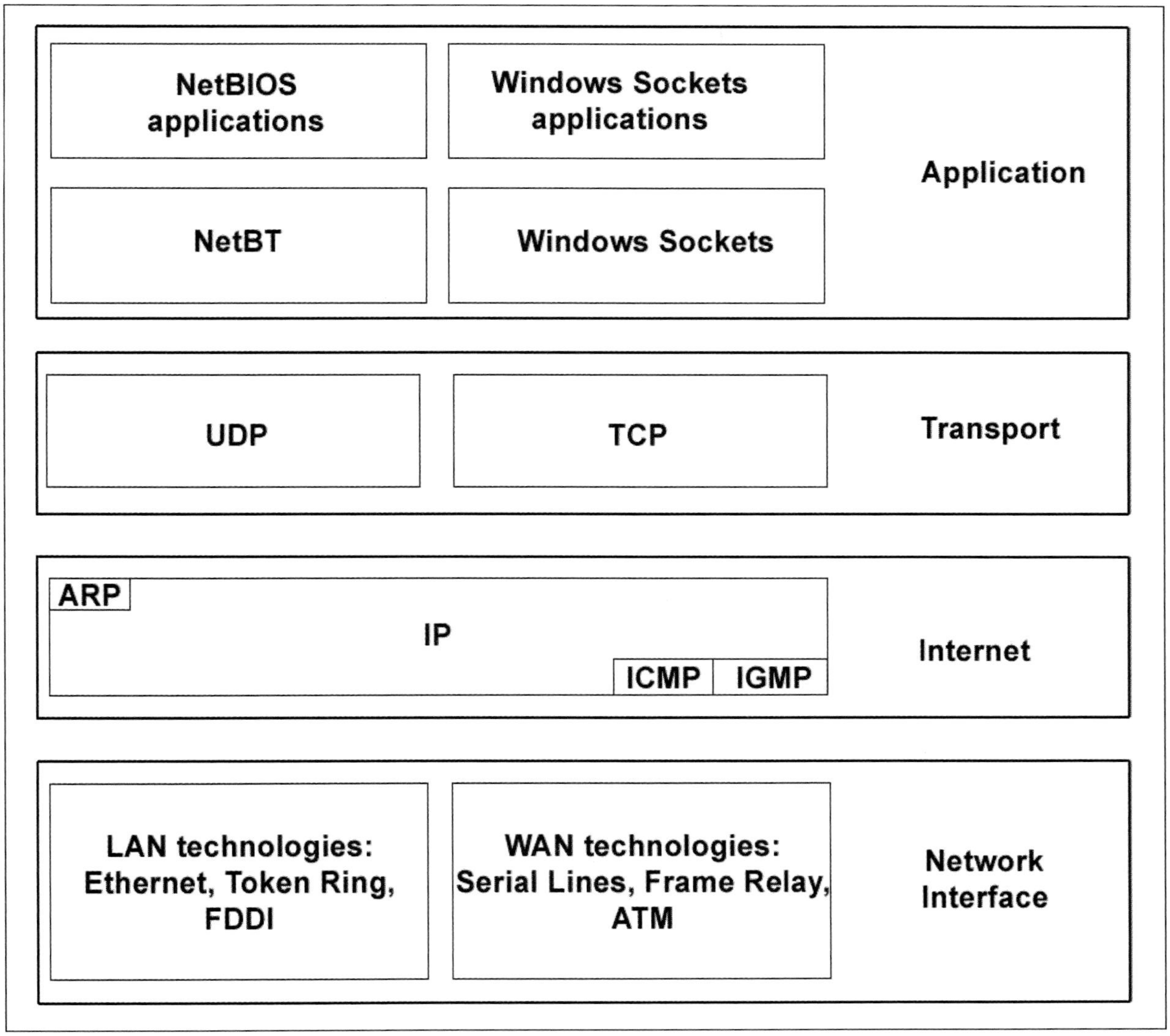

skill 1

Introducing the TCP/IP Protocol
(cont'd)

exam objective

Basic knowledge

overview

route. TCP ensures that data is reassembled in the correct sequence, with no data loss or duplication, and it reports the receipt of data. The receiver reports back to the sender whether it received all of the consecutively numbered packets, or if some need to be resent. If the sender does not receive this notification, either the acknowledgement has been lost, or the connection has been broken. The sender will then keep retransmitting the data at increasingly longer intervals, until finally, if it still receives no acknowledgement, it breaks the connection. Not all applications use TCP. However, many use UDP.

◆ **User Datagram Protocol (UDP):** UDP is used by applications to transfer small amounts of data at one time. It provides **connectionless communication**, wherein the host can send a message to the recipient without establishing a channel. This is in contrast to connection-oriented protocols which require a channel to be established between the sender and receiver before any messages are transmitted. Like TCP, UDP runs on top of IP networks, but it provides very few recovery services. Instead, it provides a direct way to send and receive datagrams on an IP network and is often used for broadcasting messages. A datagram is a unit of data similar to a packet. A connectionless protocol such as UDP is used by a host to send a message to the network with the destination address, but there is no guarantee that it will reach its destination. There is no acknowledgement that the data packets have been received and, therefore, no data retransmissions. This is why it is considered to be a less reliable protocol (**Table 6-1**).

Internet layer: This layer determines the route data will take when the data packets are transferred from the source computer to the destination computer. The Internet layer ultimately forms packets by encapsulating segments or datagrams. The term packet refers to a piece of a message transmitted over a packet-switching network. Packets contain the source computer address and the destination address in addition to the data. In IP networks, packets are often called datagrams. **Routers** are computers that interconnect the multiple computers on a network or the Internet. They use headers and a routing table to determine where packets go, and they use ICMP (Internet Control Message Protocol), an extension of IP, to communicate with each other and configure the best route between any two hosts. Routing algorithms are also sometimes used at this level to determine the best available path for the data packets, although often the paths are statically defined in the routing table.

The Internet layer consists of the following protocols:

◆ **Internet Protocol (IP):** This protocol in the TCP/IP protocol suite is responsible for addressing and routing. It provides the addressing scheme for the network and for the Internet. Packets sent between two hosts may take different routes, but IP does not ensure either the arrival of the packets or their correct sequencing. It relies on other protocols to perform these functions. Routing protocols also include several key IP protocols such as Routing Internet Protocol (RIP), Open Shortest Path First (OSPF) protocol, and Border Gateway Protocol (BGP).

◆ **Address Resolution Protocol (ARP):** This protocol is used to map an IP address to the **Media Access Control (MAC)** address. A MAC address is a unique 48-bit or 6-byte number, usually represented as 12 hexadecimal digits. It is also referred to as a hardware address, physical address, or Ethernet address. There are two types of ARP resolution:

Table 6-1   Internet Applications and Underlying Internet Protocols

Application	Application-layer protocol	Underlying transport protocol
Electronic mail	SMTP	TCP
Remote terminal access	Telnet	TCP
World Wide Web (www)	HTTP	TCP
File transfer	FTP	TCP
Remote terminal access	NFS	typically UDP
Streaming multimedia	proprietary	typically UDP
Internet telephony	proprietary	typically UDP
Network management	SNMP	typically UDP
Name translation	DNS	typically UDP

The Internet uses two transport protocols: TCP and UDP. TCP is used where reliability is more important than speed. UDP is used where speed is more important than reliability.

TCP requires the establishment of a connection between sender and receiver, and maintains a connection state that includes buffers, congestion control, sequencing of packets, and acknowledgment numbers. This makes TCP extremely reliable and manageable. UDP, in contrast, has no regulation on its send rate; it is "connectionless" in the sense that it sends data without verifying a connection—it simply blasts out data. UDP is very fast, in part because it does not have all the overhead of TCP. UDP has only 8 bytes of overhead for a data segment compared to 20 bytes for a TCP segment. For Internet phone, multimedia, and real-time Internet conferencing, UDP is preferred. Internet network managers and other users, however, do not appreciate UDP's ability to congest networks. A part of the "World Wide Wait" is due to UDP's unmanageable behavior.

skill 1

Introducing the TCP/IP Protocol
(cont'd)

exam objective   Basic knowledge

overview

local and remote. In either case, first the ARP request is initiated, and it is determined whether the IP address is local or remote. If it is local, the ARP cache is checked. Address mappings are stored in the ARP cache for future reference. In local ARP resolution, if no mapping is found in the ARP cache, an ARP request is broadcast to all hosts. When the target host validates the IP address in the request, it generates an ARP reply. The sender then updates its ARP cache. If the IP address is identified as remote, the IP address of the default gateway must be determined. The ARP cache is checked for the MAC address of the default gateway. If it is not found, an ARP request for the default gateway's hardware address is generated. After the response is received from the default gateway, the data packet is sent to the default gateway. Then the default gateway must determine if the address is local or remote. If it is local, it broadcasts an ARP request and obtains the MAC address. If it is remote, the hardware address for the next default gateway must be determined, and the process is repeated.

◆ **Internet Control Message Protocol (ICMP):** This protocol enables hosts to exchange status and error information. ICMP supports packets containing error, control, and informational messages. This information, also called an ICMP packet, is used by higher-level protocols to solve transmission problems and by network administrators to discover where network problems are located. ICMP packets are also used by the ping utility to find out if an IP device on the network is working.

◆ **Internet Group Management Protocol (IGMP):** This protocol is used so that multicast routers on a network can communicate with all member devices in a multicast group. On a network, broadcasting refers to sending data to everyone on the network, while multicasting refers to a transmission method for sending identical data to a select group of recipients. The server can transmit a single stream, regardless of how many clients have requested it. When the data stream crosses a multicast-enabled switch or router, it is copied to the paths where the clients that requested the stream are located. IGMP is used to establish memberships in certain groups on a network and to communicate group membership information to the multicast routers. It is used by a host computer to tell its local routers to send messages to it that are addressed to a particular multicast group.

Network Interface layer: This layer is at the base of the TCP/IP conceptual model. It consists of the physical media, network adapter card, and driver information. When sending data, the network interface layer encapsulates packets into frames that will be sent across the network as a series of bits. It is responsible for placing TCP/IP packets on the network medium and receiving TCP/IP packets off the network medium (**Figure 6-1A**). The Network Interface layer interacts directly with the physical medium on which the TCP/IP packets will be traveling. The Network Interface layer can connect to a wide variety of older media (like Ethernet and X.25), and also to new optical media like FDDI and Sonet (not shown). This layer makes TCP/IP communication independent of whatever phyical media evolve in the future, and provides organizations tremendous flexibility in the choice of physical media.

Figure 6-1A Network Interface Layer

Ethernet

ATM

FDDI

TCP/IP
Network
Interface Layer

ISDN

X.25

Frame
Relay

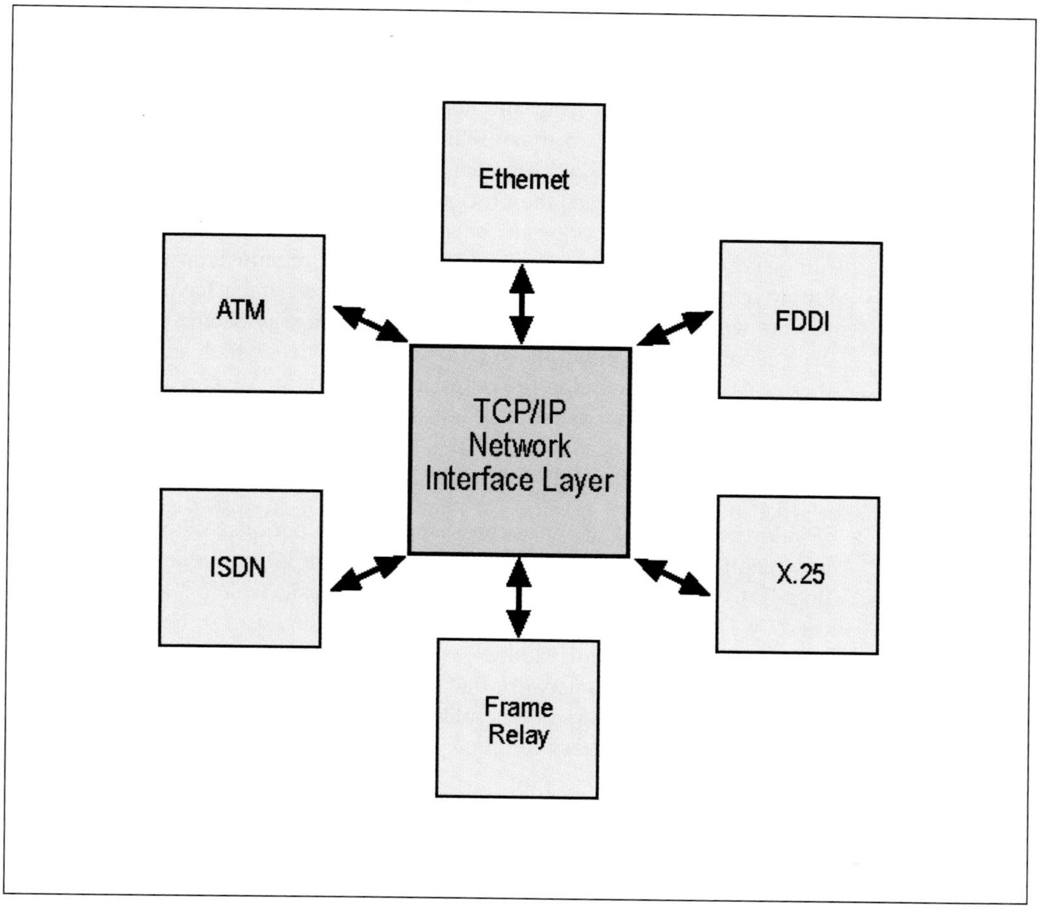

skill 2

Configuring TCP/IP to Use a Static IP Address

exam objective

Configure and troubleshoot the TCP/IP protocol.

overview

TCP/IP works in conjunction with **Dynamic Host Configuration Protocol (DHCP) service**. **DHCP** provides TCP/IP configuration information to client computers running Windows 2000 Professional, Windows 95, Windows 98, and many other types of client operating systems. The default setup in Windows 2000 Professional is that the operating system will retrieve an IP address from another computer on the network called a DHCP server. The DHCP server's job is to dynamically assign or "lease" IP addresses from a range of IP addresses to computers as they boot. This simplifies the administration of TCP/IP configuration because it automates the process of assigning IP addresses to clients. However, certain computers on the network must be assigned a static IP address. For example, a data application server may have to have an IP address that remains constant so that your customers or employees can access it. The DHCP server itself must have a constant IP address. Print servers will also have a static IP address and you may decide to assign a static IP address to each server running either the WINS or DNS service, which are discussed in the next skill. In these cases, you can assign IP addresses manually or you can use client reservations. A client reservation refers to a specific IP address within a range of permanently reserved addresses that is only leased to a specific DHCP client. In this way you can ensure that a host will always receive the same IP address.

IP addresses consist of four octets separated by periods. Within these four octets, there are two identifiers: one for the network (the network ID) and one for the computer or host (the host ID). Another number, called the **subnet mask**, which is also made up of four octets, is used by TCP/IP to divide the network ID from the host ID. For example, the subnet mask is used to determine if an IP address is on the local network or on a remote network. A subnet, therefore, is a part of a network that has a portion of the address in common. On TCP/IP networks, subnets have the same IP address prefix and the subnet mask helps to identify the subnet to which an IP address belongs.

A **default gateway** must also be set up in order to connect your network to other networks, unless your computer is using its local routing table. **Routing tables** are used to provide routers with the directions they will use to forward data packets to locations on other networks. Routing table data will determine how to send a data packet and where to send it. A router uses the destination address and the information in the table, which outlines potential routes. The routes are delineated into the steps it will take to forward the data packets from the origin and through the succeeding routers to reach the destination. You can keep a routing table that contains an entry for every computer or network that you need to communicate with, however, continually updating static routes is not practical and generally a default gateway is used instead. A default gateway is simply a router that links networks. The typical setup is that the DHCP server will dynamically assign IP addresses, subnet masks, and default gateways when a computer logs on to the network. It can also automatically assign a DNS server address.

Table 6-2 explains the elements involved in configuring a static TCP/IP address.

how to

Configure TCP/IP to use a static IP address.

1. Right-click the **My Network Places** icon on the desktop and select the **Properties** command on the shortcut menu to open the **Network and Dial-up Connections** window (**Figure 6-2**).

Table 6-2 Configuring a static TCP/IP address

Option	Description
IP address	Used to identify a TCP/IP host as a logical 32-bit address divided into four octets. Computers connected to a TCP/IP network are referred to as TCP/IP hosts. For identification purposes, you must have a unique IP address for each network adapter card in a computer running TCP/IP. An IP address consists of a network ID and a host ID. The network ID identifies all hosts on the network, while the host ID represents a specific computer. For example, in the IP address **198.154.1.207**, 198.154.1 is the network ID and 207 is the host ID.
Subnet mask	Another 32-bit number, divided into four octets, that is used to break up the IP address into the two parts: the network ID and the host ID. The subnet mask blocks or "masks" a part of the IP address in order to differentiate between the two. Companies generally either use the same subnet mask throughout their network or a VLSM (variable length subnet mask) subnetting scheme. Variable length subnetting is a method of allocating subnetted network IDs that use subnet masks of different sizes.
Default gateway	Gateways or routers are used to connect different networks. A default gateway acts as an intermediate device between hosts on different network segments. TCP/IP sends packets to the IP address for the router, which acts as a gateway to remote networks. The default gateway dispatches the data packets to the destination network. You must configure an IP address with a default gateway in order to make remote communications possible. You do not need to configure a default gateway unless you are connecting to an external network.

Figure 6-2 Network and Dial-up Connections window

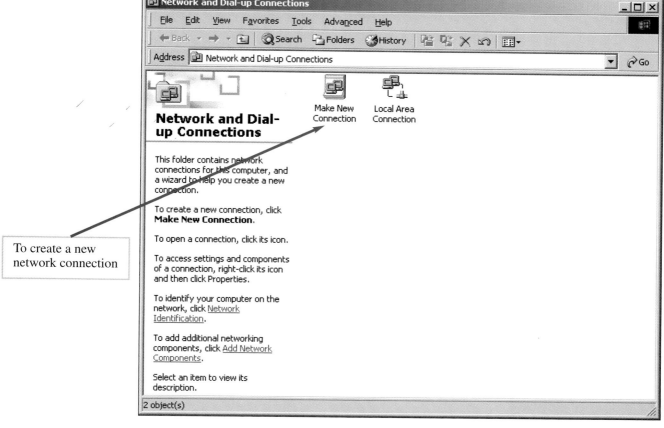

To create a new network connection

skill 2

Configuring TCP/IP to Use a Static IP Address (cont'd)

exam objective

Configure and troubleshoot the TCP/IP protocol.

how to

2. Right-click the **Local Area Connection** icon and select the **Properties** command on the shortcut menu to open the **Local Area Connection Properties** dialog box.
3. Select the **Internet Protocol (TCP/IP)** check box (**Figure 6-3**).
4. Click [Properties] to open the **Internet Protocol (TCP/IP) Properties** dialog box.
5. Click the **Use the following IP address** option button.
6. Type: **198.164.1.204** in the **IP address** text box (**Figure 6-4**).
7. Click in the **Subnet mask** text box. Windows 2000 Professional automatically assigns an appropriate subnet mask according to the given IP address.
8. Click [OK] to confirm the settings.
9. Click [OK] to close the Local Area Connection Properties dialog box.
10. Close the Network and Dial-up Connections window.

more

When TCP/IP is installed on a Windows 2000 Professional computer, it is automatically set up to be a DHCP client; a Windows 2000 Professional computer cannot be a DHCP server. The DHCP service is only included in the Windows 2000 Server products. However, a DHCP client does not necessarily need a DHCP server in order to use a dynamic IP address. If a DHCP client cannot locate a DHCP server, it will use a service called automatic private IP addressing (APIPA) to randomly choose an IP address from a private APIPA address series that is not in use on the Internet. In this way, computers on a LAN where there is no DHCP server or on a network where the DHCP server is down, can still be assigned an IP address and communicate with other computers on the same subnet. APIPA generates an address and broadcasts that address across the network. If no other computer responds to this address, the computer knows that it can assign the address to itself. The IP address will always be in the format 169.254.x.x and the subnet mask will always be 255.255.0.0. However, APIPA cannot assign a default gateway, so remote access, such as communication on the Internet or with outside networks, will not be possible. Windows 2000 computers that have used APIPA to assign themselves an IP address can usually only communicate with other Windows (98, 2000, ME or XP) computers on the same subnet that have also assigned themselves an IP address using APIPA. The IP addresses generated by APIPA are in the range from 169.254.0.0 to 169.254.255.255 because the Internet Assigned Numbers Authority (IANA) has set aside this series of addresses for this purpose. This ensures that the IP address does not conflict with any routable addresses.

tip

On a subnet where there is no DHCP server, Windows 2000 Professional computers can still use DHCP rather than APIPA if there is a router on the subnet that supports DHCP/BOOTP forwarding or if there is a Windows 2000 or NT4 Server that is running the DHCP Relay Agent service. The DHCP Relay Agent has the IP address for the remote DHCP Server and can transfer messages between subnets.

Figure 6-3 Local Area Connection Properties dialog box

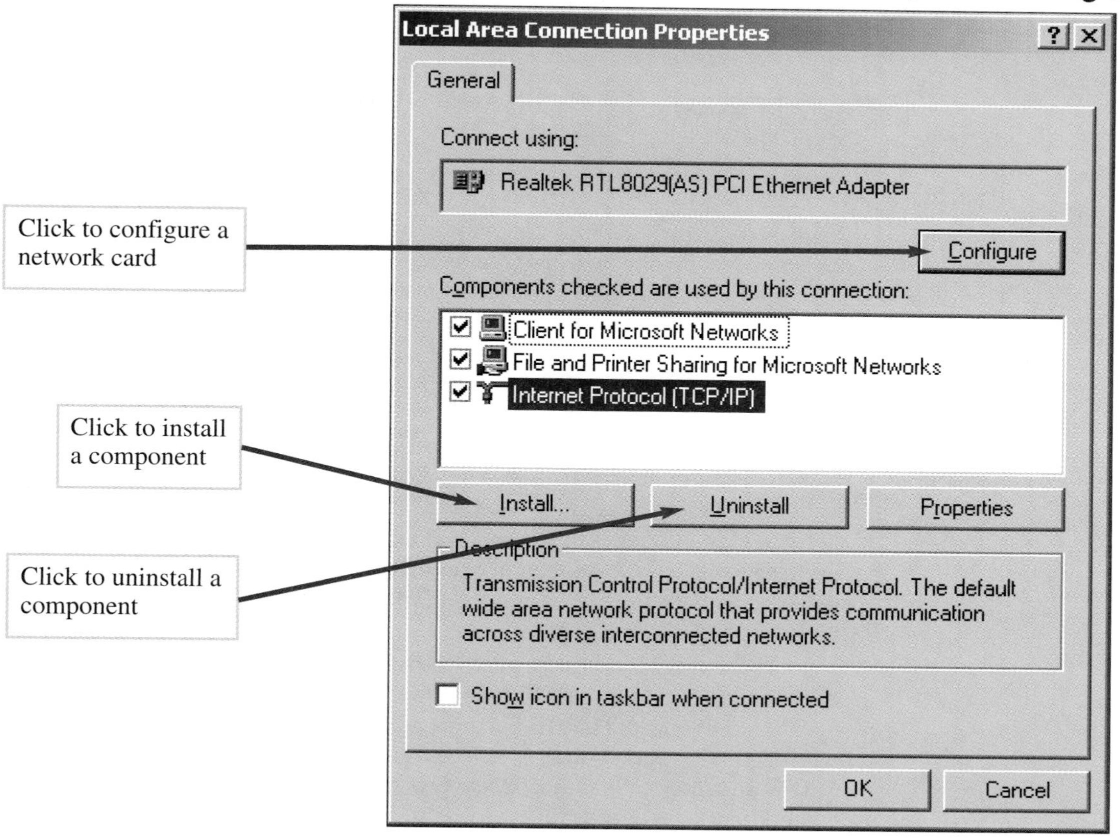

Click to configure a network card

Click to install a component

Click to uninstall a component

Local Area Connection Properties   ? X

General

Connect using:

Realtek RTL8029(AS) PCI Ethernet Adapter

Configure

Components checked are used by this connection:

☑ 🖳 Client for Microsoft Networks
☑ 🖳 File and Printer Sharing for Microsoft Networks
☑ 🖧 Internet Protocol (TCP/IP)

Install...   Uninstall   Properties

Description

Transmission Control Protocol/Internet Protocol. The default wide area network protocol that provides communication across diverse interconnected networks.

☐ Show icon in taskbar when connected

OK   Cancel

Figure 6-4 Configuring a Static IP Address

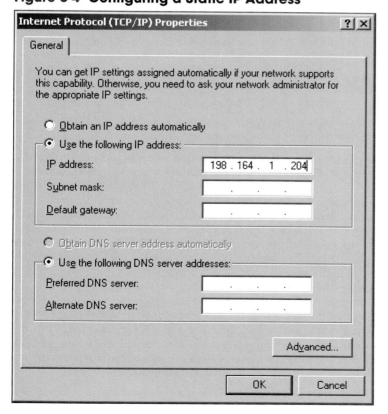

Internet Protocol (TCP/IP) Properties   ? X

General

You can get IP settings assigned automatically if your network supports this capability. Otherwise, you need to ask your network administrator for the appropriate IP settings.

○ Obtain an IP address automatically
◉ Use the following IP address:

IP address: 198 . 164 . 1 . 204

Subnet mask: .   .   .

Default gateway: .   .   .

○ Obtain DNS server address automatically
◉ Use the following DNS server addresses:

Preferred DNS server: .   .   .

Alternate DNS server: .   .   .

Advanced...

OK   Cancel

skill 3

Introducing WINS and DNS

exam objective   Basic knowledge

overview

Prior to Windows 2000, the default naming convention was NetBIOS. As you learned in Lesson 2, each computer has a computer or NetBIOS name. The NetBIOS name is used to identify the computer on a Microsoft network. When network users want to find your computer on a TCP/IP network using the NetBIOS name, there must be a method for assigning or mapping an IP address to the computer name. This method is the **WINS (Windows Internet Naming Service)** database on a WINS server which functions as the lookup directory. The WINS database in Windows 2000 is dynamically updated so that as client computers are assigned different IP addresses by the DHCP server the database stays current. Since NetBIOS was used by default in Windows NT4, setting up a WINS server is necessary if some of the client computers on your network are running that operating system or Windows 9.x or NT 3.5. If you do not set up WINS and there are no LMHOSTS files configured (see below), users can still browse on their subnet using NetBIOS names, but they cannot make connections to computers on other subnets. Furthermore, in the absence of WINS or an LMHOSTS file, NetBIOS packets must be broadcast to all computers on the network to request and announce network resources, since NetBIOS is a non-routable protocol. To configure WINS, open the Internet Protocol (TCP/IP) Properties dialog box and click the **Advanced** button to open the **Advanced TCP/IP Settings** dialog box. On the **WINS** tab, the **Enable NetBIOS over TCP/IP** option button is selected by default. You can enter a static IP address in the **WINS addresses, in order of use** text box, or you can have the DHCP server assign the address for the WINS server by selecting the **Use NetBIOS setting from the DHCP server** option button (**Figure 6-5**).

In the Advanced TCP/IP Settings dialog box, you will also see the **Enable LMHOSTS** check box selected by default. HOSTS and LMHOSTS are text files, stored on the local computer, that also contain name-to-IP address correlations. The LMHOSTS file correlates NetBIOS names to IP addresses. The HOSTS file correlates host names or fully qualified domain names (FQDNs) to IP addresses. These files must be updated manually by an administrator. Since this would be extremely difficult on a network in which IP addresses are being dynamically generated, these files are now all but obsolete as a method for mapping IP addresses to computer or domain names. However, you should know of their existence as the precursor to WINS and DNS. DNS, like the HOSTS file, correlates host names or FQDNs to IP addresses. Name resolution, which will be discussed in detail in Lesson 17, simply means the process we have been discussing of translating names into corresponding IP addresses.

DNS (Domain Name Service), which will also be discussed in detail in Lesson 17, is the main name resolution service for Windows 2000. It is a method of accessing computers on a TCP/IP network using the FQDN or host name. Fully qualified domain names consist of a host and a domain name, including a top-level domain, which is the attached Internet suffix, com, edu, gov, org, mil, net, or a country code such as ca for Canada. They look like the URLs you use to access a Web page on the Internet, for example, **www.ebay.com**. Although it is not required that TCP/IP networks use domain names, you cannot have an Active Directory domain-based network without a DNS server. The DNS service only runs on Windows 2000 Server, but you will need to know how to configure a Window 2000 Professional client computer to use the DNS server for the name resolution process. Usually, you will leave the **Obtain DNS server address automatically** option button selected in the **Internet Protocol (TCP/IP) Properties** dialog box (**Figure 6-6**). This will result in the IP address for the DNS server being automatically retrieved from the DHCP server. The other method is to manually enter a static IP address for the DNS server. First you must select the **Use the following DNS server addresses** option button and then you can type in the IP addresses for a preferred and an alternate DNS server (if applicable) in the corresponding text boxes.

**Figure 6-5 WINS tab in the Advanced TCP/IP
Settings dialog box**

Enter an IP address to
manually configure a
static IP address for the
DNS server

Select the **Use NetBIOS
setting from the DHCP
server** option button to
have the DHCP server
assign the address for the
WINS server

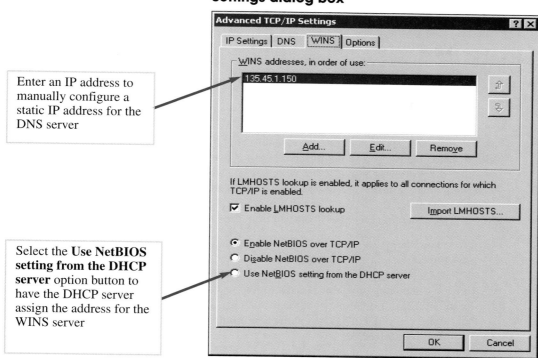

**Figure 6-6 Configuring a Windows 2000
Professional computer to be a DNS client**

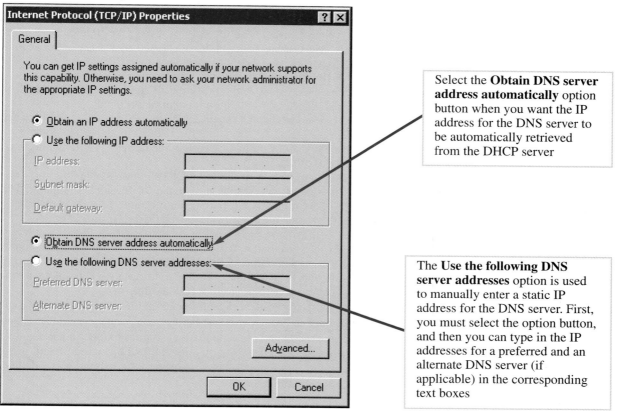

Select the **Obtain DNS server
address automatically** option
button when you want the IP
address for the DNS server to
be automatically retrieved
from the DHCP server

The **Use the following DNS
server addresses** option is used
to manually enter a static IP
address for the DNS server. First,
you must select the option button,
and then you can type in the IP
addresses for a preferred and an
alternate DNS server (if
applicable) in the corresponding
text boxes

skill 4

Troubleshooting TCP/IP Problems

exam objective

Configure and troubleshoot the TCP/IP protocol.

overview

Network administrators will find that they must frequently troubleshoot TCP/IP problems. Client configuration problems are frequent. More frequent, however, are everyday calamities such as disconnected devices and accidentally unplugged cables. Before you use any of the utilities listed below, you should troubleshoot network communication problems by making sure that everything is plugged in, switched on, and connected. Next, check the Device Manager to make sure that the driver for the network adapter is set up and functioning properly. Finally, you can use several troubleshooting utilities included in Windows 2000 Professional to inspect your network protocols. All are run from the Command Prompt window.

◆ **Ping:** The **Packet Internet Groper** utility is used to test TCP/IP configurations and identify connection failures. A packet of information is sent to check the connection between the client and the server. The Ping utility also reports the connection speed at any point in time by calculating how long it takes for the server to respond. You can use the ping utility to provide information about the availability and functionality of a particular TCP/IP host. Type the following syntax at the **Command Prompt:**

   ping IP_address

   You can also use the loopback address, 127.0.0.1 (or simply enter ping loopback) to confirm that TCP/IP is bound to your network adapter. The Reply From message will be repeated four times if the protocol is bound to the network adapter when you use the loopback address, and whenever you have successfully connected to an IP address.

◆ **Ipconfig:** This utility is used to confirm that the TCP/IP protocol is running. You can run it without any switches to get the IP address, subnet mask, and default gateway to confirm that the configuration has been initialized. You can also use the ipconfig command with the **/all** switch to include information about any DNS or WINS servers, to find out if the IP address is static or dynamic and discover the name of the host, and to make sure that there is no duplicate IP address. If there is a duplicate address, the subnet mask will be 0.0.0.0. You use the **/release** switch with ipconfig to release the IP address that has been assigned by the DHCP server. You cannot release a leased IP address in the TCP/IP Properties dialog box. The **/renew** switch is used to renew a DHCP address, which you also cannot do in the TCP/IP Properties dialog box.

◆ **ARP:** This command is used to display and modify the IP address to physical address (MAC address) translation tables used by Address Resolution Protocol.

◆ **Netstat:** This command is used to display the TCP/IP protocol statistics and network connections (**Figure 6-7**).

◆ **Nbtstat:** This utility is used to display protocol statistics and current TCP/IP connections using **NBT** (NetBIOS over TCP/IP).

◆ **Route:** This command is used to display or modify the local routing table.

◆ **Hostname:** This utility is used to validate the host name for the local computer. The Remote Copy Protocol (RCP), remote shell (RSH), and Remote Execution (REXEC) utilities will authenticate the host name after it is retrieved by the Hostname utility.

◆ **Tracert:** This utility checks the route a packet is following to reach its destination point. Tracert shows every router interface that a TCP/IP packet passes through on the path to the destination. It can be used to determine where a data transmission failure is occurring and/or where slow transmission is taking place. If data transmission is complete, it will trace the route the packets have taken to get from sender to receiver.

To find out how to use any of these commands, except Tracert and Hostname, type the command followed by **/?** in the Command Prompt window. For example, you can get information on the ARP command by typing **ARP/?** and pressing **[Enter]** (**Figure 6-7A**). To learn how to use the Tracert utility, simply type **Tracert** in the Command Prompt window and press **[Enter]**. If you enter **hostname** at the prompt, the name of the host will be returned. This command has no other switches or parameters.

Figure 6-7 Using the Netstat utility

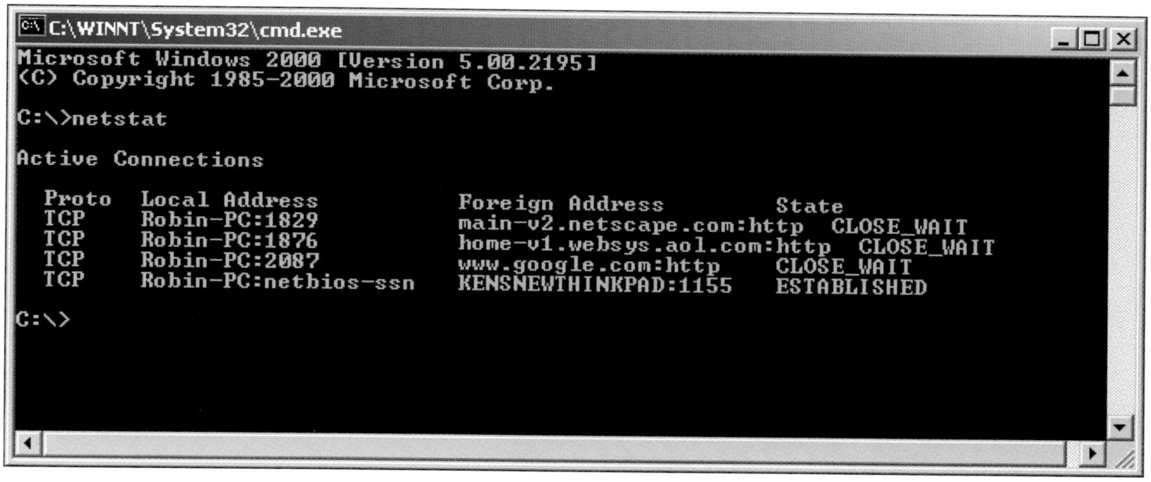

```
C:\WINNT\System32\cmd.exe                                                    _ □ ×

Microsoft Windows 2000 [Version 5.00.2195]
(C) Copyright 1985-2000 Microsoft Corp.

C:\>netstat

Active Connections

   Proto  Local Address          Foreign Address          State
   TCP    Robin-PC:1829          main-v2.netscape.com:http  CLOSE_WAIT
   TCP    Robin-PC:1876          home-v1.websys.aol.com:http  CLOSE_WAIT
   TCP    Robin-PC:2087          www.google.com:http       CLOSE_WAIT
   TCP    Robin-PC:netbios-ssn   KENSNEWTHINKPAD:1155      ESTABLISHED

C:\>
```

Figure 6-7A Using the ARP utility

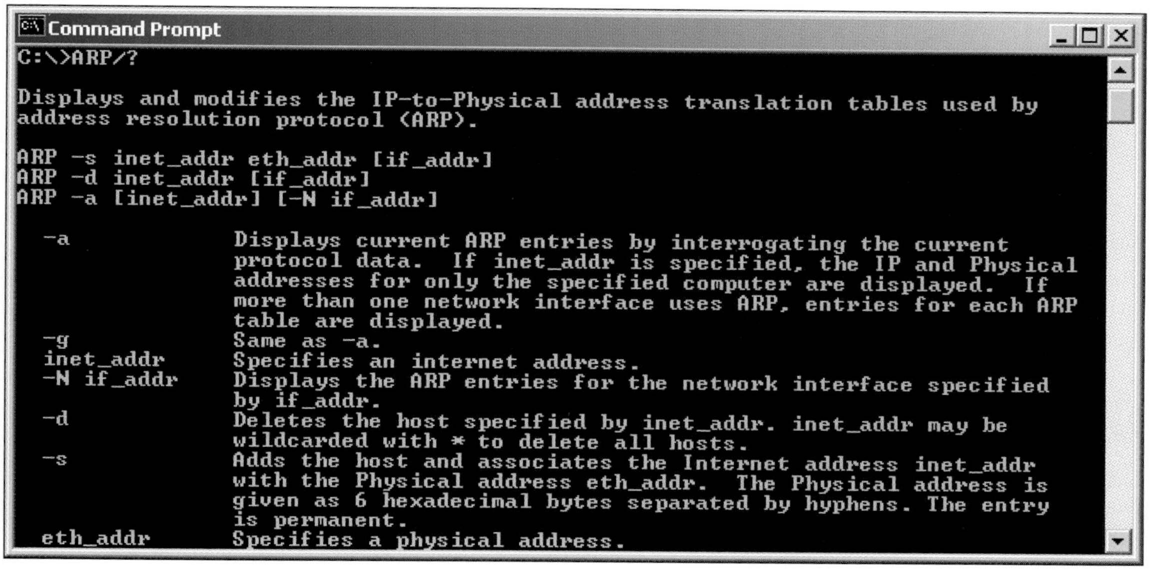

```
Command Prompt                                                              _ □ ×
C:\>ARP/?

Displays and modifies the IP-to-Physical address translation tables used by
address resolution protocol (ARP).

ARP -s inet_addr eth_addr [if_addr]
ARP -d inet_addr [if_addr]
ARP -a [inet_addr] [-N if_addr]

  -a                Displays current ARP entries by interrogating the current
                    protocol data.  If inet_addr is specified, the IP and Physical
                    addresses for only the specified computer are displayed.  If
                    more than one network interface uses ARP, entries for each ARP
                    table are displayed.
  -g                Same as -a.
  inet_addr         Specifies an internet address.
  -N if_addr        Displays the ARP entries for the network interface specified
                    by if_addr.
  -d                Deletes the host specified by inet_addr.  inet_addr may be
                    wildcarded with * to delete all hosts.
  -s                Adds the host and associates the Internet address inet_addr
                    with the Physical address eth_addr.  The Physical address is
                    given as 6 hexadecimal bytes separated by hyphens.  The entry
                    is permanent.
  eth_addr          Specifies a physical address.
```

skill 4

Troubleshooting TCP/IP Problems
(cont'd)

exam objective

Configure and troubleshoot the TCP/IP protocol.

how to

Test the TCP/IP configuration of your computer by using the **ipconfig** and **ping** commands.
1. Open the **Command Prompt** window.
2. At the Command Prompt, type **ipconfig/all** and press **[Enter]**. This displays the details of the **Ethernet adapter Local Area Connection (Figure 6-8)**. (If you want to stop the ipconfig results from scrolling off the screen, type ipconfig/all|**more**. Now you can press the **[Spacebar]** to scroll down and view further results.)
3. At the Command Prompt, type the default value, **ping 127.0.0.1** and press **[Enter]**. This IP address is called the **local loopback** address and it is used to confirm that TCP/IP is bound to your network adapter. If a "Reply from" message is repeated four times **(Figure 6-9)**, your network adapter is properly configured.

more

In addition to the troubleshooting utilities and those used to test TCP/IP connectivity, Windows 2000 Professional includes other useful utilities and protocols. For example, **File Transfer Protocol (FTP)** is used to transfer files between a computer running Windows 2000 Professional and a TCP/IP host running server software and FTP. It also provides directory and file handling services such as listing directory contents and deleting files and selecting file formats. **Trivial File Transfer Protocol (TFTP)**, a simpler form of FTP, is used to transfer files between a computer running Windows 2000 Professional and a TCP/IP host running server software and TFTP. TFTP uses the User Datagram Protocol (UDP) and thus includes no security features, acknowledgements, or data retransmissions. Servers often use it to boot diskless workstations or routers. **Remote Copy Protocol (RCP)** is used to copy files between computers running Windows 2000 Professional and hosts that support the RCP service (frequently a UNIX host), and **Remote shell (RSH)** is used to execute commands on a UNIX host.

Telnet is a terminal emulation protocol that runs over TCP/IP. When you run Telnet from a client machine and connect to a server on the network, you can enter commands which will be carried out as if you were performing them directly on the server terminal. Telnet is often used to manage a remote Web server. It is used to control the server and to communicate with other servers on the network. You can also connect to a computer on the Internet that supports Telnet to run programs from that computer. Telnet was the first way in which remote access was accomplished. **Finger** is a utility, supported by UNIX computers, that is used to retrieve information about users, including their user name and how long they have been logged on. You can find out who is logged on to a remote network by first connecting to a Telnet server and then typing **finger** at the prompt. Most Internet host computers no longer support finger due to security concerns.

Figure 6-8 Using the ipconfig/all command

```
Command Prompt                                                    _ □ ×
Microsoft Windows 2000 [Version 5.00.2195]
(C) Copyright 1985-1999 Microsoft Corp.

C:\>ipconfig/all

Windows 2000 IP Configuration

        Host Name . . . . . . . . . . . . : azimuth-08x62fk
        Primary DNS Suffix  . . . . . . . :
        Node Type . . . . . . . . . . . . : Broadcast
        IP Routing Enabled. . . . . . . . : No
        WINS Proxy Enabled. . . . . . . . : No

Ethernet adapter Local Area Connection:

        Connection-specific DNS Suffix  . :
        Description . . . . . . . . . . . : Realtek RTL8029(AS) PCI Ethernet Ada
pter
        Physical Address. . . . . . . . . : 00-C0-F0-45-85-8B
        DHCP Enabled. . . . . . . . . . . : Yes
        Autoconfiguration Enabled . . . . : Yes
        IP Address. . . . . . . . . . . . : 192.168.0.22
        Subnet Mask . . . . . . . . . . . : 255.255.255.0
        Default Gateway . . . . . . . . . : 192.168.0.1
        DHCP Server . . . . . . . . . . . : 192.168.0.1
```

Figure 6-9 Using the ping 127.0.0.1 command

```
Command Prompt                                                    _ □ ×
Microsoft Windows 2000 [Version 5.00.2195]
(C) Copyright 1985-1999 Microsoft Corp.

C:\>ping 127.0.0.1

Pinging 127.0.0.1 with 32 bytes of data:

Reply from 127.0.0.1: bytes=32 time=10ms TTL=128
Reply from 127.0.0.1: bytes=32 time<10ms TTL=128
Reply from 127.0.0.1: bytes=32 time<10ms TTL=128
Reply from 127.0.0.1: bytes=32 time<10ms TTL=128

Ping statistics for 127.0.0.1:
    Packets: Sent = 4, Received = 4, Lost = 0 (0% loss),
Approximate round trip times in milli-seconds:
    Minimum = 0ms, Maximum =  10ms, Average =  2ms

C:\>
```

skill 5

Installing NWLink on a System

exam objective

Basic knowledge

overview

The IPX/SPX (Internet Package eXchange/Sequenced Packet eXchange)/NetBIOS compatible protocol, also known more simply as **NWLink**, is used on Microsoft networks so that they can communicate with Novell Netware networks. It can also be used in exclusively Microsoft environments, but the advantages of Active Directory will be foregone because Active Directory needs TCP/IP in order to function. Therefore, NWLink is mainly used to access resources on NetWare servers. Simply configuring the NWLink protocol, however, is not always sufficient. NWLink is all you will need to connect to client/server applications (for example, SQL Server) that are running on a NetWare server. However, in order to access file and print resources on a Netware server, a software component called a redirector is needed to determine if a request for a resource should be handled locally by one of the disk drivers or by the network server. The redirector for Windows 2000 is called Client for Microsoft Networks, or the Workstation service, while the redirector for a Novell NetWare server is called Client Service for Netware (CSNW). Either a CSNW redirector or the Novell client must be installed in order for a Microsoft client to access file or print resources on a NetWare server. NWLink runs programs that use Winsock or NetBIOS-over-IPX interfaces. Configuring NWLink entails setting up three different components: the frame type, the network number, and the internal network number.

NWLink supports the following types of networking APIs that provide interprocess communication (IPC) services:

◆ **Winsock:** Winsock supports existing NetWare applications that are compatible with the IPX/ SPX socket interface in NetWare applications.
◆ **NetBIOS over IPX:** Communication with a computer running Windows 2000 Professional and NWLink NetBIOS is made possible using the **NetBIOS** protocol.

Resources on a Windows 2000 server such as Microsoft SQL Server or Microsoft SNA Server can also be accessed with NWLink. You can install **File and Print Service for Netware (FPNW)** to enable a Netware or Macintosh client to use file and print resources on a computer running Windows 2000 Server. However, FPNW is not included with Windows 2000 by default. In addition, to run FPNW, you cannot use the generic internal network number provided by Windows 2000 by default when installing NWLink. You must specify an internal network number manually.

how to

Install NWLink and Client Service for Netware (CSNW) on your computer.
1. Right-click the **My Network Places** icon on the desktop and select the **Properties** command on the shortcut menu to open the **Network and Dial-up Connections** window.
2. Right-click the **Local Area Connection** icon and select the **Properties** command on the shortcut menu to open the **Local Area Connection Properties** dialog box (**Figure 6-10**).
3. Click [Install...] to open the **Select Network Component Type** dialog box.
4. Select the **Protocol** option in the **Click the type of network component you want to install** box (**Figure 6-11**).
5. Click [Add...]. The **Select Network Protocol** dialog box opens.

tip

If you have not already installed NWLink, it will be automatically co-installed as part of installing CSNW.

**Figure 6-10 The Local Area Connection Properties
dialog box**

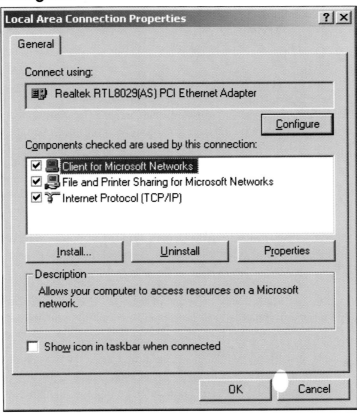

**Figure 6-11 Select Network Component Type
dialog box**

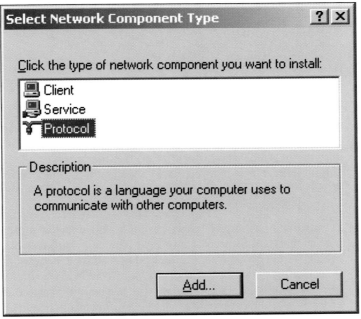

skill 5

Installing NWLink on a System (cont'd)

exam objective

Basic knowledge

how to

6. Select the **NWLink IPX/SPX/NetBIOS Compatible Transport Protocol** option in the **Network Protocol** section (**Figure 6-12**).
7. Click [OK] to apply the changes. In addition to the NWLink IPX/SPX/NetBIOS Compatible Transport Protocol, the NWLink NetBIOS protocol has been added (**Figure 6-13**). This is to ensure backward compatibility with earlier Microsoft networks. The additional protocol is needed to make IPX/SPX NetBIOS compatible.
8. Click [Install...] to open the **Select Network Component Type** dialog box again.
9. Select **Client** in the **Click the type of network component you want to install** box.
10. Click [Add...] to open The **Select Network Client** dialog box.
11. Select **Client Service for Netware** in the **Network Client** box. (This will be the only client available if the default Windows 2000 Professional installation was performed.) Click [OK]. The **Local Network** dialog box informs you that you must restart the computer. Click **Yes** to restart the computer.
12. When the computer has rebooted, the **Select NetWare Logon** dialog box opens. You must have ready the name of the NDS (Novell Directory Services) **tree** and the location of the server object (**context**) to which the client computer will be connecting. If you have access to a Netware Server and this information, enter it in the **Tree** and **Context** text boxes. If not, simply click **Cancel** and then **Yes** in the **Netware Network** dialog box to continue without setting a preferred server.
13. Close the Network and Dial-up Connections window. A **CSNW** icon ⬚ is added to the Control Panel. You can enter or change the default **NDS** tree and context settings and other **CSNW** settings by double-clicking this icon to open the Client Service for Netware dialog box (**Figure 6-14**).

more

The NWLink protocol is configured in the Properties dialog box for the protocol. You open this dialog box by opening the Properties dialog box for the connection (for example, Local Area Connection Properties), selecting the **NWLink IPX/SPX/NetBIOS Compatible Transport Protocol** in the **Components checked are used by this connection** box on the **General** tab, and clicking the **Properties** button. It is configured by setting the following three components:

◆ Frame type
◆ Network number
◆ Internal network number

Frame type: The frame type determines how the network card will format data. The frame type of the Windows 2000 computer and the Netware server must match or data will not be formatted in the same way and you will not be able to connect to the server. The default setting is AutoDetect, which means that the operating system will attempt to figure out the right frame type when you install NWLink. If it cannot do so, the default 802.2 will be used. This is the default frame type for newer versions of NetWare. You can manually set the frame type so that you do not have to rely on AutoDetect.

Network Number: The network number is a unique number for each NWLink network segment that must be specified for each frame type on a network adapter card. All computers on an NWLink network segment must have the same network number in order to be able to see each other. In this case, you can rely on Windows 2000 Professional to automatically find the network number and, for the most part, you will not need to change this setting. In fact, if there is a technical problem and you must manually assign a network number to the NWLink protocol, you must use the **Registry Editor**. This involves providing two corresponding entries:

Figure 6-12 Select Network Protocol dialog box

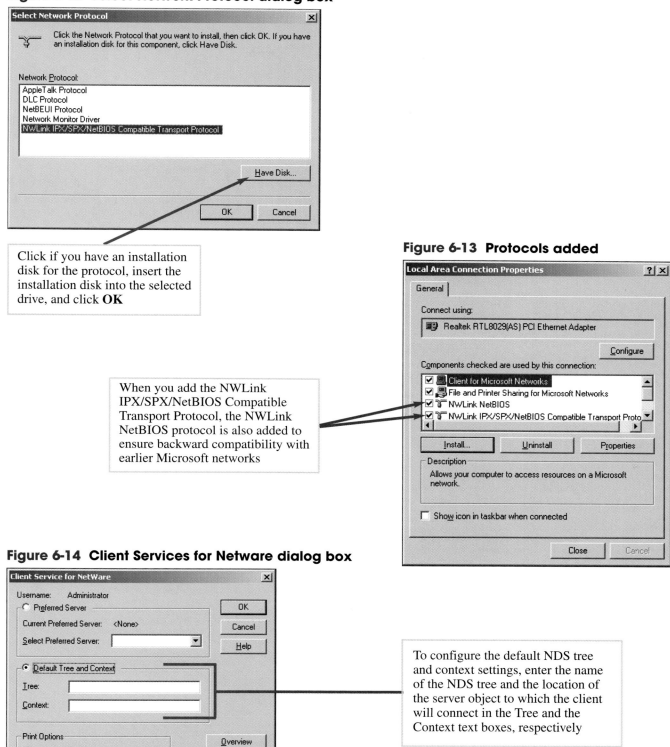

Click if you have an installation disk for the protocol, insert the installation disk into the selected drive, and click **OK**

Figure 6-13 Protocols added

When you add the NWLink IPX/SPX/NetBIOS Compatible Transport Protocol, the NWLink NetBIOS protocol is also added to ensure backward compatibility with earlier Microsoft networks

Figure 6-14 Client Services for Netware dialog box

To configure the default NDS tree and context settings, enter the name of the NDS tree and the location of the server object to which the client will connect in the Tree and the Context text boxes, respectively

skill 5

Installing NWLink on a System (cont'd)

exam objective   Basic knowledge

more

tip
If the NetWare server is functioning as a router, there can be two different frame types, but this is not the optimum setup and inefficient connections may result.

◆ **NetworkNumber:** A four-byte-long hexadecimal number used to specify the network number for the adapter. To view the network number, frame type, and device in use on a computer running Windows 2000 Professional, type **ipxroute config** as the NetworkNumber entry at the Command Prompt (**Figure 6-15**).
The NetworkNumber entry uses the **REG_MULTI_SZ** data type. If you specify the value for this entry as **zero**, NWLink takes the network number from the network. The default frame type for **NetWare 2.2** and **NetWare 3.11** on Ethernet networks is **802.3**. The default frame type for **NetWare 3.12** and later is **802.2** (**Figure 6-16**).
◆ **PktType:** The packet form (for example, Ethernet_II, SNAP, or ArcNet) is identified in the PktType.entry, and it uses the REG_MULTI_SZ data type. **Table 6-3** lists the PktType entry and packet forms supported by NWLink.

Internal Network Number: The internal network number, also called a virtual network number, is another unique number that is used for internal routing purposes to identify a specific computer on the network. It is an eight-digit hexadecimal number that by default is given a value of **00000000**. You must change this when FPNW is installed on a Windows 2000 server, when NWLink is configured on multiple adapters in the computer, when there are several different frame types on one adapter, or if an application is using the **NetWare Service Advertising Protocol (SAP)** such as **SQL Server** and **SNA Server**.

Table 6-3	NWLink supports the following Pkt Type entries and packet forms
Value	**Packet form**
0	Ethernet_II
1	Ethernet_802.3
2	Ethernet_802.2
3	SNAP
4	ArcNet
FF (default)	Auto-detect

Figure 6-15 Using the ipxroute config command

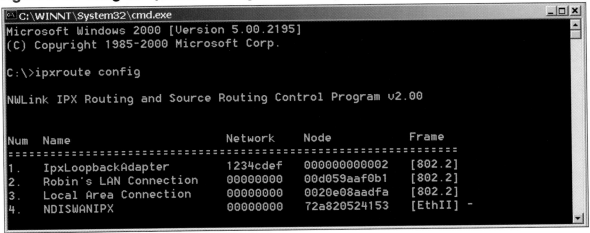

Figure 6-16 NWLink/SPX/NetBios Compatible Transport Protocol Properties dialog box

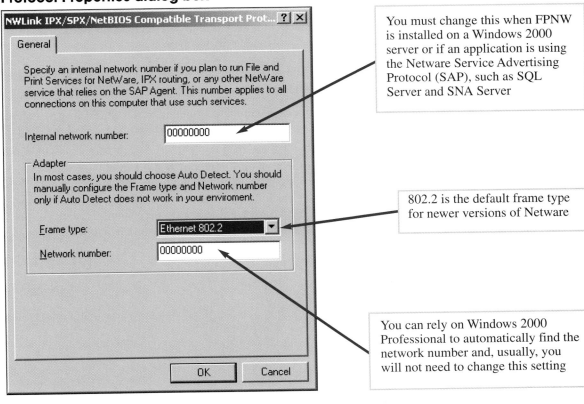

You must change this when FPNW is installed on a Windows 2000 server or if an application is using the Netware Service Advertising Protocol (SAP), such as SQL Server and SNA Server

802.2 is the default frame type for newer versions of Netware

You can rely on Windows 2000 Professional to automatically find the network number and, usually, you will not need to change this setting

skill 6

Introducing Other Protocols Supported by Windows 2000 Professional

exam objective

Basic knowledge

overview

In addition to the **TCP/IP** and **NWLink** protocol, Windows 2000 Professional supports several other protocols (**Figure 6-17**) such as:

◆ **NetBEUI (NetBios Enhanced User Interface)**
◆ **DLC (Data Link Control)**
◆ **AppleTalk**
◆ **Network Monitor Driver 2**

NetBEUI is an easy-to-install protocol that was originally used by peer-to-peer networks more than 20 years ago. Today, it is used to share resources in LANs of 20 to 200 computers. NetBEUI is smaller and faster than the newer protocols, but it is not a routable protocol, so therefore it is ineffectual for remote communications because it cannot send data packets across a router. NetBEUI is capable of communicating across bridged or switched networks; however, network size is limited both because it is non-routable and because it uses more broadcast traffic than other protocols. Communications in a NetBEUI environment use a flat naming space in which computer names cannot be reused because there are no subdivisions. This is the opposite of DNS, which, because it is hierarchical, allows computer names to be reused as long as they belong to different parent namespaces. Furthermore, in comparison to other protocols, NetBEUI creates heavy broadcast traffic because it depends on broadcasts to carry out functions such as registration and discovery.

Microsoft Data Link Control (DLC) is a non-routable protocol that is useful for connecting Windows 2000 computers to computers running the DLC protocol stack, such as IBM mainframe and minicomputers. It is also used to connect to some kinds of networked printers such as some Hewlett-Packard models with JetDirect network adapters. DLC only needs to be installed on the print server, not on each workstation that might send a print request. It runs in what is called "continuous mode", which means that until the transmission for a printing job is complete, a networked printer will be locked up and unavailable for use.

AppleTalk is used to enable computers running Windows 2000 Server to interact with computers running the Apple Macintosh OS. It is used on a Windows 2000 server, not on a Windows 2000 Professional computer.

The **Network Monitor Driver 2** protocol is used to collect statistics about the activity detected by the network card. These statistics are reported to, and can be viewed on, a Windows 2000 Server machine that is either running the Network Monitor Agent Service or the Systems Management Server. It is not a data transport protocol like the others, instead it facilitates the ability to capture data using the Network Monitor utility.

tip

DLC should not be used as the main method for communicating with Windows NT Server or NetWare networks.

Figure 6-17 Other protocols supported by Windows 2000

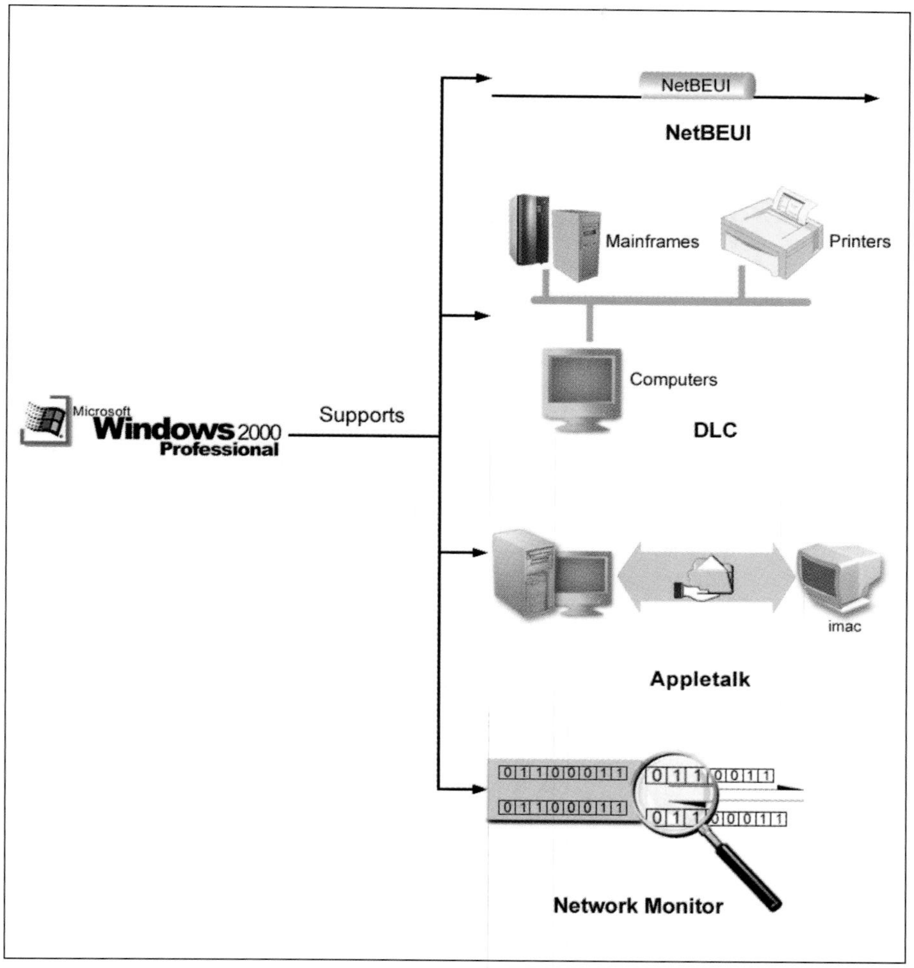

skill 6

Introducing Other Protocols Supported by Windows 2000 Professional (cont'd)

exam objective

Basic knowledge

more

Windows 2000 Professional supports several new protocols to increase authentication, encryption, and multilinking options, as shown in **(Figure 6-18)**. The new protocols are:

- ◆ Extensible Authentication Protocol (EAP)
- ◆ Remote Authentication Dial-in User Service (RADIUS)
- ◆ Internet Protocol Security (IPSec)
- ◆ Layer Two Tunneling Protocol (L2TP)
- ◆ Bandwidth Allocation Protocol (BAP)

Extensible Authentication Protocol (EAP): EAP performs arbitrary authentication of a dial-in connection and is an extension of the Point-to-Point Protocol (PPP). PPP works with Dial-Up, PPTP (Point-to-Point Tunneling Protocol), and L2TP clients. EAP uses the following to extend logon security services so that smart cards or other types of certificates can be used as part of the authentication process:

- ◆ **Generic token cards:** These are physical cards that provide passwords. They can handle several authentication methods, such as codes that change with each use.
- ◆ **MD5-CHAP (Message Digest 5 Challenge Handshake Authentication Protocol):** User names and passwords are encrypted with an MD5 algorithm using this protocol.
- ◆ **Transport Layer Security (TLS):** This protocol is used to support smart card authentication systems.

Remote Authentication Dial-in User Service (RADIUS): RADIUS is an authentication and accounting system used to facilitate the management of remote access services. It provides a suite of services designed to check user logon information to make sure it is correct in order to authorize access to a system. It is used by many ISPs to authenticate users as they dial in to the ISP. Logon data is forwarded to a RADIUS server, which verifies the data and authorizes access to the ISP system. The suite of services provided by RADIUS is referred to as **AAA** for authentication, authorization, and usage accounting. The protocol design is vendor-independent, reliable and highly scalable.

Internet Protocol Security (IPSec): To ensure secure communication over IP networks, the Internet Protocol Security (IPSec) is used. IPSec policies are used to configure IPSec security services, which provide a variable level of protection for most types of traffic in existing networks. Configuring IPSec policies can fulfill the security requirements for a user, group, application, domain, or global enterprise. You can create and manage IPSec policies using the **IP Security Policy Management** snap-in. This snap-in can be added to any custom console created with the **Microsoft Management Console**.

Layer Two Tunneling Protocol (L2TP): This is an Internet tunneling protocol used to create a channel through a network. L2TP is used with IPSec to provide a secure tunnel for the transfer of data. The encryption functions of IPSec can be used in conjunction with L2TP to create a secure VPN (Virtual Private Network). A VPN can also use only PPTP (Point-to-Point Tunneling Protocol), which provides encryption via PPP. PPP (Point-to-Point Protocol) is the default selection for dial-up connections because it is efficient, supports error-checking, and can be used on NetBEUI, TCP/IP, and IPX/SPX networks.

Bandwidth Allocation Protocol (BAP): This protocol is used when you use multilinking to combine phone lines and modems to optimize bandwidth. BAP and BACP (Bandwidth Allocation Control Protocol) are sometimes used interchangeably. They provide bandwidth-on-demand functionality and are PPP control protocols.

Figure 6-18 New protocols supported by Windows 2000 Professional

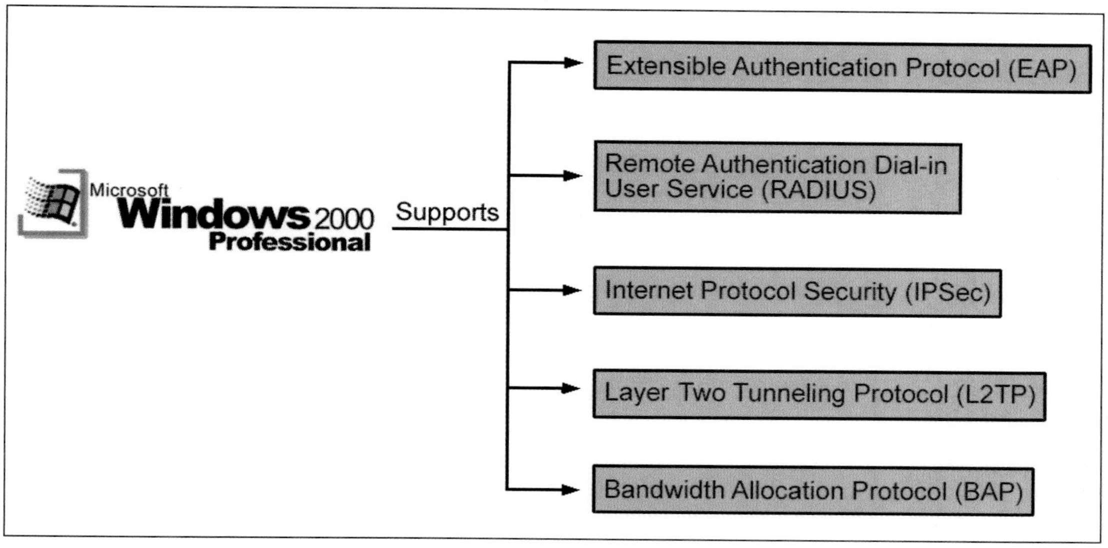

skill 7

Configuring Network Bindings

exam objective

Optimize and troubleshoot network performance.

overview

On a client computer that is using multiple protocols, you must set the **binding order** for the protocols. The binding order establishes which protocol should be used first when a network connection is initiated. Binding refers to an operational link between network layers, and it is the *client* computer that determines which protocol will be used to establish the connection. For example, if you most frequently use your computer to access a Microsoft network and the Internet, and only occasionally need to locate files on a Netware server (either 4.0 or versions that predate it) you will have both TCP/IP and NWLInk configured on your network adapter. Since your most frequent tasks involve the use of TCP/IP, you will position the protocols so that TCP/IP is the protocol of choice for the Client for Microsoft Networks (Workstation) service. However, if the client computer and the server most often accessed are on the same LAN and both use NetBEUI and TCP/IP, you will want NetBEUI to be the top protocol because NetBEUI is faster than TCP/IP.

how to

Configure the network bindings on your computer.

1. Right-click the **My Network Places** icon on the desktop and select the **Properties** command on the shortcut menu to open the **Network and Dial-up Connections** window (**Figure 6-19**).
2. Select the **Local Area Connection** icon, if necessary.
3. Open the **Advanced** menu and select the **Advanced Settings** command to open the **Advanced Settings** dialog box.
4. In the **Bindings for Local Area Connection** scrolling list box, under **Client for Microsoft Networks,** select the **NetBEUI Protocol.** Click 🔼 once to move it above the **NWLink IPX/SPX/NetBIOS Compatible Transport Protocol.** (If NetBEUI is not installed, go to step 5.)
5. Select **Internet Protocol (TCP/IP).** Click 🔽 once to position it under the **NetBEUI Protocol (Figure 6-20).** (If NetBEUI is not installed, place TCP/IP above NWLink.)
6. Click ⬚ OK ⬚ to apply the changes.
7. Close the Network and Dial-up Connections window.

more

You should disable any adapter bindings that you do not use to increase the speed of your connections and the security of your system. Simply clear the check boxes for bindings you do not need. Use the up and down arrow keys to correctly position the bindings in the protocol priority order you want used. This will also increase system efficiency because the operating system will not attempt to create unsuitable connections.

Figure 6-19 Network and Dial-up Connections window

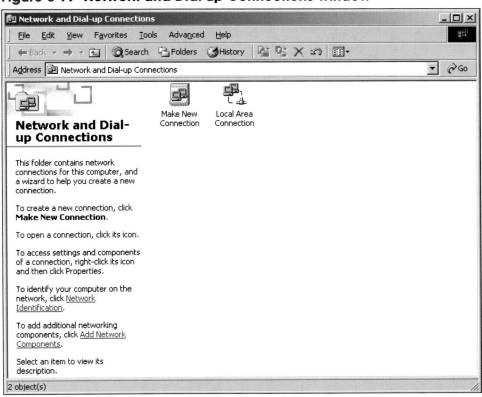

Figure 6-20 Advanced Settings dialog box

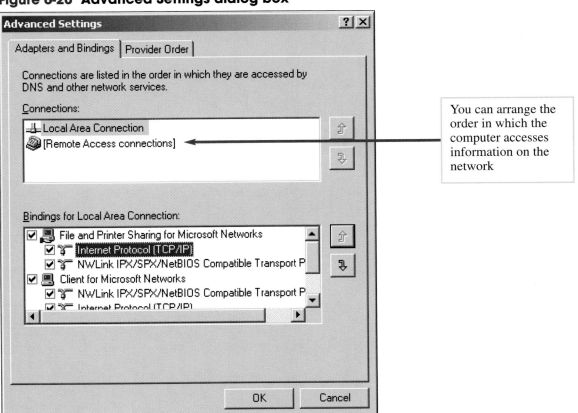

You can arrange the order in which the computer accesses information on the network

skill 8

Optimizing and Troubleshooting Network Performance

exam objective

Optimize and troubleshoot network performance.

overview

Communications between computers in a network generate network traffic. Increases in network traffic may adversely affect the performance of a network **(Figure 6-21)**. Network administrators must follow certain guidelines in order to optimize network performance. Some useful guidelines for accomplishing this and for troubleshooting common network problems are given below:

◆ If the computers on a network are communicating over Token Ring, FDDI, or switched Ethernet networks, you can balance network traffic by distributing client connections across multiple network adapters.

◆ Use adapters with the highest bandwidth available.

◆ Use adapters that support task-offloading capabilities.

◆ If your network uses multiple protocols, bind each protocol on a different adapter and make sure that the most efficient protocols are used, preferably ones that minimize broadcasts.

◆ To reduce congestion on the server, divide your network into multiple subnets or segments. Attach the server to each segment with a separate adapter.

◆ Do not reorder the server bindings. The server accepts incoming connections based on the protocol used by the client computer.

◆ Promote the use of offline files and folders for working on network applications. Offline folders make use of client-side caching and therefore reduce network traffic.

Figure 6-21 Increases in network traffic may adversely affect the performance of a network

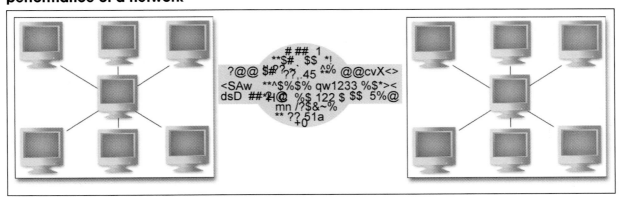

Summary

- TCP/IP is a set of protocols that enable you to route messages over a network.
- TCP/IP defines the rules for connecting networks to each other and for communication between computers on a network.
- TCP/IP consists of four layers: Network Interface, Internet, Transport, and Application.
- DHCP (Dynamic Host Configuration Protocol) provides configuration information to any standard TCP/IP DHCP-compatible client including Windows, Linux, and every other mainstream operating system on the market. The DHCP server's job is to dynamically allocate IP addresses. This simplifies the administration of the TCP/IP configuration because it automates the process of assigning IP addresses to clients.
- If a DHCP client cannot locate a DHCP server, automatic private IP addressing (APIPA) is used to randomly choose an IP address from a private APIPA address series that is not in use on the Internet. In this way, computers on a LAN where there is no DHCP server, or on a network where the DHCP server is down, can still be assigned an IP address and communicate with other computers.
- You may need to add a static IP address to selected computers on a network, such as application servers and the DHCP server.
- The IANA reserves all IP addresses that fall in the range of 169.254.0.0 to169.254.255.255.
- The Ping utility is used to test the TCP/IP configuration on your system.
- The ipconfig utility is used to confirm the TCP/IP parameters on a host computer.
- ARP is responsible for finding the MAC address associated with a known IP address.
- A MAC address is a unique 48-bit or 6-byte number, usually represented as 12 hexadecimal digits. It is also referred to as a hardware address, physical address, or Ethernet address.
- When communication is initiated between a system and a host for which the system does not have a MAC address, the system sends an ARP broadcast packet asking for a MAC address that corresponds to a local IP address or for the MAC address of the default gateway, if it is a remote host.
- Netstat displays the TCP/IP protocol statistics and the network connections related to it.
- Route displays and modifies the local routing table.
- Hostname returns the host name of a local computer for authentication by the RCP, RSH, and REXEC utilities.
- File Transfer Protocol (FTP) is used to transfer files between a computer running Windows 2000 Professional and a TCP/IP host running server software and FTP. It also provides directory and file handling services such as listing directory contents and deleting files and selecting file formats.
- Trivial File Transfer Protocol (TFTP), a simpler form of FTP, is used to transfer files between a computer running Windows 2000 Professional and a TCP/IP host running server software and TFTP. TFTP uses the User Datagram Protocol (UDP) and thus includes no security features, acknowledgements, or data retransmissions. It is often used by servers to boot diskless workstations or routers.
- Telnet is a terminal emulation protocol that runs over TCP/IP. When you run Telnet from a client machine and connect to a server on the network, you can enter commands which will be carried out as if you were performing them directly on the server terminal.
- Telnet is often used to manage a remote Web server. It is used to control the server and to communicate with other servers on the network. You can also connect to a computer on the Internet that supports Telnet to run programs from that computer. Telnet was the first way in which remote access was accomplished.
- RCP copies files between a computer running Windows 2000 Professional and a host supporting RCP.
- RSH runs commands on a Unix host.
- Finger is a utility, supported by UNIX computers, that is used to retrieve information about users, including their user name and how long they have been logged on.
- NWLink is used by Microsoft computers to access resources on Netware 4.0 servers and on servers running Netware versions that predate 4.0.
- NWLink also helps computers to communicate with network devices that use IPX/SPX socket interfaces.
- NWLink supports Winsock and NetBIOS over IPX networking APIs.
- You must install either the CSNW redirector or Novell Client for Windows 2000 on a Windows 2000 Professional machine in order to access file and print resources on a NetWare server.
- You must install FPNW to enable NetWare clients to use file and print resources on a computer running Windows 2000 Server.
- You configure three components when you install the NWLink transport protocol: Frame type, Network number, and Internal Network number.
- In addition to TCP/IP and NWLink, Windows 2000 Professional supports protocols such as NetBEUI, DLC and AppleTalk, as well as the Network Monitor Driver 2.
- The Network Monitor Driver 2 protocol is used to collect statistics about the activity detected by the network card. These statistics are reported to, and can be viewed on, a Windows 2000 Server machine that is either running the Network Monitor Agent Service or the Systems Management Server. It is not a data transport protocol

like the others; instead, it facilitates the ability to capture data using the Network Monitor utility.

◆ To increase authentication, encryption, and multilinking, Windows 2000 Professional uses some new protocols such as EAP, RADIUS, IPSec, L2TP, and BAP.

◆ Network binding links network adapter card drivers, protocols, and services by establishing an initial connection between them, allowing communication to occur at different levels.

◆ You can specify a binding order for the various protocols to optimize network performance.

Key Terms

AppleTalk
Application layer
Address Resolution Protocol (ARP)
Binding order
Connectionless Communication
Default gateways
Data Link Control (DLC)
DNS (Domain Name System)
Dynamic Host Configuration Protocol (DHCP) service
Extensible Authentication Protocol (EAP)
File Transfer Protocol (FTP)
File and Print Services for NetWare (FPNW)
Finger
Frame type
Host ID
Host Name
Hostname
Internet Control Message Protocol (ICMP)

Internet Group Management Protocol (IGMP)
Internet layer
Internal network number
Internet Protocol (IP)
Internet Protocol Security (IPSec)
IP address
Ipconfig
Layer Two Tunneling Protocol (L2TP)
Media Access Control (MAC) address
Multicasting
Nbtstat
Netstat
NetBEUI
NetBIOS over IPX
Network ID
Network Interface layer
Network Monitor Driver 2
Network number
NWLink
Ping
PktType

Remote Authentication Dial-in User Service (RADIUS)
Remote Copy Protocol (RCP)
Remote shell (RSH)
Route
Router
Routing table
Subnet mask
TCP/IP host
Tracert
Transmission Control Protocol (TCP)
Transmission Control Protocol/Internet Protocol (TCP/IP)
Transport layer
Telnet
Trivial File Transfer Protocol (TFTP)
User Datagram Protocol (UDP)
WINS (Windows Internet Naming Service)
Winsock

Test Yourself

1. Which of the following protocols is responsible for providing the addressing scheme for networks and for the Internet?
   a. TCP
   b. IP
   c. UDP
   d. DHCP

2. Which of the following is a function of the Internet layer in the TCP/IP conceptual model?
   a. Responsible for placing TCP/IP packets on the network medium and receiving TCP/IP packets off the network medium
   b. Determines the route the data packets will take
   c. Enables applications to gain access to the network
   d. Makes sure that messages are delivered in the correct sequence without errors, and with no data duplication or data loss

3. Which of the following protocols enables hosts to exchange status and error information over the network?
   a. UDP
   b. ICMP
   c. IGMP
   d. ARP

4. The Internet Group Management Protocol provides:
   a. Multicasting.
   b. Automatic IP address assignment.
   c. Connectionless packet delivery.
   d. Passwords for accounts.

5. Which protocol ensures the delivery of data packets in the correct sequence to the destination computer?
   a. Transmission Control Protocol
   b. User Datagram Protocol
   c. Address Resolution Protocol
   d. Internet Control Message Protocol

6. Which of the following utilities enables you to check the route a packet is following to reach its destination point?
   a. Netstat
   b. Route
   c. Tracert
   d. ARP

7. Which of the following protocols will you use to enable clients running Microsoft operating systems to access resources on NetWare 4.0 or earlier servers?
   a. AppleTalk
   b. DLC
   c. NWLink
   d. NetBEUI

8. The Ping utility is used to:
   a. Test TCP/IP configurations and identify connection failures.
   b. Validate the host name for the local computer.
   c. Display protocol statistics and current TCP/IP connections using NBT.
   d. Check the route a packet is following to reach its destination point.

9. Transport Layer Security is used by EAP to:
   a. Be the authentication standard when a smart card is in use.
   b. Provide passwords for accounts.
   c. Encrypt user names and passwords.
   d. Create an encrypted tunnel through a network.

10. Which of the following is used to divide the network ID from the host ID?
    a. IP address
    b. Subnet mask
    c. Default gateway
    d. BAP

11. Which of the following is used to optimize network performance?
    a. Frame type
    b. Binding order
    c. Network Monitor Driver 2
    d. Subnet mask

Projects: On Your Own

1. Verify the configuration of a computer.
   a. Open the **Command Prompt.**
   b. Type **ipconfig/all | more** at the Command Prompt.
   c. Press **[Enter]**.

2. Install NWLink on your computer.
   a. Access the **Network and Dial-up Connections** window.
   b. Access the **Local Area Connection Properties** dialog box.
   c. Display the **Select Network Component Type** dialog box.
   d. Select the **Protocol** option from the dialog box and access the **Select Network Protocol** dialog box.
   e. Select the **NWLink IPX/SPX/NetBIOS Compatible Transport Protocol** option from the Network Protocol section.

   f. Apply the changes.
   g. Close the Local Area Connections Properties dialog box.
   h. Close the Network and Dial-up Connections window.

3. Configure the network bindings in your computer.
   a. Access the **Network and Dial-up Connections** window.
   b. Access the **Advanced Settings** dialog box.
   c. Select the **Internet Protocol (TCP/IP)** check box from the Advanced Settings dialog box.
   d. Apply changes.
   e. Close all the windows.

Problem Solving Scenarios

Your company, Bay View Architects, has just landed a large project from a client in Philadelphia. To service this client, Bay View has purchased a new print server. Outline in a memo the specific steps you would take to assign a static IP address to this print server.

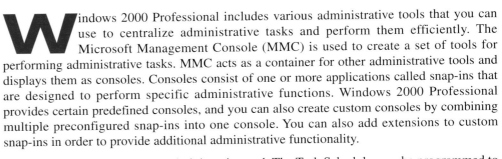

LESSON

7

Performing Administrative Tasks

Windows 2000 Professional includes various administrative tools that you can use to centralize administrative tasks and perform them efficiently. The Microsoft Management Console (MMC) is used to create a set of tools for performing administrative tasks. MMC acts as a container for other administrative tools and displays them as consoles. Consoles consist of one or more applications called snap-ins that are designed to perform specific administrative functions. Windows 2000 Professional provides certain predefined consoles, and you can also create custom consoles by combining multiple preconfigured snap-ins into one console. You can also add extensions to custom snap-ins in order to provide additional administrative functionality.

The Task Scheduler is another administrative tool. The Task Scheduler can be programmed to carry out certain routine tasks, such as performing a backup every Friday or a virus check on all systems at the start of each day. You can use the Task Scheduler to schedule system tasks and programs, such as the Disk Cleanup utility, to run at specific time intervals.

Goals

In this lesson, you will learn about the MMC console and snap-ins. You will also learn to create a custom console, add an extension snap-in to a console, and schedule administrative tasks.

Lesson 7	Performing Administrative Tasks	
Skill	**Exam 70-210 Objective**
1. Introducing the Microsoft Management Console	Basic knowledge
2. Creating Custom Consoles	Basic knowledge
3. Adding Extensions to Snap-Ins	Basic knowledge
4. Working with Scheduled Tasks	Configure, manage, and troubleshoot the Task Scheduler.
5. Troubleshooting Tasks	Configure, manage, and troubleshoot the Task Scheduler.

Requirements

To complete the skills in this lesson, you will need a computer with Windows 2000 Professional installed on it.

skill 1

Introducing the Microsoft Management Console

exam objective

Basic knowledge

overview

The primary administrative tool in Windows 2000 Professional is the **Microsoft Management Console (MMC),** which is the foundation for all of the management tools in the operating system. The MMC, which provides a simple, uniform, user-friendly interface, is used to manage hardware, software, and network components. It provides a framework for creating, saving, and opening a collection of tools, called **consoles.** A console consists of management applications called **snap-ins** that integrate applications, information, and views of your network and enable you to perform administrative tasks. For example, the Computer Management console combines various administration utilities into a single console tree. Using this console, you can manage a local or remote computer and view the list of users connected to the computer. You can also start and stop system services such as the Task Scheduler and view device configurations.

The MMC management interface is used to create consoles with which you can easily perform administration tasks. The benefits of the MMC are listed below:

◆ Provides a single interface from which to administer tasks and troubleshoot problems. For example, the **Disk Management** snap-in is used to create, delete, and format partitions on a basic disk and lets you create simple, spanned, or striped volumes on dynamic disks.

◆ You can use consoles to perform administrative tasks on all of the computers in a network through a central machine as long as you have administrative access to each of the target computers.

◆ Snap-ins can administer tasks and troubleshoot problems on remote computers. Most, but not all snap-ins, such as the **Remote Storage** snap-in, are designed for remote administration.

◆ You can create custom consoles to perform the tasks you most often undertake. Your custom consoles are saved as .msc files which can be reused on the computer on which you create them or transferred to other computers.

The MMC has two types of console modes: **Author mode** and **User mode**. You choose between these two modes to designate the operating mode and functionality for each console.

Author mode: In this mode, you have complete access to the MMC functionality of the saved console. You can save the console, view all portions of the console tree, add or remove snap-ins, and create new windows. Author mode is the default mode for new consoles that you save.

User mode: When you save a console in User mode you can distribute it to other administrators. There are three User mode types: Full Access; Limited Access, Multiple Windows; and Limited Access, Single Window. **Table 7-1** provides a description of the three user mode types.

To set the console mode, open the **Console** menu and click the **Options** command to open the **Options** dialog box. Select the console mode in the **Console Mode** list box. Even if you save a console in one of the User modes, you can right click it and select **Author** on the context menu at any time to open it in Author mode.

Table 7-1 *User Mode Types*

Full Access mode	Allows users to: • View the entire console tree. • Add and delete new windows. Prevents users from: • Adding/removing snap-ins. • Changing console properties.
Limited Access, Multiple Windows	Allows users to: • Create new windows. • Add and delete new windows. • Access only those areas that were visible when the console was saved. Prevents users from: • Closing existing windows. • Changing console properties.
Limited Access, Single Window	Allows users to: • Access only one window. Prevents users from: • Opening new windows. • Gaining access to other portions of a console tree.

skill 2

Creating Custom Consoles

exam objective

Basic knowledge

overview

Consoles contain snap-ins that facilitate management of system services, processes, and applications. Each console is saved with an **.msc** extension. Note that some important snap-ins, including the Group Policy, Security Templates, and Security Configuration and Analysis snap-ins, are not supplied in any of the preconfigured consoles. You will have to build a custom console in order to use them.

Each console window is divided into a **console tree** and a **details pane**. The console tree organizes the snap-ins that are available in the console in hierarchical order. The details pane displays the contents of the snap-in that is selected in the console tree.

Windows 2000 Professional supports two types of consoles, preconfigured and custom. The predefined consoles are installed on your system during the installation of Windows 2000 Professional. Preconfigured consoles contain commonly used snap-ins, such as the Computer Management, Event Viewer, and Local Security snap-ins, which are used to perform administrative tasks. You cannot modify a preconfigured console or add any new snap-ins to it.

You can also create your own **custom consoles** by combining multiple preconfigured snap-ins into one console. For example, you can create the **Administering Events** custom console by combining the **Computer Management** and **Component Services** snap-ins. You can then view and manage all of the services running on a particular system rather than searching for specific services.

After you create custom consoles, you can:

◆ Save them and use them in the future.
◆ Distribute them to other administrators to meet their administrative needs.
◆ Use them to carry out remote administration. This centralizes and unifies administrative tasks.

tip

When you add items to the console tree, they are displayed under the console root.

tip

Custom consoles are saved in the **Administrative Tools** folder by default. The preconfigured MMCs are also saved in this folder, which can be accessed from the Control Panel.

how to

Create a custom console named **Administering Events** and add the **Computer Management** snap-in to it to manage your computer.

1. Click [🏴Start] and then click the **Run** command to open the **Run** dialog box.
2. Type **MMC** in the **Open** list box (**Figure 7-1**).
3. Click [OK]. MMC is initialized and displays the default empty console.
4. Open the **Console** menu and click the **Add/Remove Snap-in** command to open the **Add/Remove Snap-in** dialog box with the **Standalone** tab active by default. The **Console root** option is selected by default in the **Snap-ins added to** list box.
5. Click [Add...] to open the **Add Standalone Snap-in** dialog box. This dialog box lists all available snap-ins.
6. Click the **Computer Management** snap-in to select it to be added to the custom console (**Figure 7-2**).
7. Click [Add]. The **Computer Management** dialog box prompts you to select the computer you want the snap-in to manage (**Figure 7-3**).
8. Most of the time you will select the local computer. Make sure that the **Local computer: (the computer this console is running on)** option button is selected.
9. Click [Finish] to close the **Computer Management** dialog box.
10. In the Add Standalone Snap-in dialog box, click the **Component Services** snap-in and then click [Add]. This adds this snap-in to the Add/Remove Snap-in dialog box.

tip

The Console1 window is the default MMC window. It does not contain any snap-ins.

Figure 7-1 Opening a blank MMC

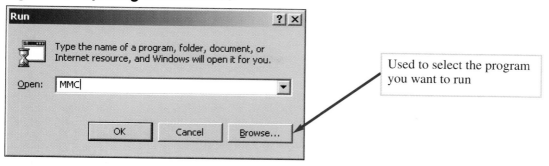

Used to select the program you want to run

Figure 7-2 Windows 2000 stand-alone snap-ins

Select the snap-in that you want to add to the console

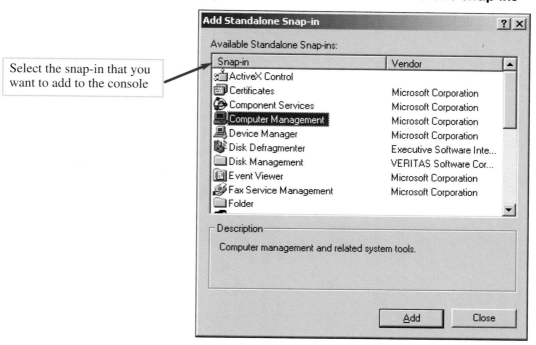

Figure 7-3 Selecting the computer to manage

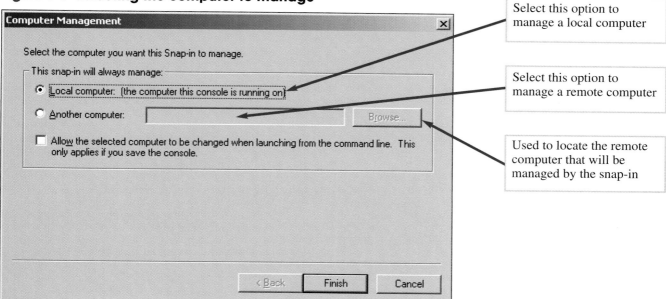

Select this option to manage a local computer

Select this option to manage a remote computer

Used to locate the remote computer that will be managed by the snap-in

skill 2

Creating Custom Consoles *(cont'd)*

exam objective

Basic knowledge

how to

11. Click [Close] to close the Add Standalone Snap-in dialog box.
12. Click [OK] to close the **Add/Remove Snap-in** dialog box.
13. In order to use the console again, you must save it. Open the **Console** menu and click the **Save As** command to open the **Save As** dialog box.
14. To save the console on the desktop, select **Desktop** in the **Save in** list box.
15. Type **Administering Events** in the **File Name** text box (**Figure 7-4**).
16. Click [Save]. The console name appears in the MMC title bar (**Figure 7-5**).
17. **Close** the **Administering Events** console. The Administering Events icon is added to the desktop (**Figure 7-6**).

more

Custom consoles are, by default, stored in the Administrative Tools folder. In contrast to Windows 2000 Server, the Start menu for Windows 2000 Professional does not contain a shortcut to the Administrative Tools folder. However, you can add the folder to the Start menu by dragging the Control Panel icon to the Start menu. When you move an icon you are prompted to create a shortcut. You can also right-click the taskbar and click **Properties** on the shortcut menu to open the **Taskbar and Start Menu Properties** dialog box. On the **Advanced** page, select the **Display Administrative Tools** check box at the bottom of the dialog box. (Alternatively, click **Start**, point to **Settings**, and click the **Taskbar & Start Menu** command to open the dialog box.)

Figure 7-4 Saving a console on the desktop

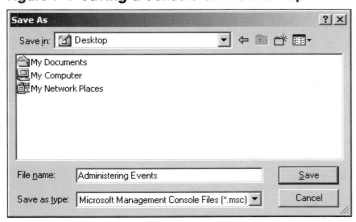

Figure 7-5 New Administering Events console

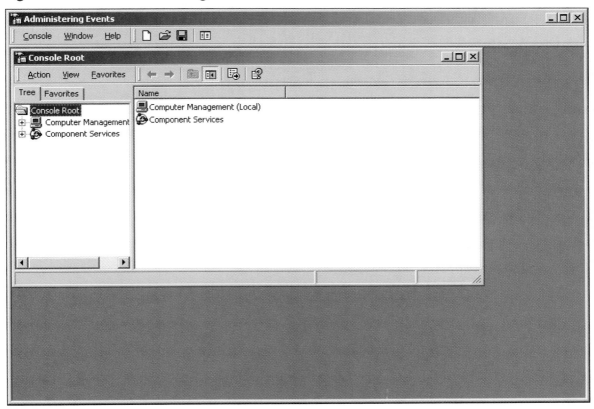

Figure 7-6 Administering Events icon on the desktop

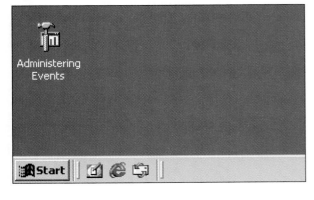

skill 3

Adding Extensions to Snap-Ins

exam objective

Basic knowledge

overview

MMC provides an interface and the architecture for adding snap-ins to a console. You can combine snap-ins from various vendors, such as Microsoft or ISVs, and those created by in-house developers, into a single console. MMC acts as a common link between the snap-ins provided by different vendors. Windows 2000 Professional supports two types of snap-ins:

◆ **Stand-alone snap-ins:** These snap-ins are used to perform administration tasks. They are simply referred to as snap-ins.

◆ **Extension snap-ins:** These are referred to as extensions. Extension snap-ins expand the administrative functionality of other snap-ins. For example, you can add the **Event Viewer Extension** snap-in to the **Computer Management** snap-in to view the task processing results on a system. Extension snap-ins are designed to work with one or more stand-alone snap-ins or other extension snap-ins, depending on the function of the parent snap-in. An extension provides functionality only when you are in the parent snap-in. When a snap-in is added to a console, all the available extensions of that snap-in are added to the console by default. However, you can remove an extension from a snap-in as needed. When you add an extension to a snap-in, Windows 2000 Professional displays only those extensions that are compatible with the stand-alone snap-in.

You can add the preconfigured consoles for Windows 2000 Server to Windows 2000 Professional by running the **Adminpak.msi** program. This application can be found on the Windows 2000 Server installation CD.

tip

The complete set of standard Windows 2000 snap-ins is included in Windows 2000 Server. A smaller set of snap-ins is included in Windows 2000 Professional.

how to

Add the **Event Viewer Extension** snap-in to the **Administering Events** custom console.

1. Double-click **the Administering Events** icon on the desktop to open the **Administering Events** console.
2. Open the **Console** menu and click the **Add/Remove Snap-in** command to open the **Add/Remove Snap-in** dialog box.
3. Click the **Extensions** tab to display the extension snap-ins available in the Administering Events console.
4. In the **Snap-ins that can be extended** list box, select **Computer Management**.
5. Clear the **Add all extensions** check box.
6. Clear all of the check boxes except the **Event Viewer Extension** option in the **Available extensions** list box (**Figure 7-7**).
7. Click   OK   to add the **Event Viewer Extension** snap-in to the console tree.
8. Expand the **Computer Management (Local)** node. Expand the **System Tools** node. The Event Viewer extension has been added to the Computer Management snap-in (**Figure 7-8**).
9. **Close** the **Administering Events** window. The **Microsoft Management Console** message box prompts you to save the changes.
10. Click   Yes   to save the console settings to the Administering Events console window.

Figure 7-7 Adding snap-in extensions

Select the snap-in to which you are adding the extension

Select the extension to be added to the snap-in

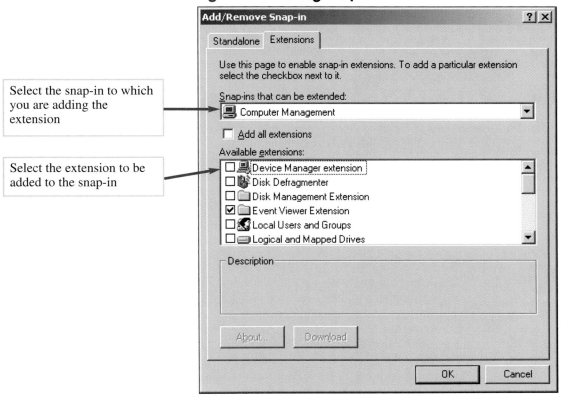

Figure 7-8 Adding snap-in extensions

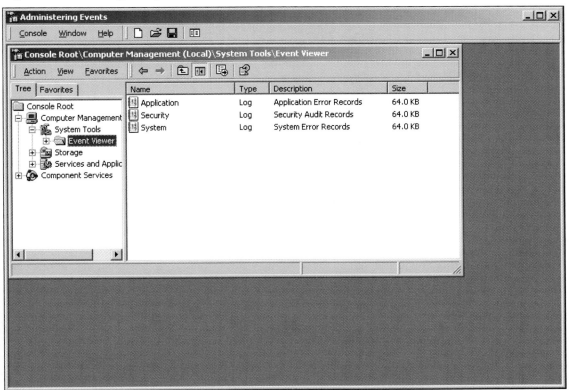

skill 4

Working with Scheduled Tasks

exam objective

Configure, manage, and troubleshoot the Task Scheduler.

overview

As a network administrator, you will need to perform certain tasks at regular intervals. For example, you might run the backup application on the first Monday of every month. You can use **Scheduled Tasks** to run any application, script or document at specified time intervals. Virus scans, disk cleanups and other administrative utilities can be configured to run daily, weekly, monthly, at system startup, at logon, or when the system is idle. You can also use Scheduled Tasks to:

tip

Scheduled tasks are saved in the **Scheduled Tasks** folder in the **Control Panel.**

◆ Schedule maintenance utilities at specific time intervals.
◆ Customize the running of a task at a specified time.
◆ Stop a scheduled task from running.
◆ Run tasks on remote computers.

The following options can be configured in the Scheduled Task Wizard:

◆ **Application:** You can select the program you want to schedule from a list of applications that are registered with Windows 2000 Professional. You can also specify any program or batch file that is available on the network.
◆ **Task Name:** You can give the scheduled task a logical name. For example, you can name the task that starts the virus check utility, Virus Check.
◆ **Frequency:** You can specify the number of times the task should be performed by Windows 2000 Professional and whether the task should be performed daily, weekly, monthly, one time only, when the computer starts, or when you log on.
◆ **Time and Date:** You can specify the start time and start date for the task. Where appropriate, you can also specify the days on which the task should be repeated.
◆ **Name and Password:** You can enter a user name and password and specify that a particular task be run under the security settings for that user.

The **Task Scheduler** also includes some advanced options that can be set in the **Properties** dialog box for the scheduled task **(Figure 7-9)**. **Table 7-2** lists the tabs in the Properties dialog box and their descriptions.

how to

Configure your system to run the **Backup** application on the first **Monday** of every month at **9:00 AM**.

1. Click **Start**, point to **Settings,** and click the **Control Panel** command to open the Control Panel window.
2. Double-click the **Scheduled Tasks** icon to open the Scheduled Tasks window.
3. Double-click the **Add Scheduled Task** icon to open the **Scheduled Task Wizard**.
4. Click **Next >**. A list appears showing the programs you can schedule.
5. Scroll down and select the **Backup** option to schedule the backup application **(Figure 7-10)**.
6. Click **Next >** to open the next **Scheduled Task Wizard** screen.
7. Type **Running Backup** in the **Type a name for this task** text box.
8. In the **Perform this task** section, click the **Monthly** option button and then click **Next >** **(Figure 7-11)**.
9. Type **9:00 AM** in the **Start time** spin box. You can also use the spin arrows to set the time.

Table 7-2 Advanced Properties of the Task Scheduler

Task	The Task tab allows you to configure command-line programs that run tasks. You can also enter information or comments about the task, assign a different user and password to run the task, or disable the task by clearing the check box.
Schedule	Using the Schedule tab, you can set multiple schedules for a particular task or change when a task is scheduled to run.
Settings	On the Settings tab, you can change the options that affect the execution of a task. For example, you can specify that the task be run only when the computer is idle, or you can specify that the task be disabled if the computer starts in the battery mode.
Security	The Security tab is only present on an NTFS partition. Normally Scheduled Tasks can be managed only by administrators, but you can assign tasks to other users who will need permissions to run the task. The Access Control List (ACL) contains a list of all users who can manage the task.

Figure 7-9 Running Backup dialog box

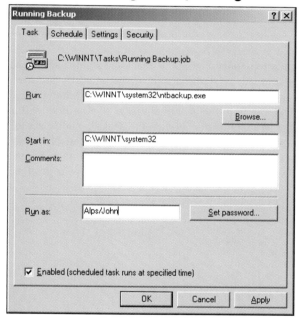

Figure 7-10 Scheduling a task

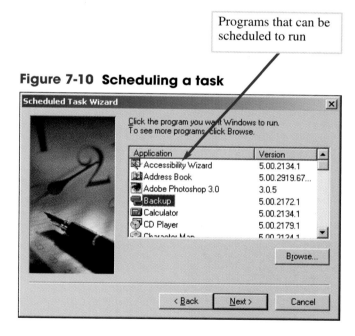

Programs that can be scheduled to run

Figure 7-11 Setting the name and frequency for the task

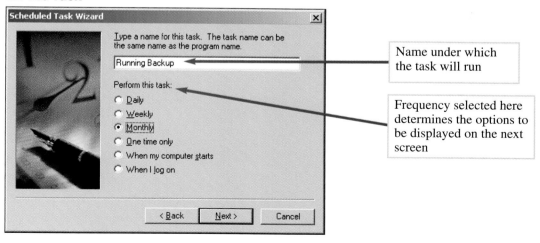

Name under which the task will run

Frequency selected here determines the options to be displayed on the next screen

skill 4

Working with Scheduled Tasks (cont'd)

exam objective   Configure, manage, and troubleshoot the Task Scheduler.

how to

10. Click the **The** option button. By default, the Wizard displays **the first Monday** of each month option. Click [Next >] **(Figure 7-12)**.
11. The wizard displays the name of the user who is currently logged on to the system. Enter the password for the user account in the **Enter the password** text box. Re-type the password in the **Confirm password** text box **(Figure 7-13)**. You can specify a user account and password that is different from the administrative account that you used to log on as long as that user is a member of either the **Backup Operators** or **Administrators** group. Only members of these groups have the right to perform backups.
12. Click [Next >]. A summary of the settings you have entered for the Backup application is displayed **(Figure 7-14)**.
13. Click [Finish] to add the **Running Backup** task to the list of scheduled tasks. The task is saved with a **.job** file extension and added to the **Scheduled Task** window.

more

You cannot schedule, run, or modify a task if the Task Scheduler service is stopped. You can use the **Services** snap-in in the **Administrative Tools** window to check the status of the Task Scheduler service. The service can be stopped, started, paused, or resumed by the user. Alternatively, you can check which services are running in the Computer Management console. The Computer Management console is in the Administrative Tools folder in the Control Panel. You can also right-click the **My Computer** icon on the desktop and select the **Manage** command on the shortcut menu to open the **Computer Management** console. In the **details** pane, double-click the **Services and Applications** node to display its contents. Double-click the **Services** snap-in to view all the services that are running on your machine and their status.

Figure 7-12 Selecting the time and day for the task

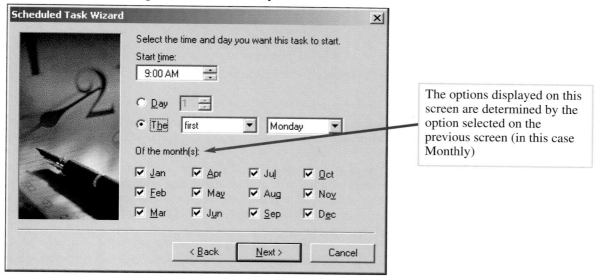

The options displayed on this screen are determined by the option selected on the previous screen (in this case Monthly)

Figure 7-13 Specifying the user account details

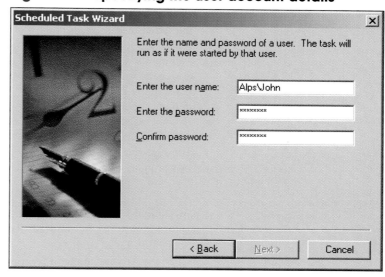

Figure 7-14 Summary of the scheduled task

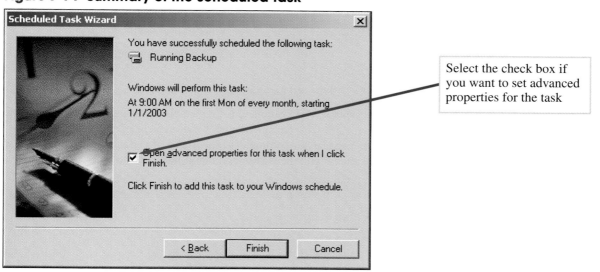

Select the check box if you want to set advanced properties for the task

skill 5 *Troubleshooting Tasks*

exam objective

Configure, manage, and troubleshoot the Task Scheduler.

overview

If you find that the Task Scheduler service is not functioning properly and that scheduled tasks are not running as programmed, you can explore several possible reasons. Some troubleshooting measures are given below:

◆ Incorrect time/date setting on the computer. The system checks the date and time on the local computer before starting a task. If the date or time settings on the computer are different from the actual date and time, the task will not run on schedule. You can check the system date and time in the system tray. When you double-click the clock (**Figure 7-15**), the **Date/Time Properties** dialog box opens. You can correct the time, if necessary, in the Date/Time Properties dialog box (**Figure 7-16**).

◆ The path for the tool or program that is supposed to be launched is not correct. You can check the path for the task by right-clicking the task in the **Scheduled Tasks** window and clicking **Properties** on the shortcut menu to open the **Properties** dialog box for the task. Here, you can check to see if the displayed path is correct.

◆ The Task Scheduler service has been stopped or paused. You can check this by opening the **Advanced** menu in the Scheduled Tasks window. If the Task Scheduler service has been stopped, the Advanced menu will display the **Start Using Task Scheduler** command. Usually the Advanced menu displays the **Stop Using Task Scheduler** command because the service runs by default. If the Task Scheduler service has been paused, the Advanced menu will display the **Continue Task Scheduler** command. By default, the menu displays the **Pause Task Scheduler** command.

◆ If you create several scheduled tasks and all but one of them runs, you may have a user rights conflict. When you enter a user name and password in the Scheduled Task Wizard, you must be sure that this user has the right to perform the specific system task. Many tasks require administrative rights.

tip

The system tray is the toolbar in the right corner of the taskbar.

how to

Troubleshoot the **Running Backup** task.

1. Double-click the **Scheduled Tasks** icon in the **Control Panel** window to open the Scheduled Tasks window.
2. Open the **Advanced** menu (**Figure 7-17**) and click the **Stop Using Task Scheduler** command to stop the Task Scheduler service.
3. Right-click the **Running Backup** task and click **Run** on the context menu.
4. A message box informs you that the service is currently stopped and that no services will run unless it is started. Click [Yes] to start the Task Scheduler service (**Figure 7-18**).
5. Close the Task Scheduler.

more

The other commands on the **Advanced** menu in the Scheduled Tasks window are:

◆ **Notify Me of Missed Tasks:** This command is toggled off by default. When you activate this command a check mark will indicate that the service has been turned on.

◆ **AT Service Account:** You use this command to specify the user account that will be used for all tasks that are created with the AT.exe command-line utility (discussed below).

Figure 7-15 The system tray

Figure 7-16 Date/Time Properties dialog box

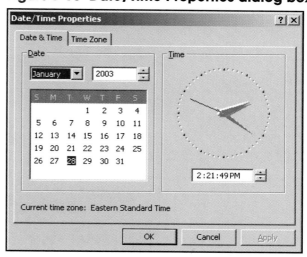

Figure 7-17 Stopping the Task Scheduler service

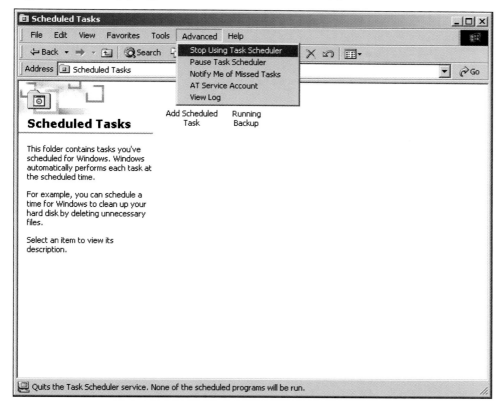

Figure 7-18 Restarting the Task Scheduler service

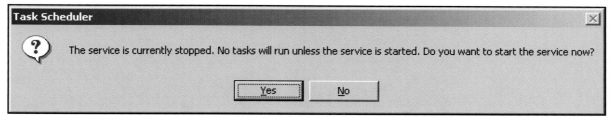

skill 5

Troubleshooting Tasks (cont'd)

exam objective

Configure, manage, and troubleshoot the Task Scheduler.

more

◆ **View Log:** This command is used to open **SchedLgU.Txt** in Notepad (**Figure 7-19**). This file contains the actions of the Scheduled Tasks utility and can be used to troubleshoot problems. Specific error messages will be recorded when a task fails to execute.

The command-line version of the Scheduled Tasks tool is **AT.exe**. When you create tasks using the command-line tool, those tasks must all run under the account that you specify in the AT Service Account Configuration dialog box (AT Service Account command on the Advanced menu). The graphical tool is more user-friendly and you can run different tasks under different user accounts. To learn about the syntax for the AT command, type: **at /?** at the command line (**Figure 7-20**).

Figure 7-19 SchedLgU.Txt file in Notepad

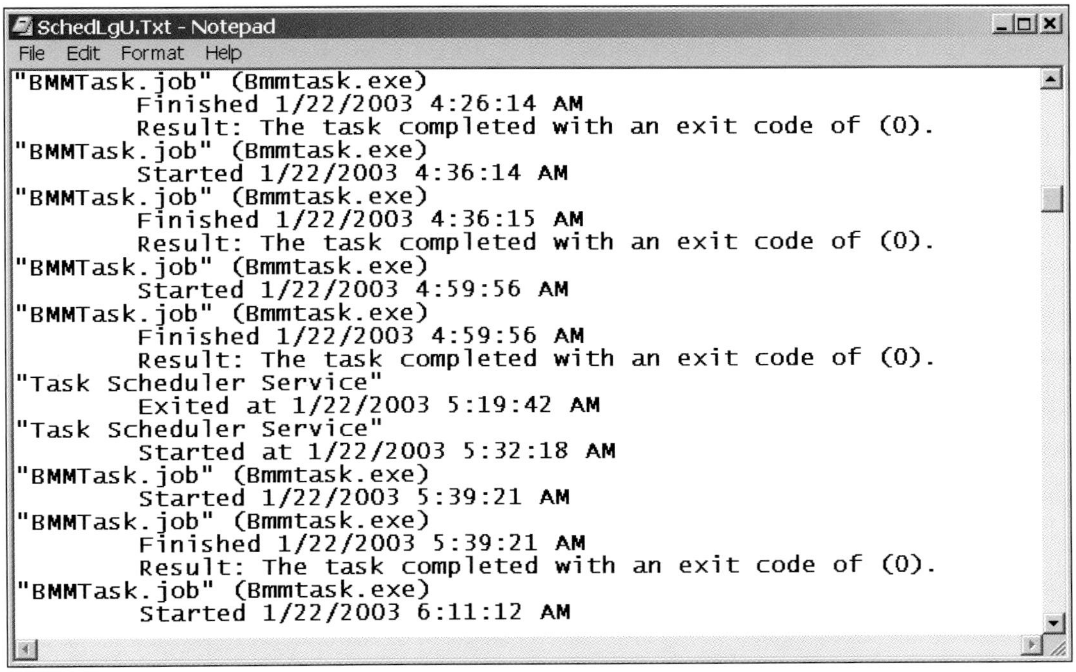

```
SchedLgU.Txt - Notepad
File Edit Format Help
"BMMTask.job" (Bmmtask.exe)
        Finished 1/22/2003 4:26:14 AM
        Result: The task completed with an exit code of (0).
"BMMTask.job" (Bmmtask.exe)
        Started 1/22/2003 4:36:14 AM
"BMMTask.job" (Bmmtask.exe)
        Finished 1/22/2003 4:36:15 AM
        Result: The task completed with an exit code of (0).
"BMMTask.job" (Bmmtask.exe)
        Started 1/22/2003 4:59:56 AM
"BMMTask.job" (Bmmtask.exe)
        Finished 1/22/2003 4:59:56 AM
        Result: The task completed with an exit code of (0).
"Task Scheduler Service"
        Exited at 1/22/2003 5:19:42 AM
"Task Scheduler Service"
        Started at 1/22/2003 5:32:18 AM
"BMMTask.job" (Bmmtask.exe)
        Started 1/22/2003 5:39:21 AM
"BMMTask.job" (Bmmtask.exe)
        Finished 1/22/2003 5:39:21 AM
        Result: The task completed with an exit code of (0).
"BMMTask.job" (Bmmtask.exe)
        Started 1/22/2003 6:11:12 AM
```

Figure 7-20 Syntax of the AT command

```
Command Prompt
The AT command schedules commands and programs to run on a computer at
a specified time and date. The Schedule service must be running to use
the AT command.

AT [\\computername] [ [id] [/DELETE] | /DELETE [/YES]]
AT [\\computername] time [/INTERACTIVE]
    [ /EVERY:date[,...] | /NEXT:date[,...]] "command"

\\computername     Specifies a remote computer. Commands are scheduled on the
                   local computer if this parameter is omitted.
id                 Is an identification number assigned to a scheduled
                   command.
/delete            Cancels a scheduled command. If id is omitted, all the
                   scheduled commands on the computer are canceled.
/yes               Used with cancel all jobs command when no further
                   confirmation is desired.
time               Specifies the time when command is to run.
/interactive       Allows the job to interact with the desktop of the user
                   who is logged on at the time the job runs.
/every:date[,...]  Runs the command on each specified day(s) of the week or
                   month. If date is omitted, the current day of the month
                   is assumed.
/next:date[,...]   Runs the specified command on the next occurrence of the
                   day (for example, next Thursday).  If date is omitted, the
                   current day of the month is assumed.
"command"          Is the Windows NT command, or batch program to be run.
```

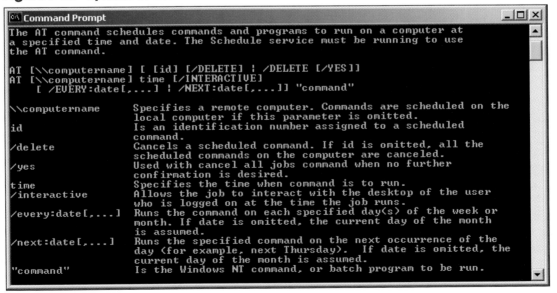

Summary

- The Microsoft Management Console (MMC) is a default administrative tool that you use to manage hardware, software, and network components. It provides a framework that you can use to create, save, and open a collection of administrative tools, called consoles.
- There are two types of consoles: predefined and custom.
- Predefined consoles are installed on a system during the installation of Windows 2000 Professional. You cannot modify a preconfigured console or add any new snap-ins to it.
- Custom consoles are created by combining multiple preconfigured snap-ins into one console. You can save and reuse custom consoles, distribute them to other administrators, and use them to carry out remote administration.
- A custom console can be saved in either of the two modes: Author or User.
- A console tree organizes the available snap-ins in hierarchical order.

- Snap-ins are management applications that are used to perform specific administrative tasks.
- There are two types of snap-ins: Stand-alone snap-ins and Extension snap-ins.
- Stand-alone snap-ins are used to perform administration tasks.
- Extension snap-ins provide additional administrative functionality to other snap-ins.
- The Scheduled Tasks tool can be used to schedule programs and batch files to run at specified intervals.
- You can troubleshoot tasks that are not running by checking the system date and time, checking the path for the task that has been scheduled, checking to see if the Task Scheduler service has been stopped or paused, and checking for a user rights conflict. You can also check the log file, SchedLgU.txt, to view the error messages for the Scheduled Task utility.

Key Terms

Author mode	Disk Management snap-in	Snap-in
Console tree	Extension snap-in	Stand-alone snap-in
Console	Microsoft Management Console (MMC)	Task Scheduler
Custom console	Preconfigured console	User mode
Details pane	Scheduled Tasks	

Test Yourself

1. Which of the following statements about a console are correct?
   a. A stand-alone snap-in can be used to administer only a local computer.
   b. An extension snap-in provides functionality only when you invoke the parent snap-in.
   c. You can add the preconfigured consoles of Windows 2000 Sever to Windows 2000 Professional.
   d. To use the predefined consoles, you need to install them on your system from the Windows 2000 Professional Installation CD.

2. Which of the following types of console modes allows users to create new windows, but does not grant access to close the existing windows?
   a. Full Access
   b. Limited Access, Single Window
   c. Limited Access, Multiple Windows
   d. Author

3. Console snap-ins that are designed to work only in conjunction with one or more stand-alone snap-ins and that can only provide functionality when added to a parent snap-in are called:
   a. Extensions
   b. Supplements
   c. Add-on snap-ins
   d. Supplements

4. Microsoft Management Console:
   a. Is stored in an administrative template file.
   b. Is a framework to which management tools can be added.
   c. Contains a comprehensive list of applications for which a task can be scheduled.
   d. Is saved with a .job extension.

5. Which of the following statements about a console is correct?
   a. You can create a custom console by combining multiple preconfigured snap-ins in one console.
   b. When you add a snap-in to a console, you need to select the extensions that should be included in that snap-in.
   c. Stand-alone snap-ins provide additional administrative functionality to other snap-ins.
   d. You can add or remove an extension from a preconfigured console.

6. You are logged on to a Window 2000 Professional machine as an administrator and you create a scheduled task to run a backup of the C: drive after business hours. You enter the user name and password for the workstation user, who is a member of the Users group, in the Scheduled Task Wizard. The next day you discover that the backup did not run. What happened?
   a. You can only create a backup task when you are logged on as a member of the Backup Operators group.
   b. You must change the user name and password for the task to a member of the Backup Operators or Administrators groups because only members of these groups have the right to perform backup jobs.
   c. You forgot to start the Task Scheduler service.
   d. You must use the AT.exe command to create a backup task.

Projects: On Your Own

1. Create a custom console, add a Computer Management snap-in, and save it with the name Managing System.
   a. Access the **Run** dialog box.
   b. Type **MMC**.
   c. Access the **Add/Remove Snap-in** in the Console1 dialog box.
   d. Select the **Computer Management** option.
   e. Save the console.
2. Schedule a disk cleanup task to run once a week on Friday.
   a. Access the **Control Panel** window.
   b. Run the **Scheduled Task Wizard**.
   c. Select the **Disk Cleanup** utility.
   d. Set the task to run once a week.
   e. Set the start time for the task as **6:00 AM** on **every Friday**.
   f. Set the security context for the task (Enter the user name and password for the task to run under.)
   g. Click **Finish**.

Problem Solving Scenarios

1. You are the coordinator at Expert Trainers Center. You have 20 computers at the training center. The training at the center requires students to access the network frequently. Therefore, many temporary files are created on each workstation, unnecessarily using up disk space. You decide that every morning when the computers are switched on, the Disk Cleanup utility should be run. Outline in a memo the steps you would take to run Disk Cleanup every morning, on each of the 20 client computers.

2. The System Administrator at CarbonTec Inc., a fabricator of carbon fiber parts for aircraft, would like help in administering the Windows 2000 network. Write a memo explaining how he can configure the Microsoft Management Consoles that will allow him to do so.

Administering User Accounts and Groups

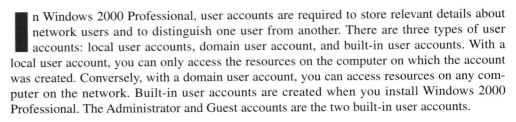

In Windows 2000 Professional, user accounts are required to store relevant details about network users and to distinguish one user from another. There are three types of user accounts: local user accounts, domain user account, and built-in user accounts. With a local user account, you can only access the resources on the computer on which the account was created. Conversely, with a domain user account, you can access resources on any computer on the network. Built-in user accounts are created when you install Windows 2000 Professional. The Administrator and Guest accounts are the two built-in user accounts.

In a peer-to-peer or workgroup network, where there is no dedicated server and no central logon authority, resources such as printers, disks, and folders are shared using local user accounts and group names. Microsoft recommends that workgroup networks contain no more than 10 computers. Windows 2000 Professional is all you will need to create a workgroup network. However, if you want to create a domain-based network, you will have to create at least one central server (domain controller) that stores Active Directory. Active Directory is the database that stores all of the information about users, groups, and access permissions, and manages logging on to the network. In order to create a domain controller you must have Windows 2000 Server installed. You only use domain user accounts in a domain-based network.

Setting up user accounts in either type of network is the first line of defense against unauthorized access to network resources. You create local user accounts and groups to allow multiple users to access resources on a particular stand-alone or workgroup computer. Then you assign permissions to the groups and to individual users so that they can access only certain resources and folders on the machine. A group is therefore a collection of user accounts with similar permissions and rights. To create local user accounts, you use the Computer Management console, which is one of the Administrative Tools in the Windows 2000 Professional operating system. You can also modify existing user accounts by changing their properties.

Goals

In this lesson you will identify the user accounts and groups available in Windows 2000 Professional, plan and create user accounts, explore the user's Properties dialog box, and set properties for user accounts. You will also create local groups, add members to a group, and put built-in groups into operation.

Lesson 8   Administering User Accounts and Groups

Skill	Exam 70-210 Objective
1. Introducing User Accounts	Implement, configure, manage, and troubleshoot local user accounts. Implement, configure, manage, and troubleshoot local user authentication.
2. Planning User Accounts	Create and manage local users and groups.
3. Creating User Accounts	Create and manage local users and groups.
4. The Users and Passwords Utility	Create and manage local users and groups.
5. Identifying User Properties	Implement, configure, manage, and troubleshoot local user accounts. Configure and troubleshoot domain user accounts. Implement, configure, manage, and troubleshoot account settings. Configure and manage user profiles.
6. Setting User Account Properties	Configure and troubleshoot local user accounts.
7. Creating Local Groups	Create and manage local users and groups.
8. Adding Members to a Group	Create and manage local users and groups.
9. Implementing Built-in Groups	Implement, configure, manage, and troubleshoot user rights.
10. Application Installation and Recovery	Manage applications by using Windows Installer packages.

Requirements

Administrative rights on a Windows 2000 Professional computer.

skill 1

Introducing User Accounts

exam objective

Implement, configure, manage, and troubleshoot local user accounts. Implement, configure, manage, and troubleshoot local user authentication.

overview

A **user account** is an account that contains all of the personal information related to a user. It also identifies a user on the network. The personal information includes the **user name** and **password**, which is required for logon, the names of **groups** to which the user belongs, and the **rights** that the user has for interacting with system resources.

The types of user accounts supported by Windows 2000 are:

- Local
- Domain
- Built-in

tip

It is not a good practice to create local user accounts on computers running Windows 2000 Professional that are part of a domain, because domains do not recognize local user accounts and local users cannot access domain resources.

A **local user account** is used to access resources on the computer where the account was created. You cannot replicate local user accounts to any other computer in a workgroup. For example, if you have created a local user account named **user1** on a computer named **comp1**, you can log on to this computer as user1 and access the local resources. If this computer is part of a workgroup that consists of three more computers, **comp2**, **comp3**, and **comp4**, and you want to use the local user account user1 on the other computers in the workgroup, you will have to create the account on each computer. Furthermore, if you want to change the password for the user1 account, you must change the password on each of the computers on which it was created, because each computer maintains its own **local security database**. Local user accounts are created in the local security database and all information pertaining to local user accounts and groups is stored there.

A **domain user account** is used to access the resources of a computer in a domain. A domain can be defined as a group of computers on a network that access a common directory database (**Active Directory** in Windows 2000) for authentication purposes. Domains have common rules and procedures, such as password policies and account policies. Domain user accounts are created in Active Directory in Windows 2000. Domain user accounts do not need to be created on multiple computers on the network because Active Directory serves as the central storage area for all account information on the network. To gain access to resources on the network, a user must enter his or her user name and password and the domain name during the logon process. Windows 2000 Professional verifies that the user is authorized to access the domain and creates an **access token**. The access token stores the user information and the security settings so that it can be used by the operating system to identify the user on the network.

There are actually two logon procedures. First the user must log on to the local computer where they are physically located, using their user name, password, and the name of the domain to which they belong or the name of the computer to which they are logging on. If you enter a domain name, it is sent to the domain controller for network authentication. In order to access network resources, the user must be authenticated on the network. If you log on to a domain, both processes (local and network) occur at the same time, but when accessing domain resources, the user name and password must be confirmed using the ACL (Access Control List) for the resource the user is attempting to access on the server. As long as a user has permission for the resource, this second authentication will occur imperceptibly. If you do not have permission to access the resource, you will receive an Access denied message (**Figure 8-1**). If you log on locally first (i.e., you select the local computer name in the first logon dialog box) and then attempt to access network resources, you will have to be authenticated in a second process. On a workgroup network, users log on locally and access shared resources on other computers in the workgroup seamlessly only if they have an account with the same username and password on the computer they are accessing. When a user attempts to access another computer, the **Enter Network Password** dialog box (**Figure 8-2**) will open

Figure 8-1 Access denied message

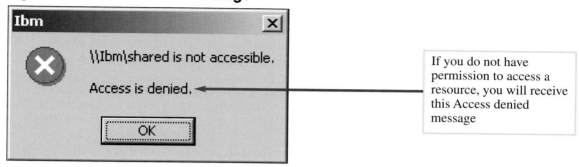

If you do not have permission to access a resource, you will receive this Access denied message

Figure 8-2 The Enter Network Password dialog box

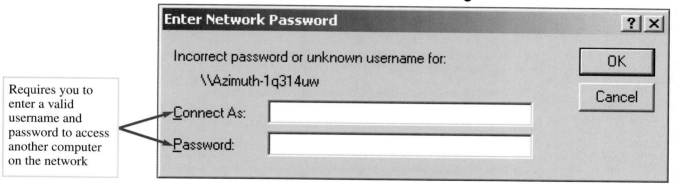

Requires you to enter a valid username and password to access another computer on the network

skill 1

Introducing User Accounts *(cont'd)*

exam objective

Implement, configure, manage, and troubleshoot local user accounts. Implement, configure, manage, and troubleshoot local user authentication.

overview

and he or she will be required to enter a user name and password with permission to access that computer.

The logon process can be customized to include such features as not displaying the last user name on the logon screen, adding a logon security warning, enabling or disabling the Shutdown button, allowing automated logons, and automatically locking a user account from use after a specific number of invalid logon attempts. These changes to the logon process are accomplished locally through the use of local security policies (see Lesson 12), although they can also be accomplished in the Registry (see Lesson 15) in the HKEY_LOCAL_ MACHINE\SOFTWARE\Microsoft\Windows NT\Current Version\Winlogon key. Setting security policies is the preferred method because it is far safer and easier than making manual changes to a Registry key. In a domain environment these types of security settings are set using a Group Policy.

Built-in user accounts are the default accounts created by Windows 2000. The two built-in user accounts are the **Administrator** and **Guest** accounts (**Figure 8-3**). You can rename these accounts (and should always do so for the Administrator account), but you cannot delete them.

The **Administrator account** is used to manage the overall functioning of a computer. You use it to manage and configure the local computer or a domain. The Administrator account should always be renamed and you should not use it for any other work besides administrative tasks, so that you do not run the risk of inadvertently harming your system. The Administrator account cannot be deleted, it cannot be locked out due to invalid logon attempts, and it cannot be disabled in order to be by-passed during logon. You also cannot remove it from the Administrators local group to which it automatically belongs. The administrative tasks you can perform include:

◆   Creating and modifying user accounts and groups.
◆   Managing security policies.
◆   Assigning rights and permissions to user accounts.
◆   Installing printers.
◆   Installing hardware devices and drivers.
◆   Changing system date and other system settings.

The **Guest account** can be used by people who only need to access computer resources infrequently or on a temporary basis. The Guest account has limited rights, which restrict users from changing the system date and other system settings. Guests cannot perform any administrative tasks and have only limited access to resources. For example, a student who sits for an online exam will likely be assigned the Guest account so that they can answer the questions on the exam, but cannot change any questions or tamper with any other resources on the computer. A new password should always be set for the Guest account, which is blank by default. The guest account also cannot be deleted or locked out due to invalid logon attempts, but it can be disabled and in fact is disabled by default. You can rename the Guest account if you do not want it to be used.

more

The prerequisite for creating a domain user account is a domain. This means that at least one computer on the network must be running one of the Windows 2000 Server products and be configured as a domain controller.

Administrator and Guest accounts are the two built-in local user accounts

Figure 8-3 The built-in local user accounts

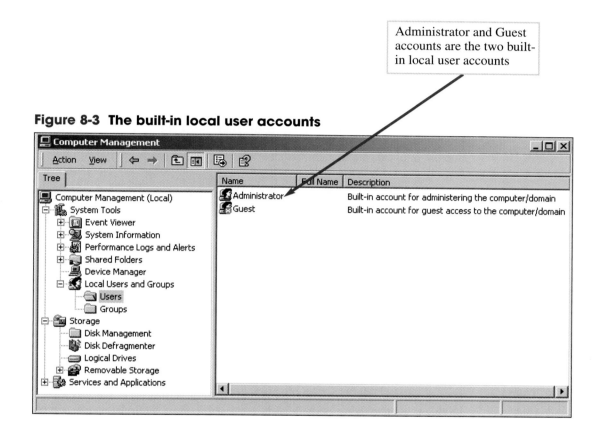

skill 2

Planning User Accounts

exam objective

Create and manage local users and groups.

overview

tip

Using a naming convention might not seem imperative in a small network, but small networks often end up growing, sometimes rapidly. If you use a naming convention from the beginning, you will be prepared for network expansion and it will be easier to keep track of user names on your network.

tip

Typically, the best practice is to let users control their own passwords.

Before you start creating user accounts, you should determine the naming convention you will use and plan how you will assign and structure the passwords on the network. The **naming convention** is a pattern that users will follow to identify themselves on the network. Following a specific naming convention will make it easier for network users to remember their logon names. For example, as an administrator, you may create user accounts for the employees in your organization using the first name and last initial of each employee, such as **JoeyM** for **Joey Mathews**. When planning your naming convention, there are specific guidelines you should follow. First, local user account names must be unique. There cannot be two accounts with the same name in a local security database. Likewise, each domain user account name stored in Active Directory must be unique. Second, logon names can contain a maximum of **20** characters, which can be either upper or lower case. You can actually enter more than 20 characters in the user logon field, but the operating system only accepts the first 20. Third, some characters, including " / \ [ ] : ; | = , + * ? < > are not acceptable. You cannot use these characters in a user logon name. Fourth, although the operating system saves the case when you create a logon name, it is not case sensitive. In other words, Joey Mathews can enter either JoeyM or joeym in the user logon field. Alphanumeric and special characters can also be used to create unique logon names. Finally, if two users have the same name, you must determine a method for differentiating between the two users. You may decide to use the second letter in the last name for one user or you can add a number to each user name. For example, if two users are named **Erin Williams**, the user names can be **ErinW** and **Erin Wi**, or **Erin W1** and **ErinW2**.

Next, you must decide how you will assign and structure the passwords on your network. The password is used in conjunction with the user name to log on to the network. It is imperative that the Administrator account be renamed and assigned a password in order to prevent unauthorized access. Next, you must decide who will be responsible for controlling passwords—the Administrator or the users. If the Administrator controls the passwords, only he or she will be able to change them. Passwords should be difficult for hackers to guess. Employees should be warned against using birth dates, children's names, street names and numbers, college names, and other easily available identifying information in their passwords. Passwords can have a maximum length of **128** characters. It is a good practice to have at least **8** characters in every password. Valid password characters include all upper and lower case letters, numbers, and many non-alphanumeric characters. The same set of characters that are invalid for logon names are recommended for use in passwords (` ~ ! @ # $ % ^ & * ( ) _ + - = { } | [ ] \ : " ; ' < > ? , . /). **Table 8-1** sets forth some useful guidelines to follow with respect to the creation of logon names and password.

Table 8-1   Guidelines for Logon Names and Passwords

Guidelines for Logon Names

1. **Must be Unique:** Local user logon names must be unique on the local computer on which they are created. Domain user logon names must be unique in the directory. That is, they must be unique within a specific parent container. No two user logon names in the same parent container can have the same RDN (relative distinguished name) or common name. (See Lesson 17).

2. **Maximum of 20 characters:** You can enter more than 20, but Windows only recognizes the first 20.

3. **Cannot use invalid characters:** " / \ [ ] : ; | = , + * ? < >

4. **Not case sensitive:** Windows 2000 saves the case in which a user logon name was created, but the letters in the logon name can be entered in either upper or lower case when the user is logging on.

5. **Have a system for handling duplicate names:** Devise a consistent system for differentiating between users with the same name. This might involve using the second letter in the last name for one user or adding a number to each user name. You can also use department names in the user name to cut down on this type of conflict.

Guidelines for Passwords

1. **Rename and assign a password to the Administrator account.**

2. **Create passwords that are difficult for hackers to guess.** Strong passwords contain characters from three groups: letters (both uppercase and lower case), numbers, and the non-alphanumeric characters: ` ~ ! @ # $ % ^ & * ( ) _ + - = { } | [ ] \ : " ; ' < > ? , . /

3. **Minimum length of 8 characters.**

4. **Use at least one symbol in the second through sixth spots.**

5. **Keep them different from previously used passwords.**

6. **Can have a maximum of 128 characters.**

7. **Do not use easily available identifying information:** Avoid using common words or names and do not use birth dates, children's names, street names and numbers, or college names.

8. **If your network includes Windows 95 or 98 computers, keep password length to no more than 14 characters.** These operating systems do not support passwords longer than this.

9. **Decide who will control passwords:** If the Administrator controls the passwords, only he or she will be able to change them.

skill 3

Creating User Accounts

exam objective

Create and manage local users and groups.

overview

When you are setting up a workgroup network, you will want to create local user accounts for the primary user of each computer and for anyone else who shares the computer. Local user accounts will not have the unrestricted access of the Administrator account, but will allow broader access than the Guest account. One way to create local user accounts on a workgroup workstation is in the **Local Users and Groups** snap-in in the **Computer Management** console **(Figure 8-4)** using the **New User** dialog box **(Figure 8-5)**.

In the New User dialog box you enter the user information, including the user's logon name (which cannot be left blank), the user's full name (first and last, with a middle initial if desired), a description of the user (for example, their job title or department), and the user's password. The password text is entered as a series of asterisks. Although this is an optional field and it can be left blank when you are first creating an account, all users should be instructed to create a password for their account to ensure network security. The password must be reentered in the **Confirm password** text box to make sure that it has been entered correctly. You can also set a temporary password when you create the account and specify that the user can change the password the first time they log on. This option is selected by default. If the network administrator is going to control the passwords, you can select the **User cannot change password** option to disallow users from changing their own passwords. If you want the password to remain unchanged (for example, passwords that a particular program will use), you will set the **Password never expires** option. If you are setting up an account that will not be put into use immediately, or you have an employee who is going on a long leave, you can select the **Account is disabled** option to prevent the account from being used until it is needed.

how to

Create and test a local user account, **Usr1**, on your machine.

1. Log on as an **Administrator**.
2. Click 🔳Start on the Taskbar, point to **Settings,** and click the **Control Panel** command to open the **Control Panel** window **(Figure 8-6)**.
3. Double-click the **Administrative Tools** icon to open the **Administrative Tools** window **(Figure 8-7)**.
4. Double-click the **Computer Management** icon to open the **Computer Management** snap-in.
5. Double-click the **Local Users and Groups** console to open it. There are two folders in the console tree: **Users** and **Groups**.

Figure 8-4 Computer Management snap-in

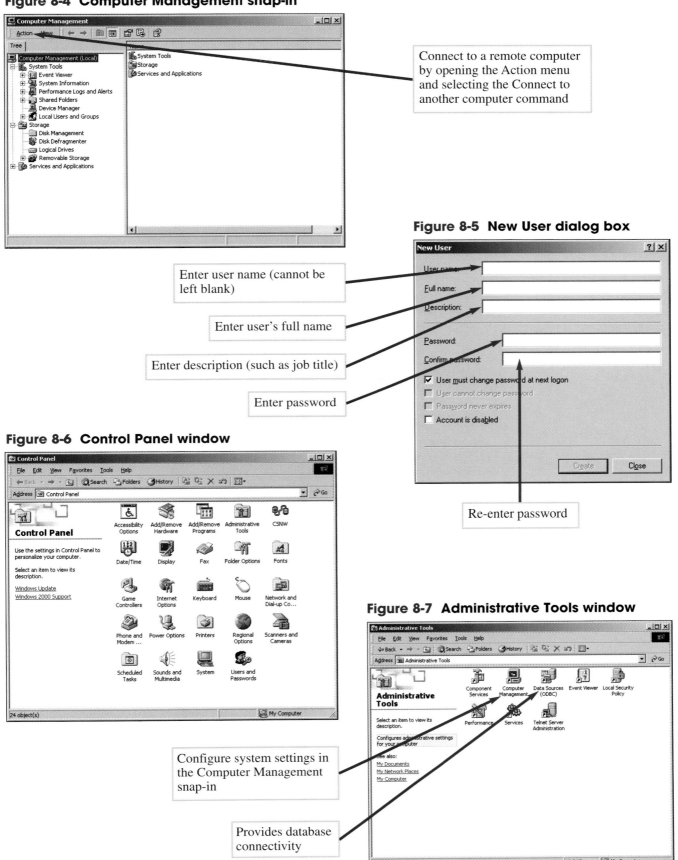

Connect to a remote computer by opening the Action menu and selecting the Connect to another computer command

Figure 8-5 New User dialog box

Enter user name (cannot be left blank)

Enter user's full name

Enter description (such as job title)

Enter password

Re-enter password

Figure 8-6 Control Panel window

Figure 8-7 Administrative Tools window

Configure system settings in the Computer Management snap-in

Provides database connectivity

skill 3

Creating User Accounts (cont'd)

exam objective

Create and manage local users and groups.

how to

6. Right-click **Users** and click the **New User** command on the shortcut menu (**Figure 8-8**) to open the **New User** dialog box.
7. Type **Usr1** in the **User name** text box.
8. Type **Joe Forester** in the **Full name** text box.
9. Type **daylight** in the **Password** text box. Notice that the password appears as a series of asterisks.
10. Re-type the password in the **Confirm password** text box.
11. The **User must change password at next logon** check box is selected by default. **Figure 8-9** illustrates steps **7** to **10**.
12. Click ⬚ Create ⬚. A local user account is now created. The New User dialog box remains open so that you can create another user account if necessary.
13. Close the New User dialog box.
14. Close the Computer Management snap-in and the Administrative Tools window.
15. To test the local user account, log off of the Administrator account (**Start**, **Shut Down**, select **Log off administrator** in the **What do you want the computer to do?** list box, and click ⬚ OK ⬚, or press [Ctrl] + [Alt] + [Del] to open the **Windows Security** dialog box and select the **Log Off** button). The **Welcome to Windows** dialog box opens.
16. Press [Ctrl] + [Alt] + [Del]. The **Logon to Windows** dialog box opens.
17. Type **Usr1** in the **User name** text box and **daylight** in the **Password** text box.
18. Click ⬚ OK ⬚. The Logon Message, **You are required to change your password at first logon** appears. Click ⬚ OK ⬚. The **Change Password** window opens.
19. Type a new password, such as **night**, in both the **New Password** and **Confirm New Password** text boxes.
20. Click ⬚ OK ⬚. The Change Password window displays the message, **"Your password has been changed."**
21. Click ⬚ OK ⬚. You are now successfully logged on as Usr1.

tip

Always have new users change their passwords the first time they log on to ensure that their password is known only to them.

Figure 8-8 Computer Management snap-in

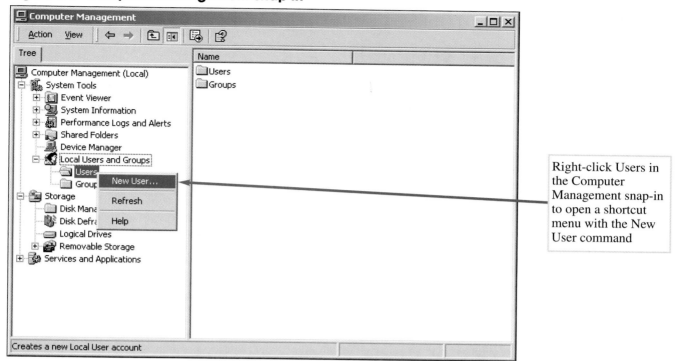

Right-click Users in the Computer Management snap-in to open a shortcut menu with the New User command

Figure 8-9 New User dialog box

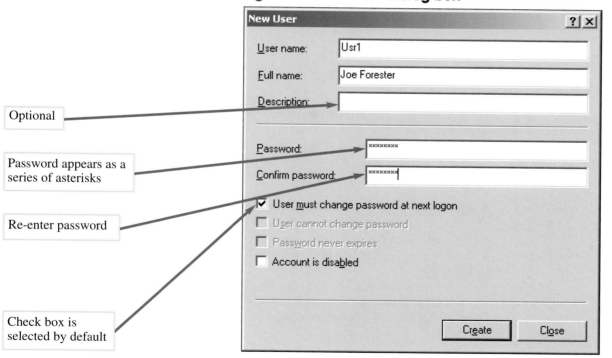

Optional

Password appears as a series of asterisks

Re-enter password

Check box is selected by default

skill 4

The Users and Passwords Utility

exam objective

Create and manage local users and groups.

overview

The other tool you can use to create and manage user accounts is the **Users and Passwords** utility in the Control Panel. You will only be able to open this utility if you log on with the Administrator account or another user account that is a member of the Administrators group. If you are not currently logged on as an Administrator, when you attempt to open the applet, the **Users and Passwords** dialog box will prompt you to enter the user name and password of an Administrator on the computer. The **Users** tab in the Users and Passwords tool lists all local user accounts, the groups to which they belong, and the domain if the account is part of a domain. You can add local users to the computer, add users to a group, create or change local user passwords, and, if the computer is on a network, you can add network user accounts to local groups on the computer so that those users can use their network password to log on. However, you will not be able to change the password for a network user and you can only put a user into one group in the Users and Passwords tool. Furthermore, you can only create groups in the Local Users and Groups snap-in. You must also use the Local Users and Groups snap-in if you want to make a user a member of several groups.

If your computer belongs to a domain, when you add a new user, you will be granting permission to an existing domain user account to access resources on the local computer. In fact, for computers in a domain, you can only perform this function in the Users and Passwords tool. To add a new local user, open the **Advanced** tab and click the **Advanced** button to open the Local Users and Groups snap-in. Then follow the procedure in the previous skill. You can also open the **Action** menu with the **Users** node selected to access the **New User** command.

how to

Create a local user account using the Users and Passwords utility.
1. Click [🏁Start], point to **Settings,** and click the **Control Panel** command to open the Control Panel.
2. Double-click the **Users and Passwords** icon. If you are still logged on as Usr1, you will be prompted to enter the user name and password of an Administrator on the computer. Do this and click [OK] to open the **Users and Passwords** dialog box (**Figure 8-10**).
3. Click [Add...] to open the **Add New User Wizard**.
4. Type **Usr2** in the **User name** text box.
5. Type **Jim Simmons** in the **Full name** text box (**Figure 8-11**) and click [Next >].
6. Type a password in the **Password** and **Confirm Password** text boxes and click [Next >].
7. The next dialog box asks you to specify the level of access you want to grant to the user. Select the **Restricted user** option button to place this user in the **Users** group. The default selection is a **Standard user**, which will be a member of the **Power Users** group.

Figure 8-10 Users and Passwords dialog box

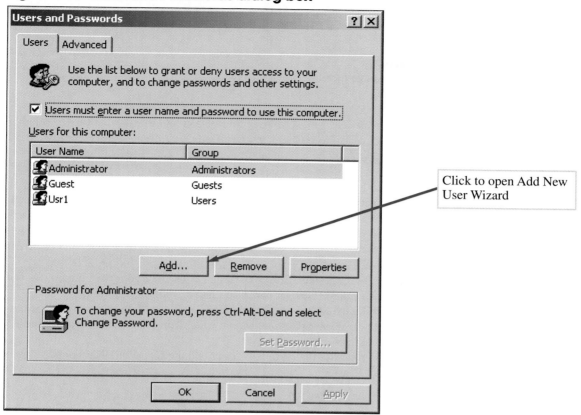

Click to open Add New User Wizard

Figure 8-11 The Add New User Wizard

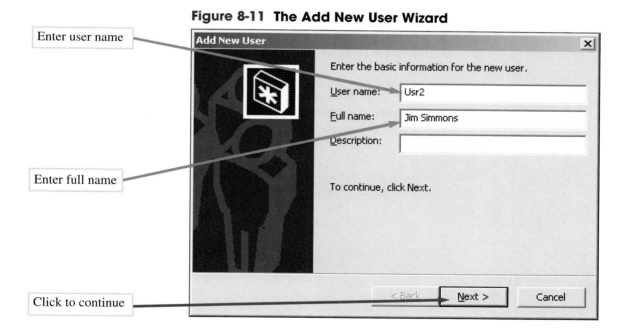

Enter user name

Enter full name

Click to continue

skill 4

The Users and Passwords Utility
(cont'd)

exam objective

Create and manage local users and groups.

how to

You can also select the **Other** option button and use the list box to select a different group, such as Backup Operators, Replicator, or Administrators (**Figure 8-12**).

8. Click [Finish]. The new local user account is added to the Users and Passwords tool.

9. Open the **Advanced** tab. Here you can use the **Certificate Management** section to import and manage certificates that will be used to prove the identity of users. A certificate authority is an organization that assigns a certificate to a user and authenticates the user's identity. You can also select the **Require users to press Ctrl+Alt+Delete before logging on** check box to set the Secure Boot settings. If you select this setting, users will have to use the Ctrl+Alt+Delete key combination before the logon dialog box will appear (**Figure 8-13**).

10. Return to the **Users** tab. Select **Usr2** and click the **Properties** button. On the **General** tab, you can change the user name, full name, or the description.

11. Open the **Group Membership** tab. Here, you can change the group membership you assigned to the user in the same way in which you selected the level of access in the Add New User Wizard.

12. Close the Properties dialog box for Usr2 and the Users and Passwords dialog box. Close the Control Panel.

more

The [Advanced...] button on the **Advanced** tab in the **Users and Passwords** dialog box opens the Local Users and Groups snap-in, which you will use to set account properties, add and remove members to and from groups, create new groups, and perform other administrative tasks that you will be learning as you proceed through the lesson.

If your computer is part of a domain, when you click the Add button to open the Add New User Wizard, you can either enter the name of an existing domain user account and the domain to which it belongs, or you can use the Browse button to view a list of user accounts in the domain. What you will be doing is importing a user account that can be used to access resources over the network that are stored on the local computer. When you import a user account, the user can access resources whether the computer is part of the domain or not. Domain users must have a user account in the local security database of a non-domain computer in order to access shared resources on that computer. This is also useful in cases where the local administrator of the computer wants to create a local security configuration that is different from the security settings in effect on the domain. Domain user accounts that are imported to a local computer cannot be used to log on locally. They can only be used to access resources on the local computer over the network.

Figure 8-12 Selecting the level of access

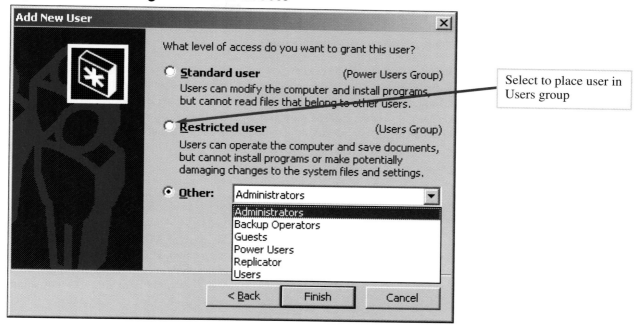

Select to place user in Users group

Figure 8-13 The Advanced tab in the Users and Passwords dialog box

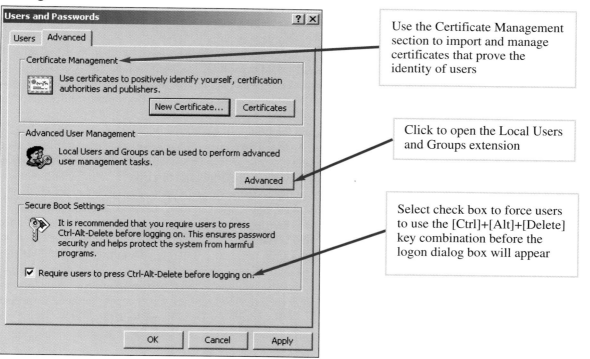

Use the Certificate Management section to import and manage certificates that prove the identity of users

Click to open the Local Users and Groups extension

Select check box to force users to use the [Ctrl]+[Alt]+[Delete] key combination before the logon dialog box will appear

skill 5

Identifying User Properties

exam objective

Implement, configure, manage, and troubleshoot local user accounts. Configure and troubleshoot domain user accounts. Implement, configure, manage, and troubleshoot account settings. Configure and manage user profiles.

overview

Every local user account you create has a set of default properties which can be modified in the **Properties** dialog box for that user. To access the Properties dialog box for a specific user account, first open the **Computer Management** console (right-click My Computer and click Manage). Select the **Local Users and Groups** extension and double-click the **Users** folder in the details pane to view all of the local user accounts. Double click the **user account name** to open the Properties dialog box. The Properties dialog box contains three tabs **(Figure 8-14)**:

◆   General
◆   Member Of
◆   Profile

On the **General** tab you can change the full name or the description for a user, configure the account so that the user must change his or her password at their next logon, set the password so that it cannot be changed by the user, set the password to never expire, or, if the account has been locked out of the system, you can clear the **Account is locked out** check box. Account lockout happens when the user has surpassed a set number of invalid logon attempts. The check box will be activated if the user has been unable to log on within this specified number of attempts. This is a security feature that helps prevent unauthorized users from accessing the resources on the network. Only an administrator can clear the check box to reactivate the account.

On the **Member Of tab**, you can add or remove user accounts from a group.

On the **Profile tab**, you can set the path for the user profile, logon script, and home folder **(Figure 8-15)**. A **user profile** is created the first time a user logs on to a particular computer. It stores directories that contain user-specific data for applications, the user's cookies from their Web-surfing activities, the history list of URLs from Internet Explorer, all of their network and printer mappings, their Microsoft Office templates, and their desktop settings. This includes many settings that the user can specify such as the color scheme, resolution, and application settings, as well as the location of their My Documents folder and user-specific Registry data. Also included in the user profile are directories that store the user's history list of files recently accessed and temporary files, their Start menu layout, and the links they have used with the Send To command. There are two main types of user profiles, either local or roaming. **Local user profiles** are stored locally and are accessed from the logon computer. When a user logs on to a computer, their individual desktop settings and connections are accessed. Different users can log on to the same computer and each can access their own individualized desktop environment, application settings, network connections, and history and most recently used lists. When a user logs on to a computer running Windows 2000 Professional for the first time, a user profile for that user is created by default and is stored in a folder named after the user logon name under **C:\Documents and Settings**. A **My Documents** folder is created for each user profile and an icon for that folder is included on the desktop. This folder is the default location for the **Open** and **Save As** commands on the **File** menu. When the user modifies their desktop settings, the changes are saved in the user profile. For example, if a user adds a file to the My Documents folder and logs off, the file will be incorporated into the user profile and it will be available the next time the user logs on.

tip

It is a good practice to store home folders on an NTFS volume and to use NTFS permissions for security because this is superior to the shared folder permissions available on a FAT volume.

Figure 8-14 Usr1 Properties dialog box

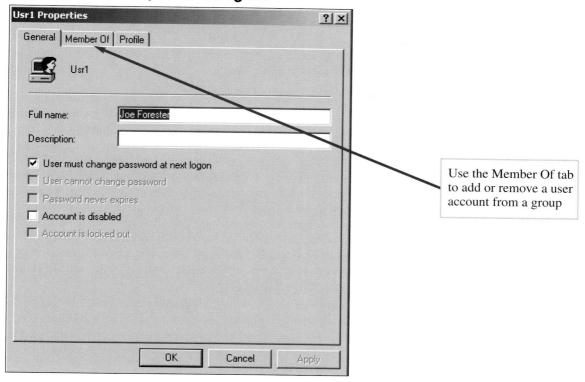

Use the Member Of tab to add or remove a user account from a group

Figure 8-15 Profile tab of Usr1 Properties dialog box

Enter the path to the user profile

Enter the path to the logon script you want a user to use. Logon scripts run executable files (e.g., anti-virus applications) every time users log on, and for mapping drive letters, initiating programs, and executing command-line operations when the system boots

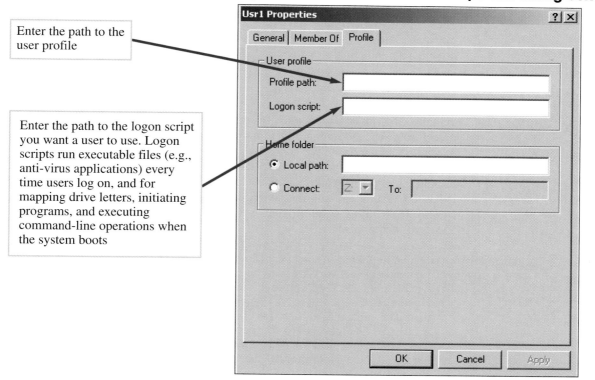

skill 5

Identifying User Properties (cont'd)

exam objective

Implement, configure, manage, and troubleshoot local user accounts. Configure and troubleshoot domain user accounts. Implement, configure, manage, and troubleshoot account settings. Configure and manage user profiles.

overview

As an Administrator, you can delete, copy, or change the type of user profile. For instance, a user profile can be changed from a local user profile to a **roaming user profile**. A roaming user profile sets up the same desktop environment for a user, no matter which computer he or she is using to log on to the domain. Roaming user profiles are one of the distributed computing technologies that Windows 2000 groups under the name **IntelliMirror**, along with offline files and the improved Add Remove Program Wizard, which now includes Windows Installer technology. The objective behind the IntelliMirror concept is to create an environment in which users can easily move between computers while still being able to access their own data, applications, and settings. A complete IntelliMirror system will include both server-side and client-side features on a domain-based system that includes using Active Directory and Group Policy to centrally mange users' desktops. When you create a roaming user profile, the user can log on to any computer in the domain and a server will automatically download all of their customized user settings to the local computer.

There are also read-only user profiles called **mandatory user profiles**. Users of mandatory profiles cannot save any changes that are made to the desktop while they are logged on. Mandatory user profiles are generally used when many users share the same profile. Desktop settings can be changed during each session, but the changes will not be available when the user logs on for their next session.

Logon Script: In earlier versions of Windows, logon scripts were used to set the desktop environment. User profiles have largely replaced them in this function. However, **logon scripts** are still used to create compatibility with non-Windows 2000 client computers on the network. In such cases the logon script file is used to configure the user's work environment. The script is run each time the user logs on. They can also be useful for running particular executable files, such as anti-virus applications every time a user logs on, and for mapping drive letters, initiating programs, and executing command-line operations when the system boots.

Home folder: A **home folder** is a private network location in addition to the My Documents folder where users can store their personal files. The home folder can be located on a client computer, but its true function is to serve as a storage area on the network that users can access from any workstation, so it is more appropriately stored in a shared folder on a network server. When you create the home folder on a network server, users can access it from any computer on the network. Administrators can use this centralized storage area to easily backup important network files instead of going from client computer to client computer to make sure that all relevant files are backed up. Users of client computers running any of the Microsoft operating systems, such as MS-DOS, Windows 95/98, or Windows 2000, can access the home folder.

how to

Create a **home folder** on a network file server.
1. Log on to the network file server as an **Administrator**.
2. Double-click the **My Computer** icon on the desktop to open the **My Computer** window.
3. Double-click the **Local drive C** icon to display the folders and files on the C: drive. Open the **File** menu, point to **New**, and click the **Folder** command to create a new folder on the local drive C (**Figure 8-16**). The new folder displays the default name **New Folder**.
4. Type **Home** to replace the default name.
5. Right-click the **Home** folder and click the **Properties** command to open the **Home Properties** dialog box.
6. Click the **Sharing** tab. Select the **Share this folder** option button. The Sharing page is shown in **Figure 8-17**.

Figure 8-16 Local drive (C:) window

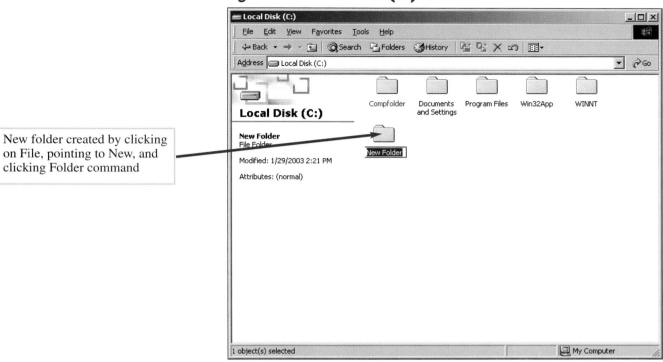

New folder created by clicking on File, pointing to New, and clicking Folder command

Figure 8-17 Home Properties dialog box

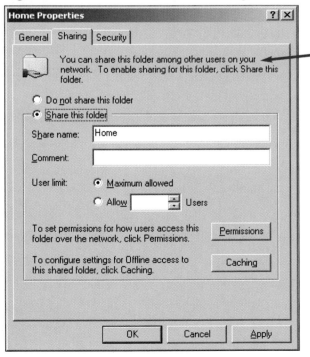

This refers to copying files to a local workstation so that, if a network connection fails, a user can continue working with a shared folder

skill 5

Identifying User Properties (cont'd)

exam objective

Implement, configure, manage, and troubleshoot local user accounts. Configure and troubleshoot domain user accounts. Implement, configure, manage, and troubleshoot account settings. Configure and manage user profiles.

how to

7. Click Permissions to open the **Permissions for Home** dialog box.
8. Select the **Everyone** group, if necessary **(Figure 8-18)** and click Remove.
9. Click Add to open the **Select Users, Computers, or Groups** dialog box.
10. Click the **Users** group in the **Name** section **(Figure 8-19)**, and then click Add. The Users group is added to the bottom section of the Select Users, Computers, or Groups dialog box. Click OK to close the dialog box and add the Users group to the Permissions for Home dialog box. This way, only users with a valid domain user account will be able to access the folder.
11. Click the **Allow** check box to the right of **Full Control** in the **Permissions** section **(Figure 8-20)**. Then, click OK.
12. Click OK to close the Home Properties dialog box. Close the C: drive window and the My Computer window.
13. On the client workstation, click Start on the Task bar. Point to **Settings** and click **Control Panel** to open the **Control Panel** window.
14. Double-click the **Administrative Tools** icon to open the **Administrative Tools** window.
15. Double-click the **Computer Management** icon to open the **Computer Management** window.
16. Double-click the **Local Users and Groups** snap-in to expand it.
17. In the right pane of the Computer Management window, double-click the **Users** folder to display a list of users on the network.
18. Select a user for whom you would like to create a home folder in the shared Home directory **Usr1**.
19. Right-click **Usr1** and click the **Properties** command to open the **Usr1 Properties** dialog box.
20. Click the **Profile** tab.
21. Select the **Connect** option button.

Figure 8-18 Permissions for Home dialog box

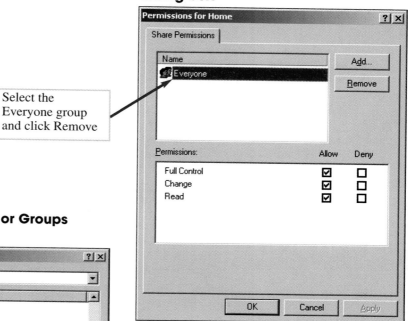

Select the Everyone group and click Remove

Figure 8-19 Select Users, Computers, or Groups dialog box

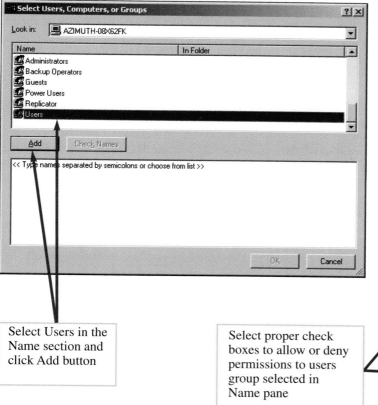

Select Users in the Name section and click Add button

Figure 8-20 Permissions for Home folder

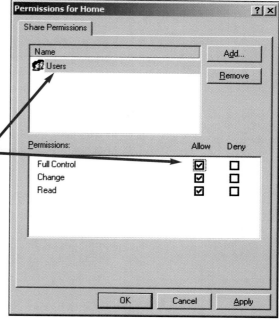

Select proper check boxes to allow or deny permissions to users group selected in Name pane

skill 5

Identifying User Properties (cont'd)

exam objective

Implement, configure, manage, and troubleshoot local user accounts. Configure and troubleshoot domain user accounts. Implement, configure, manage, and troubleshoot account settings. Configure and manage user profiles.

how to

22. In the **To:** text box, specify the UNC (Universal Naming Convention) path for the home folder. The UNC path contains the name of the server (the NetBIOS name for the computer where it is stored), the folder name and a **%username%** variable, such as **\\bethserver\home\Usr1 (Figure 8-21).** When you use the username variable, each user's home folder will be given the user logon name automatically.

23. Click [OK]. Close all open windows. You have now successfully created a Home folder on a network file server.

more

Windows 2000 contains a hidden file known as **Ntuser.dat** for each user account. This file contains the system settings for an individual user account, along with the environment settings for the user. Log on as **Administrator** and create a user account that you can use to create user profiles. Log off and log on again using the account you have just created. Configure the desktop environment that you want, for example, select wallpaper, a screen saver, and screen resolution. Log off and log on again using the **Administrator** account. Locate the Ntuser.dat file in **C:\Documents and Settings\user_logon_name (Figure 8-22).** Make this file a mandatory roaming user profile by changing its name from Ntuser.dat to **Ntuser.man**. Now you can copy this file and apply the mandatory user profile to any user account.

Although this lesson deals mainly with local user accounts, at this point there are several concepts you must understand about domain accounts. They are created in the **Active Directory Users and Computers** console. This console will be created by default on a domain controller. However, you can install it on a Windows 2000 Professional computer if you have the Windows 2000 installation CD. Simply perform a search for .msi files on the CD-ROM drive and double-click **ADMINPAK.MSI** to start the **Administration Tools Setup Wizard**. You configure domain user accounts by opening the Users node, right-clicking the user account icon in the details pane, and selecting Properties to open the Properties dialog box for the user. For a domain user account, you can also specify the location of a roaming user profile on a domain server (**Profile** tab), as previously discussed; and on the **Account** tab, you can designate certain logon hours to restrict the times the user will be allowed to log on to the domain. On the **Sessions** tab, you can set the **Idle** session limit to log off a user after a set amount to time. As with local user accounts, you can use the **Member of** tab to change the group memberships for a user, and you can also use the **Dial-in** tab to designate if a user has permission to dial in to a Remote Access Server (RAS). Administrators can also disable accounts, change passwords, move domain user accounts to different OUs (organizational units), and delete and rename domain user accounts, just as the Local Administrator can do for local user accounts. On a domain-based network, it will often take some time for new domain user accounts to be replicated to the other domain controllers on the network. Therefore, if a new user cannot log on, simply waiting a bit may solve the problem. Another common reason users may report an inability to log on is that they have inadvertently selected an incorrect domain in the list box in the logon dialog box. Other logon problems include the setting needing to be adjusted on the Account tab or users attempting to log on during hours that have been placed off limits. If the user cannot connect to a remote server, check to make sure that permission has been granted on the Dial-in tab. In Lesson 12, you will learn about group policies. Domain group policies take precedence over local group policies. If a user is having trouble logging on, you may need to open the Active Directory Users and Computers console (in the Administrative Tools folder), right-click the domain to which the user belongs, and open the Properties dialog box for the domain on the **Group Policy** tab. Here, you can select a Group Policy object and click the **Edit** button to open the Group policy snap-in, where you can view the policy settings to determine if a policy setting for the domain is overriding a local computer policy and is affecting the ability of the user to log on.

Figure 8-21 Usr1 Properties dialog box

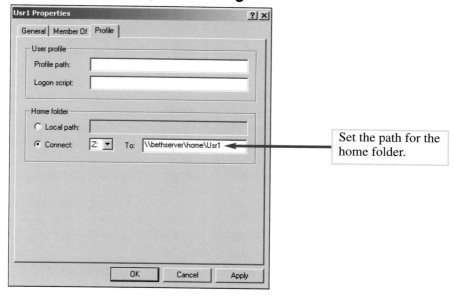

Set the path for the
home folder.

Figure 8-22 Ntuser.dat file

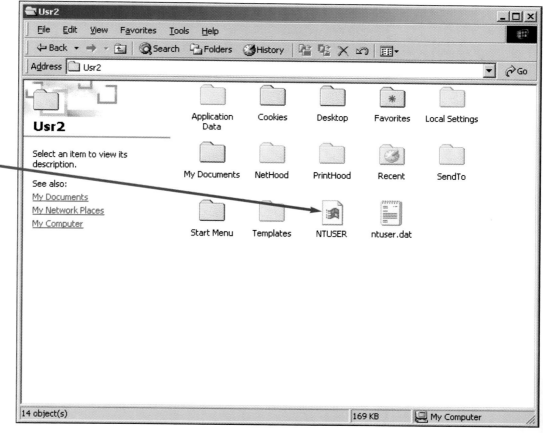

Ntuser.dat file
containing system
settings for Usr2

Setting User Accounts Properties

exam objective

Implement, configure, manage, and troubleshoot local user accounts. Implement, configure, manage, and troubleshoot account settings.

overview

If you need to modify the properties of a user account after you have created it, you use the **Properties** dialog box for the user. For example, you may want to change the password property from **User must change Password at next logon** to **User cannot change password.** Modifying a user account is also necessary when a user becomes a member of an additional group or when they no longer need to belong to a certain group. You access the Properties dialog box for a user in the **Computer Management** snap-in.

how to

Set the **User cannot change password** property for **Usr1**.
1. Log on as an **Administrator**.
2. Right-click **My Computer** and click **Manage** to open the **Computer Management** window.
3. Double-click **Local Users and Groups** to expand it.
4. Click **Users** to display a list of users in the Details pane.
5. Right-click the user (**Usr1**) for whom you want to set the **User Cannot Change Password** property, and select the **Properties** command (**Figure 8-23**) to open the **Usr1 Properties** dialog box.
6. Select the **User cannot change password** check box (**Figure 8-24**) and click   OK . Close the Computer Management window.
7. Log off as Administrator and log on as **Usr1**.
8. Press the **[Ctrl] + [Alt] + [Del]** keys. The **Windows Security** dialog box opens.
9. Click the **Change Password** button.
10. Type **night** as the password in the **Old Password** text box, and then type **noon** in the **New Password** and **Confirm New Password** text boxes.
11. Click   OK . The **Change Password** message box informs you that you do not have permission to change your password. Click   OK   to close the Change Password message box.
12. Click **Cancel** to close the Change Password dialog box.
13. Click **Log Off** in the Windows Security dialog box. Click **Yes** to confirm that you want to log off.

more

If a user is having trouble with his or her account, open the Properties dialog box for that user and check the settings. For example, if the user wants to change the password but is unable to do so, open that user's **Properties** dialog box and make sure that the **User cannot change password** check box is not selected. Similarly, if a user is unable to access his or her account, make sure that the **Account is disabled** or **Account is locked out** check boxes are not selected.

Figure 8-23 Computer Management window

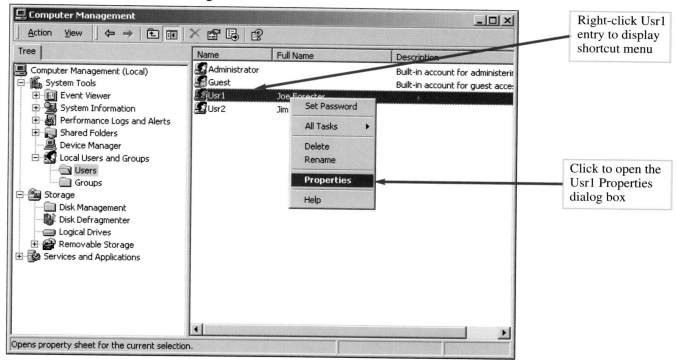

Right-click Usr1 entry to display shortcut menu

Click to open the Usr1 Properties dialog box

Figure 8-24 Setting the User cannot change password property

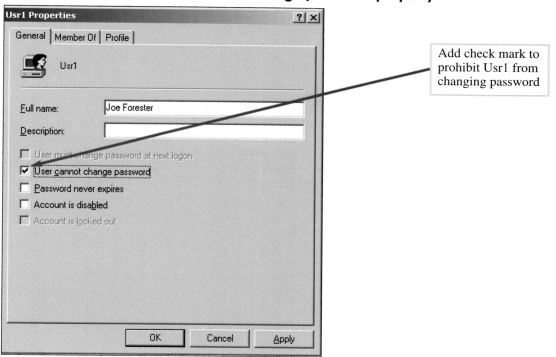

Add check mark to prohibit Usr1 from changing password

skill 7   *Creating Local Groups*

exam objective

Create and manage local users and groups.

overview

Groups are used to make it easy to assign permissions and rights to users with similar needs. It is much easier to assign permissions and rights to a group of users rather than having to assign permissions and rights on an individual basis. **Permissions** are used to assign the capabilities a user has when he or she gains access to a resource. For example, students in a class would likely be assigned permission to read the files in a professor's folder, but would not be able to modify them. First, to assign permissions to such a group, you create a Students group and give that group Read-only permission. Then, you add the user accounts for these students to the Students group. **Rights** give users the ability to perform system tasks, such as changing the time on the computer or shutting down the system. A member of a group receives all the permissions and rights that are given to a group. Users can belong to multiple groups, and one group can belong to another group in a domain.

Local Groups: A **local group** resides in the local security database on a single computer and is a used to assign permissions and rights to local user accounts for the resources on that computer. Local groups are used in peer-to-peer or workgroup networks. For the most part, they should not be used on domain-based networks. Windows 2000 Professional can only create and manage local groups. A local group cannot be a member of any other group.

On a domain-based network, you can create **global groups** that can be added to a local group to access resources in the domain. If you use local groups in a domain-based network, they will not appear in Active Directory, so you will have to administer them individually.

On a domain-based network **domain local groups** are used to assign rights and permissions to users in a particular domain. Like domain local groups, global groups can have members only from the domain in which they were created, but they can be granted permissions in any domain within a forest of domains (See Lesson 17). Domain local groups can only be assigned permissions in a single domain.

tip

Windows 2000 Professional cannot create or manage global groups unless you have installed **adminpak.msi**. Global groups always are stored on a domain controller, but can be used to assign permissions and rights to a Windows 2000 Professional system.

how to

Create a local group called **Employees**.

1. Log on as an **Administrator**.
2. Right-click **My Computer** and click **Manage** to open the **Computer Management** window.
3. Double-click **Local Users and Groups** to expand it.
4. Right-click the **Groups** folder to open a shortcut menu. Click the **New Group** command to open the **New Group** dialog box as shown in **Figure 8-25**.
5. Enter the group name **Employees** in the **Group name** text box.
6. Enter the group description **Employees of Blossoms Creations** in the **Description** text box (**Figure 8-26**).
7. Click [Create]. Close the New Group dialog box and the Computer Management window.

more

If you want to delete a group, for example, when a group of freelancers in your organization has completed their project, you simply open the **Computer Management** window, open the **Groups** folder, right-click the group name listed on the right side of the window, and select the **Delete** command or select the group and press the Delete key.

You can also delete a group by selecting the group and clicking the Delete ⊠ button on the toolbar. This will terminate the rights and permissions assigned to the Freelancers group, but will not delete their individual user accounts. Every group you create is assigned a unique **SID** (security identifier) that is used by the operating system to recognize the group and its permissions. When a group is deleted, the SID will not be reused even if you create another group with the same name. In order to recreate the group, you must reassign the rights and permissions.

Figure 8-25 New Group dialog box

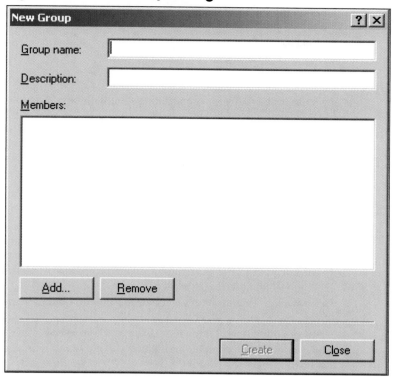

Figure 8-26 New Group dialog box showing the group name and description

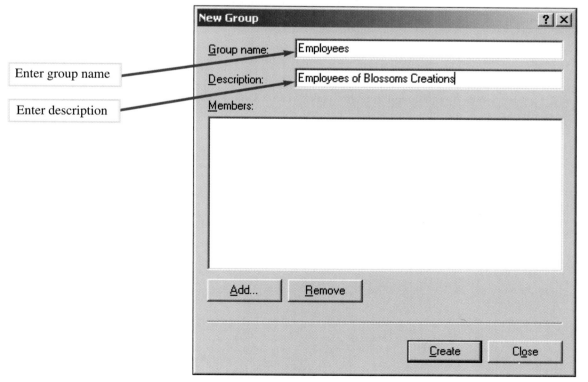

Enter group name

Enter description

skill 8   *Adding Members to a Group*

exam objective

Create and manage local users and groups.

overview

As new employees join your organization, you will have to add their user accounts to various groups that are relevant to the projects they will be working on. This will help you to effectively manage the rights and permissions of employees working on different projects or in different departments. To add members to a group, you use the Select Users and Groups dialog box, which is accessed in the Computer Management snap-in.

how to

Add a user, **Usr1**, to the **Power Users** group.

1. Open the **Computer Management** window and expand the **Local Users and Groups** node.
2. In the left pane of the Computer Management window, click **Groups** to display a list of all the available groups in the details pane.
3. Double-click **Power Users** to open the **Power Users Properties** dialog box (**Figure 8-27**).
4. Click `Add...`. **The Select Users or Groups** dialog box opens.
5. Make sure that the computer on which you are working is selected in the **Look in** list box.
6. Select **Usr1** in the **Name** section (**Figure 8-28**) and click `Add...`. The user ID is displayed in the lower pane of the Select Users or Groups dialog box.
7. Click `OK`. The Power Users Properties dialog box displays the selected user's name in the **Members** section, as shown in **Figure 8-29**.
8. Click `OK` to close the Power Users Properties dialog box. Close all other open windows.

tip

You can add multiple user accounts at the same time by using either the [**Shift**] or the [**Ctrl**] key while you select other accounts.

more

When an employee is transferred or promoted to a different department, you may have to remove his or her user account from a particular group. To remove a member from a group, open the **Properties** dialog box for the group, select the member, and click `Remove`. The selected user or users will be removed from the group. Click `OK` to close the Properties dialog box.

tip

You can use the **Member Of** tab in the **Properties** dialog box for the user to add a user account to multiple groups.

Figure 8-27 Power Users Properties dialog box

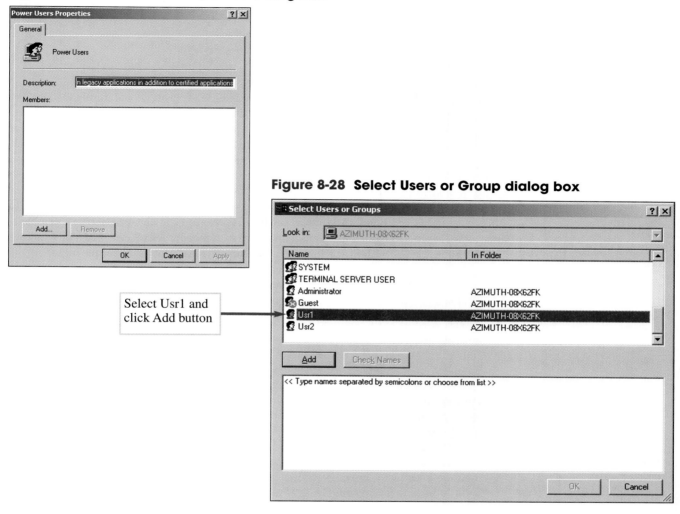

Figure 8-28 Select Users or Group dialog box

Select Usr1 and click Add button

Figure 8-29 Adding a user to a group

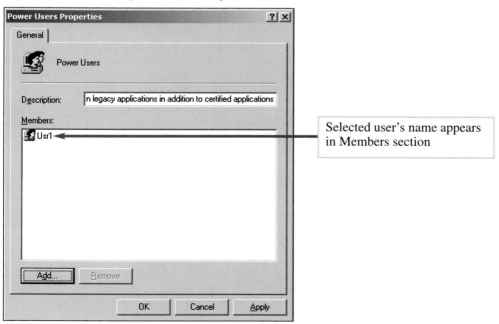

Selected user's name appears in Members section

skill 9

Implementing Built-in Groups

exam objective

Implement, configure, manage, and troubleshoot user rights.

overview

Built-in groups are created automatically by Windows 2000 Professional during installation. There are two types of built-in groups, either local or system. **Built-in local groups** are found on all Windows 2000 Professional computers and on Windows 2000 servers that are not domain controllers. They have preset rights or privileges for the local computer, such as modifying the desktop, installing a program, sharing a folder, or backing up the hard drive. You can view the rights that each built-in group has by opening the **Local Security Policy** console in the Administrative Tools folder. Expand the **Local Policies** node and double-click **User Rights Assignment (Figure 8-30)**. For example, only Administrators will have the right to **Increase quotas** and **Load and unload device drivers**. You can change the rights that built-in groups are granted by default by applying security templates (See Lesson 12). In Windows 2000 Professional, the built-in local groups can be found in the **Groups** folder in the **Computer Management** window **(Figure 8-31)**. You add users to these built-in local groups to give them the appropriate level of interaction with the operating system. A list of the built-in local groups and their capabilities is given below:

◆ **Users:** Also called **Restricted Users** in some dialog boxes (the Add New User Wizard, for example), these users cannot share folders, install programs that other users will be able to run, create local printers, or modify system settings in the operating system, the Registry, or in applications. All local user accounts you create automatically become members of this group, which enables them to run all Windows 2000 applications but may not allow them to run some older Window NT 4.0 applications. The compatible security template **(compatws.inf)** reduces some of the user rights restrictions on the Users group so that members can run older Windows NT 4.0 applications.

◆ **Administrators:** Users with unlimited access, rights, and permissions. The built-in local user account, Administrator, is automatically added to this group.

◆ **Guests:** Users with restricted access who cannot change the desktop environment. The built-in local user account, Guest, is automatically made a member of this group. These users will generally have to be given individual rights in order to perform even the most basic tasks.

◆ **Power Users:** Also called **Standard Users** in some dialog boxes, notably the Add New User Wizard, these users can create local user accounts, install applications that do not involve operating system services or change operating system files, run and halt system services that did not start automatically, and remove users from the Guests, Users, and Power Users groups. They cannot, however, change or delete user accounts that they did not create, change the memberships in the Administrators or Backup Operators groups, or take ownership of files.

◆ **Backup Operators:** These users can back up and restore any file on the system. Members of the Users group can only do so if they have the proper file access permissions.

◆ **Replicators:** These users can perform file replication in a domain.

Built-in system groups are found on all computers that run Windows 2000, either Professional or Server. Built-in system groups do not have any specific members. Therefore, you cannot add, modify, or remove users from this group. Members of a built-in system group are based upon how a user gains access to the computer or the network rather than on which user is accessing the computer. You may recognize the names of the built-in system groups

Figure 8-30 User rights assignments for built-in local groups

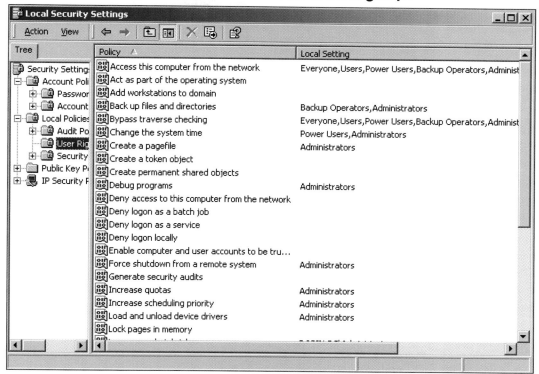

Figure 8-31 Groups node in the Local Users and Groups snap-in

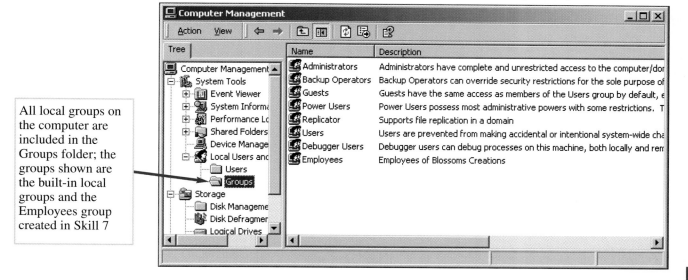

All local groups on the computer are included in the Groups folder; the groups shown are the built-in local groups and the Employees group created in Skill 7

skill 9

Implementing Built-in Groups (cont'd)

exam objective

Implement, configure, manage, and troubleshoot user rights.

overview

from the **Select Users or Groups** and **Select Users, Computers, and Groups** dialog boxes **(See Figure 8-32)**. The commonly used system groups are:

◆ **Everyone:** All users who are accessing the computer, including the Guest account. If you have activated the Guest account, a user who does not have a valid user account will be authenticated as a Guest and will automatically inherit all rights and permissions assigned to the Everyone group. This can pose a security risk, so do not liberally assign rights and permission to this group.

◆ **Authenticated Users:** All users who have been authenticated either on the local computer or in the domain (those with valid user accounts in the local security database or in the domain database in Active Directory). In contrast to the Everyone group, this excludes anonymous users.

◆ **Creator Owner:** Users who create or take ownership of a resource, for example, a folder.

◆ **Interactive:** Users who are accessing local resources on the computer with which they are physically interacting.

◆ **Network:** Users who are accessing a shared resource on a computer via a network connection.

◆ **Anonymous Logon:** Users with accounts that were not authenticated by Windows 2000 Professional.

◆ **Dialup:** Users who are accessing a shared resource on a computer via a dial-up connection or virtual private network (VPN).

Figure 8-32 Built-in system groups in the Select Users, Computers, or Groups dialog box

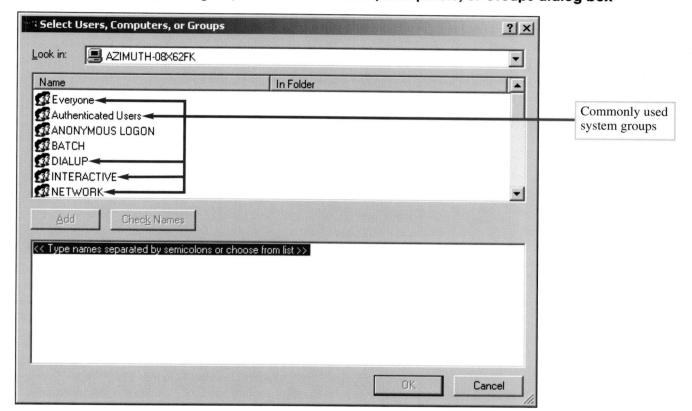

skill 10 *Application Installation and Recovery*

exam objective

Manage applications by using Windows Installer packages.

overview

Windows Installer is an application installation technology that now augments the Add/Remove Programs Wizard. It is touted by Microsoft as one of the main features that reduces the TCO (Total Cost of Ownership) of a Windows 2000 network and, as previously mentioned, one of the IntelliMirror technologies that facilitates users moving from computer to computer. Microsoft's other applications and many other application providers now include this technology to manage user installation options and to ensure the complete and safe removal of applications. Windows Installer is also useful for its diagnostic capabilities for malfunctioning applications. It can find which key files have been deleted or corrupted and easily repair them to restore functionality. It also includes the ability to take a snapshot of the current system configuration so that the computer can return to its original state in the event of an aborted or failed application installation. Windows Installer packages are autonomous databases that contain a set of rules and instructions for application program interfaces (APIs), which software developers must follow in order for Windows Installer to process the commands they present for installation. The benefits of the Windows Installer service include improved management facilities, such as advertising features without installing them, user customization, and installing software on demand.

In order for applications to use the Windows Installer service, the installation routines must be written in an MSI file. MSI stands for Microsoft Installer, which is the name given to the previous version of the service. Installing applications on a Windows 2000 Professional computer simply involves double-clicking an .msi file or right-clicking it and selecting the Install command on the shortcut context menu. For example, if you have a Windows-Installer-"aware" application on a CD-ROM on your D: drive, you can simply search for .msi files on the D: drive and install only those components of the application that you want. Each one will display as a separate .msi file in the search results window (**Figure 8-33**). This is in contrast to the setup.exe files that you are probably more familiar with. You can also use the Microsoft Installer Executive, MSIEXEC.EXE, at the command prompt or in the Run dialog box. To install an application, you would add the command line parameter /I. Some of the other command line parameters you can use with MSIEXEC.EXE are outlined in **Table 8-2**. Windows Installer is one of the services listed when you open the **Services** node in the **Administrative Tool**s window (click **Start**, point to **Settings**, click **Control Panel**, double-click **Administrative Tools**, double-click **Services**).

However, the true capabilities of Windows Installer can only be taken advantage of on a domain-based Active Directory system where the .msi files can be copied to a network share and a Group Policy can be created to manage the installation of applications. When MSI files are deployed via a GPO (Group Policy Object), they can be stored on a member server, or on any other server that is given the appropriate UNC path and permissions. This process is a bit more complex and involves deciding whether to publish an application for users or whether to assign it to users or computers. When you publish an application, it is made available to any user who wants it and will appear in the Add/Remove Programs control panel. Users will simply have to run the Add/Remove Programs Wizard to install the application. Applications are published only to specific users, not to computers. On the other hand, when you assign an application, you designate the users *or computers* to which it will be made available. If the application is assigned to a user, he or she will simply have to open the application from the Start menu or attempt to open a file created using the application and it will be automatically installed. The application will always be included on the user's Start menu and cannot be deleted. If the program is removed, it will reappear on the Start menu. If it is assigned to a computer, it will install the next time the computer is started. Administrators generally choose

Figure 8-33 Windows Installer Package files on a CD-ROM

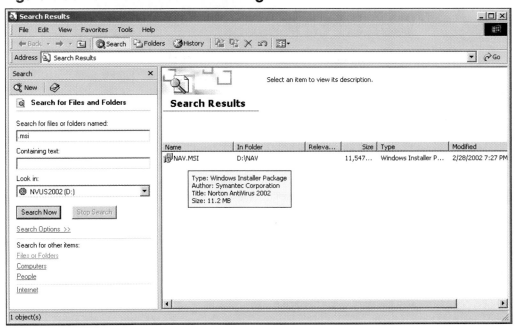

Table 8-2   Command Parameters for MSIEXEC.EXE

Variable	Function
/I	Installs or configures a product. For example, to install an application from the D: drive, you would type: **msiexec /I D:\\<*filename*>.msi**
/F	Fix or repair. This is the command-line version of the Repair option. It is used with a number of other variables that designate exactly what to repair. For example, **p** is used to designate that you only want to reinstall if a file is missing, **o** is used to reinstall if a file is missing or if an older version is installed, **e** is used to reinstall if a file is missing or an equal or older version is installed, and **d** is used to reinstall if a file is missing or a different version is installed.
/L	Log: Windows Installer automatically logs noteworthy events in the Application event log by default. If you want to designate other events that you want recorded, you will use this variable in conjunction with other variables to specify the events you want the log file to include. For example, **i** is used to record Status messages, **w** is used to record nonfatal warnings, **e** is used to record all error messages, **a** is used to record the startup of actions, and **u** is used to record user requests.
/P	Patch: This variable modifies an existing administrative image on a server that client workstations will use to install the application. For example, if you want to apply a patch to an administrative installation package, type: **msiexec /p <*PatchPackage*> /a <*filename*>.msi**
/X	Extract or Uninstall: This is the command line version of the Remove option in the Add/Remove Programs Wizard.
/J	This variable is used to advertise an application. It is used with a number of other variables to designate how you want the application to be advertised. For example, **u** is used to advertise to the current user, and **m** is used to advertise to all users of the computer. For example, to advertise a package to all users of this computer you would type: **msiexec /jm <*filename*>.msi**

skill 10

Application Installation and Recovery (cont'd)

exam objective

Manage applications by using Windows Installer packages.

to assign applications to computers when several users share a workstation and they will all need the same program or if an application is only needed on one or several computers.

overview

The benefits that are conveyed to the Add/Remove Program Wizard (**Figure 8-34**) include the repair process, which can replace any necessary application or system files that may have been unintentionally deleted or lost in a system crash. This is where the IntelliMirror capability comes in. Users can reconfigure their computers with the same applications and settings they had previously. The Add/Remove Program Wizard can also perform a more thorough un-installation than was previously possible. Registry entries, shortcuts, and other odds and ends files are now removed from the system. To repair an application, users simply have to open the **Add/Remove Programs** window, select the application in question, and click either the **Change** or the combined **Change/Remove** button and a **Repair** option will generally be available (**Figure 8-35**).

Figure 8-34 Add/Remove Programs Wizard

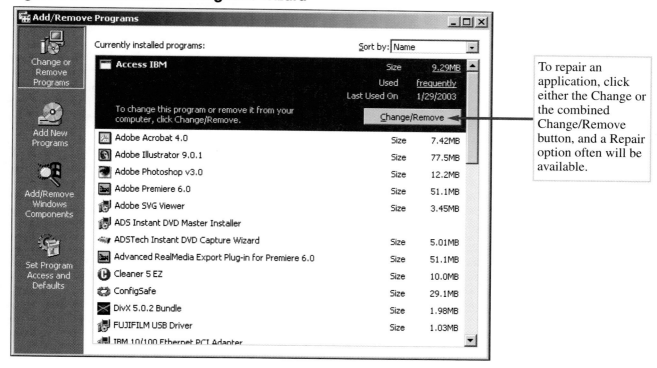

To repair an application, click either the Change or the combined Change/Remove button, and a Repair option often will be available.

Figure 8-35 Repairing an application

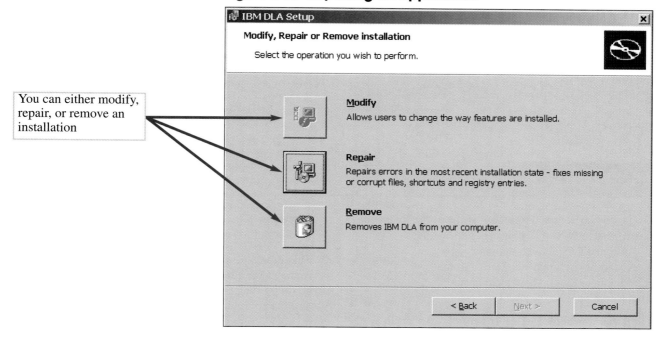

You can either modify, repair, or remove an installation

Summary

- A user account stores the personal information for a user and is used to identify the user on the network.
- There are three types of user accounts in Windows 2000 Professional: local user accounts, domain user accounts, and built-in user accounts.
- You create user accounts in the Computer Management snap-in, which is found in the Administrative Tools window.
- Local user accounts are used to access the local resources on a computer.
- Local user accounts cannot be replicated in a work-group.
- Domain user accounts are used to logon to a domain and gain access to resources on computers on the network.
- In domain-based network, Windows 2000 Professional assigns an access token to the user, which identifies the user on the network.
- Built-in user accounts are default accounts created by Windows 2000 Professional.
- There are two built-in user accounts: Administrator and Guest.

- The Administrator account is used to manage the overall functioning of a computer.
- The Guest account is assigned to users who use the computer only occasionally or on a temporary basis, and thus the account has very limited rights.
- Windows Installer is an application installation technology that now augments the Add/Remove Programs Wizard.
- The benefits of the Windows Installer service include improved management facilities, such as advertising features without installing them, user customization, and installing software on demand.
- In order for applications to use the Windows Installer service, the installation routines must be written in an MSI file.
- You can also use the Microsoft Installer Executive, MSIEXEC.EXE, at the command prompt or in the Run dialog box.
- Windows Installer is one of the services listed when you open the Services node in the Administrative Tools window.

Key Terms

Access token
Administrator account
Assigned application
Built-in local groups
Built-in system groups
Built-in user accounts
Domain local group
Domain user account
Global group
Group
Guest account

Home folder
IntelliMirror
Local group
Local user account
Local user profile
Logon script
Mandatory user profile
Member Of tab
My Documents
Naming convention
Ntuser.dat

Password
Permissions
Profile tab
Publishing an application
Rights
Roaming user profile
User account
User account properties
User profile
Windows Installer

Test Yourself

1. Users who do not need to access the resources of a computer frequently, would typically be:
   a. Assigned a local user account.
   b. A member of a built-in system group.
   c. A member of a built-in local group.
   d. Assigned a Guest account.

2. Carol has transferred to a different department in your organization and you must remove her account from the Accounting group. Which of the following tabs will you use?
   a. General
   b. Member Of

   c. Profile
   d. Sharing

3. This type of user profile sets up the same desktop environment for a user no matter which computer he or she is using to log on to the domain.
   a. Mandatory user profile
   b. Local user profile
   c. Roaming user profile
   d. Home folder user profile

4. You set these to assign the capabilities a user will have after they gain access to a resource:

a. User profile
b. Passwords
c. Permissions
d. Logon script

5. Your company has recruited new Instructional Designers who are required to work on a project on Windows 2000 Server. To make their storyboards, they need to take screenshots and edit them using Adobe Photoshop. Your company has only one licensed copy of Adobe Photoshop, so it can be installed only on one computer. The Instructional Designers will have to work in shifts to use Photoshop. The computer on which you have installed Photoshop has critical files stored on it, so you cannot give Full Control to the Instructional Designers. You need to make a collection of their accounts on this computer and then assign them permissions. Which of the following options best describe this collection?
a. Local group
b. Domain
c. User profile
d. Power user

6. A group which does not have any specific members is known as a:
a. Built-in system group.
b. Built-in local group.
c. Local group.
d. Domain local group.

7. A group that can create or modify a local user account is known as:
a. A Replicator.
b. Power Users.
c. Authenticated Users.
d. Creator Owner.

8. A roaming user profile enables you to:
a. Create a group of computers on a network sharing a common directory database.
b. Store user-specific settings on a computer on which the user has logged on.
c. Set up the same desktop environment, application settings, network connections, and history and most recently used lists for a user in a domain no matter which computer they use to log on.

d. Store information for a user that defines him/her on the network.

9. To gain access to resources on a domain, a user must enter his or her user name and password and the domain name during the logon process. Windows 2000 Professional verifies that the user is authorized to access the domain and creates a/an _____, which stores the user information and the security settings so that it can be used by the operating system to identify the user on the network.
a. IntelliMirror
b. User profile
c. Access token
d. Local security database

10. Which of the following best describes a group of computers on a network that use a common directory database to authenticate users who attempt to log on?
a. User accounts
b. Domain
c. Access tokens
d. Security database

11. The account that is created in the local security database of a computer is the:
a. Domain user account.
b. Guest account.
c. Local user account.
d. Built-in system account.

12. You can have a maximum of 25 characters in user logon names.
a. True
b. False

13. The Password never expires option is useful if you have more than one user accessing the same account.
a. True
b. False

14. To add members to a group, you use the Select Users and Groups dialog box, which is accessed from the Computer Management window.
a. True
b. False

Projects: On Your Own

1. Create a local user account.
   a. Log on as **Administrator**.
   b. Click **Start** in the taskbar of your computer. Point to **Settings** and click **Control Panel**.
   c. Click the **Administrative Tools** icon.
   d. Click the **Computer Management** icon.
   e. Expand **Local Users and Groups** by double-clicking it.

   f. Right-click **Users** and click **New Users**.
   g. Type **Usr1** in the **User Name** text box.
   h. Type **Joe Forester** in the **Full Name** text box.
   i. Type any password, such as **daylight**, in the **Password** text box if you wish to assign a password to the user.
   j. Type the same password in the **Confirm Password** text box.

k. Select the check box to specify whether the user can change the password or not.
l. Click **Create**.

2. Set the User cannot change password property.
    a. Log on as **Administrator**.
    b. Click **Start** in the taskbar of your computer. Point to **Settings** and click **Control Panel**.
    c. Click the **Administrative Tools** icon.
    d. Click the **Computer Management** icon.
    e. Expand **Local Users and Groups** by double-clicking it.
    f. Click **Users**.
    g. Right-click the user for which you want to set the **User cannot change password** property.
    h. Click the **Properties** option.
    i. Check the **User cannot change password** option from the user's **Properties** dialog box and click **OK**.

Problem Solving Scenarios

1. You have just been hired as an Assistant Network Administrator by Sureflow Baggage Inc., a company in Pewaukee, Wisconsin that manufactures computer-controlled baggage handling equipment for the airlines. There are 140 employees, all of whom will be given access to the shared resources stored on workstations on the company's Windows 2000 peer-to-peer network. You want to ensure that executives, managers, and regular employees are assigned permissions giving them access to only the information they require, as determined by senior management. You will need to establish three local groups and assign different rights and permissions to each group. Outline in a memo the steps you will take to create the three local groups. Include information on how you will structure users' logon names and passwords.

2. Senior management at Sureflow Inc. is very concerned about the security of data on the company's network. They want executives and managers to be required to enter a new password every time they logon, but regular employees to have just one password. Executives and managers will be issued a small password generator that generates a unique eight-character password each time it is activated. Outline the steps you will take to create this capability.

Working with Shared Folders

Since the main function of any network of computers is to share resources, providing accessibility to files and folders and making sure that the correct levels of access are granted is crucial to a functional and secure system. Shares are segments of a computer's resources that are made available to other users on a network. If you do not grant sufficient access, users may be hampered in performing their duties. On the other hand, if the access you grant is too liberal, you risk the inadvertent or even intentional loss or destruction of vital enterprise data. There are three levels of control in a Windows 2000 environment: local, network, and Internet. You must control access to shared resources on a local computer and resources that are shared over the network, and you can also control network access to an intranet or the Internet using the Internet Information Service (IIS) snap-in. Network sharing is controlled by the File and Print Sharing for Microsoft Networks service (also known more simply as the Server service), which is automatically configured on all Windows 2000 Professional computers and starts as soon as the operating system is initiated. The Server service uses the Server Message Block (SMB) protocol to communicate with other Windows computers so that file and print resources can be shared between network users.

As you have learned, access to both a local PC and networked computers can be controlled by setting group policies. Beyond that, the type of local and network access that can be granted depends upon the type of disks in use. On FAT, FAT32, and NTFS partitions and volumes, you can use what are called **share permissions**, or shared folder permissions, to control access to network resources. On NTFS volumes, you also can use NTFS permissions to control access to both files and folders on the local computer. You can use share permissions in conjunction with NTFS permissions to control network access if a folder resides on an NTFS partition. Using share permissions, you can permit particular users to access only certain folders and, to some degree, you can control the level of access or the tasks they will be able to perform after they have opened the folder. In this lesson, we will concentrate on how to create share permissions.

After you assign permissions, you will also need to monitor user access to shared folders to maintain and secure the data. To do this, you can view a list of open files that are located in the shared folders and the users who are currently using the files. Additionally, you can make the shared folders available offline by storing copies of the files in a reserved portion of disk space on the client machine called the cache. This enables you to work on the latest version of files even when you are not connected to the network.

Goals

In this lesson, you will learn how to share folders, assign permissions to shared folders, and connect to a shared folder. You will also learn how to monitor access to shared folders and how to configure offline files and folders.

Lesson 9   Working with Shared Folders

Skill	Exam 70-210 Objective
1. Introducing Shared Folders	Basic knowledge
2. Sharing a Folder	Create and remove shared folders, Connect to shared resources on a Microsoft network.
3. Introducing Types of Permissions for Shared Folders	Control access to files and folders by using permissions. Control access to shared folders by using permissions.
4. Accessing Shared Resources on a Windows Network	Connect to shared resources on a Microsoft network.
5. Monitoring Access to Shared Folders	Manage and troubleshoot access to shared folders. Monitor, manage, and troubleshoot access to files and folders.
6. Configuring and Managing Offline Files and Folders	Manage and troubleshoot the use and synchronization of offline files.Optimize access to files and folders.

Requirements

To complete this lesson, you will need a system with Windows 2000 Professional installed on it.

skill 1

Introducing Shared Folders

exam objective

Basic knowledge

overview

In Windows 2000 Professional, members of the Administrators or Power Users groups can create shared folders on FAT and FAT32 partitions, or on NTFS volumes using one of three methods. They can use Windows Explorer, the Shared Folder utility, or the NET SHARE command. This type of access control is only for folders. Individual files within the folders cannot be given their own sets of permissions. To control who can access a particular file, you must grant the appropriate privileges to the folder in which it is stored. Unless a contradictory group policy has been set, shared folders can be made available on removable disks and CD-ROM drives. However, shared folder permissions are not applicable at the local computer level. It is very important that you understand this. They cannot be used to control what users can access locally. By default, all local resources can be accessed by any user, except on NTFS volumes where many system folders and files are protected from access by users. In contrast, shared folders are used for networks and share permissions must be set up or these folders cannot be accessed by anyone.

When you set up shared folder permissions, you grant different levels of access to individual users or to groups. As you have learned, using groups is the best method, because it is much easier for administrators to set permissions for groups of users. After you determine which folders will be shared and which groups or individuals will be able to access them, you set permissions to control what these users will be allowed to do, depending on the type of resource. For example, you can assign the Change permission for a folder to allow users to modify the data in the folder and delete files in the folder. On the other hand, the Manage Printers permission allows users to have administrative control over a printer so that they can change the properties for the printer, pause and restart it, and share and remove sharing permissions from the printer.

You set share permissions in the ACL (Access Control List) for that resource. Most objects in Windows 2000 Professional have an ACL. The ACLs you will access to set share permissions are for folders, Registry keys, and printers. The default permission for a shared resource is Full Control for the Everyone group. Generally, you will remove this permission and set your own according to your organizational needs. You can also organize the shared folders according to their function in order to make it easy for users to locate them. You can store different types of content, such as applications or data, in a shared folder. Based on the contents, you can categorize shared folders in the following ways **(Figure 9-1)**:

◆ **Shared Application Folders:** These folders contain the applications that users can access over the network. Storing applications in one place is an organizationally sound design because it creates a single location from which programs can be installed and upgraded. This way you will not have to install applications on each system separately. Shared Application folders are stored on a network server where they can be used by the client systems.

◆ **Shared Data Folders:** A Shared Data folder is used to store either Working Data or Public Data. Working data folders contain centralized information that a select group of users needs to perform their duties. Public data folders contain more general centralized data that is used by a large group of users.

tip

In a domain, the **Administrators** and **Server Operators** groups can share folders on any computer in the domain. The local **Power Users** group can only share local resources.

more

Windows 2000 Professional automatically shares certain folders, whose contents are available only to Administrators. These **administrative shares** are appended with a **dollar** sign (**$**) to

Figure 9-1 Shared Application folders and Shared Data folders

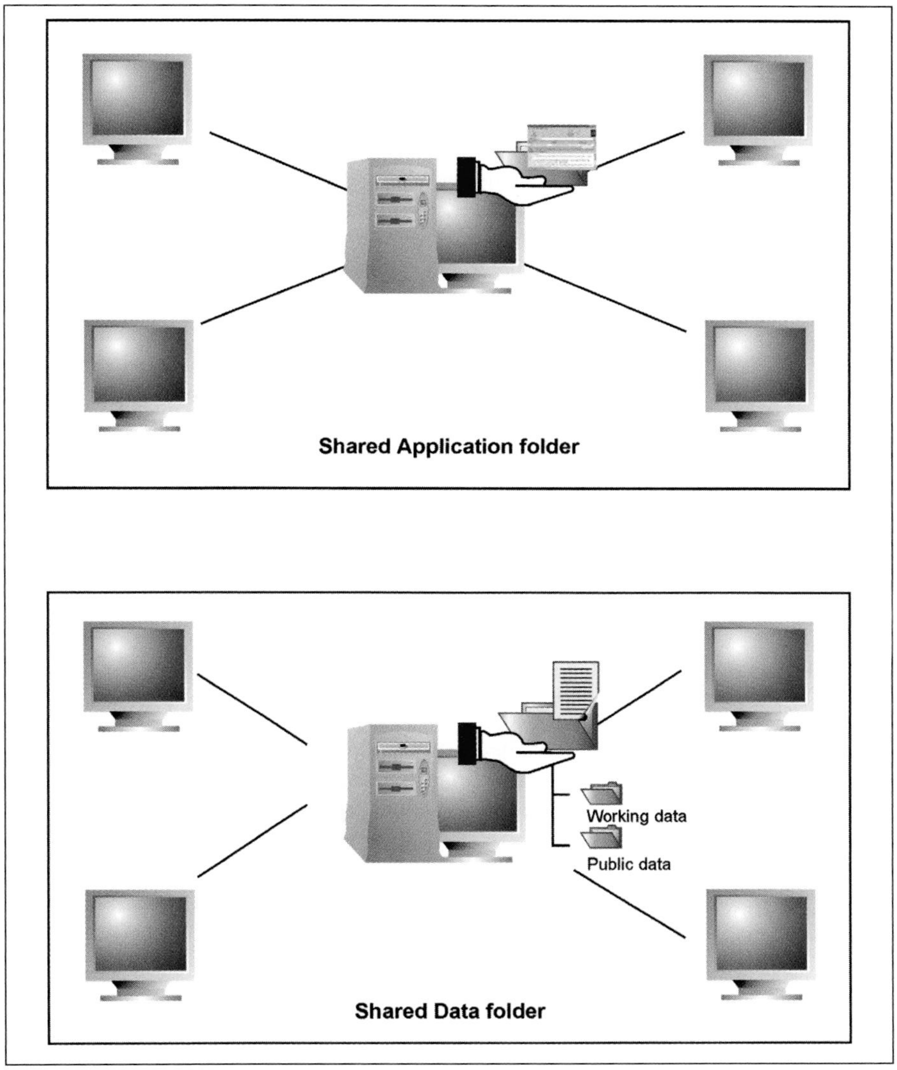

Shared Application folder

Working data

Public data

Shared Data folder

skill 1

Introducing Shared Folders (cont'd)

exam objective

Basic knowledge

more

hide them from other users on the network **(Figure 9-2)**. For example, the %systemroot% folder, the root of each volume, and the location of the printer drivers are hidden administrative shares.

Some of the administrative shared folders that Windows 2000 automatically creates are:

◆ **Admin$:** Admin$ is the shared folder used by Administrators to administer Windows 2000 Professional. By default, **C:\Winnt**, the system root folder, is shared as **Admin$** **(Figure 9-3)**. Only members of the **Administrator** group have **Full Control** permission to access this folder. Members of other groups such as Everyone, Power Users, and Server Operators have no rights to access these folders.

◆ **C$, D$, E$:** The drive letter administrative shares point to the roots of the corresponding logical drive. For example, D$ is the shared folder name for the shared D: drive. The administrator accesses these shared folders to connect to the entire volume of a remote computer to perform administrative tasks.

◆ **Print$:** The Print$ administrative share is used by Administrators to monitor shared printers remotely by providing access to the printer driver files. Members of the **Administrators**, **Server Operators**, and **Print Operators** groups have **Full Control** permission for this folder. The **Everyone** group is given only Read permission.

◆ **IPC$ (Interprocess Communications):** The IPC$ administrative share is used to facilitate IPC communication between systems. Interprocess communications refers to the capacity supported by multiprocessing systems that allows one process, or executing program, to exchange information with another process that is either executing on the same computer or on another computer on a network. It allows client computers to submit requests for service to servers and enables servers to answer those requests.

Only members of the Administrators and Backup Operators local groups have the right to use the administrative shares on Windows 2000 Professional and Windows 2000 Server member servers. Users in the Administrators, Backup Operators, and Server Operators groups can access administrative shares on a domain controller.

You can also create shared hidden folders. You can share folders and append a dollar sign to the end of the share name. This will enable only users who know the folder name and have appropriate permissions to gain access to the folder. You can use this to share applications with other Administrators so that other users will not be able to see these folders when they use My Network Places to access shared resources.

Figure 9-2 Built-in administrative shares in Shares node in Shared folders snap-in

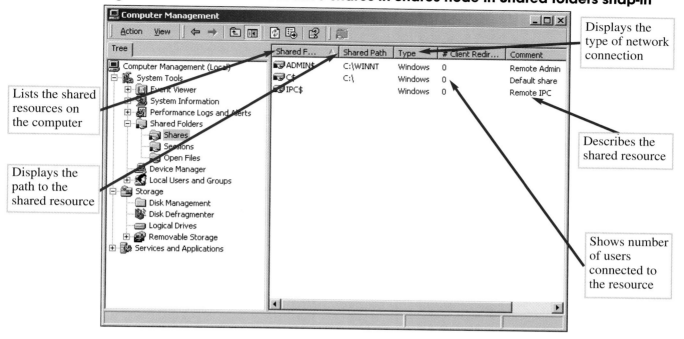

Lists the shared resources on the computer

Displays the path to the shared resource

Displays the type of network connection

Describes the shared resource

Shows number of users connected to the resource

Figure 9-3 The WINNT Properties dialog box

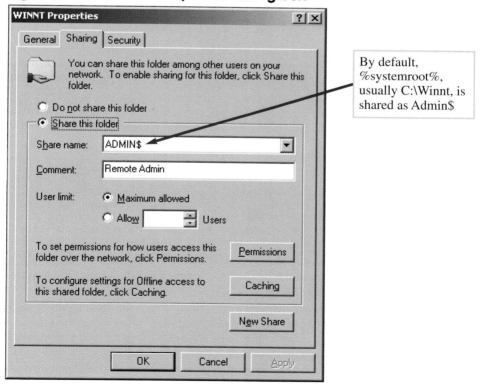

By default, %systemroot%, usually C:\Winnt, is shared as Admin$

skill 2

Sharing a Folder

exam objective

Create and remove shared folders. Connect to shared resources on a Microsoft network.

overview

To create a shared folder, you use the **Sharing tab** on the Properties dialog box for that folder. By default, the name that is given to the shared folder will be the original folder name, but you can change this if you want. This way you can use one name for opening the folder locally and another name for accessing it over the network. On the Sharing tab, you can set various options for sharing the folder, as well as set the properties for the shared folder. Some of the options are:

◆ **Share this folder:** This option makes the contents of the folder available to network users.

◆ **Share name:** This is the name assigned to the folder that you want to share. Network users will use this name to access the shared folder.

◆ **Comment:** This is a description of the shared folder.

◆ **User limit:** This option is used to set the number of users who can simultaneously access a shared folder over a network. If you click the **Maximum allowed** option button, Windows 2000 Professional will allow ten users to connect to the shared folder, or you can specify a lower number. A maximum of ten simultaneous users is allowed because Windows 2000 Professional is designed for workgroup or peer-to-peer networks. Windows 2000 Server, on the other hand, allows a maximum number of users to simultaneously access a shared folder, based on licensing terms.

◆ **Permissions:** This button is used to assign access permissions to ensure that only authorized users can connect to the shared folder.

◆ **Caching:** This button is used to designate how the contents of a shared folder can be accessed offline.

You can also disallow the sharing of a folder to make its contents unavailable over the network. To do this, click the **Do not share this folder** option button on the **Sharing** tab.

You can also create a shared folder using the **Create Shared Folder Wizard**. This wizard guides you through the process of selecting the folder you want to share, making it available to network users, and assigning permissions to the various users who will be accessing it. You access the Create Shared Folder Wizard in the **Computer Management** window.

how to

Share a folder named **General**.

1. Right-click [🍂 Start], and click the **Explore** command on the shortcut menu to open the **Windows Explorer** window.

2. Right-click the folder that you want to share, for example **General**. Then click the **Properties** command on the shortcut menu to open the **General Properties** dialog box.

3. Click the **Sharing** tab.

4. Click the **Share this folder** option button to make the contents of the folder accessible to other users on the network (**Figure 9-4**). The name of the folder you have chosen to share, in this case **General**, appears by default in the **Share name** text box, and the **Maximum allowed** option button is selected by default.

5. Accept the defaults and click [OK] to close the **General Properties** dialog box.

Figure 9-4 Sharing tab in General Properties dialog box

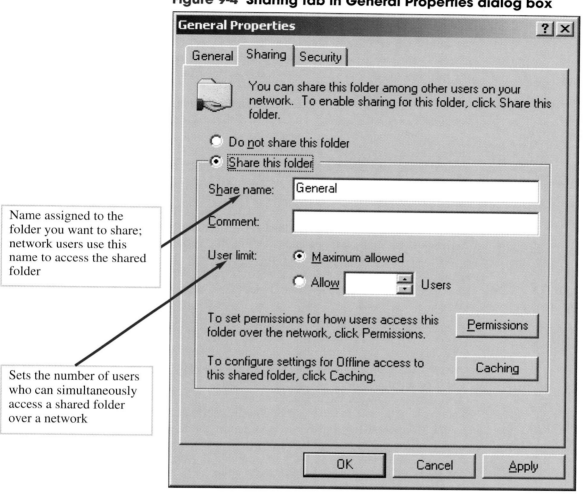

Name assigned to the folder you want to share; network users use this name to access the shared folder

Sets the number of users who can simultaneously access a shared folder over a network

skill 2

Sharing a Folder (cont'd)

exam objective

Create and remove shared folders. Connect to shared resources on a Microsoft network.

more

In order to create shortcuts for your users to connect to a shared folder, you use one of the following methods:

- **My Network Places:** The **My Network Places** icon on the desktop can be used to map a network location. First, double-click the **Add Network Place** icon in the My Network Places window to open the **Add Network Place Wizard (Figure 9-5)**. Then, in the **Type the location of the Network Place** text box, enter the **UNC (Universal Naming Convention) pathname** for the shared folder. The UNC path is used to connect to any resource on the network for which you have permission. The syntax for the UNC path is: *\\computername\sharename*. The *computername* is the name of the computer or server (the NetBIOS name) you are going to connect to and the *sharename* is the name of the shared folder. Make sure you understand that the UNC path is not the same as the pathname you use to open a local resource. The MS-DOS pathname uses the familiar C:*foldername**subfoldername**filename* syntax. The UNC pathname does not include a drive letter or a hierarchical path. You can also enter just *\\computername* to view all of the shares on any computer. After you have entered the UNC, click **Next** to open the **Completing the Add Network Place Wizard** dialog box. **Enter a name for this new Network Place** in the text box and click **Finish**. My Network Places serves as a network resources browser for your users, providing them with an easy way to connect to any shared folders you have added as a network place. All that your users will see are the shortcuts you have created—shared folder icons. They will never have to know the UNC pathname.

- **Map Network Drive dialog box:** Right-click either My Computer or My Network Places on the desktop and select the **Map Network Drive** command. In the **Drive** list box, choose any drive letter that is not already being used for the network connection. Enter the UNC pathname for the folder or use the **Browse** button to locate the folder and it will be automatically entered in the **Folder** list box. Select the **Reconnect at logon** check box if you want the mapped connection to be included in a user's user profile so that they will be able to see it in Windows Explorer each time they log on. You can also use the **Connect using a different user name** link to specify a different user name for making this connection **(Figure 9-6)**. After you have mapped a network drive, users will see it as another drive letter in My Computer and Windows Explorer. This is what is called a logical drive, as opposed to an actual physical drive.

- **Run command:** You can also specify the UNC path to a shared resource in the Open text box in the Run dialog box **(Figure 9-7)**, or you can enter *\\computername* to view a list of the shared folders on that computer **(Figure 9-8)**. Then, double-click the share to connect to it over the network.

- **NET USE command:** At the command prompt, type: **NET USE (drive letter):** *\\computername\sharename*. In other words, type the drive letter you are going to use for the mapped connection and the UNC for the shared folder.

Mapping a network drive to a shared resource creates a shortcut to the resource. Once this shortcut is created, your users can access the shared resource directly through the shortcut instead of having to use the NET USE or Map Network Drive utilities again.

tip

You can also use a URL path to a Web folder or an FTP (File Transfer Protocol) path to an FTP site.

tip

You can also map a network drive to a shared network folder (not a local folder) by right-clicking the folder and selecting the **Map Network Drive** command on the shortcut menu.

Figure 9-5 Add Network Place Wizard

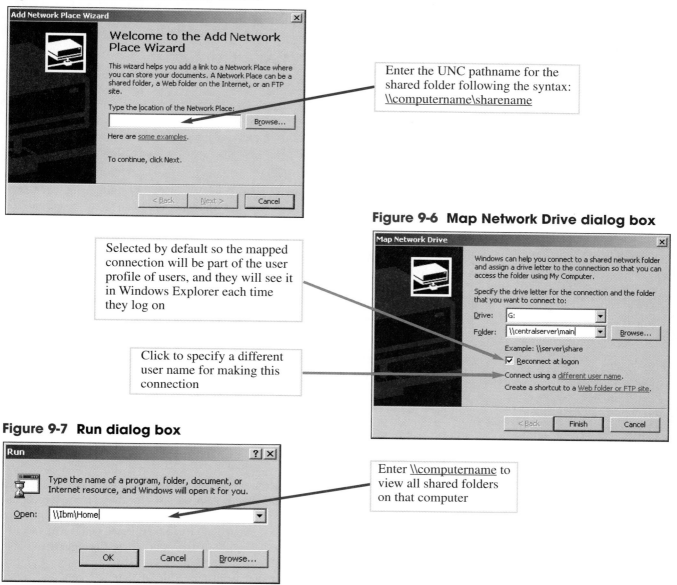

Enter the UNC pathname for the shared folder following the syntax: \\computername\sharename

Figure 9-6 Map Network Drive dialog box

Selected by default so the mapped connection will be part of the user profile of users, and they will see it in Windows Explorer each time they log on

Click to specify a different user name for making this connection

Figure 9-7 Run dialog box

Enter \\computername to view all shared folders on that computer

Figure 9-8 Viewing network resources

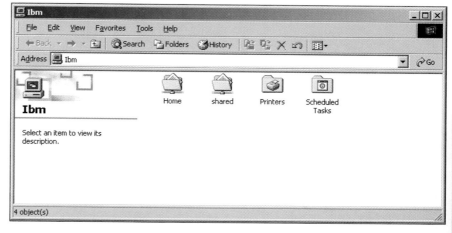

skill 3

Introducing Types of Permissions for Shared Folders

exam objective

Control access to files and folders by using permissions. Control access to shared folders by using permissions.

overview

When you create shares, you can control the level of access network users have to some extent. As you will see in the next lesson, you have much more latitude in setting the level of control users will have when you use NTFS permissions. For shared folders there are only three levels of access **(Figure 9-9)**.

◆ **Read:** The Read permission allows users to display folder names, file names, file data, and the attributes of folders shared on remote systems. Users can also run programs that are in shared application folders.

◆ **Change:** The Change permission allows users to create folders, add files to folders, modify data in files, add data to files, modify file attributes, and delete files and folders, in addition to the actions permitted by the Read permission.

◆ **Full Control:** The Full Control permission allows full access to the shared folder, including all actions permitted by the Read and Change permissions, and users can change permissions on the share.

These three levels of access are controlled by two conditions: allow and deny. The default setting is Allow, which gives users the specific permission for the shared folder. Deny, on the other hand, blocks the permission. The Deny setting should not be used very often, because it supersedes the Allow condition; however, it can be useful in cases where you want to deny a specific user in a group the same level of access granted to the group. It is also possible to grant the Change permission while at the same time denying the Read permission, so that a user will be able to delete files based on the file name, but will not be able to read the file before deleting it **(Figure 9-10)**. Some important guidelines for assigning shared folder permissions are listed below:

◆ If you assign a specific permission to a user and the user is a member of a group that has a different set of permissions, then the effective permissions for the user are the combination of the user and group permissions. In other words, you add the two permissions together. For example, if a user has been granted the **Read** permission and is a member of a group that has the **Change** permission, the cumulative effect is the **Change** permission, which includes the **Read** permission.

◆ If you deny a permission to a user, it specifically overrides the allow condition for that permission. Allow gives users the specific permission for the shared folder. Deny *blocks* the permission. For example, if a user has been granted the Read permission by virtue of his or her membership in Group A, but he or she also belongs to Group B, which has been specifically denied the Read permission, the user will not be allowed to access the file.

◆ When you copy or move a shared folder to a new location, the shared folder does not remain shared in the new location.

◆ Organize folders with the same security requirements within a single folder. For example, you can store the folders of various applications within a single folder. Then, you can share the folder containing all of the application folders, instead of sharing each application folder individually.

◆ Assign relevant share names to folders to enable users to locate them easily. Share names should also be short so that they are easier to remember and so that other operating systems can use them. MS-DOS, Windows 3.x, and Windows for Workgroups use 8.3 character names.

Figure 9-9 Shared folder permissions

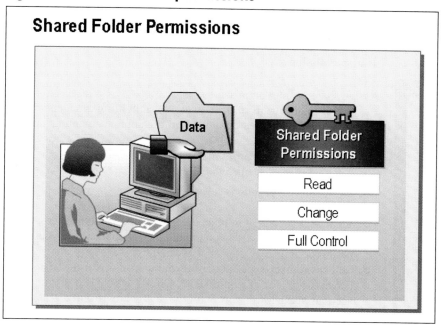

Figure 9-10 Share permissions

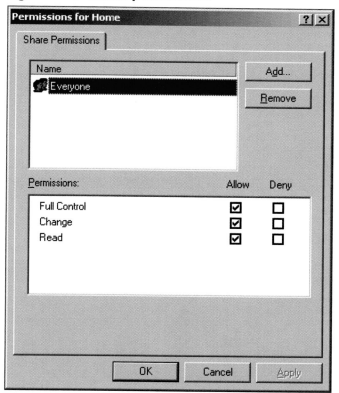

skill 3

Introducing Types of Permissions for Shared Folders (cont'd)

exam objective

Control access to files and folders by using permissions. Control access to shared folders by using permissions.

how to

Assign shared folder permissions.

1. In the **Windows Explorer** window, right-click the General folder in the C: drive and click the **Properties** command on the shortcut menu to open the **General Properties** dialog box.
2. In the General Properties dialog box, click the **Sharing** tab.
3. Click [Permissions] to open the **Permissions for General** dialog box.
4. By default, **Everyone** is selected in the **Name** list. Click [Remove] to remove this group from the Name list.
5. Then click [Add] to open the **Select Users, Computers, or Groups** dialog box. Here you can select a user, a computer, or a group to which you want to assign shared folder permissions.
6. Select the user accounts and groups on the **Name** list to which you want to assign permissions, for example **Usr2**. Click [Add] to display the selected user or group account in the lower portion of the dialog box **(Figure 9-11)**.
7. Click [OK] to open the **Permissions for General** dialog box. The **Name** list displays the selected user name **Usr2 (Figure 9-12)**.
8. Select the user **Usr2** and select the **Allow** check box next to the **Read** permission to allow Usr2 to read the data in the General folder.
9. Click [OK] to close the **Permissions for General** dialog box.
10. Close the General Properties dialog box.

Figure 9-11 Selecting a user to assign permissions

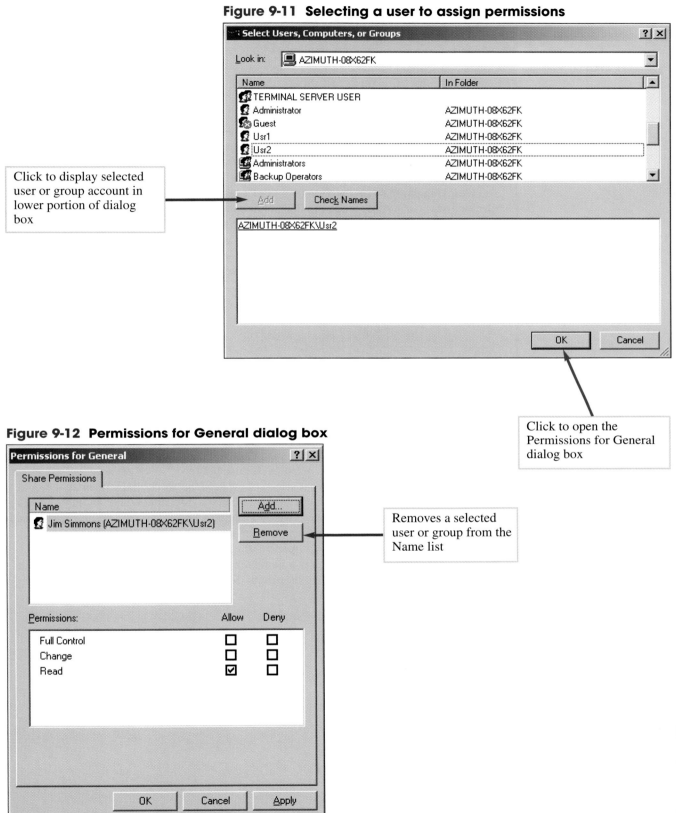

Click to display selected user or group account in lower portion of dialog box

Click to open the Permissions for General dialog box

Figure 9-12 Permissions for General dialog box

Removes a selected user or group from the Name list

skill 4

Accessing Shared Resources on a Windows Network

exam objective

Connect to shared resources on a Microsoft network.

overview

As you have learned, you can use My Network Places to create shortcuts to shared folders, Web folders, and File Transfer Protocol (FTP) sites on a remote network. FTP is a protocol that is used to make file transfers between local and remote computers possible. Local workstations upload files to an FTP server and remote users can then download them. When a URL contains *ftp*, it means that you are accessing an FTP server rather than a Web server. When you view Web pages in your browser, HTTP (Hypertext Transfer Protocol) is used to transmit files so that you can read them, or to transfer or copy them to a local drive. On the other hand, you use FTP to transfer files from a workstation to the file server and vice versa, and on each end they are stored on the hard drive of the receiving computer. Usually you can only access these sites by specifying a user name and password. However, if anonymous access is enabled, you can also gain limited access to the files and folders on an FTP site by logging on anonymously.

how to

Use **My Network Places** to access an ftp site. The path address of the site is: **ftp://ftp.netscape.com.** Log on anonymously to the FTP site and name the new network place **Netscape FTP**.

1. Open the **Windows Explorer** window.
2. Click the **My Network Places** icon to open the **My Network Places** window (**Figure 9-13**).
3. Double-click the **Add Network Place** icon to start the **Add Network Place Wizard**.
4. Type **ftp://ftp.netscape.com** in the **Type the location of the Network Place:** text box to indicate the path to the shared resource (**Figure 9-14**).
5. Click [Next >] to open the next screen of the **Add Network Place Wizard**.
6. The **Log on anonymously** check box is selected by default. When you log on anonymously, you do not need to specify a user name and password, and you can use limited resources on the FTP site. However, anonymous logon is not always possible.
7. Click [Next >] to open the **Completing the Add Network Place Wizard** screen.
8. Type **Netscape FTP** in the **Enter a name for this Network Place:** text box to indicate a name for the new network place (**Figure 9-15**).
9. Click [Finish] to save the settings and close the **Add Network Place Wizard**.
10. Close Windows Explorer.

Figure 9-13 Selecting the My Network Places icon

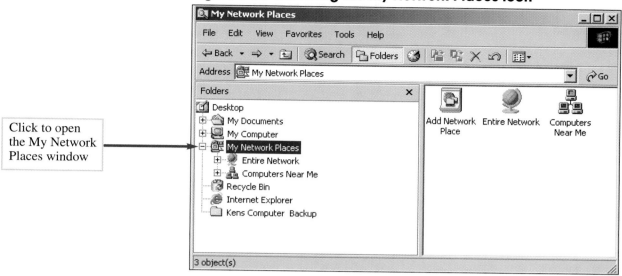

Click to open
the My Network
Places window

Figure 9-14 Specifying the location of the ftp folder

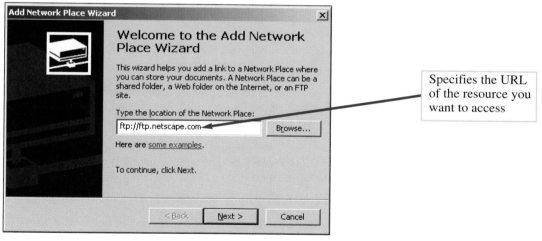

Specifies the URL
of the resource you
want to access

Figure 9-15 Specifying a name for the new network place

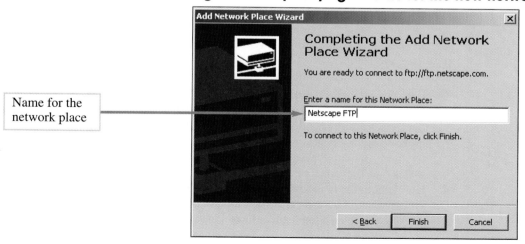

Name for the
network place

skill 5

Monitoring Access to Shared Folders

exam objective

Manage and troubleshoot access to shared folders. Monitor, manage, and troubleshoot access to files and folders.

overview

tip

Members of the Administrators or Server Operators groups in a domain have the right to monitor all systems in the domain. Members of the local Administrators and Power Users groups can monitor a local system in a workgroup.

tip

The default maximum user limit is 10 in Windows 2000 Professional. You can set this to a lower value.

tip

The list of shared folders and open files does not update automatically. To update the list, you must click the Refresh command on the Action menu in the Computer Management window.

In an organization, there are certain confidential resources that must be safeguarded. Restricted access by only select users must be assigned in order to keep those resources secure. It is also important to monitor such resources at regular intervals. Apart from security reasons, you monitor and manage user access to shared network resources for the following reasons:

◆ **Maintenance:** While performing maintenance tasks on network resources, you may be required to make certain resources unavailable to some or all connected users. You can monitor who is using the resources and notify them before making the resources unavailable.

◆ **Planning:** As the number of users on a network grows, you need to plan for new resources and monitor the usage of existing resources.

You can use the **Shared Folders snap-in** to monitor user access to shared resources in the following ways:

Determining the number of users accessing a shared folder: You can view the maximum number of users who can gain access to a folder at one time by selecting the shared folder in the details pane of the Shared folder snap-in. Then open the **Action** menu and select the **Properties** command to open the **Properties** dialog box for the shared folder. On the **General** tab you can see the number of users who are allowed to concurrently gain access to the folder (**Figure 9-16**).

Monitoring Open Files: You can view a list of the open files in the shared folders and the users who are accessing the files. To do this, you need to access the **Open Files** folder in the **Shared Folders** snap-in, which is in the Computer Management console. Administrators can also disconnect users from one open file or from all open files when required. You disconnect users from all open files by selecting **Open Files** in the Shared Folders snap-in. Then, open the **Action** menu and select the **Disconnect All Open Files** command or you can simply right-click Open Files and select Disconnect All Open Files on the context menu (**Figure 9-17**). You close a particular open file by selecting the open file, opening the Action menu, and selecting the **Close Open File** command or by right-clicking the file you want to close and selecting Close Open File.

Administrators also can use the Shares or Shared Folders nodes to contact users when the user limit has been met and another user must access the open file, or the Administrator must shut down the system for maintenance. To do this, right-click either node, point to **All Tasks**, and click the **Send Console Message** command to open the **Send Console Message** dialog box (**Figure 9-18**). Alternatively, with either node selected, open the **Action** menu, point to **All Tasks**, and click the **Send Console Message** command.

more

tip

Windows 2000 also includes a feature called Auditing, which you can use to monitor access to shared folders over a network. Auditing can provide you with information like the number of unauthorized attempts to log on or access folders, what folders were accessed when and by whom, and what actions they tried to perform.

At times users might experience difficulty in accessing a shared folder. This can be due to various reasons, including improper access permissions. You must identify the cause of these problems and follow corrective measures. Some common problems, their probable causes, and the solutions are listed below:

◆ **User access denied to the Admin$ folder:** This problem arises for non-members of the Administrators or Backup Operators groups. Only members of the Administrators and Backup Operators local groups can access the administrative shares on Windows 2000 Professional computers and Windows 2000 Server member servers. Users in the Administrators, Backup Operators, and Server Operators groups can access administrative shares on a domain controller.

◆ **User is not able to modify the contents of a shared folder:** This problem may arise when you only have the Read permission for a shared folder. So that the user can modify the content of a folder, an administrator must assign the Change or Full Control permission.

Figure 9-16 Determining the user limit

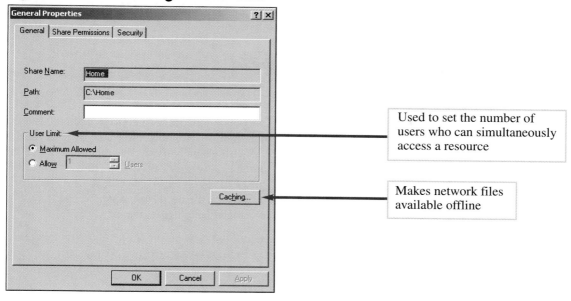

Used to set the number of users who can simultaneously access a resource

Makes network files available offline

Figure 9-17 The Shared Folders node, disconnecting all open files

Contains commands used to monitor user access

Used to view and monitor shared folders, open files, and open sessions

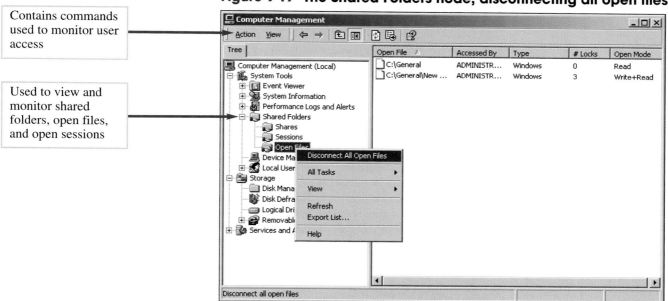

Figure 9-18 The Send Console Message dialog box

Allows Administrator to to contact users when the user limit has been met

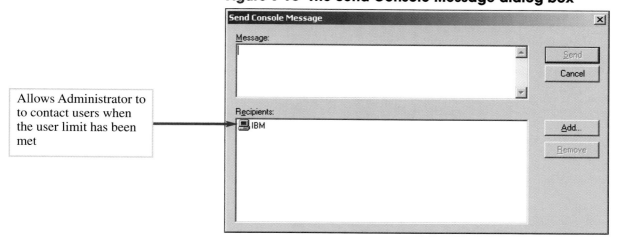

skill 6

Configuring and Managing Offline Files and Folders

exam objective

Manage and troubleshoot the use and synchronization of offline files. Optimize access to files and folders.

overview

The purpose of offline files and folders is to allow you to work with network documents even when the system is down. If granted permission to do so, Administrators and users can select certain network files and folders to be cached. **Caching** simply means that the data is copied to the local workstation. Network files that are stored locally are called **Offline files**. Offline files are stored in a reserved portion of your system's disk space called the **Cache**. If the network connection malfunctions, users can continue working on the local copy. Then, when the system is restored, Windows 2000 can synchronize or automatically update the network file.

Caching offline folders is a two-stage procedure. First, you must configure your computer to be able to use offline folders and files. Then you must configure your computer so that you can make the shared folders stored on your computer available offline to other users on the network.

You give your computer the ability to use offline folders and files on the **Offline Files** tab in the **Folder Options** dialog box. There are two ways to access this dialog box. You can select the **Folder Options** command on the **Tools** menu in the **My Computer** window or you can double-click **Folder Options** in the **Control Panel**. Then, on the **Offline Files** tab, **(Figure 9-19)** you must make sure that the **Enable Offline Files** check box is selected. In Windows 2000 Professional this check box and the **Synchronize all offline files before logging off** check box are selected by default, while in Windows 2000 Server you must set them yourself.

Next, you must select the resource that you want to be made available offline. In order to do this, you must use the Map Network Drive Wizard to assign a drive letter to a shared network resource. You must have a link to a network drive in order to make those files available offline. After you have created a link to a network drive, open the **My Computer** window, right-click the drive icon, and select the **Make Available Offline** command **(Figure 9-20)**. The first time you create an offline folder, the **Offline Files Wizard (Figure 9-21)** will open. You will have to answer questions about how the synchronization of the folders should take place and, if you want, you can have a desktop icon added. Then the offline files will be copied to your hard drive and a double-arrow icon will be added to the drive icon. Next time you create an offline folder, the wizard will not be necessary.

To configure shared folders stored on your computer so that network users can cache them, you must open the **Caching Settings** dialog box from the Properties dialog box for the shared folder. To open the Caching Settings dialog box, click the **Caching Settings** button on the **Sharing** tab in the Properties dialog box for the shared folder. The options in the **Setting** list box are:

- ◆ **Automatic Caching for Documents:** This option automatically downloads and caches (or copies) all files in a folder as users open them. Old copies of the file that are already stored on the user's hard disk will be automatically replaced with the newer version.
- ◆ **Automatic Caching for Programs:** This option makes offline copies of all files from shared folders that have been read, run, or referenced without being modified. Automatic caching for programs enables you to read and execute read-only programs that run from the server without connecting to the network. You cannot change the content of these files.
- ◆ **Manual Caching for Documents:** This is the default setting, which lets users manually specify the documents they want to be available offline.

When you reconnect to the network, the changes that you made to the offline files are updated to the network files. This process is called **synchronization**. To configure the synchronization

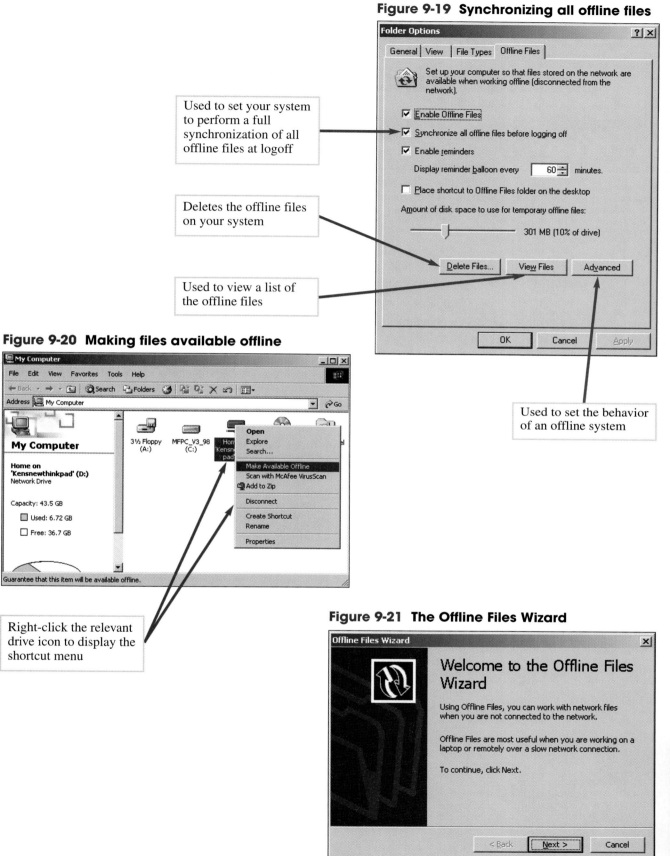

Figure 9-19 Synchronizing all offline files

Used to set your system to perform a full synchronization of all offline files at logoff

Deletes the offline files on your system

Used to view a list of the offline files

Used to set the behavior of an offline system

Figure 9-20 Making files available offline

Right-click the relevant drive icon to display the shortcut menu

Figure 9-21 The Offline Files Wizard

skill 6

Configuring and Managing Offline Files and Folders *(cont'd)*

exam objective

Manage and troubleshoot the use and synchronization of offline files. Optimize access to files and folders.

overview

process, open the **My Computer** window and select the mapped network drive. Then open the **Tools** menu and select the **Synchronize** command to open the **Synchronization Manager Items to Synchronize** dialog box **(Figure 9-22)**. Click the **Setup** button to open the **Synchronization Settings** dialog box. On the **Scheduled** tab, click the **Add** button to start the **Scheduled Synchronization Wizard**. You can schedule synchronization tasks to take place daily, only on weekdays, or you can set a schedule for a set number of days between synchronization. The Synchronization Manager is used to update offline files and folders:

◆ Every time you log on or log off your system.
◆ At specific intervals when your system is idle.
◆ At scheduled times.

You have two options for synchronizing files. If you want to perform a full synchronization, leave the **Synchronize all offline files before logging off** check box selected on the Offline Files tab in the Folder Options dialog box. If you only want to perform a quick synchronization, clear the check box.

◆ **Full synchronization:** This ensures that you have the latest version of the offline files on the network.
◆ **Quick synchronization:** This ensures that you have a complete set of offline files on your system, but does not guarantee that they are the latest version.

Computers on a Microsoft network use a file-sharing protocol called Server Message Block (SMB) for network communication. The File and Print Sharing for Microsoft Networks service (the Server service) used by the computer that hosts the share and the client computer running the Workstation service (the client redirector) that accesses the share, use this protocol to communicate. This means that non-Microsoft networks, such as Novell NetWare, are not compatible and you cannot set up offline files with them.

how to

Configure a folder so that network users can cache the files in the share.
1. Log on to your system as an **Administrator**.
2. Open the **Windows Explorer** window.
3. Right-click a folder on your system, for example **Folder1**, and click the **Sharing** command on the shortcut menu to open the **Folder1 Properties** dialog box with the **Sharing** tab active.
4. Click the **Share this folder** option button to make the contents of the folder accessible to users over the network.
5. Click [Caching] to open the **Caching Settings** dialog box. Make sure that the **Allow caching of files in this folder** check box has not been cleared. (It is selected by default on Windows 2000 Professional computers.)
6. In the **Setting** list box, select the **Automatic Caching for Documents** option **(Figure 9-23)**.
7. Click [OK] to close the **Caching Settings** dialog box.
8. Click [OK] to close the **Folder1 Properties** dialog box.

Figure 9-22 Synchronizing selected offline files

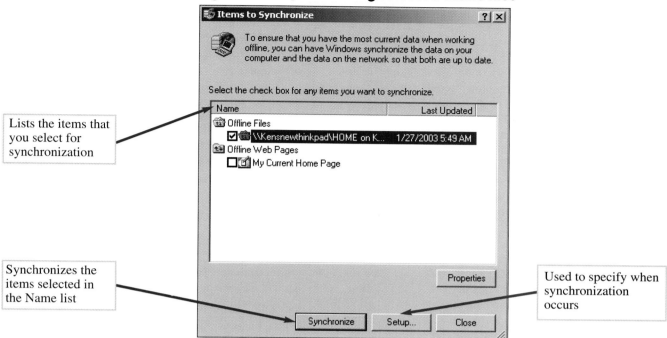

Lists the items that you select for synchronization

Synchronizes the items selected in the Name list

Used to specify when synchronization occurs

Figure 9-23 Caching Settings dialog box

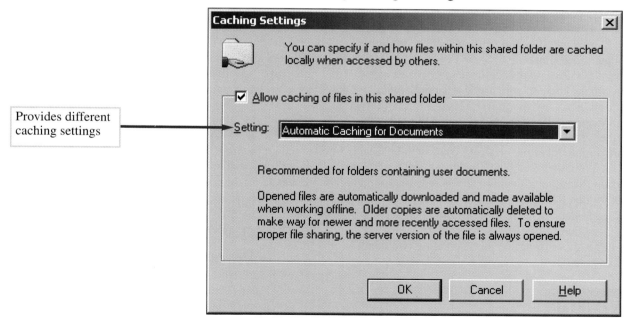

Provides different caching settings

Summary

◆ A folder that is shared on a computer and is accessible to users over a network is called a Shared Folder or a share.

◆ On FAT, FAT32, and NTFS partitions and volumes, you can use what are called share permissions or shared folder permissions to control access to network resources.

◆ This type of access control is only for folders. Individual files within the folders cannot be given their own sets of permissions. To control who can access a particular file, you must grant the appropriate privileges to the folder in which it is stored.

◆ Shared folder permissions are not applicable at the local computer level. They cannot be used to control what users can access locally. By default, all local resources can be accessed by any user, except on NTFS volumes where many system folders and files are protected from access by users. In contrast, shared folders are used for networks and share permissions must be set up or these folders cannot be accessed by anyone.

◆ After you determine which folders will be shared and which groups or individuals will be able to access them, you set permissions to control what these users will be allowed to do.

◆ You set share permissions in the ACL (Access Control List) for that resource.

◆ The default permission for a shared resource is Full Control for the Everyone group. Generally, you will remove this permission and set your own according to your organizational needs.

◆ Windows 2000 Professional automatically shares certain folders, whose contents are available to only Administrators and Backup Operators. These administrative shares are appended with a dollar sign ($) to hide them from other users on the network.

◆ To share a folder over the network, you use the Sharing tab on the Properties dialog box for the folder.

◆ You assign permissions to a user in the Permissions dialog box for that folder.

◆ For shared folders there are three levels of access: Read, Change, and Full Control.

◆ These three levels of access are limited by two conditions: allow and deny.

◆ Allow gives users the specific permission for the shared folder. Deny blocks the permission. The Deny setting should not be used very often, because it supersedes the Allow condition.

◆ If you assign a specific permission to a user and the user is a member of a group that has a different set of permissions, then the effective permissions for the user are the combination of the user and group permissions. For example, if a user has been granted the Read permission for a shared folder and is a member of a group that has the Change permission, the cumulative effect is the Change permission, which includes the Read permission.

◆ Shared folders that are copied or moved to another location are not shared at the new location.

◆ You connect to a shared folder using the Map Network Drive Wizard.

◆ Offline files enable you to work on the latest version of network files when you are not connected to the network.

◆ Caching offline folders is a two-stage procedure. First, you must configure your computer to be able to use offline folders and files. Then you must configure your computer so that you can make the shared folders stored on your computer available offline to other users on the network.

◆ You give your computer the ability to use offline folders and files on the Offline Files tab in the Folder options dialog box. On the Offline Files tab, you must make sure that the Enable Offline Files check box is selected. In Windows 2000 Professional, this check box and the Synchronize All Offline Files check box are selected by default, while in Windows 2000 Server you must set them yourself.

◆ To configure folders stored on your computer so that network users can cache them, you must open the Caching Settings dialog box from the Properties dialog box for the shared folder.

◆ Users who belong to the Administrator and Server Operators group can share folders on any system in a domain.

◆ You use the Shared Folders snap-in in the Computer Management window to monitor user access to network resources.

Key Terms

Administrative shared folders
Admin$
C$, D$, E$
Caching
Change permission
Create Shared Folder Wizard
Full Control permission
ICP$ (Interprocess Communications)

My Network Places
Offline files
Offline folders
Open Files folder
Print$
Read permission
Shared Application Folder
Shared Data Folder

Shared Folder permissions
Shared folder
Shared Folders snap-in
Synchronization
UNC (Universal Naming Convention)
   pathname

Test Yourself

1. John is the member of two groups, HR Recruitment and HR Strategic Planning at Spearhouse Corp. You assign Read Permission to the HR Recruitment group to access a shared folder named Employee Details. You also assign the Change permission to the HR Strategic Planning group to access the Employee Details folder. The effective permission for John to access Employee Details is:
   a. Read
   b. Write
   c. Full Control
   d. Change

2. Which of the following types of permissions can you assign to local users for a file system directory on a Windows 2000 Professional computer if the hard disk is formatted with the FAT32 file system?
   a. Shared folder permissions
   b. File-and-folder permissions
   c. NTFS permissions
   d. None of the above

3. You are the Administrator of a peer-to-peer network at a family-run pharmacy and you have created a shared folder named Drug Efficacy. The owner asks you to move the folder to a new, more powerful Windows 2000 computer. After you have moved the folder, the pharmacist complains to you that she can no longer access it. What happened?
   a. You have moved it to an NTFS volume and the share permissions that you had set are no longer applicable. You must set NTFS permissions for the folder.
   b. The pharmacist must log off and log back on in order to access the folder in its new location.
   c. Folders that are copied or moved to another location are not shared in the new location.
   d. You forgot to allow caching of files in the shared folder after you moved it.

4. Which of the following symbols is used to identify a share created automatically by Windows 2000 for administrative purposes?
   a. %
   b. &
   c. $
   d. #

5. Suzanne has the Full Control permission for a shared folder on Bill's computer. She also belongs to the Sales group, which has been denied the Full Control permission. What is Suzanne's effective permission?
   a. Full Control
   b. Read
   c. None
   d. Change

6. John is a freelancer working for Pixel Inc. He uses a Windows 2000 Professional laptop and a dial-up connection to a Windows 2000 server on the network to access the files that he needs. He uses Offline Files so that when he is traveling he can work on his files without a network connection and can then synchronize his files. He wants to make sure that the cached version on his laptop is always in full synchronization with the network version. What should he do?
   a. In the Settings list box in the Caching Settings dialog box, he should select, Automatic Caching for Documents.
   b. On the General tab in the Synchronization Settings dialog box, he should select the Synchronize all offline files before logging off check box.
   c. On the Offline Files tab in the Folder Options dialog box, he should leave the Synchronize all offline files before logging off check box selected.
   d. On the On Idle tab in the Synchronization Settings dialog box, he should select the Schedule a full synchronization check box.

7. Which of the following is used to view all open files in the shared folders on the network?
   a. Shared folders snap-in
   b. Admin$ folder
   c. Caching Settings dialog box
   d. The Properties dialog box for the shared folder

8. Which of the following do you use to make the content of a folder available to users over a network?
   a. Caching Settings dialog box
   b. Sharing tab
   c. Permissions button
   d. APM tab

9. You can set up offline files with Novell Netware servers running versions 4.0 and higher.
   a. True
   b. False

Projects: On Your Own

1. Sharing a folder.
   a. Access the **Properties** dialog box of a folder.
   b. Click the **Sharing** tab.
   c. Click the **Share this Folder** option button.
   d. Type the name in the **Share Name** text box.
   e. Share a folder with the specified name.
2. Assign shared folder permissions.
   a. Select a folder and access the **Permissions** dialog box.
   b. Remove the **Everyone** option.
   c. Access the **Select Users, Computers or Groups** dialog box.
   d. Select a user or group account and click **Add**.

   e. Access the **Permission** dialog box again and select the user.
   f. Select the **Allow** check box to assign the Full Control permission.
3. Configure Caching to access network files offline.
   a. Log on as **Administrator**.
   b. Access the **Properties** dialog box for a shared folder.
   c. Access the **Caching Settings** dialog box.
   d. Select the **Allow caching of files in this folder** check box.
   e. Select the **Manual Caching for Documents as** option.
   f. Accept the settings.

Problem Solving Scenarios

1. You work as a project manager at Excelerate, Inc., a fashion industry design house in New York City. You manage a team of 10 assistant designers who share resources on a workgroup network. You are very concerned about security; therefore, you want all team members to keep a local copy of their work on their hard drives, but to back up their files at the end of every day on your machine as well. Describe in a memo to your instructor how you will create a shared folder named Team Share on your system and assign permissions to the assistant designers this capability.

2. As a Network Administrator at Excelerate, Inc., you have been asked to assign different share folder permissions to various departments to access a folder named Software on the file server. The departments in the company are divided into groups—for example, the Market Research group, Human Resources group, and Production group. Management wants the following functionality:

◆ The Market Research group must be able to edit files in the folder and assign permissions to new users.
◆ The Human Resources group should not have access to the Software folder.
◆ The Production group must be able to add and delete file folders, but should not be able to change permissions on the share.

Describe in a memo how you will achieve these objectives.

Just as you provide accessibility to files and folders and make sure that the correct levels of access are granted, you can also share print resources and assign different levels of access to different sets of users. Although Microsoft's printing terminology is somewhat counterintuitive, it can help you to understand how sharing print resources works. In Windows 2000, a **printer** is considered to be the software that delivers the requests for service from the operating system to the physical print device. A **print device**, therefore, is the physical hardware that you think of as a printer, which creates the hard copies of your digital files. It is then easy to understand how another resource stored on a disk on the hard drive, (the printer) can be shared with other network users. It is also easy to understand why the ability to configure shared printers is so valuable to a business. Each client does not need its own expensive hardware device.

A **print server** handles the requests for service for a shared printer. A print server can either administer these requests through a print device that is physically connected to it, or through a print device connected to the network. Network connected print devices are called network-interface print devices and they have their own NIC (network interface card) and network address or an external network adapter connection. The main point, however, is that a print server receives the requests, queues them, uses a printer driver to translate the digital documents into printer code, and sends the instructions to the print device. Windows 2000 Professional computers, and even Windows 9.x computers, can be configured as print servers. However, this ability is limited by the fact that they can, for the most part, only be used on exclusively Microsoft networks. An exception to this is that a Linux system running the SMB (Server Message Block) client can print to a Windows 2000 or 9.x print server. However, Microsoft recommends that, if any of the client computers on your network are either Macintosh or Netware and the print server must support more than ten simultaneous clients, you should use Windows 2000 Server instead.

As a Network Administrator you must know how to install and configure new printers, how to manage and share print resources, and how to maintain printer security. You should also know how the printing process works, how to monitor user access to network printers, how to ensure the optimum usage of your print resources, and how to troubleshoot printer problems.

Goals

In this lesson, you will learn to set up the environment for network printing, add a local printer to your computer, share a printer over a network, connect to a network printer, and configure a network printer. You will also learn to manage printers, troubleshoot printer problems and control access to network printers by assigning permissions.

Lesson 10   Setting Up, Configuring, and Administering Network Printers

Skill	Exam 70-210 Objective
1. Setting up an Environment for Printing	Basic knowledge
2. Adding a Local Printer	Connect to local and network print devices. Connect to a local print device.
3. Connecting to a Network Printer	Connect to local and network print devices. Connect to an Internet printer.
4. Configuring a Network Printer	Monitor, configure, and troubleshoot I/O devices, such as printers, scanners, multimedia devices, mouse, keyboard, and smart card reader.
5. Assigning Access Permissions to Network Printers	Control access to printers by using permissions.
6. Managing Printers	Manage printers and print jobs. Monitor, configure, and troubleshoot I/O devices, such as printers, scanners, multimedia devices, mouse, keyboard, and smart card reader.
7. Troubleshooting Printer Problems	Monitor, configure, and troubleshoot I/O devices, such as printers, scanners, multimedia devices, mouse, keyboard, and smart card reader.

Requirements

To complete this lesson, you will need a computer with Windows 2000 Professional installed on it and a network environment. You will need printers named Printer1 and Printer2, and a printer at a remote location.

skill 1

Setting Up an Environment for Printing

exam objective

Basic knowledge

overview

Before you can share your print resources, you must set up an environment for network printing and ensure that you have a sufficient number of print devices to meet the needs of all users. The print environment also includes some other utilities and devices besides the printer (the software interface), the physical print device, and the print server (the computer that provides access to the shared printer).

The terminology used in the printing communication environment is described below:

◆ **Printer port:** A **printer port** is the software interface that a computer uses to communicate with a printer. The printer port does not refer to the physical hardware port, but rather to the software that communicates with it. Local connections to a print device can be made using a parallel, serial, infrared, or USB port. Remote connections can be made using either a network cable or a print device that has a NIC called a network-interface print device. The printer port communicates with any of these types of physical connections. In Windows 2000 you can use the LPT (line printer), COM, and USB interfaces, or IR (Infra Red) interfaces if available.

◆ **Printer driver:** A **printer driver** is the software that contains the information used by the operating system to convert the print commands for a particular model of print device into a printer language, such as PostScript. It tells the operating system what attributes the print device has and what print commands it follows so that documents can be properly printed.

◆ **Printer pool:** A **printer pool** is a single printer (that is the software that delivers the requests for service from the operating system) that can queue print jobs to multiple ports and their associated print devices. Print pooling is used when there are many print devices on a network that can receive instructions from the same type of print driver. Print jobs will be allocated by the printer pool to the first available print device.

When you are setting up your network printing environment, there are several important considerations you must keep in mind (see **Figure 10-1**). First, if a print server must handle many requests for service from many printers or for many large documents, it is important that you add enough RAM to the print server to ensure that it can accommodate the load. Insufficient RAM can adversely affect printing performance. Second, you must make sure that you have enough disk space on the print server to store the documents to be printed until they can be sent to the print device. Error messages will be generated if there is insufficient disk space on the print server.

You must also estimate what you expect the printing requirements for your organization to be. Note how many users you have, how often they print and in what quantity, and the length of a typical document. Then you can determine the type and number of print devices you think you will need in order to accommodate the quantity of requests for service. Next, you must estimate how many print servers your network will need for this number of print devices. Finally, you will need to decide how to place the print devices in the organization so that users can easily collect their printouts. For each computer, you can also define a default printer to be used for requests that are initiated from that workstation.

Figure 10-1 Requirements for setting up network printing

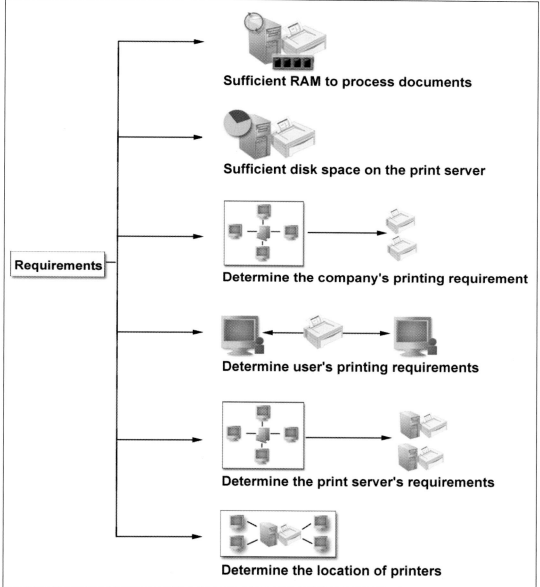

Sufficient RAM to process documents

Sufficient disk space on the print server

Determine the company's printing requirement

Determine user's printing requirements

Determine the print server's requirements

Determine the location of printers

skill 2

Adding a Local Printer

exam objective

Connect to a local print device.

overview

Local print devices are used to print documents from stand-alone computers that are not on a network or when a single individual, for example, the CEO, requires exclusive use of a printer. First, you must attach the print device to the computer using a physical port on the computer. A local print device usually uses a parallel (LPT), serial (COM), or USB port. The port enables your computer to communicate with the attached print device. Since most print devices today support Plug and Play, the operating system automatically detects them. You must use the **Add Printer Wizard** to create the logical printer, that is, the software interface that delivers the requests for service from the operating system to the physical print device. When you make a request for a print job, the document is spooled (or stored) on the logical printer before it is sent to the actual print device. Only members of the local Administrators or Power Users groups can install a local printer.

how to

Add a local printer to your computer.

1. Click 🔳**Start**, point to **Settings**, and click the **Printers** command to open the **Printers** window.
2. Double-click the **Add Printer** icon to start the **Add Printer Wizard**. The **Welcome to the Add Printer Wizard** screen opens.
3. Click [**Next >**], to open the **Local or Network Printer** screen.
4. The **Local Printer** option button and the **Automatically detect and install my Plug and Play printer** check box are selected by default (**Figure 10-2**). Click [**Next >**] to accept the defaults and open the **New Printer Detection** screen.
5. The computer searches for any new Plug and Play devices on your computer. When it detects a Plug and Play device, it displays the **Found New Hardware** message box for a few seconds showing the name of the attached hardware device, for example, **HP Color LaserJet 5P (Figure 10-3)**. Then the computer automatically installs the attached Plug and Play device.
6. The **New Printer Detection** screen appears again, this time to let you know that the printer has been installed.
7. Click the **Yes** option button on the New Printer Detection screen to print a test page so that you can confirm that the print device is installed properly.
8. Click [**Next >**] to open the **Printer Sharing** screen. The **Do not share this printer** option button is selected by default
9. Click [**Next >**] to accept the default and open the **Completing the Add Printer Wizard** screen (**Figure 10-4**).
10. Click [**Finish**] to add the local printer to your computer. The **<Printer Name>** icon appears in the Printers window.

Figure 10-2 Adding a local printer

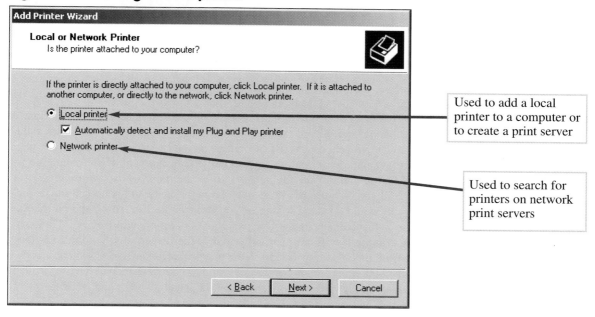

Figure 10-3 Detecting a Plug and Play device

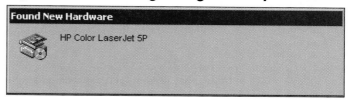

Figure 10-4 Completing the local printer installation

skill 3

Connecting to a Network Printer

exam objective

Connect to an Internet printer.

overview

The other way you can access a print device is by using a network connection. When you do this, the Add Printer Wizard creates the logical printer that will connect you to the shared print device. When you choose **Network printer** on the Local or Network Printer page, the Locate Your Printer page will open next. You can either enter the UNC pathname for the shared printer, or you can browse the network to locate the *printservername\sharename* of your choice. You can also use My Network Places to locate and connect to a shared print device just as you would a shared folder, or you can use the Run command on the Start menu and enter the UNC pathname in the Open text box. If your client is running Windows 2000, NT, or 9.x, the computer will automatically install the driver needed to deliver the requests for service from the operating system to the physical print device, as long as a copy of the driver is stored on the print server. Windows 3.x and MS-DOS users will have to manually install the print driver and, if your network includes Macintosh, UNIX, and Netware clients, additional services will have to be installed on the print server.

If you are on an Active Directory network, the Locate Your Printer page will include the **Find a printer in the Directory** option button. When you click Next, a dialog box will open in which you can search the Active Directory for a printer based on its name, location, capability, or a comment.

You can also connect to remote print devices, such as a print device at a branch office of your company, by connecting to it over the Internet or on your intranet. As long as you have permission for an Internet printer, you can connect to it using its URL. In this case, on the Locate Your Printer page, you will select this option and enter the URL.

Many organizations today have network-interface print devices which connect to the Internet using a network interface card (NIC). For these devices, you usually have to configure a TCP/IP port. You will select the **Create a new port** option button on the **Select Printer Port** page and select a port type in the **Type** list box. The default choice is a Standard TCP/IP port. When you click the Next button, the **Add Standard TCP/IP Printer Port Wizard** opens. On the **Add Port** page, you will have to enter either the IP address or FQDN (fully qualified domain name) for the print device in the **Printer Name or IP Address** text box. When you enter an IP address, the operating system automatically enters a port name in the **Port Name** text box. (**Figure 10-5**).

Note that if you are connecting to a Hewlett Packard network-interface print device, you will often have to add the DLC (Data Link Control) protocol in the **Network and Dial-up Connections** control panel before you run the Add Printer Wizard. Although many HP network printers no longer use DLC, older models do, and this protocol is not installed with Windows 2000. In fact, any network protocol besides TCP/IP will have to be added, along with ports that use the protocol.

Figure 10-5 Specifying the printer to which to add a port

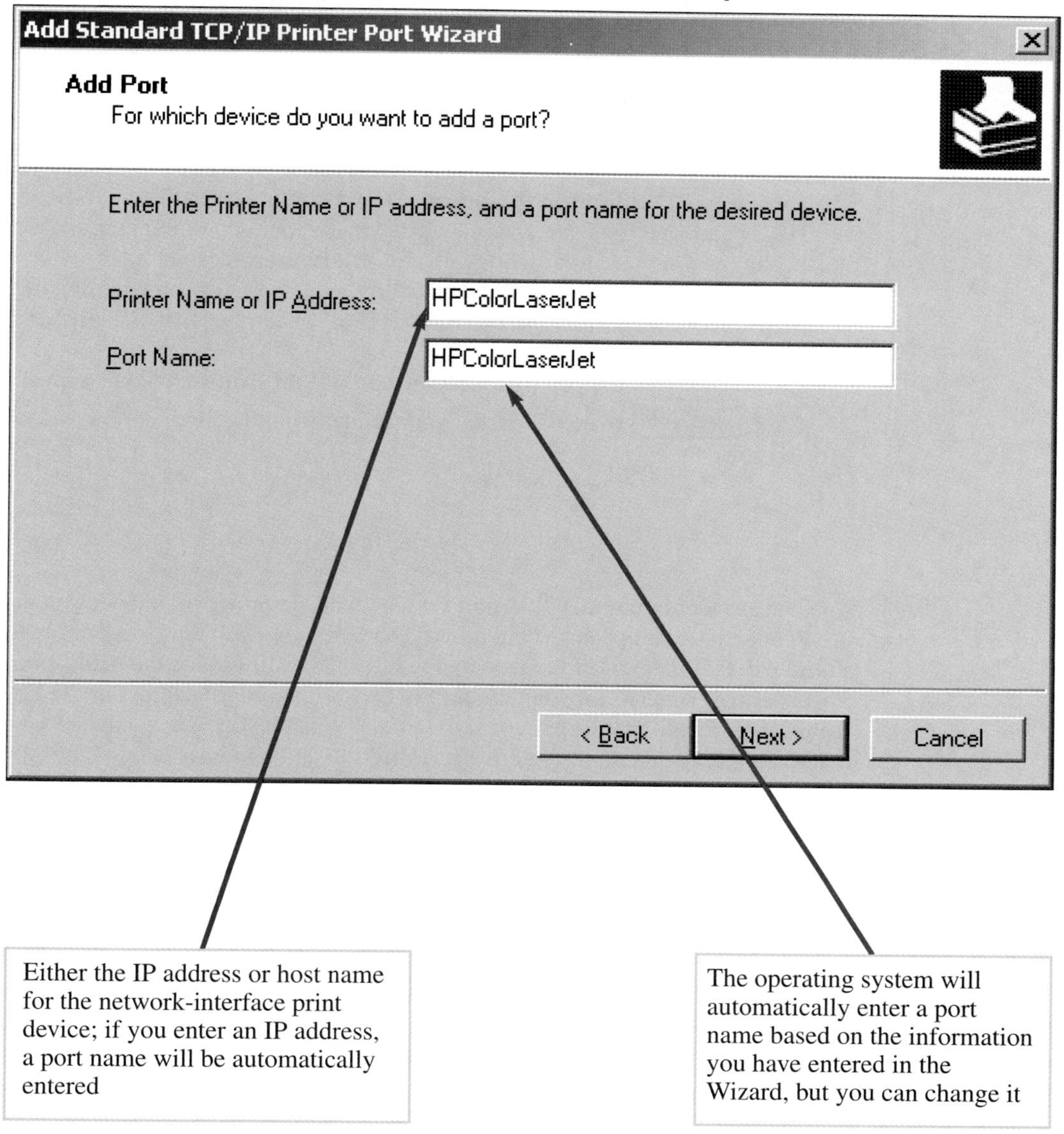
Add Standard TCP/IP Printer Port Wizard
Add Port
For which device do you want to add a port?
Enter the Printer Name or IP address, and a port name for the desired device.
Printer Name or IP Address:
HPColorLaserJet
Port Name:
HPColorLaserJet
< Back
Next >
Cancel
Either the IP address or host name for the network-interface print device; if you enter an IP address, a port name will be automatically entered
The operating system will automatically enter a port name based on the information you have entered in the Wizard, but you can change it

skill 3

Connecting to a Network Printer
(cont'd)

exam objective

Connect to an Internet printer.

how to

Connect to a network printer.
1. Open the **Printers** window.
2. Double-click the **Add Printer** icon to start the **Add Printer Wizard**. The **Welcome to the Add Printer Wizard** screen opens.
3. Click `Next >` to open the **Local or Network printer** screen.
4. Click the **Network printer** option button **(Figure 10-6)**.
5. Click `Next >` to open the **Locate Your Printer** screen. This is where you enter the UNC pathname for a share, or the URL for an Internet or intranet print device.
6. Select the **Connect to a printer on the Internet or on your intranet** option button. In the URL text box, type the path for the network printer, following the syntax, **http://*printservername/printername/*.** For example: **http://PrintSrv1/HPColor2/** **(Figure 10-7)**.
7. Click `Next >` to open the **Completing the Add Printer Wizard** screen.
8. Click `Finish` to install the network printer from the Internet on your computer.

tip

If IIS (Internet Information Services), Microsoft's Web server software, has been installed on the print server that is servicing the request, you can connect to a printer on the intranet by specifying the path of the printer in the URL text box. You can also locate the printer by browsing the network.

more

You can also configure a TCP/IP port for a network-interface print device on the **Ports** tab in the **Properties** dialog box for the print device. Simply click the **Add Port** button and select **Standard TCP/IP** port in the next dialog box. This will initiate the **Add Standard TCP/IP Port Wizard**. Once again you will have to enter either the IP address or the FQDN name for the print device. In the final dialog boxes of the Wizard, you will install and set up the port so that the logical printer will send its instructions to an IP address rather than a local port.

Figure 10-6 Connecting to a network printer

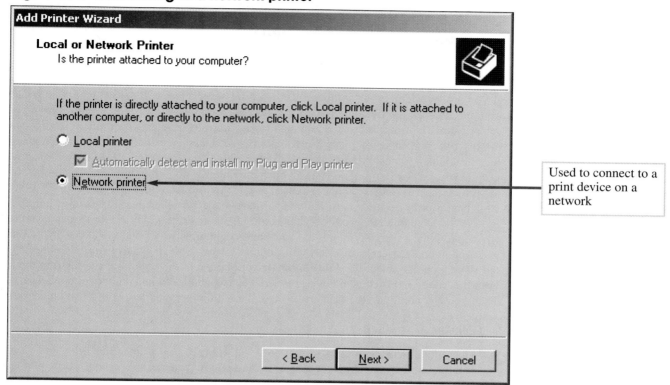

Add Printer Wizard

Local or Network Printer
Is the printer attached to your computer?

If the printer is directly attached to your computer, click Local printer. If it is attached to another computer, or directly to the network, click Network printer.

○ Local printer
   ☑ Automatically detect and install my Plug and Play printer
● Network printer ◀──────────── Used to connect to a print device on a network

〈 Back   Next 〉   Cancel

Figure 10-7 Entering the URL for a printer

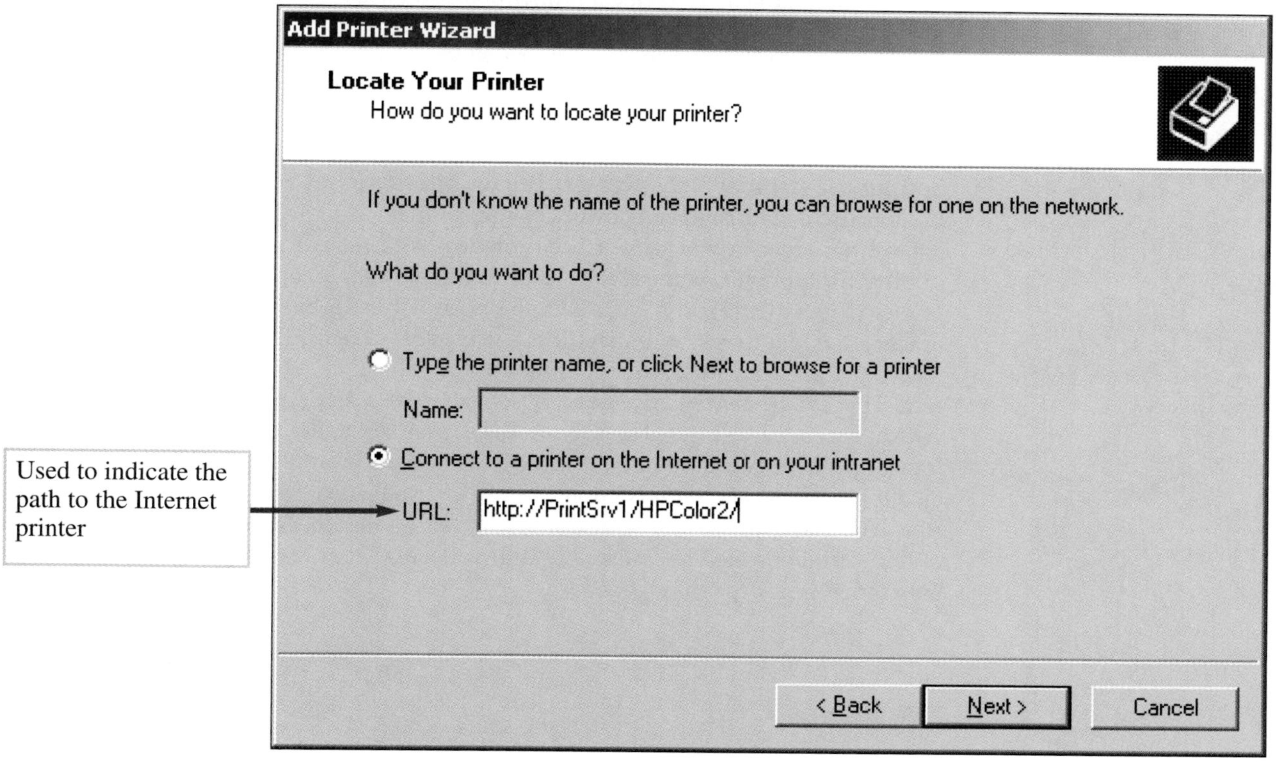

Add Printer Wizard

Locate Your Printer
How do you want to locate your printer?

If you don't know the name of the printer, you can browse for one on the network.

What do you want to do?

○ Type the printer name, or click Next to browse for a printer
   Name: [   ]

● Connect to a printer on the Internet or on your intranet

Used to indicate the path to the Internet printer ──────▶ URL: [http://PrintSrv1/HPColor2/]

〈 Back   Next 〉   Cancel

skill 4 *Configuring a Network Printer*

exam objective

Monitor, configure, and troubleshoot I/O devices, such as printers, scanners, multimedia devices, mouse, keyboard, and smart card reader.

overview

If you are setting up your computer to be a print server, you will select the Local Printer option button on the Local or Network Printer page in the Add Printer Wizard. When you select Network printer, all you can do is *locate* a network printer; you cannot create a new printer. You can connect as many print devices as your hardware configuration will allow and then install their logical printers. If you have not already done so in the wizard, after you have installed the printer or printers, you can open the Sharing tab in the Properties dialog box for the printer, and make it a shared resource, just as you did for a folder **(Figure 10-8)**. When you share a print resource, you must set a share name for other users to locate when they browse the available resources on your server. By default, the only driver that is installed when you create a shared printer is the one that is compatible with Windows 2000. If you want to add additional drivers so that they will automatically download when clients first connect to the share, you can select the **Additional Drivers** button at the bottom of the Sharing tab to open the Additional Drivers dialog box where you can choose from a number of other drivers. Then you can configure the printers to meet the requirements of your organization. If your server will be required to handle a large quantity of printing jobs, several features are useful, including Printer Pooling and Print Priorities.

♦ **Creating a printer pool:** A printer pool is a single logical printer on a print server that is associated with multiple physical print devices. You can use printer pooling when you have a number of the same type or similar types of print devices which all use the same driver so that they can all understand the same sets of commands. Print jobs that are sent to a printer pool will be directed to the least busy print device in the pool. This is a benefit to the administrator because he or she can manage multiple print devices from a single printer. To create a printer pool, you use the **Ports** tab on the **Properties** dialog box for the printer. At the bottom of the tab, select the **Enable printer pooling** check box and select all of the ports to which you want the logical printer to print. When you enable printer pooling, you cannot control which print device will receive the job, so it is helpful to have the print devices near each other so your employees can easily find their documents.

♦ **Setting the priority of a printer:** Printer priority is set when multiple configured printers use a common print device. You set printers as high-priority or low-priority to control the order in which their print jobs will be sent to the print device. To set the priority for a printer, you use the **Advanced** tab on the **Properties** dialog box for the printer **(Figure 10-9)**. You can rank the priority of the printer from 1 through 99. The number 1 is the lowest rank, and it is selected by default. If you leave the default in place, any printer with a priority from 2-99 will have its jobs sent to the print device first. This can be particularly useful if you have one user or group whose print jobs are critical and must be printed as soon as they are ordered. For example, if you have two logical printers and only one print device, and you want one printer's documents to take priority, you can set this printer's rank to 2 so that its print jobs will be completed first. You can also use the **Available from** option button to make a printer available only at certain times. This can be useful if you have a user or group that has a large volume of low-priority printing jobs.

Figure 10-8 Sharing a printer

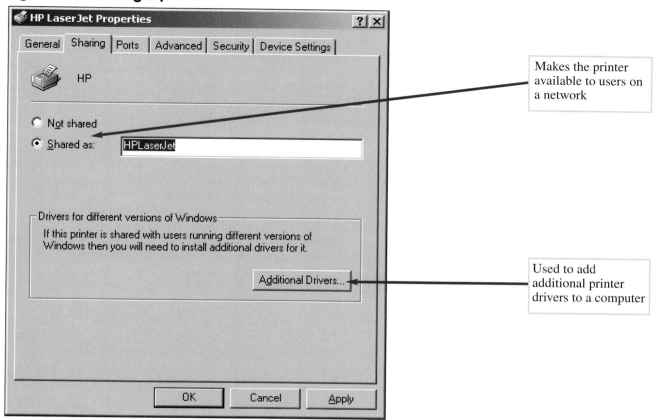

Makes the printer available to users on a network

Used to add additional printer drivers to a computer

Figure 10-9 Setting the priority of a printer

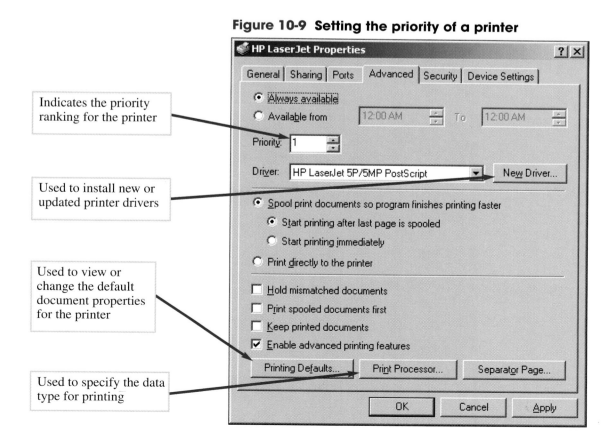

Indicates the priority ranking for the printer

Used to install new or updated printer drivers

Used to view or change the default document properties for the printer

Used to specify the data type for printing

skill 4

Configuring a Network Printer (cont'd)

exam objective

Monitor, configure, and troubleshoot I/O devices, such as printers, scanners, multimedia devices, mouse, keyboard, and smart card reader.

how to

Configure a print server to create a printer pool.

1. Log on to the print server as an **Administrator**.
2. Open the **Printers** window and right-click the printer icon for a print device that is attached to the print server, for example, HP LaserJet 4050 Series PCL 6. Then click the **Properties** command to open the **Properties** dialog box for the printer.
3. Click the **Ports** tab and select the **Enable printer pooling** check box.
4. Select the ports for the print devices that you want to include in the printer pool. For example, click **LPT1**, **LPT2**, and **LPT3** in the Port list box **(Figure 10-10)**. These multiple print devices connected to the computer will form the printer pool. All will receive their instructions from the one logical printer.
5. Click [OK] to create a printer pool on a computer.

Figure 10-10 Creating a printer pool

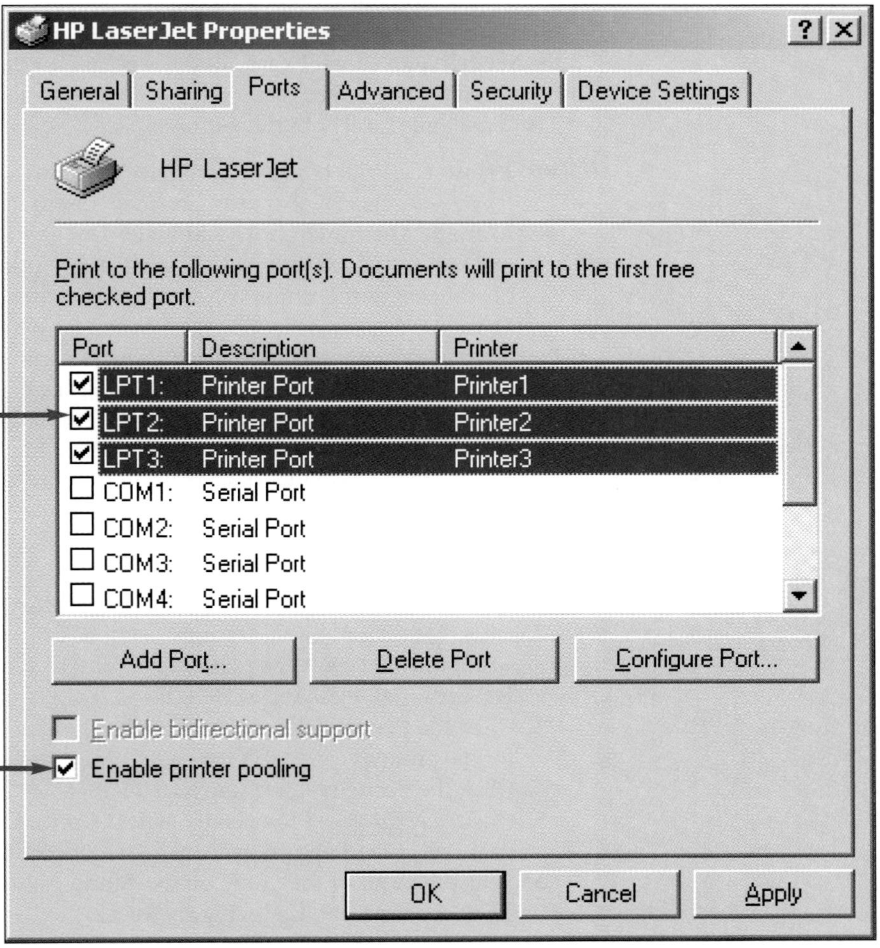

Used to select all of the ports to which you want the logical printer to print

To create a printer pool you must have a number of the same type or similar types of print devices which all use the same driver

HP LaserJet Properties   ? ✕

| General | Sharing | Ports | Advanced | Security | Device Settings |

HP LaserJet

Print to the following port(s). Documents will print to the first free checked port.

Port	Description	Printer
☑ LPT1:	Printer Port	Printer1
☑ LPT2:	Printer Port	Printer2
☑ LPT3:	Printer Port	Printer3
☐ COM1:	Serial Port	
☐ COM2:	Serial Port	
☐ COM3:	Serial Port	
☐ COM4:	Serial Port	

[Add Port...]   [Delete Port]   [Configure Port...]

☐ Enable bidirectional support
☑ Enable printer pooling

[OK]   [Cancel]   [Apply]

skill 5

Assigning Access Permissions to Network Printers

exam objective

Control access to printers by using permissions.

overview

When you install a printer on a network, by default, the Everyone group has the Print permission. Since this is the most restrictive print permission you can assign, you will generally not have to spend much time on printer security. However, you can use printer permissions to limit access to a particular network printer for certain users, and you can allow users who are not administrators to manage a particular printer. You set print permissions on the **Security** tab on the **Properties** dialog box for the printer. Just like any other permissions, print permissions can be either allowed or denied and denials override allowed permissions. There are three levels of print permissions:

◆ **Print:** The Print permission enables a user to connect to a printer and send print jobs to it. These users can also pause, resume, restart, and cancel their own print jobs.
◆ **Manage Documents:** The Manage Documents permission enables a user to pause, resume, restart, and cancel all other users' printing jobs. However, a user cannot send documents to the printer or control the status of the printer. Members of the **Creator Owner** group have the Manage Documents permission by default.
◆ **Manage Printers:** The Manage Printers permission grants a user administrative control over a printer. Users with this permission can pause and restart the printer, share a printer, adjust printer permissions, change printer properties, delete a printer, and cancel all other users' documents or all queued documents. Members of the **Administrators** and **Power Users** groups have the Manage Printers permission by default.

how to

Assign access permissions to a user named James, for accessing a Network Printer.

1. Log on to your computer as an **Administrator**.
2. Click ![Start], point to **Settings,** and click the **Printers** command to open the **Printers** window. Right-click the printer icon for which you want to set permissions; for example, **HP LaserJet 4050 Series PCL 6.**
3. Click the **Properties** command on the shortcut menu to open the **Properties** dialog box for the printer.
4. Click the **Security** tab **(Figure 10-11).**
5. Click Add... to open the **Select Users, Computers, or Groups** dialog box. All of the users and groups on the network are listed in the **Name** box.
6. Select the user or the group on the **Name** list to whom you want to assign print permissions, for example, **Usr1 (Figure 10-12).**
7. Click Add... to display the selected user, **James** in the lower portion of the dialog box.
8. Click OK to close the **Select Users, Computers, or Groups** dialog box. The name/s you selected now appear in the Name list.
9. Select **Usr1** (Joe Forester) on the **Name list (Figure 10-13).**
10. Select the **Allow** check box for the **Manage Printers** permission to assign it to James. To view or change the permissions assigned to a printer, click Advanced... in the Properties dialog box for the printer. This opens the **Access Control Settings** dialog box for the printer, which displays a list of the permissions assigned to users. Any user with the Manage Printers permission can view, remove, or edit a selected permission
11. Click OK to close the printer's **Properties** dialog box.

tip

To remove a user or a group from the permissions list, select the user on the Name list in the Properties dialog box for the printer, and click Remove.

Figure 10-11 Assigning printer permissions

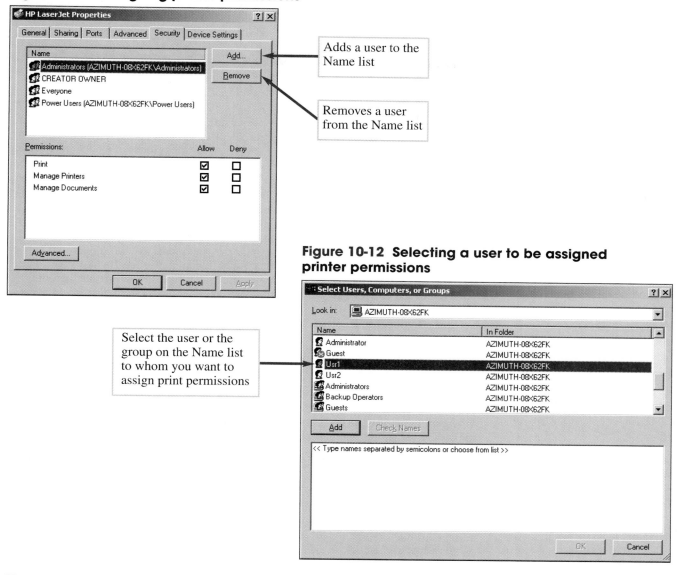

Figure 10-12 Selecting a user to be assigned printer permissions

Adds a user to the Name list

Removes a user from the Name list

Select the user or the group on the Name list to whom you want to assign print permissions

Figure 10-13 Assigning printer permissions

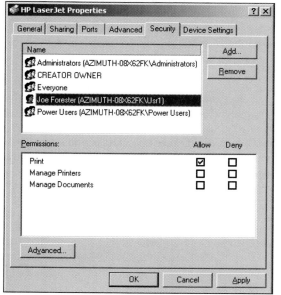

skill 6

Managing Printers

exam objective

Manage printers and print jobs. Monitor, configure, and troubleshoot I/O devices, such as printers, scanners, multimedia devices, mouse, keyboard, and smart card reader.

overview

Managing printers and print jobs involves pausing and resuming printing; canceling documents; pausing, resuming, or canceling specific documents; restarting print jobs; scheduling documents to print at a later time; and changing the priority of a document, so that the printing requirements of your organization can be met. For example, if you urgently need a particular document for a meeting and you have a problem with the default printer on your computer, you can redirect the print job to another printer.

Managing printers involves performing a variety of administrative tasks, such as:

♦ **Specifying paper sizes for paper trays:** A printer has multiple paper trays that hold paper of different sizes, so you must specify the paper size. You do this on the **Device Settings** tab in the Properties dialog box for the printer **(Figure 10-14)**. When a user selects a paper size and gives a print command, Windows 2000 automatically routes the print job to the correct paper tray. Some common paper sizes are Legal, A4, Envelope #10, and Letter Small.

♦ **Setting a Separator Page:** A Separator page, also called a banner page, is a file that identifies a printed document, usually with the name of the user who requested it and the date and time. It is printed between documents so that you can easily identify the start and end of each print job. You can choose from the four default separator pages by using the **Separator Page** button Separator Page... on the **Advanced** tab in the Properties dialog box **(Figure 10-14)** for a printer to locate your *systemroot* \System32 folder **(Figure 10-15)**, where these pages are stored.

♦ **Performing printing tasks:** A user may need to perform a variety of printing tasks such as pausing, resuming, and canceling the printing of documents. For example, if you send the wrong document to be printed, you can cancel the print job; or if a printer is malfunctioning, you can pause it while you fix the problem and resume printing when it is resolved. To pause all print jobs, open the Printers folder, right-click the printer icon, and select the **Pause Printing** command. To resume all print jobs, select the **Pause Printing** command again to toggle it off. To pause a particular document, double-click the printer icon, right-click the document, and select Pause Printing. Use the Shift or Ctrl key to select multiple documents. To resume printing specific documents, double-click the printer icon, right-click the documents you want to resume and select **Resume**. To cancel all documents, right-click the printer icon and select the **Cancel All Documents** command. To cancel one or more specific documents, double-click the printer icon, right-click the documents, and select the **Cancel** command. To restart a print job, right-click the documents and select the **Restart** command.

♦ **Sending documents to a different printer:** If a print device is malfunctioning, you might decide to redirect all queued print jobs. You can do this by adding a port on the **Ports** tab in the Properties dialog box for the printer. First, if there is a working printer of the same type on another local port on the same print server, select the check box for the port, and click OK. Alternatively, if there is a working printer of the same kind on a different print server, click the **Add Port** button. In the **Printer Ports** dialog box, click the **New Port** button. In the **Port Name** dialog box, enter the UNC pathname for the redirect printer in the **Enter a port name** box.

♦ **Changing ownership of a printer:** If the owner of a printer (the person who installed it) leaves the organization and you must pass on the administrative responsibility to a new user, you can change its ownership. Users with the Manage Printers permission and members of the Administrators and Power Users groups can take ownership of a printer on the **Owner** tab on the ACL for the printer. First, open the Properties dialog box for the printer. On the **Security** tab, click the **Advanced** button to open the **Access Control Settings for <printername>** dialog box. Then, open the Owner tab and select your user account under **Name** in the **Change owner to** box.

Figure 10-14 Specifying paper sizes

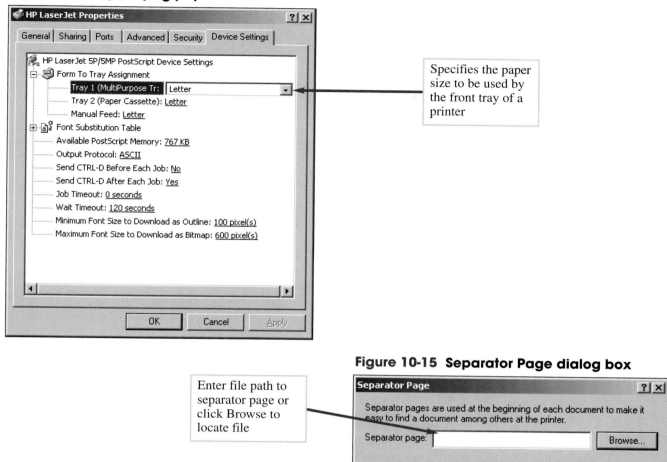

Specifies the paper size to be used by the front tray of a printer

Figure 10-15 Separator Page dialog box

Enter file path to separator page or click Browse to locate file

Figure 10-16 Browsing to locate separator page files in the system32 folder

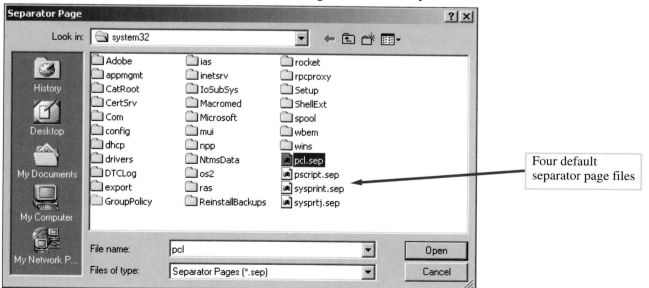

Four default separator page files

skill 6

Managing Printers (cont'd)

exam objective

Manage printers and print jobs. Monitor, configure, and troubleshoot I/O devices, such as printers, scanners, multimedia devices, mouse, keyboard, and smart card reader.

how to

Redirect a document from one printer to another, from Printer1 to Printer2.

1. Click [Start], point to **Settings** and click the **Printers** command to open the **Printers** window. Minimize the window.
2. Create a test document in Word and save it as Printjob1.doc. Send Printjob1.doc to the printer.
3. Maximize the Printers window.
4. Double-click the **Printer1** icon to open the **Printer1** window. This displays a list of the documents that were sent to Printer1 for printing.
5. Select the document **Printjob1.doc** in the displayed list, as the document you want to redirect to Printer2.
6. Open the **Printer** menu and click the **Properties** command to open the **Printer1 Properties** dialog box (**Figure 10-17**).
7. Click the **Ports** tab to display a list of available ports.
8. Click the port **LPT2**, to which **Printer2** is assigned (**Figure 10-18**).
9. Click [OK]. You have redirected the document, **Printjob1.doc** from Printer1 to Printer2.

tip

To redirect documents to a printer on a different print server, the printer must already exist on the network and it must be shared on the print server. You can then add a local port for the second print server and provide the print server name and the appropriate share name for the printer.

more

There are also tools you can use to manage documents that are in the printing queue. These are found on the General tab in the Properties dialog box for a document. To open the Properties dialog box for a document, open the Printers folder and right-click the document. You can also select more than one document. A notification is used when you want someone other than the person who sent the print job to know that the job is complete. Simply enter the user name in the **Notify** text box. You can also use the **Priority** slider to adjust the priority that was assigned to the document. Finally, you can restrict print times to specific hours by selecting the **Only from** option button and setting a schedule in the **Only from** and **To** spin boxes. You can also manage printers using any computer with a Web browser, even if it is not a Windows 2000 computer and does not have the correct print driver. When you manage your printers using a Web browser, you can create your own home page containing the location and links to the printers, and you will have access to a page that lists the status of every printer on a print server. Crucial data that does not display in the Printers window, which can be used to correct print device problems, will display instantaneously on this summary page. You can also access all of the printers, or a specific printer, on a print server by entering the path to the print server or to the particular printer in the **Address** text box in the Web browser.

caution

To access a printer using a Web browser, the print server on which the printer resides must have Internet Information Server (IIS) installed. IIS is a Web server that runs on the Windows 2000 platform and responds to user requests from a browser.

Figure 10-17 Selecting the Properties command

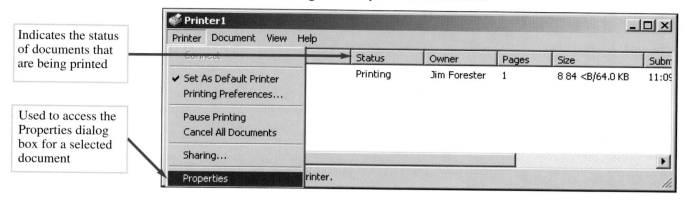

Indicates the status of documents that are being printed

Used to access the Properties dialog box for a selected document

Figure 10-18 Specifying the port for a printer

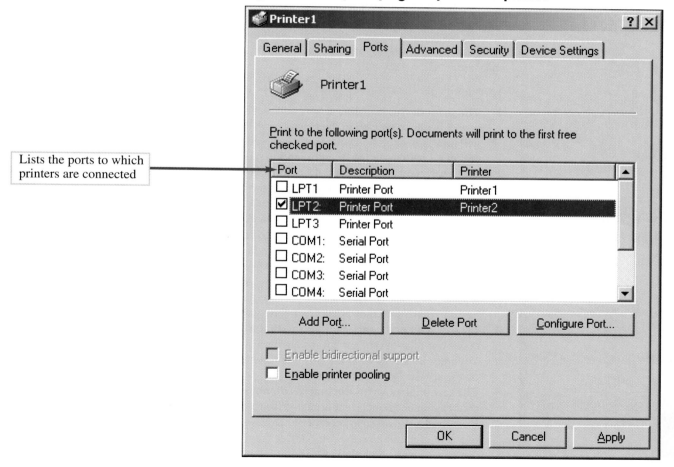

Lists the ports to which printers are connected

skill 7 | *Troubleshooting Printer Problems*

exam objective

Monitor, configure, and troubleshoot I/O devices, such as printers, scanners, multimedia devices, mouse, keyboard, and smart card reader.

overview

Troubleshooting printer problems can occupy more time than an administrator would like. The first thing you should check, as you would when troubleshooting any hardware device, is whether the local devices are plugged in and hooked up. You should check the cables, make sure the power is on, and check the paper and toner. Then, you can try recreating the logical printer on the client, reinstalling the print driver, and terminating and re-sharing the printer on the print server. Check the print queue for stalled print jobs (click **Start**, point to **Settings**, click **Printers**, double-click the **Printer** icon). If nothing is listed under Status (waiting, paused, or printing) it is likely the print job has stalled. You must also make sure that the print spool service is running (Open the **Services** snap-in in the **Administrative Tools** console). Stop and restart the Print Spooler service **(Figure 10-19)**. Make sure that there is enough disk space for spooling on the print server (75 MB is recommended.). If the print device is operational and other users can print, the print server is probably not the problem. If other users also cannot print, make sure that the printer on the print server is using the correct driver, and make sure that you have installed the correct drivers for other operating systems on the print server. If you are using a network-interface print device, you should first make sure that there is a network connection between the device and the print server. Make sure that you can see and connect to the print server from the workstation. PING the IP address for a TCP/IP printer to make sure it is operational.

Some problems you may encounter, and their causes and solutions, are described below:

◆   **The print device is offline:** Users will receive this error message when the physical print device is not connected to the network or is turned off or has gone offline. Usually there will be a light or an LCD message to tell you whether the printer is online. Press the Reset or Online button to cycle the printer into online mode.

◆   **The user receives an Access Denied or No Access Available message**: This is usually caused by improper permissions. Check the permissions assigned to both the user and the groups to which he or she is a member and check for any denied permissions. Sometimes a user will try to configure a printer from an older application and will receive this message when they do not have permission to change printer configurations. You must either change the user's permissions or ask an administrator to reconfigure the printer.

◆   **A Test page does not print:** This can happen if you select the wrong port when you add a printer. You can solve this problem by configuring the printer again using the correct port. If the printer is using a network-interface print device, check the IP address or DNS name to make sure they are correct.

◆   **User gets an error message stating that a printer driver must be installed:** When the correct printer drivers are not installed on a print server, you will get this error message. You must make sure that the correct printer drivers for each client computer are installed on the server.

◆   **The test page or print documents do not print completely:** The cause of this problem could again be an incorrect printer driver. Install the printer again with the correct driver.

◆   **Documents do not print correctly:** Documents may not print correctly on some printers in a printer pool when the print devices in the pool do not use the same driver. You must use either identical or similar print devices that use the same printer driver.

◆   **Documents do not reach the print server:** This problem may arise as a result of insufficient hard disk space on a computer. To solve this problem, free some space on the hard disk **(Figure 10-20)**.

Figure 10-19 The Print Spooler service

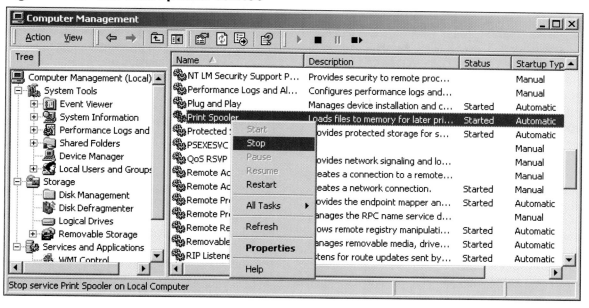

Figure 10-20 Various printer problems

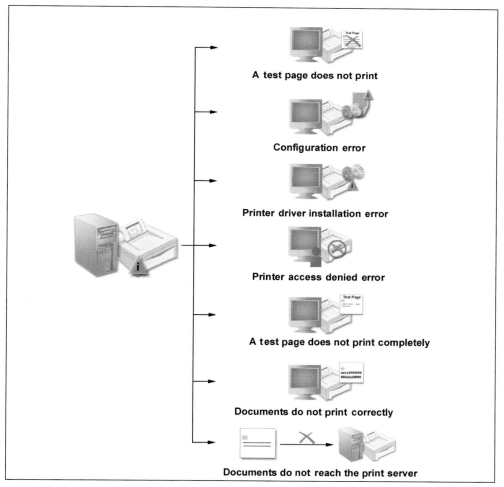

Summary

◆ In Windows 2000, a printer is considered to be the software that delivers the requests for service from the operating system to the physical print device.

◆ A print device, therefore, is the physical hardware that you think of as a printer, which creates the hard copies of your digital files.

◆ A print server handles the requests for service for a shared printer. A print server can either administer these requests through a print device that is physically connected to it or through a network-connected print device.

◆ Network-connected print devices are called network-interface print devices and they have their own NIC (network interface card) and network address or an external network adapter connection.

◆ Windows 2000 Professional computers and even Windows 9x computers can be configured as print servers.

◆ A printer port is the software interface that a computer uses to communicate with a printer. Once again, the printer port does not refer to the physical hardware port, but rather to the software that communicates with it.

◆ A printer driver is the software that contains the information used by the operating system to convert the print commands for a particular model of print device into a printer language.

◆ A printer pool is a single printer (that is, the software that delivers the requests for service from the operating system) that can queue print jobs to multiple ports and their associated print devices.

◆ Print pooling is used when there are many print devices on a network that can receive instructions from the same type of print driver. Print jobs will be allocated by the printer pool to the first available print device.

◆ Printer priority is set when multiple configured printers use a common print device. You set printers as high-priority or low-priority to control the order in which their print jobs will be sent to the print device.

◆ Only members of the local Administrators or Power Users groups can install a local printer.

◆ You can access a print device using a network connection. You use the Add Printer Wizard to create the logical printer that will connect you to the shared print device. On the Locate Your Printer page, you either enter the UNC pathname for the share or browse the network to locate it.

◆ You can also use My Network Places to locate and connect to a shared print device, just as you would a shared folder, or you can use the Run command on the Start menu and enter the UNC pathname in the Open text box.

◆ If you are on an Active Directory network, you can use the Find a printer in the Directory option on the Locate Your Printer page to search the Active Directory for a printer based on its name, location, capability, or a comment.

◆ You can also connect to remote print devices, by connecting to the printer over the Internet or on your intranet. As long as you have permission for an Internet printer you can connect to it using its URL.

◆ You can configure a TCP/IP port for a network-interface print device on the Ports tab in the Properties dialog box for the print device. Click the Add Port button and select Standard TCP/IP port in the next dialog box to initiate the Add Standard TCP/IP Port Wizard.

◆ If you are setting up your computer to be a print server, you will select the Local Printer option button on the Local or Network Printer page in the Add Printer Wizard. When you select Network printer, all you can do is *locate* a network printer; you cannot create a new printer.

◆ There are three levels of printer permissions: Print, Manage Printers, and Manage Documents.

◆ The Print permission enables a user to connect to a printer and send it print jobs. These users can also pause, resume, restart, and cancel their own print jobs.

◆ The Manage Printers permission grants a user administrative control over a printer. Users with this permission can pause and restart the printer, share a printer, adjust printer permissions, change printer properties, delete a printer, and cancel all other users' documents or all queued documents.

◆ Members of the Administrators and Power Users groups have the Manage Printers permission by default.

◆ The Manage Documents permission enables a user to pause, resume, restart, and cancel all other users' printing jobs. However, a user cannot send documents to the printer or control the status of the printer.

◆ Members of the Creator Owner group have the Manage Documents permission by default.

Key Terms

Add Printer Wizard
Local print device
Manage Documents permission
Manage Printers permission
Network printer

Print permission
Print device
Printer
Printer driver
Printer pool

Printer port
Print server
Separator page

Test Yourself

1. You are installing a local printer using the Add Printer Wizard. Which of the following options do you need to specify during the installation process?
   a. Share Name
   b. Security settings
   c. Location
   d. Port

2. Which of the following converts print commands into a printer language?
   a. Printer port
   b. Print device
   c. Printer driver
   d. Print server

3. You have multiple identical print devices located in close proximity to the server where the logical printer is configured, and you want print jobs to be sent to the least busy print device so that your print jobs can be serviced as quickly as possible. Which of the following will you use?
   a. Printer pooling
   b. Printer priorities
   c. Redirecting
   d. Printing preferences

4. You want to send your print jobs to a network-interface print device that is connected to your network. Which of the following will you have to enter in the Add Printer Wizard when you are configuring the logical printer? (Choose all that apply.)
   a. Name of the manufacturer
   b. A TCP/IP port
   c. Printer name
   d. IP address
   e. URL of the printer

5. You have multiple printers using a single print device. What rank would you assign to a printer to make it the lowest priority printer in the group?
   a. 99
   b. 999
   c. 89
   d. 1

6. You are the network administrator at SpringHead Corp. Mary, the Project Manager at your company, is unable to print her documents using the printer that is configured on her computer. She wants you to redirect her documents to a different printer. Which of the following sequences of steps will you follow in order to do this?
   a. Right-click the Printer icon → click Properties → click Advanced tab
   b. Right-click the printer icon → click Printing Preferences
   c. Right-click the printer icon → click Properties → click Port tab
   d. Right-click the printer icon → click Sharing → click Device Setting tab

7. You work for a large dog food manufacturer. Jane has connected to a printer and sent a print job for a document that she and her partner Samuel need for a meeting after lunch. She has left for lunch and the printer has run out of ink. Samuel rushes over to ask you to pause the printer so that he can refill it. What permission must you have in order to do this?
   a. Printer Pooling
   b. Manage Documents
   c. Print
   d. Manage Printers

8. The Systems Manager of your company, Susan, is allowed to print, pause, resume and restart print jobs sent by other users to a network printer; however, she cannot control the status of the printer. Which of the following permissions does Susan have?
   a. Manage Documents
   b. Print
   c. Manage Printers
   d. Full Control

9. Which of the following can you configure so that documents are sent to the least busy print device in a group of print devices that all use the same driver?
   a. Print Server
   b. Network Printer
   c. Printer Pool
   d. Printer Port

Projects: On Your Own

1. Add a local printer on a computer.
   a. Access the **Add Printer Wizard**.
   b. Click the **Local Printer** option button.
   c. Access the **New Printer Detection** screen.
   d. The computer automatically detects the attached Plug and Play device and installs it.
2. Add a network printer on a computer.
   a. Access the **Add Printer Wizard**.
   b. Click the **Network Printer** option button.
   c. Access the **Browse for Printer** screen.
   d. Click the network printer on the **Shared Printers** list box.
   e. Access the **Completing the Add Printer Wizard** screen to add a network printer on a computer.
3. Assign Access Permissions to a user for accessing a Network Printer.
   a. Access the **Properties** dialog box of a printer.
   b. Click the **Security** tab.
   c. Access the **Select Users, Computers, or Groups** dialog box.
   d. Select a user or a group from the **Name** list box.
   e. Assign the **Print** permission in the **Permissions** section.

Problem Solving Scenarios

1. You are working as a Systems Administrator at Pitch Inc., a marketing firm in New York City. John Williams, a senior designer, requires color printing of advertising campaign sample pages for several of his projects. Therefore, he wants you to add and configure a color laser jet printer on his computer. Additionally, he wants this printer to be available to his workgroup members. Outline the steps you would take in a memo to add and configure a color printer on John's computer and then share it over a network.

2. Your company has recently purchased Hewlett Packard laser printers with enhanced features. These printers have been added and configured on all employee computers. Your company management requires that only managers must be allowed to change the print status of the documents sent to printers, and regular employees must be allowed to print documents only. Outline in a memo to company management how you will assign the appropriate print permissions to managers and employees.

11 Working with NTFS Permissions

O n NTFS disks you can use **NTFS permissions**, either alone or in combination with share permissions, to control access to network resources. Unlike shared folder permissions, NTFS permissions can also be used to control access to resources that are stored on the computer where the user is physically logged on. Although you will generally choose a file system during the installation of Windows 2000 Professional, you can convert a drive to NTFS after installation. One reason that NTFS is considered to be superior to the other file systems is that NTFS permissions can be set for both files and folders, and you have many more options for controlling what users can do with a file or folder once they have opened it. This progressive file system also supports large data storage, long file names, compression, encryption, and ownership of files and folders. Each file or folder on an NTFS volume has a set of attributes, including the compression attribute, the encryption attribute, and the owner attribute. NTFS attributes also include the security permissions you set for groups or individual users.

If you are unsure whether you are working with an NTFS volume, you can open Windows Explorer and check the properties for the drive (right-click the drive letter and select the Properties command), or you can open the Properties dialog box for any file or folder to see if the dialog box has a Security tab. When you set NTFS permissions, you do not have to specifically share the file or folder first; you simply open the Security tab to configure the ACL (Access Control List). The Security tab displays the standard NTFS permissions. Setting them involves the same process as configuring the ACL permissions for shared folders; you allow or specifically deny the appropriate level of access. Like share permissions, the Deny condition overrides the Allow condition. By default the Everyone group is granted the Full Control NTFS permission for the root of a drive, although not for the system subfolders. As with share permissions, you will generally remove this permission and set your own according to your organizational needs.

Goals

In this lesson, you will learn how to assign NTFS file and folder permissions, and how to assign Special Access permissions to users to control user access to objects. Finally, you will learn how to troubleshoot problems related to NTFS permissions.

Lesson 11   Working with NTFS Permissions

Skill	Exam 70-210 Objective
1. Identifying Types of NTFS Permissions	Basic knowledge
2. Assigning NTFS Permissions	Monitor, manage, and troubleshoot access to files and folders. Control access to files and folders by using permissions.
3. Using Special Access Permissions	Monitor, manage, and troubleshoot access to files and folders. Control access to files and folders by using permissions.
4. Troubleshooting NTFS Permissions	Monitor, manage, and troubleshoot access to files and folders. Control access to files and folders by using permissions.

Requirements

To complete this lesson, you will need a computer with Windows 2000 Professional installed on it and a volume formatted with NTFS. You will also need a folder named General on the NTFS volume or partition. The exercises will assume it is stored on the C: drive.

skill 1
Identifying Types of NTFS Permissions

exam objective

Basic knowledge

overview

One of the most important things to remember about NTFS permissions is that they can be configured for both files and folders. While share permissions are configured at the folder level, and any subfolders or files within the folder inherit the shared folder permissions, different NTFS permissions can be assigned to a file than for the folder in which it is stored. File permissions take precedence over folder permissions.

Another important concept is that NTFS permissions, like share permissions, are cumulative, or added together. If a user has the NTFS Read permission granted through membership in one group and the NTFS Modify permission granted through membership in another group, his or her effective permission is Modify.

However, when NTFS permissions are used in combination with share permissions, the most restrictive permission applies. For example, if a user has the Read share permission granted through membership in one group and the NTFS folder Modify permission granted through membership in another group, his or her effective permission when accessing the network share would be Read. Remember, share permissions apply only to users who are connecting over the network, so if users connect to the folder on the computer on which it is being hosted, they will have the NTFS Modify permission locally.

One effective way of handling this contradiction is to create shared folders and leave the default permission, Full Control for the Everyone group, intact. Then, instead of applying any share permissions, use NTFS permissions to secure the resources. Since the most restrictive permission applies, as long as you have fine-tuned your NTFS permissions so that groups have the appropriate level of access, your resources will be secure. Additionally, since NTFS permissions operate locally, you can be confident that security for files and folders on the computers on which they are stored is effective even when more than one user accesses the computer.

The standard NTFS folder permissions are (Figure 11-1):
- **Read:** Users can open and view the content of files, folders, and subfolders. They can also view the ownership of objects, permissions assigned to objects, and the various folder attributes such as Read-Only, Hidden, Archive, and System.
- **Write:** Users can create new files and subfolders in a folder. This permission also allows users to view folder ownership, the assigned permissions, and to use the **Properties** dialog box to change folder attributes.
- **List Folder Contents:** Users can only view the names of subfolders and files in a folder.
- **Read and Execute:** This permission includes the tasks permitted by the Read and List Folder Contents permissions and gives users the ability to navigate through folders for which they do not have permission, to get to files and folders for which they do have permissions.
- **Modify:** Users can view, create, delete, and modify the content of folders, as well as change attributes. This permission includes all tasks permitted by the Read, Write, and Read and Execute permissions.
- **Full Control:** Users can change permissions and take ownership of folders. This permission includes all actions that are permitted by all other NTFS permissions.

The standard NTFS file permissions are (Figure 11-2):
- **Read:** Users can read the file and view the file attributes, file ownership, and permissions.
- **Write:** Users can change the file, change file attributes, and view file ownerships and permissions.
- **Read and Execute:** Users can view the contents of files and run program applications.
- **Modify:** Users can modify and delete the file, run applications, change attributes, and perform all other actions permitted by the Write and Read and Execute permissions.
- **Full Control:** Users can change permissions, take ownership, and perform all actions permitted by the other NTFS permissions.

tip

When you assign NTFS permissions to a folder, all files and subfolders in the folder inherit the same permissions by default (This default action can be changed.). On the other hand, NTFS permissions assigned to files cannot be further inherited because files do not contain any object that can inherit these permissions.

Figure 11-1 NTFS folder permissions

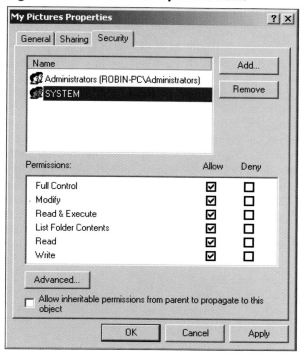

Figure 11-2 NTFS file permissions

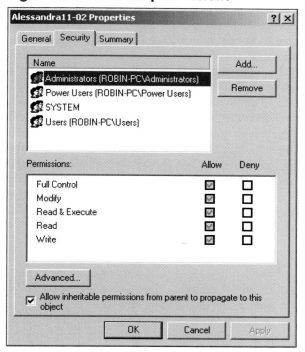

skill 2

Assigning NTFS Permissions

exam objective

Monitor, manage, and troubleshoot access to files and folders. Control access to files and folders by using permissions.

overview

When you assign NTFS permissions, you must understand not only how they work when combined with other NTFS permissions and how they work when combined with share permissions, but also how they are inherited from the parent folders. By default, whatever permissions you assign to the parent folder are inherited by the subfolders and files stored in that folder. This is true for both share permissions and NTFS permissions. You will know that an NTFS permission has been inherited if it is grayed out and inactive on the Security tab in the Properties dialog box. This indicates that there is no need to assign this permission to the subfolder or file because it has already been inherited. However, for certain files you may want to prevent the inheritance of some of the permissions granted to the parent folder. This can be accomplished easily by removing the check from the **Allow inheritable permissions from parent to propagate to the object** check box at the bottom of the Security tab. At this point, you can either copy the previously inherited permissions or you can remove the inherited permissions and keep only those that are explicitly set for the object. The best practice is to copy the existing permissions because then you can reconfigure the ACL by removing or adding the necessary permissions. If you remove all of the permissions, you will have to reconfigure the entire Security tab.

The important rules for assigning NTFS permissions are recapped and outlined below:

◆ When you assign multiple permissions to a user, the effective permission for the user is the combination of all the assigned permissions. For example, if a user has the Read permission for a file, and he/she is a member of another group that has the Write permission for that file, the effective permission for the user is both Read and Write.

◆ When you set the Deny condition, it overrides an allowed permission the user has for accessing the file or folder. For example, if a user named John has the Modify permission for the **Client** folder, which contains two files, Feedback.doc and Requirements.doc, and John is also a member of the Sales group, which has been denied the Modify permission for the Feedback.doc file, John can read and write to only Requirements.doc **(Figure 11-3)**.

◆ When you assign both shared folder permissions and NTFS permissions, the effective permission will be the most restrictive one. For example, if Kelvin is a member of the Team Leaders group and the QA group, and the Team Leaders group has been assigned the Read shared folder permission for the Standards folder, but the QA group has been assigned the Full Control NTFS permission for the Standards folder, the effective permission when Kelvin access the folder over the network is Read **(Figure 11-4)**.

◆ NTFS file permissions override NTFS folder permissions. For example, if a user, James, does not have access permissions for a folder named Sales, but James has permission to access a file named data.doc that is stored in the Sales folder, he can access data.doc, but he must do so by specifying the path for that file in the **Run** dialog box. Without permission to read the folder, he cannot view the folder or open it to look for the file.

◆ When you assign NTFS permissions to a folder, the files and subfolders contained in that folder inherit the assigned permissions. However, you can prevent permissions from being inherited by the files and subfolders of a folder.

◆ When you copy or move files or folders, the NTFS permissions often change. When you copy a file from one folder to another, the permissions change because now the file will inherit a new set of NTFS permissions from the new parent folder. When you copy a file, you become the owner of the file. Once you take ownership of a file, you can change the NTFS permissions.

tip

Remember you can assign NTFS permissions to both files and folders, unlike the shared folder permissions which can be assigned only at the folder level.

caution

You must have the Write permission for the destination folder in order to copy or move an NTFS object to its destination folder. You must have at least the Modify permission for the source file or folder in order to move it.

tip

The NTFS permissions for a file or folder copied or moved from an NTFS volume to any other volume, such as FAT or FAT32, are lost because other volumes do not support NTFS permissions.

Figure 11-3 Denying the Modify permission

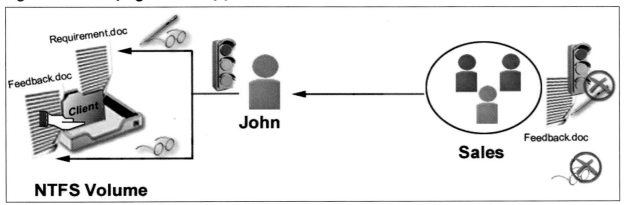

Figure 11-4 Combining shared folder permissions and NTFS permissions

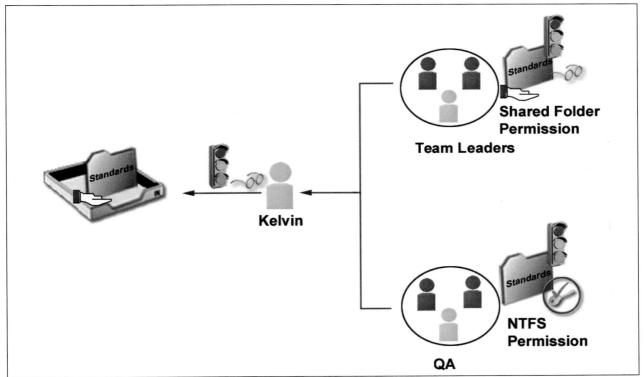

skill 2

Assigning NTFS Permissions (cont'd)

exam objective

Monitor, manage, and troubleshoot access to files and folders. Control access to files and folders by using permissions.

overview

◆ When you move a file, the NTFS permissions may change, subject to the directory into which you are moving it. When you move a file or folder within an NTFS volume, the permissions are not changed in the new location because the owner of the object remains the same. However, when you move a file or folder to a different NTFS volume, the NTFS permission changes because the ownership of the moved file changes in the new location. Ownership changes because the operating system treats a move to a different volume as if it were a copy and then a delete.

how to

Assign the Read and Write NTFS permissions to a user for accessing the General folder.

1. Right-click the **General** folder, and click the **Properties** command to open the **General Properties** dialog box.
2. Click the **Security** tab.
3. Click [Add...] to open the **Select Users or Groups** dialog box (on a domain network the **Select Users, Computers, or Groups** dialog box opens).
4. Select the **Usr1** on the **Name** list.
5. Click [Add...]. The name of the selected user appears in the lower section of the dialog box **(Figure 11-5)**.
6. Click [OK] to close the Select Users or Groups dialog box.
7. The user name is added to the **Name** box in the General Properties dialog box. The dialog box will show **Joe Forester**, the full name you used when you created the **Usr1** account in Lesson 8.
8. Select **Joe Forester** in the Name list, and select the **Allow** check box for the Write permission. The Read & Execute, List Folder Contents, and Read permissions should be selected by default **(Figure 11-6)**.
9. Click [OK] to close the General Properties dialog box.

tip

If the allow or deny check box for a specific permission is grayed out, it indicates that this permission is inherited from the parent object.

more

In order to effectively assign permissions to multiple users in a large organization, you should follow the guidelines described below:

◆ Assign permissions at the group level rather than at an individual level, according to the level of access that the group requires for each object. This simplifies monitoring access to shared objects over a network. For example, if you have a folder named Sales that contains confidential information, and members of the **Managers** group need to modify it regularly, but members of the **Executive** group only need to view and read its contents, assign the **Modify** permission to the Managers group and the **Read** permission to the Executive group rather than assigning permissions to individual members.

◆ Organize folders with the same NTFS permissions within a single folder. For example, you can store the folders of similar applications within a single folder. Then, you can share and assign appropriate access permissions to this single folder, instead of sharing and assigning permissions for each application folder individually.

Figure 11-5 Selecting a user for assigning permissions

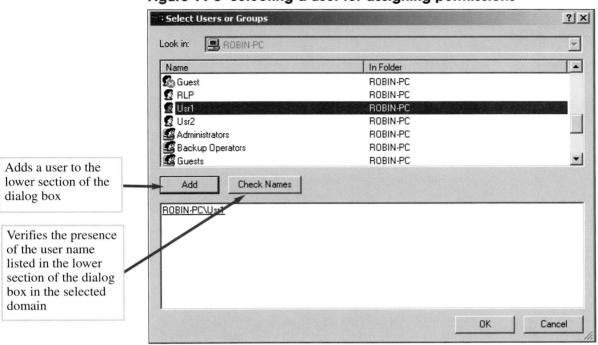

Adds a user to the lower section of the dialog box

Verifies the presence of the user name listed in the lower section of the dialog box in the selected domain

Figure 11-6 Assigning permissions to a user

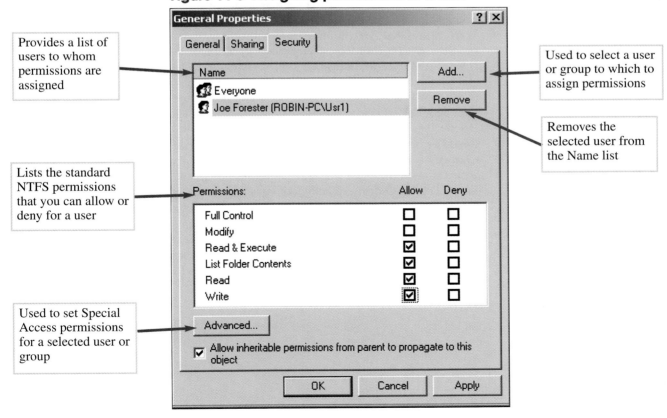

Provides a list of users to whom permissions are assigned

Used to select a user or group to which to assign permissions

Removes the selected user from the Name list

Lists the standard NTFS permissions that you can allow or deny for a user

Used to set Special Access permissions for a selected user or group

skill 3   *Using Special Access Permissions*

exam objective

Monitor, manage, and troubleshoot access to files and folders. Control access to files and folders by using permissions.

overview

As you have learned, on an NTFS volume you can decide precisely what level of control users will have. This is accomplished using the fourteen **special access permissions** to fine-tune your security. These special access permissions are additional security attributes that can be configured on the ACL for a resource. After you assign standard NTFS permissions, you can view the available special access permissions by clicking the **Advanced** button on the **Security** tab. The **Change Permissions** and **Take Ownership** permissions are commonly used to further regulate access to files and folders.

The Special Access permissions are described below (**Figure 11-7**):

◆ **Traverse Folder/Execute Files:** Users can view the directory structure of folders and work on files in those folders.

◆ **List Folder/Read Data:** Users can view folders and read their content.

◆ **Read Attributes:** Users can view and read the attributes of folders, for example, Read-only, Archive, and Hidden.

◆ **Read Extended Attributes:** Users can read the extended attributes of files that are defined by programs.

◆ **Create Files/Write Data:** Users can create new files on a directory and write data on an existing file on your computer.

◆ **Create Folders/Append Data:** This permission allows you to create folders and add data to folders.

◆ **Write Attributes:** Users with this permission can change the system-generated attributes associated with a folder or file such as Read-only, Hidden, Archive, compressed, or encrypted.

◆ **Write Extended Attributes:** Users with this permission can change the program-generated extended attributes associated with a file.

◆ **Delete Subfolders and Files:** Users can delete subfolders and files in a folder. For example, consider a situation where you need to restrict a user from deleting subfolders in a folder to which he/she has full access. To do this, you deny the Delete Subfolders and Files permission to the user in the Permissions Entry dialog box for the folder.

◆ **Delete:** Users can delete files and folders.

◆ **Read Permissions:** Users can view the permissions assigned to a file.

◆ **Change Permissions:** Users can change permissions for an object.

◆ **Take Ownership:** Users who are granted this permission can take ownership of a file or folder. They must then explicitly take ownership. Ownership of a resource can be taken, but it cannot be assigned to others. The current owner of a file or folder, an administrator, or any user with the Full Control permission can assign the Take Ownership permission to another user. That user can then take ownership of the resource on the Owner tab in the Access Control Settings dialog box. For example, an employee named Keith leaves your organization and you want to assign ownership of his files to another employee, Ryan. First you must assign the Take Ownership attribute to Ryan, and then Ryan must take ownership of each resource.

tip

The Take Ownership permisson can be assigned only by the owner of the object, an administrator, or a user with the Full Control permission for that object.

Figure 11-7 Various Special Access permissions

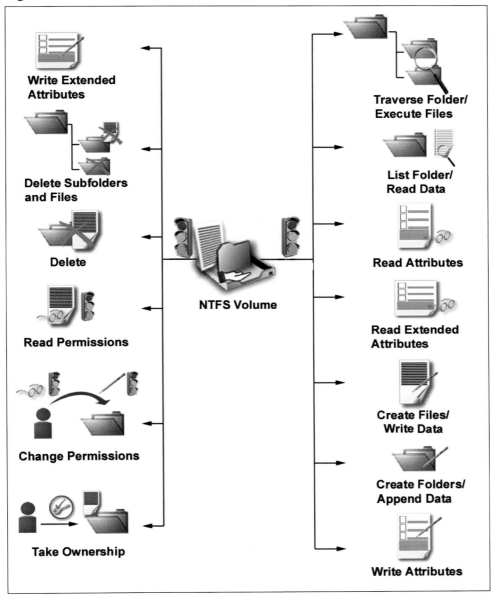

skill 3

Using Special Access Permissions
(cont'd)

exam objective   Basic knowledge

how to

Set Special Access Permissions for a user.

1. Right-click the **General** folder on the C: drive of your computer, and then click the **Properties** command to open the **General Properties** dialog box.
2. Click the **Security** tab.
3. Select **Joe Forester** in the **Name** list, and then click [Advanced..] to open the **Access Control Settings for General** dialog box. By default, the user name is selected in the **Permission Entries** section (**Figure 11-8**).
4. Click [View/Edit..] to open the **Permission Entry for General** dialog box. A list of the Special Access permissions appears.
5. Select the **Allow** check boxes for the **Change Permissions** and **Take Ownership** permissions in the **Permissions** section (**Figure 11-9**). This allows Usr1 to change the access permissions for the folder and to take ownership of the folder.
6. Click [OK] to close the Permissions Entry for General dialog box.
7. Click [OK] to close the Access Control Settings for General dialog box.
8. Click [OK] to close the General Properties dialog box.

Figure 11-8 Access Control Settings for General dialog box

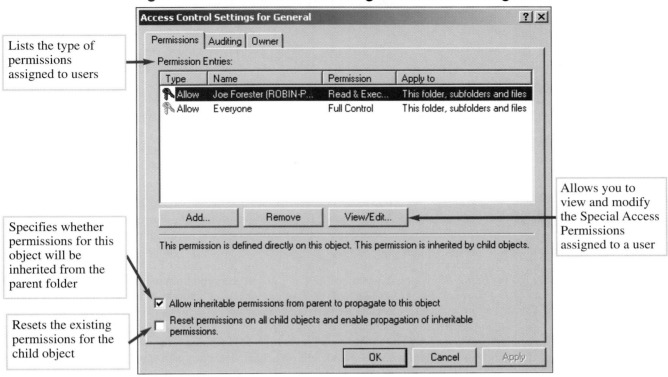

Lists the type of permissions assigned to users

Specifies whether permissions for this object will be inherited from the parent folder

Resets the existing permissions for the child object

Allows you to view and modify the Special Access Permissions assigned to a user

Figure 11-9 Assigning Special Access Permissions

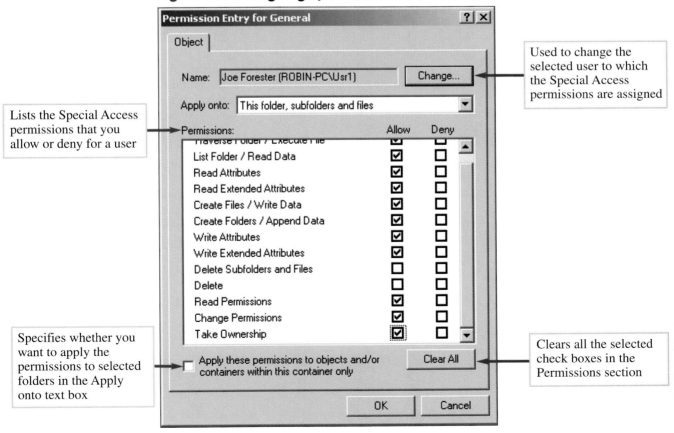

Lists the Special Access permissions that you allow or deny for a user

Used to change the selected user to which the Special Access permissions are assigned

Specifies whether you want to apply the permissions to selected folders in the Apply onto text box

Clears all the selected check boxes in the Permissions section

skill 4

Troubleshooting NTFS Permissions

exam objective

Monitor, manage, and troubleshoot access to files and folders. Control access to files and folders by using permissions.

overview

After you assign NTFS permissions, certain problems can occur. For example, a user that you thought would be able to access a folder may be unable to do so. You can troubleshoot such problems by identifying their causes and modifying the permissions accordingly. Some of the problems related to NTFS permissions and their solutions are described here:

◆ **A user added to a group is unable to access files or folders:** You add a new user, Charles, to a group named Core. Charles needs to view the content of the Ratings folder, but he is denied access to it. To solve this problem, you may need to update the access permissions for the Core group by adding the Read permission for the Ratings folder to the Core group. If the Core group already has this permission assigned, check the other group permissions and the individual permissions set for Charles to make sure that he has not been denied access to the folder. Most importantly remember that when you add a user to a group, they must log off and log back on before they become part of that group, or they must close all network connections to the computer where the file is stored and make new connections.

◆ **A user is unable to access a file on an NTFS volume:** If a user is unable to access a file on an NTFS volume, you should first check the location of the file to find out whether it has been copied or moved from one NTFS volume to another. Remember, when you copy or move a file to another NTFS volume, the permissions for the file may change, so you may need to reassign permissions for that user or for an appropriate group to which he or she belongs. If appropriate access permissions were never set, you will also have to reconfigure the ACL for the resource so that the individual or a group to which he or she belongs is assigned the correct level of access. Always check to see whether the user or a group to which the user belongs has been denied access.

◆ **A user is not allowed to delete the existing content of a file:** If you do not want a user to delete the existing content of a file, you can assign the **Create Folders/Append Data** permission to the user so that he or she can only add data to the file and cannot delete or modify the existing content. To do this, you use the Permissions Entry dialog box for the file.

◆ **A user with Full Control permission for a folder can delete a file in the folder even though they do not have permission to delete the individual file:** Consider a situation where a user named John has Full Control permission for the **Report** folder. He deletes a file named Monthly Status that is stored in the Report folder, even though he does not have permission to delete the individual file. To prevent this problem from recurring, you must remove the special access permission **Delete Subfolders and Files** so that John will not be able to delete any more files in the folder (**Figure 11-10**).

Figure 11-10 Troubleshooting Problems with NTFS Permissions

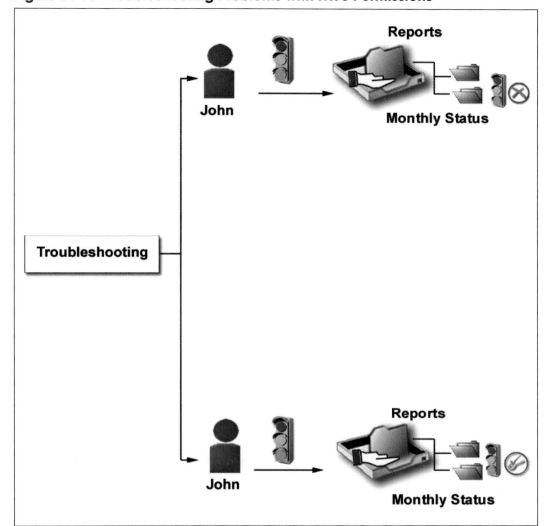

Summary

◆ NTFS permissions are used to control access to objects on an NTFS volume, such as files and folders, and to ensure the security of data on an NTFS volume.

◆ NTFS permissions determine the tasks that users can perform on the content of files and folders.

◆ NTFS permissions can be configured for both files and folders.

◆ NTFS folder permissions are assigned to folders and subfolders on an NTFS volume.

◆ The NTFS folder permissions are: Read, Write, List Folder Contents, Read and Execute, Modify, and Full Control.

◆ NTFS file permissions are assigned to files on an NTFS volume.

◆ The NTFS file permissions are: Read, Write, Read and Execute, Modify, and Full Control.

◆ NTFS file permissions override NTFS folder permissions.

◆ The effective NTFS permission for a user with multiple permissions is the sum of all the assigned NTFS permissions.

◆ When NTFS permissions are used in combination with share permissions, the most restrictive permission applies when the folder is accessed over the network.

◆ The Deny condition overrides a specifically allowed permission.

◆ By default, the files and subfolders in a folder inherit the permissions that are assigned to that folder.

◆ NTFS permissions often change when files or folders are copied or moved to a new location.

◆ You assign permissions to groups according to the level of access they require for each resource.

◆ Permissions should be assigned to a group rather than to individual users.

◆ The Special Access permissions allow you to fine-tune a specific level of access that users have to objects on the NTFS volume.

◆ The Access Control List (ACL) for a file or folder is used to assign the Special Access permissions.

◆ Troubleshooting NTFS permission problems involves identifying the causes of the problems and then solving them accordingly.

Key Terms

NTFS file permissions
NTFS folder permissions

NTFS permissions
Special access permissions

Test Yourself

1. You want to disallow some network users from accessing a file on your computer by setting the attribute for the file to read-only. Which of the following permissions must you have in order to modify the attributes for the file?
   a. Read
   b. Read & Execute
   c. Write
   d. List Folder Content

2. Harry is a member of two groups, Sales and Managers, at Kemp Corp. For a file named Requirements, you assign the Read and Execute Permission to the Sales group, and the Modify permission to the Managers group. The effective permission for Harry for the Requirements file is:
   a. Read.

   b. Modify.
   c. Read and Execute.
   d. Write.

3. Mary has the Read permission for accessing a folder named Reports on an NTFS volume. This folder contains two files, Monthly.doc and Final.doc. Mary is also a member of two groups, Sales and Managers. The Managers group has the Write permission for the Reports folder. The Sales group is denied the Write permission for the Final.doc file. The effective permission for Mary allows her to:
   a. Write to only Monthly.doc.
   b. Read and Write to both the files.
   c. Read only the Monthly.doc file.
   d. Write to both the files.

4. Which of the following special permissions allows you to view the directory structure of folders and work on the files in that directory structure?
   a. Read Attributes
   b. Create Folders/Append Data
   c. List Folder Contents
   d. Traverse Folder/Execute Files

5. Peter is working as a Marketing Manager at Vector Inc. He has the NTFS Read permission for a folder named Client.As an administrator, you create a file named Schedule.doc in this folder and assign Peter the Modify permission to change the content of the file. The effective permission for Peter on the file Schedule.doc is:
   a. Write.
   b. Modify.
   c. Read.
   d. Full Control.

6. You have the Change shared folder permission for a folder named Analysis, while all other network users only have the Read shared folder permission for this folder. What is your effective permission for the Analysis folder when you log on to the computer where the file is stored?
   a. Full Control
   b. Change
   c. Modify
   d. Read

7. Which of the following permissions do you use to fine-tune a specific level of access users can have for files and folders on an NTFS volume?
   a. Shared folder permissions
   b. Special Access permissions
   c. NTFS permissions
   d. Read and Execute permission

Projects: On Your Own

1. Assign the Read and Write NTFS permissions to a user named Harry, for accessing the Project folder.
   a. Open the **Project Properties** dialog box.
   b. Open the **Select Users, Computers, or Groups** dialog box.
   c. Select the user name, **Harry**, in the **Name** list.
   d. Select the **Allow** check box for the Read and Write permissions.
   e. Close the **Project Properties** dialog box to assign the Read and Write NTFS permissions to Harry.

2. Set the Special Access permission known as Change Permissions, for a user, Jack, to access a folder named Meeting.
   a. Open the **Meeting Properties** dialog box.
   b. Open the **Select Users, Computers, or Groups** dialog box.
   c. Select the user name, **Jack,** in the **Name** list.
   d. Open the **Access Control Settings for Meeting** dialog box.
   e. Open the **Permission Entry for Meeting** dialog box.
   f. Select the **Allow** check box of the Special Access permission **Change Permissions**.
   g. Close the **Properties** dialog box to set the Special Access permission, **Change Permissions**, to access the Meeting folder.

Problem Solving Scenarios

1. You are working as an administrator at a sporting goods company called Dukes Corporation. Harry Blackmun, Sales Manager at Dukes, has a folder named Sales on the NTFS drive of his computer. The files in the Sales folder contain information that should be modified by only the Sales Manager. The Sales Representatives who work under Harry will, however, need to have read access to the files in the Sales folder. He wants you to assign the NTFS Read permission to his team members, and NTFS Write and Modify permission to the Sales Manager. Write a memo describing how you would achieve these capabilites. Include how you will handle the combination of shared folder permissions and NTFS permissions and how you will handle the default permissions.

2. You are working as a regional Sales Manager at Dukes Corporation. The members of your sales team have Read permission to access a folder named Regional Sales that you create on the NTFS volume of your computer. You want your Administrative Assistant, Susan Olson, to create subfolders and add data to the Regional Sales folder regularly. You also want Susan to be able to set appropriate permissions for the team members to access the Regional Sales folder. Write a report describing the steps you would take to assign appropriate special access permissions to Susan to enable her to perform these tasks.

12 Configuring Local Security Policies

Setting group policies is another important part of your overall network security strategy. Group policies are used to manage many different settings for both computers and users, including the desktop appearance, the allocation of software applications, and password limitations. Group policies are most often implemented when you are working with a domain-based network that combines Windows 2000 Servers and Windows 2000 Professional clients in an Active Directory environment. You set group policies for sites, domains, and OUs (organizational units) to manage computer configuration, the user environment, and account policies such as minimum password length and length of time a password can be used. Since Windows 2000 Professional can only be used to set up a peer-to-peer or workgroup network, when you are studying this topic, the emphasis is on setting group policies for individual computers. Group policies for local computers that do not use Active Directory are set using the Local Security Policy console and the Group Policy MMC snap-in. There are four categories of local security policies in the Local Security Policy console: account policies, local policies, public key policies, and IP security policies.

Account policies consist of the password policy and the account lockout policy. Password policies are used to implement specific rules for how all users who log on to a computer must structure their passwords, the frequency with which they must change them, and the length of time they can use their passwords before they must be changed. These policies are not set individually. They apply to all users on a local computer. Account lockout policies are used to set how many invalid logon attempts will be allowed before the account is barred from use. You can also set a specific time period during which the account will remain locked out or configure the policy so that an Administrator must unlock it.

Local security policies are classified as audit policies, user rights assignments, or security options. For example, you can set a security option to prevent the name of the last user that logged on to the computer from displaying in the logon dialog box. User rights assignments prescribe what actions a user can execute. For example, Increase quotas and Load and unload device drivers user rights are assigned to the built-in Administrators group by default. You can add a user to this group so that they can perform these and other administrative tasks, or you can create your own groups and assign specific rights to them for interacting with the operating system.

Public key policies include the Encrypting File System (EFS) recovery policy. Files and folders are encrypted using a security algorithm and a file encryption key to change the contents into unreadable characters. Either the user who encrypted the file or a user who has been designated as the recovery agent can recover an encrypted file using this policy. When other users try to access an encrypted file, they will receive an Access Denied message.

IPSec (Internet Protocol Security) policies are used to protect data as it travels on a TCP/IP network. IPSec policies ensure the security of data packets by encrypting them before sending them to another computer on a public network.

Security templates can simplify the administration of your local security policies in a workgroup setting. Instead of having to set many different policies on each workstation, you can use a security template to apply a group of security settings all at once.

Goals

In this lesson, you will learn to secure your computer by setting password policies, specifying an account lockout policy, and setting various security options such as preventing the last user name that logged on to the computer from appearing in the logon dialog box. You will also learn how to encrypt and decrypt files using both the Properties dialog box and the Cipher utility, how to add a recovery agent, and how to use IP Security policies to protect data as it travels over a public network. Finally, you will learn how to use the pre-configured security templates in Windows 2000, how to perform a security analysis, and how to apply a group of security settings all at once to the local computer.

Lesson 12   Configuring Local Security Policies

Skill	Exam 70-210 Objective
1. Introducing Local Security Policies	Implement, configure, manage, and troubleshoot local security policy.
2. Securing Passwords Using Password Policy	Implement, configure, manage, and troubleshoot account policy.
3. Enhancing Computer Security Using Account Lockout Policy	Implement, configure, manage, and troubleshoot account policy.
4. Securing Data Using Security Options	Implement, configure, manage, and troubleshoot local security policy.
5. Increasing Security Using EFS (Encrypting File System)	Encrypt data on a hard disk by using Encrypting File System (EFS).
6. Encrypting and Decrypting Files and Folders Using the Cipher Utility	Encrypt data on a hard disk by using Encrypting File System (EFS).
7. Recovering Encrypted Files Using Recovery Agents	Implement, configure, manage, and troubleshoot local security policy.
8. Securing Data on a Network Using IPSec Policies	Implement, configure, manage, and troubleshoot local security policy.
9. Working with Security Templates	Implement, configure, manage, and troubleshoot a security configuration.

Requirements

To complete this lesson, you will need administrative rights on a Windows 2000 Professional computer with an NTFS volume. You will also need a file named Wages.doc stored in the Employees folder and a file named Metadata.doc stored in the Data folder. Both folders must be saved on an NTFS volume. The exercises will assume this is the C: drive. Substitute the correct drive letter in the exercises if necessary. You will also need a file named Accountinfo that was created on the NTFS drive with a Standard or Restricted User account.

Introducing Local Security Policies

exam objective

Implement, configure, manage, and troubleshoot local security policy.

overview

Group Policies are used to administer and manage the security of an entire network. They are used at the local level to manage the security of workgroup or stand-alone computers. Group policies for local computers that do not use the Active Directory are set using **local security policies** in the **Local Security Settings** console and in the **Group Policy** snap-in. Local security policies are used to set certain conditions which all users operating the computer will have to abide by. For example, account policies set the rules for the logon process, such as the settings for passwords and the procedures that will be followed to lock user accounts after invalid logon attempts. These policies apply to a local computer that is not part of an Active Directory network. If the computer becomes part of a **domain**, higher-level security policies will be set by the Administrator which may override any local security policies that have been set.

The domain security policies set by the Domain Administrator are applied to sites, domains, and organizational units. Site policies override local policy, domain policies override site policies, and OU policies override domain policies. This default behavior can be controlled using the Block Inheritance and No Override settings.

There are four categories of local security policies: account policies, local security policies, public key policies, and IP Security (IPSec) policies (**Figure 12-1**).

Account policies consist of the password policies and the account lockout policies that are used to secure passwords (**Figure 12-2**). Locking an account will ensure that further logon attempts will not be permitted until a specified time period has passed. In this way you can help to secure your computer from unauthorized access. You can set the number of invalid logon attempts that will be permitted and the time period during which the account will be locked out after this number has been exceeded, or you can lock the account indefinitely until an Administrator unlocks it.

Local security policies are used to set various security options for your computer, such as preventing the last user name that logged on to the computer from appearing in the logon dialog box, or you can force users to use the key combination Ctrl+Alt+Delete before they can logon so that only Windows, and not a Trojan horse program, can read the password. You set security options to protect your computer from viruses and unauthorized user access (**Figure 12-3**). For example, you can configure a local security policy so that the local Guest account will not be able to log on to your computer.

Using **public key policies (Figure 12-4)**, you can set additional recovery agents for a system so that if the owner of an encrypted file forgets his or her password, the recovery agent can copy the encrypted file to that user's computer and decrypt the file by clearing the **Encrypt contents to secure data** checkbox in the Properties dialog box for the file. Files are encrypted using a session key and then versions of the file are encrypted using both the user's public key and the recovery agent's public key. The recovery agent has a file recovery certificate and his or her own private key that corresponds to the certificate. EFS requires that a recovery agent be designated before encryption can proceed. The local Administrator is automatically designated as the recovery agent on stand-alone or workgroup computers and a recovery key is placed in his or her personal certificate store on the computer. In a domain, the Domain Administrator account is the default recovery agent for the domain. You can reassign this responsibility or designate additional recovery agents. Recovery agents are required so that encrypted data will never be unrecoverable.

Finally, you use **IP Security policies** to define security rules for data transmitted across a network so that the data cannot be intercepted or stolen during transit.

Figure 12-1 The Local Security Settings console

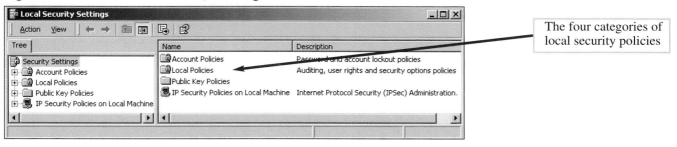

The four categories of local security policies

Figure 12-2 Account policies

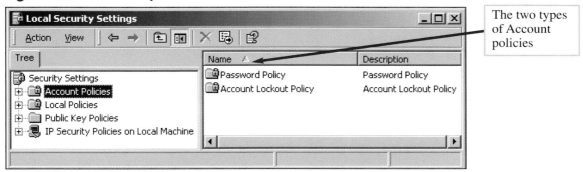

The two types of Account policies

Figure 12-3 Local policies

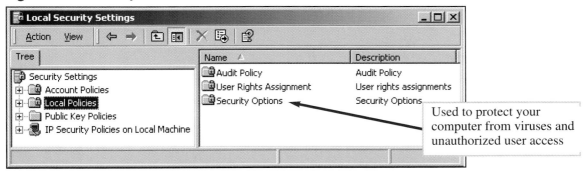

Used to protect your computer from viruses and unauthorized user access

Figure 12-4 Public key policies

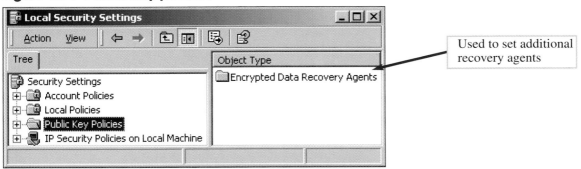

Used to set additional recovery agents

skill 1

Introducing Local Security Policies
(cont'd)

exam objective

Implement, configure, manage, and troubleshoot local security policy.

overview

To configure some of the local security policies, you use the Local Security Settings console. However, in order to see all the policy settings that are available in Windows 2000, you must create a custom Microsoft Management Console (MMC). MMC is the primary administrative tool in Windows 2000 Professional that provides a method to create, save, and open other administrative tools that are called **snap-ins**. In order to put account policies into operation, you must add the Group Policy snap-in to the MMC.

how to

Create a custom Microsoft Management console by adding the Group Policy snap-in to an MMC.

1. Click [Start], and then click the **Run** command to open the **Run** dialog box.
2. Type **mmc** in the **Open** text box, and click **OK** to open the **Console Root** window (**Figure 12-5**).
3. Open the **Console** menu and click the **Add/Remove Snap-in** command to open the **Add/Remove Snap-in** dialog box.
4. Click [Add] to open the **Add Standalone Snap-in** dialog box. Click the list arrow to scroll down the **Available Standalone Snap-ins** list and select the **Group Policy** option. (**Figure 12-6**).
5. Click [Add] to initiate the **Select Group Policy Object Wizard**.
6. Click [Finish] to add the Group Policy snap-in as a **Local Computer Policy** in the Console Root window (**Figure 12-7**). This will be used to configure the Local Group Policy for the computer.
7. Click [Close] to close the Add Standalone Snap-in dialog box.
8. Click [OK] to close the Add/Remove Snap-in dialog box.
9. In the Console Root window, click the plus sign ⊞ beside the Local Computer Policy node to expand the node.
10. Click the plus sign to expand the **Computer Configuration** node.
11. Click the plus sign beside the **Windows Settings** node and then the **Security Settings** node to expand the nodes.
12. Expanding the Security Settings node displays the four categories of local security policies in the Details pane of the Console Root window (**Figure 12-8**).
13. Open the **Console** menu and select the **Save** command to open the **Save As** dialog box. Type **Local Group Policy** in the **File name** text box and click the **Save** button to save your new custom console. Close the Local Group Policy console.

Figure 12-5 The Run dialog box

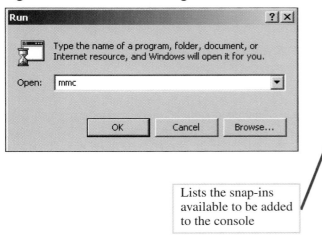

Figure 12-6 Selecting the Group Policy snap-in

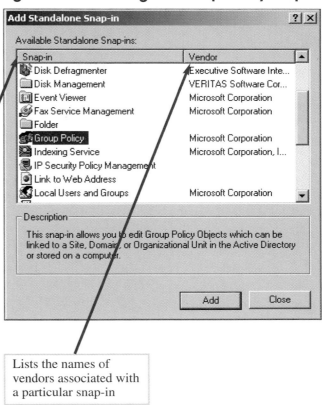

Lists the snap-ins
available to be added
to the console

Lists the names of
vendors associated with
a particular snap-in

Figure 12-7 Console root window

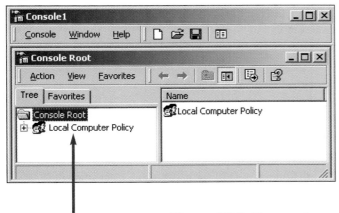

The Group Policy
snap-in has been added
to the console root
window as a Local
Computer Policy

Figure 12-8 Four categories of local security policies

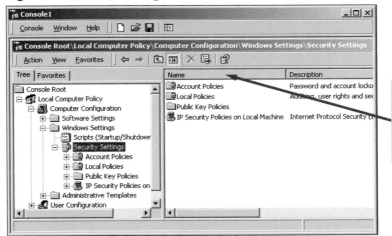

List of local
security policies
that can be applied
on the local
computer

skill 2

Securing Passwords Using Password Policy

exam objective

Implement, configure, manage, and troubleshoot account policy.

overview

Account policies are used to set the user account properties that control the logon process. They include password policies and account lockout policies. **Password policies** are used to supplement the security of your computer by requiring users to change their passwords at specific time intervals, requiring passwords to be a certain length, and by making users keep a password history so that they cannot simply switch back and forth between two passwords. The various password policy options in Windows 2000 Professional are listed in the **Password Policy** node (**Figure 12-9**). The Password Policy node is under the **Account Policies** node. Password policies for a local computer are set on the computer itself. However, if the local computer is logged on to a domain, the domain password policies will apply to the local computer.

The password policy options that can be set are: Enforce password history, Maximum password age, Minimum password age, Minimum password length, Passwords must meet complexity requirements, and Store password using reversible encryption for all users in the domain.

The **Enforce password history** option is used to set the number of passwords that will be stored in a password history. You can store up to 24 old passwords so that users can refer to their password history and avoid repeating old passwords. This will also help them to create new passwords that are distinctly different from the old ones. You can also leave the value set to the default of 0 if you do not think that maintaining a password history is necessary.

The **Maximum password age** option is used to set the maximum number of days users can keep a particular password. You can set this option as high as 999, although Windows 2000 Professional allows you to use a password for 42 days by default. Setting a value of 0 indicates that a password will never expire.

The **Minimum password age** option is used to set the minimum number of days during which users must keep the same password. This option can also be set as high as 999 days. Setting a value of 0 indicates that a password can be changed on the same day on which it is set. This setting is particularly useful when a user is compelled to change his or her password by the system so that you can prevent that user from immediately changing it back. The **Minimum password length** option is used to set the minimum number of characters a password must have. You can set the minimum password length as high as 14 characters.

The **Passwords must meet complexity requirements** option, which is disabled by default, is enabled when you want to require users to follow a minimum password length and a consistent password structure that will require them to construct passwords that contain a combination of capital letters, lower case letters, numbers, or punctuation marks. This policy requires passwords to be at least 6 characters long and to contain characters that include at least three of the following four different types of characters: upper case letters, lower case letters, digits, or non-alphanumeric characters (such as !,$,#,%). The password also cannot include all or part of the user's account name (**Table 12-1**).

The **Store password using reversible encryption for all users in the domain** option is used by Network Administrators so that a reversibly encrypted password is stored for all users in a domain.

Figure 12-9 Listing the password policy options

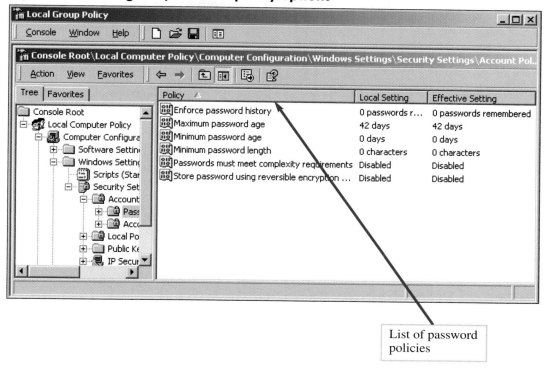

List of password
policies

Table 12-1 Passwords must meet complexity requirements	
Requirement	**Explanation**
Minimum password length	Must be at least six characters long
Character complexity	Must have characters from three of the four categories: (a) Upper case letters (English) (b) Lower case letters (English) (c) Numbers (base 10) (d) Non-alphanumeric characters (`~!@#$%^&*()_+-={}|:";'<>,./)
No duplication of user	Cannot contain all or even part of the user's account name

skill 2

Securing Passwords Using Password Policy (cont'd)

exam objective

Implement, configure, manage, and troubleshoot account policy.

how to

Set a password policy that requires users to set passwords with at least 14 characters.

1. Open the **Start** menu, point to **Programs**, point to **Administrative Tools**, and click **Local Group Policy.msc** to reopen the new custom console you created in the previous skill.

2. Expand the **Local Computer Policy** node and then expand the **Computer Configuration** node.

3. Expand the **Windows Settings** node and then the **Security Settings** node.

4. Double-click the **Account Policies** node under the Security Settings node, then double-click the **Password Policy** node under the Account Policies node to list the password policies.

5. Double-click the **Minimum password length** option to open the **Local Security Policy Setting** dialog box. You can set the password policy in the Local Security Policy Setting dialog box.

6. In the Local Security Policy Setting dialog box, enter **14** in the **Password must be at least** spin box to set a password policy that requires users to set passwords with at least 14 characters (**Figure 12-10**).

7. Click [OK] to save the password policy and close the Local Security Policy Setting dialog box.

8. Double-click **Enforce password history**. Enter **15** in the **Keep password history** spin box (**Figure 12-11**).

9. Click [OK] to save the password policy and to close the **Local Security Setting** dialog box.

10. Double-click **Maximum password age**. Enter **60** in the **Passwords expire in** spin box.

11. Click [OK] to save the password policy and to close the Local Security Setting dialog box. The policies will take effect when you close the console and save the settings.

12. Close the **Local Group Policy** console. Click **Yes** to save the console settings.

Figure 12-10 Setting the minimum password length

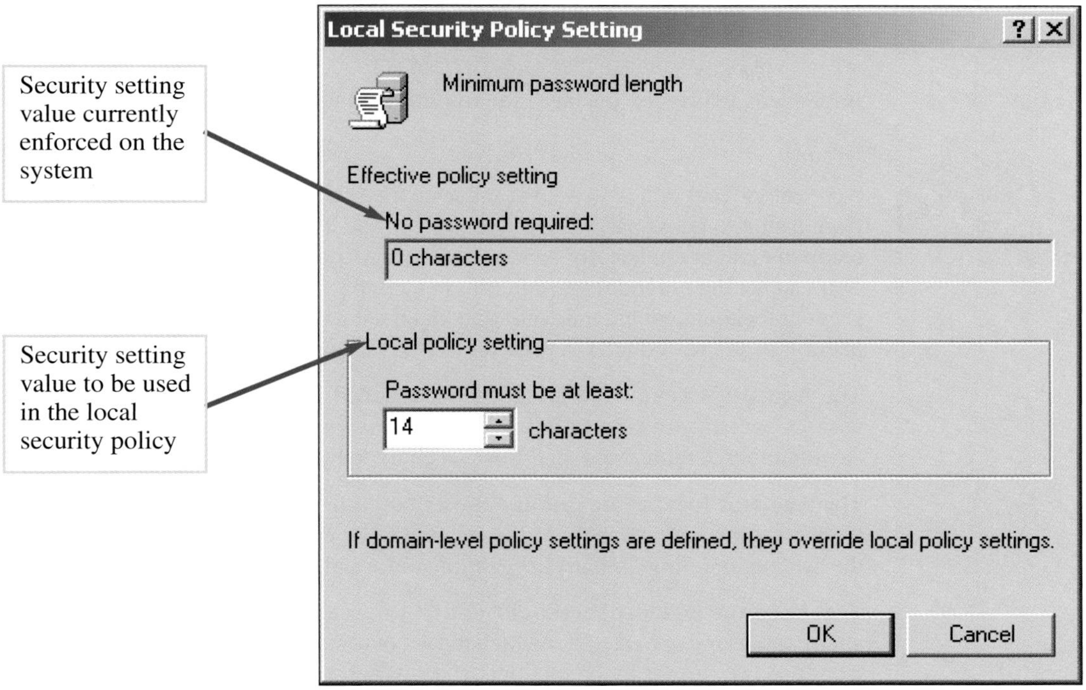

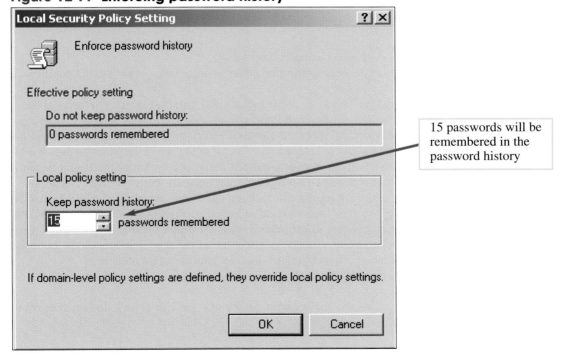

Figure 12-11 Enforcing password history

skill 3

Enhancing Computer Security Using Account Lockout Policy

exam objective

Implement, configure, manage, and troubleshoot account policy.

overview

Account lockout policy is used to enhance the security of your computer by preventing users from trying to guess passwords. If a user repeatedly attempts to log on to your computer, the computer can automatically lock out the user account according to the specifications you set. You can set the number of invalid logon attempts you will tolerate, the time duration for the account lockout, and the time duration that must pass after an invalid logon attempt before the bad logon attempt counter is reset to 0.

The **Account Lockout Policy** node is contained in the **Account Policies** node. It lists the various account lockout policies. The options you can set are: Account lockout duration, Account lockout threshold, and Reset account lockout counter after **(Figure 12-7)**.

The **Account lockout duration** option is used to set the time duration (minutes from 0 to 99999) during which you want the account to be disabled. You can set the value to 0 to lock the account indefinitely until the Administrator unlocks it.

The **Account lockout threshold** option is used to specify the number of invalid logon attempts a user can make after which the account will be locked and the user will be prevented from making further logon attempts. The default value for this option is 0, meaning that the account will never be locked no matter how many invalid logon attempts are made. You can set the account lockout threshold between 0 and 999.

The **Reset account lockout counter after** option sets the time duration that must elapse after an invalid logon attempt before the account lockout counter is reset to 0. You can reset the bad logon attempt counter between 1 and 99999 minutes.

how to

Set an account lockout policy so that a user account is locked out after three invalid logon attempts.

1. Open the **Local Group Policy** console.
2. Expand the **Local Computer Policy** node and then expand the **Computer Configuration** node, if necessary.
3. Expand the **Windows Settings** node and then the **Security Settings** node, if necessary.
4. Double-click the **Account Policies** node under the Security Settings node, if necessary, then, double-click the **Account Lockout Policy** node under the **Account Policies** node. The account lockout policies are listed in the right pane of the window **(Figure 12-12)**.
5. Double-click the **Account lockout threshold** option in the Policy heading in the right pane of the window to open the **Local Security Policy Setting** dialog box.
6. Type **3** in the **Account will lock out after** spin box in the **Local policy setting** section to specify that the account should be locked after three invalid logon attempts **(Figure 12-13)**.
7. Click OK to open the **Suggested Value Changes** window **(Figure 12-14)**. The Suggested Value Changes window shows the suggested values for the **Account lockout duration** and **Reset account lockout counter after** policies.
8. Click OK to apply the settings and close the Local Security Policy Setting dialog box.
9. Either leave the console open for the next skill, or close it and save the console settings.

tip

The Suggested Value Changes window appears each time the Account lockout duration is changed to or from zero [0]. It also will appear when the Account lockout duration is set to a number lower than the Reset lockout counter after value, or when the Account duration or Reset lockout duration after value is changed from Not Defined.

Figure 12-12 The various account lockout policies

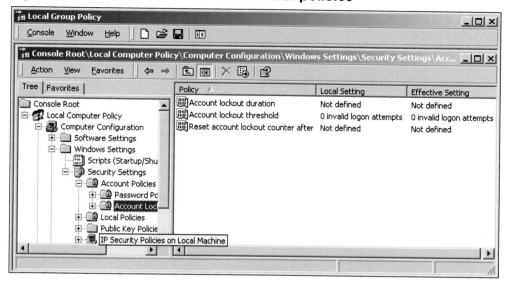

Figure 12-13 Setting an account lockout threshold policy

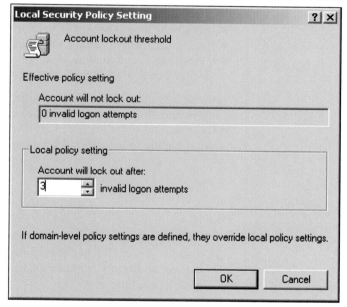

Figure 12-14 The Suggested Value Changes window

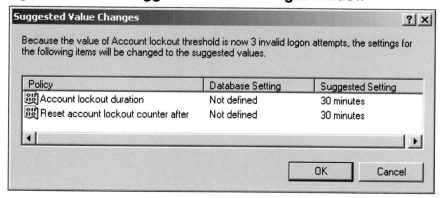

skill 4

Securing Data Using Security Options

exam objective

Implement, configure, manage, and troubleshoot local security policy.

overview

There are many security options you can use to further enhance the security of the data on your computer. For example, you can **Restrict CD-ROM access to the locally logged-on user only** or you can **Prevent users from installing printer drivers**. You can also set the behavior for installing unsigned drivers (**Unsigned driver installation behavior**). You can either set the system to **Silently succeed**, to **Warn but allow installation**, or to disallow the installation of unsigned drivers (**Do not allow installation**). Other security options include allowing automatic administrative log on to the Recovery Console (**Recovery Console: Allow automatic administrative logon**) and shutting down the system immediately if the system is unable to log security audits.

The **Security Options** node, which is found under the **Local Policies** node in the Local Security Policy console, is used to set about 40 types of security options for your computer (**Figure 12-10**). You can set restrictions such as denying unknown connections to your computer, logging off users when the logon time expires, and prompting users to change passwords before the password expires. Some of the commonly used security options include:

◆ Disabling the Allow system to be shut down without having to log on setting.
◆ Additional restrictions for anonymous connections.
◆ Preventing users from installing printer drivers.
◆ Automatically logging off users when the logon time expires.

You can use these options to configure security settings for a computer according to your requirements. For example, if you do not want anybody to be able to shut down your computer unless they have logged on, you need to disable the **Allow computer to be shut down without having to log on** local policy setting.

caution

By default, Windows 2000 Professional does not require users to log on in order to shut down the computer. You must open the Local Security Policy Setting dialog box for this policy and select the Disabled option button to prevent unauthorized users from shutting down the system.

how to

Set the **Do not display last user name in logon screen** security option.

1. Open the **Local Group Policy** console, if necessary.
2. Expand the **Local Computer Policy** node and then expand the **Computer Configuration** node, if necessary.
3. Expand the **Windows Settings** node and then the **Security Settings** node, if necessary.
4. Double-click the **Local Policies** node under the Security Settings node. Then double-click the **Security Options** node to display the security options in the right pane of the window (**Figure 12-15**).
5. Double-click the option **Do not display last user name in logon screen** in the right pane of the window, to open the **Local Security Policy Setting** dialog box.
6. In the **Local policy setting:** section, click the **Enabled** option button to program the computer not to display the last user name on the logon screen (**Figure 12-16**).
7. Click <u> OK </u> to set the security option and close the Local Security Policy Setting dialog box.
8. Close the Local Group Policy console and save the console settings.

Figure 12-15 List of security options

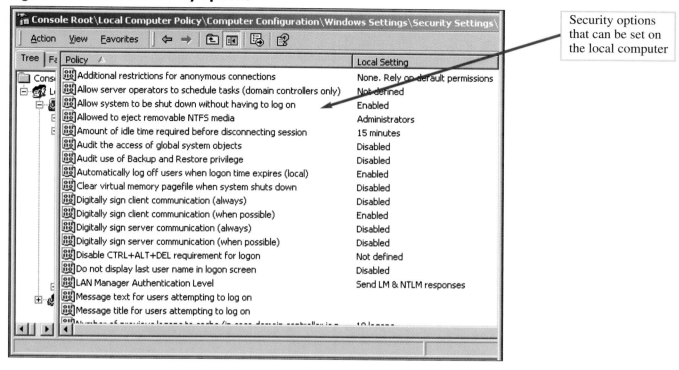

Security options that can be set on the local computer

Figure 12-16 Disabling the display of the last user name on the logon screen

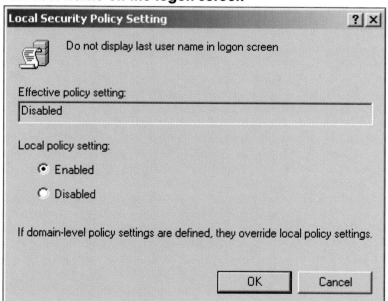

skill 4

Securing Data Using Security Options *(cont'd)*

exam objective

Implement, configure, manage, and troubleshoot local security policy.

more

The **User Rights Assignment** node under **Local Policies** is used to specify what actions a user can execute within the operating system. Users belong to different groups, such as **Administrators**, **Users**, **Guests**, and **Backup Operators**. The User Rights Assignment defines the rights enjoyed by a particular user within a specific group. For example, the Backup Operators have the right to back up and restore any file on the computer, but they are not given any access to those files, such as opening them or taking ownership of them, unless specifically granted *permissions* to do so.

The various user rights are listed under the User Rights Assignment node under Local Policies security policy (**Figure 12-17**). You can configure user rights according to your requirements in the **Local Security Policy Setting** dialog box (**Figure 12-18**). For example, you can grant all groups the right to change the system time.

tip

While certain rights are granted to certain groups by default, no rights are granted explicitly to any particular user account.

Figure 12-17 List of user rights on a computer

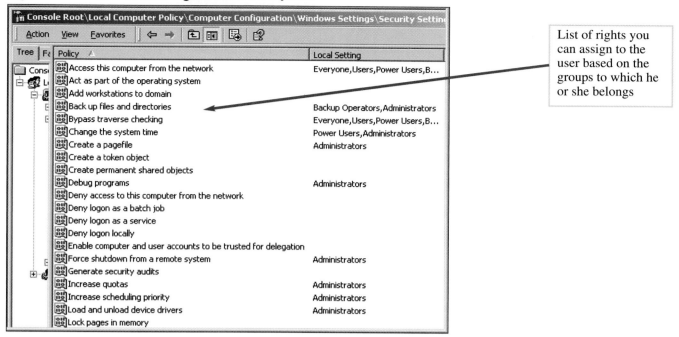

List of rights you can assign to the user based on the groups to which he or she belongs

Figure 12-18 Configure user rights

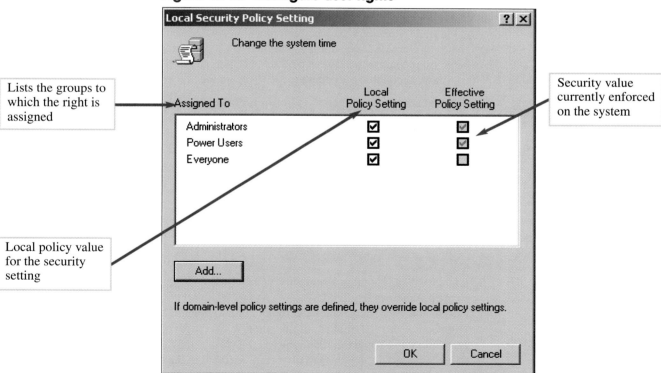

Lists the groups to which the right is assigned

Security value currently enforced on the system

Local policy value for the security setting

skill 5

Increasing Security Using EFS (Encrypting File System)

exam objective

Encrypt data on a hard disk by using Encrypting File System (EFS).

overview

As you have learned, the most effective way to protect local resources is to use an NTFS volume and apply NTFS permissions, because share permissions are not effective locally. However, local NTFS permissions can be bypassed by users if they access them by using an operating system other than Windows NT or Windows 2000 and use another utility such as NTFSDOS. In many organizations, such as defense establishments or in the banking sector where security is of primary concern, the **Encrypting File System** (EFS) can be used to rule out this possibility. You can encode data that is stored on NTFS partitions so that it is non-readable. Other users will not be able to access encrypted files even if they have access to your computer. For example, if Linda and John share the same computer and John does not want Linda to view the files that he uses, he can encrypt them. Linda will receive an Access Denied message if she tries to open one of John's files.

In the EFS encryption technique, important data is secured using a cryptographic key pair: a public key and a private key. Data is encrypted using a session key (file encryption key – FEK). The session key is then encrypted using the user's public key and later decrypted using the user's private key. If the user who encrypted the file leaves the company and deletes his or her certificate, or has his or her user account deleted, or if a certificate becomes corrupt, another user, who is designated as the recovery agent, can open the file. The recovery agent has a file recovery certificate and his or her own EFS recovery agent private key to decrypt the file so that it can be recovered.

At least one user account in Windows 2000 Professional must be designated as the recovery agent. On stand-alone computers or computers in a workgroup, Windows 2000 automatically designates the local Administrator as the recovery agent and places the appropriate recovery key in the Administrator's personal certificate store on the computer. In a domain, the Domain Administrator account is the default recovery agent for the domain.

New files created in an encrypted folder or files copied to an encrypted folder are automatically assigned the encryption attribute. Modifications made to an encrypted file or folder are also automatically encrypted. Backup versions and copies of encrypted files will also be encrypted automatically as long as they are stored on another NTFS volume.

You can set the encryption attribute for a file or a folder by selecting [Advanced...] in the **Properties** dialog box for the file or folder. You can access the Properties dialog box by right-clicking the file or folder in the **Windows Explorer** window.

how to

Encrypt a folder.
1. Click [Start], point to **Programs**, point to **Accessories**, and click **Windows Explorer** to open Windows Explorer.
2. Locate and then double-click the folder **Data** to open it. The **metadata** file appears.
3. Right-click the file **metadata** and then click the **Properties** command to open the **metadata.doc Properties** dialog box.
4. Click [Advanced...] to open the **Advanced Attributes** dialog box (**Figure 12-19**). In this dialog box, you can set the encryption attribute for the metadata file.
5. Select the **Encrypt contents to secure data** check box to encrypt the contents of the file **metadata (Figure 12-20)**. Note that if you select this check box, you cannot select the **Compress contents to save disk space** check box to compress the data in the file. An encrypted file cannot be compressed, nor can a compressed file be encrypted.
6. Click [OK] to close the **Advanced Attributes** dialog box.

Figure 12-19 Properties dialog box for the metadata file

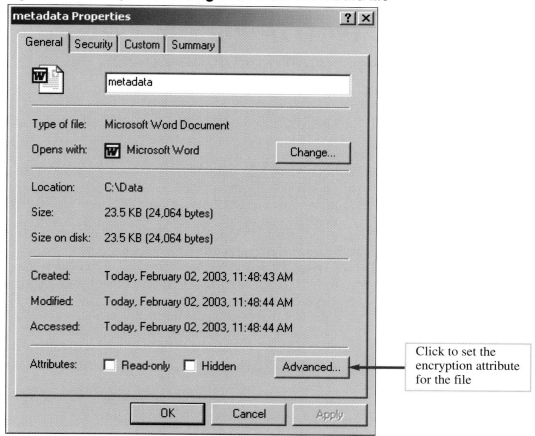

Figure 12-20 Encrypting a file

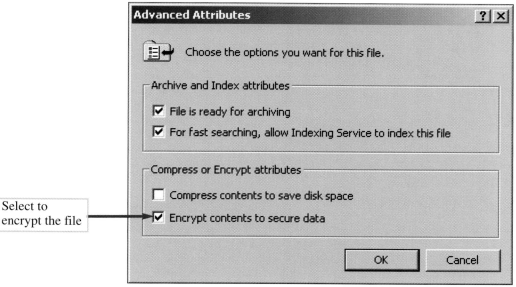

skill 5

Increasing Security Using EFS (Encrypting File System) *(cont'd)*

exam objective

Encrypt data on a hard disk by using Encrypting File System (EFS).

how to

7. Click [Apply] in the *metadata* **Properties** dialog box to apply the encryption.
8. In the **Encryption Warning** dialog box (**Figure 12-21**), click the **Encrypt the file only** option button.
9. Click [OK] to close the Encryption Warning dialog box.
10. Click [OK] to close the metadata Properties dialog box.
11. Right-click the Data folder and then click the Properties command to open the **Data Properties** dialog box.
12. Click [Advanced...] to open the **Advanced Attributes** dialog box.
13. Select the **Encrypt contents to secure data** check box.
14. Click [OK] to close the Advanced Attributes dialog box.
15. Click [Apply] in the Data Properties dialog box to apply the encryption.
16. The **Confirm Attribute Changes** dialog box appears (**Figure 12-22**).
17. Click the **Apply changes to this folder**, **subfolders**, **and files** option button to encrypt the folder and all of its contents, including all subfolders and files.
18. Click [OK] to close the Confirm Attribute Changes dialog box.
19. Click [OK] to close the Data Properties dialog box.

more

An encrypted file or folder remains encrypted if it is copied or moved to:

◆ The same NTFS partition on the same computer.
◆ A different NTFS partition on the same computer.
◆ An NTFS partition on a different computer that runs Windows 2000.

However, if you move an encrypted file or folder to a File Allocation Table (FAT) partition or another computer running an NTFS version earlier than NTFS 5, the encrypted file or folder does not retain its attributes. This is because FAT and FAT32 partitions, and NTFS partitions lower than version 5, do not support EFS.

Figure 12-21 Confirming encryption for a particular file

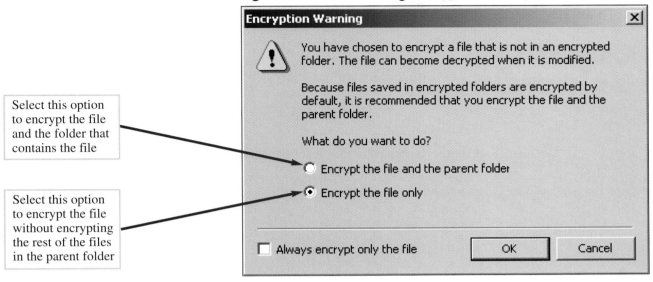

Select this option to encrypt the file and the folder that contains the file

Select this option to encrypt the file without encrypting the rest of the files in the parent folder

Figure 12-22 Applying attributes to files and folders

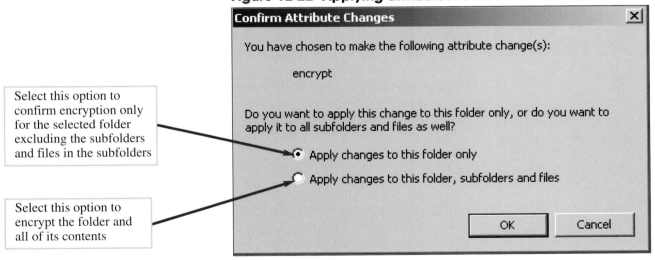

Select this option to confirm encryption only for the selected folder excluding the subfolders and files in the subfolders

Select this option to encrypt the folder and all of its contents

skill 6

Encrypting and Decrypting Files and Folders Using the Cipher Utility

exam objective

Encrypt data on a hard disk by using Encrypting File System (EFS).

overview

Instead of using Windows Explorer and the Properties dialog box for a file or a folder, you can use the Cipher command-line utility to enable encryption. You can also use the **Cipher** utility to view the encryption settings for files and folders, as well as to encrypt and decrypt them.

You can execute the Cipher command by typing the following at the command prompt:

Cipher / [command parameter] [pathname...]

In the syntax of the Cipher command, **[pathname ...]** denotes the location of the file or folder that you want to encrypt or decrypt. The various parameters that are used with the Cipher command designate various encryption and decryption requirements. **Table 12-2** lists the variables used with the Cipher command.

When using multiple parameters with the command, you must insert a single space between the variables. You can also execute the Cipher command by specifying only the path name.

You can encrypt multiple files at a time using this utility. You can also use wildcards with the **Cipher** utility to specify a group of files with a common attribute, such as the same file extension.

tip

You can open the command prompt window by typing cmd in the Open: text box in the Run dialog box.

how to

Encrypt a file using the Cipher command-line utility.

1. Click **Start** and click the **Run** command to open the **Run** dialog box.
2. Type **cmd** in the **Open:** text box and click **OK** to open the command prompt window (**Figure 12-23**).
3. Type **cd employees** to access the **Employees** folder.
4. Type **cipher /e /a wages.doc** and press the **[Enter]** key. A message **Encrypting files in C:\employees**appears. The /e variable is used to denote that the operation used is encryption. The /a variable denotes that the encryption operation is performed on a specific file in a folder.
5. After a few seconds, your file is encrypted and a message appears: **1 file(s) [or directorie(s)] within 1 directorie(s) were encrypted**. You are also warned that converting files from plaintext to ciphertext may leave sections of old plaintext on the disk volume(s). It is recommended to use **CIPHER /W**:directory to clean up the disk after all converting is done. The **/w** switch,which requires an update to the **Cipher.exe** tool or **SP3**, removes data from available unused disk space on the entire volume. The directory specified can be anywhere on a local volume. (**Figure 12-24**).
6. Type **exit** to close the command prompt window. You have successfully encrypted the file **wages.doc** in the **employees** folder.

Table 12-2 Variables used with Cipher command

Variable	Use
/e	The /e parameter is used to encrypt a folder. Encrypted folders are marked so that any file added to the folder will be automatically encrypted.
/d	The /d parameter is used to decrypt an encrypted folder. Files added to a decrypted folder will be automatically decrypted.
/s	The /s parameter is used to perform the encryption or decryption operation on a folder and all its subfolders.
/a	The /a parameter is used to perform the encryption or decryption operation on a specific file. Files in a folder can be decrypted during editing or file modification if the parent folder has not been encrypted. Therefore, it is important to encrypt both the file and the parent folder.
/i	The /i parameter is used to ignore any errors that may occur during the encryption/decryption operation and continue the process.
/f	The /f parameter is used to force the encryption operation on all files and folders, even if they have already been encrypted. If they are already encrypted, they will be skipped.
/q	The /q parameter is used to run the operation in quiet mode so that only the most important information, such as errors that occur during the process, will be displayed.
/h	The /h parameter is used so that files with the hidden or system attributes will be listed, which does not occur by default.
/k	The /k parameter is used to create a new file encryption key.
pathname	The pathname parameter is used to specify the path to the file or folder to be encrypted or decrypted.

Figure 12-23 Accessing the command prompt window

Used to enter the location or path for the file or program that you want to open

Run ? X

Type the name of a program, folder, document, or Internet resource, and Windows will open it for you.

Open: cmd

OK   Cancel   Browse...

Figure 12-24 Using the cipher utility to encrypt a file

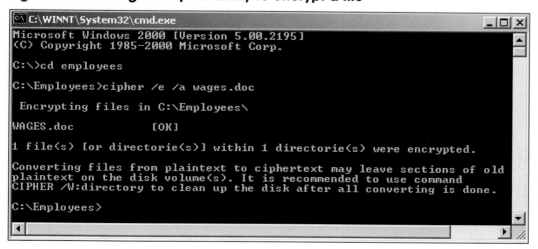

```
C:\WINNT\System32\cmd.exe                          _ □ X
Microsoft Windows 2000 [Version 5.00.2195]
(C) Copyright 1985-2000 Microsoft Corp.

C:\>cd employees

C:\Employees>cipher /e /a wages.doc

 Encrypting files in C:\Employees\

WAGES.doc          [OK]

1 file(s) [or directorie(s)] within 1 directorie(s) were encrypted.

Converting files from plaintext to ciphertext may leave sections of old
plaintext on the disk volume(s). It is recommended to use command
CIPHER /W:directory to clean up the disk after all converting is done.

C:\Employees>
```

skill 7

Recovering Encrypted Files Using Recovery Agents

exam objective

Implement, configure, manage, and troubleshoot local security policy.

overview

Files encrypted using EFS can only be opened and used by the user who encrypted them or by an account that has been designated as the **recovery agent**. The recover agent has a file recovery certificate, which is needed to decrypt the file or folder. All other users will receive an Access Denied message when they try to open the file. Private keys can be lost or damaged during disk crashes or while formatting disks. This is why Windows 2000 Professional requires that at least one user account be designated as the recovery agent so that encrypted data will never be unrecoverable. By default, the Administrator account on the local PC is the recovery agent.

To add a recovery agent to a stand-alone or workgroup computer, you can use the Add Recovery Agent Wizard. To open the Recovery Agent Wizard, open the Control Panel, open the **Administrative Tools** folder, open the **Local Security Policy** snap-in, expand the **Public Keys Policies** node, right-click **Encrypted Data Recovery Agents** and select **Add** on the context menu **(Figure 12-25)**. However, the Add Recovery Agent Wizard will ask you for a **file recovery** certificate (**.cer** file) and you must use **Certificate Services** on a Windows 2000 Server to create alternate recovery agent certificates.

If the computer joins a domain, the Domain Administrator account becomes the recovery agent, by default. However, any other user can also be designated as a recovery agent if he or she is provided with a file recovery certificate (.cer file).

To recover encrypted files or folders, the best method is to copy them to the recovery agent's computer where the file recovery certificate and the private key are located. It is not a good idea to have the recovery agent copy his or her private key to the computer where the file is stored, because this can compromise the security of a network. Then the recovery agent simply clears the **Encrypt contents to secure data** check box in the **Advanced Attributes** dialog box to recover the file. The Advanced Attributes dialog box is accessed by selecting the **Advanced** button in the Properties dialog box for the encrypted file or folder.

First, the recovery agent should use Backup or a different backup utility to restore the user's backup version of the encrypted file to the computer where their recovery agent certificate is located. Then he or she can use the Properties dialog box for the file or folder, or the Cipher utility, to decrypt the file. Finally, the recovery agent should make a backup copy of the decrypted file and send the backup version back to the user/owner.

tip

You cannot share encrypted files with other users.

how to

Recover a file.

1. Log on to your computer as **Usr1** (or any other standard or restricted user account you have created on your computer). Create and save a file named **Accountinfo** on the C: drive of the computer (This must be an NTFS disk.). Encrypt the file.
2. Log off and log back on as **Usr2** (or any other standard or restricted user account you have created on the computer).
3. Open **Windows Explorer**. Double-click **My Computer**. Double-click the **C:** drive in the contents window. Locate the **Accountinfo** file. Right-click **Accountinfo** and click **Properties**.
4. On the General tab, click [Advanced...] to open the **Advanced Attributes** dialog box. Clear the check from the **Encrypt contents to secure data** check box in the **Compress or Encrypt attributes** section. Click [OK].
5. Click **OK** to close the Accountinfo Properties dialog box.
6. The **Error Applying Attributes** dialog box opens to inform you that access has been denied **(Figure 12-26)**.
7. Click [Ignore].

tip

If you are not the owner of an encrypted file or the designated recovery agent, you will receive the message shown in **Figure 12-27** when you attempt to open the file.

Figure 12-25 Add Recovery Agent Wizard

Figure 12-26 The Error Applying Attributes dialog box

Access is denied to an encrypted file for a user who is not the owner or a designated recovery agent

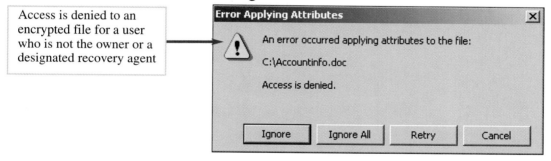

Figure 12-27 User does not have access privileges

skill 7

Recovering Encrypted Files Using Recovery Agents (cont'd)

Implement, configure, manage, and troubleshoot local security policy.

how to

8. Click `Advanced...`. Replace the check in the **Encrypt contents to secure data** check box.
9. Click **OK** to close the Advanced Attributes dialog box.
10. Click **OK** to close the Accountinfo Properties dialog box and close Windows Explorer.
11. Log off and log back on using the local Administrator account.
12. Open Windows Explorer. Double-click **My Computer**. Double-click the C: drive and locate the **Accountinfo** file.
13. Right-click the encrypted file **Accountinfo** and click the **Properties** command to open the Accountinfo Properties dialog box **(Figure 12-28)**.
14. On the **General** tab, click `Advanced...` to open the **Advanced Attributes** dialog box.
15. Clear the **Encrypt contents to secure data** check box to decrypt the file **(Figure 12-29)**.
16. Click `OK` to close the Advanced Attributes dialog box.
17. Click `Apply` to apply the changes.
18. Click `OK` to close the Accountinfo Properties dialog box. You have successfully recovered an encrypted file.

Figure 12-28 Accessing the properties dialog box for the encrypted file

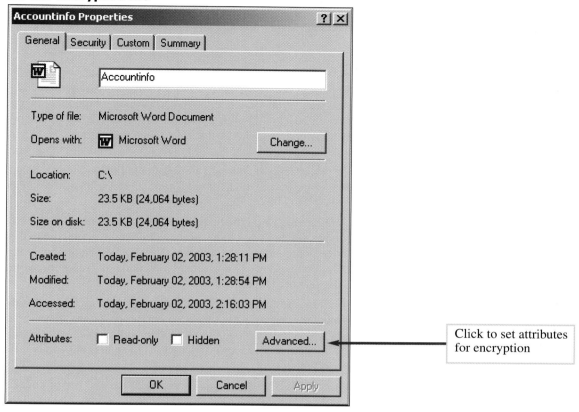

Click to set attributes for encryption

Figure 12-29 Recovering an encrypted file

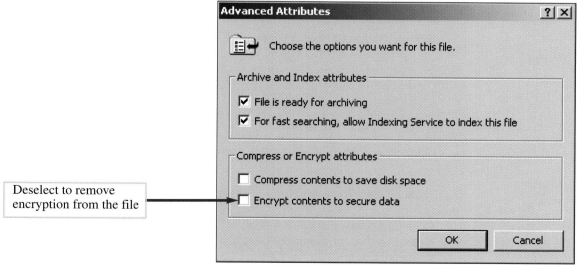

Deselect to remove encryption from the file

skill 8

Securing Data on a Network Using IPSec Policies

exam objective

Implement, configure, manage, and troubleshoot local security policy.

overview

Internet Protocol Security (IPSec) policy settings are used to protect confidential data on a public network. Data packets are encrypted before they are sent to a destination computer to make sure that they are secure and cannot be intercepted, stolen, or modified in transit. IPSec policies are functional on a **Transmission Control Protocol/Internet Protocol (TCP/IP)** network and you can transfer data packets between computers regardless of the type of partitions that are used.

IPSec policies ensure that encrypted files that are transmitted from a source computer reach the destination computer in the same encrypted form and are decrypted at the destination computer.

IPSec policies are configured in the **IP Security Policies on the Local Machine** node in the Local Security Settings snap-in. There are three preconfigured policy templates you can choose from: Client (Respond Only), Secure Server (Require Security), and Server (Request Security). You set IPSec Policies based on whether your computer is performing the role of a client or a server on the network **(Figure 12-30)**.

Of the three policy options, the **Client (Respond Only)** policy is used to provide maximum flexibility when negotiating security with the server computers on the network. By default, this policy sends data packets to server computers without applying security measures such as encryption. However, if specifically requested by a server, the policy ensures that the data will be encrypted before it is sent.

The **Secure Server (Require Security)** option minimizes the number of client computers with which you can communicate over a network, because all communications must be secured using Kerberos trust. When the number of computers with which you can communicate decreases, security is greatly enhanced. When you set this policy, unsecured communications with untrusted client computers are blocked. Whether or not a client is trusted is determined by the authentication mechanism used by the client. Windows 2000 Professional provides several authentication mechanisms, notably Kerberos V5. When a user attempts to access a network service, authentication mechanisms such as Kerberos V5 confirm the identification of the user to the network service.

The **Server (Request Security)** option helps provide secure communication by requesting security using Kerberos trust from client computers. This means that, for all IP traffic, clients will be requested to provide security using authentication mechanisms, but communication with unsecured clients will not be denied. Data packets will still be exchanged, even if Kerberos trust is not established.

It is important to note that none of the IPSec policy options are assigned to the computer by default. For an existing IPSec policy option, you can either add a new IP security rule or edit an existing IP security rule in the **<policy name> Properties** dialog box.

tip

Using EFS, you can move or copy data only from one NTFS 5 partition to another. Moving or copying the data to a different version of NTFS or to a FAT partition is not possible because data does not remain encrypted. EFS encrypted files are not encrypted as they traverse a network.

how to

Assign the **Client (Respond Only)** IPSec policy option and add a new security rule to the policy.

1. Open the **Local Group Policy** console.
2. Expand the **Local Computer Policy** node and then expand the **Computer Configuration** node, if necessary.
3. Expand the **Windows Settings** node and then the **Security Settings** node, if necessary.
4. Double-click the **IP Security Policies on Local Machine** node. The IPSec policy options appear in the right pane of the window.
5. Right-click the **Client (Respond Only)** policy option and then click the **Assign** command on the shortcut menu to assign the policy **(Figure 12-31)**.

Figure 12-30 The IP security policies options in the console root window

Click to view a list of actions

Click to list options to customize the window

Click to organize Favorites folder and view list of Favorites

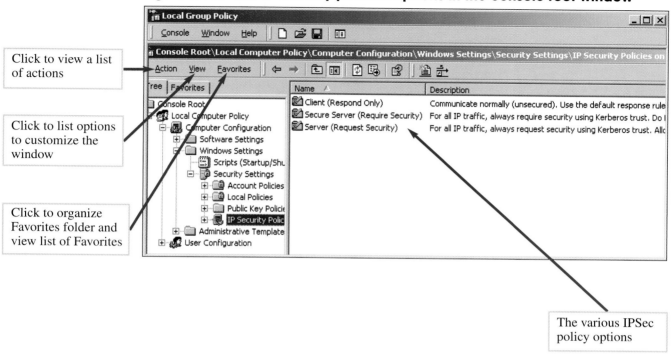

The various IPSec policy options

Figure 12-31 Assigning the Client (Respond Only) policy

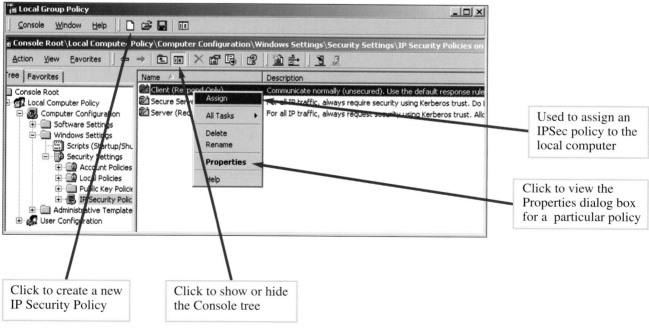

Used to assign an IPSec policy to the local computer

Click to view the Properties dialog box for a particular policy

Click to create a new IP Security Policy

Click to show or hide the Console tree

skill 8

Securing Data on a Network Using IPSec Policies (cont'd)

exam objective

Implement, configure, manage, and troubleshoot local security policy.

how to

6. Right-click the **Client (Respond Only)** policy option and then click the **Properties** command to open the **Client (Respond Only) Properties** dialog box to configure the policy. You can also open the **Client (Respond Only) Properties** dialog box by double-clicking the Client (Respond Only) policy option.

7. Click [Add] to initiate the **Security Rule Wizard (Figure 12-32)**. The Security Rule Wizard is used to add a new IP security rule.

8. Click [Next >] to open the **Tunnel Endpoint** screen.

9. The **This rule does not specify a tunnel** option button is selected by default. Click [Next >] to open the **Network Type** screen.

10. In the **Select the network type**: section, click the **Local area network (LAN)** option button to apply the security rule to computers on the local area network (LAN) only **(Figure 12-33)**.

11. Click [Next >] to open the **Authentication Method** screen.

12. The **Windows 2000 default (Kerberos V5 protocol)** option button is selected by default. Click [Next >] to open the **IP Filter List** screen.

13. In the **IP filter lists**: section, click the **All IP Traffic** option button to apply the security rule to all IP traffic. The IP filter list shows the list of IP traffic, such as all ICMP (Internet Control Message Protocol) or all IP. The IP security rule applies to the IP traffic that is selected on the IP filter list.

14. Click [Next >] to open the **Filter Action** screen.

15. Click the **Request Security (Optional)** option in the **Filter Actions** section **(Figure 12-34)** to provide secure communication by requesting security from clients.

16. Click [Next >] to move to the last screen of the Security Rule Wizard.

17. Click [Finish] to save the settings and exit the Security Rule Wizard.

18. Click [Close] to close the Client (Respond Only) Properties dialog box.

19. Close the Local Group Policy console and save the console settings.

caution

Kerberos is only used for network authentication on a domain-based network. If you are on a workgroup network, a Warning dialog box to this effect will open. Click Yes to continue and save the rule properties. You will have to remove the rule after you complete the exercise.

Figure 12-32 Adding a security rule

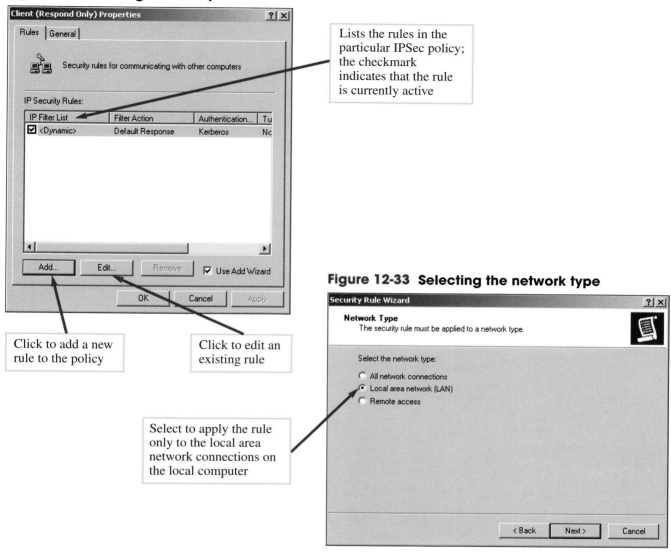

Lists the rules in the particular IPSec policy; the checkmark indicates that the rule is currently active

Click to add a new rule to the policy

Click to edit an existing rule

Figure 12-33 Selecting the network type

Select to apply the rule only to the local area network connections on the local computer

Figure 12-34 Selecting the filter action

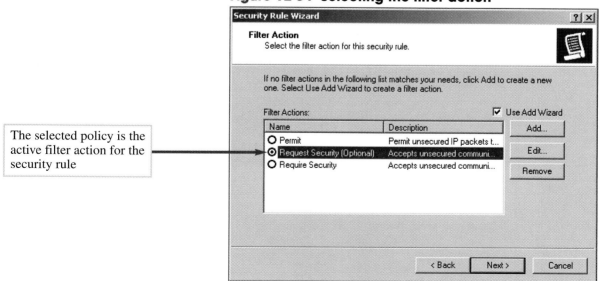

The selected policy is the active filter action for the security rule

skill 9 *Working with Security Templates*

exam objective

Implement, configure, manage, and troubleshoot a security configuration.

overview

Security templates are valuable on a workgroup network because rather than configuring your local security policies and local group policies one by one, you can use a security template to apply a whole range of security configuration settings all at once. You can create a custom MMC with the **Security Templates** and **Security Configuration and Analysis** snap-ins to provide a centralized tool where all of the security attributes are organized in one place and you can analyze the security configuration of the computer. A security template can include password and account lockout policies, local security policies, user rights assignments, registry key security, group memberships, and permissions for the local file system. On a domain-based network, you can apply a security template to a Group Policy object so that all of the settings are put into operation on a site, a domain, or an OU (organizational unit). You use the Import Policy command on the shortcut menu for the Security Settings node to import a security template to a Group Policy object so that you can configure the security settings for multiple computers at one time. Security templates are saved as .inf files. You can copy, paste, import, and export some or all of the security settings from these text files to apply them to a Group Policy object. All security attributes, except IPSec and Public Key policies, can be stored in a security template. The Security and Configuration Analysis snap-in is used to compare the current security configuration of the computer to one of the security templates, to create custom templates, and to apply a template to either the local computer or to a Group Policy object.

how to

Create a custom Security Templates console and use the Security and Configuration Analysis tool to analyze the current security configuration of the local computer. Customize one of the predefined security templates and apply it to the local computer.

1. Click **Start** and then click the **Run** command to open the **Run** dialog box.
2. Type: **mmc** in the **Open** text box and click **OK** to open the **Console Root** window.
3. Open the **Console** menu and click the **Add/Remove Snap-in** command to open the **Add/Remove Snap-in** dialog box.
4. Click **Add** to open the **Add Standalone Snap-in** dialog box. Scroll down the **Available Standalone Snap-ins** list to locate and select the **Security Templates** snap-in. Click **Add**.
5. Select the **Security Configuration and Analysis** snap-in and click **Add**.
6. Click **Close** to close the Add Standalone Snap-in dialog box.
7. Click **OK** to close the Add/Remove Snap-in dialog box.
8. Open the **Console** menu and click the **Save** command to open the **Save As** dialog box.
9. Type **Security Templates** in the File name text box and click **Save**. By default, the console will be saved in the Administrative Tools folder.
10. Expand the **Security Templates** node. Expand the **C:\WINNT\Security\Templates** node. The pre-configured security templates appear as shown in **Figure 12-35**. The predefined templates are explained in **Table 12-3**.
11. Right-click the **Security Configuration and Analysis** node and select the **Open database** command on the shortcut menu to open the **Open database** dialog box.
12. Type **Local PC** in the **File name** text box and click **Open** to open the **Import Template** dialog box.
13. Select **securews.inf** in the Content window and click **Open** to open the template for a high-security workstation.

Figure 12-35 The predefined Security Templates

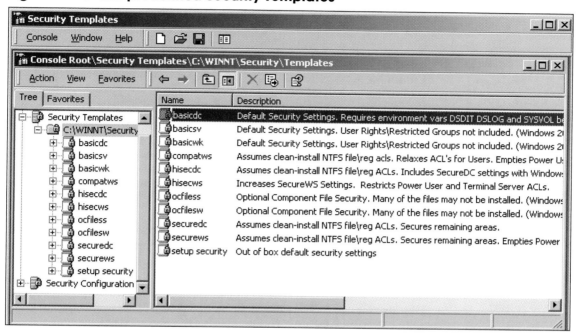

Table 12-3	The Predefined Security Templates
basicdc	The default template for a domain controller.
compatws	Compatible workstation: Used on workstations that must be compatible with older applications. Users group access controls are less stringent for certain files, folders, and registry keys that older applications often need to access so that they can be run with no problem by members of the Users group.
hisecws	The template for a maximum security workstation.
hisecdc	The template for a maximum security domain controller.
securedc	The template for a high security domain controller.
securews	The template for a high security workstation.
basicwk	The default template for a workstation.
basicsv	The default template for a member server.

skill 9

Working with Security Templates
(cont'd)

Implement, configure, manage, and troubleshoot a security configuration.

how to

14. Right-click the **Security and Configuration Analysis** node and select the **Analyze Computer Now** command. Click [OK] in the **Perform Analysis** dialog box to confirm the path to the log file.

15. When the analysis is complete, open the **Security Configuration and Analysis** node. Open the **Account Policies** node and select **Password Policy**. Policies with a green check mark indicate that the local computer policy meets the requirements for a high-security workstation. Policies with a red X do not, as shown in **Figure 12-36**.

16. Double-click **Enforce password history** to open the **Analyzed Security Policy Setting** dialog box. The current setting is for 15 passwords to be remembered. The database setting for a high-security workstation is 24. Click [OK] to close the dialog box and maintain the setting in the database.

17. Double-click **Minimum password length**. In the **Password must be at least** spin box, enter **14** to make the policy setting in the database match the current computer setting. Click [OK]. Note that there are four password policies on the computer that still do not match the database setting.

18. Click the **Account Lockout Policy** node. Double-click **Account lockout threshold**. Note that the current computer setting allows 3 invalid logon attempts, while the database setting for a high-security workstation allows 5 invalid logon attempts.

19. Change the setting in the **Account will lock out after** spin box to match the current computer setting. Click [OK] to define the policy in the database.

20. Expand the **Local Policies** node and select **Audit Policy**. Open the **Analyzed Security Policy Setting** dialog box for the **Audit account logon events** policy. Remove the check mark from the **Define this policy in the database** check box and click [OK] to remove this policy setting from the database. You will be configuring this audit policy in the next lesson.

21. Select the **Security Options** node. Double-click **Do not display last user name in logon dialog box**. Click the **Enabled** option button and click [OK] to define this policy in the database. Note that there are a number of security options that do not meet the requirements for a high-security workstation.

22. Right-click the **Security Configuration and Analysis** node and select the **Configure Computer Now** command. In the **Configure System** dialog box, click **OK** to confirm the path to the log file. The system is configured with the custom template you designed in the exercise.

23. Right-click the **Security and Configuration Analysis** node and select the **Analyze Computer Now** command. Click [OK] in the **Perform Analysis** dialog box to confirm the path to the log file. You will now be able to view the information in the database and compare it with the new computer settings.

24. Expand the **Account Policies** node and select **Password Policy**. Notice that now the current computer settings match the database settings for all of the password policies (**Figure 12-39**).

25. Expand the **Local Policies** node and select **Security Options**. Note that all of the computer settings now match the database settings for the custom high-security workstation template you designed in the exercise.

26. Close the Security Templates console and save the console settings.

more

There is also a command line tool called SECEDIT.EXE that you can use to perform most of the same functions as the Security Template and Security Configuration and Analysis snap-ins. This utility works from a batch file, script, or automatic task scheduler; for example, you

Figure 12-36 Performing a security analysis

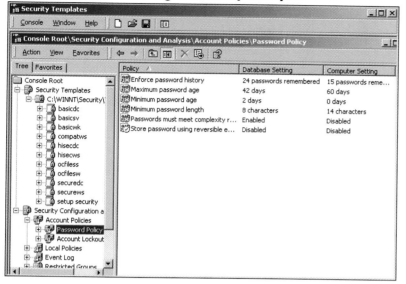

Figure 12-37 Analyzed Security Policy Setting dialog box

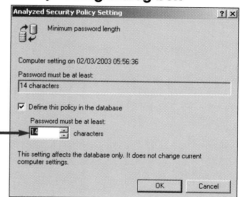

Enter 14 to make the policy setting in the database match the current computer setting

Figure 12-38 Defining a policy setting in the database

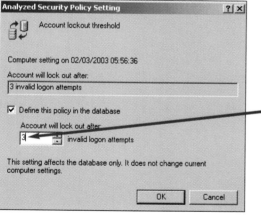

Enter 3 to make the database setting match the current computer setting

Figure 12-39 Password policies configured using custom Security Template

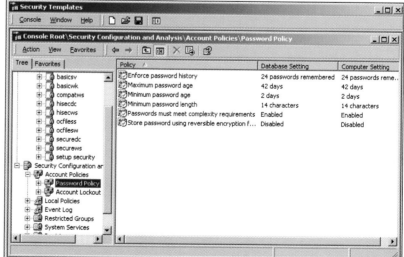

skill 9

Working with Security Templates
(cont'd)

exam objective

Implement, configure, manage, and troubleshoot a security configuration.

more

can use a SECEDIT command in a logon script that is used for the entire system. SECEDIT can also be run from the command line to create templates, analyze security, and apply a security template. The SECEDIT tool is particularly useful on a domain-based system to perform analyses on a large number of computers at the same time. The results of the analysis can either be viewed in the Security Configuration and Analysis snap-in or from the command line. Some of the most commonly used command parameters for SECEDIT are explained in **Table 12-4**.

Security templates can only be applied to Windows 2000 computers and some of the security settings are not compatible with earlier versions of the operating system, particularly those related to encryption. This means that when you use one of the high-security or maximum security templates, you may not be able to communicate with computers which are not running Windows 2000. Use either the default or compatible templates on a network that includes Windows 9x or Windows NT computers.

Table 12-3 SECEDIT Command Parameters	
/analyze	Analyzes the current security settings against the /DB and /CFG parameters you enter. (See below.)
/configure	Configures the security settings on the computer based on the /DB and /CFG parameters you enter.
/export	Exports a template from a security database to an .inf template file using the /DB and /CFG parameters you enter.
/DB *filename*	The path to the database that contains the security configuration settings you want SECEDIT to use to perform the analysis or that you want to be applied.
/CFG *filename*	The path to the security template that you want SECEDIT to use to analyze or configure the database you specified with the /DB parameter. You can only use this argument in conjunction with the /DB parameter. If you do not specify a security template, the template that is already stored in the database will be applied, or the analysis will be performed against the configuration settings that are already stored in the database.
/refreshpolicy	Reapplies the security settings to the local computer or to the Group Policy object. This is particularly useful if you want to reapply the security settings for the currently logged-on user on the local computer without waiting for a policy change to take effect on its own. Group Policy updates occur by default when the computer is restarted, and every 60 to 90 minutes thereafter.
/validate *filename*	Validates the syntax of a security template that you want to import into a database for analysis or apply to the system.

Summary

- Group policies are used to manage many different settings for both computers and users, including the desktop appearance, the allocation of software applications, and password limitations.
- Group policies are usually implemented when you are working with a domain-based network that combines Windows 2000 Servers and Windows 2000 Professional clients in an Active Directory environment.
- Group policies for local computers that do not use the Active Directory are set using local security policies. Local security policies are used to configure the settings for a local computer, which can be a workgroup or a stand-alone computer, so that the data can be safeguarded.
- There are four categories of local security policies that can be used to safeguard a computer: account policies, local security policies, public key policies, and IP security policies.
- Account Policies consist of the password policy and the account lockout policy.
- Password policies are used to implement specific rules for how all users who log on to a computer must structure their passwords, the frequency with which they must change them, and how long they can use them before the passwords must be changed. These policies are not set individually; they apply to all users on a local computer.
- Account lockout policies are used to set how many invalid logon attempts will be allowed before the account is barred from use. You can also set a specific time period during which the account will remain locked out, or configure the policy so that an Administrator must unlock it.
- Local security policies are classified as audit policies, user rights assignments, or security options.
- User rights assignments are used to prescribe what actions a user can execute within the operating system.
- Public Key Policies include the Encrypting File System (EFS) recovery policy. Files and folders are encrypted using a security algorithm and a file encryption key to change the contents into unreadable characters. Either the user who encrypted the file or a user who has been designated as the recovery agent can recover an encrypted file. When other users try to access an encrypted file, they will receive an Access Denied message.
- IPSec (Internet Protocol Security) policies are used to protect data as it travels on a TCP/IP network. They ensure the security of data packets by encrypting them before sending them to another computer on a public network.
- You can specify and customize your password settings by using various password policy options available in the Password Policy node. For example, you can set a

- minimum length for passwords or assign a password age to ensure that passwords are changed frequently.
- You can encrypt your files and folders on an NTFS disk using the Encrypting File System (EFS) so that they cannot be read or modified by unauthorized users.
- You can encrypt files and folders in Windows Explorer or by using the Cipher command-line utility.
- Either the user who encrypted the file or a user who has been designated as the recovery agent can recover an encrypted file.
- Windows 2000 Professional requires that at least one user account be designated as the recovery agent so that encrypted data will never be unrecoverable. By default, the Administrator of the local PC is the recovery agent.
- You can set additional recovery agents for a system so that, if the owner of an encrypted file forgets the password, the recovery agent can copy the encrypted file to his or her computer and decrypt the file by clearing the Encrypt Contents to Secure Data checkbox in the Properties dialog box for the file.
- The Domain Administrator account is, by default, designated as the recovery agent for a domain.
- You can set security rules related to data communication on a TCP/IP network using IPSec Policies. IPSec Policies are used to ensure the integrity, confidentiality, and authentication of data packets traveling over a TCP/IP network.
- When you log on to your Windows 2000 Professional computer as a member of a domain, the local security policy settings on your computer may be overridden by the security policies of the domain.
- Site policies override local policy, domain policies override site policies, and OU policies override domain policies. This default behavior can be controlled using the Block Inheritance and No Override settings.
- Security Templates are valuable on a workgroup network because, rather than configuring your local security policies and local group policies one by one, you can use a security template to apply a whole range of security configuration settings all at once.
- The Security and Configuration Analysis snap-in is used to compare the current security configuration of the computer with one of the security templates, to create custom templates, and to apply a template to either the local computer or to a Group Policy object.
- A security template can include password and account lockout policies, local security policies, user rights assignments, registry key security, group memberships, and permissions for the local file system.
- There is also a command-line tool called SECEDIT.EXE that you can use to perform most of the same functions as the Security Template and Security Configuration and Analysis snap-ins.

Key Terms

Account lockout duration
Account lockout policy
Account lockout threshold
Account policies
Cipher utility
Client (Respond Only)
Console
Encrypting File System (EFS)
Encryption
Enforce password history
Group policies
IP filter rule

IP security policies
Kerberos V5
Local policies
Maximum password age
Minimum password age
Minimum password length
Password
Password history
Password policy
Passwords must meet complexity
   requirements
Public key policies

Recovery agent
Reset account lockout counter after
Secure Server (Require Security)
Security Configuration and Analysis
   snap-in
Security Template snap-in
Server (Request Security)
Store password using reversible
   encryption for all users in the
   domain
User rights assignment

Test Yourself

1. You want to set a password policy for your computer so that the password can be changed on the same day on which it is set. Which of the following policies will you use?
   a. Enforce password history
   b. Maximum password age
   c. Minimum password age
   d. Minimum password length

2. You are the Network Administrator at Healthcare Inc., a pharmaceutical company. Details of drugs the company carries are stored on a computer. Which of the following settings will enable you to minimize the chances of an unauthorized person accessing the computer?
   a. Setting values of 8 and 1 for the Account lockout threshold policy and Account lockout duration policy respectively.
   b. Setting a value of 3 for the Minimum password age policy.
   c. Setting values of 1 and 8 for the Account lockout threshold policy and the Account lockout duration policy.
   d. Setting a value of 1 for the Account lockout threshold policy and a value of 0 for the Account lockout duration policy.
   e. Setting a value of 3 for the Maximum password age policy.

3. You want to implement a policy that enforces complexity requirements for passwords so that they are more secure. Kelly, Joe, George, Sam, and Michael want to set their passwords as kirstenkelly, #59USA, 29974, SamEmaNuaL, and Boeing29 respectively. Passwords can be set for which of the following people?
   a. Kelly
   b. Joe

   c. George
   d. Sam
   e. Michael

4. Which one of the following settings will you use to lock an account indefinitely if invalid logon attempts take place?
   a. Set a value of 0 for the Account lockout duration option.
   b. Set a value of 0 for the Account lockout threshold option.
   c. Set a value of 99,999 for the Account lockout duration option.
   d. Set a value of 999 for the Account lockout threshold option.

5. The Encrypting File System (EFS) is used to secure:
   a. Passwords.
   b. Data files on local computers.
   c. Data packets traveling on a network.
   d. FAT partitions.

6. Which of the following commands would you use with the Cipher utility to decrypt an encrypted folder and its sub folders?
   a. cipher /e /s folder_name
   b. cipher /d /s folder_name
   c. cipher /d folder_name
   d. cipher /e /f folder_name

7. A folder named Misc is saved on the NTFS 5 partition of your computer. You have encrypted the folder using Encrypting File System. Which one of the following statements is true?
   a. If you move the encrypted folder to a FAT partition on a different computer running Windows 2000 Professional, the folder still remains encrypted.

b. Any file that is added to the folder would have to be encrypted.

c. If a file from the Misc folder is transmitted across the network to a computer running Windows 2000 Professional on an NTFS volume that was formatted using NTFS 4, the file is decrypted when it reaches the destination computer.

d. If you move the encrypted folder to an NTFS 5 partition on a different computer that runs Windows 2000 Professional, the folder is decrypted.

8. Which one of the following statements is true about encrypting files and folders using Encrypting File System (EFS)?

a. You can encrypt a compressed file.

b. You can choose to encrypt a specific file within a folder.

c. You can encrypt files and folders stored on FAT partitions.

d. Files and folders encrypted using EFS cannot be recovered if the user's private key is lost.

9. Which one of the following conditions holds true when you are implementing a security policy in an organization?

a. You can enable a security policy at the local and domain level and disable it if the computer is not logged on to the domain.

b. Policies at the domain level can be applied to sites, domains, and Organizational Units.

c. You set the various audit policies, user rights assignments, and security options using Account Policies.

d. You set the minimum number of logon attempts using Security Options.

10. You want to encrypt a folder My data on your computer and also force encryption on all the sub folders even if they are encrypted. Which of the following Cipher commands will you use?

a. cipher /e /s:folder_name /k

b. cipher /e /s:folder_name /f

c. cipher /e /s:folder_name /q

d. cipher /e /s:folder_name /h

11. You have kept the Allow system to be shut down without having to log on local security policy enabled, and gone out on personal work. Your friend Joe thinks that you have left for the day and he wants to shut down the computer. Joe can shut down your computer.

a. True

b. False

12. The /i variable used with the Cipher command is used to:

a. Perform the encryption or decryption operation on a folder and all its sub folders.

b. Force the encryption operation on all files and folders even if they have been encrypted.

c. Display files with the hidden or system attributes during an encryption or decryption operation.

d. Continue the encryption or decryption operation in spite of errors that may occur during the operation.

13. Which IP Sec policy minimizes the number of computers with which you can communicate on a network?

a. Client (Respond Only)

b. Secure Server (Require Security)

c. Server (Request Security)

d. Password

14. Which one of the following statements is true about recovery agents?

a. The recovery agent has a file recovery certificate and his or her own private key so that encrypted files will always be recoverable.

b. Backup Operators are by default recovery agents.

c. To recover an encrypted file, the recovery agent should first uncheck the Encrypt contents to secure data check box in the Advanced Attributes dialog box for the encrypted file.

Projects: On Your Own

1. Set up a local security policy so that any user accessing a computer has the right to change the system time.

a. Open the **Run** dialog box.

b. Open the **Console Root** window.

c. Open the **Add/Remove Snap-in** dialog box.

d. Open the **Add Standalone Snap-in** dialog box.

e. Initiate the Select Group Policy Object Wizard.

f. Close the Add Standalone Snap-in dialog box.

g. Close the Add/Remove Snap-in dialog box.

h. Access the User Rights Assignment options and open the Local Security Policy Setting dialog box.

i. Set the user right and close the Local Security Policy Setting dialog box.

2. Set a security option so that the user is prompted to change the password a day before the expiration date.

a. Open the **Run** dialog box.

b. Open the **Console Root** window.

c. Open the **Add/Remove Snap-in** dialog box

d. Open the **Add standalone Snap-in** dialog box.

e. Initiate the Select Group Policy Object Wizard.

f. Close the Add Standalone Snap-in dialog box.

g. Close the Add/Remove Snap-in dialog box.

h. Access the Security Options and open the **Local Security Policy Setting** dialog box.

i. Set the security option and close the Local Security Policy Setting dialog box.

3. Encrypt a folder named **Personal** and all its contents from the Windows Explorer.
   a. Open the Windows Explorer.
   b. Open the Properties dialog box of the **Personal** folder.
   c. Open the **Advanced Attributes** dialog box.
   d. Set the encryption property for the folder.
   e. Close the Advanced Attributes dialog box.
   f. Accept and confirm the changes.
   g. Select the option to encrypt the folder along with its contents, such as sub folders and files.
   h. Close the Confirm Attribute Changes dialog box.
   i. Close the Personal Properties dialog box.

Problem Solving Scenarios

1. Rodman Auto Supply is an automobile wholesaler operating in Pennsylvania and Ohio. Located in Pittsburgh, Rodman has 75 employees on a Windows 2000 network, and three remote locations. As the Network Consultant, you would like to institute a new password policy for the network. You would like to force users to change their passwords every thirty days, not allow them to re-use old passwords, and to use passwords that have at least six characters including three of the four different types of characters. Outline in a written report how you would achieve these objectives.

2. The Senior Network Administrator at Rodman Auto Supply has expressed concern that files in the Finance department are open to all employees in Finance. The Financial Manager also is concerned and wants to encrypt selected files. He would like you to ensure that these files can be opened by only himself or his Assistant Financial Manager. In a memo to the Senior Network Administrator, explain how you would achieve this objective. Be sure to include your thinking about designating recovery agents.

A network administrator's job includes making sure that the computers on the network function optimally, that resources are secure, that the proper people are accessing the correct resources, and that users who should not be accessing resources are not doing so. Auditing is used to observe and record the events that occur on the network, including logons—both successful and unsuccessful—and access to files, folders, the Registry, and printers. These events are recorded in the Security event log which you can view using the Event Viewer snap-in in the Computer Management console. These tools are used to keep administrators informed of such occurrences as a user who is attempting to access a computer by repeatedly guessing account names and/or passwords, users who are accessing files at unusual times of the day, and users who are accessing resources that they should not have access to.

Auditing does not take place automatically. You must configure a local security policy to track the events you think are important, given your environment and the specifics of your situation. Then you must decide whether you want to track the success or failure of the events. The events you choose will be recorded in the Security event log. The entries in the log will identify the events that are occurring, the users who are performing the actions, and the success or failure, or both, of the events, depending on what you have chosen to record. As a general rule of thumb, you will want to monitor unsuccessful events if you are concerned about possible security breaches and successful events if you are evaluating the capacity or overall functioning of your system.

In addition, administrators need to monitor the performance of the computers on a network and take corrective actions if the performance is not up to par. The **System Monitor** in the Performance console is used to display data from current activity on the network or from log files, so that you can evaluate the day-to-day usage of the system. Administrators can monitor the performance of the memory of the system and the processors, find out if the disks are operating optimally, and evaluate overall network performance by monitoring how well the network cards are functioning and what volume of traffic they are able to handle. The Performance console is also used to create logs that record information about the performance of the resources on a computer and to configure alerts that perform certain actions based on the captured data.

Goals

In this lesson, you will learn how to audit various events that occur on a computer, such as logging on, accessing files and folders, and shutting down and restarting a computer. You will also learn to monitor resources of a computer, such as the processors and memory. Additionally, you will learn to create logs and alerts using the Performance console.

Requirements

To complete this lesson, you will need a computer that has Windows 2000 Professional installed on it. Additionally, you will need two folders, Reports and Projects, stored on the C: and D: drives of this computer, respectively. This computer must be connected to another computer named Computer1.

skill 1

Introducing Auditing

exam objective

Basic knowledge

overview

Each time a user logs on to a computer or to a network, he or she performs a number of activities, including the logon process itself, and accessing files, folders, printers, and the Registry. These activities are called events. As a network administrator, you will want to track and monitor some of these events on a regular basis in order to ensure the security and seamless functioning of the computers on the network. **Auditing** is used to track user activities and object access on the computers on a network. First, you will need to determine which events need to be audited on each computer. Auditing must be set up for each computer.

Auditing can be used to track exactly who logged on to a computer and when, what files were accessed or folders were created, what printers were used, and what registry keys were accessed when and by whom and what actions the users attempted to perform on them. In order to audit who is accessing which objects and what actions they are performing on those objects, you must first activate the audit object access policy because there is no auditing set up for workstations and servers by default. Then, you configure the audit object access policy in the Properties dialog box and the System ACL editor for the object. At this point it might be helpful to distinguish between a System ACL (SACL) and a Discretionary ACL (DACL). A System ACL (SACL) is used to allow the system administrator to log any attempts to gain access to an object. The list of ACEs (Access control entries) in the SACL will determine which users and groups will be audited. A discretionary ACL (DACL), which is used to set permissions, determines which users and groups can and cannot access the object, and it is controlled by the owner of the object or anyone that has been granted the right to change the permissions for the object.

In an organization, auditing is used to help prevent security breaches by allowing you to track unauthorized attempts to log on or access folders. Auditing is also used to help conduct resource planning for the computers on your network. For example, you may discover that too many users are accessing a particular printer on the network, and that this printer is overtaxed. Based on this finding, you may decide to install another printer.

In order to monitor a particular event, you must define an **audit policy** in the Audit Policy folder under the **Local Policies** node in the **Local Security Settings** window. The audit policy tells the operating system what to record in the Security event log on each computer. The events you can audit in Windows 2000 Professional are listed in **Table 13-1**. When you define an audit policy, you select the events you want to track and decide whether to track the success or failure, or both, for the event. For example, if you want to audit the system events that occur on your computer such as when a user restarts or shuts down their computer, you will activate the **Audit system events** policy and specify whether to audit successes or failures or both.

Audited events are stored in the **Security event log**. You can view the Security log using the **Event Viewer** snap-in in the Computer Management console.

caution

Auditing increases the overhead on a computer. File system reads take place frequently, which can overload the Security event log and cause both disk space and performance shortfalls. Therefore, you need to decide which events are important to track for your situation.

how to

Set audit policies for logon and object access events on a computer. Track only failed logon attempts, but track both successful and failed access attempts for objects.
1. Log on to your computer as an **Administrator**.
2. Click **Start**, point to **Programs**, point to **Administrative Tools**, and click the **Local Security Policy** command to open the **Local Security Settings** window.
3. Double-click the **Local Policies** folder to access the **Audit Policy** folder.
4. Click the Audit Policy folder to display the list of audit policies in the details pane (**Figure 13-1**).

Table 13-1   Events that can be audited on a computer

Event	Description
Logon Events	Users log on or off a computer, or make or cancel a network connection.
Account Management	An account or group is created, deleted, or modified, or a user account is renamed, has a new password set, or was activated or disabled.
System Events	A computer is shut down or restarted or some event that concerns the Security log has taken place.
Object Access	A file, folder, or printer is accessed.
Policy Change	User rights, audit policies, or user security options are changed.
Privilege Use	A right, such as Take Ownership or Print, is exercised by a user.
Account Logon Events	The computer has joined a domain and a request to log on to the domain is sent to the domain controller.
Process Tracking	A program is executed by a user.
Directory Service Access	The computer has joined a domain and an Active Directory object, such as a computer or domain, is accessed.

Figure 13-1 Audit policies for a local computer

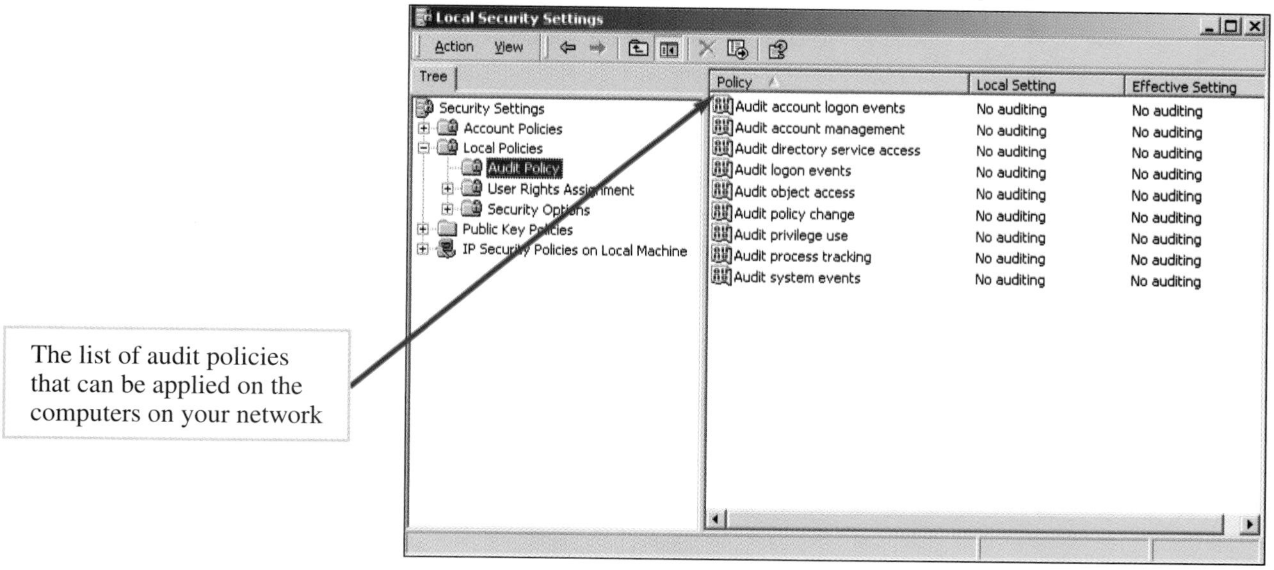

The list of audit policies that can be applied on the computers on your network

skill 1

Introducing Auditing *(cont'd)*

exam objective

Basic knowledge

how to

tip

Audit account logon events is used to monitor either successful or failed attempts to log on to a domain controller.

5. Double-click the **Audit logon events** audit policy to open the **Local Security Policy Settings** dialog box.
6. Select the **Failure** check box to track failed logon attempts **(Figure 13-2)**.
7. Click [OK] to save the settings and close the Local Security Policy Setting dialog box.
8. Double-click the **Audit object access** audit policy to open the Local Security Policy Settings dialog box.
9. Select the **Success** check box to track successful access attempts for objects on the computer.
10. Select the **Failure** check box to track failed object access attempts **(Figure 13-3)**.
11. Click [OK] to save the settings and close the Local Security Policy Setting dialog box. This simply enables auditing object access on the computer. Next, you will have to choose which files and folders you want the operating system to monitor.
12. Restart the computer to activate auditing. Once you have restarted the computer, the Local Security Setting window displays the status of the Audit logon events and Audit object access audit policies as **Success** or **Failure**, respectively **(Figure 13-4)**.

Figure 13-2 Tracking failed logon attempts

Used to track
successful attempts
for an event

Used to track
failed attempts
for an event

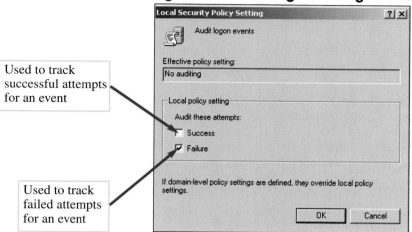

Figure 13-3 Tracking object access

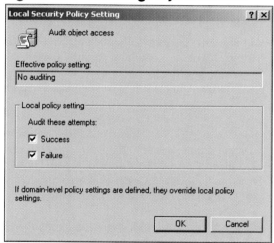

Figure 13-4 Configured audit policies

After you have restarted the
computer, the Effective
Setting column shows that
audits have been enabled
for failed logon events and
for both successful and
failed object access

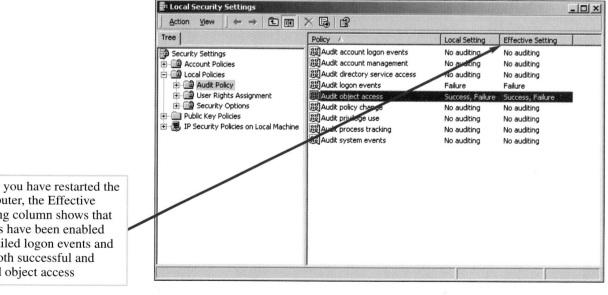

skill 2

Auditing Access to Files and Folders

exam objective

Implement, configure, manage, and troubleshoot auditing.

overview

Now that you have activated object access auditing, you must choose which files and folders you want the operating system to track. Certain files and folders on any computer or network will contain sensitive data that you will want to make sure are only being accessed by authorized users. For example, generally only the Finance Manager and certain other managers will be given access to the files containing the capital expenditures for the company. It is these types of files you will want to monitor so that you can view unauthorized attempts to access them. You will have to activate the audit object access policy on each computer on which sensitive data that must be tracked is stored. Next, you select the users whose actions you want to audit. You can audit local users or local groups, and if the Windows 2000 Professional computer joins a domain, domain users, and domain groups. After you select who you are going to audit, you must choose what file system actions you want to monitor in the ACL editor for the file or folder. For example, you can audit who is viewing a folder, creating a file, changing permissions, or viewing permissions.

tip

You can enable auditing only for a file or a folder that is stored on an **NTFS** drive.

You can also specify whether or not the subfolders within a folder should inherit the auditing settings. If you are enabling auditing for a subfolder, you can specify whether or not it should inherit the auditing settings of its parent folder. Remember, in order to enable auditing for a file or folder, you must first activate the **Audit object access audit policy** on that computer.

how to

Enable auditing for a folder named **Reports** located on the **C:** drive of your computer. Log an event every time a user in the Everyone group creates or deletes a file in the **Reports** folder.

1. Open **Windows Explorer** to display the files and folders on your computer.
2. Double-click the **C: drive** icon to display the folders on the drive.
3. To open the context menu, right-click the folder for which you want to enable auditing, for example **Reports**.
4. Click the **Properties** command to open the **Reports Properties** dialog box.
5. Click the **Security** tab, and then click [Advanced...] to open the **Access Control Settings for Reports** dialog box (**Figure 13-5**).
6. Click the **Auditing** tab; the **Allow inheritable auditing entries from parent to propagate to this object** check box is selected by default. This default means that the auditing settings for the parent folder will be inherited by this folder.
7. Select the **Reset auditing entries on all child objects and enable propagation of inheritable auditing entries** check box so that any pre-existing auditing settings on the subfolders in the **Reports** folder will be reset and will now inherit the settings you are making for the Reports folder (**Figure 13-6**).
8. Click [Add...] to open the **Select User**, **Computer**, **or Group** dialog box.
9. In the **Name** text box, type the name of the user or group for which you want to enable auditing. For example, type: **Everyone**, to indicate that you want to enable auditing for the **Everyone** group (**Figure 13-7**).
10. Click [OK] to close the **Select User**, **Computer**, **or Group** dialog box and open the **Auditing Entry for Reports** dialog box where you can select the actions to be audited.
11. Select the **Successful** check box next to the **Create Files/Write Data** option to indicate that you want to track each time a file is successfully created or when data is added to a file.
12. Select the **Successful** check box next to the **Delete Subfolders and Files** option to indicate that you want to track each time a file or subfolder is successfully deleted (**Figure 13-8**).
13. Click [OK] to save the settings and close the **Auditing Entry for Reports** dialog box.
14. Click [OK] to close the **Access Control Settings for Reports** dialog box.
15. Click [OK] to close the **Reports Properties** dialog box.

Figure 13-5 The Reports Properties dialog box

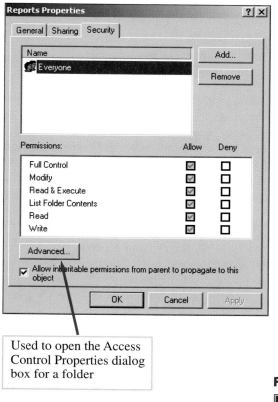

Used to open the Access Control Properties dialog box for a folder

Figure 13-6 Specifying auditing settings for subfolders

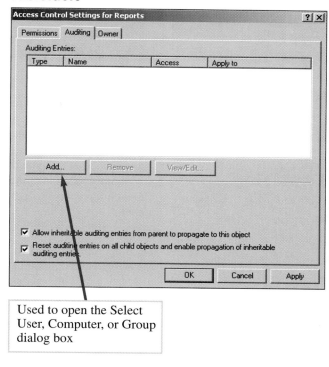

Used to open the Select User, Computer, or Group dialog box

Figure 13-7 Selecting the users to be audited

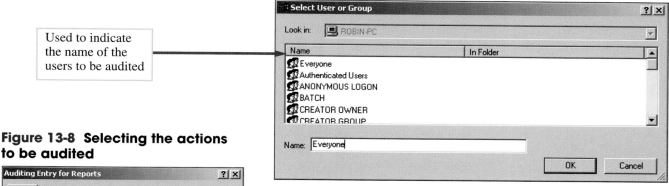

Used to indicate the name of the users to be audited

Figure 13-8 Selecting the actions to be audited

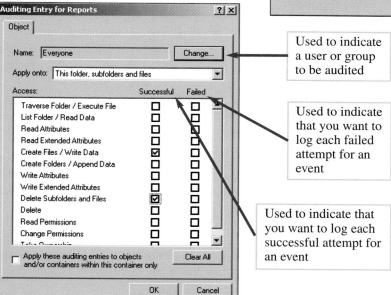

Used to indicate a user or group to be audited

Used to indicate that you want to log each failed attempt for an event

Used to indicate that you want to log each successful attempt for an event

skill 3

Managing Auditing

exam objective

Implement, configure, manage, and troubleshoot auditing.

overview

When you implement audit policies, you must understand that auditing increases the overhead on a computer. The CPU will be frequently reading file systems and the Security event log can become inundated with entries that can cause problems with both disk space and performance. Therefore, you need to decide which events are important to track for your circumstances. Once you have carefully chosen the events you think are important to monitor, for whom you want to monitor them, and what actions you want to track, you must set a schedule for yourself to check the security log regularly. You can also manage the auditing activities for your organization by managing the operation of the Security event log, which stores the details of the events that are audited.

One important aspect of managing the Security log involves maintaining its size. When events are being regularly recorded, the Security log can become very large. This can quickly use up disk space on your computer. You can control the size of the Security log by specifying a maximum file size in the Event Viewer. When the Security log reaches the maximum file size, you can choose to either overwrite old events as needed, set a specific age for the events you want to be overwritten, or prevent events from being overwritten. If you choose the first option you could lose data if the log becomes full before you archive it. If you choose the second option, you could lose data that is at least as many days old as you have chosen if you do not archive the log soon enough. If you choose the final option, you must make sure that you monitor the Event Viewer often enough to archive or clear the logs before they become full, because when the log is full the operating system will stop recording events. Archiving is the process you use to save a history of the security events you are auditing so that you can track trends in resource usage. You also use the Event Viewer to archive old log files and store them for future reference.

When you open Event Viewer, the following logs are displayed in addition to the Security log by default:

◆ **Application log:** This log captures the details of events that occur when an application, such as a database application, is run on a computer. Errors, warnings, or information related to these events are recorded automatically.
◆ **System log:** This log records errors, warnings, and information generated by Windows 2000 Professional, such as a service starts or stops. These events are recorded automatically.

how to

View events in the Security Log of your computer, set the maximum size of the Security log to **384 KB**, and indicate that events older than **5** days should be overwritten.

1. Log off of the Administrator account and attempt to log back on as **Usr1** (or any other User account you have created on the computer). Enter an incorrect user name on your first logon attempt. Enter an incorrect password on your second logon attempt. Log on successfully on your third attempt.
2. Create a file named **Expenses.doc** and save it in the **Reports** folder. Close the file.
3. Log off as **Usr1** and log back on as an Administrator.
4. Click [Start], point to **Programs**, point to **Administrative Tools**, and click the **Event Viewer** command to open the **Event Viewer** window.
5. Click **Security Log** in the left pane of the **Event Viewer** window to open the events in the Security log.
6. Scroll down the list and locate the two **Failure Audits (Figure 13-9)**. Double-click the first Failure Audit to open the **Event Properties** dialog box to display the details of the selected event **(Figure 13-10)**.

Figure 13-9 The Security log

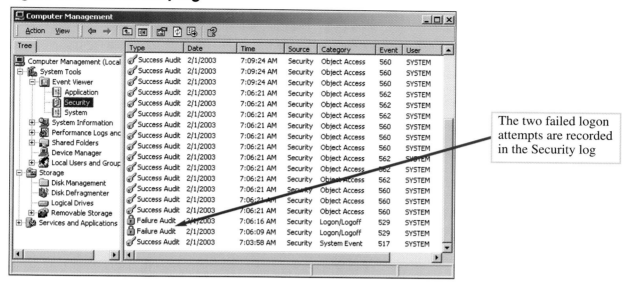

The two failed logon attempts are recorded in the Security log

Figure 13-10 Details of an event recorded in the Security log

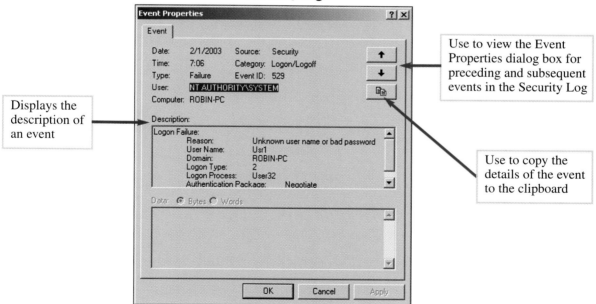

Use to view the Event Properties dialog box for preceding and subsequent events in the Security Log

Displays the description of an event

Use to copy the details of the event to the clipboard

skill 3

Managing Auditing *(cont'd)*

exam objective

Implement, configure, manage, and troubleshoot auditing.

how to

7. Use the up and down arrow buttons to view the next and previous Event Properties dialog boxes for the events in the Security Log. Locate the Event Properties dialog box for the Success Audit in which the Expenses file was saved in the Reports folder **(Figure 13-11)**. Close the Event Properties dialog box.

8. Right-click **Security Log** and select the **Properties** command on the context menu to open the **Security Log Properties** dialog box.

9. Indicate the maximum size for the log file in the **Maximum log size** text box. For example, type **384**.

10. The **Overwrite events older than** option button is selected by default. To set the number of days old you want events that are overwritten to be, type **5**, in the **Overwrite events older than** text box **(Figure 13-12)**.

11. Click [OK] to save the settings and close the Security Log Properties dialog box.

12. Close the Event Viewer.

tip

The file size can be entered in any multiple, but it will be resized to the closest multiple of 64.

more

You must remember to examine the Security event log regularly because the process of auditing will not warn you if security infringements are occurring. Your sensitive files should always be monitored by first setting an audit policy and then following up to see if unauthorized users are either attempting to access them or succeeding in accessing them. Do not audit events that are not essential either for enhancing the security of your system or for tracking developments in system usage.

Figure 13-11 Events Properties dialog box

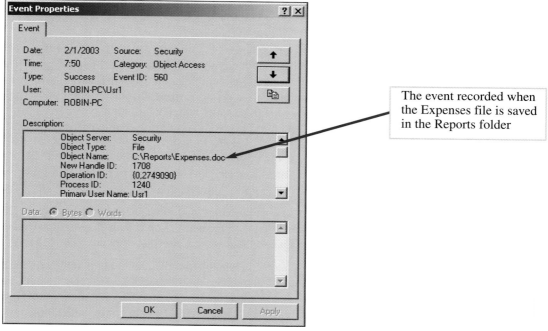

The event recorded when the Expenses file is saved in the Reports folder

Figure 13-12 Security Properties dialog box

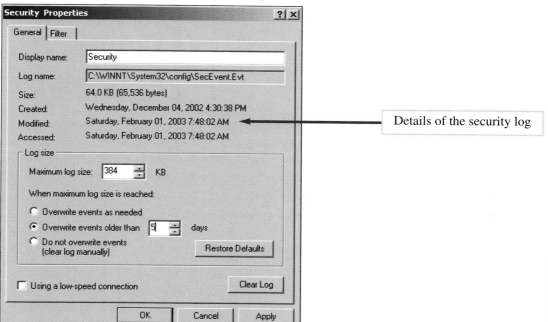

Details of the security log

skill 4

Monitoring System Performance

exam objective

Optimize and troubleshoot performance of the Windows 2000 Professional desktop. Optimize and troubleshoot processor utilization.

overview

At times, the performance of your computer may not be satisfactory. For example, the processing speed may have noticeably decreased so that you are experiencing delays in opening applications. This happens due to bottlenecks, which reduce the speed of the computer system as a whole. A **bottleneck**, in computer parlance, refers to any resource, such as memory or disk space, which causes other resources to delay while it completes its assigned function. For example, if your computer has insufficient memory, memory is the bottleneck that is likely holding up computer functions. The solution to bottlenecks in most situations is to upgrade your system. You may need to add more RAM, get a newer, faster network interface card, buy a more powerful processor, or upgrade your drives.

However, you can use the tools in Windows 2000 Professional to monitor the resources of a computer and determine where and what the bottlenecks are and how they are adversely affecting the computer's performance. You can also configure alerts to perform actions based on the performance of the resources on your computer.

First, you must ascertain what the normal operating parameters for the computer are. This is referred to as establishing a baseline or benchmarking the system. The idea is that in order to detect anomalous system behavior, you must first know what level of performance you have during normal usage and under typical workloads. In particular, you should establish baseline behavior when a computer first begins to run on the network and when the hardware or software configuration has been modified. For example, to determine the baseline behavior for the processors, you can create a counter log using the Processor—%Processing Time counter and the System—Processor Queue Length counter, which you should run for a few weeks to a month **(Figure 13-13)**. This way, at a later date when you make system modifications, you will have a benchmark range of values to evaluate against the new range of values you get after modification **(Figure 13-14)**. Sporadic spikes in the values recorded by a counter are generally discarded. The idea is to get a reliable range of values against which future performance can be compared. As a general rule, baselines should be established for all of the important servers on the network.

You monitor the resources on your computer, either to establish a baseline or to diagnose a bottleneck, in the **Performance** console. The **Performance** console consists of the **System Monitor** and the **Performance Logs and Alerts** tools. The System Monitor is used to view a graphical representation of the performance of the resources on your computer. The Performance Logs and Alerts tool is used to record the performance of resources in logs and to configure alerts, which are activated based on threshold values that you set to perform specific actions.

When you open the Performance console, the empty System Monitor appears by default. It will display the performance of your computer based on objects and counters that you configure. An **object** is a system resource, such as a processor, disk, network interface, or memory, whose performance you can monitor. **Counters** are performance measures for the object that can be calculated and related as numeric figures. For example, if you want to monitor the performance of the processor object, you can monitor counters, such as the percentage of time the processor is busy (%Processor Time) and the number of times each second that it is interrupted by service requests (Interrupts/Sec). Counters can have multiple instances. For example, if a computer has two processors there can be three instances for the %Processor Time counter, one for each processor and one for the total processing time.

Processors are not frequently the cause of a bottleneck, but if the %Processor Time counter is consistently above 80%, it will confirm this is the problem area. You can also use the Processor-Interrupts/Sec counter to find out the average number of times the processor is

Figure 13-13 The System Monitor

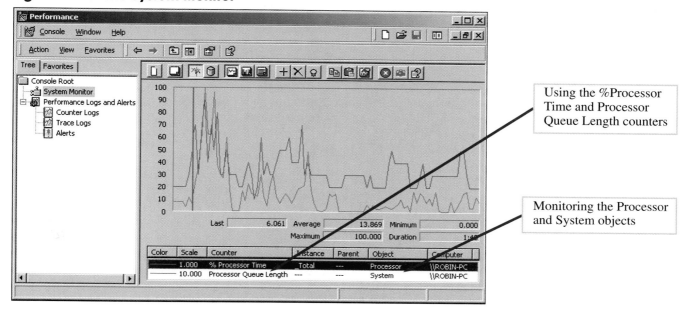

Using the %Processor Time and Processor Queue Length counters

Monitoring the Processor and System objects

Figure 13-14 Processor Baseline counter log

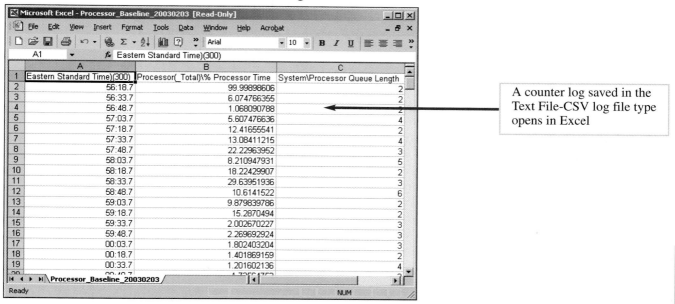

A counter log saved in the Text File-CSV log file type opens in Excel

skill 4

Monitoring System Performance
(cont'd)

exam objective

Optimize and troubleshoot performance of the Windows 2000 Professional desktop.

overview

interrupted by hardware device requests for attention. When the system is not in use, the only interrupts are caused by the processor hardware timer which will produce approximately 66 to 100 interrupts per second. First, establish a baseline for normal workloads. This value will depend on the number of disk I/0 operations per second and the number of network packets per second and will generally run between 200 and 300 on Windows 2000 Professional. Then monitor for values that exceed this range.

In order to monitor performance measures for system objects, you must use the **Add Counters** dialog box to add instances of counters for certain objects to the current graph in the System Monitor. The System Monitor tool captures the data from the counters and displays it as a chart, a histogram, or a report.

how to

Monitor the average time each of the processors in your computer spends processing service requests and the average number of times per second they are interrupted by device requests. Display the data as a histogram.

1. Click ⊞Start, point to **Programs**, point to **Administrative Tools**, and click the **Performance** command to open the **Performance** console (**Figure 13-15**).
2. Click ⊞ to open the **Add Counters** dialog box.
3. Select the **Use local computer counters** option button to indicate that you want to monitor objects on the local computer.
4. **Processor** is selected by default in the **Performance object** list box.
5. Select **%Processor Time** in the **Select counters from list** box.
6. Select the **All instances** option button to monitor all instances of the selected object (**Figure 13-16**).
7. Click Add to add the selected counter.
8. Select **Interrupts/sec** in the **Select counters from list** box.
9. Select the **All instances** option button and Click Add .
10. Click Add to add the selected counter to the Performance console.
11. Click Close to close the Add Counters dialog box and save the data (**Figure 13-17**).
12. Click the Histogram button 📊 to display the captured data as a histogram (**Figure 13-18**). The histogram indicates the amount of time all the processors in your computer have spent processing.
13. Close the Performance console.

tip

Some devices that may cause interrupts are adapters, network adapters, the system clock, and the mouse.

more

There are many other counters you can track with the System monitor. Since it would be impossible to memorize the purpose of each one, you can select the counter you want to find out about in the Add Counter dialog box and use the **Explain** button Explain to open the **Explain Text** section which provides a description of what the counter measures.

Figure 13-15 The System Monitor in the Performance console

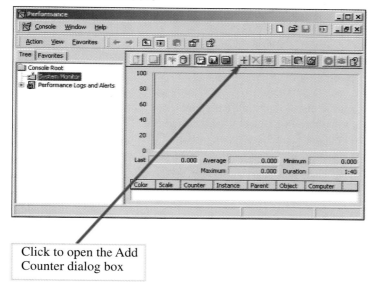

Click to open the Add Counter dialog box

Figure 13-16 Monitoring all instances of an object

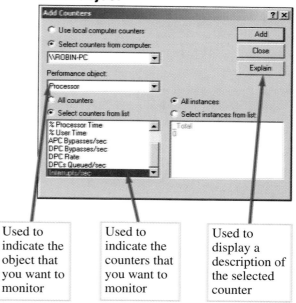

Used to indicate the object that you want to monitor

Used to indicate the counters that you want to monitor

Used to display a description of the selected counter

Figure 13-17 Captured data displayed as a chart

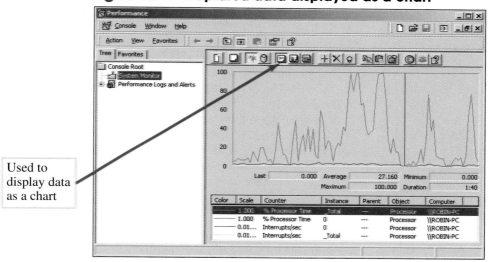

Used to display data as a chart

Figure 13-18 Histogram for processor monitoring

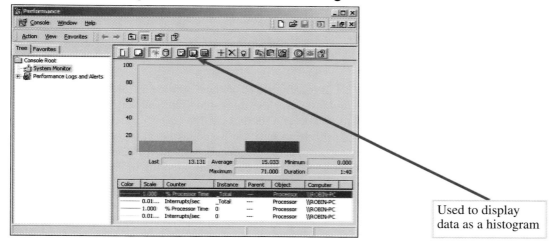

Used to display data as a histogram

skill 5

Configuring Alerts

exam objective

Basic knowledge

overview

While the **System Monitor** tool displays graphical representations of the performance measures for various objects, **Performance Logs and Alerts (Figure 13-19)** are used to store the data for future reference. You can create two types of logs, Counter logs and Trace logs. **Counter logs** use the GUI data from the System monitor to create a log file, which is by default in the *.**BLG** format (Binary LoG). **Trace logs** survey events that take place on the system **(Figure 13-20)**. They do not track performance data, so you do not select counters when you configure them. Instead, you choose the events logged by a system provider or you can add a non-system provider **(Figure 13-21)**. Both logs store data pertaining to resource usage for a specified time period. You can set begin and end times, or you can start and stop them manually. While Counter logs record the state of object counters at specific intervals of time that you set, Trace logs monitor a particular value continuously.

Based on the performance of resources on your computer, you must take certain actions to enhance the performance of your computer. For example, the most frequent cause of system bottlenecks is memory. There are several counters you can use to evaluate how much memory your system is using. The **Available Mbytes** counter calculates how much memory is left to run a process after all other running processes and the cache are taken care of. The **Pages/sec** counter measures the number of times the processor had to ask for data that was not in RAM (physical memory), but rather had been stored in the page file. The page file is a logical memory location on the root drive where the operating system was installed. If the page file is habitually being called upon, system delays are most likely already perceptible. The Paging file counter **%Usage** will tell you how much of the page file is currently being used. You can use these three counters to monitor the memory on your system and configure an **alert** to send you a message when the value is either under or over certain thresholds. For example, if the available megabytes of memory dips below 4 MB, the paging file usage is consistently more than 99 percent, or if you see frequent peaks over 20 being recorded by the Pages/Sec counter, it is probably time to add more memory to your system. The average number of times per second that the processor has to ask for data that is not in RAM should not exceed 5.

You can also automate actions to be performed when the value of a counter surpasses the threshold value for that particular counter, and you can configure an alert to monitor a particular counter at a scheduled time or when you manually start the scan. You can configure alerts to perform the following actions:

◆ **Send a message:** Alerts can send messages to computers that are connected to the computer being monitored. For example, you can set up an alert on a computer on your network to send a message to your computer when the available disk space is less than a certain value.

◆ **Run a program:** Alerts can be programmed to run a program. For example, you can configure an alert to run a disk defragmenting program when the available disk space is below a certain limit.

◆ **Start a new log:** Alerts can be configured to create a new log to record events when the counter value is either under or over the threshold you have set. Starting a new log enables you to view events that occur after the alert has been triggered.

◆ **Create an entry in the Application log:** Alerts can create an entry in the Application log. The Application log records events that occur when an application is run. Logging an entry in the Application log enables you to determine the time when an alert was triggered.

You configure alerts by using the **Alert** dialog box in the **Performance** console.

Figure 13-19 Performance Logs and Alerts node

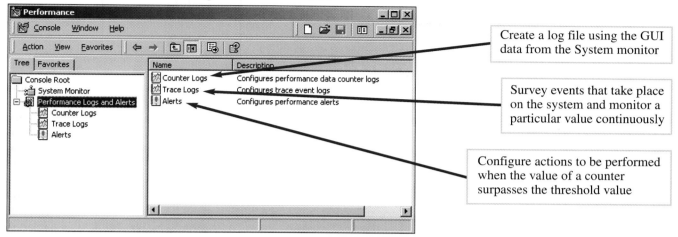

Create a log file using the GUI data from the System monitor

Survey events that take place on the system and monitor a particular value continuously

Configure actions to be performed when the value of a counter surpasses the threshold value

Figure 13-20 Creating a Trace log

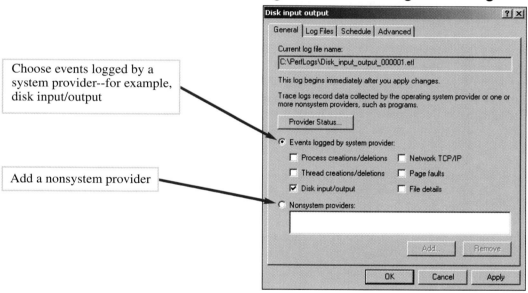

Choose events logged by a system provider--for example, disk input/output

Add a nonsystem provider

Figure 13-21 Add Nonsystem Providers dialog box

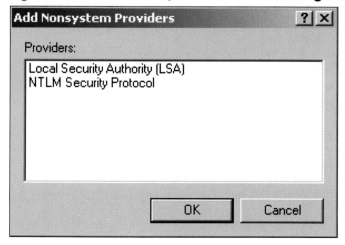

skill 5

Configuring Alerts (cont'd)

exam objective

Basic knowledge

how to

Create a counter log named **Memory Log** to evaluate how much memory your system is using at particular points in time. The log should record data every **30 minutes**. Save the counter log in the PerfLogs folder on the **C:** drive of your computer as a text file that has values separated by commas and do not allow the log file size to exceed **1024 Kb**. Manually start and stop the counter log so that you can monitor peak usage times. Also, configure an alert named **Memory Alert** to send a message to a computer named **Computer1** when the available memory falls below **4MB**, the **Pages/Sec exceeds 5**, or the **%Usage** of the page file reaches 99%. Make sure that the alert will monitor the memory of your computer when you manually start and stop the scan.

1. Click ![Start], point to **Programs**, point to **Administrative Tools**, and click the **Performance** command to open the **Performance** console.
2. Click the plus (+) symbol next to the **Performance Logs and Alerts** node to display the **Counter Logs**, **Trace Logs**, and **Alerts** nodes.
3. Right-click the Counter Logs node to open the shortcut menu.
4. Click the **New Log Settings** command to open the **New Log Settings** dialog box to indicate a name for the new log.
5. Type **Memory Log**, in the **Name** text box to name the new log.
6. Click [OK] to open the **Memory Log** dialog box.
7. Click [Add] to open the **Select Counters** dialog box.
8. In the **Performance object** list box, select **Memory**.
9. Make sure that the **Select counters from list** option button is selected. Hold down the Ctrl key and select the **Available Mbytes** and **Pages/sec** counters in the scrolling list box **(Figure 13-22)**.
10. Click [Add] to add the selected counter to the Performance console.
11. In the **Performance object** list box, select **Paging File**.
12. In the **Select counters from list** box, select, **%Usage** and click [Add].
13. Click [Close] to close the Select Counters dialog box.
14. Indicate the time interval at which the log should record data related to the selected counters. For example, type **30** in the **Interval** spin box at the bottom of the Memory Log dialog box.
15. Select the unit of the time interval from the **Units** list box. For example, select **minutes** **(Figure 13-23)**.
16. Click the **Log Files** tab. Indicate the location where you want the log file to be saved if different from the default, **C:\PerfLogs**, in the **Location** text box.
17. Select **mmddhh** from the **End file names with** list to append the month, day and hour of the day to the name of the log file. You can also add the month, day, year, and hour or a serial number to the name of the log file.
18. Select **Text File – CSV** from the **Log file type** drop-down list to indicate that the log file should be a comma-separated text file.
19. Select the **Limit of** option button to specify a size limit for the log file.
20. Indicate the size limit for the log file. For example, type **1024** in the **Limit of** text box **(Figure 13-24)**.
21. Click the **Schedule** tab to access the options for scheduling the log file. If you accepted the default location and the **PerfLogs** folder has not yet been created, the Memory Log message box will prompt you to create it. Click **Yes**.
22. Select the **Manually** option button in the **Start log** section to indicate that you will manually start the log.

Figure 13-22 Adding counters to the Performance console

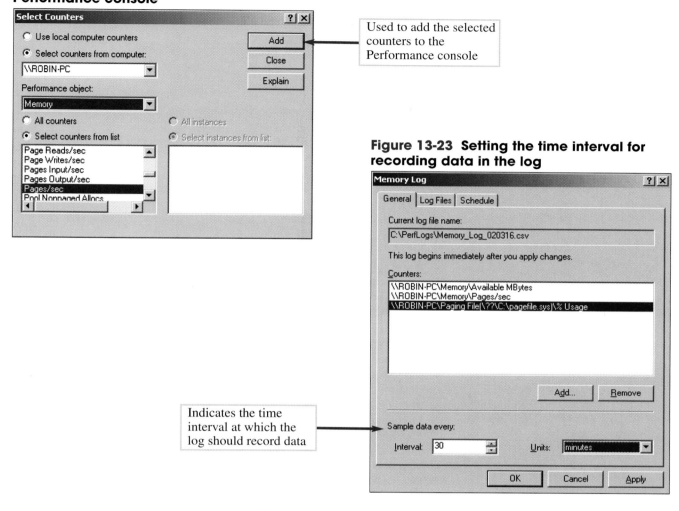

Used to add the selected counters to the Performance console

Figure 13-23 Setting the time interval for recording data in the log

Indicates the time interval at which the log should record data

Figure 13-24 Setting Log File properties

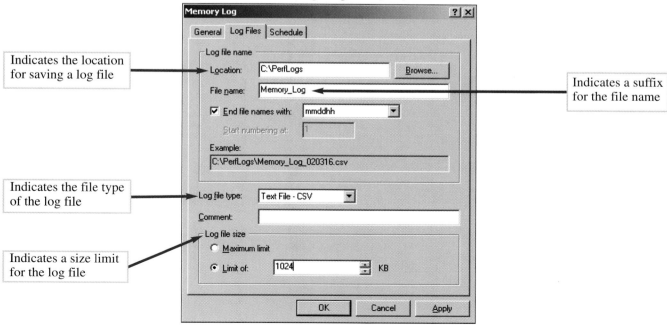

Indicates the location for saving a log file

Indicates a suffix for the file name

Indicates the file type of the log file

Indicates a size limit for the log file

skill 5

Configuring Alerts (cont'd)

how to

23. Select the **Manually** option button in the **Stop log** section, if necessary, to indicate that you will manually stop the log.
24. Click [OK] to save the configuration and close the Memory Log dialog box.
25. Right-click the Alerts node to open the shortcut menu.
26. Click the **New Alert Settings** command to open the **New Alert Settings** dialog box.
27. Indicate a name for the new alert in the **Name** text box. For example, type **Memory Alert**.
28. Click [OK] to open the **Memory Alert** dialog box.
29. In the **Comment** text box on the **General** tab of the Memory Alert dialog box, specify a comment for the alert. This comment will be displayed in the message that the alert sends. For example, type: **You need to add memory**.
30. Click [Add...] to open the **Select Counters** dialog box.
31. In the **Performance object** list box, select **Memory**.
32. Make sure that the **Select counters from list** option button is selected. Hold down the **Ctrl** key and select the **Available Mbytes** and **Pages/sec** counters in the scrolling list box.
33. Click [Add] to add the selected counter to the Performance console.
34. In the **Performance object** list box, select **Paging File**.
35. In the **Select counters from list** box, select **%Usage** and click [Add] to add the selected counter to the Performance console.
36. Click [Close] to close the Select Counters dialog box.
37. Select the **Memory\Available Mbytes** counter in the **Counters** scrolling list box. In the **Alert when value is** list box, select **Under**, if necessary. In the **Limit** text box, enter the threshold value **4 (Figure 13-25)**.
38. Select the **Memory\Pages\sec** counter in the **Counters** list box. In the **Alert when value is** list box, select **Over**. In the **Limit** text box, enter the threshold value **5**.
39. Select the Paging File\%Usage counter in the Counters list box. In the **Alert when value is** list box, select **Over**. In the **Limit** text box, enter the threshold value, **99**.
40. Click the **Action** tab to display the check boxes that you use to specify the action that the alert should perform.
41. Select the **Send a network message to** check box.
42. Indicate the name of the computer to which you want the alert to send a message. For example, type **\\Computer1 (Figure 13-26)**.
43. Click the **Schedule** tab to display the options for starting the alert scan.
44. Select the **Manually (using the shortcut menu)** option button to indicate that you will manually start monitoring. **Manually** should also be automatically selected in the **Stop scan** section.
45. Click [OK] to save the configuration and close the Memory Alert dialog box. Close the Performance console.

Figure 13-25 Setting the threshold value for an alert

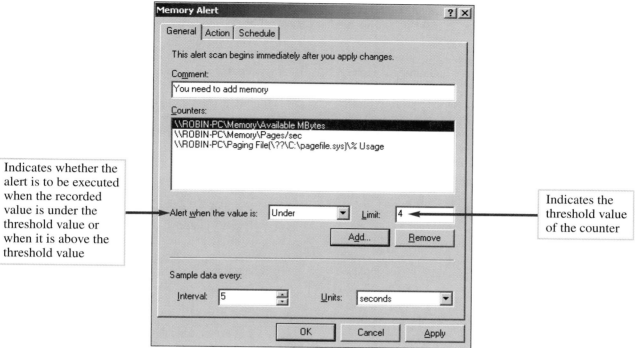

Indicates whether the alert is to be executed when the recorded value is under the threshold value or when it is above the threshold value

Indicates the threshold value of the counter

Figure 13-26 Location for sending the Alert message

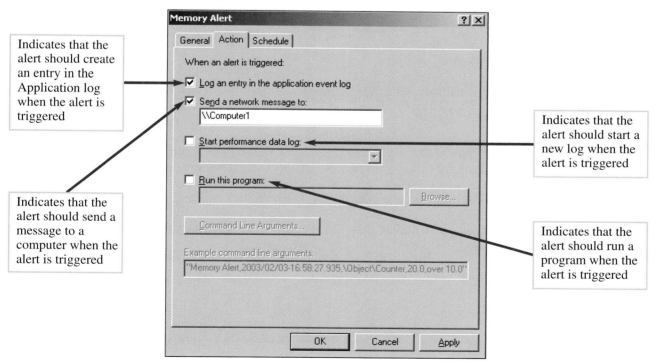

Indicates that the alert should create an entry in the Application log when the alert is triggered

Indicates that the alert should send a message to a computer when the alert is triggered

Indicates that the alert should start a new log when the alert is triggered

Indicates that the alert should run a program when the alert is triggered

Summary

- Auditing is used to track user activities and object access on the computers on a network. It must be set up for each computer.
- Auditing is used to help prevent security breaches by allowing you to track unauthorized attempts to log on or access folders.
- It is also used to help conduct resource planning for the computers on your network.
- When you define an audit policy, you select the events you want to track and whether to track the success or failure, or both, for the event.
- Events are activities such as logging on to a computer or a network, and accessing files, folders, printers, and the Registry.
- The success and failure of events that occur on a computer are recorded in the Security log. You use the Event Viewer to view the Security log.
- You can only audit access to files and folders on NTFS disks.
- In order to audit access to files and folders, you must first activate object access auditing on the computer on which the resource is stored. Then you must choose which files and folders you want the operating system to track.
- Next you select the users whose actions you want to audit and what file system actions you want to monitor in the System ACL editor for the file or folder. For example, you can audit who is viewing a folder, creating a file, changing permissions, or viewing permissions.
- Auditing increases the overhead on a computer. The CPU will be frequently reading file systems and the Security event log can become inundated with entries, which can cause problems with both disk space and performance.
- You can control the size of the Security log by specifying a maximum file size in the Event Viewer. When the Security log reaches the maximum file size, you can choose to either overwrite old events as needed, set a specific age for the events you want to be overwritten, or prevent events from being overwritten.
- The Event Viewer is also used to archive old log files and store them for future reference.

- You monitor the resources on your computer, either to establish a baseline or to diagnose a bottleneck, in the Performance console.
- First, you must determine what the normal operating parameters for the computer are. This is referred to as establishing a baseline or benchmarking the system and it is used to ascertain the level of performance you have during normal usage and under typical workloads.
- The idea is to get a reliable range of values against which future performance can be compared. As a general rule, baselines should be established for all of the important servers on the network.
- A bottleneck refers to any resource, such as memory or disk space, which causes other resources to delay while it completes its assigned function.
- The Performance console consists of System Monitor and the Performance Logs and Alerts tools.
- The System Monitor displays the performance of your computer based on objects and counters that you configure.
- An object is a system resource, such as a processor, disk, network interface, or memory, whose performance you can monitor.
- Counters are performance measures for an object that can be quantified, such as the percentage of time the processor is busy (%Processor Time).
- Performance Logs and Alerts are used to store system performance data for future reference. You can create two types of logs, Counter logs and Trace logs.
- Counter logs use the GUI data from the System monitor to create a log file.
- Trace logs survey events that take place on the system. They do not track performance data, so you do not select counters when you configure them. Instead, you choose the events logged by a system provider.
- While Counter logs record the state of object counters at specific intervals of time that you set, Trace logs monitor a particular value continuously.
- Alerts are used to inform you when a counter has either gone above or below a threshold that you have set, or to perform actions when a threshold value has been crossed.

Key Terms

Alert

Application log

Audit object access audit policy

Audit policy

Auditing

Bottleneck

Counter

Counter log

Event Viewer

Object

Performance Logs and Alerts

Security event log

System log

System Monitor

Trace log

Test Yourself

1. Which one of the following options is a benefit of Auditing?
   a. Runs programs based on the performance of a computer.
   b. Helps prevent security breaches on computers.
   c. Decreases the overhead on a computer.
   d. Records events in the System log.

2. Which one of the following actions is audited using the Audit system events audit policy?
   a. Logging on to a computer.
   b. Accessing a printer.
   c. Sending a logon request to a domain controller.
   d. Shutting down a computer.

3. You are setting up auditing for a folder on your computer. The audit policy that you select in the Local Security Settings dialog box is:
   a. System events.
   b. Process tracking.
   c. Privilege use.
   d. Object access.

4. Which one of the following statements is true about auditing access to files and folders on a computer?
   a. You can select the users to be audited.
   b. The file or folder must be on a FAT drive.
   c. Auditing for privilege use events should be enabled.
   d. You set up auditing for a folder using the Event Viewer.

5. The Security event log records events:
   a. Such as the failure of a driver or other system component to load.
   b. For which an audit policy has been configured.
   c. That are generated by Windows 2000 Professional.
   d. As information, warnings, or errors.

6. The Security log of your computer is occupying a large amount of disk space. You want to reduce disk space usage, but you also want to save old events in the log for future reference. Which one of the following actions do you need to perform?
   a. Create a Counter log to record audited events.
   b. Archive the Security log.
   c. Reduce the size of the Security log and archive old events.
   d. Configure the Security log to overwrite events older than 1 day.

7. You need to monitor the memory utilization of your computer. To do so, you will use:
   a. Event Viewer.
   b. Performance console.
   c. Local Security Policy window.
   d. Security log.

8. Counters are:
   a. System resources.
   b. Resources that slow down a computer.
   c. Performance measures for an object.
   d. Logs that record data continuously.

9. Which one of the following logs records data on the performance of a computer at specific intervals of time?
   a. Security log
   b. Application log
   c. Counter log
   d. Trace log

10. You can configure alerts using the:
   a. Event Viewer.
   b. Event Properties dialog box.
   c. Local Security Settings window.
   d. Performance console.

Projects: On Your Own

1. Enable auditing for a folder named **Pictures** located on the **D:** drive of your computer. Ensure that an event is logged every time users in the Administrators group create a file in **Pictures**.
   a. Log on as an **Administrator**.
   b. Open the **Local Security Policy** window.
   c. Open the **Local Security Policy Setting** dialog box for the **Audit object access** policy.
   d. Select the **Success** check box.
   e. Restart the computer.
   f. Open **Windows Explorer**.
   g. Open the **Pictures Properties** dialog box.
   h. Click the **Security** tab.
   i. Click **Advanced**.
   j. Click the Auditing tab.
   k. Click **Add**.
   l. In the **Name** text box , indicate the name of the user or group for which you want to enable auditing. For example, type **Administrators**.
   m. Click **OK**.

n. Select the **Successful** check box next to the **Create Files/ Write Data** option.

o. Close the **Pictures Properties** dialog box.

2. Set the maximum size of the Security log on your computer to **320 KB**. Also, indicate that events older than **4** days should be overwritten.

a. Open **Event Viewer**.

b. Right-click **Security Log** in the left pane of the **Event Viewer** window.

c. Select the **Properties** command in the shortcut menu.

d. Type **320** to indicate the maximum size for the log file in the **Maximum log size** text box.

e. The **Overwrite events older than** option button is selected by default. Indicate the number of days after which the events should be overwritten. For example, type **4** in the **Overwrite events older than** text box.

f. Click **OK** to save the settings and close the **Security Log Properties** dialog box.

Problem Solving Scenarios

1. As Network Administrator for Turco's Food Emporium, a regional food distributor in Bedford, New Jersey, you manage a Windows 2000 network for 150 employees in a single location. There are many confidential corporate files on the network. You are particularly concerned about files stored in a shared directory on the Financial Manager's machine (the Finance sub-directory). In fact, the Financial Manger has asked you to take steps to secure files in the Finance sub-directory, to audit access to this directory, and to keep track of who is using the files. Outline, in a report, the steps you will take to achieve these objectives.

2. When discussing security issues with the Financial Manager of Turco's Food Emporium, you discover that her computer is not performing well. It seems to be very slow at accessing files and even slower at launching programs. Outline in a brief memo the steps you will take to continuously monitor her computer for one week to try to determine the cause of the problem. What counters will you use?

14 Backing Up and Restoring Data

You have carefully planned your network, created user accounts and assigned those users to specific groups, created shared folders, assigned permissions, and set password and account lockout policies. Auditing has been configured to monitor unsuccessful events that could indicate possible security breaches and successful events that will help you to evaluate the capacity and overall functioning of your system. You have encrypted sensitive files and assigned recovery agents so that encrypted data will always be recoverable. IPSec policies have been configured to protect data that is sent over the network and security options have been set to further protect the computers on your network from unauthorized user access and viruses. You are monitoring important system performance measures so that you can anticipate bottlenecks and you have configured alerts to warn you when these resources are either under or over certain thresholds. But what if your system fails? What will you do if a disk drive crashes, or if a virus or power outage wipes out all of the data on the hard drive of one of your computers? How will you recover the operating system and all of that data you have so carefully safeguarded?

There are several tools and utilities that are used to protect your data in the event of such a catastrophe, starting with Windows Backup. The Backup utility consists of the Backup Wizard, the Restore Wizard, and the Emergency Repair Disk (ERD).

You use the Backup Wizard to create copies of vital enterprise data that are either stored in a backup file on a different hard disk, a Zip or Jaz drive, or other removable storage media such as a CD-RW or other writable optical disk, or magnetic tape. If data is lost or damaged, you can use the Restore Wizard to recover it from the backup copies. You must also back up all system files, the startup environment files, the partition boot sector, and the Registry because they can also be accidentally deleted or become corrupt. The Emergency Repair Disk will be used to back up these files so that you can rebuild your system if the system files become corrupt or the operating system will not start.

Before making backups, you should create a backup plan so that you can retrieve lost data quickly and efficiently. First, you must identify the data that needs to be backed up and the medium you are going to use. Then you must decide upon a backup schedule and a backup type. Backup types differ depending on how the *archive attribute or backup marker* (also called the archive bit) is treated. The archive attribute is set on a file when it has changed. Some backup types will remove the archive bit when the file has been backed up, while others will ignore it. You must also decide whether to perform network or local backup jobs.

Goals

In this lesson, you will learn to plan for data backup, decide on the type of backup, and perform the backup operation using the Backup Wizard. You will learn about the different types of backups and how to use them to develop a comprehensive backup and restore strategy. You will also learn to restore data and create an Emergency Repair Disk.

Lesson 14 Backing Up and Restoring Data

Skill	Exam 70-210 Objective
1. Planning Data Backups	Basic knowledge
2. Introducing Backup Types	Basic knowledge
3. Backing Up Data	Basic knowledge
4. Restoring Data from a Backup	Recover system state data. Recover system state data and user data by using Windows Backup.
5. Changing the Default Backup and Restore Options	Basic knowledge
6. Creating an Emergency Repair Disk	Basic knowledge

Requirements

To complete this lesson, you will need a computer running Windows 2000 Professional that is connected to a network. You will need administrative permissions and a folder named **accounts** on the **C:** drive.

skill 1

Planning Data Backups

exam objective

Basic knowledge

overview

Since data can be the most important asset of an organization, you must make sure that it is protected from losses due to viruses, disk drive failures, or user deletion. You can safeguard data by creating copies, or **backups**, of the files and folders on client computers or on servers on the network. Lost or damaged data can be retrieved if you have conscientiously designed and implemented a comprehensive backup plan.

You can back up files and folders as well as an entire disk; however, first you must decide what data must be backed up and how frequently it will be backed up. Usually data that is essential to the operation of an organization, such as financial statements and sales reports, should be backed up daily. Employee records should be backed up whenever they are modified. If reports are created on a weekly, monthly or quarterly basis and do not change during the interim, they can be backed up accordingly. Data on individual client systems should be backed up regularly or as often as the files are changed.

Next, you must decide on the media you will use. You can back up files to Zip or Jaz drives, CD-RW or other writeable optical drives, or to the hard drive on a remote file server. Magnetic tape has been the most widely used backup medium because it is inexpensive and you can store large amounts of data on it; however, tape can deteriorate over time.

You must also decide whether to implement a network backup or a local backup. When you perform a **network backup**, you can combine essential data from multiple computers on a single disk or tape. This is obviously the most efficient method for Administrators because they will not have to physically visit each client computer and server, possibly dragging the removable storage device with them. **Local backups** can work on small networks where an organizational policy is in effect that requires users to back up their own data on a regular schedule. However, unless you are going to circulate the storage device, each client will need its own Zip, CD-RW, or tape drive, and this cost can be prohibitive. You can also adopt a hybrid method that combines both network and local backups. Users can backup data on the local hard drive of their PCs to a network file server and the Administrator can backup the network drive on the file server locally with a removable storage device.

tip

You must make sure that the files and folders you are backing up are not in use by any application or user on the network. Open files and folders will not be backed up.

tip

You must make sure that your storage media device is listed in the Windows 2000 Hardware Compatibility List.

more

In order to back up data, you must have the appropriate user rights. Any user can back up files and folders that they have created (files they own) and files for which they have the **Read**, **Read and Execute**, **Modify**, or **Full Control** permission. Local **Administrators** and **Backup Operators** can backup any file or folder on the local computer. Domain Administrators and Backup Operators can backup any file or folder in the domain or in other trusted domains because they are granted the **Back up files and directories** user right by default.

Similarly, to restore a backed up file or folder, you must have the appropriate user rights and permissions. File or folder owners can restore the backup copy. Other users can restore files or folders if they have the **Write**, **Modify**, or **Full Control** permission. Members of the local Administrators and Backup Operators groups can restore any file or folder on the local computer. Administrators and Backup Operators on the domain controller have the **Restore files and directories** user right by default and can restore any backup file or folder on the domain.

Figure 14-1 Making backups using the Backup Wizard

Initiates and guides you through the backup process

Initiates and guides you through the restore process

Used to backup system files, the Registry, the partition boot sector, and the startup environment

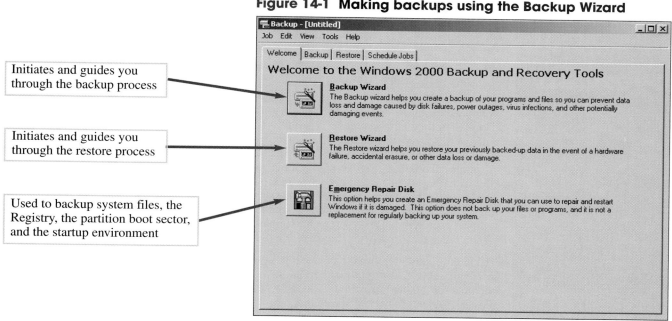

Figure 14-2 Planning data backups

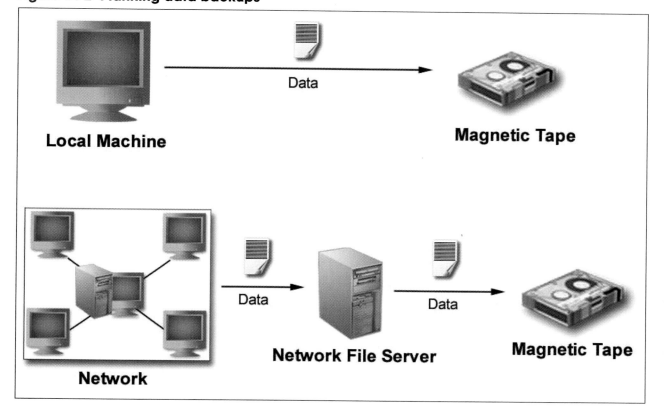

skill 2   *Introducing Backup Types*

exam objective

Basic knowledge

overview

There are five different backup types from which you can choose either in the Backup Wizard or on the Backup Type tab in the Options dialog box. In order to choose one of these types, first you must understand what the **archive attribute** or **archive bit** is and how each backup type handles it. The archive attribute is a property for files and folders that is used to identify them when they have changed. When a file has changed, the **Archive** attribute is automatically selected on the **General** tab in the **Properties** dialog box on a FAT32 partition. **(Figure 14-3).** On an NTFS partition, the Archive Attribute can be found in the Advanced Attributes dialog box **(Figure 14-4)**. Some backup types remove the archive attribute to mark files as having been backed up, while others do not. For example, in a **Normal backup** the archive attribute is removed to denote that the file has been backed up, but in a **Copy backup,** the archive attribute is not removed to mark files as having been backed up. Copy backups are used between Normal and Incremental or Normal and Differential backups (discussed below) so that when they take place the process will not be affected by the removal of the archive bit.

The archive attribute is used by some types of backups and not by others. Sometimes it is used to identify files that need to be backed up, sometimes it is removed to denote that a file has been backed up, and sometimes it is ignored. For example, in a Normal backup, all selected files and folders are backed up whether they have the archive attribute or not; however, as noted above, the attribute is then removed from any files on which it has been set. Copy backups do not use the archive attribute. All selected files and folders with or without the archive attribute are backed up and, as noted above, the archive bit is not removed. The Copy backup type essentially "ignores" the archive attribute, creating a representation of your data at a particular point in time. An **Incremental backup** backs up only the selected files and folders that have the archive attribute, which is then removed. Thus, if a file has not changed since the previous backup, it will be skipped during the next Incremental backup. A **Differential backup,** on the other hand, backs up only selected files and folders with the archive attribute, which is not removed. Therefore, even if a file has not changed since the previous Differential backup, it will be backed up again because it still has the archive attribute. A **Daily backup** is used to back up all selected files and folders that have changed on that day, but the archive bit is not removed. The different types of backup and their characteristics are explained in **Table 14-1**.

more

Organizations use a blend of the different backup types in order to optimize the time spent on both the backup and the restore processes. For example, a Normal backup will take longer than an Incremental backup because all selected files are backed up whether or not they have the archive attribute. However, with a Normal backup you can quickly restore all of your files using the most recent copy of the backup file or tape. On the other hand, if you used only Incremental backups you would not be able to recover all of your data. Since an Incremental backup only backs up files and folders with the archive attribute, you would not be starting with a full set of files. Furthermore, you would have to restore a whole series of backup tapes in order to recapture all of your files because each backup would only include changed files. Therefore, although the backup process would be quick, the restore process would be unwieldy, if not impossible.

For these reasons, you should use a combination of Normal and other backup types to effectively manage your backup and restore times and ensure that all lost data can be recovered. For example, if you create a backup schedule that uses a combination of the Normal and Differential backup types, you will only have to restore the last Normal backup and the last Differential backup. On the other hand, if you use a combination of Normal and Incremental backups, you will have to restore the last Normal backup and all Incremental backups in the interim. A Normal/Incremental strategy will take less time to back up files because each Incremental backup will only capture changed files, whereas each Differential backup will capture all files that have changed since the last Normal backup. However, a Normal/Incremental strategy will take more time to restore files.

Figure 14-3 The Archive attribute (FAT32 partition)

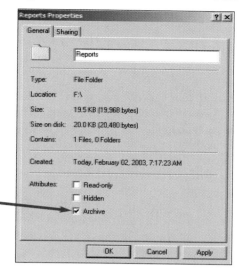

Files and folders that have changed are marked with the archive attribute

Figure 14-4 The Archive attribute (NTFS partition)

On an NTFS partition, click the Advanced button on the General tab in the Properties dialog box for a file or folder to access the archive attribute

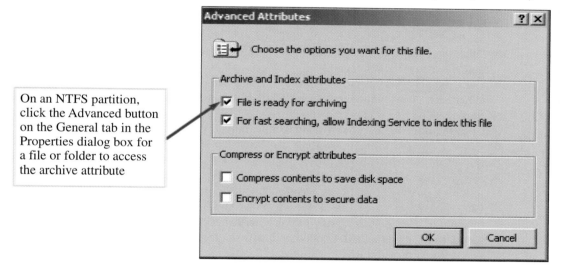

Table 14-1	Characteristics of the different types of backups
Type of Backup	**Criteria for Backing Up Files**
Normal	All selected files/folders are backed up whether or not they have the archive attribute.
Copy	All selected files/folders are backed up whether or not they have the archive attribute.
Differential	Only the selected files/folders with the archive attribute are backed up.
Incremental	Only the selected files/folders with the archive attribute are backed up.
Daily	All selected files/folders that have been modified that day are backed up.

skill 3

Backing Up Data

exam objective

Basic knowledge

overview

Once you have planned your backup strategy and decided which backup types to perform at what time intervals, you can use the **Backup Wizard** to configure your backup schedule. You can also manually set backup jobs on the Backup tab. First, you must decide which files to back up. You can either back up all the files and folders on your computer or only specific files and folders. You can also back up the **System State**, which includes such files as the **Registry** and **boot.ini** files, so that you can restore the operating system to its original state in the event of a system failure. A System State backup would be performed on a clean installation of the operating system to recover all of the configuration changes. System State backups should also be part of the backup process when any affected system component, such as the Registry, has changed, which can happen quite frequently. Next, you must choose the media you are going to use and the location where you are going to store the data. Finally, you can either start the backup or select advanced backup settings.

how to

Back up the **accounts** folder on the **C:** drive of your computer.

1. Log on to the computer as an **Administrator**.
2. Click **Start**, point to **Programs**, point to **Accessories**, point to **System Tools**, and click the **Backup** command to open the **Backup** window.
3. Click the Backup Wizard button to open the **Welcome to the Windows 2000 Backup and Recovery Tools** screen.
4. Click **Next >** to open the **What to Back Up** screen. On this screen you can choose to either back up everything; only selected files, drives or network data; or only the System State data.
5. Click the **Back up selected files, drives, or network data** option button.
6. Click **Next >** to open the **Items To Back Up** screen. This screen prompts you to select the local and network drives and files and folders to be backed up.
7. Double-click **My Computer** and expand the **C:** drive to select the required folder. Select the check box to the left of the **accounts** folder (**Figure 14-5**).
8. Click **Next >** to open the **Where to Store the Back Up** screen to choose the target medium to use, such as tape or backup file. A backup file can be located on any disk-based media, either a hard disk, a shared network folder, or removable media.
9. In the **Backup media or file name** text box, type **C:\accountfolderbackup.bkf**, which is the path where the backup file will be stored (**Figure 14-6**).
10. Click **Next >** to open the **Completing the Backup Wizard** screen. This screen summarizes the information for the backup operation, including the creation date and time, media type, and your other choices.
11. Click **Advanced...** to open the **Types of backup** screen. This is where you select the type of backup you want performed.
12. Select the **Normal** backup type on the **Select the type of backup operation to perform** list (**Figure 14-7**).
13. Click **Next >** to open the **How to Back Up** screen.
14. The **Verify data after backup** option button is selected by default. This option tells the system to verify the backed up data to make sure it is the same as the original data.
15. Click **Next >** to open the **Media Options** screen.
16. The **Append this backup to the media** button option is selected by default. This option is used to add the current backup job to an existing backup file or tape (**Figure 14-8**). If you select the second option, **Replace the data on the media with this backup,** previous backups, if any, will be replaced.
17. Click **Next >** to open the **Backup Label** screen.

tip

You can also open the Backup window by typing **ntbackup** in the Run dialog box.

caution

Files that you are going to back up must be closed. The Backup Wizard does not back up open files.

Figure 14-5 Selecting the items to be backed up

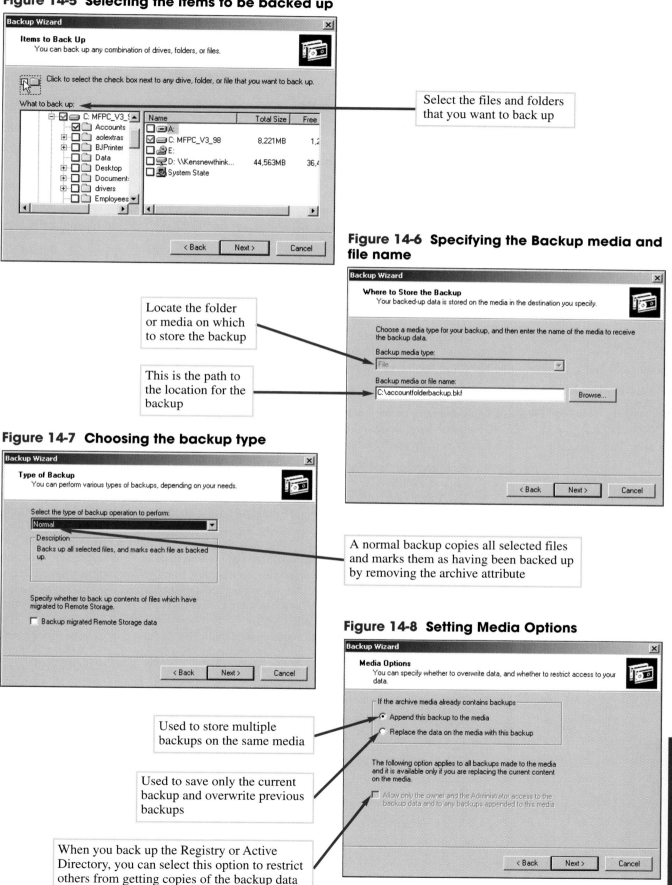

Select the files and folders that you want to back up

Figure 14-6 Specifying the Backup media and file name

Locate the folder or media on which to store the backup

This is the path to the location for the backup

Figure 14-7 Choosing the backup type

A normal backup copies all selected files and marks them as having been backed up by removing the archive attribute

Figure 14-8 Setting Media Options

Used to store multiple backups on the same media

Used to save only the current backup and overwrite previous backups

When you back up the Registry or Active Directory, you can select this option to restrict others from getting copies of the backup data

skill 3

Backing Up Data (cont'd)

exam objective   Basic knowledge

how to

18. Accept the default backup label, **Set created mm/dd/yyyy At hh:mm (AM/PM)**, in the **Backup label** text box.
19. Click Next > to open the **When to Back Up** screen.
20. Click the **Now** button to start the backup operation immediately.
21. Click Next > to open the **Completing the Backup Wizard** screen (**Figure 14-9**).
22. Click Finish to back up the selected folder.
23. The **Selection Information** dialog box appears for a short period of time giving the status of the backup.
24. The **Backup Progress** dialog box opens to inform you that the backup is complete (**Figure 14-10**). After completing the backup process, you can click Report... to view the **backup log.** The backup log is a text file that records backup operations and is stored on the hard disk of the computer. It gives detailed information regarding the backup operation, such as the number of files backed up, total size of the backup, and the start and end time of the backup.
25. Click Close to close the Backup Progress dialog box.
26. Close the Backup window.

more

The advanced backup settings you can select by clicking the Advanced... button on the Completing the Backup Wizard screen can be used to change the default settings for the current backup job. You can select from the following options:

◆ **Backup migrated Remote Storage data:** This option is used to specify that you want to back up files that have been transferred to **Remote Storage**.

◆ **Use hardware compression, if available:** This option increases the available data storage space on a tape device. If the tape device supports hardware compression, the option is available; otherwise it is not.

◆ **Allow only the owner and the Administrator Access to the backup data and to any backups appended to this media:** This option is used to control access to the backup file or tape. However, you can use this option only when you are replacing an existing backup on a backup medium. It is not available if you are appending data to the existing backup. It is particularly useful when you are backing up the Registry or Active Directory so that other users cannot access the files.

◆ **Backup label:** This is used to replace the default Set Created *date* At *time* label with a name and description.

◆ **Media label:** This is used to specify a name and label for the backup media, such as the tape name instead of the default Media Created *date* At *time* label.

◆ **When to Back Up:** You use this option to schedule your backups. The **Now** option starts the backup operation immediately. When you select **Later**, you can schedule unattended backups to run after working hours when all files are closed. You can also name the backup job, set the start date, and schedule your backup jobs for different days of the week, or you can schedule them to occur weekly, monthly, or at system startup.

tip

Windows 2000 Professional does not include Remote Storage. In Windows 2000 Server, infrequently accessed files are moved from local storage to a defined area on the hard drive known as Remote Storage.

Figure 14-9 Completing the backup process

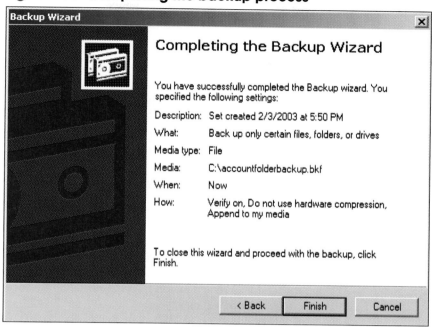

Figure 14-10 Details of a backup

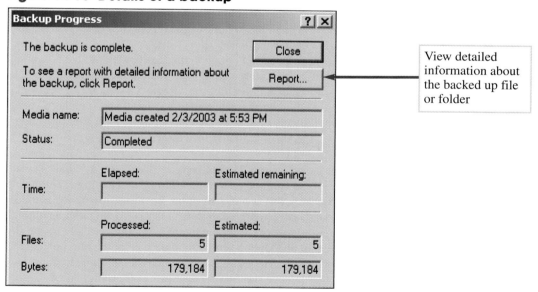

View detailed information about the backed up file or folder

skill 4

Restoring Data from a Backup

exam objective

Recover system state data. Recover system state data and user data by using Windows Backup.

overview

In the event of a hard disk crash, the accidental erasure of data, or damage due to a virus, you will need to restore your backed up data. Experts recommend that you test the restoration process regularly to ensure that you will be able to restore your data to its original state in the event of such a catastrophe. The **Restore Wizard** will help you to make this a painless procedure. You can restore individual drives, folders and files, or an entire backup set. A **backup set** is the compilation of files and folders from one volume that you have backed up and stored in a file or on one or more tapes. The backup set is displayed as a hierarchical tree that you can use to open drives and folders to find the files you want to restore.

how to

Restore the **accounts** folder backup named **Media created mm/dd/yyyy At hh:mm**.
1. Open the **Backup** window.
2. Click the **Restore Wizard** button [icon] to initiate the **Restore Wizard**. The **Welcome to the Restore Wizard** screen appears.
3. Click [Next >] to open the **What To Restore** screen. This screen lists the backed-up files and folders.
4. Click the **plus** sign ⊞ beside the **File** node to expand the node.
5. Click the plus sign beside the **Media created m/d/yyyy At hh:mm** node to expand the node.
6. Double-click the **C:** node to expand it. Click in the check box next to Accounts to select it for restoration (**Figure 14-11**).
7. Click [Next >] to restore the entire folder. The Completing the Restore Wizard screen opens.
8. Click [Advanced...] to open the **Where to Restore** screen to specify the location where the restored file is to be located.
9. Click the **Alternate Location** option in the **Restore files to** list box to select an alternate location for storing the restored data. Type **C:\Restored Data** in the **Alternate location** box. When you select this option, the directory structure of the backed-up files and folders is preserved in the alternate folder. It is used when you need some of the files, but you do not want to overwrite or change any of the current files or folders on your disk.
10. Click [Next >] to open the **How to Restore** screen (**Figure 14-12**). This screen lists various options for the restore operation.
11. Accept the default selection: **Do not replace the file on my disk (recommended)**. This option is used to prevent the restored data from overwriting existing data. The **Replace the file on disk only if it is older than the backup copy** option is used when you want the restored data to overwrite existing data if the existing data is older than the backup copy. This option will preserve the changes you have made to the file. The **Always replace the file on disk** option is used to replace all of the files on your hard disk with the files in the backup set. Any changes since the backup will be lost.
12. Click [Next >] to open the **Advanced Restore Options** screen. You will be prompted to select security options for the restore operation. Clear all of the check boxes.
13. Click [Next >] to open the **Completing the Restore Wizard** screen. This screen summarizes the restore options you have chosen, such as the media selected for the restore operation and the location for the restored data.
14. Click [Finish] to start the restore operation.

Figure 14-11 Selecting items to be restored

Opens Backup File Name dialog box to specify the path and file name of the backup file you want to catalog

Select the file or folder that you want to restore

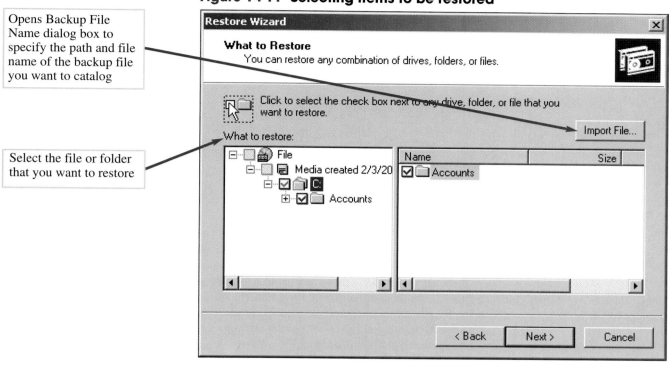

Prevents the restored data from overwriting existing data

Used when you want the restored data to overwrite existing data if the existing data is older than the backup copy; preserves the changes you have made to the file

Figure 14-12 Selecting options for restoring data

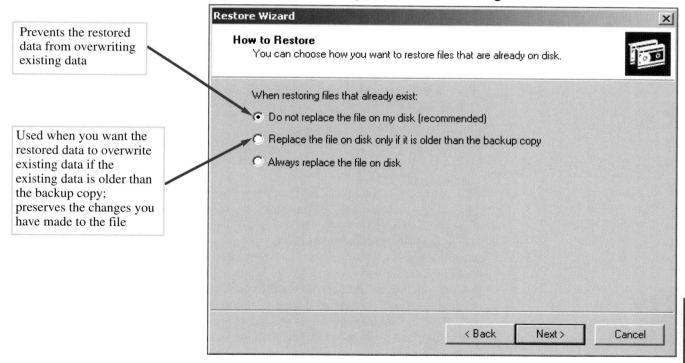

skill 4

Restoring Data from a Backup (cont'd)

exam objective

Recover system state data and user data by using Windows Backup.

how to

15. The **Enter Backup File Name** dialog box asks you to specify the path for the backed-up file that you want to restore. The **C:\accountfolderbackup.bkf** path is entered by default in the **Restore from backup file** text box (**Figure 14-13**).
16. Click [OK]. The **Selection Information** dialog box opens. Depending on the amount of data you have selected to back up and the efficiency of your hardware, this screen may appear only briefly or for a more extended period.
17. Next, the **Restore Progress** dialog box opens showing the status of the operation, the estimated and actual amount of data being restored, the time that has passed, and the time left until the operation is complete (**Figure 14-14**).
18. When, the operation is complete, you can click [Report...] in the Restore Progress dialog box to view information on the restore process. The restore log, which will open in Notepad, shows the number of files that have been restored, the duration of the restore process, the total size of the files restored, the start and end time for the restore operation, the backup destination, and the media type and label. This information will be appended to the backup log. The report log can prove useful at a later date to confirm what files were restored (**Figure 14-15**).
19. Click [Close] to close the Restore progress dialog box. Close the Backup window.

more

The [Advanced...] button on the **Completing the Restore Wizard** screen can be used to display the **Where to Restore** page. Here, you can choose from the following options:

◆ **Original location:** This option is used to replace the original data, which is now corrupted or lost, with the restored data.

◆ **Single folder:** This option is used to recover backed up data in a single separate folder without retaining the directory structure of the backed up files and folders. You can specify the path of the folder in the **Alternate location** text box.

◆ **Restore security:** This option is used to restore all the original security settings including the permissions, audit entries, and file ownerships. However, this applies only if you have backed up data from a Windows 2000 NTFS volume and you are restoring it to a Windows 2000 NTFS volume.

◆ **Restore Removable Storage database:** This option is used to restore the Removable Storage database. You only need to select this if you are using Removable Storage to manage your storage media. It will restore the Removable Storage database to **%systemroot%\System32\Ntmsdata**, deleting the existing database. Removable Storage is a service used to manage your tapes and disks and storage devices, which applications can use to access and share media resources.

◆ **Restore junction points, and restore file and folder data under junction points to the original location:** This option is used to restore the junction points on your hard disk along with the data they refer to. If you do not select this option, the junction points will be restored, but you still may be unable to access the data they point to. Junction points are locations on a hard disk that point to data in another location. This can be another location on the hard disk or on another storage device. They are created when you create a mounted drive, so you must always select this option when you are restoring a mounted drive. Mounted drives are drives attached to an empty folder on an NTFS volume that are assigned a label or name rather than a drive letter.

Figure 14-13 Specifying the name for the file to be restored

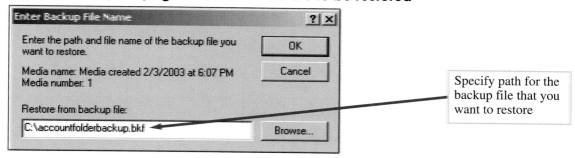

Specify path for the backup file that you want to restore

Figure 14-14 The progress of the restore operation

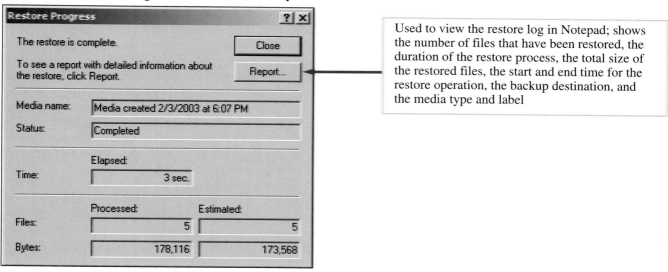

Used to view the restore log in Notepad; shows the number of files that have been restored, the duration of the restore process, the total size of the restored files, the start and end time for the restore operation, the backup destination, and the media type and label

Figure 14-15 The Backup/Restore log

skill 5

Changing the Default Backup and Restore Options

exam objective

Basic knowledge

overview

You can change the default settings for all backup and restore operations in the **Options** dialog box for the Backup utility. The tabs in the dialog box are:

◆ **General:** On this tab, you can change the default status information for the backup and restore processes, and send alert messages, verify data, and list the items being backed up by default. The **Compute selection information before backup and restore operations** option estimates the number of files and bytes being backed up and displays this information before the backup or restore begins. The **Verify data after the backup completes** option checks the backed-up data and the original data on your hard disk to make sure they are identical. If the data does not match, it indicates a problem with either the media or the file you are using to back up the data and you will need to use a different media or another file and run the backup again. If you often back up data on a mounted drive, you should select the **Back up the contents of mounted drives** option to make sure that the data, and not just the path information for the mounted drive, are backed up. The **Show alert message when I start Backup and Removable Storage is not running** option is used when your main backup medium is tape or other media that you use Removable Storage to manage. If you primarily use some kind of removable disk or if you back up data to a file or a hard disk, you do not need to select this option.

◆ **Restore:** On this tab you can specify the default setting for how to replace existing files with restored files.

◆ **Backup Type:** On this tab, you can change the default backup type that will be chosen in the Backup Wizard.

◆ **Backup Log**: Here you can specify the amount of information you want to include by default in the backup log.

◆ **Exclude Files:** Here you can specify the files that you want to exclude from the backup process by default. You can exclude a type of file for a specific user or for all users for security purposes.

how to

Change the default backup type to **Differential**.
1. Open the **Backup** window.
2. Open the **Tools** menu and click the **Options** command to open the **Options** dialog box Click the **General** tab (**Figure 14-16**). Select the **Verify data after backup completes** check box.
3. Click the **Backup Type** tab (**Figure 14-17**).
4. In the **Default Backup Type** list, click the **Differential** backup type to select it.
5. Click [OK] to accept the changes. Close the Backup window.

more

The **Tools** menu in the **Backup** window also contains the **Backup Wizard**, **Restore Wizard**, and **Create an Emergency Repair Disk** commands. These commands will open the welcome screens for the Backup and Restore Wizards or the **Emergency Repair Diskette** dialog box, respectively. From here, you can proceed to create a backup, restore a backup, or create an ERD.

Figure 14-16 The Options dialog box

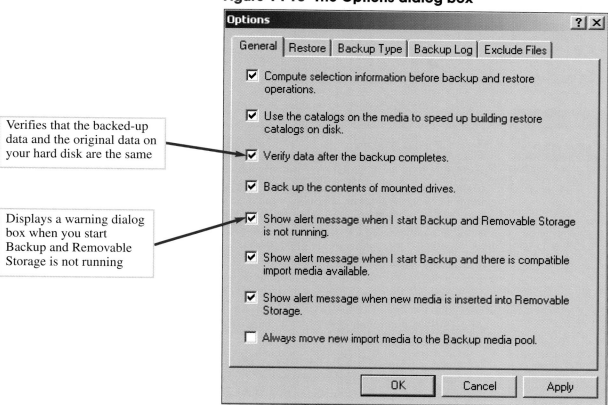

Verifies that the backed-up data and the original data on your hard disk are the same

Displays a warning dialog box when you start Backup and Removable Storage is not running

Figure 14-17 Selecting the Default Backup Type

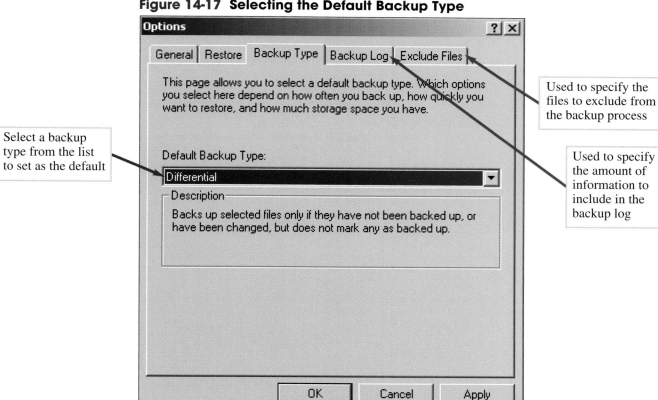

Used to specify the files to exclude from the backup process

Select a backup type from the list to set as the default

Used to specify the amount of information to include in the backup log

skill 6

Creating an Emergency Repair Disk

exam objective

Basic knowledge

overview

Unexpected circumstances can cause system files to be deleted or damaged, or become corrupt. The Backup utility is also used to create an **Emergency Repair Disk** (ERD), which will be used in such emergencies to repair and restart the operating system. An ERD should be created immediately following the successful installation of the operating system and updated whenever you change any part of the system configuration, such as adding a new device driver. The ERD cannot be used to boot a Windows 2000 system, but if you can boot the computer using the installation CD-ROM or the setup floppies you created using the Setup CD, you can use the ERD to begin the Emergency Repair process. The Emergency Repair process compares the system file **checksums** on the hard drive with the checksums on the ERD. Checksums are numerical values that are assigned to files based on their contents. If there are missing files or files that do not match because they are corrupt, you will be prompted to reinstall them from the installation CD. The Emergency Repair process can also be effective if you are receiving boot error messages indicating that the operating system is not found. This usually indicates a defect in the boot sector, which the ERD can fix.

tip

Before setting the option to back up the Registry, make sure that it will fit on the floppy; otherwise, it will not be backed up.

You create the Emergency Repair Disk in the **Backup** window **(Figure 14-18)**. You can create the ERD with or without the Registry. If you choose to include the Registry, the ERD will include the system files, the startup environment, the partition boot sector, and the Registry.

how to

Create an ERD that does not include the Registry.

1. Open the **Backup** window.
2. Click the **Emergency Repair Disk** button 🖫 in the **Backup** window to open the **Emergency Repair Diskette** dialog box.
3. The Emergency Repair Diskette dialog box prompts you to insert a blank floppy.
4. After you have inserted the floppy, click [OK] to start the ERD creation process **(Figure 14-19)**.
5. The Emergency Repair Diskette dialog box displays the progress of the operation.
6. After all the data is copied, the Emergency Repair Diskette dialog box indicates that the ERD has been successfully saved. You should label and date the diskette and store it in a safe location **(Figure 14-20)**.
7. Close the Backup window.

tip

You should select the Also backup the registry to the repair directory option. You may need a second floppy disk.

Figure 14-18 Creating an Emergency Repair Disk

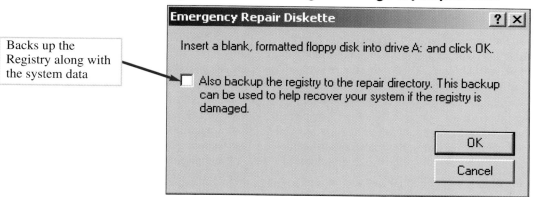

Backs up the Registry along with the system data

Figure 14-19 Copying the system data

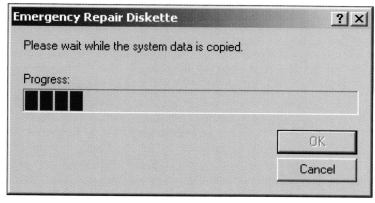

Figure 14-20 Successful creation of an ERD

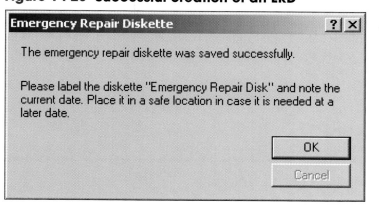

Summary

◆ You use the Backup Wizard to create copies of vital enterprise data that are either stored in a backup file on a different hard disk, a Zip or Jaz drive, or other removable storage media such as a CD-RW or other writable optical disk, or magnetic tape.

◆ Regular data backups ensure that a copy of the data is always present to replace the original damaged or lost data.

◆ The Backup Wizard in Windows 2000 Professional can be used to manually back up data or to schedule unattended data backups at regular intervals.

◆ There are five backup types from which you can choose: Normal, Copy, Incremental, Differential, and Daily.

◆ The archive attribute is a property for files and folders that is used to identify when they have changed. When a file has changed, the Archive attribute is automatically selected on the General tab in the Properties dialog box for the file.

◆ The archive attribute is used by some types of backups and not by others. Sometimes it is used to identify files that need to be backed up, sometimes it is removed to denote that a file has been backed up, and sometimes it is ignored.

◆ In a Normal backup, all selected files and folders are backed up whether they have the archive attribute or not; however, the archive attribute is removed to denote that the file has been backed up.

◆ Copy backups do not use the archive attribute. All selected files and folders with or without the archive attribute are backed up and the archive bit is not removed.

◆ An Incremental backup backs up only the selected files and folders that have the archive attribute, which is then removed. Thus, if a file has not changed since the previous backup, it will be skipped during the next Incremental backup.

◆ A Differential backup backs up only selected files and folders with the archive attribute, which is not removed. Therefore, even if a file has not changed since the previous Differential backup, it will be backed up again because it still has the archive attribute.

◆ Organizations use a blend of the different backup types in order to optimize the time spent on both the backup and the restore processes.

◆ If you create a backup schedule that uses a combination of the Normal and Differential backup types, you will only have to restore the last Normal backup and the last Differential backup.

◆ If you use a combination of Normal and Incremental backups, you will have to restore the last Normal backup and all Incremental backups in the interim. This will take less time to back up files than a Normal/Differential strategy, but more time to restore files.

◆ A backup set is the compilation of files and folders from one volume that you have backed up and stored in a file or on one or more tapes.

◆ The Restore Wizard uses the backup copies to recover data that has been lost or damaged.

◆ When the backup or restore operation is complete, you can view the backup and restore logs respectively in Notepad to view detailed information such as the number of files that have been backed up or restored, the duration of the backup/restore process, the total size of the files backed up or restored, the start and end time for the operation, the backup destination, and the media type and label.

◆ Unexpected circumstances can cause system files to be deleted or damaged, or become corrupt. The Backup utility is also used to create an Emergency Repair Disk (ERD), which will be used in such emergencies, to repair and restart the operating system.

◆ An ERD should be created immediately following the successful installation of the operating system and updated whenever you change any part of the system configuration, such as adding new device drivers.

◆ The ERD cannot be used to boot a Windows 2000 system, but if you can boot the computer using the installation CD-ROM or the setup floppies you created using the Setup CD, you can use the ERD to begin the Emergency Repair process.

◆ The Emergency Repair process can also be effective if you are receiving messages that the operating system is not found. This usually indicates a defect in the boot sector, which the ERD can fix.

◆ The ERD will include the system files, the startup environment, the partition boot sector, and the Registry if you choose to include it.

Key Terms

Archive attribute	Checksums	Incremental backup
Backup	Copy backup	Local backup
Backup log	Daily backup	Network backup
Backup set	Differential backup	Normal backup
Backup Wizard	Emergency Repair Disk (ERD)	Restore Wizard

Test Yourself

1. Which of the following statements is true?
   a. You can only backup data to the hard disk of a computer.
   b. You can back up files and folders, but not an entire disk.
   c. Only Administrators and Backup Operators can back up files.
   d. File or folder owners and users with the Write, Modify, or Full Control permission for a file or folder can restore files and folders.

2. Which of the following statements is true about the archive attribute? (Choose all that apply)
   a. The archive attribute is also called the backup marker or the archive bit.
   b. In a Normal backup, all selected files and folders are backed up whether they have the archive attribute or not, and the attribute is removed to denote that a file has been backed up.
   c. The archive attribute is used to mark files that have been modified since the last backup.
   d. In a Copy backup, all selected files and folders with or without the archive attribute are backed up and the archive attribute is removed.
   e. A Differential backup backs up all selected files and folders and the attribute is not removed.

3. In a Normal backup:
   a. All selected files/folders are backed up whether or not they have the archive attribute. The archive attribute is removed.
   b. Only the selected files/folders with the archive attribute are backed up. The archive attribute is removed.
   c. Only the selected files/folders with the archive attribute are backed up. The archive attribute is not removed.
   d. All selected files/folders are backed up whether or not they have the archive attribute. The archive attribute is not removed.

4. Which one of the following backup types clears the archive attribute?
   a. Daily
   b. Incremental
   c. Differential
   d. Copy

5. Which of the following statements is true?
   a. If you create a backup schedule that uses a combination of the Normal and Differential backup types, you will have to restore the last Normal backup and all Differential backups in the interim.
   b. If you use a combination of Normal and Incremental backups, you will have to restore the last Normal backup and the last Incremental backup.
   c. A Normal/Incremental backup strategy will take less time to back up files than a Normal/Differential strategy, but more time to restore files.

   d. A Normal/Differential backup strategy will take less time to back up files than a Normal/Incremental strategy, but more time to restore files.

6. You created a file on 5/8/2002 on the FAT partition of your system and backed up the file on 12/8/2002. A week later, you realize the file is corrupt and needs to be restored. While restoring the file, you have selected the advanced options of replacing the file on disk only if it is older than the backup copy, restoring security, and restoring removable storage database. Which one of the following actions can occur as a result of selecting these options?
   a. The restored file replaces the original file on the FAT partition.
   b. All the permissions given to the file originally are present even after the file is restored.
   c. The link to the remote path, and the data referred to, are restored on your hard disk.
   d. The restored file is created in a separate single folder on the same partition.

7. Susan has updated device drivers for several devices attached to her Windows 2000 Professional computer. She wants to update the Emergency Repair Disk. What tool will she use?
   a. makeboot.exe
   b. The ERD command line utility
   c. Winnt32/cmdcons
   d. The Windows 2000 Backup utility

8. Which one of the following statements is true about the Emergency Repair Disk (ERD)?
   a. When you create the ERD, the Registry files are backed up by default in the ERD creation process.
   b. The ERD contains only backup copies of the partition boot sector and all system files.
   c. Whenever the system configuration of a computer changes, the ERD should be updated.
   d. The ERD is created only once, immediately after the installation of Windows 2000 Professional on a computer.

9. You are the Network Administrator for a financial services company. Several key files that are updated on a daily or almost daily basis are stored on a share. The share and all of its subfolders total 3 gigabytes in size. You decide that since these files are so crucial, it is necessary to perform a backup every day. You want the backups to take the least amount of time possible, but you also want to be able to restore the files as quickly as possible in the event of a disaster. What backup strategy will you use?
   a. Incremental backups
   b. Differential backups
   c. Normal
   d. Normal and Differential

Projects: On Your Own

1. Back up the **My data** folder on the **C:** drive of your computer. Use the **Copy** backup type, verify the backed up folder for data integrity, and specify the backup label as **backup of my data**.
   a. Open the **Backup** window.
   b. Initiate the **Backup Wizard**.
   c. Select the **Back up selected files, drives, or network data** option.
   d. Select the source folder that you want to back up.
   e. Set the default location as the destination of the backup media.
   f. Select the type of backup operation.
   g. Select the option for verifying the data after backup.
   h. Append the backup to the media.
   i. Specify the backup label.
   j. Set the backup time as **Now**.
   k. Complete the backup process.

2. Restore the folder **My data**. Select the alternate location **C:\Restored data** to restore the data.
   a. Initiate the **Restore** Wizard in the **Backup** window.
   b. Select the folder that you want to restore.
   c. Select the backup media from which you want to restore the file.
   d. Restore the desired folder.
   e. Specify the alternate location where you want to restore the data.

   f. Accept the default option of always replacing the file on disk with the restored file.
   g. Clear all the checkbox options pertaining to the advanced restore options.
   h. Complete the restoration process.

3. While specifying backup and restore options, in the **Options** dialog box, set the default backup type as **Daily**. Also, set options to always verify the data after the backup operation is completed and show detailed information in the log files.
   a. Open the **Options** dialog box in the **Backup** window.
   b. Select the option for verifying the data after completion of backup.
   c. Set the backup type.
   d. Select the option to view detailed information in the log file.
   e. Confirm the changes.
   f. Close the dialog box.

4. Create an **Emergency Repair Disk (ERD)** on a blank formatted floppy disk and include the Registry as part of the ERD creation process.
   a. Open the **Emergency Repair Diskette** dialog box in the **Backup** window.
   b. Select the option for including the registry in the backup.
   c. Insert a blank formatted floppy.
   d. After creating the ERD, specify a name and the date of creation of the ERD on the floppy disk label.

Problem Solving Scenarios

1. Blackmun's Coffee is an importer of Latin American coffee beans to the United States. Located in Baltimore, Blackmun's has 32 workstations on a Windows 2000 network. You have recently been hired as the Information Systems Administrator. You have discovered that the company has no backup policy, and it is left up to individuals to backup and secure their data. The Accounting department seems particularly vulnerable because its computers store all the financial information for the company. You have decided to implement a firm-wide back up policy. You would also like to backup system data on all the clients. Since the amount of data is quite large, you want an inexpensive external source to store this data, and reduce load on your hard disk. Explain in a memo how you would implement a regular backup of all the company's important data.

15 Working with the Registry and Boot Process

The Registry is a database that stores information that Windows 2000 uses to monitor the software and hardware configurations on a computer. Everything from display settings to NIC settings, user profiles, group policies, and hardware profile information is stored in the Registry. The Registry is crucially important to the operation of the operating system, functioning in the areas of security, file location, remembering user preferences, tuning parameters, and device configuration. For instance, when you make changes to the display settings on your desktop or add new hardware to your computer, Windows 2000 Professional stores the display settings or the settings for the new drivers in the Registry. When the operating system or an application you are running malfunctions, you may be able to use the Registry to remedy the problem.

The Registry is organized in a hierarchical structure, which you can view with either of the two Registry Editors, regedit.exe or regedt32.exe. As with Windows Explorer, you use the plus sign buttons to expand the hierarchical tree to display more branches in the tree. You can also use the Registry Editor to edit information in a Registry file. After you make changes in the Registry Editor, they are automatically saved and applied immediately.

The settings in the Registry file are read during the boot process (the process followed by a computer as it starts). When you are booting your computer and any type of problem occurs that prevents the operating system from starting, you can try to use the Last Known Good Configuration, which is stored in the Registry, to resolve the problem. As its name indicates, the Last Known Good Configuration contains settings saved in the Registry the last time a user successfully logged on to the computer. You can also try to boot the computer in Safe Mode. When you start up in Safe Mode, only the basic drivers and files are loaded and the Registry is activated. You can use Safe Mode to remove corrupt drivers, fix driver conflicts, or uninstall and reinstall applications to resolve possible autostart difficulties. If Safe Mode and the Last Known Good Configuration do not work, you can try the Recovery Console. The Recovery Console enables you to start the operating system when all else has failed. It provides you with a set of administrative command-line tools that can be used to repair your Windows 2000 Professional installation.

Goals

In this lesson, you will learn about the Registry and its components and how the Registry is edited. You will also learn about the boot process, control sets, and the various advanced boot options that can be used to troubleshoot and correct problems.

Lesson 15   Working with the Registry and Boot Process

Skill	Exam 70-210 Objective
1. Introducing the Registry	Basic knowledge
2. Identifying the Components of the Registry Structure	Basic knowledge
3. Working with the Registry Editor	Basic knowledge
4. Working with Control Sets	Basic knowledge
5. Introducing the Boot Process	Basic knowledge
6. Identifying Advanced Boot Options	Troubleshoot system restoration by using Safe Mode.
7. Modifying the Boot.ini File	Basic knowledge
8. Using the Recovery Console to Troubleshoot and Recover Tasks	Recover system state data and user data by using the Recovery Console.

Requirements

To complete this lesson, you will need a Windows 2000 Professional computer and administrative rights on the computer.

skill 1

Introducing the Registry

exam objective

Basic knowledge

overview

When you configure or change the settings on your computer, most of the information related to the hardware and software settings is stored in a database on your computer called the **Registry**. For example, if you change the color settings, screen saver, or wallpaper, these changes are saved in the Registry. However, although the Registry looks like a single database when you view it in the Registry editor, settings are stored in several different files, mainly C:\windows\system32\Config, and profile folders in C:\Documents and Settings. The Registry stores all of the information related to the configuration of the software and hardware devices on a computer. The information stored in the Registry can be divided into the following basic categories:

◆ **User Profiles:** When you customize your desktop environment, which includes the various display settings, network and printer connections, and other specified settings, the information is first copied to the Registry and then to the user profile. This information is recreated each time you boot your computer.

◆ **Device Drivers:** Device drivers use the data in the Registry to configure the hardware peripherals attached to a computer. They also provide information to the Registry about the system resources, which are currently used by the drivers.

◆ **Setup programs:** When you install a program on a computer, the configuration data for the program is added to the Registry and the setup program can search the Registry to find out if the necessary components have been installed.

◆ **Hardware Profiles:** If a computer has multiple hardware configurations, different hardware profiles are created for each configuration. Hardware profiles contain information about the devices that must be started when the computer is booted up and the settings with which the devices will be started. Hardware profiles are updated in the Registry. **(Figure 15-1)**.

◆ **General System Configuration:** Control panel parameter configuration and information about all services that are installed on the computer are also stored in the Registry. This includes what services are installed, the services they are reliant upon, and the order in which the services should be initiated.

◆ **Applications:** Configuration data on all software in use on the computer is stored in the Registry.

◆ **Network Protocols and NIC settings:** NIC settings stored in the Registry include the IRQ (Interrupt request) number, memory base address, I/O channel ready, I/O port base, address, and transceiver type.

You view the information in the Registry using the **Registry Editor**. You can also use the Registry Editor to modify the configuration information. To access the Registry Editor window, you can use either the **regedit.exe** command or **regedt32.exe** in the **Run** dialog box **(Figure 15-2)**. Regedit is used to access the Windows 9.x version of the Registry Editor and Regedt32 is used to access the Windows NT version. Regedit has a Windows 9.x style interface and you can view the entire Registry in one window, while Regedt32 has separate windows for each key root. Regedit has more expansive search capabilities. You can search almost the entire Registry using key names, value names, and value contents, while in Regedt32 you can only search by key names. However, Regedt32 is considered to be the more secure of the two because you can open it in Read-only mode so that changes that could result in disruption to the system cannot be accidentally committed. Regedt32 also supports access control and auditing and is the recommended Registry Editor for Windows 2000.

caution

Incorrectly modifying the Registry can have serious results, including making the computer completely non-functional. Therefore, you should always back up the Registry before making any changes.

Figure 15-1 The HKEY_CURRENT_CONFIG root key in Regedit

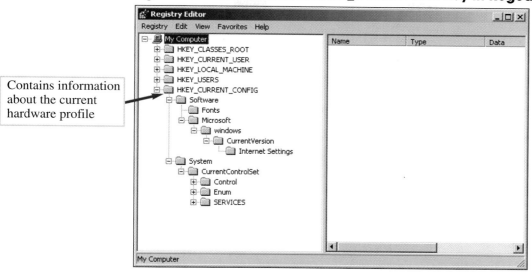

Contains information about the current hardware profile

Figure 15-2 The structure of the Regedt32 Registry

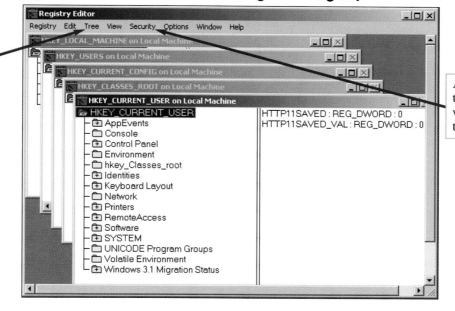

Select between the tree and data views

Assign permissions to determine who will have access to the Registry key

<table>
<tr><td>

skill 2

</td><td>

Identifying the Components of the Registry Structure

</td></tr>
<tr><td>

exam objective

</td><td>

Basic knowledge

</td></tr>
<tr><td>

overview

</td><td>

When you open the Registry Editor window, the data is organized in a hierarchical tree format. Regedt32 displays the five root keys in separate windows. The root keys, also called **subtrees** or **subtree keys**, are the primary nodes in the Registry structure. Root keys are similar to root folders on a disk. They store other keys and values just as the root folder stores other folders and files. The five root keys in the Registry are displayed in **Figure 15-3** and are outlined below:

</td></tr>
</table>

- **HKEY_LOCAL_MACHINE:** This subtree contains the configuration data for the installed hardware and software and the operating system. It does not change, regardless of what user is logged on to the computer. Data includes the startup parameters, and the drivers that will be used. The keys in the HKEY_LOCAL_MACHINE subtree are described in **Table 15-1**.

- **HKEY_CLASSES_ROOT:** This subtree contains information about the file types that are associated file extensions in Windows Explorer so that the correct application will be used to open a file. For example, a .bmp file is associated with the Paint program, an .mdb file with Access, and an .xls file with Excel. This key is copied from the HKEY_LOCAL_MACHINE/Software/Classes subkey and is not necessary for the operation of Windows 2000, but rather is preserved for compatibility with older programs and device drivers.

- **HKEY_USERS:** This subtree contains information about the default user profile settings on a computer. It does not pertain to any particular user, but rather is the container for profiles for all users who have ever logged on to the computer as well as the default user profile. This key is rebuilt each time the computer boots using the default user profile and either Ntuser.dat or Ntuser.man.

- **HKEY_CURRENT_USER:** This subtree contains information about the profile of the user who is currently logged on to a Windows 2000 Professional computer. The data in this key is copied from the relevant subkey in the HKEY_USERS key when a particular user logs on.

- **HKEY_CURRENT_CONFIG:** This subtree contains information about the hardware profile that is currently in use and it is used when you boot up the computer so that the correct device drivers are loaded and the appropriate system settings are configured. This key is also preserved for compatibility with older programs and device drivers. It is the same data that is now stored in the HKEY_LOCAL_MACHINE\System\CurrentControlSet\Hardware Profiles\Current subkey.

- ◆ **Keys:** In the Registry structure hierarchy, keys are like folders on a hard disk. They are simply containers in which other keys and values are stored, and they are displayed as folders in the left pane of the Registry window. Keys correspond to hardware or software objects and the information is stored in sections. For example, the HKEY_LOCAL_MACHINE subtree expands to display five **subkeys**: Hardware, SAM,

Table 15-1 Subkeys in the HKEY_LOCAL_MACHINE Subtree

Hardware	Contains the configuration information about the physical devices attached to a computer, such as network cards and CD drives. This key is recreated each time you boot the computer.
SAM	SAM, or Security Accounts Manager, contains data related to the local security database of the computer. It defines the user account and group membership for a computer.
Security	Contains information about the security policies on the computer. It defines the control parameters, such as password and user rights.
Software	Contains information about the software installed on the computer, and the mapped file extensions.
System	Contains information that is required to boot a Windows 2000 computer. This information includes the startup parameters, loading order for device drivers, and behavior of the operating system.

Figure 15-3 The five root keys in the Registry

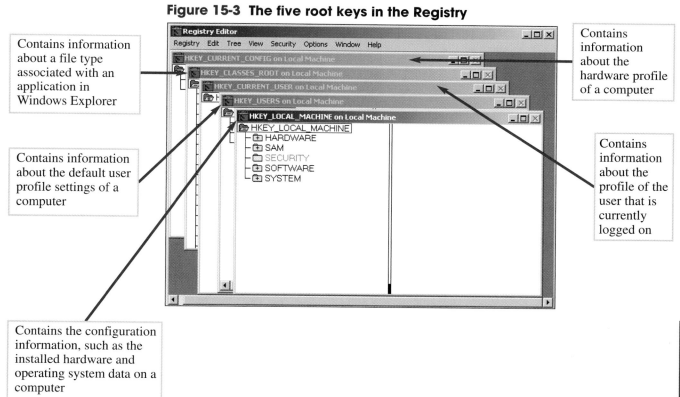

Contains information about a file type associated with an application in Windows Explorer

Contains information about the default user profile settings of a computer

Contains the configuration information, such as the installed hardware and operating system data on a computer

Contains information about the hardware profile of a computer

Contains information about the profile of the user that is currently logged on

skill 2

Identifying the Components of the Registry Structure *(cont'd)*

exam objective

Basic knowledge

overview

Security, Software, and System. These subkeys are further divided. For example, the System subkey is divided into the subkeys ControlSet001, ControlSet002, etc., which are used for setting the computer configuration **(Figure 15-4)**. **Values** or **value entries** are the extremities of the tree. They are the endpoints of a Registry path that serve as parameters to control the configuration settings **(Figure 15-5)**. Value entries are composed of a name, a data type, and a value.

- **Name:** The name looks like a capitalized multi-word phrase without spaces, for example, AutoRestartShell or CurrentUser.
- **Data type:** The data type determines the format, such as string, binary, or numerical, in which the value will be stored in the Registry. The data types supported by Windows 2000 Professional are explained in **Table 15-2**.
- **Value:** The value is the actual data in the currently selected subkey. The value may be a single binary digit, a string of ASCII characters, or hexadecimal values.

Hive: A hive is a distinct group of keys, subkeys, and value entries with its own Registry file and .LOG file. By default, most hive files are stored in the %systemroot%\System32\Config folder.

Figure 15-4 The HKEY_LOCAL_MACHINE root key and subkeys

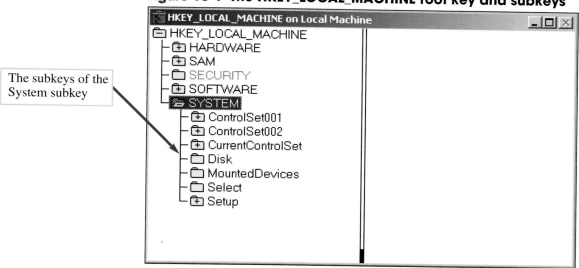

The subkeys of the System subkey

Figure 15-5 Value entries

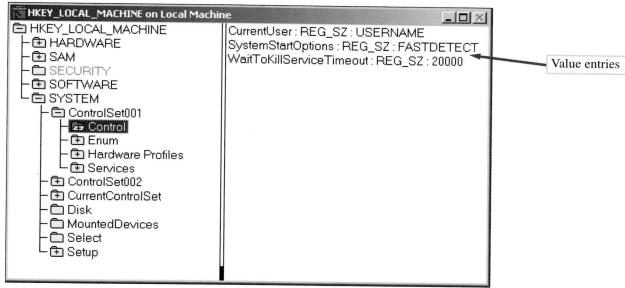

Value entries

Table 15-2 Data types supported by Windows 2000 Professional

Data Type	Description
REG_DWORD	Stores data in a binary or hexadecimal format. It is a four-byte binary value structured with 0x at the beginning and eight hexadecimal digits with no spaces.
REG_SZ	Stores data in string format. It is the most common type of value and it can include letters and numbers.
REG_EXPAND_SZ	Stores data in string format, which can contain replaceable parameters.
REG_BINARY	Stores data in hexadecimal format. It is a series of two-digit, base 16 (one byte) numbers that are divided with spaces.
REG_MULTI_SZ	Stores data as list of strings that contain values separated by null characters.

skill 3

Working with the Registry Editor

exam objective

Basic knowledge

overview

As a user, you might never need to use or even access the Registry on your computer. However, as an Administrator, it is important that you be familiar with the Registry and understand functions such as viewing, editing, backing up, and restoring the Registry. You can accomplish these functions using the Registry Editor. Both Registry Editors are automatically installed when you install Windows 2000 Professional. Microsoft recommends Regedit for searching, and Regedt32 for editing. Regedt32.exe is stored in the %systemroot%\System32 folder. As you make changes in the Registry Editor, these changes are automatically saved and applied immediately, and they cannot be undone. Read-only mode in the Regedt32.exe Registry Editor is recommended for viewing the Registry so that you will not be able to do any irreversible damage. The Registry and View menus contain useful commands that you can use to view and modify Registry information. Some of the commands on these menus are listed and described in **Table 15-3**.

how to

View the **SystemBiosVersion** in the Registry.

1. Click ![Start] and then click the **Run** command to open the **Run** dialog box.
2. Type **regedt32.exe** in the **Open** text box and then click [OK] to open the **Registry Editor** window.
3. Open the **Options** menu and click the **Read Only Mode** command to switch to read-only mode.
4. Open the **View** menu and make sure that the **Tree and Data** command is selected.
5. Maximize the **Registry Editor** window and then maximize the **HKEY_LOCAL_MACHINE on Local Machine** window.
6. Double-click the **HARDWARE** node and then the **DESCRIPTION** node to expand them.
7. Select the **System** subkey to view the information related to the **SystemBios (Figure 15-6)**.
8. Close the **Registry Editor** window.

caution

Making even a slight error while using the Registry Editor can lead to serious problems on your computer.

Table 15-3   Registry Editor commands

Command	Menu	Description
Save Key	Registry	This command saves the currently selected key and all the corresponding subkeys.
Restore	Registry	This command loads data in the selected file under the currently selected key.
Save Subtree As	Registry	This command saves the currently selected keys and all corresponding subkeys in a text file. You can then search for a newly added or modified value using a text editor.
Select Computer	Registry	This command opens the Registry of a remote computer on a network. You can modify remote access permissions for the operating system of a remote computer by creating the HKEY_LOCAL_MACHINE\SYSTEM\CurrentControlSet\Control\securePipeServers\winreg Registry key of the type REG_DWORD, with a value of 1.
Find Key	View	You can search the Registry for a specific key using this command. The search is limited to the subtree in which the search began. You can view the key names you searched for in the left pane of the Registry Editor.

Figure 15-6 Viewing the SystemBios values

Contains information related to the SystemBios and VideoBios

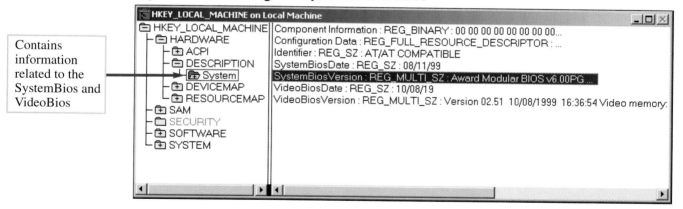

skill 4

Working with Control Sets

exam objective

Basic knowledge

overview

When you are booting a computer, certain configuration information, such as the startup parameters and a list of the installed device drivers and hardware components, must be accessed. This data is stored in **control sets**. The Registry will include more than one control set if you have changed system settings or experienced difficulties with your system settings.

The control sets are stored as subkeys in the **HKEY_LOCAL_MACHINES\SYSTEM** Registry key. The subkeys contain complete information about the boot process and the settings for the storage devices. The subkeys required for booting a Windows 2000 Professional computer are **ControlSet001**, **ControlSet002**, **CurrentControlSet**, and **Select**. The CurrentControlSet subkey points to one of the ControlSet00x keys.

The **Select** subkey contains value entries with the names: **Current**, **Default**, **Failed**, and **LastKnownGood**. The Current value entry lists the configuration that was used to boot the current session. If you make changes in the Control Panel or modify the Registry, you are changing the CurrentControlSet. The Default value entry contains the control set that will be used when you next boot up your computer, provided you do not choose Last Known Good Configuration on the Hardware Profile/Configuration Recovery or Windows 2000 Advanced Options menus. It is generally identical to the CurrentControlSet. The Failed value entry contains the control set that was unsuccessful the last time you started the computer, causing you to resort to the Last Known Good Configuration. Finally, the LastKnownGood value entry contains the control set that was saved after the last successful logon (**Figure 15-7**).

After every successful logon, an identical copy of the CurrentControlSet, which contains the data used for configuring the computer, is copied to the LastKnownGood value entry in the Select subkey. When you start your computer, there are two configurations that can be used: the **Default Configuration** or the **Last Known Good Configuration**. The configuration information that is saved when a computer shuts down normally is contained in the default configuration, and the configuration data that was saved after the last successful logon is saved in the Last Known Good Configuration. If your computer is configured for dual booting, you simply select Windows 2000 on the Please Select the Operating System to Start menu to choose the default configuration. Possible causes of startup failures which might instigate the use of the Last Known Good Configuration are:

◆ Incorrectly editing the Registry.
◆ Adding a new driver that is either not compatible with your hardware or is defective.
◆ Disabling a critical device driver (such as the SCSIPORT driver).

more

The Last Known Good Configuration cannot help you to restart the computer if:

◆ There are corrupt or missing files.
◆ A new driver is copied onto an old driver that is still active, the configuration does not change and reverting to the Last Known Good Configuration will not help.
◆ There are any improper operating system modifications that are not related to the control set (for example, incorrectly configured user profiles or improper file permissions).
◆ A hardware device problem is occurring and you forget to choose Last Known Good Configuration, and then you successfully log on. When you make configuration changes, they are saved in the CurrentControlSet. When you reboot the computer, the kernel copies that information to what people often refer to as the CloneControlSet. The CloneControlSet information ultimately is stored in one of two Registry keys, either ControlSet001 or ControlSet002. On a successful logon, the location of the CloneControlSet is copied to the LastKnownGood value entry in the Select subkey. As such, when a user chooses to boot using the Last Known Good Configuration option, the computer looks to the LastKnownGood value entry in the Registry, and then boots using the ControlSet that it specifies.

caution

If you run into difficulties due to a configuration change on your computer and you forget to use the Last Known Good Configuration when you reboot, **do not** log on. The LastKnownGood value entry will be overwritten if you log on.

Figure 15-7 Value entries in the Select subkey

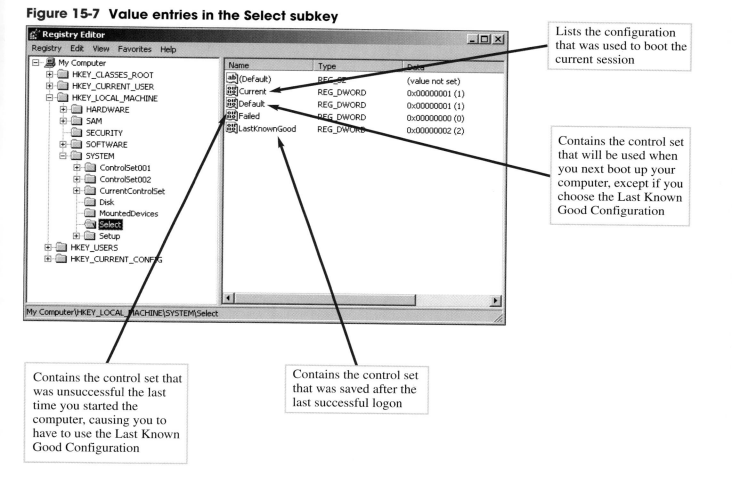

skill 5 | *Introducing the Boot Process*

exam objective   Basic knowledge

overview

When you start up a computer, the various configuration files and drivers are accessed in sequential order. This series of steps in which files are accessed is known as the **boot process**. Being familiar with the normal boot process will help you to understand the areas where things can be going wrong when startup fails. The boot process consists of the following phases:

◆ **Power-on Self Test (POST):** First, the computer runs the POST, which is a built-in diagnostic program that checks the hardware to ensure that the basic hardware components, such as the keyboard and the mouse, are present. POST also checks the amount of physical memory available on the computer **(Figure 15-8)**.

◆ **Startup:** Next, if the computer has a Plug and Play BIOS (Basic Input Output System), it locates the system board hardware devices. Then the BIOS finds the boot device and locates and runs the **Master Boot Record (MBR)**, which locates the boot sector on the active partition, loads the boot sector into memory and loads the hidden system file **Ntldr**.

◆ **Boot Loader:** Next, the **Ntldr** file (the boot loader) puts the CPU into 32-bit memory mode and loads the FAT and NTFS mini-file drivers so that the OS can be located and loaded from any type of partition.

◆ **Selecting the Operating System:** Ntldr then reads the **Boot.ini** file. If there are other operating systems on the computer, it is at this point that you will be asked to choose between them on the **Select the Operating System to Start** screen. If you choose a DOS-based OS, Ntldr must run **Bootsect.dos**, because this is where the boot sector for the previous OS is stored. If an alternative selection is not made, Ntldr loads the default operating system specified in Boot.ini.

◆ **Detecting the Hardware:** If you select Windows 2000, **Ntdetect.com** takes over. This utility performs most of the hardware detection functions, including distinguishing the Bus/adapter type and locating the parallel ports, SCSI adapters, video adapters, communication ports, floppy disks, keyboard, and the mouse/pointing device. The Ntldr utility compiles a list of the installed hardware components and later updates the Registry under the **HKEY_LOCAL_MACHINE\HARDWARE** key.

◆ **Selecting the Configuration:** At this point in the boot process, Ntldr takes over again and you will be asked to choose a hardware profile on the **Hardware Profile/Configuration Recovery** menu if more than one exists on the machine. You will also now be able to press **[L]** to choose the **Last Known Good Configuration**. This will start the computer using the Registry information that Windows saved after the last successful logon. If your computer is configured for dual-booting, you can also access the Last Known Good Configuration by pressing F8 when the **Select the Operating System to Start** screen displays to open the **Windows 2000 Advanced Options Menu**. Or, if your computer is not configured for dual-booting and it does not have multiple hardware profiles, you can press F8 at boot time when the Starting Windows text prompt appears to view the **Windows 2000 Advanced Options Menu**. You navigate on any of these menus using the arrow keys. If you do not select a hardware profile during the specified time period, the computer will start with the default hardware profile. If there is only one hardware profile configured on the computer, the Hardware Profile/Configuration Recovery menu does not appear and Windows 2000 Professional loads using the default hardware configuration.

◆ **Kernel Load Phase:** Next, as the Starting Windows 2000 screen opens, Ntldr loads the **Ntoskrnl.exe** and **hardware abstraction layer (Hal.dll)** utilities and the **control set**. Hal.dll contains code that interfaces the OS with the hardware devices. The control set, as you will learn, is simply a list of device drivers, services, and settings for the Registry key

caution

If the MBR is missing or corrupt, you will not be able to boot the computer.

tip

You can change the settings in the boot.ini file to change the default operating system or the amount of time the computer should wait before automatically loading the default operating system.

caution

The Last Known Good Configuration option will not solve problems caused by missing or corrupt drivers or files. Also, any changes made since the last successful startup can be restored only if the user has not logged on again and overwritten the old control set.

Figure 15-8 The POST screen

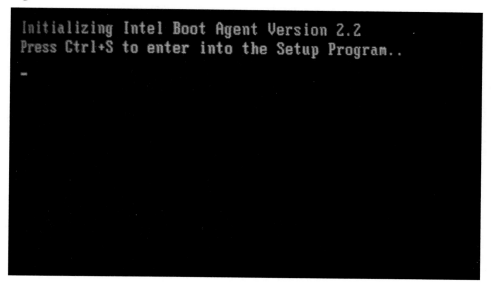

```
Initializing Intel Boot Agent Version 2.2
Press Ctrl+S to enter into the Setup Program..

_
```

Table 15-4 Files initiated during the boot process

File	Location	Function
Ntldr	System partition root	The Boot loader for Windows 2000 Professional computers.
Boot.ini	System partition root	Provides the boot menu information.
Bootsect.dos	System partition root	Provides the DOS boot information for computers that are configured for dual-booting.
Ntdetect.com	System partition root	Detects the hardware attached to the machine.
Ntbootdd.sys	System partition root	Allows Windows 2000 Professional to access the SCSI drive on a computer on which the onboard BIOS is disabled.
Ntoskrnl.exe	%systemroot%\System32	The kernel for the Windows 2000 Professional operating system (%systemroot% refers to the folder on the boot partition where the OS files are stored).
Hal.dll	%systemroot%\System32	The code for the hardware abstraction layer.
System key	%systemroot%\System32\Config	The key that contains the Windows 2000 Professional Registry data.
Device drivers	%systemroot%\System32\Drivers	The programs that allow the device drivers to communicate with the operating system.

skill 5

Introducing the Boot Process (cont'd)

exam objective

Basic knowledge

overview

tip

If errors are reported during the boot process, the System log can be checked for details after the boot process is complete.

HKEY_LOCAL_MACHINE\SYSTEM, which is loaded into the system from the *%systemroot %*\System32\Config\System file.

◆ **Kernel Initialization Phase:** Now, as the **Starting up** progress bar displays, **Ntoskrnl.exe (Figure 15-9)** creates the **HKEY_LOCAL_MACHINE\HARDWARE** Registry key, which contains information about hardware components on your computer. The kernel also creates something known as the CloneControlSet, which is an identical copy of the CurrentControlSet and contains the data used for configuring the computer. The CloneControlSet is ultimately stored in either the ControlSet001 or the ControlSet002 Registry key. After a user successfully logs on, the location of the CloneControlSet is copied to the LastKnownGood value entry in the Select subkey. The basic device drivers that were loaded during the boot loader phase are now initialized by the kernel and more device drivers are detected and loaded. If anything goes wrong when the drivers are loading and initializing, an error message is sent to the kernel. These messages are saved in the **System log**, which can be viewed in the **Event Viewer**. After the device drivers are loaded and initialized, the **Session Manager (Smss.exe)** starts the services. The Session Manager is responsible for creating the user-mode environment that provides the visible interface with Windows 2000 Professional. The set of instructions executed by the Session Manager is listed in **Table 15-5**.

◆ **Logon Process:** Finally, the logon dialog box is displayed as a result of **Winlogon.exe** and **Lsass.exe (Local Security Authority)** and a final last group of high-level services is started, including the Workstation service and the Server (File and Printer Sharing for Microsoft Networks) service. After logon, Windows 2000 Professional builds the new version of the Last Known Good Configuration.

Table 15-5   Instructions executed by the Session Manager

Instructions	Description
BootExecute data item	Executes the various commands mentioned in the BootExecute data item and then loads the various services. The BootExecute data item appears under the Registry KEY_LOCAL_MACHINE\SYSTEM\CurrentControlSet\Session Manager \BootExecute.
Paging file	Creates the paging file information that holds parts of programs and data files that do not fit in the computer's memory.
Symbolic links	Creates the symbolic links that direct some commands to the correct component in the file system.
Win32 subsystem	Starts the Win32 subsystem. The Win32 subsystem controls all I/O and access to the video screen.

Figure 15-9 Ntsokrnl in the System32 folder

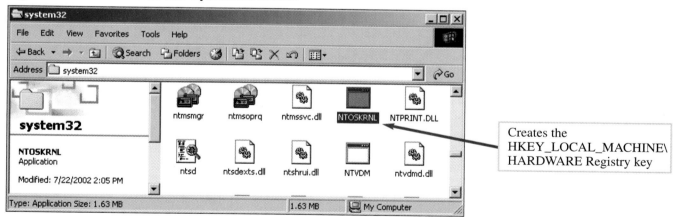

Creates the HKEY_LOCAL_MACHINE\ HARDWARE Registry key

skill 6

Identifying Advanced Boot Options

exam objective

Troubleshoot system restoration by using Safe Mode.

overview

If you are having trouble starting the operating system, you can also restart and press F8 when the **Starting Windows** progress bar is displayed. On the black screen, below the progress bar, a text prompt will indicate: **For troubleshooting and advanced startup options for Windows 2000, press F8**. When you press F8, the **Windows 2000 Advanced Options Menu** will appear. You can use the arrow keys on your keyboard to select from several **Safe Mode** commands. Safe mode is used to resolve problems that result from faulty device drivers, faulty programs, system service failures, or services that start automatically. When you boot in Safe Mode, the operating system will only load a basic set of files and drivers for the keyboard, mouse, basic VGA monitor, default system services, and disk. **Safe Mode with Networking** includes networking drivers and services if you must have network access to fix the problem, and **Safe Mode with Command Prompt** opens the command prompt instead of the **Graphical User Interface (GUI)** environment **(Figure 15-10)**. The other options on the menu are as follows:

Enable Boot Logging: This command will record the loading and initialization of drivers and services in the **Ntbtlog.txt log** file, which is located in the %windir% folder. Data pertaining to drivers and services that successfully load, as well as those that do not load or initialize, will be stored here, creating a constructive foundation for your troubleshooting efforts. This option is automatically enabled when you start the computer in any of the safe modes.

Enable VGA mode: This command boots the OS with only a basic VGA driver and is useful when your monitor display has been configured at a setting that your monitor does not support.

Last Known Good Configuration: This command starts the computer using the Registry information that Windows saved after the last successful logon.

tip

Safe Mode and Safe Mode with Networking also load the basic VGA driver, **vga.sys**.

how to

Start your computer in **Safe Mode** and restore the **Display settings**.
1. Shut down and restart your computer.
2. When the **Starting Windows** progress bar displays on the black screen, a text prompt at the bottom of the screen will indicate: **For troubleshooting and advanced startup options for Windows 2000, press F8**. Follow the prompt to open the **Windows 2000 Advanced Options Menu** screen.
3. Use the down arrow key to select **Safe Mode** and press the **[Enter]** key to open the screen showing a list of drivers used in the safe mode **(Figure 15-11)**.
4. Log on as an **Administrator** and press the **[Enter]** key.

Figure 15-10 The Advanced startup options

The advanced boot options available after pressing the F8 key while booting the computer

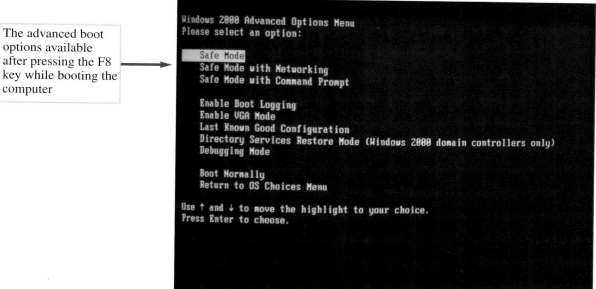

Figure 15-11 List of drivers loaded in Safe Mode

The drivers loaded in Safe Mode

skill 6

Identifying Advanced Boot Options
(cont'd)

exam objective

Troubleshoot system restoration by using Safe Mode.

how to

5. The **Desktop** dialog box informs you that Windows is running in the safe mode and that some devices may not be available **(Figure 15-12)**.
6. Click [OK] to continue with Startup. When Startup is complete, your desktop will be displayed with no wallpaper and Safe Mode will appear in all four corners of the screen.
7. Click [Start], point to **Settings** and click the **Control Panel** command to open the **Control Panel** window.
8. Double-click the **Display** icon to open the **Display Properties** dialog box.
9. Open the **Settings** tab where you can change the screen resolution.
10. Drag the **Screen area** slider to set it at **800 by 600** pixels **(Figure 15-13)**.
11. Click [Apply] to open the **Display Properties** dialog box, which informs you that the settings will be applied and the screen may flicker.
12. Click [OK]. After the monitor flickers, the **Monitor Settings** dialog box opens asking you whether you want to keep the settings.
13. Click **Yes**. The screen flickers again and the setting is loaded.
14. Close the Display Properties dialog box and the Control Panel.
15. Restart the computer.

Figure 15-12 Desktop in Safe Mode

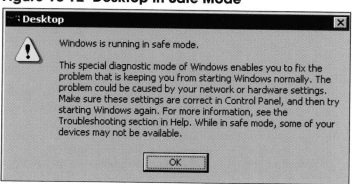

Figure 15-13 Changing the screen resolution

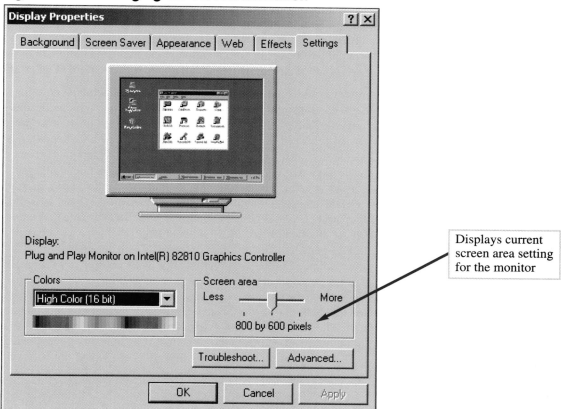

Displays current screen area setting for the monitor

skill 7

Modifying the Boot.ini File

exam objective

Basic knowledge

overview

tip

The **boot.ini** file, by default, contains the path to the default operating system.

The **boot.ini** file is created during the installation of Windows 2000 Professional and, as you have learned, it is accessed during the selecting the operating system phase of the boot process to find out if any other operating systems are stored on the computer. The boot.ini file is saved in the root of the system partition and it tells the computer what OS choices to display during startup. It is a hidden, read-only, system file with two sections, **boot loader** and **operating systems**, as explained in **Table 15-6**.

At this point, it is important to make the distinction between the system partition and the boot partition. The system partition is the disk volume that stores the files needed to boot the OS, Ntldr, boot.ini, Ntdetect, etc. The boot partition is the partition where the actual OS files (typically \Winnt) and the OS support files (typically \Winnt\System32) are stored. The boot partition can be the same partition as the system partition. (Refer back to Table 15-4.)

Boot.ini will generally not need to be modified, but you can use a text editor, such as Notepad, to manually change the boot.ini file if necessary. For example, you may want to change the "timeout" time period. This is the time you will have to choose between alternative operating systems on a dual boot system when the Please Select the Operating System to Start menu appears. There are also a number of switches you can append to the entries in the operating systems section to modify the boot process. In addition, the file attributes for boot.ini can be changed using My Computer or Windows Explorer. In order to edit the boot.ini file, you must use one of these utilities first to remove the Hidden and Read-Only attributes. Then you can either open the file in Notepad directly or use the command prompt to open it in Notepad. To use the command prompt, type **cmd** in the **Open** text box in the **Run** dialog box; then, at the command prompt, type **boot.ini**. You can also use the command prompt to remove the system, hidden, and read-only attributes by typing: **attrib –s –r –h boot.ini (Figure 15-14)**.

tip

Always create a backup copy of the **boot.ini** file before you modify it. Even minor errors in the boot.ini file can result in your computer not booting.

You might want to make other changes to the boot.ini file, including changing the default OS and changing the parameters for one of the listed operating systems. In this case, the term parameters refers to the particular features that will be used to start this Windows version. Sometimes when you add a controller or a hard disk, you may have to edit the **ARC path**. The term ARC path (Advanced RISC [reduced instruction set] Computing) refers to the path that points to a valid boot partition containing the Windows 2000 operating system files. As you will see when you open the boot.ini file, this path has four parts: multi, disk, rdisk, and partition. Multi tells the computer which disk controller to use–0, 1, 2 and so forth. Multi refers to an IDE disk controller or a SCSI type controller with BIOS enabled. There is also a special case in which the disk controller is SCSI without BIOS enabled and, in this case, you will see scsi (x) instead of multi (x). The disk part of the ARC path designates which disk to use on the disk controller indicated in the first section. If a SCSI controller without BIOS enabled is indicated, the disk portion will tell the computer what SCSI address to boot to on the disk. The disk value will always be 0 if the controller is multi. The rdisk component designates which disk to use on the disk controller indicated in the multi section. It will always be 0 if the controller is SCSI. The partition section designates which partition to use on the disk that was pointed to in the first two elements of the path, not including the zeros entered to nullify a possibility. (The disk partitions run from 1 upward. Zero would not be a valid entry here.) When you add switches, they are appended to the end of the ARC path.

Table 15-6   Sections of boot.ini file

Boot loader	Also known as Ntldr. Contains entries for the default operating system to be loaded, and the time that the computer should wait for an action from you before loading the default operating system. If the timeout is set to zero, Ntldr loads the default operating system as soon as the computer boots. If you want the computer to wait indefinitely for you to make a selection, set the timeout to –1. The computer will not boot unless you select an operating system and press the [Enter] key.
Operating systems	Contains entries for all of the operating systems installed on the computer. Each entry for an operating system contains the path to the boot partition for that operating system. The entry also contains the text that will appear on the boot loader screen.

Figure 15-14 Using the command prompt to remove file attributes

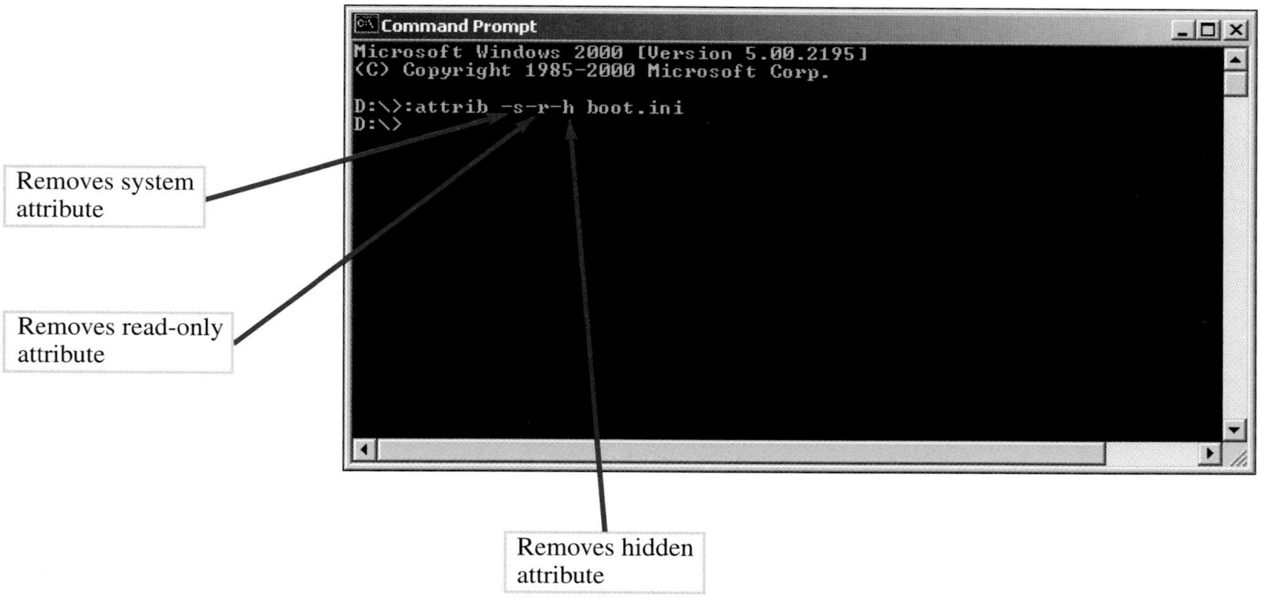

Removes system attribute

Removes read-only attribute

Removes hidden attribute

skill 7

Modifying the Boot.ini File (cont'd)

exam objective

Basic knowledge

how to

Edit the boot.ini file on your computer to remove the entry for the Windows 98 operating system.

1. Open **Windows Explorer**. Select the drive containing the boot.ini file (the drive where the operating system is installed).
2. Open the **Tools** menu and select the **Folder Options** command to open the Folder Options dialog box.
3. Open the **View** tab. In the **Advanced settings** box, under the **Hidden files and folders** icon, select the **Show hidden files and folders** option button.
4. Click   OK . Open the **View** menu and select the **Refresh** command.
5. Locate the boot.ini file in the Windows Explorer window. Right-click it and select the **Properties** command on the shortcut menu. On the **General** tab, in the **Attributes** section at the bottom of the dialog box, remove the check mark from the Read-Only check box. Click   OK .
6. Close Windows Explorer.
7. Click Start , point to **Programs**, point to **Accessories**, and click the **Notepad** command to open the **Notepad** window.
8. Open the **File** menu and select the **Open** command to open the **Open** dialog box.
9. Select the system root drive in the **Look in** list box to view the files and folders on the drive. For example, select the **C:** drive. If the boot.ini file does not appear in the Contents window, you can type boot.ini in the **File Name** list box and select the **All Files** option in the **Files of type** list box (**Figure 15-15**).
10. Select the **Boot.ini** file and then click   Open   to open the file (**Figure 15-16**).
11. In the Boot.ini file, select the text entry for Windows 98 under the **operating systems** section.
12. Press the **[Delete]** key to remove the entry.
13. Click the **Save** command on the **File** menu to save the configuration.
14. Close Notepad.

caution

Do not update the **boot.ini** file if you are unsure of the repercussions of the change. Always back up the boot.ini file before making any changes.

more

A few of the switches, which are predefined parameters that you can add to the operating systems section to provide additional functionality, are:

◆ **/basevideo:** Boots the computer using the standard VGA video driver. This is useful if you receive a message telling you that your video driver is missing or corrupt, or that an invalid driver was installed for the hardware.

◆ **/fastdetect=[com$x$ | comx,y,z.]:** Disables the detection of the serial mouse.

◆ **/maxmem:n:** Specifies the maximum amount of RAM used by Windows 2000 Professional. This is useful if you are trying to find out if you have a faulty memory chip.

◆ **/noguiboot:** Boots the computer without showing the graphical boot status screen.

◆ **/sos:** Displays the names of the device drivers as they load. This is a useful troubleshooting tool.

Figure 15-15 Opening boot.ini

Type boot.ini if the file name is not displayed in the contents window

Select All Files if you must type boot.ini in the File Name text box

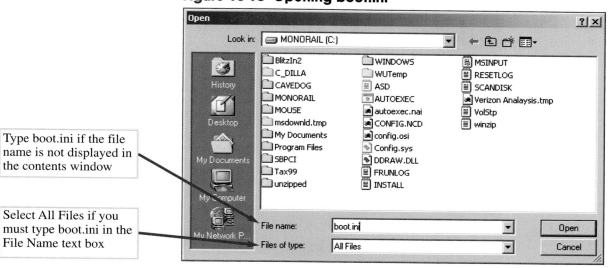

Figure 15-16 Editing boot.ini

The time that the computer should wait for an action from you before loading the default operating system

Tells the computer which disk controller to use (0,1,2) if it is either an IDE disk controller or a SCSI disk controller with BIOS enabled

Tells the computer what SCSI address to boot to on the disk if the disk controller is SCSI without BIOS enabled. This value will always be 0 if the controller is multi

Specifies which disk to use on the disk controller indicated in the multi section. This value will always be 0 if the controller is multi

Selects the disk partition that contains the operating system files

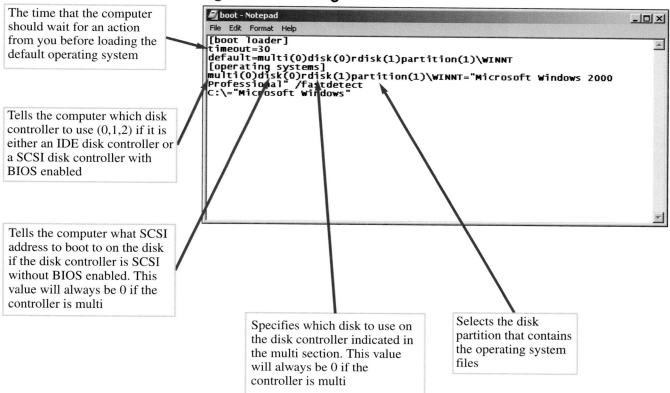

skill 8

Using the Recovery Console to Troubleshoot and Recover Tasks

exam objective

Recover system state data and user data by using the Recovery Console.

overview

If you are unable to fix boot problems using either Last Known Good Configuration or Safe Mode, the final tool you can turn to is the **Recovery Console**. It allows you to start the operating system when you cannot get it to start using the other methods. You can use the Recovery Console to stop the specific software or driver causing the problem. The Recovery Console does not start the Registry so you can use it to copy your Registry backup to C:\Winnt\System32\Config to restore the Registry. It is a command-line interface used to perform a variety of functions, including the following:

- Troubleshoot and recover tasks.
- Copy, rename, or replace operating system files and folders.
- Format hard disks.
- Repair the file system boot sector or the Master Boot Record (MBR).
- Read and write data on the local drive of your computer.

The Recovery Console provides you with a limited set of administrative commands that can be used to repair your Windows 2000 Professional installation. **Table 15-7** lists and describes a few of these commands.

You start the Recovery Console by booting your computer with a Windows 2000 Professional CD or from the Windows 2000 Professional Setup disks. Remember, you run the Makeboot.exe tool from the Bootdisk folder on the Windows 2000 CD-ROM, or Makebt32.exe if accessing the tool from within Windows 2000 to make the set of Setup floppy disks. Before deciding whether to start from a CD or floppy disks, you should first try booting the computer in the Safe Mode. The Recovery Console method is recommended only if you are an advanced user or Administrator who can use basic commands to identify and locate problems relating to drivers and files.

how to

Start the Recovery Console from the Windows 2000 Professional CD-ROM.

1. Insert the **Windows 2000 Professional CD** into the CD-ROM drive of your computer. You can also use the four Startup Disks to boot the computer.
2. Restart the computer and press **[Enter]** to start booting the computer from the CD. The computer will inspect the computer's configuration, load the relevant files, and open the **Setup Notification** screen. It takes a few minutes to load the files. If the Setup disks are used, the computer prompts you to insert disks.
3. Press **[Enter]** to open the **Welcome to Setup** screen.
4. Press **[R]** to select the **To repair a Windows 2000 installation, press R** option and open the **Windows 2000 Repair Options** screen.
5. Press **[C]** to activate the **Recovery Console**.
6. You will be asked which Windows 2000 installation you want; usually there will only be one installation. Type: **1**, and press **[Enter]**.
7. You will be prompted to log on using the Administrator password. Enter the password and press **[Enter]** to open a command prompt.
8. Type **Help**, and press **[Enter]** to view a list of the Recovery Console commands.
9. After you have reviewed the commands, type **Exit**, and press [Enter] to restart the computer.

Table 15-7   Recovery Console commands

Commands	Description
Attrib	Changes attributes of a file or folder.
Chdir (cd)	Displays the name of the current folder or enables you to change to a different directory by specifying the directory name.
Chkdsk	Checks and displays the status of a disk.
Cls	Clears the screen.
Copy	Copies a file to a given location.
Delete (del)	Deletes specific file or files.
Dir	Displays all the files and sub folders under a folder.
Disable	Disables a device driver or a system service.
Enable	Enables or starts a device driver or a system service.
Exit	Exits the recovery console and restarts your computer.
Fdisk	Manages partitions on your hard disk.
Fixboot	Writes a new partition boot sector on the system partition.
Fixmbr	Fixes the Master Boot Record of the system partition.
Format	Formats a disk.
Help	Displays the list of commands that can be used in the Recovery Console.
Logon	Allows you to log on to Windows 2000 installation.
Map	Displays the drive letter mapping.
Type	Displays the specified text file.
Mkdir (md)	Creates a folder.
Rename (ren)	Renames a file.
Rmdir	Removes a directory.
Systemroot	Sets the current folder to the system root folder.

Summary

- The Registry is a database that stores information that Windows 2000 uses to monitor the software and hardware configurations on a computer.
- The information stored in the Registry can be divided into several basic categories: user profiles, device drivers, setup programs, and hardware profiles, general system configurations, applications and network protocols and NIC settings.
- You view and modify the configuration information in the Registry using the Registry Editor.
- There are actually two Registry Editors included with Windows 2000 Professional, regedit.exe and regedt32.exe.
- To open them, you enter either regedit.exe or regedt32.exe in the Run dialog box.
- Regedit.exe is used to access the Windows 9.x version of the Registry Editor and regedt32.exe is used to access the Windows NT version.
- Regedt32 is considered to be the more secure of the two because you can open it in Read-only mode so that changes that could result in disruption to the system cannot be accidentally committed. Regedt32 also supports access control and auditing and is the recommended Registry Editor for Windows 2000.
- Regedt32 displays the five root keys in separate windows. The root keys, also called subtrees or subtree keys, are the primary nodes in the Registry structure.
- The root keys are: HKEY_CLASSES_ROOT, HKEY_CURRENT_USER, HKEY_LOCAL_MACHINE, HKEY_USERS, and HKEY_CURRENT_CONFIG.
- The root keys contain subkeys and values.
- Keys are like folders on a hard disk. They are containers in which other keys and values are stored, and they are displayed as folders in the left pane of the Registry window.
- Values or value entries are the extremities of the tree. They are the endpoints of a Registry path that serve as parameters to control the configuration settings.
- Value entries are composed of a name, a data type, and a value.
- A set of Registry files that contains keys, subkeys, and value entries is called a hive.
- When you start up a computer, the various configuration files and drivers are accessed in sequential order. This series of steps in which files are accessed is known as the boot process.
- The boot process consists of a set of distinct phases, starting with the Power-on Self Test (POST), which is a diagnostic tool that runs under the control of the BIOS (Basic Input/Output System).
- Next the BIOS finds the system board hardware devices and runs the MBR (Master Boot Record).
- The MBR locates the boot sector on the active partition and loads the Ntdlr file, which in turn puts the computer into 32-bit mode and loads the FAT and NTFS mini-file drivers.
- Ntldr then reads boot.ini to find out what operating systems are stored on the computer.
- After the OS is chosen, NTDETECT.COM detects most of the hardware.
- Ntdlr then presents a list of hardware profiles and the Last Known Good Configuration option.
- Ntoskrnl.exe and the HAL (Hardware Abstraction Layer) are then loaded, along with the control set and some low-level device drivers. This is the kernel load phase.
- In the kernel initiation phase, Ntoskrnl.exe builds the HKEY_LOCAL_MACHINES\HARDWARE Registry key, loads more drivers, and initializes the low-level drivers.
- Finally, the logon dialog box is displayed by using Winlogon.exe and Lsass.exe (Local Security Authority) and a final last group of high-level services is started, including the Workstation service and the Server (File and Printer Sharing for Microsoft Networks) service.
- When you are booting a computer, certain configuration information, such as the startup parameters, and a list of the installed device drivers and hardware components must be accessed. This data is stored in control sets.
- The control sets are stored as subkeys in the HKEY_LOCAL_MACHINES\SYSTEM Registry key.
- Windows 2000 Professional includes advanced boot options that you can use if you have problems booting your computer. These are: Safe Mode, Enable boot logging, Enable VGA mode, and Last Known Good Configuration.
- The boot.ini file is created during the installation of Windows 2000 Professional and contains information related to the operating system(s) installed on your computer.
- You can modify the boot.ini parameter values by accessing the System Properties program in the Control Panel. You can also edit the parameters manually using a text editor.
- Windows 2000 Professional also includes the Recovery Console, a command-line interface that can be used to perform a variety of troubleshooting and recovery tasks.

Key Terms

Advanced RISC Computing (ARC)
   path
Boot loader (Ntldr)
Boot process
Boot sector
Boot.ini
Control set
Enable boot logging
Hardware profile

Hive
Keys
Last Known Good Configuration
Master Boot Record (MBR)
Power-on Self Test (POST)
Recovery Console
regedit.exe
regedt32.exe
Registry

Registry Editor
Safe Mode
Session Manager (Smss.exe)
Subkey
Subtree
Systemroot
Timeout
Value entries

Test Yourself

1. When you boot up your computer, what is the first task that is executed?
   a. Ntldr gathers configuration information.
   b. The boot portion of the hard disk is located.
   c. The POST routines are executed.
   d. BIOS runs the MBR.

2. What is a control set?
   a. Configuration information, such as the startup parameters and a list of the installed device drivers, hardware components, and services that is stored in a Registry key.
   b. A record of the master boot.
   c. A file that contains the information about the operating systems installed on the computer.
   d. A file that detects hardware installed on the computer.

3. What happens when a computer is started in Safe Mode?
   a. The computer does not allow you to execute any application other than System Tools.
   b. Drivers and services for networking are added.
   c. The computer loads information saved in the Registry during the last shutdown.
   d. The computer loads only basic files and drivers.

4. When is the boot.ini file created?
   a. During the installation of Windows 2000.
   b. After kernel initialization.
   c. After the operating system is selected.
   d. When the Ntdetect and Ntoskrnl files detect hardware.

5. A hive is a component of the ___.
   a. Boot.ini file.
   b. Registry.
   c. Subtree.
   d. Control Set.

6. What kind of information does the subtree HKEY_LOCAL_MACHINE contain?

   a. Hardware and software configuration settings.
   b. User settings.
   c. File type to application mapping data.
   d. Currently active hardware.

7. Which of the following files detects the hardware installed on the computer during the boot sequence phase of the booting process?(Choose all that apply.)
   a. Boot.ini
   b. Ntldr
   c. Ntdetect.com
   d. Lsass.exe
   e. Ntoskrnl

8. What does the Master Boot Record (MBR) do?
   a. Locates the boot sector on the active partition, loads the boot sector into memory, and loads the hidden system file **Ntldr**(the boot loader).
   b. Checks the hardware to make sure that the basic hardware components are on the computer.
   c. Reads the boot.ini file to find out what operating systems are on the computer.
   d. Detects the hardware installed on the computer.

9. Under which of the following conditions can you use the Last Known Good Configuration to boot your computer?
   a. You have incorrectly edited the Registry and you are not able to reboot the computer.
   b. Any problem occurring in the computer due to a change in the user profiles.
   c. The drivers for a device are corrupted.
   d. Any change that was made before the last successful logon needs be reversed.

10. The Registry stores information related to the user and hardware profiles only.
   a. True
   b. False

Projects: On Your Own

1. View the **System Bios Version** in the Registry.
   a. Open the **Registry Editor** window.
   b. Access the **System** subkey in the **HKEY_LOCAL_MACHINE on Local Machine** window.
   c. View the information related to the **System Bios**.
   d. Close the **HKEY_LOCAL_MACHINE on Local Machine** window.
2. Start your computer in **Safe Mode** and change the **Display settings**.

   a. Open the **Windows 2000 Advanced options menu** screen and select the **Safe Mode** option.
   b. Log on as an **Administrator**.
   c. Open the **Control Panel** window.
   d. Open the **System Properties** dialog box.
   e. Modify the screen resolution to be **800 by 600** pixels.
   f. Accept the changes.

Problem Solving Scenarios

1. You have received a call from a person in your company saying that his Windows 2000 professional desktop system is no longer starting up. After discussing the situation, you discover that the screen goes blank during the initial boot process after he selects the operating system on his dual-boot system. You also discover that he recently installed a new NIC and a new VGA Driver. However, he failed to restart his machine after each installation although the system had prompted him to do so. Write down the steps you would take to diagnose and solve the problem.

2. One of the workstations on your network is configured for a dual-boot with Windows 98 and Windows 2000 Professional. The workstation user mainly uses Windows 2000 Professional, which is the default operating system for her machine. The user reports that recently the computer has been taking an inordinately long time to boot up. Now, she cannot boot it at all. When you go to the workstation, you find that you cannot boot to the Last Known Good Configuration or into Safe Mode, because the POST successfully runs, but then the boot process simply stops. Describe what you think the problem might be and outline the steps you will take to fix both the critical problem and the original secondary problem reported by the user. Include 2 methods for fixing the secondary problem and the specific command you will use to fix the critical problem.

16

Configuring Remote Access and Dial-Up Networking

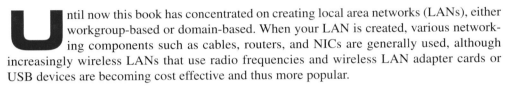

Until now this book has concentrated on creating local area networks (LANs), either workgroup-based or domain-based. When your LAN is created, various networking components such as cables, routers, and NICs are generally used, although increasingly wireless LANs that use radio frequencies and wireless LAN adapter cards or USB devices are becoming cost effective and thus more popular.

However, when you want to make long distance connections, the Public Switched Telephone Network (PSTN), also referred to as Plain Old Telephone Service (POTS) is accessed. The telephone system is a circuit switched network: it establishes a dedicated link from the caller to the receiver. Your local TCP/IP network uses dial-up networking or Remote Access Services (RAS) and virtual private networks (VPNs) to connect to this established infrastructure. For example, you might need to access resources on your PC or on your organization's LAN when you are traveling to another state or country, or you might want to make a resource on your computer available to a branch office or even to a single user in another city or state. Your employees might also need Internet access on your local LAN if you do not yet have a continuous connection, or they may need to access their e-mail while on the road. Network and Dialup software or Remote Access Services are used to connect to an ISP (Internet Service Provider) or to your company's network. Users dial in to a RAS server, connect to it through a modem, and the RAS server routes the connection to the LAN via a network interface card. Internet Connection Sharing (ICS) is used to share an Internet link with other computers on your LAN so that just one computer on the LAN functions as the gateway to the Web. This is particularly useful for small networks where it may not be feasible to have separate dial-up connections for different computers on a network.

Security is an important consideration when you access resources over a public network. In order to create secure connections, Windows 2000 Professional supports several protocols that provide security, authentication, and encryption for RAS connections. Virtual Private Networks (VPNs) are used to create secure connections over an untrusted public network. VPNs use tunneling protocols to create a secure tunnel within the public Internet through which the corporate LAN can be accessed.

Goals

In this lesson, you will learn how to use RAS to connect a Windows 2000 PC to a remote computer or a remote network. You will learn to configure both outbound and inbound connections, as well as how to share an Internet link using Internet Connection Sharing (ICS). You will also learn about the protocols that are used to enhance security and how to create a VPN.

Lesson 16 Configuring Remote Access and Dial-Up Networking

Skill	Exam 70-210 Objective
1. Introduction to the Protocols in Windows 2000 Professional	Basic knowledge
2. Configuring Outbound Connections	Basic knowledge
3. Creating a Dial-Up Connection to a Remote Access Server	Connect to computers by using dial-up networking. Create a dial-up connection to connect to a remote access server.
4. Connecting to the Internet by Using a Dial-Up Connection	Connect to the Internet by using dial-up networking.
5. Setting up a VPN Connection	Connect to computers by using a virtual private network (VPN) connection.
6. Configuring Inbound Connections	Basic knowledge
7. Configuring Internet Connection Sharing	Configure and troubleshoot Internet Connection Sharing.

Requirements

To complete this lesson, you will need a Windows 2000 Professional machine with a standard 56.6 Kbps modem and the TCP/IP protocol installed. It must also be configured with a static IP address.

skill 1

Introduction to the Protocols in Windows 2000 Professional

exam objective

Basic knowledge

overview

Remote Access Services (RAS) or Network and Dial-Up Connections software is used to extend your local network by enabling you to access the LAN from a remote location and by allowing you to access resources that are located on remote computers or on the Internet from the LAN. Connections between remote computers are established using RAS connections. The computer that establishes the RAS connection is called the **RAS client** and the computer with which the connection is established is called the **RAS server**. Every RAS connection has a RAS client and a RAS server.

When you create remote connections, the most important task is to prevent unauthorized users from accessing your resources. Windows 2000 Professional supports several protocols that are used in conjunction with TCP/IP to ensure the security of data transfers, either by encryption or authentication **(Figure 16-1)**.

◆ **Extensible Authentication Protocol (EAP):** EAP uses a negotiated authentication method to extend the logon security process using smart cards or certificates. It is an extension of the **Point-to-Point Protocol (PPP)**, which is used by Windows 2000 to ensure cross-functionality with other remote access software. PPP settles configuration issues between other networking protocols, including TCP/IP, IPX, and AppleTalk. When EAP is used to support smart cards or other certificate authentication, an authentication method that both the RAS client and the RAS server support is negotiated and agreed upon. For authentication, EAP uses generic token cards, Transport Level Security (TLS), and Message Digest 5 Challenge Handshake Authentication Protocol (MD5-CHAP).

- **Generic token cards** are physical cards that provide PIN numbers for authentication. These cards use codes that change every time the PIN is used so that the PIN cannot be easily decoded.
- **TLS** supports smart cards and certificates. It is composed of two layers: the TLS Record Protocol, which uses symmetric data encryption to ensure that connections are private, and the TLS Handshake protocol, which negotiates an encryption algorithm and cryptographic key before the application protocol can transmit or receive any data. Algorithms are mathematical formulas with a clearly defined end-point that are used to solve a particular problem. They can be written in any language from English to programming languages. Smart cards store user certificates and public/private keys that are used for authentication purposes in conjunction with a PIN number. Certificates are digital signatures that validate users and networks.
- **MD5-CHAP** uses a **Message Digest 5 (MD5)** algorithm to encrypt user names and passwords. MD5 is a hashing algorithm. Hashing algorithms transform data in such a way that the resulting data is unique and cannot be converted back to its original form. Hence, a client can be authenticated, without sending the password over the network.

When you use Extensible Authentication Protocol (EAP) to set up a smart card, the other protocols listed below (CHAP, MS-CHAP, PAP, and SPAP) are no longer available **(Figure 16-2)**. For a smart card, you only need EAP; the client and the server will negotiate the authentication method, for example, TLS (Transport Level Security).

- **Challenge Handshake Authentication Protocol (CHAP):** CHAP is a protocol that provides authentication on the basis of a value that is calculated using an algorithm. CHAP sends a challenge message to the client as soon as the client dials in. The client applies an algorithm to the message to calculate a hash value (a fixed-length number), and sends the value to the server. The server also calcu-

Figure 16-1 Protocols in Windows 2000 Professional

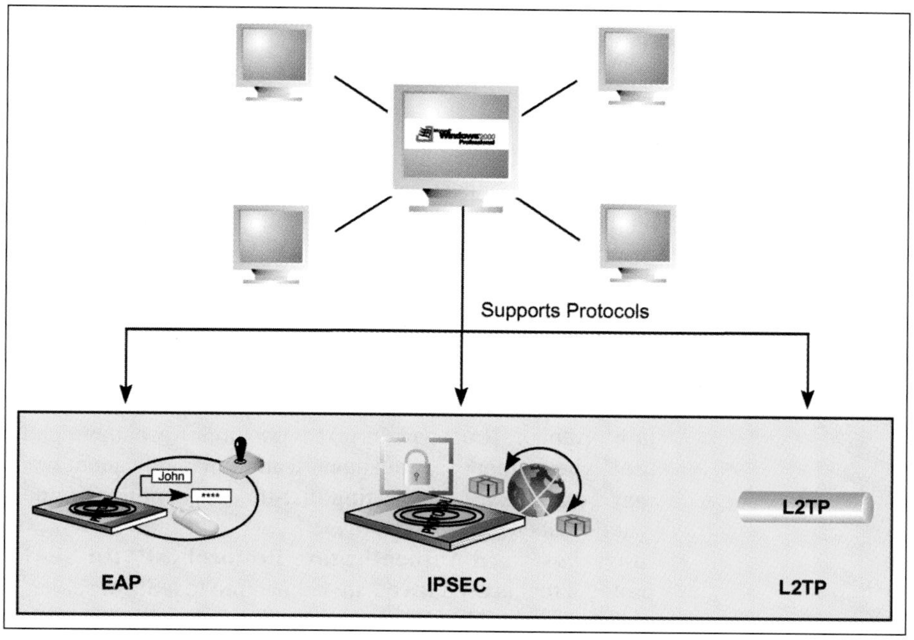

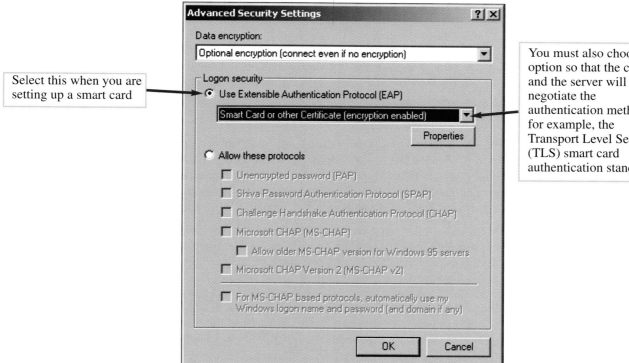

Figure 16-2 Setting up a Smart Card

Select this when you are setting up a smart card

You must also choose this option so that the client and the server will negotiate the authentication method, for example, the Transport Level Security (TLS) smart card authentication standard

skill 1

Introduction to the Protocols in Windows 2000 Professional *(cont'd)*

exam objective Basic knowledge

overview

lates a value and compares this value to the value sent by the client. If the value matches, the connection is established and the user can access shared resources on the server.

- **Microsoft CHAP (MS-CHAP):** MS-CHAP is Microsoft's version of CHAP. The challenge message is specifically designed for Windows operating systems and one-way encryption is used. MS-CHAP is used with Windows 9.x and NT and only the client is authenticated. In the extended version, MS-CHAP2, both the client and the server are authenticated.
- **Password Authentication Protocol (PAP):** PAP is the least secure authentication protocol. It uses plain text passwords for authentication. However, PAP is used when a more secure authentication method cannot be used and this protocol may be necessary for creating dial-up connections with non-Windows networks that do not encrypt passwords.
- **Shiva Password Authentication Protocol (SPAP):** SPAP is an authentication protocol that is used if you are connecting to a Shiva server. This protocol is more secure than PAP but less secure than CHAP or MS-CHAP. Data is not encrypted **(Figure 16-3)**.

◆ **Internet Protocol Security (IPSec):** This protocol ensures the secure exchange of data packets in the IP layer. IPSec is a set of security protocols that is widely used for VPNs. Data packets are encrypted in one of two ways: Transport mode or Tunnel mode. Transport mode encrypts only the data, while Tunnel mode encrypts both the data and the message header.

◆ **Layer Two Tunneling Protocol (L2TP):** Tunneling protocols create a virtual tunnel between two computers or networks connected across an untrusted communication channel. L2TP is an Internet Engineering Task Force (IETF) standard that provides security over untrusted IP links by creating a tunnel for the data, but it does not provide encryption.

caution

You need to use L2TP in conjunction with an encrypting technology such as IPSec to provide encryption as well as tunneling.

more

Windows 2000 Professional also supports **Bandwidth Allocation Protocol** (BAP), which is used to augment the use of multilinked devices. The term multilinked devices refers to combining several ISDN (Integrated Services Digital Network) lines or modem links to obtain greater bandwidth. (ISDN simply refers to the international data transfer format for sending voice, video, and data over digital telephone lines or normal telephone wires.)

Multilinking means that multiple physical links are combined to create one logical link. All of the links are pooled and the load is balanced among the physical connection components. BAP is used to dynamically add or drop links on demand so that only as much bandwidth as is required for the current network traffic is used. BAP dynamically provides optimum bandwidth and helps in reducing connection costs **(Figure 16-4)**. However, as the price of broadband decreases, multilinking will become increasingly less cost effective because the cost of extra phone lines and modems will exceed the cost of broadband access, which will yield many times the bandwidth.

Figure 16-3 Protocols used for remote connections

The least secure authentication protocol; uses plain text passwords for authentication

Used if you are connecting to a Shiva server; data is not encrypted

Provides authentication on the basis of a value calculated using an algorithm

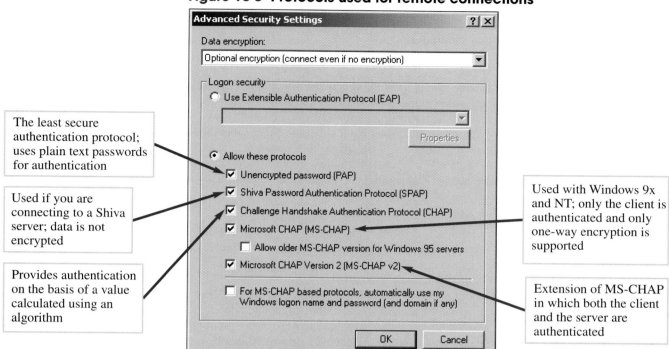

Used with Windows 9x and NT; only the client is authenticated and only one-way encryption is supported

Extension of MS-CHAP in which both the client and the server are authenticated

Figure 16-4 Configuring BAP options

Select multiple devices on the General tab in the Properties dialog box for a connection to configure a multilink connection. On the Options tab, select Dial devices only as needed in the Multiple devices section and click Configure. This is the dialog box you will then see; it will allow you to set these options so that Windows can dynamically add or drop links

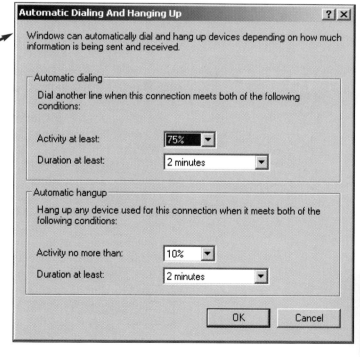

skill 2 | *Configuring Outbound Connections*

exam objective

Basic knowledge

overview

All connections in Windows 2000 Professional are configured in the Network and Dial-up Connections window. **Outbound connections** are used to dial out and connect to another computer or network, and **inbound connections** are used so that other computers can connect to yours via phone line, the Internet, or direct cable. You can use the **Network Connection Wizard** to set up and configure both outbound and inbound connections. In the Network Connection Wizard, you select the type of connection you want to configure depending upon your needs **(Figure 16-3)**. For outbound connections, you will choose from the following three types:

◆ **Connections to a private network:** These are connections using a regular or ISDN modem to a private network that are established by dialing in to a RAS server. A private network is a **Local Area Network** (LAN) of any organization.

◆ **Connections to the Internet:** These are connections from a computer to the Internet through a modem or an ISDN line.

◆ **Connections to a Virtual Private Network (VPN):** These are connections to private networks, such as a LAN, through an untrusted public network. These connections use tunneling and encryption protocols to create a virtual tunnel over an untrusted network, such as the Internet, to exchange information securely.

You can also use the **Connect directly to another computer** option to establish a physical connection to another computer using a serial, parallel, or infrared port. Next, you must specify whether you want your computer to act as the host or the guest. Shared resources are stored on host computers, while guest computers need to access the shared resources on the host.

how to

Set up a guest computer and establish a remote connection from another computer. Assign the name **Shared1** to the connection.

1. Click **Start**, point to **Settings**, and click the **Network and Dial-up Connections** command to open the **Network and Dial-up Connections** window.
2. Double-click the **Make New Connection** icon to open the **Network Connection Wizard**.
3. Click **Next >** to open the **Network Connection Type** screen.
4. Select the **Connect directly to another computer** option button **(Figure 16-5)**.
5. Click **Next >** to open the **Host or Guest** screen **(Figure 16-6)**.
6. Select the **Guest** option button to specify that the computer is to act as a guest.
7. Click **Next >** to open the **Select a device** screen.
8. Select the device that is to be used for the connection. For example, select **Direct Parallel (LPT1)** if you want to use the parallel port on the computer.
9. Click **Next >** to open the **Connection Availability** screen.
10. Select the **For all users** option button **(Figure 16-7)**.
11. Click **Next >** to open the **Completing the Network Wizard** screen.
12. Indicate a name for the connection in the **Type the name you want to use for this connection**: text box, for example, type **Shared1**.
13. Click **Finish** to save the settings and close the Network Connection Wizard.
14. The **Connect** window opens automatically. Close it.

Figure 16-5 Selecting the type of network connection

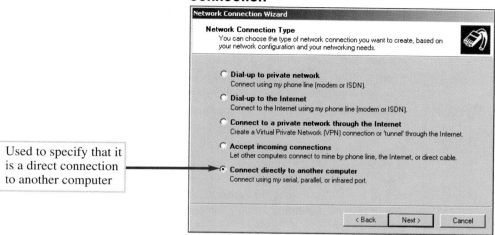

Used to specify that it is a direct connection to another computer

Figure 16-6 Selecting a role for the computer

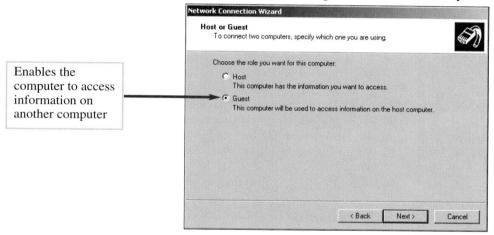

Enables the computer to access information on another computer

Figure 16-7 Setting connection availability to all users or only yourself

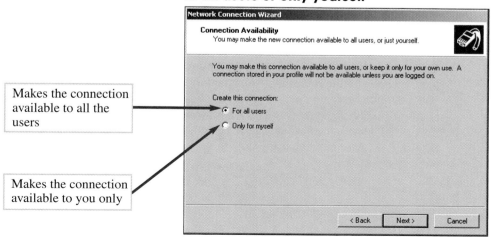

Makes the connection available to all the users

Makes the connection available to you only

skill 3

Creating a Dial-Up Connection to a Remote Access Server

exam objective

Connect to computers by using dial-up networking. Create a dial-up connection to connect to a remote access server.

overview

RAS can be used to make a connection to a local area network (LAN) from a remote location. For example, if you are traveling to another city as part of your job and you need to access resources on your office computer, you can do so using RAS.

You can configure a Windows 2000 Professional computer as a RAS client so that it can dial out to the RAS server, or you can configure a Windows 2000 Professional computer to be the RAS server to which other computers will connect using dial-up. RAS clients connect to a RAS server using a configured access device, such as a modem. Modems change outgoing digital signals from a computer into analog signals that can be transmitted over wires, and they transform incoming analog signals into digital signals that the computer can use. The RAS server and the RAS client must use the same connection medium when you are creating a dial-up connection. If the RAS server uses an Integrated Services Digital Network (ISDN) modem, the RAS client must also use one, and if one uses a regular modem the other must do the same.

Using RAS, you can connect to a LAN by dialing the phone number of the RAS server. When you dial in to the RAS server, it receives the data from the modem and sends it to the LAN through the network interface card (NIC).

tip

You can add a shortcut to your desktop for any dial-up connection you create in the Network Connection Wizard so that you can easily access the connection.

how to

Set up a dial-up connection with a remote network for only yourself named **My Connection**.
1. Click **Start**, point to **Settings**, and click the **Network and Dial-up Connections** command to open the **Network and Dial-up Connections** window.
2. Double-click the **Make New Connection** icon to start the **Network Connection Wizard**.
3. Click **Next >** to open the **Network Connection Type** screen, and select the **Dial-up to private network** option button (**Figure 16-8**).
4. Click **Next >** to open the **Select a Device** screen.
5. Select the device to be used for the connection, for example, **Modem—Standard 2400 bps Modem (COM1)**.
6. Click **Next >** to open the **Phone Number to Dial** screen (**Figure 16-9**).
7. Type the phone number in the **Phone number**: text box to indicate the phone number of the network.
8. Click **Next >** to open the **Connection Availability** screen.
9. Select the **Only for myself** option button to indicate that the connection can be used only by you. You can select the **For all users** option button to make the connection accessible to all users (**Figure 16-10**).
10. Click **Next >** to open the **Completing the Network Connection Wizard** screen.
11. Type the name **My Connection** in the **Type the name you want to use for this connection**.
12. Click **Finish** to save the settings and close the Network Connection Wizard.
13. The Connect window opens automatically. Close it.

Figure 16-8 Selecting the connection type

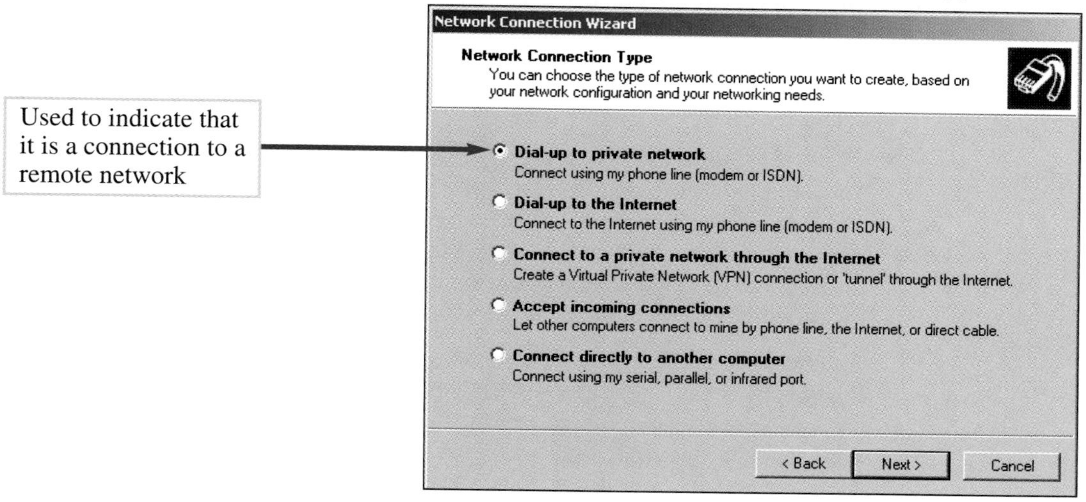

Used to indicate that it is a connection to a remote network

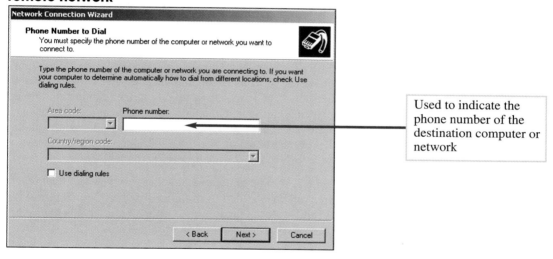

Figure 16-9 Specifying the phone number of the remote network

Used to indicate the phone number of the destination computer or network

Figure 16-10 Specifying that the connection can be used only by your profile

Makes the connection available to all users

Makes the connection available to you only

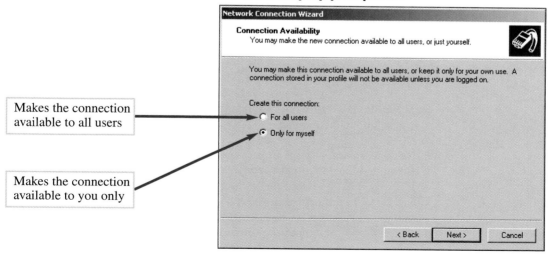

skill 4

Connecting to the Internet by Using a Dial-Up Connection

exam objective

Connect to the Internet by using dial-up networking.

overview

You can establish a connection to the Internet using one of several methods. The most common way is through a modem. You connect to the Internet using a modem if you have a stand-alone computer or if you are on a small LAN. If you connect to the Internet through a modem, it will either be installed on your computer or you can share a connection to the Internet that is configured on one of the computers on the LAN.

Another method of establishing a connection with the Internet is through a **proxy server**. Proxy servers have two purposes. They provide a connection to the Internet for computers on a LAN. Second, they provide a means for controlling in-coming and out-going requests for service. For instance, a proxy server can be used by an employer to prevent employees from accessing certain Web sites. A proxy server can also be set to allow (or disallow) access from unauthorized computers outside a LAN. Proxy servers can also be configured to improve network performance because Web pages that have been requested by network users are saved for a specified time period (if you have a caching server) . This means that when a second user requests the same Web page, the request can be fulfilled by the proxy server instead of being forwarded to the Web server. The proxy server is usually on the LAN, so the request for the page can be carried out more quickly.

When you set up an Internet connection through a modem, you can sign up for a new Internet account or transfer an existing Internet account to the computer on which you want to establish the dial-up connection. If you are setting up an Internet connection through a modem, Windows 2000 automatically detects the modems on your computer and displays a list from which you can select the one you want to use. After you have selected the modem, Windows dials the phone number of the Microsoft Internet Referral Service and displays a list of ISPs. You can then select your ISP from this list and connect to the Internet.

If your computer is on a LAN that is using a proxy server, you will have to specify the IP address for the proxy server. You can do this using the **Internet Connection Wizard**. You can either indicate the IP address of the proxy server manually or let Windows detect the proxy server.

When you set up an Internet account, you can also set up an Internet mail account. To set up an Internet mail account you must specify a mail server, which can either be a Post Office Protocol 3 (POP3) server, an Internet Mail Access Protocol (IMAP) server, or a Hypertext Transfer Protocol (HTTP) server.

how to

Set up a dial-up connection with the Internet from your computer by using a modem.

1. Open the **Network Connection Wizard**.
2. Click [Next >] to open the **Network Connection Type** screen.
3. Select the **Dial-up to the Internet** option button to indicate that you want to create a connection to the Internet.
4. Click [Next >] to open the **Internet Connection Wizard**.
5. Select the **I want to set up my Internet connection manually, or I want to connect through a local area network [LAN]** option button (**Figure 16-11**).
6. Click [Next >] to open the **Setting up your Internet connection** screen.
7. Select the **I connect through a phone line and a modem** option button to specify that you want to connect to the Internet using a modem (**Figure 16-12**).
8. Click [Next >] to open the Choose Modem screen. If you have more than one modem, select the one you want to use for this connection (**Figure 16-13**).

Figure 16-11 Selecting the type of Internet connection

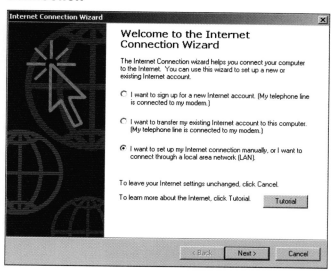

Figure 16-12 Selecting the medium for connecting to the Internet

Used to indicate whether you want to connect to the Internet using a modem or through a LAN

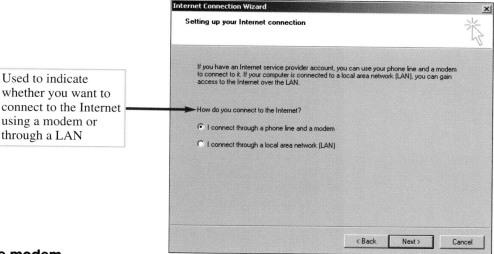

Figure 16-13 Choosing the modem

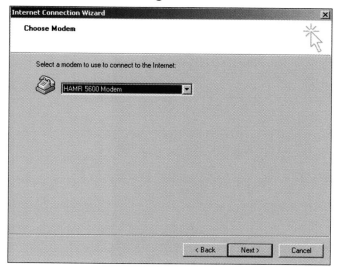

skill 4

Connecting to the Internet by Using a Dial-Up Connection (cont'd)

exam objective

Connect to the Internet by using dial-up networking.

how to

9. Click Next > to open the **Internet account connection information** screen.

10. Enter the telephone number of the ISP you want to use in the **Area code** and **Telephone number** text boxes. Select the **Use area code and dialing rules** check box if you want the connection to follow dialing rules, for example, dialing 9 to access an outside line that you have already configured in the **Phone and Modem Options** dialog box in the Control Panel **(Figure 16-14)**. Click the **Advanced** button. In the **Advanced Connection Properties** dialog box you can create a **SLIP** or **C-SLIP** (Serial Line or Compresed Serial Line Internet Protocol) connection rather than the default PPP connection and set a logon procedure **(Figure 16-15)**.

11. Click Next > to open the second **Internet account logon information** screen.

12. Type a user name for the connection, for example, type **Steve**.

13. Type a password for the connection, for example, type **password (Figure 16-11)**.

14. Click Next > to open the **Configuring your computer** screen.

15. Indicate a name for the connection in the **Connection name** text box; for example, type **conn1**.

16. Click Next > to open the **Set Up Your Internet Mail Account** screen. If you are setting up an Internet mail account, you will need to indicate a name and address for the account. You will also have to enter the name or IP address of the mail server that you want to use. This server can be an **Internet Mail Access Protocol (IMAP)**, **Post Office Protocol l (POP3)**, **Hyper Text Transfer Protocol (HTTP)**, or **Simple Mail Transfer Protocol (SMTP)** server.

17. Select the **No** option button to specify that you do not want to set up an Internet mail account.

18. Click Next > to open the **Completing the Internet Connection Wizard** screen.

19. Click Finish to save the configuration and close the Internet Connection Wizard.

20. Close all open windows (such as the Web browser and Connect window that will automatically open).

Figure 16-14 Entering Internet account information

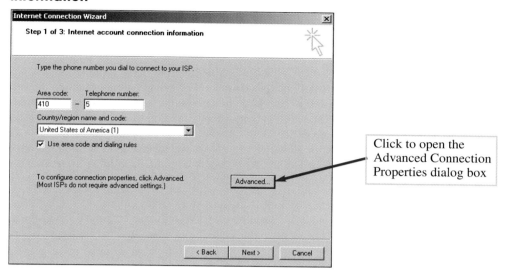

Click to open the Advanced Connection Properties dialog box

Figure 16-15 The Advanced Connection Properties dialog box

Figure 16-16 Entering a User name and Password for the Internet connection

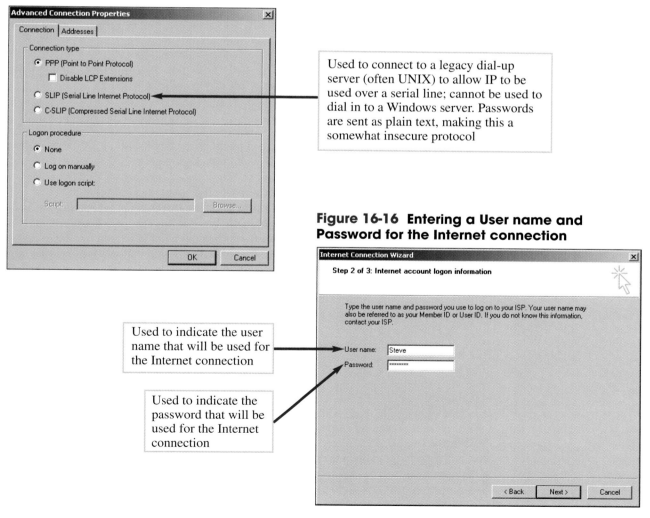

Used to connect to a legacy dial-up server (often UNIX) to allow IP to be used over a serial line; cannot be used to dial in to a Windows server. Passwords are sent as plain text, making this a somewhat insecure protocol

Used to indicate the user name that will be used for the Internet connection

Used to indicate the password that will be used for the Internet connection

skill 5

Setting up a VPN Connection

exam objective

Connect to computers by using a virtual private network (VPN) connection.

overview

A **Virtual Private Network (VPN)** is a secure connection across an **untrusted network**. An **untrusted network** is an open public network that can be accessed by all, i.e. the Internet. This is how a VPN works. First, a remote client creates a connection with the Internet through a dial-up connection, modem, cable, or digital subscriber line (DSL). Then, tunneling and encryption protocols are used to establish a secure channel through the established infrastructure to the LAN. The protocols keep the data flow private even though it is traveling through the public Internet.

Suppose you want to connect two distant offices. Before VPN technologies were introduced, you would have had to create a Wide Area Network (WAN), which is expensive. Using a VPN, the cost is greatly reduced because you can use the existing infrastructure of the Internet.

A computer must be configured as the VPN server, which will be the terminus of the secure tunnel. Many different types of computers can be configured as a VPN server, including Windows 2000 server computers, Linux computers, and even a Windows 2000 Professional computer for a single connection. Secure connections in VPNs are created using either **Point-to-Point Tunneling Protocol (PPTP)** or **Layer Two Tunneling Protocol (L2TP)**. Both of these protocols work over dial-up lines, public TCP/IP networks (the Internet), local network links, and WAN links. If you use L2PT, a "tunnel" will be created, but data will not be encrypted. L2TP must be used in conjunction with IPSec which will provide data encryption. When you use L2TP, the message header is compressed, while PPTP does not use header compression. PPTP uses Microsoft Point-to-Point Encryption (MPPE) to furnish encryption.

how to

Create a VPN connection named **VPN1** to a computer having the IP address **135.3.45.1**. Make sure that the connection can be used only by your profile.

1. Open the **Network Connection Wizard**.
2. Click [Next >] to open the **Network Connection Type** screen.
3. Select the **Connect to a private network through the Internet** option button to indicate that you want to create a **VPN**.
4. Click [Next >] to open the **Public Network** screen.
5. Select the **Automatically dial this initial connection** option button. Usually when you create a VPN, you use one connection icon to connect to the Internet and another one to set up the VPN tunnel. Typically, the Internet connection has already been created and it will be automatically placed in the list box. The **Do not dial the initial connection** option is generally selected when you have a cable or DSL link that is continuously connected so you do not need to create a dial-up link to an ISP.
6. Click [Next >] to open the **Destination Address** screen where you must enter the IP address or a Fully Qualified Domain Name (FQDN) for the computer (the VPN server) you want to connect to. Type **135.3.45.1** in the **Host name or IP address** text box **(Figure 16-17)**.
7. Click [Next >] to open the **Connection Availability** screen. Select the **Only for myself** option button to indicate that only your profile should be able to access the VPN **(Figure 16-18)**.
8. Click [Next >] to open the **Completing the Network Connection Wizard** screen.
9. Type a name for the new connection in the **Type the name you want to use for this connection**: text box. For example, type **VPN1 (Figure 16-19)**.
10. Click [Finish] to save the configuration and close the Network Connection Wizard.
11. You will be prompted with a message asking if you want to initiate the connection now. Click No.

Figure 16-17 Indicating the IP address of the network

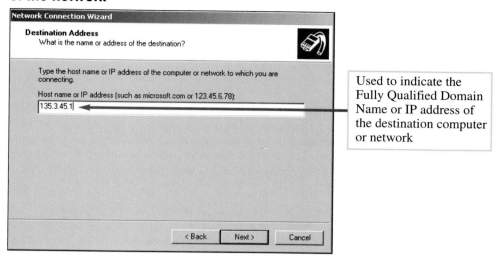

Used to indicate the Fully Qualified Domain Name or IP address of the destination computer or network

Figure 16-18 Specifying that the connection can only be used by your profile

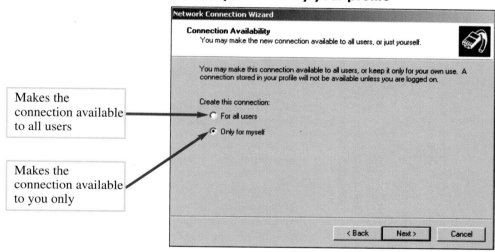

Makes the connection available to all users

Makes the connection available to you only

Figure 16-19 Specifying a name for the VPN connection

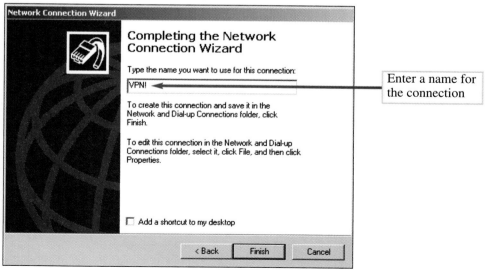

Enter a name for the connection

skill 6

Configuring Inbound Connections

exam objective

Basic knowledge

overview

Inbound connections are used to allow other computers to connect to yours via either a phone line, the Internet, or through a direct cable. In the Network Connection Wizard, you can select the networking components (the protocols, services, and clients) that you will use to establish connections from different kinds of computers. Only the users you select will be able to dial in to the computer. You can accept incoming VPN connections if your computer has a FQDN and unique IP address.

caution

You can have a maximum of 256 inbound connections on a computer.

Users must be given the phone number they will dial to connect to your computer, and call back options can be set for each user. If you set a callback number, your computer will authenticate the incoming user, disconnect, and call him or her back at the number you specify. This enhances security because, if an unauthorized user calls in, this number will be called back to establish the connection, not the number of the unauthorized user. You can also use callback options to avoid long distance charges for the connection. The bill will be charged to your phone number, instead of to the client who is calling in.

There are three callback options that define how a computer responds when a user dials in. You configure callback options on the **Callback** tab in the Properties dialog box for a user who is allowed to access the connection. To reconfigure callback options after you have created an incoming connection, right-click **Incoming Connections** in the Network and Dial-up Connections window and click **Properties** to open the **Incoming Connections Properties** dialog box. On the **Users** tab, select the user for whom you want to configure callback options and click the Properties button. On the **Callback** tab, set one of the following:

◆ **Allow the caller to set the callback number:** If you select this option, the computer disconnects as soon as a user dials in and calls them back on the number that they indicate. This setting is useful when users need to dial in from different locations because they can indicate a different number to call back each time they connect.

◆ **Always use the following callback number:** If you select this option, the computer calls back only a specified number. Selecting this option enhances the security of your network because users can establish a connection to the computer using only one number.

◆ **Do not allow callback:** If you select this option, there is no callback. Once the connection is established, the computer stays connected and allows the user to access resources.

When you configure inbound connections, you can select network components, such as the TCP/IP protocol, to be used for the connection. You must also specify the names of the devices, such as the modem, that will be used for the connection and whether or not the computer should allow incoming VPN connections.

how to

Set up an inbound connection that uses a modem and can be accessed only by the Administrator. Enable callback for the users so that they can use the connection from different locations, and make sure that the connection uses the TCP/IP protocol.

1. Open the **Network Connection Wizard**.
2. Click [Next >] to open the **Network Connection Type** screen.
3. Select the **Accept incoming connections** option button to enable the computer to receive inbound connections.
4. Click [Next >] to open the **Devices for Incoming Connections** screen.
5. Select a **modem** check box in the **Connection devices** list box to indicate the device to be used for the inbound connection (**Figure 16-20**). Click the Properties button to view the properties of the modem, then close the dialog box (**Figure 16-21**).

Figure 16-20 Selecting a device for an inbound connection

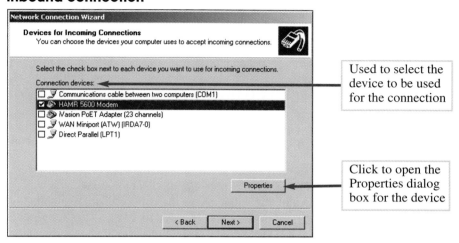

Used to select the device to be used for the connection

Click to open the Properties dialog box for the device

Figure 16-21 The Properties dialog box for a modem

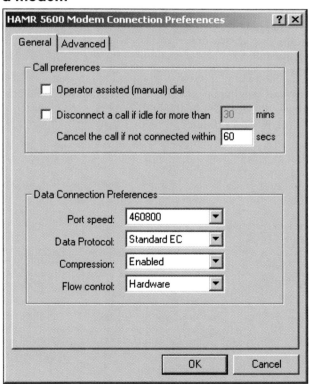

skill 6

Configuring Inbound Connections
(cont'd)

exam objective

Basic knowledge

how to

tip

Users will specify this phone number when they connect to the computer.

6. Click [Next >] to open the **Incoming Virtual Private Connection** screen. You can accept incoming VPN connections if your computer has a unique Internet domain name or IP address.
7. Select the **Do not allow virtual private connections** option button to restrict inbound VPN connections.
8. Click [Next >] to open the **Allowed Users** screen.
9. Select the **Administrator** check box in the **Users allowed to connect** list box (**Figure 16-22**).
10. Click [Properties] to open the **Administrator Properties** dialog box.
11. Click the **Callback** tab to set the **Callback** properties.
12. Select the **Allow the caller to set the callback number** option button so that they can dial in from different locations (**Figure 16-23**).
13. Click [OK] to save the callback setting.
14. Click [Next >] to open the Networking Components screen. The **Internet Protocol (TCP/IP)** check box in the **Networking components:** list box is selected by default, as are NetBEUI, the Server service and the Workstation service (**Figure 16-24**).
15. Click [Next >] to open the **Completing the Network Connection Wizard** screen.
16. Click [Finish] to save the configuration and close the **Network Connection Wizard**.

more

After you have created an inbound connection, the devices to be used for that connection are converted to answer mode so that, when a user dials in, the computer immediately answers and authenticates the connection. In answer mode, devices can be used by only one inbound connection at a time.

After you have set up either outbound or inbound connections, you can modify the properties for those connections, such as the name of the connection or the IP address of the destination network in the **<Connection name> Properties** dialog box.

Figure 16-22 Selecting users who can access the inbound connection

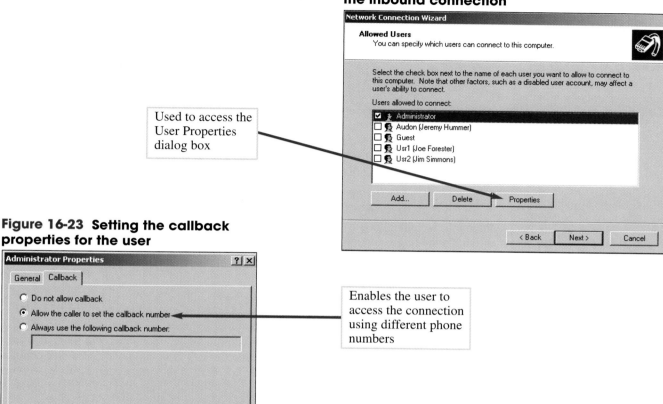

Used to access the User Properties dialog box

Figure 16-23 Setting the callback properties for the user

Enables the user to access the connection using different phone numbers

Figure 16-24 Selecting network components

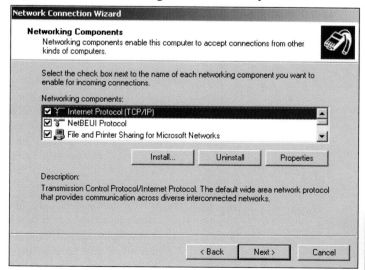

skill 7

Configuring Internet Connection Sharing

exam objective

Configure and troubleshoot Internet Connection Sharing.

overview

After you set up an Internet connection on a computer, you can configure **Internet Connection Sharing** so that you can share the link with other computers on your LAN. This computer will then provide the single Internet connection for all computers on the LAN. ICS is most useful for small networks where you want all the computers to use one Internet connection that is shared in the same way as a shared folder.

The other computers on the LAN must be configured to get their IP addresses automatically (in the TCP/IP Properties dialog box). Furthermore, if they have previously established an Internet connection, they will have to open the **Tools** menu in **Internet Explorer** and select the **Internet Options** command to open the Internet Options dialog box. On the **Connections** tab, they will have to select the **Never dial a connection** option button.

If you are on a LAN, the computer on which ICS is configured is assigned a static IP address; thus any previously established TCP/IP connections will be lost and will have to be reconfigured. It will assign IP addresses and subnet masks to the other computers on the LAN just like a DHCP server. The default gateway for the other computers on the LAN will be the IP address for the ICS computer. The network adapter in the ICS computer will serve as a dedicated (reserved for this purpose) router for the network. ICS should not be used on a domain-based network where there is a domain controller, a DHCP server, a DNS server, or any other computer with a static IP address. Instead, domain-based networks will use Network Address Translation (NAT), which is included with Windows 2000 Server.

You configure Internet Connection Sharing in the **Connection Properties** dialog box. It is important to note that Internet Connection Sharing automatically assigns unregistered non-routable IP addresses to the client computers on the network. Any network can use these private address ranges as long as some type of NAT facility is available for translation. Remember, in order to use Internet Connection Sharing, you must make sure that all the computers on the LAN obtain their IP addresses automatically.

how to

You have a network of five computers. Configure a dial-up Internet connection, **Conn1**, on one of them and enable Internet Connection Sharing so that all the computers on the network can share the same connection.

1. Open the **Network and Dial-up Connections** window to access the list of connections configured on the computer.
2. Right-click the **Conn1** icon to display the shortcut menu (**Figure 16-25**).
3. Click the **Properties** command on the shortcut menu to display the **Connection Properties** dialog box.
4. Click the **Sharing** tab to access the Internet Connection Sharing options.
5. Select the **Enable Internet Connection Sharing for this connection** check box to enable Internet Connection Sharing (**Figure 16-26**).
6. If you are not on a DSL or cable continuous connection, the **Enable on-demand dialing** check box will be selected automatically. This will instruct the ICS computer to call the ISP when any computer on the network initiates a connection to the Internet.
7. Click [OK] to save the configuration and close the **Connection Properties** dialog box. (If you are not really going to configure ICS, click **Cancel**.)

Figure 16-25 Selecting the connection to be configured

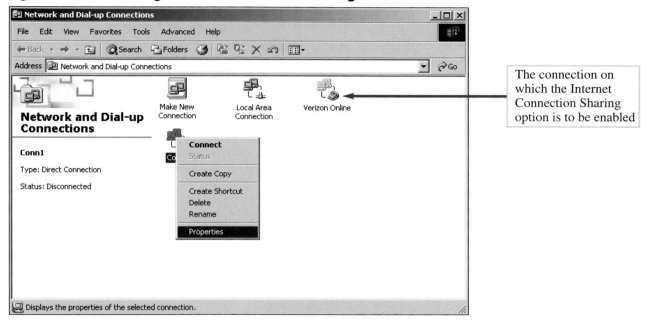

The connection on which the Internet Connection Sharing option is to be enabled

Figure 16-26 Selecting the Internet Connection Sharing option

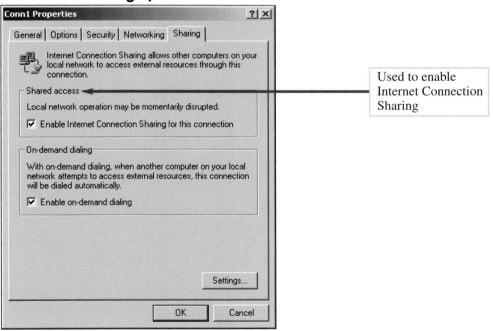

Used to enable Internet Connection Sharing

skill 7

Configuring Internet Connection Sharing (cont'd)

exam objective

Configure and troubleshoot Internet Connection Sharing.

more

If after enabling Internet Connection Sharing on your computer, other computers on your LAN cannot access the Internet, check the following:

◆ **TCP/IP is not enabled on all the computers:** Internet Connection Sharing will not function if the TCP/IP protocol is not installed on the client computers **(Figure 16-27)**.

◆ **The Internet Connection Sharing service has stopped:** If the Internet Connection Sharing service has stopped, you must start it again. You can check the status of the Internet Connection Sharing service in the **Services** window. You open the **Services** window by opening the **Start** menu, pointing to **Administrative Tools**, and clicking the **Services** command **(Figure 16-28)**.

◆ **Internet Connection Sharing is configured for the wrong connection:** Internet Connection Sharing must be configured for the connection to the Internet. If it has been accidentally configured for a connection with the LAN or for any other connection, users will not be able to connect to the Internet.

Figure 16-27 Checking to make sure TCP/IP is enabled on all computers sharing the Internet connection

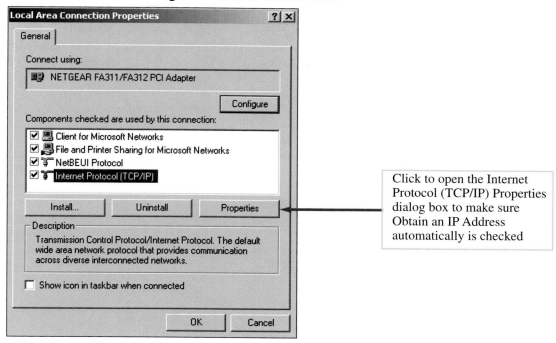

Click to open the Internet Protocol (TCP/IP) Properties dialog box to make sure Obtain an IP Address automatically is checked

Figure 16-28 The Services window

Make sure the Internet Connection Sharing service has not been stopped

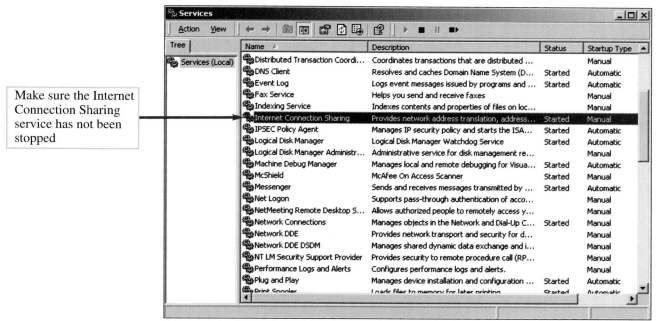

Summary

◆ Windows 2000 Professional supports EAP, IPSec, L2TP, and BAP to enhance security, authentication, and multi-linking of connections.

◆ EAP uses generic token cards, Message Digest 5 Challenge Handshake Authentication Protocol (MD5-CHAP), and Transport Level Security (TLS) for authentication of users who try to establish a connection.

◆ You can configure a Windows 2000 Professional computer as a Remote Access Service (RAS) client, a RAS server, or both.

◆ Outbound connections enable a computer to dial out and connect to a remote computer or network and exchange data.

◆ You can set up three types of outbound connections: connections to a network through a RAS server, connections to the Internet, and connections to a Virtual Private Network (VPN).

◆ The Internet Connection Wizard is used to sign up for a new Internet account, transfer an existing Internet account to a computer, or to connect to the Internet using a LAN.

◆ A Virtual Private Network (VPN) is a secure connection across an untrusted network.

◆ VPNs are created using tunneling protocols, either Point-to-Point Tunneling Protocol (PPTP) or Layer Two Tunneling Protocol (L2TP).

◆ Inbound connections enable users to dial-in to a computer. You configure all connections using the Network Connection Wizard.

◆ The Callback feature for inbound connections is used to authenticate the user, hang up, and call the client back at a pre-specified phone number to prevent unauthorized user access, or to localize long distance or other carrier charges for a remote user.

◆ Internet Connection Sharing is used to establish a single Internet connection for multiple computers on a LAN.

Key Terms

Bandwidth Allocation Protocol (BAP)
Callback
Challenge Handshake Authentication Protocol (CHAP)
Extensible Authentication Protocol (EAP)
Generic token card
Inbound connection
Internet Connection Sharing
Internet Protocol Security (IPSec)

Internet Service Provider (ISP)
Layer Two Tunneling Protocol
MD5-CHAP
Microsoft CHAP (MS-CHAP)
Multilinked device
Outbound connection
Password Authentication Protocol (PAP)
Point-to-Point Protocol (PPP)
Point-to-Point Tunneling Protocol (PPTP)

Proxy server
RAS client
RAS server
Remote Access Service (RAS)
Shiva Password Authentication Protocol (SPAP)
Transport Level Security (TLS)
Tunneling protocol
Untrusted network
Virtual Private Network (VPN)

Test Yourself

1. Which of the following option buttons on the Network Connection Type screen in the Network Connection Wizard will you select to set up a connection to a LAN using a RAS connection?
   a. Dial-up to private network
   b. Dial-up to the Internet
   c. Connect to a private network through the Internet
   d. Accept incoming connections

2. You are configuring the callback options for users of an inbound connection on a computer on your network. Which of the following will you achieve by using the Always use the following callback number option button?

   a. Both security and accessibility from all locations.
   b. Only Security.
   c. Only Accessibility from all locations.

3. Which of the following protocols is used to set up a Virtual Private Network?
   a. Bandwidth Allocation Protocol (BAP)
   b. Point-to-Point Tunneling Protocol (PPTP)
   c. Extensible Authentication Protocol (EAP)

4. You are the Network Administrator for a small LAN and you are configuring a Windows 2000 Professional computer for an employee who telecommutes from her home 70 % of the time. Since this employee sometimes

works on a file containing confidential company financial information, you want to make sure she has a secure connection for transmitting that data to the LAN. Which protocols will you use?

a. NW Link and EAP
b. IPSec and BAP
c. PPTP and L2TP
d. L2TP and IPSec

5. To set up a dial-up RAS connection, you need to make sure that:

a. An outbound connection is configured on the RAS server.
b. A POP3 server is present at one end of the connection.
c. The RAS server and RAS client use the same communication medium.
d. A proxy server is present on your LAN.

6. You have a small office network with five computers and a single dial-up Internet connection. What will you do to make sure that client computers on the network can access the Internet?

a. Set up a Virtual Private Network (VPN).
b. Set up inbound connections on all the computers.
c. Set up Internet Connection Sharing.
d. Set up outbound connections on all the computers.

7. When you configure Internet Connection Sharing on a computer with a dial-up Internet connection, you need to make sure that the computers on the network:

a. Are configured with an inbound connection.
b. Obtain IP addresses automatically.
c. Use tunneling protocols.
d. Are connected directly to a modem.

8. You need to set up a network to connect the two offices of your company located in New York and New Jersey. The marketing divisions located at the two offices need to exchange confidential data. However, the cost of setting up a WAN connection is prohibitive. Which of the following can you use to exchange data securely without setting up a WAN connection?

a. A dial-up connection to the Internet.
b. A Virtual Private Network.
c. Multilinked devices.
d. A proxy server.

9. Transport Level Security (TLS) protocol is associated with:

a. Smart cards.
b. A cryptographic system.
c. Codes that change every time a password is used.

10. You are an Administrator at Spirits Unlimited. You run the Network Connection Wizard on your computer and create a dial-up connection to a private network. Your office mate logs on to your computer, but he cannot find the connection. What is wrong?

a. Only an Administrator will be able to see the connection because you created the connection as an administrator.
b. You forgot to create a desktop icon for the connection.
c. On the Sharing tab in the Properties dialog box for the connection, you selected the Enable on-demand dialing check box.
d. You created the connection only for yourself by selecting the Only for myself option on the Connection Availability page.

Projects: On Your Own

1. Set up a dial-up connection named **Dial-up1** with a private network that has the phone number **3345222**. Also ensure that all users on the network can use the connection.

a. Open the **Network Connection Wizard**.
b. Select the **Dial-up to private network** option button.
c. Select **Modem—Standard 2400 bps Modem (COM1)** as the device to be used for the connection.
d. Type **3345222** in the **Phone number**: text box.
e. Click the **For all users** option button.
f. Type **Dial-up1** in the **Type the name you want to use for this connection**: text box.
g. Click **Finish** to save the configuration.

2. Create a VPN connection named **VPN4** to a computer having an IP address **120.9.47.51**. Ensure that the connection can be used only by your profile.

a. Open the **Network Connection Type** screen of the **Network Connection Wizard**.

b. Select the **Connect to a private network through the Internet** option button.
c. Type **120.9.47.51** in the **host name or IP address** text box.
d. Select the **Only for myself** option button.
e. Type **VPN4** in the **Type the name you want to use for this connection**: text box.
f. Click **Finish** to save the configuration.

3. Set up an inbound connection that uses a **Standard 2400 bps modem**. In addition, the connection should be accessible only by the Administrator profile. Also ensure that callback is disabled.

a. Open the **Network Connection Type** screen of the **Network Connection Wizard**.
b. Click the **Accept incoming connections** option button.
c. Select the **Standard 2400 bps modem** check box from the **Connection devices** list box.

d. Select the **Administrator** check box from the **Users allowed to connect**: list box.

e. Click the **Callback** tab of the **Administrator Properties** dialog box.

f. Click the **Do not allow callback** option button.

g. Click **OK** to save the callback properties.

h. Click **Finish** to save the configuration.

Problem Solving Scenarios

1. MidWest Paint and Wallpaper, Inc. is a regional wholesaler and distributor for paint, wallpaper, and other decorating supplies. It sells products to retail stores in the upper-Midwest region from Wisconsin, Minnesota, and the Dakotas, to Montana. Located in St. Paul, Minnesota, MidWest has ten sales reps in the field all the time. They have recently been equipped with laptop computers with Windows 2000 Professional installed. The laptops have built-in 56k modems. The Sales Director wants to link the sales reps into the company's Windows 2000 network from the field so they can enter orders directly to the order entry system, report sales, and download price files. As Network Administrator, write a document that describes how you will provide remote dial-up access as well as security for the data.

2. Media Solutions in Ossining, New York, builds multimedia presentations for New York advertising firms. Media Solutions employs twelve artists and programmers in a single office. As a Technical Consultant, you have helped Media Solutions install a Windows 2000 workgroup network. Now the firm's managers want you to connect the LAN to the Internet so they can share files easily with their customers. In addition they want you to make it possible for all the employees to share a single Internet connection. They would like you to write a memo describing how you will connect their firm to the Internet and permit sharing of a single Internet connection.

DNS, Active Directory Services and Web Server Resources

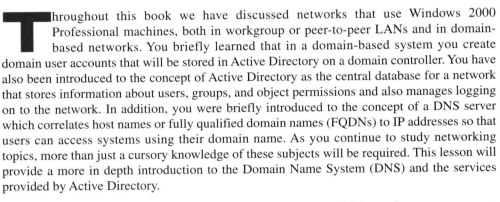

Throughout this book we have discussed networks that use Windows 2000 Professional machines, both in workgroup or peer-to-peer LANs and in domain-based networks. You briefly learned that in a domain-based system you create domain user accounts that will be stored in Active Directory on a domain controller. You have also been introduced to the concept of Active Directory as the central database for a network that stores information about users, groups, and object permissions and also manages logging on to the network. In addition, you were briefly introduced to the concept of a DNS server which correlates host names or fully qualified domain names (FQDNs) to IP addresses so that users can access systems using their domain name. As you continue to study networking topics, more than just a cursory knowledge of these subjects will be required. This lesson will provide a more in depth introduction to the Domain Name System (DNS) and the services provided by Active Directory.

DNS is the main name resolution service for Windows 2000 and it is used to access computers on a TCP/IP network using the hostname instead of an Internet Protocol (IP) address based on a 32-bit number consisting of four octets. Each octet represents a binary numbering the range 0 to 255 and is separated by a period. Name resolution is the translation of computer names to IP addresses and vice-versa. Name resolution is required so that a user can enter the name of the target computer, and the connection to the other computer can be established using computer language based on binary digits.

As you have learned, user accounts can be stored in one of two places: the local security database on a local machine or the domain database on a domain-based network. In addition to serving as the central security database, Active Directory, which is the domain database for Windows 2000, also stores all of the information about how the network is structured and organized. Users access it to identify and locate all of the resources on a network.

On most networks, computers are connected to the Internet so that users can access information and services from Web sites. Sometimes a separate computer, known as a Web server, is set up by the System Administrator so that users can share resources with other users who are running Web browsers or FTP (File Transfer Protocol) utilities. Web servers are packaged with Internet- and intranet-related programs for sending e-mails, downloading requests for File Transfer Protocol (FTP) files, uploading files, and building and publishing Web pages.

Goals

In this lesson, you will learn about the DNS service, the name resolution process, and how to configure a Windows 2000 Professional computer as a DNS client. Additionally, you will learn about the various concepts associated with Active Directory services. This lesson will also introduce the concept of managing Web server resources and teach you how to set up a Web server.

Lesson 17   DNS, Active Directory Services, and Web Server Resources

Skill	Exam 70-210 Objective
1. Examining DNS Service	Basic knowledge
2. Examining the Name Resolution Process	Basic knowledge
3. Configuring Windows 2000 as a DNS Client	Basic knowledge
4. Introducing Active Directory Structure	Basic knowledge
5. Introducing Active Directory Concepts and Services	Basic knowledge
6. Managing Web Server Resources	Manage and troubleshoot Web server resources.

Requirements

To complete this lesson, you need a Windows 2000 Professional computer with TCP/IP configured, running on a Windows 2000 Server network that has DNS service installed.

skill 1 | *Examining DNS Service*

exam objective

Basic knowledge

overview

Computers on a network must uniquely identify each other in order to communicate with one another. Lesson 6 introduced you to the Internet Protocol (IP) addressing system, which is responsible for addressing and routing data. You learned that it provides the addressing scheme for a network and for the Internet. IP addressing involves assigning each computer a unique identifier, which is a 32-bit number consisting of four octets separated by periods (an octet is an 8-bit value). An IP address contains two identifiers: one for the network and one for the computer or host. The subnet mask is used to divide the network ID from the host ID. It also consists of four octets and is seen by the computer as a string of 32 binary digits (i.e., a series of ones and zeros). The ones identify which of the 32 ones and zeros in the IP address make up the network ID, and the zeros in the subnet mask identify the host ID.

This series of ones and zeros representing "off" and "on" is called machine code and it is the only language that a computer can understand. However, humans prefer names to numbers and find it much easier to access another user's computer by specifying the computer name. Therefore, a system is required for converting computer names to numbers, in other words into IP addresses. Windows 2000 uses Domain Name System (DNS) servers to perform the task of **name resolution**. Name resolution simply refers to the process by which a name is translated into a corresponding number; in the case of a DNS server, the host name is converted to an IP address. The DNS server maintains a database containing IP addresses mapped to their corresponding names. To access a computer on the network, users need only specify its name.

DNS has a hierarchical structure. The nodes in this hierarchical structure are called domains. Each domain has a name associated with it, for example, domain1. As you add more domains to the DNS hierarchy, the name of the parent domain is added to the child domain or sub-domain. For example, in the domain name **exams.courses.com**, exams represents a sub-domain of the **courses.com** domain, and **courses** is a sub-domain of the **com** domain.

The domain at the top of the DNS hierarchy is called a **root domain**. The child domain of the root domain is called a **top-level domain**, and the child domain of a top-level domain is a **second-level domain**. The root domain is represented by a period. The top-level domains are the two- and three-character names you are familiar with in surfing the Web, such as com, net, edu, org, gov, and the various country codes such as uk for Great Britain. Second-level domains have two parts, a top-level name and a second-level name, for example, ebay.com, yale.edu, usmint.gov, and royal.gov.uk (the official Web site of the British monarchy). A **host name** is at the bottom of the DNS hierarchy and it designates a particular computer either on the Internet or on a private network **(Figure 17-1)**.

By default, TCP/IP uses the name of the computer on which resources are located as the host name. For example, the complete path to the location of a computer named **courses** on the **domain1** domain is **courses.domain1.com**.

A **Fully Qualified Domain Name (FQDN)** includes a **domain name** (i.e a name that follows Internet naming conventions that use dots to separate parts of a name) in addition to the host name. For example, **server1** may be the alias for a computer on a TCP/IP network, whereas **server1.finance.redhen.com.** is the FQDN for the computer. The trailing period means that this is an FQDN; but even if the period were missing, it is assumed to be there. Com is the top-level domain, designating that this is a commercial organization. Redhen is the second-level domain, indicating the organization name. Finance is a sub-domain of Redhen.com (or third-level domain) indicating the Finance department, and server1 is the name of the computer in the Finance department. The host name is the leftmost part of a FQDN **(Figure 17-1)**. The

tip

DNS is most commonly associated with the Internet, but is also extensively used by LANs and WANs to resolve and locate computer names on the network.

caution

A host name might be different from a computer name if the site developer or the administrator changes the default name given to the computer by the TCP/IP protocol.

Figure 17-1 DNS hierarchy

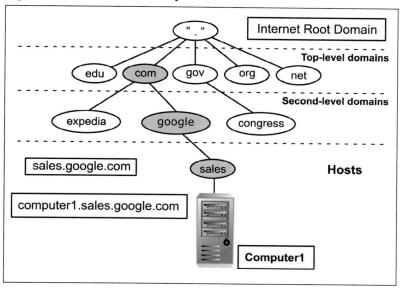

Figure 17-2 A FQDN

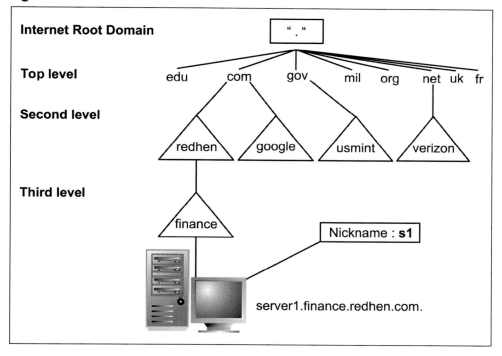

skill 1

Examining DNS Service *(cont'd)*

exam objective   Basic knowledge

overview

FQDN represents the exact location of the resource on the network, while the host name can be used by the user at this computer rather than typing the entire FQDN.

On a small network, a DNS server may contain just one database file that stores all of the name-to-IP-address resolution data. However, on larger networks it becomes necessary to divide administrative control and DNS functions into zones. **Zones** are distinct, contiguous segments of the DNS namespace that make a large domain manageable by enabling different administrators to manage different zones. For example, if the resources in **domain1** are related to marketing and finance, the domain can be divided into the zones marketing and finance. The names of the marketing and finance zones will be **marketing.domain1.com** and **finance.domain1.com**, respectively. This partitions or subdivides the DNS namespace to make it easier to manage. Servers in the marketing zone will store all records for the marketing zone and servers in the finance zone will store all records for that zone.

There must be at least one **DNS name server** for each zone. When multiple DNS servers are created in a zone, there are two kinds of DNS database files: primary and secondary. One DNS name server in the zone will store the primary zone database file and the others will store copies of it called secondary zone database files. Modifications and updates can only be made to the primary zone database file. **Zone transfers** occur to replicate any changes to the primary zone database file to the secondary zone database files. The server where the primary zone database file is housed is called the **authoritative server** because it has authority over the other DNS servers in the zone. The purpose of the secondary database file servers is to reduce the traffic and query load on the primary database zone server. Secondary database file servers also provide redundancy; that is, if the authoritative server is down, the secondary database file servers can service requests instead (**Figure 17-3**).

Keep in mind that because DNS is fully integrated with Windows 2000, a FQDN such as **www.ebay.com** can also be the name of a local network. Active Directory is based on DNS, so all Active Directory names are DNS names. For example, redhen.com is a valid DNS name. It can also be used as a Windows 2000 domain name, and **TParks@redhen.com** can function as both an Internet e-mail address and a user name on your LAN. This way, your network users can locate things on the local network in the same way that they locate them on the Internet.

more

It is advisable to keep domain names simple and precise. Using simple names makes it easier for people to remember them. For example, a site containing information about music with the name **music.com** is easier to remember and relate with music. Domain names are not case-sensitive and can be up to 63 characters long. However, a FQDN can have a maximum length of 255 characters. The standard characters supported by the DNS service in Windows 2000 are A-Z, a-z, 0-9, and the hyphen. The DNS service also supports the Unicode character set, which contains characters not included in the ASCII (American Standard Code for Information Interchange) character set to support languages other than English. You can use these characters only if all the DNS servers that you are using to administer your site or network support Unicode.

It is also advisable to restrict the FQDN to 3 or 4 domain levels. The more domain levels there are, the more administrative effort will be required to maintain them.

Figure 17-3 DNS Namespace Subdivided into Zones

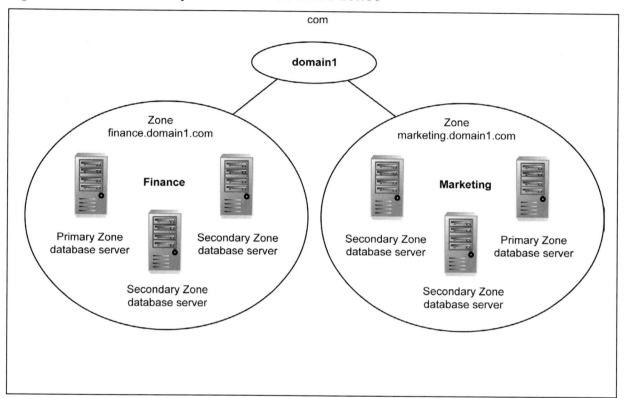

skill 2

Examining the Name Resolution Process

exam objective

Basic knowledge

overview

To resolve names to IP addresses and vice-versa, DNS uses the name resolution process. There are two types of name resolution queries: **forward lookup queries** and **reverse lookup queries**. A computer initiates a forward lookup query when a user attempts to access another computer using a name. These queries resolve names to IP addresses **(Figure 17-4)**, while reverse lookup queries resolve IP addresses to names. For example, if a computer named Computer1 has an IP address 142.13.55.2, the forward lookup query will translate Computer1 to 142.13.55.2. The reverse lookup query for the same computer will translate 142.13.55.2 to Computer1.

Forward Lookup query: When a user enters a name to access a resource, a forward lookup query is initiated. For example, suppose you attempted to access **www.prenhall.com** from your computer, a host inside the **www.school.edu** domain. Your client computer first sends a query to its primary DNS name server. That DNS name server first checks to see if it is authoritative for the zone. If so, it searches its zone database file for an IP address corresponding to the specified name. If not, the server checks its cache. If the server still cannot resolve the name, it sends a query to one of the preset root servers. The root server cannot respond authoritatively for prenhall.com, but it sends a referral to the primary DNS name server for a .com name server. The primary DNS name server then sends a query to the .com server, which sends a referral for a name server that is authoritative for prenhall.com. The primary DNS name server then contacts that name server, which finds the correct host-to-IP address mapping and returns the results to the primary DNS name server, which then relays them to your client computer.

Reverse Lookup query: When an IP address needs to be translated into its corresponding name, a reverse lookup query is initiated. A reverse lookup query is required when a computer needs the name of a computer which has a particular IP address. Since the DNS database is indexed by name and not by IP addresses, the process would be complex, involving an extensive search of all domain names if it were not for **in-addr.arpa**. This second-level domain was expressly created to simplify this task. This domain contains name-to-IP address mappings indexed by IP addresses **(Figure 17-5)**.

more

On a network like the Internet, millions of queries are passed from one name server to another, causing a lot of network traffic. To reduce network traffic, DNS name servers cache query results. A query result can be cached for a specific amount of time called the **Time to Live (TTL)**, after which it is deleted. Updated information will not be sent in response to client requests until the TTL expires. Longer TTL values will increase network efficiency, because requests will be able to be answered more quickly, but shorter TTL values ensure that current data is accessed. The default TTL is 60 minutes.

Figure 17-4 Forward Lookup queries

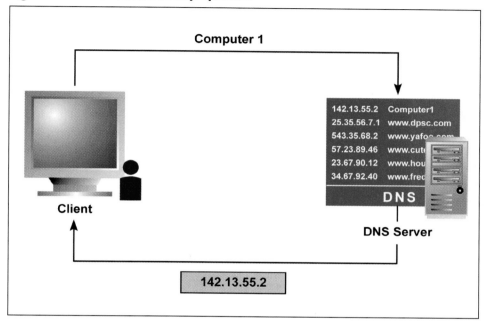

Figure 17-5 in-addr.arpa

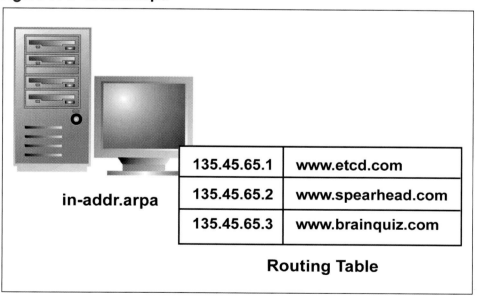

skill 3

Configuring Windows 2000 as a DNS Client

exam objective

Basic knowledge

overview

In order to use the DNS name resolution process, there must be a Windows 2000 Server on your network running the DNS service. First, you must make sure that the Transmission Control Protocol/Internet Protocol (TCP/IP) is configured on your computer, and then you can configure your Windows 2000 Professional computer as a DNS client.

how to

Configure your Windows 2000 Professional computer as a DNS client.

1. Right-click the **My Network Places** icon to open the shortcut menu.
2. Click the **Properties** command on the shortcut menu to open the **Network and Dial-up Connections** window, where you configure the properties for a connection.
3. Right-click **Local Area Connection** to open the shortcut menu.
4. Click the **Properties** command to open the **Local Area Connection Properties** dialog box **(Figure 17-6)**, where you configure the properties of the components used by the local area connection.
5. Select **TCP/IP** in the **Components checked are used by this connection** box, and then click   Properties   to open the **Internet Protocol (TCP/IP) Properties** dialog box.
6. Select the **Use the following DNS server addresses** option button to specify the name of a DNS server. If you are on a network, you will have to ask the network administrator for the IP address of the DNS server.
7. Type the IP address of the primary DNS server for the client in the **Preferred DNS server** text box. For example, type **135.85.42.2 (Figure 17-7)**. If another DNS server is available on the network, you can type its IP address in the Alternate DNS server text box. This DNS server is used if the primary DNS server is not available.
8. Click   OK   to save the configuration and close the Internet Protocol (TCP/IP) Properties dialog box.
9. Click   OK   to close the **Local Area Connection Properties** dialog box.
10. Close the **Network and Dial-up Connections** window.

**Figure 17-6 Local Area Connection
Properties dialog box**

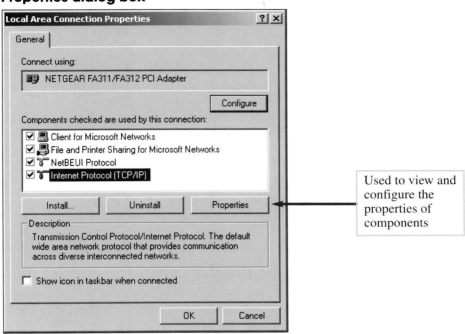

Used to view and
configure the
properties of
components

**Figure 17-7 Internet Protocol (TCP/IP)
Properties dialog box**

Used to specify
the IP address of
the primary DNS
server

Used to specify
the IP address of
a secondary DNS
server

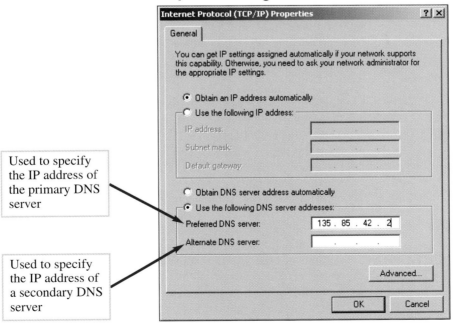

skill 4

Introducing Active Directory Structure

exam objective   Basic knowledge

overview

On a Windows 2000 domain-based network, Active Directory stores information about network objects such as users and groups, printers, and computers **(Figure 17-8)**. Users access Active Directory to locate the resources they need on the network. Active Directory is a searchable database that employs a hierarchical folder structure so that network users can easily find any resource, no matter what server it is located on. Active Directory serves as the central repository for network objects and as a central administrative location so that network administrators do not have to individually manage multiple servers. User and group accounts, permissions, and network resources can all be managed in Active Directory.

Active Directory is based on the domain system. Domains are logical groups of users, computers, and resources. Objects in Active Directory are organized in a logical and a physical structure. Within the logical structure, you can locate any object by name, regardless of its physical location. The physical structure, on the other hand, is used to modify how Active Directory works. If your network is faced with bandwidth limitations that adversely affect replication and authentication processes, you can create additional **sites**. Sites are defined by creating subnets for each of the physical locations on the network. Additional subnets will be used to establish which server clients will use to log on to the network and locate resources. Additional sites are created when your WAN connections do not have adequate bandwidth to support replication and communication between servers.

The logical Active Directory structure consists of the following organizational units:

◆ **Object:** Any tangible or intangible thing stored in Active Directory. It can be a physical object such as a computer or a virtual object such as a share. Objects include resources on a network. All objects have attributes or characteristics that are associated with them which define their properties and behaviors **(Figure 17-9)**. Objects in Active Directory include users, printers, servers, shares, and organizational units (described below).

◆ **Organizational unit (OU):** A subdivision of a domain that is used to group objects in Active Directory. For example, you could have a Finance OU that contains the Cost Accounting OU and the Fiscal Policy OU. Each OU will contain the users, groups, printers, computers, shares, etc., for that OU. The purpose of OUs is to create administrative segments within Active Directory that can be managed by their respective administrators. For example, the head of the Finance department would be the Administrator of the Finance OU and he or she in turn would delegate administrative responsibility for Cost Accounting and Fiscal Policy OUs to their department heads. In this way, administrative control is apportioned without giving any one Administrator access to the entire Active Directory. In Windows 2000, OUs are used to reduce the number of domains on a network. Now, unlike in Windows NT, one domain rather than many can be created with numerous OUs that mimic your organizational structure. Control over the OUs can then be delegated to one or more Administrators.

◆ **Domain:** Domains are logical groups of objects that can have their own security policies, can establish trust relationships with other domains, and can hypothetically contain millions of users. Multiple domains in Windows 2000 are used mainly when security requirements necessitate multiple domain-wide security policies, such as account policies. Active Directory is stored on a computer that is referred to as a **domain controller**. You

tip

Domains are the building blocks of Active Directory and they use the DNS naming convention.

Figure 17-8 Active Directory

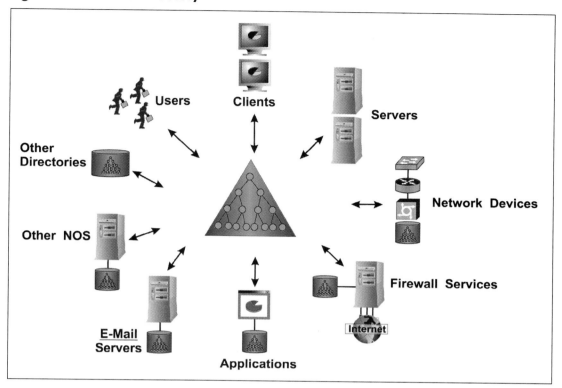

Figure 17-9 Objects and their Attributes

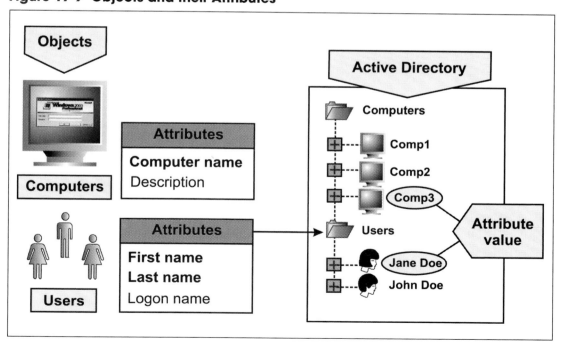

skill 4

Introducing Active Directory Structure (cont'd)

exam objective

Basic knowledge

overview

only need to have one domain controller for a domain to exist, but most networks have several domain controllers which store replicas of Active Directory. All domain controllers in a Windows 2000 network are equals and directory data is replicated through a process known as **multimaster replication**. This means that all domain controllers replicate Active Directory data rather than having a single master replicator server which is responsible for updating Active Directory on all of the domain controllers. Therefore, when you make changes to Active Directory on any domain controller, they are automatically replicated to all other domain controllers in the domain. All domain controllers are responsible for keeping Active Directory up to date.

◆ **Tree:** Domains are grouped in a hierarchical structure called a **tree**. A tree is composed of a contiguous namespace. Trees are used by organizations to create logical domain structures which can be efficiently managed. For example, if you have a domain named *courses.com* and you are going to add a new domain named exams, you can either add the new domain to the existing domain to create a single tree with a parent domain and a child domain, or you can create a new tree, *exams.com*. If you add the new domain to the existing domain, you would create *exams.courses.com*, in which exams is the child domain of courses.com **(Figure 17-10)**.

◆ **Forest:** A **forest** is a group of one or more trees. A forest is the fundamental security boundary on a Windows 2000 network. All computers that must share a single Active Directory must be in the same forest, and all domains in a forest share a common schema and global catalog. The **schema** is the database design, which can be extended by adding new object classes or new attributes. A class is the pattern for a set of objects that share a definable set of characteristics. For each class, the schema defines the permanent set of characteristics the class *must* have and the optional attributes that it *may* have. Every object in Active Directory is an instance of one or more classes in the schema. The **global catalog** is a partial read-only copy of all objects in Active Directory that stores commonly used object attributes. Its functions are to respond to logon requests and search queries. All trees in a forest have established transitive trust relationships via the Kerberos V5 security protocol. **Transitive trust** means that if a domain has established a trust relationship with another domain, it can also communicate and connect to the domains that that domain trusts and vice versa. The trust relationship is extended to include all other domains that are trusted by that domain. In other words, if domain1 trusts domain2, which trusts domain3, then domain1 and domain3 can communicate because they share a trust relationship with domain2. Domains that do not share a common domain name can be grouped together in a forest and a forest can contain multiple trees. For example, Redhenacct.com and Redhenfinance.com are two different trees because they do not share a contiguous namespace, but they can both be in the same forest in the Active Directory configuration so that users can access resources in the domains in each of the trees.

Figure 17-10 Trees

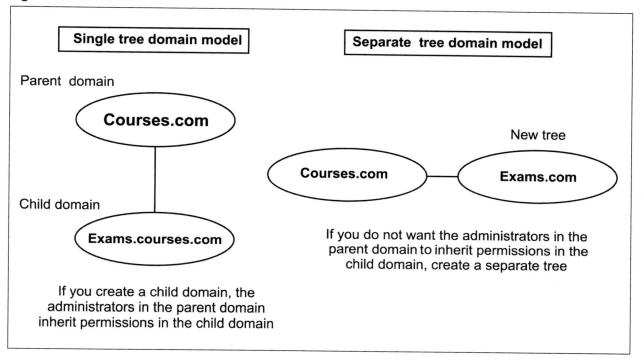

skill 4

Introducing Active Directory Structure (cont'd)

exam objective

Basic knowledge

overview

The physical Active Directory structure refers to where objects are located on the network, for example, where a certain computer, server, or printer is located. It outlines, for example, what servers are connected on a LAN and which clients are connected via WANs.

◆ **Sites:** Sites are defined by creating subnets for each of the physical locations on the network. A **site** is a group of TCP/IP subnets with dependable and consistent connections, generally meaning a high-speed link (10Mbps+). **Subnets** are a grouping of devices that share a common network prefix (**Figure-17-11**). Computers in close physical proximity (i.e., on a LAN) are grouped together to form a subnet. When a user logs on to a domain, his or her client computer is automatically associated with a site according to the subnet on which it exists. Additional sites are typically created when administrators think that the domain controllers are inadequately responding to user requests. Multiple sites are used to control the authentication and replication processes so that network traffic across WAN links can be minimized.

more

When you create additional sites, connections are automatically generated among the various sites. However, the clients on those sites must be **site aware**, or able to recognize the site-related data that Active Directory is imparting. Windows 2000 Professional and Server machines are, by design, site responsive, but on Windows NT 4.0 and Windows 9.x machines, you must install the Active Directory client extensions to give them site awareness. Installing client extensions will also allow these machines to log on to the domain controller that is nearest to them and to change passwords on any Windows 2000 domain controller, as long as the computer is a member of a Windows 2000 domain.

Figure 17-11 Subnets

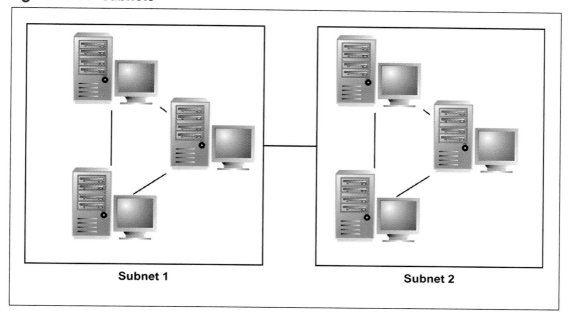

Subnet 1   Subnet 2

skill 5

Introducing Active Directory Concepts and Services

exam objective

Basic knowledge

overview

To further understand the contents and structure of Active Directory, you must have a broader understanding of the term schema. Schema in general defines the contents and organizational structure of Active Directory. For all objects in Active Directory, such as computers, users, and groups, the schema defines the attributes of these objects, their classes, and class properties. For example, for the user object, a schema defines the user attributes, such as the first name, last name, and logon name. For each object class, the schema defines the attributes an instance of the class must have, such as the object name, object identifier, and additional optional attributes that it may have. Furthermore, the schema defines the parent object class from which the current object class is derived. The schema is created automatically when the Active Directory service is installed. The schema initially contains the definition and attributes of objects supported by default, such as user accounts, computers, and groups. You can create new classes and assign new attributes to existing objects, thereby extending the schema.

You must also have a broader understanding of the global catalog, as well as be familiar with the concepts of a namespace and a naming convention (**Figure 17-12**).

Global Catalog: The global catalog stores information about objects in a forest. On networks where there is only one domain controller, the global catalog will be stored on the single domain controller and will perform both functions: domain controller and global catalog server. On networks which have several domain controllers, the global catalog will be stored on at least one of them and you can designate additional domain controllers as global catalog servers in order to provide quicker responses to user requests. The global catalog allows users to find directory information no matter which domain it is stored on. The global catalog stores a replica of each object, but not all of its attributes. Only the attributes that will be needed for searches to locate the full copy of the object are stored. This is called a partial replica. Because the global catalog holds a partial replica of every object in Active Directory, all domain data does not have to be replicated to all other domain controllers in order for users to locate data anywhere on the network. When information about objects is updated, a global catalog server exchanges this information with other global catalog servers in a forest. This ensures that users have access to the latest information about objects. The global catalog also allows users to locate logon servers on the network by providing universal group membership information to the domain controller when they begin the logon process. There must be a global catalog server on the network, or else users—unless they are members of the Domain Administrators group—will not be able to log on to the network; they will only be able to log on to the local computer.

Namespace: A naming system is the system by which names are connected with objects and objects are located based on their names. In other words, the system follows the same set of naming conventions (see below). A naming system supplies a naming service to its users for all functions related to naming objects. Directory services, such as Active Directory, extend the naming service so that objects can also be assigned attributes. When objects are also associated with attributes, users can search for objects based on their attributes instead of only being able to perform straight object name searches. DNS is the naming system for Active Directory. The namespace is simply the set of names in the naming system, so a DNS namespace, such as Active Directory, contains the names of the DNS domains. It is the conceptual delimited area in which object names are looked up or resolved. There are two types of namespaces, contiguous and disjointed. In a **contiguous namespace**, the name of the child object always contains the name of the parent domain. Domains that form a single domain tree share a contiguous namespace. In a **disjointed** or **non-contiguous namespace**, the names of a parent object and of a child of the same parent do not have a direct relationship.

tip

The domain is also created when the Active Directory service is installed.

Figure 17-12 Global Catalog

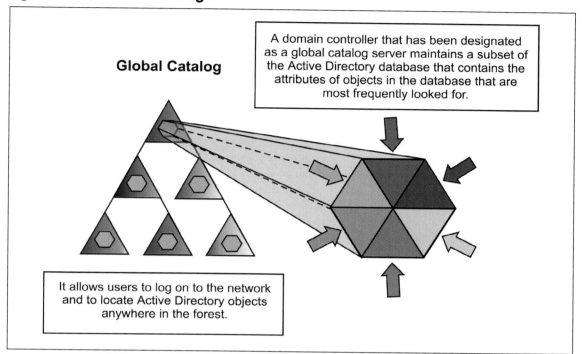

Global Catalog

A domain controller that has been designated as a global catalog server maintains a subset of the Active Directory database that contains the attributes of objects in the database that are most frequently looked for.

It allows users to log on to the network and to locate Active Directory objects anywhere in the forest.

skill 5

Introducing Active Directory Concepts and Services (cont'd)

exam objective

Basic knowledge

overview

Naming Conventions: Active Directory uses four naming conventions: distinguished names, relative distinguished names, globally unique identifiers, and user principal names. The **distinguished name**, or **DN**, is a unique identifier for an object that contains the name of the domain where the object is stored and the full path to the object, including every level of the container objects in which it is stored. An example of this would be: **CN=Ted Parks**, **CN=Users**, **DC=domain1**, **DC=com**. If you do not know the exact DN of an object, you can still locate it by searching for one of its attributes. The **relative distinguished name (RDN)** is part of the object name. It is the attribute that identifies it as unique from its peers, usually its "common name", for example a user account name such as TedParks. RDNs are unique within a specific parent container, meaning that no two objects in the same parent container can have the same RDN or common name. A **globally unique identifier** or **GUID** is another unique identifier that is assigned to an object when it is created. A GUID is a 128-bit number that never changes, regardless of changes in the location or the name of the object. The GUID is used internally by Active Directory and by applications so that they can locate the object again even if it has been moved or renamed. The GUID is one of the attributes of an object that is stored in the global catalog. **User principal names**, or **UPNs** contain the user account name, plus the DNS name of the domain where the user account object is stored, separated by a @ sign. For example, **TParks@redhen.com** could be the UPN for the TedParks user account in the redhen.com tree **(Figure 17-13)**.

Figure 17-13 Active Directory concepts and services

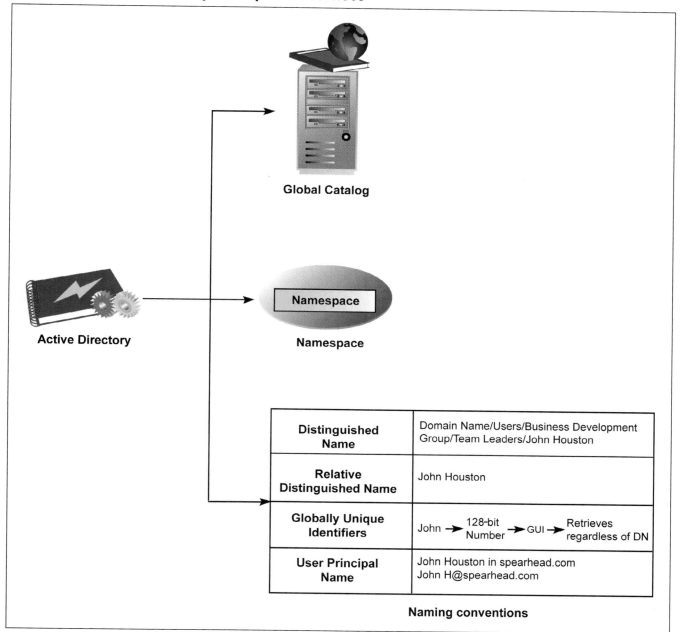

Distinguished Name	Domain Name/Users/Business Development Group/Team Leaders/John Houston
Relative Distinguished Name	John Houston
Globally Unique Identifiers	John → 128-bit Number → GUI → Retrieves regardless of DN
User Principal Name	John Houston in spearhead.com John H@spearhead.com

Naming conventions

skill 6

Managing Web Server Resources

exam objective

Manage and troubleshoot Web server resources.

overview

If you want users on your network to be able to share resources with other users who are running Web browsers or FTP (File Transfer Protocol) utilities, you can install **Internet Information Server (IIS)** version 5, which comes with Windows 2000 Professional. Sharing Web resources involves publishing your files using HTTP (HyperText Transfer Protocol) rather than the SMB (Server Message Blocks) protocol that is used by the Server service (File and Print Sharing for Microsoft Networks) when you share folders and printers. However, TCP/IP must be installed before you can install IIS.

Like any other resources on your network, shared Web resources must have access controls configured to keep them secure. One simple tip is to disable services which you do not want users to be able to run. This is done in the Internet Information Services snap-in to the Computer Management console. You can also change the default TCP/IP port for a service so that users will have to know the port number in order to access it. The default port for a Web server is 80, while the default port number for an FTP server is 21. If you change these, users will have to add a colon and the port number to the URL in order to gain access. Furthermore, you can limit the number of incoming connections, restrict which users will be allowed to have Operator privileges, restrict access to the home directory for either the WWW or the FTP service by setting permissions. In addition, you can either restrict the access allowed by or deny all access to the anonymous user account. You can also only grant access to a specific range of IP addresses or you can deny access for specific IP or DNS addresses or a range of addresses. Another method for restricting access is to open the Advanced TCP/IP Property dialog box for the Local Area Connection and set filters so that only certain TCP or UDP (User Datagram Protocol) ports can be used. You can also set specific IP protocols that you want to be used for incoming traffic.

how to

Install IIS on your computer.

1. Click [🔊 Start], point to **Settings**, and then click the **Control Panel** command to open the **Control Panel** window.
2. Double-click the **Add/Remove Programs** icon to open the **Add/Remove Programs** window.
3. Click the **Add/Remove Windows Components** icon in the left panel to open the **Windows Components Wizard** screen (**Figure 17-14**).
4. Click the **Internet Information Services (IIS)** check box in the **Components** list box. (**Figure 17-15**).
5. Click [Next >]. The **Insert Disk** window appears asking you to insert the **Windows 2000 Professional CD** into the **CD drive**.

Figure 17-14 The Add/Remove Windows Components icon in the Windows Components Wizard screen

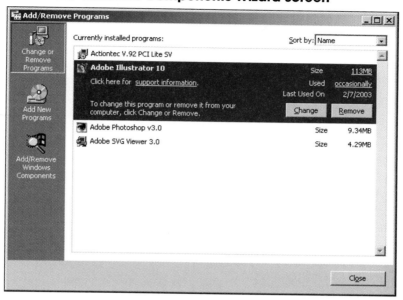

Figure 17-15 Installing IIS on a computer

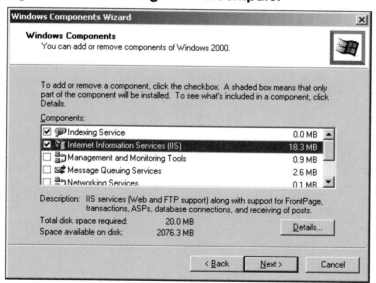

skill 6

Managing Web Server Resources
(cont'd)

exam objective   Manage and troubleshoot Web server resources.

how to

tip

Double-clicking the Administrative Tools icon in the Control Panel window will open the Administrative Tools window.

6. Insert the Windows 2000 Professional CD and click [OK] to open the **Configuring Components** screen. This screen shows the progress of relevant IIS files as they are copied to the system.

7. After all of the files are copied onto the system, the **Completing the Windows Components Wizard** screen opens to inform you that the Windows Components Wizard has successfully finished **(Figure 17-16)**.

8. Click [Finish] to exit the Wizard.

9. Close the Add/Remove Programs window.

10. Close the Control Panel window. After you have installed IIS on your computer, two new tools, **Internet Information Services Manager** and **Personal Web Manager** are added in the **Administrative Tools** window **(Figure 17-17)**. You can use these tools to configure and manage your Web site.

Figure 17-16 Completing the Windows Components Wizard

Figure 17-17 New tools added to the Administrative Tools window

Personal Web Manager and Internet Information Services Manager can be used to configure and manage your Web site

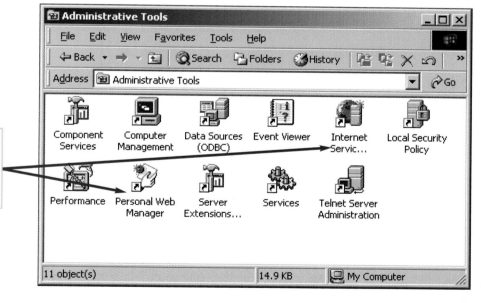

Summary

◆ Computers on a network uniquely identify each other by using Internet Protocol (IP) addresses.

◆ An IP address is a 32-bit number consisting of four octets separated by periods (an octet is an 8-bit value).

◆ Windows 2000 uses the Domain Name System (DNS) service to convert host names or FQDNs to IP addresses (name resolution).

◆ DNS is a large database containing IP addresses and their corresponding names.

◆ DNS has a hierarchical structure. The nodes in this hierarchical structure are called domains.

◆ The domain at the top of the DNS hierarchy is called the root domain (represented by a period). Underneath the root domain are the top-level domains, and underneath the top-level domains are the second-level domains.

◆ A Fully Qualified Domain Name (FQDN) includes a domain name in addition to a host name.

◆ Zones are distinct, contiguous segments of the DNS namespace that make a large site manageable by enabling different administrators to manage different zones.

◆ To resolve IP addresses to names and vice-versa, DNS uses the name resolution process, which consists of forward lookup queries and reverse lookup queries. Forward lookup queries are used for resolving names to IP addresses while reverse lookup queries resolve IP addresses to names.

◆ in-addr.arpa is a special second-level domain that contains name-to-IP-address mappings indexed by IP addresses.

◆ In order to use the DNS name resolution service you need to configure your computer as a DNS client.

◆ To configure your computer as a DNS client, Transmission Control Protocol/Internet Protocol (TCP/IP) must be running on your computer.

◆ Active Directory organizes objects in a structured hierarchical order. The domain is a logical group of users, computers, and resources.

◆ Domains are grouped in a hierarchal structure called a tree. A tree is composed of a contiguous DNS namespace.

◆ A forest is a group of one or more trees that do not share a contiguous namespace. All computers that must share a single Active Directory must be in the same forest, and all domains in a forest share a common schema and global catalog.

◆ The schema defines the contents and organizational structure of Active Directory. For all objects in Active Directory, such as computers, users, and groups, the schema defines the attributes of these objects, their classes, and class properties.

◆ Computers in close physical proximity are grouped together to form a subnet. On TCP/IP networks, subnets are a grouping of devices that share a common network prefix.

◆ Sites are defined by creating subnets for each of the physical locations on the network. A site is a group of TCP/IP subnets with dependable and consistent connections, generally meaning a high-speed link (10Mbps+).

◆ The global catalog is a partial read-only copy of all objects in Active Directory that stores commonly used object attributes. Its functions are to respond to logon requests and search queries.

◆ The global catalog stores a replica of each object, but not all of its attributes. Only the attributes that will be needed for searches to locate the full copy of the object are stored. This is called a partial replica.

◆ Because the global catalog holds a partial replica of every object in Active Directory, all domain data does not have to be replicated to all other domain controllers in order for users to locate data anywhere on the network.

◆ On networks where there is only one domain controller, the global catalog will be stored on the single domain controller and will perform both functions: domain controller and global catalog server.

◆ On networks which have several domain controllers, the global catalog will be stored on at least one of them and you can designate additional domain controllers as global catalog servers in order to provide quicker responses to user requests

◆ A namespace is a conceptual delimited area in a domain in which an object name is resolved.

◆ There are two types of namespaces, contiguous and disjointed.

◆ In a contiguous namespace, the name of the child object always contains the name of the parent domain. Domains that form a single domain tree share a contiguous namespace.

◆ In a disjointed or non-contiguous namespace, the names of a parent object and of a child of the same parent do not have a direct relationship.

◆ If you want users on your network to be able to share resources with other users who are running Web browsers or FTP (File Transfer Protocol) utilities, you can install Internet Information Server (IIS) version 5 which comes with Windows 2000 Professional.

◆ Sharing Web resources involves publishing your files using HTTP (HyperText Transfer Protocol) rather than the SMB (Server Message Blocks) protocol that is used by the Server service (File and Print Sharing for Microsoft Networks) normally when you share folders and printers.

Key Terms

Active Directory
Authoritative server
Contiguous namespace
Directory service
Disjointed namespace
Distinguished name (DN)
DNS name server
Domain
Domain controller
Forest
Forward lookup query
Fully Qualified Domain Name (FQDN)
Global catalog

Global catalog server
Globally unique identifier (GUID)
Host
Host name
in-addr.arpa
Internet Information Server (IIS)
Multimaster replication
Name resolution
Object
Organizational unit (OU)
Relative Distinguished Name (RDN)
Replication
Reverse lookup query
Root Domain

Schema
Second-level domain
Site
Site aware
Subnet
Top-level domain
Transitive trust
Tree
Time to Live (TTL)
User Principal Names (UPN)
Web server
Zones
Zone transfers

Test Yourself

1. Which of the following are involved in the name resolution process?
   a. Forward lookup queries
   b. Reverse lookup queries
   c. The in-addr.arpa domain
   d. All of the above

2. Names are translated into IP addresses using:
   a. Reverse lookup queries.
   b. in-addr.arpa.
   c. Forward lookup queries.
   d. Time to Live (TTL).

3. In the domain name reviews.networks.com., which of the following is the root domain?
   a. reviews
   b. com
   c. the final period
   d. networks.com

4. You need to configure your computer as a DNS client. To do so, you need to use the:
   a. Add/Remove Programs window.
   b. Internet Protocol (TCP/IP) Properties dialog box.
   c. Internet Information Services Manager.
   d. Windows Components Wizard.

5. Which one of the following components must be installed on your computer in order to configure it as a DNS client?
   a. Personal Web Manager.
   b. The in-addr.arpa domain.
   c. TCP/IP.

6. A directory service:
   a. Is a database containing IP addresses and their corresponding names.
   b. Is a database of resources and services available on a network.
   c. Is a group of domains.

   d. Contains information regarding all objects contained in a tree.

7. Which of the following defines the contents and organizational structure of Active Directory, particularly the attributes, classes, and class properties for all objects?
   a. Schema
   b. Domain
   c. Domain Controller
   d. Site

8. Which of the following stores information about objects in a forest, and helps users to locate logon servers on the network by providing universal group membership information to the domain controller?
   a. Schema
   b. Global catalog
   c. Namespace
   d. Site

9. Which one of the following naming conventions contains the complete path leading to an object, including the name of the domain that holds the object?
   a. Distinguished name
   b. Relative distinguished name
   c. Globally unique identifier (GUID)
   d. User principal name

10. When an IIS Web server is installed on a computer running Windows 2000 Professional: [Choose all that apply.]
    a. The installed Web server is able to manage heavy network traffic.
    b. Two new tools, Server Extensions and Services are added to the Administrative Tools window.
    c. The Web server is packaged with Internet- and intranet-related programs for sending e-mail, downloading requests for FTP files, and building and publishing Web pages.

Projects: On Your Own

1. Configure your computer as a DNS client.
   a. Open the **Network and Dial-up Connections** window.
   b. Open the **Local area connection Properties** dialog box.
   c. Open the **Internet Protocol (TCP/IP) Properties** dialog box.
   d. Select the **Use the following DNS server addresses** option button.
   e. Type the IP address of the primary DNS server for the client in the **Preferred DNS Server** text box.
   f. Close the **Internet Protocol (TCP/IP) Properties** dialog box.
   g. Close the **Local area connection Properties** dialog box.

2. Install IIS on a computer running Windows 2000 Professional.
   a. Log on as **Administrator**.
   b. Open the **Control Panel** window.
   c. Open the **Add/Remove Programs** window.
   d. Start the **Windows Components Wizard**.
   e. Install **Internet Information Services** (IIS) on the computer.
   f. Close the **Windows Components Wizard**.
   g. Close the **Add/Remove Programs** window.
   h. Close the **Control Panel** window.

Problem Solving Scenarios

1. Grey Polymers Inc. is an industrial supplier of polymer products to small and medium businesses located in Atlanta, Georgia. Grey purchases large quantities of basic polymers from large chemical suppliers. It then re-sells the polymers to smaller firms who use the products in extrusions, moldings, and fabrications. Grey Polymers expanded rapidly in the last two years, from a small firm with only ten employees to 150 employees at last count. The Network Administrator has asked you to install a DNS server to speed up the name resolution process on the TCP/IP network. There are about 100 clients. Write a memo describing how you go about configuring each of these clients as a DNS client.

2. Your boss, Sharon Tims, the Systems Administrator at Eagle Sporting Goods Inc., has read about other firms moving various employee human resource applications to corporate intranets. A corporate intranet is a Web site built to run on an internal TCP/IP corporate network. Users access the information on an intranet using their computer's browser. Sharon has asked you to install an Internet Information Server on the company's Windows 2000 network. Write a plan in the form of a memo describing how you will install this server.

Glossary

Access control entry (ACE) Entry in an access control list. Contains a set of access rights and a security identifier (SID) that identifies a trustee (ex: user or group) for whom the rights are allowed, denied, or audited.

Access control list (ACL) A list of security protections that apply to an object such as files and printers. Two types: discretionary and system.

Access Control Settings dialog box Provides options to assign Special Access permissions to objects.

Access token Contains the security information for a logon session and identifies the user, the user's groups, and the user's privileges.

Account lockout duration Used to set the time duration an account will remain locked out once the account lockout threshold has been reached.

Account lockout policy Used to set policies relating to locking out user accounts due to invalid logon attempts.

Account lockout threshold Number of invalid logon attempts that will be tolerated before a user account is locked out.

Account policies Used to set user account properties that control the logon procedure, such as password and account lockout rules.

ACE See Access control entry.

ACL See Access control list.

ACPI See Advanced Configuration and Power Interface.

Action log Contains information about the events that have transpired during Setup, including the copying of files, the creation of registry entries, and any errors that may have occurred.

Active Directory (AD) Stores information about network objects; used by network users to locate resources.

Active partition Partition used to boot the computer.

AD See Active Directory.

Add Printer Wizard Used to add and share a local or network printer on your computer.

Add/Remove Hardware Wizard Used to add, delete, upgrade, and troubleshoot computer peripherals.

Address Resolution Protocol (ARP) Used to map an IP address to a Media Access Control (MAC) address.

Admin$ A hidden administrative share that points to the %systemroot% directory.

Administrative shared folders Folders available only to Network Administrators and hidden from other users.

Administrator account Built-in account used to manage the overall functioning of a computer.

Advanced Configuration Power Interface (ACPI) Power management standard that allows the operating system to control and manage power consumption.

Advanced Power Management (APM) BIOS controlled method of power management. Uses activity timeouts to determine when to transition devices to low power states.

Advanced RISC Computing (ARC) path Points to a valid boot partition containing the Windows 2000 operating system files.

Alert Generated when a specific counter exceeds or falls below a specified value.

Answer file File that contains the inputs required for the Windows Setup program.

AppleTalk Protocol that enables computers running Windows 2000 Server and Apple Macintosh to share resources such as files and printers.

Application layer Layer of TCP/IP used by applications to gain access to the network.

Application log Records events that occur when an application is run.

Application response setting Setting that can be accessed in the Performance Options dialog box that enables you to optimize processor performance for foreground applications or background services.

Archive attribute Property for files and folders that is used to identify them when they have changed. Also known as an archive bit or backup marker.

Archive bit See archive attribute.

ARP See Address Resolution Protocol.

Assigned application Application that is automatically installed when the user opens the application from the Start menu or attempts to open a file created using the application. If assigned to a computer, will install the next time the computer is started.

Audit object access audit policy Policy that must be activated in order to enable auditing for a file or folder.

Audit policy Sets the types of events you want to monitor in the Security event log of a computer.

Auditing Used to monitor events that occur on a computer, such as who has accessed, or attempted to access, a file.

Author mode Type of console mode that provides users complete access to MMC functionality.

Authoritative server Server where the primary zone database file is located.

Backup Copies of data are created for the purpose of disaster recovery.

Backup log Text file that records backup operations on a computer and is stored on the hard disk of the computer.

Backup marker See archive attribute.

Backup set Collection of backed up files and folders you have stored in a file or on one or more tapes.

Backup utility Prevents accidental loss of data due to hardware, software failure or user error. Can be used to schedule automatic backups at regular intervals.

Backup Wizard Used to configure backup jobs by selecting files, drives, or network data, and choosing where to store the data. You can manually back up data or schedule unattended backup jobs.

Bandwidth Allocation Protocol (BAP) Dynamically provides optimum bandwidth by adding and dropping connections and helps in reducing connection costs during remote access.

BAP See Bandwidth Allocation Protocol.

Basic storage Data storage type in which the hard disk is divided into partitions that function as logically separate units of storage.

Binding order Used to establish which protocol should be used first when a network connection is initiated.

Boot loader Known as Ntldr in Windows 2000. Responsible for reading information from boot.ini and then loading the appropriate operating system based on user selection or a default timeout.

Boot process Process by which a computer starts.

Boot sector Portion of the hard disk which contains the program that loads the Windows 2000 Professional operating system and the information about the file system.

Boot.ini Contains information relating to the operating systems(s) installed on the computer.

Bottlenecks System resources that slow down the performance of a computer.

Built-in local groups Used to assign rights to perform system tasks on a single computer.

Built-in system groups Groups whose membership is controlled by the operating system.

Built-in user accounts Default accounts that are created by Windows 2000.

Caching Enables you to access the contents of a shared folder offline.

Callback Feature that can be used for inbound connections to increase security for your network and localize long distance charges.

Change permission Allows users to create folders, add files to folders, modify data in files, add data to files, modify file attributes, and delete files and folders, in addition to actions permitted by the Read permission.

Checksums Numerical values that are assigned to files based on their contents. The Emergency Repair process compares the system file checksums on the hard drive with the checksums on the ERD. If there are missing files or files that do not match because they are corrupt, you will be prompted to reinstall them from the installation CD.

Checkupgradeonly switch Used with the Winnt32 command to generate a hardware compatibility report.

Chkupgrd.exe Utility that immediately generates hardware compatibility report; is much faster compared to checkupgradeonly switch.

C$ D$ E$ Drive letter hidden administrative share that points to the root of the corresponding logical drive.

CDFS See Compact Disk File System.

Challenge Handshake Authentication Protocol (CHAP) Provides authentication when a user attempts to establish a connection, based on values calculated using an algorithm.

CHAP See Challenge Handshake Authentication Protocol

Cipher utility Command-line utility used to encrypt and decrypt files and folders under specified conditions or requirements.

Client (Respond Only) IPSec policy used to provide maximum flexibility when negotiating security. Communication will occur with untrusted servers, but encryption will be used when requested by a server.

Compact Disk File System (CDFS) File system format used to store data on CD-ROMs.

Computer name See NetBIOS name.

Connectionless communication Communication in which the host can send a message to the recipient without establishing a channel.

Console Administrative tools made up of programs called snap-ins that are used to perform various management tasks.

Console tree Organizes the snap-ins available in a console in hierarchical order.

Contiguous namespace Namespace in which the name of the child object contains the name of the parent domain. Domains that form a single domain tree share a contiguous namespace.

Control set Contains data about the configuration settings used to control the computer.

Copy backup Backs up all selected files and folders with or without the archive attribute and does not remove the archive attribute.

Counter Performance measure for an object that can be quantified, such as the percentage of time the processor is busy (%Processor Time).

Counter logs Uses GUI data from System Monitor to create a log file.

Create Shared Folder Wizard Guides you through the process of selecting the folder you want to share, making it available to network users, and assigning permissions to the users who will be accessing it.

Custom console Created by combining preconfigured snap-ins. Used to perform common administrative tasks.

Daily backup Backs up the selected files and folders that have been modified during the day and does not remove the archive bit.

Data Link Control (DLC) Special-purpose and non-routable protocol designed to access IBM mainframe or minicomputers and certain networked printers.

Default gateway Acts as an intermediate device between hosts on different network segments.

Defragmentation Process that rearranges files, programs, and unused space to ensure that all related components of files and programs are placed in adjacent sectors of the hard disk, enabling files to open more quickly.

Details pane Displays the contents of the snap-in that is selected in the console tree.

Device driver Software that enables a specific device such as a printer, modem, or network card to communicate with an operating system.

Device Manager Utility in Windows 2000 Professional that you use to view and change device properties, update device drivers, configure device settings, and uninstall devices.

DHCP See Dynamic Host Configuration Protocol.

Differential backup Backs up selected files and folders on which the archive bit has been set, but the attribute is not removed.

Digital signature Code attached to driver files to assure the file is from the correct source—typically the hardware manufacturer or Microsoft.

Directory database Central database shared by a group of computers that form a Windows 2000 domain.

Directory service Provides a directory that stores information about resources and services available on a network.

Disjointed namespace Name of a parent object and the name of a child of the same parent are not directly related.

Disk cleanup A tool used to free space on the hard drives by removing deleted, orphaned, temporary, or downloaded files

Disk defragmenter A utility that rearranges files, programs, and unused space to ensure that all related components of files and programs are placed in adjacent sectors of the hard disk, enabling files to open more quickly.

Disk limit Value for disk quota set on the Quotas tab in Properties dialog box for an NTFS volume or partition. Designates the amount of space a user is allowed to use.

Disk management snap-in Used to create, delete, and format partitions on a basic disk; lets you create simple, spanned or striped volumes on dynamic disks.

Disk mirroring All or part of a hard disk is duplicated onto one or more hard disks. Any change made to the original disk is copied to the other disk.

Disk properties Attributes of a hard disk.

Disk quotas Used to track and control disk usage on a per-user, per-volume basis.

Disk striping A technique that divides data into 64K blocks and spreads it equally in a fixed rate and order among all disks in an array.

Distinguished Name (DN) A unique identifier for an object that contains the name of the domain where the object is stored and the full path to the object including every level of the container objects in which it is stored.

Distribution server Network server that stores the installation files for distribution over a network.

DLC See Data Link Control.

DN See Distinguished Name.

DNS See Domain Name System.

DNS name server Server containing a zone database file.

Domain Logical group of computers on a network that access a common directory database for authentication purposes and that follow common rules and procedures. Domains are the fundamental building block in a Windows 2000 network.

Domain controller Computer running Windows 2000 server on which Active Directory resides.

Domain local group Used to assign rights and permissions to users in a particular domain.

Domain Name System (DNS) Main name resolution service for Windows 2000. Correlates host names and fully qualified domain names (FQDNs) to IP addresses.

Domain user account Used to access the resources of a computer in a domain.

Dynamic Host Configuration Protocol (DHCP) Protocol that automatically assigns IP addresses.

Dynamic disk Disk that is initialized for dynamic storage.

Dynamic storage Storage type only supported by Windows 2000 Professional and Server that uses volumes instead of partitions.

Emergency Repair Disk (ERD) Utility used to create an emergency disk that can be used to repair and restart a Windows 2000 Professional computer if the computer cannot be started on its own.

Enable boot logging Enabled automatically when a computer is started in Safe Mode. Logs all events related to the loading of drivers and services.

Encrypting File System (EFS) Feature of Windows 2000 Professional that enables users to encrypt and decrypt files on a hard disk.

Encryption The process of encoding the contents of a file, or all of the files in a folder, so that it is unreadable unless the reader possesses the appropriate key.

Enforce password history Used to set the number of passwords that will be stored in the password history.

ERD See Emergency Repair Disk.

Error log Stores a description of the errors that have occurred and an entry indicating the magnitude of each error.

Event Viewer Computer Management console snap-in that allows you to view the Security log.

Extended partition A partition in a basic disk created out of any available free space. Only one extended partition can be created on a hard disk.

Extensible Authentication Protocol (EAP) Used to extend the logon security process using smart cards or certificates.

Extension snap-in Provides additional administrative functionality to other snap-ins.

FAT See File Allocation Table.

FAT16 See File Allocation Table

FAT32 file system The 32-bit version of the FAT file system. Enables the operating system to keep track of the status of various segments of disk space used for file storage.

Fault tolerance The ability of a computer or operating system to respond to a crisis without loss of data.

File Allocation Table (FAT) A table or list maintained by the operating system that keeps track of the status of various segments of disk space used for file storage. Also referred to as FAT16.

File and Print Services for NetWare (FPNW) Enables a NetWare client to use the file and print resources on a computer running Windows 2000 Server.

File Transfer Protocol (FTP) Used to transfer files between a computer running Windows 2000 Professional and a TCP/IP host running server software and FTP. It also provides directory and file handling services such as listing directory contents and deleting files and selecting file formats.

FilterKeys Accessibility option that programs the system to ignore repeated keystrokes.

Finger Used to retrieve information about users, including their user name and how long they have been logged on.

Forest Group of trees that share a common schema, global catalog, and configuration.

Forward lookup query Resolves a name to an IP address.

FPNW See File and Print Services for Netware.

Frame type Defines how the network adapter card formats data.

FTP See File Transfer Protocol.

Full Control permission Allows full access to the shared folder, including all actions permitted by the Read and Change permissions; users can also change permissions on the share.

Fully Qualified Domain Name (FQDN) Includes a domain name in addition to the host name.

Generic token card Physical card that provides authentication.

Global catalog A partial read-only copy of all objects in Active Directory that stores commonly used object attributes.

Global catalog server A domain controller that stores a copy of a global catalog.

Global group Used to assign permissions for accessing resources in a domain; are stored in Active Directory.

Globally Unique IDentifier (GUID) A unique identifier that is assigned to an object when the object is created. A GUID is a 128-bit number that never changes, regardless of changes in the location or the name of the object.

Group A collection of user accounts that have similar rights and permissions.

Group policies Used to administer and manage a wide range of network environment settings, including password restrictions, software distribution, and the desktop appearance.

Guest account A built-in account that can be assigned to users who limited access to a system on a temporary basis.

GUID See Globally Unique IDentifier.

Hardware Compatibility List (HCL) List of devices verified by Microsoft to be compatible with Windows 2000 Professional.

Hardware profile Contains information about the devices that need to be started when you boot the computer and the settings with which the devices should be started.

HCL See Hardware Compatibility List.

Hibernate mode See Hibernation.

Hibernation Enables Windows 2000 Professional to save your current system state to your hard disk and then shuts down the system while you are not working on it. Also referred to as Hibernate mode.

Hive Set of files that contains keys, subkeys, and value entries of the Registry.

Home folder Folder used to store personal files that can be stored on a client computer, but is usually stored on a shared folder on a network server so that it serves as a centralized storage area that users can access from any workstation.

Host Computer where a resource resides.

Host ID Part of IP address that represents a specific computer.

Host name Name of a specific computer on a given network.

Hostname Utility used to validate the host name for a local computer

Hot plugging See Hot swapping.

Hot swapping Ability to add and remove devices without shutting down and restarting the system. Also called hot plugging.

ICMP See Internet Control Message Protocol.

ICS See Internet Connection Sharing.

IGMP See Internet Group Management Protocol.

in-addr.arpa Second-level domain expressly created so that a reverse lookup query need not carry out an extensive search of all domain names.

Inbound connection Used so that other computers can connect to yours via phone line, the Internet or direct cable.

Incremental backup Backs up only the selected files and folders that have the archive attribute, which is then removed.

Installation script Script that enables you to specify the variations in the hardware and software configuration of your computer.

IntelliMirror Group of distributed computing technologies that includes roaming user profiles, offline files, and Windows Installer. Allows users to easily move between computers while still being able to access their own data, applications, and settings.

Internal network number Unique number is used for internal routing purposes to identify a specific computer on the network. Also referred to as a virtual network number.

Internet Connection Sharing (ICS) Feature that enables multiple computers on a local area network to share a single Internet connection.

Internet Control Message Protocol (ICMP) Enables hosts to exchange status and error information.

Internet Group Management Protocol (IGMP) Protocol that enables multicast routers on a network to communicate with all member devices in a multicast group.

Internet Information Server (IIS) Enables users on a network to share resources with others who are running Web browsers or FTP utilities.

Internet layer Layer of TCP/IP that determines the route data will take when data packets are transferred from source computer to destination computer.

Internet Protocol (IP) Protocol within TCP/IP protocol suite responsible for addressing and routing.

Internet Protocol Security (IPSec) Set of security protocols and cryptographic protection services that are used to encrypt data packets in the IP layer and provide secure communications over IP networks.

Internet Protocol (IP) security policies Used to configure IPSec security services, which provide a variable level of protection for most types of traffic in existing networks.

Internet Service Provider (ISP) Company that provides individuals and organizations access to the Internet.

IP See Internet Protocol.

IP address A 32-bit number consisting of four octets and containing two identifiers, one for the network and one for the computer or host.

Ipconfig Used to confirm TCP/IP configuration parameters on a host.

IPC$ (Interprocess Communications) Administrative share used to facilitate IPC communication between systems.

IPSec See Internet Protocol Security.

IrDA Agreed-upon formats for transmitting data over infrared connections, thus allowing other programs and devices to interact with Windows 2000.

ISP See Internet Service Provider.

Kerberos V5 Internet standard security protocol for handling authentication of user or system identity.

Keys Correspond to hardware or software objects on a computer and store the information in sections.

Last Known Good Configuration (LKGC) Enables you to start your computer using the information saved in the Registry after the last successful logon.

Layer Two Tunneling Protocol (L2TP) Tunneling protocol that creates a secure tunnel across an untrusted communication channel.

Local backup Backup method that must be performed at each client and server computer.

Local group A collection of local user accounts stored in the local security database on a single computer.

Local policies Used to set group policies for local computers that do not use the Active Directory.

Local print device Print device that is physically connected to a computer through a physical port.

Local security database Lists user accounts and resource security information for the computer on which the database resides.

Local user account A user account that is stored in a local security database on a particular computer. It can only be used to access resources on the computer on which it was created.

Local user profile Stored locally and accessed from the logon computer.

Log files Information files generated during Setup process. Include action log and error log, among others.

Logical drive A volume you create within an extended partition on a basic disk.

Logon script A set of command-line operations that are performed when a user logs onto a system.

Manage Documents permission Gives users the ability to pause, resume, restart, and delete documents from all users that have been spooled to be printed.

Manage Printers permission Grants administrative control over a printer. Users can pause and restart the printer and change printer properties.

Mandatory user profile Read-only roaming user profile. In this type of profile, Windows 2000 does not save the changes a user makes to the desktop environment after the user logs off.

Master Boot Record (MBR) First sector on a hard disk. Contains a partition table with information on the primary and extended partitions including which primary partition is active.

Master disk image Used to copy the installation to other computers.

Maximum password age Used to set the maximum number of days users can keep a particular password.

MD5-CHAP See Message Digest 5 Challenge Handshake Authentication Protocol.

Media Access Control (MAC) address Unique 48-bit or 6-byte number also called the hardware address, physical address, or Ethernet address.

Member Of tab Tab in the User Properties dialog box where a user can be added or removed from a group.

Member server Computer that is not a domain controller of a Windows 2000 domain but runs Windows 2000 Server.

Message Digest 5 Challenge Handshake Authentication Protocol Uses the Message Digest 5 (MD5) algorithm to encrypt user names and passwords.

Microsoft CHAP (MS-CHAP) Microsoft version of CHAP.

Microsoft Management Console (MMC) A built-in administrative tool used to manage hardware, software, and network components.

Minimum password age Used to set the minimum number of days during which users must keep the same password.

Minimum password length Used to set the minimum number of characters a password must have.

Mini-Setup Wizard Starts the first time that a computer starts from a disk that has been duplicated by the Sysprep utility. The wizard gathers any information that is needed to further customize the computer installation.

Modem Device used to communicate between two computers, over a telephone line.

MouseKey Enables users to perform mouse functions using the numeric keypad.

Multicasting Transmission method for sending identical data to a select group of recipients. The server can transmit a single data stream, regardless of how many clients have requested it. When the data stream crosses a multicast-enabled switch or router, it is copied to the paths where clients that requested the stream are located.

Multilinked device Combines several ISDN lines or modem links to create one logical link and obtain greater bandwidth.

Multimaster replication Feature of Active Directory that enables changes to Active Directory on any domain controller to be automatically replicated to all other domain controllers in the domain.

Multiple displays Enables you to expand the size of your desktop across more than one monitor.

Multiprocessing Two or more CPUs carry out one or more processes simultaneously, with each processing unit working on a different set of instructions or on different parts of the same process.

My Documents Folder that provides an area for the users to store their personal files.

My Network Places Serves as a network resource browser for users, providing an easy way to connect to shared folders added as a network place.

Name resolution Process that resolves names into IP addresses and vice-versa in a domain name system.

Naming convention Pattern that is followed for all user logon names on a network to make it easy for users to remember their account names.

NBT NetBIOS over TCP/IP.

Nbtstat Displays protocol statistics and current TCP/IP connections using NBT (NetBIOS over TCP/IP).

NetBEUI Protocol used to share resources in a small LAN.

NetBIOS Fifteen-character, or fewer, name given to a computer that must be different from all other computer, workgroup, or domain names. Sometimes referred to as computer name.

NetBIOS over IPX Enables a NetWare client running NetBIOS to communicate with a computer running Windows 2000 Professional and NWLink NetBIOS.

Netstat Displays TCP/IP protocol statistics and its network connections.

Network backup Backup method in which data from multiple network computers are backed up on a single removable backup medium.

Network Connection Wizard Used to select the networking components required to establish connections with different kinds of computers.

Network ID Identifies all hosts on the network.

Network Interface Card (NIC) Expansion board you insert into a computer so that you can connect to a network.

Network Interface layer Layer of TCP/IP conceptual model that consists of physical media.

Network Monitor Driver 2 Protocol used to collect and displays statistics about the activity detected by the network card on a computer running Windows 2000 Professional.

Network number Unique hexadecimal number that must be specified for each frame type on a network adapter card.

Network printer Printer shared with other network users.

NIC See Network Interface Card.

Normal backup Backs up all selected files and folders whether an archive bit has been set or not, but removes the archive attribute as necessary to denote that a file has been backed up.

NTFS compression Feature that enables the compression of files and folders on an NTFS volume.

NTFS folder permissions NTFS permissions configured for folders. Includes Read, Write, List Folder Contents, Read and Execute, Modify, and Full Control.

NTFS file permissions NTFS permissions configured for files. Includes Read, Write, Read and Execute, Modify and Full Control.

NTFS file system Advanced file system designed for use specifically within the Windows 2000 operating system.

NTFS permissions Permissions used on NTFS disks to control access to network resources.

Ntldr See boot loader.

Ntuser.dat File that contains the system settings for an individual user account, along with environment settings for the user.

NWLink Protocol that enables clients running Microsoft operating systems to access resources on NetWare servers.

Object Any tangible or intangible thing stored in Active Directory. Can be a physical object such as a computer or a virtual object such as a share. In the context of system monitoring, a system resource such as a processor, disk, network interface card (NIC), or memory whose performance can be monitored.

Octet An 8-bit value.

Offline files and folders Network files that are stored locally so that they are available even if the user is not connected to the network.

Open Files folder Used to view a list of open files located in shared folders, and the users who are accessing these files.

Organizational unit (OU) Subdivision of a domain used to group objects in Active Directory.

Outbound connection Used to dial out and connect to another computer or network.

PAP See Password Authentication Protocol.

Partition Part of a hard disk drive that has been formatted to act as a logically separate unit of storage.

Password Security feature that is used in combination with a logon name to control access to network and local resources.

Password Authentication Protocol (PAP) Protocol that uses plain text passwords for authentication.

Password history Stores the passwords previously used by a user account.

Passwords must meet complexity requirements Used to require users to follow a minimum password length and a consistent password structure to ensure that a combination of capital letters, lower case letters, numbers, or punctuation marks are used.

PCMCIA card See Personal Computer Memory Card International Association card.

Peer-to-peer network All computers in a network share resources as equals without a dedicated server. Also referred to as a workgroup.

Performance logs and alerts Used to record the performance of resources in logs and to configure alerts, which are activated based on threshold values that you set to perform specific actions.

Permissions Used to assign the capabilities users have when they gain access to a resource; for example, the Change permission enables users to change and delete data in a file.

Personal Computer Memory Card International Association (PCMCIA) card Removable credit-card-sized devices that are plugged into an expansion slot (PCMCIA slot) or a port, generally on a portable computer. Used to add a NIC, modem, or hard disk drive to the portable computer.

Ping Utility used to test TCP/IP configurations and identify connection failures.

PktType Identifies the packet form (such as Ethernet_II, SNAP, or ArcNet) that must be used.

Plug and Play Gives Windows 2000 Professional the capability to configure newly connected hardware automatically and dynamically, to load appropriate drivers, to register device notification event, and to use removable and changeable devices.

Point-to-Point Protocol (PPP) Used by Windows 2000 to ensure cross-functionality with other remote access software. PPP settles configuration issues between other networking protocols, including TCP/IP, IPX, and AppleTalk.

Point-to-Point Tunneling Protocol (PPTP) Tunneling protocol that creates secure connections to corporate networks over the Internet.

POST See Power-on Self Test.

Power options Enable the system to control and manage all the power requirements of a system in order to manage power consumption.

Power schemes Enable Windows 2000 Professional to automatically switch off a monitor and hard disk when the user is not working on the system.

Power-on Self-Test (POST) Built-in diagnostic program that checks the hardware to ensure that basic hardware components are present; also checks amount of physical memory available on the computer.

PPP See Point-to-Point Protocol.

PPTP See Point-to-Point Tunneling Protocol.

Preconfigured console Console that is a part of the Windows 2000 Professional operating system by default.

Primary partition Volume created using the unallocated space on a basic disk.

Print$ Used by administrators to monitor shared printers remotely by providing access to the printer driver files.

Print device Hardware that creates the hard copies of your digital files.

Print permission Enables users to connect to a network printer and print documents.

Print server Computer that manages the print requests for a shared printer.

Printer Software that delivers the requests for service from the operating system to the physical print device.

Printer driver Software that contains the information used by the operating system to convert the print commands for a particular model of print device into a printer language, such as PostScript.

Printer pool Used to associate a single printer with multiple print devices, which can be either local or network-interface print devices.

Printer port Printer software interface that a computer uses to communicate with a printer.

Profile tab Tab in the Properties dialog box where you set the path for user profile, logon script, and home folder.

Protocol binding Process of establishing communication between network components on different levels.

Proxy server Provides a connection to the Internet for computers on a LAN, and a means for controlling in-coming and out-going requests for service.

PSTN See Public Switched Telephone Network.

Public key policies Used to configure Encrypting File System (EFS) recovery agents.

Public Switched Telephone Network (PSTN) A collection of the world's interconnected public telephone systems.

Publishing an application Makes application available to any user who wants it; application will appear in the Add/Remove Programs control panel. Applications are published only to specific users, not to computers.

RADIUS See Remote Authentication Dial-in User Service.

RAS See Remote Access Service.

RAS client Computer that establishes RAS connection with RAS server.

RAS server Computer with which RAS client establishes RAS connection.

RCP See Remote Copy Protocol.

RDN See Relative Distinguished Name.

Read permission Enables users to display folder names, file names, file data and the attributes of folders shared on remote systems; also run programs that are in shared application folders.

Recovery agent Account configured with a recovery agent certificate and a private key that can be used to open and use an encrypted file.

Recovery Console Command-line interface that can be used to perform a variety of troubleshooting and recovery tasks.

Regedit.exe Windows 9x version of Registry editor.

Regedt32.exe Windows NT version of Registry editor.

Registry Database in which the Windows 2000 Professional operating system stores information relating to the hardware and software settings on a computer.

Registry editor Used to view and modify the configuration information in the Registry.

Relative distinguished name (RDN) Part of the object name; the attribute that identifies object as unique from its peers, usually its "common name."

Remote Authentication Dial-in User Service (RADIUS) Protocol with a remote user authentication design that is vendor-independent and highly scalable.

Remote Access Service (RAS) Enables you to share and access resources on a computer or a network from remote locations.

Remote Copy Protocol (RCP) Copies files between a computer running Windows 2000 Professional and an RCP host.

Remote installation Enables an administrator to install Windows 2000 Professional on client computers throughout a network from a central location.

Remote Installation Services (RIS) server Windows 2000 server which stores RIS image used for remote installation.

Remote shell (RSH) Runs commands on a Unix host.

Removable media Devices that can be removed from your system while the system is still on.

Replication Process of creating and managing duplicate versions of any database.

Reset account lockout counter after Used to set the time duration that must pass after an invalid logon attempt before the bad logon attempt counter is reset to 0.

Restore Wizard Used to restore data.

Reverse lookup query Resolves an IP address to a name.

Rights Give users the ability to perform an action that inter-acts with the operating system, for example, changing the system time or shutting the system down.

RIS server See Remote Installation Services (RIS) server.

Roaming user profile Profile that sets up the same desktop environment for a user, no matter which computer the user is using in a domain.

Root Domain The top of the domain hierarchy, represented by a period.

Root key See Subtree key.

Route Displays and modifies the local routing table.

Router Computers that interconnect the multiple computers on a network or the Internet. They use headers and a forwarding table to determine where packets go, and ICMP (Internet Control Message Protocol), an extension of IP, to communicate with each other and configure the best route between any two hosts.

Routing table Used to provide routers with directions they will use to forward data packets to locations on other networks.

RSH See Remote shell.

Safe Mode Starts the computer by loading only a set of basic files and drivers.

Scheduled Tasks Utility used to schedule programs and scripts to run at a specific time.

Schema The database design, which includes the object classes and attributes that are stored in Active Directory.

Second-level domain The names that organizations register for the Internet. They have two parts, a top level name and a unique second-level name, for example yale.edu.

Secure Server (Require Security) IPSec policy that minimizes the number of clients with which you can communicate over a network, thereby enhancing security. Unsecured communications with untrusted clients will be blocked.

Security Configuration and Analysis snap-in Used to compare the current security configuration of a computer or Group Policy object with one of the predefined security templates, to create custom security templates and to apply a template either to the local computer or to a Group Policy object.

Security event log Records the success and failure of events you have chosen to audit.

Security Template snap-in Used to create a centralized tool where all of the available templates and all of the available security attributes are organized in one place.

Separator page Contains printer commands and is used to identify and separate different documents that are going to be printed.

Server (Request Security) IPSec policy that always requests security using Kerberos trust, but does not block communications from unsecured clients.

Session Manager (Smss.exe) Responsible for creating the user-mode environment that provides the visible interface with Windows 2000 Professional.

Setup Program that is executed to prepare the hard disk for later stages of installation. Copies the files required to run the Setup program.

Setup Wizard Collects setup information such as names, passwords, and regional settings for the computer on which you are installing Windows 2000 Professional

Share permissions See Shared folder permission.

Shared Application Folder Contains applications that network users can access from a central location.

Shared Data Folder Stores either working or public data. Working data is needed by a select group of users, while public data is more general and used by a large group of users.

Shared folder Resources that are made available to other computers on a network.

Shared Folder permission Used to control access to network resources. Also known as share permissions.

Shared Folders snap-in Enables an Administrator to monitor access to network resources.

Shiva Password Authentication Protocol (SPAP) An authentication protocol used when you connect to a Shiva server.

ShowSounds Accessibility function that displays captions for the speech and sounds generated by programs.

Simple volume Dynamic disk volume that contains disk space from a single disk.

Site Group of TCP/IP subnets with dependable and consistent connections.

Site aware Ability of clients on a site to recognize site-related data that Active Directory is imparting.

Slipstreaming Process of integrating service packs with the Windows 2000 installation files.

Smart card Credit card-sized devices used to store passwords, public and private keys and other types of identifying data.

SMP See Symmetric Multiprocessing System.

Smss.exe See Session Manager.

Snap-in Application present in MMC that enables you to perform administrative tasks.

SoundSentry Accessibility function that programs Windows 2000 to generate visual warnings when the system's built-in speaker plays a sound.

Spanned volume Dynamic disk volume that can include disk space from up to 32 disks.

SPAP See Shiva Password Authentication Protocol.

Special Access permissions Used to assign a specific level of access to users for objects on an NTFS disk.

Stand-alone snap-in Used to perform administrative tasks.

Standby Helps conserve the power used by computer by shutting down power to peripheral devices that are not in use.

StickyKeys Accessibility function that configures the system so that users do not have to hold down multiple keys simultaneously.

Striped volume Dynamic disk volume that combines areas of free space from multiple hard disks—32 is the maximum number of disks—into one logical volume.

Store password using reversible encryption for all users in the domain Used by Network Administrators so that a reversibly encrypted password is stored for all users in a domain.

Subkey Key within a key.

Subnet Grouping of devices that share a common network prefix.

Subnet mask 32-bit, four-part number used to break up an IP address into the network ID and host ID

Subtree Primary node within the Registry structure. Similar to the root folder of a disk, and contains the grouped information of the Registry. Also called root key or subtree key.

Subtree key See subtree.

Symmetric Multiprocessing System (SMP) Description for process in which multiple processors execute instructions of an application. The same memory space and the same applications are used.

Synchronization Process by which changes to offline files

are updated to network files.

Sysdiff Utility used with Setup Manager to perform automated installations of applications that do not support scripted installation routines. Includes Sysdiff.exe and Sysdiff.inf.

Sysprep See System Preparation tool.

System Preparation tool (Sysprep) Used to create disk image of the Windows 2000 installation and copy that image to various computers.

System service Creates unique SID when computer to which master image is copied is started for first time.

System log Records errors, warnings, and information generated by Windows 2000 Professional.

System Monitor Used to view a graphical representation of the performance of resources on your computer.

Systemroot Path to the Windows 2000 Professional installation folder.

Task Scheduler Administrative tool that can be used to schedule and carry out routine tasks at specified intervals.

TCP See Transmission Control Protocol.

TCP/IP Standard suite of protocols that enables you to exchange information across networks.

TCP/IP host Computer that is connected to a TCP/IP network.

Telnet Terminal emulation protocol often used to manage a remote Web server or another type of server. When you run Telnet from a client machine and connect to a server on the network you can enter commands which will be carried out as if you were performing them directly on the server terminal.

TFTP See Trivial File Transfer Protocol.

Timeout Time that the computer should wait for an action from you before loading the default operating system.

ToggleKeys Accessibility function that causes computer to generate sounds when certain locking keys are pressed.

Top-level domain The two- or three-character names used to designate the type of organization or its geographic location (com, gov, edu, org, net, uk, au, nz, etc.).

Trace log Surveys events that take place on the system.

Tracert Checks the route a packet follows to reach its destination.

Transmission Control Protocol (TCP) Protocol within TCP/IP protocol suite used to establish a connection between two hosts so they can exchange streams of data. Operates in Transport layer.

Transport layer Layer of TCP/IP that sets up communication sessions between computers and makes sure that messages are delivered in the correct sequence without errors.

Trivial File Transfer Protocol (TFTP) Uses UDP to transfer files between a computer running Windows 2000 Professional and a TCP/IP host running server software and TFTP.

Transitive trust Relationship established between domains so that if a domain has established a trust relationship with another domain, it can also communicate and connect to the domains that that domain trusts and vice versa.

Tree Group of domains that share a contiguous namespace.

TTL Time to live, after which the name server deletes the query result from its cache.

Tunneling protocol Creates a virtual tunnel between two computers or networks through the established Internet infrastructure.

UDF See Universal Disk Format

Universal Disk Format (UDF) File systems used to access DVD drives.

Universal Serial Bus (USB) External bus device (communication line) used to transfer data among the components in a computer system.

UNC (Universal Naming Convention) pathname Used to connect to any resource on the network for which you have permission. The syntax for the UNC path is: *\\computername\sharename.*

Uninterruptible Power Supply (UPS) Supplies backup battery power to a system when there is a sudden loss of electrical power.

Untrusted network Open public network that can be accessed by anyone.

Update.exe Utility used to replace existing Windows 2000 files with the appropriate new files from the service pack.

UPS See Uninterruptible Power Supply.

User account Contains all the required information about a user that is needed to identify the user on the network.

User account properties Set of properties associated with a user account.

User Datagram Protocol (UDP) Used by applications to transfer small amounts of data at one time.

User mode Enables you to distribute a console to other administrators.

User principal names User account name plus the DNS name of the domain where the user account object is stored, separated by a @ sign.

User profile Collection of folders that stores the current desktop environment for a user, application settings, and the user's personal data.

User rights assignment Used to prescribe what actions a user can execute within the operating system.

Value entries Data or values that are contained by the subkeys of the Registry.

Verbose mode A mode for running a command that causes messages generated to be displayed to the user.

Video adapter Expansion board that plugs into a computer to give it display capabilities.

Virtual memory Temporary storage used by a computer to run programs that need more memory than is available at any given point in time.

Virtual Memory Manager (VMM) Coordinates the use of physical and virtual memory.

Virtual network number See Internal network number.

Virtual Private Network (VPN) A secure connection established using tunneling and encryption to transfer data securely over the Internet.

VMM See Virtual Memory Manager.

VPN See Virtual Private Network.

WDM See Win32 Driver Model.

Win32 Driver Model (WDM) Common model for device drivers that works across Windows 98 and Windows 2000 operating systems.

Windir Command to display names and paths of Windows directories.

Windir\comsetup.log Registers the Optional Component Manager and Com+ setup routines.

Windir\debug\netSetup.log Registers information about joining a domain or a workgroup, including the network computer name, workgroup, and domain validation.

Windir\mmdet.log Registers multimedia device installation information and the port range for each device.

Windir\setupapi.log Registers an entry when a line from an **.INF** file is executed and error information if the execution was unsuccessful.

Windows Installer Application installation technology that now augments the Add/Remove Programs Wizard. One of the main features that reduces the TCO (Total Cost of Ownership) of a Windows 2000 network, and one of the IntelliMirror technologies that facilitates users moving from computer to computer.

Windows Internet Naming Service (WINS) Service used to map IP addresses to NetBIOS or computer names.

Windows 2000 Advanced Server Advanced version of Windows 2000 server that can support high-end network applications.

Windows 2000 Datacenter Server Microsoft's most powerful server operating system.

Windows 2000 Professional Main Microsoft desktop operating system for businesses of all sizes.

Windows 2000 Readiness Analyzer Generates a compatibility report about your computer's current hardware and software.

Windows 2000 Server Operating system for client/server networks.

WINS See Windows Internet Naming Service.

Winsock Provides support to existing NetWare applications that are compatible with the IPX/ SPX socket interface.

Winnt.exe Program used to install Windows 2000 Professional over a network on a target computer running a Windows 3.x operating system.

Winnt32.exe Program used to install Windows 2000 Professional over a network on a target computer running Windows 2000, 98, 95, NT 4.0 or 4.0.

Workgroup A logical group of users who work on a common project and share information and resources, on computers that are interconnected, generally over a local area network (LAN). Also known as a peer-to-peer network.

Zone transfers Replicate any changes in the primary zone database file to the secondary zone database files.

Zones Distinct, contiguous segments of the DNS namespace that make a large domain manageable by enabling different administrators to manage different zones.

Index

X-Y-Z